EGYPT
IN TRANSITION

EGYPT
IN TRANSITION

by
Jean and Simonne
Lacouture

TRANSLATED BY
FRANCIS SCARFE

CRITERION BOOKS · NEW YORK

L'Égypte en mouvement *was first published*
by Editions du Seuil, Paris
This translation, incorporating later revisions
and additions by the authors, was first published in 1958

Copyright in all countries signatory
to the Berne Convention

English translation © 1958 by Methuen & Co Ltd

Library of Congress Catalog Card Number 58-10614

PRINTED IN GREAT BRITAIN

Contents

Illustrations

*Except where otherwise acknowledged, the photographs
are by Simonne Lacouture*

9

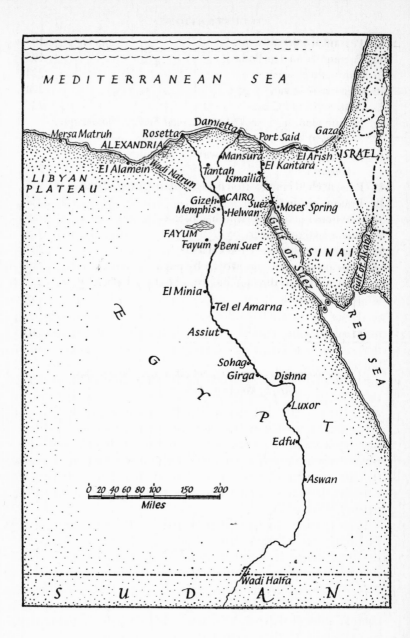

MEDITERRANEAN SEA

Mersa Matruh
Rosetta
Damietta
Port Said
Gaza
ALEXANDRIA
El Arish
ISRAEL
El Alamein
Wadi Natrun
Tantah
Mansura
El Kantara
LIBYAN
Ismailia
PLATEAU
Gizeh
CAIRO
Suez
Moses' Spring
Memphis
Helwan
FAYUM
SINAI
Fayum
Beni Suef
Gulf of Suez
Gulf of Akaba
El Minia
Tel el Amarna
RED SEA
Assiut
E
G
Sohag
Y
Girga
Dishna
P
Luxor
Edfu
T
Aswan

0 20 40 60 80 100   150   200
Miles

Wadi Halfa

S   U   D   A   N

INTRODUCTION

Egyptian Continuity and Revolutions

In about A.D. 2000 a Pharaoh of the twelfth dynasty showed a *fellah's* prudence by building a wall across the Sinai peninsula, which came to be known as 'The Prince's Wall'. According to New Kingdom scribes he hoped to 'prevent Asian plunderers from coming to water their flocks in the river Nile'. He failed. The Prince's Wall has vanished, but the Asian plunderers and their flocks, the Shepherd Kings, Saint Mark, the Prophet's horsemen, have left their imprint on Egypt. In vain did de Lesseps sunder the two continents with his canal, or Zionism raise a thicker wall than the Prince's between Beit-Hanun and Elath: the highway is still open, the interflow of life goes on.

The swing-bridges at Ferdan and El Kantara—though so flimsy that a tanker once swept one away—are enough to anchor Africa to Asia. The sand and stone of Sinaïtic Egypt stretches to the east and green and brown Nilotic Egypt to the west. Two unsatisfied continents are linked by a single country, two-faced, porous, permeable, which explains the one to the other. Egypt forms the hinge between the two clamouring halves of the world. It is here that Africa's muddled and almost dumb misery meets the clear-sighted, struggling poverty of Asia.

India is more strongly installed at Suez, the black races more enduringly rooted at Aswan, than Europe is in Alexandria. For thirteen hundred years torrid Islam, swarming from Asia, has lived side by side with the gods of earth, water and death that ride the old Nile. A crude streak of brownish-grey mud of almost the same colour as the peasants it supports and feeds, Egypt lies across the long charred crescent that joins Senegal to the Punjab—not cutting it, but deflecting it a little as thick glass refracts sunlight.

In Cairo the great lay and religious universities, the teeming prisons and the young Trades-Union movement are all silently

11

preparing upheavals just as radical as those which ten times over transformed the aspect and structure of the Egyptian nation in the past, or which are now changing Asia, her fascinating neighbour. Egypt has often been held up as a model of historical stability, yet despite its unchanging framework the land and its people have known the most violent breaks with tradition, from the so-called 'social revolution' that swept away the Old Empire down to the introduction of all-the-year-round irrigation which modified the relationship between man and the Nile.

Egypt is a shifting land, made of mud and as malleable as mud, whose changes of appearance and outlook have taken the most diverse forms. Maybe its most striking revolutions were of a spiritual order, for instance that of Amenophis IV, the short-lived opponent of polytheism, or that of Caliph Omar's devout warriors. But its renewals more often take a technical or administrative turn, for instance Imhotep's invention of stone architecture, or the adoption of the Hyksos' chariots which enabled the Middle Kingdom to change the course of Egyptian history by throwing her armies towards the Euphrates, to return with Mitanni princesses, metals hitherto unknown, fresh ideas. Equally 'materialistic' revolutions were the redistribution of land by Sultan Selim, Mohamed Ali and Mohamed Neguib, or the complete reorganization of agriculture in the nineteenth century when cotton-growing was introduced, or the gradual domestication of the Nile.

More sharply determined than any other nation by its remarkable geographical setting—a tomb-like river-bed hemmed in between two deserts—Egypt has undergone such deep changes that she is hard put to recognize her past self. Perhaps this is because Egyptian revolutions, so profound and always fraught with other changes to come, were most often the work of foreign hands. Yet long internal tension is always at the root of movement: the revolution that overthrew the sixth dynasty came before the Bedouin invasion; while the Bey's power was already undermined before the Battle of the Pyramids.

None the less, it was the Greek Alexander who drove out Darius's satraps; the invading Arabs who threw out the hated Byzantines; Bonaparte who, by crushing the Mamelukes, opened the way for the Albanian Mohamed Ali. The conqueror is usually received in Egypt with open arms; defeat is 'nationalized' and as often as not treated as a 'liberation'. This seeming opportunism does not mean that Egyptian patriotism is of no account, it still remains to be considered. What is really involved is this people's inner dynamism, which is the less inclined to rise against tyranny as the land and river makes it dependent on whoever controls the dykes and dams, though Cairo twice revolted against Bonaparte and Kléber, and Arabi against a Khedive who was in the grip of foreigners, while on 23 July 1952 Egyptian officers contrived a *coup d'état* of uniformed peasants.

Too many winds have blown against those old stones, too many thrones and dominations have crushed this nation, for it to be able to recognize itself in Luxor or Memphis. Anyone sharing the life of Modern Egyptian citizens must often wonder how the name given by Greek travellers to the Nile peasantry (*aiguptioi*, which most philologists agree to be made up of *ka*, meaning the life principle, and Ptah, one of the great gods of Memphis) can be related to the name given by foreigners to the 'Misriyin', the people of Misr or Misra, the feverish, Arabic-speaking Egypt of today?

Everything in Egypt goes to show that history has been done away with, if by history we mean a collection of privileged moments and a chronicle of collective dramas rather than a building up of a society and the evolution of manners. The thread of historical continuity is certainly more marked from the rapers of the Sabine women down to Signor Gronchi, than it is from the Saïte kings down to Colonel Nasser. It was the intrusion of Islam rather than that of Christianity that snapped the Ariadne's thread which for thirty centuries ensured the well-known continuity of Egyptian life in spite of invasions and the dethroning of dynasties.

But it was not success in war that gave Islam its superior revolutionary value. It was, rather, the linguistic change that went with it. Why should there have been three thousand years of Pharaonism? Did the form of the State itself dictate such a long game of patience? Not at all, since nothing remained intact in the change from the Old to the New Kingdom—neither the conception of the monarchy, nor the relationship between the king and the different social orders, nor the site of the capital, nor diplomatic policy. How could it be blood or race, when from east to west and from north to south the valley was constantly swept by invasions, while black-skinned Pharaohs followed on the sons of Asiatic princesses? Religion offers a more likely explanation, although Snefru and Seti I, rulers of the third and nineteenth dynasties, had not even the same gods and did

13

not observe the same rites: all they had in common was their burial-magic.

But, stronger even than religion, the language was ancient Egypt's most enduring feature. Being the inventors of writing, which they associated closely with the country's soil, flora and fauna, the Egyptians were able to pass from the hieroglyphic to the more abstract hieratic script without sacrificing the wonderful link which the former system gave between themselves—the living—and the dead. It is remarkable that the boldest innovator in Egyptian history, Amenophis IV, realized that this was a fundamental necessity and therefore, instead of merely destroying the old gods, reformed yet in a sense preserved the language itself by substituting a kind of popular slang for the hieroglyphs. In this way he perpetuated the very key and totem of the old civilization of hoe and stone, as well as that of the scribe himself.

In the fourth century A.D. six million Egyptians—that is to say the bulk of the population—were converted to Christianity. But the new religion as advanced by Saint Mark in the first century was unable to thrust its essential, explosive qualities on Egypt. It was at once adapted, nationalized, moulded in diluted form on to the Egyptian tradition, though of course it gave an opening into the Mediterranean additional to that already offered by Hellenism. Like Pharaonism, Egyptian Christianity was mainly confined to the Nile Valley. Though expressed in Greek at Alexandria, its prayers were in Coptic everywhere else, that is to say in an hellenic transcript of the old language. While there was a break-away from the hieroglyph, the Coptic tongue orally carried on the language of the Pharaohs. Thus Egyptian Christianity failed to snap the essential link in the chain of tradition.

On the other hand the Moslems, more tolerant than the Christians, while showing a greater respect for Coptic faith and practices than the Copts had had for Graeco-Roman 'paganism', brought not only their triumphant, lucid and hygienic religion, but with it a language that was to prove their most lasting instrument of power. The Moslems disliked the idea of forced conversion, for the Prophet had said 'There must be no religious constraint', and, perhaps partly because the Christians paid useful taxes, went no further than imposing Arabic as the official language, less than fifty years after settling in the valley of the Nile.

In a sense, the prefect Abdullah ibn al-Malik's ordinance of the year 706 may be regarded as a sabre-stroke slashing across Egyptian history. In replacing Coptic by Arabic for official documents, the conqueror ended four thousand years of a civilization that had been identified with its language, and substituted another civilization which was equally based on a Holy Book and on the spoken word.

But this was not enough to make peasant Egypt turn Arab. At the most it became *arab-speaking*. In the lingo of the valley peasantry the word 'arab' means no more than a shady beachcomber, a vagrant and pilferer. Egyptian Islam has ever been tinged with heresy: the Ulema, wherever they come from, cannot feel too happy as they pass through the famous 'Cities of the Dead' which lie all round Cairo, those scalped cities where the tombs are walled but not roofed, where the Moslem dead are surrounded by an almost physical atmosphere of survival not unworthy of the priests of Osiris.

No matter: sparsely Arab but markedly Moslem, the Egypt which dates from the Amr conquest has no share, either, in that rational, materialistic, aesthetic world whose axis should run through the Nile, Thebes, Alexandria, Crete and Athens—what we would now call the Western World. It partakes, rather, of a turbanned, imaginative, squatting, discontinuous world, a world both hedonist and ascetic, intellectually rootless, as intensely given to pleasure as to spirituality, and which makes the Houris of Paradise into the most exquisite idealizations of womanhood as well as the most lascivious visions—that world of the Moslem East which Gobineau and Massignon saw so differently yet so accurately.

After the Arab invasion the only link that Egypt had with the Theban empires was through the Christian minority which strove to base its right to survival on its attested Pharaonic origins. It is not the least unusual feature of this unusual people that, especially within the Coptic community, there is some physical resemblance to the gods and men shown on the friezes of ancient tombs, with their long eyes, tanned skin, heavy features, straight nose and strong square shoulders. The explanation is not that religion shapes faces or colours their skins, but that most of the Christians who refused to renounce their faith for Islam were thrust back into Upper Egypt, where they kept their typical physique; whereas the Moslems, settling in the north, intermarried with Turks, Circassians, Albanians and the peoples of fair-skinned Islam.

But there is no need to be taken in: the attachment shown today by the modern replicas of Isis, Rameses and Iskandar is somehow artificial and over-insistent. Unlike the gay familiarity of the Neapolitans of Pompeii, the Provençaux at Vaison-la-Romaine or the Athenians on the Acropolis, it is little more than a claim to legitimacy.

It is only too easy to bring out the differences, and useless to contrast the splendour of olden times and today's uncertainties, thus isolating archaeology from everyday life. To all appearances the hieratic giants who could not divorce their godhead from politics have nothing in common with the makers of modern Egypt, fumbling strategists of an 'International' of under-developed countries . . .

But at a different level certain constants cannot be ignored—on the plane of the land itself, human types, family life and farming. Bearing this in mind we can see many characteristics which the various phases of Egypt have in common. They were all formed in the same mould, far more exacting a mould than the hexagon of France or the 'boot' of Italy, the mould of a valley that certain political policies might stretch as far as the second or fourth Cataract, or which a military defeat would cut off from Nubia; but in the hollow of which, deep and narrow as a sarcophagus, a people has to carry on its brave struggle for existence.

The geographical data of Egypt are extremely simple but compelling. A line of water and verdure that widens near the sea runs between two deserts, flat on the west, hilly on the east, and joins Africa to the Mediterranean with its stroke of black. This lay-out cannot be said to explain Egypt's past or to decide its evolution once and for all. But it would be foolish to deny the emphasis with which it suggests her destiny, even more strongly perhaps than insularity does in the case of England or Japan. Egypt's uniqueness springs from its isolation between two deserts which cut her off as much from the Maghrib as from Palestine and the Sudan. It springs from a constant battle between river and desert, fertile Osiris and barren Seth, black soil and red sand.

A land which is expected to give so much, which yields two harvests a year in certain zones of Middle Egypt and whose frontier can hardly be extended towards the desert, has gradually taken on a kind of mythological meaning, an obsessional value. The over-valuation of land is one of the chronic vices of private domestic economy in Egypt, as well as being one of the most dangerous germs of stagnation. To own and join up little strips of land, to

16

have more and more *feddans* (acres) and quarrel and kill each other over a handful of soil, such is the common pattern of life, and it makes for a Shylock mentality. It often turns dramatic situations into farce. While it has been proved that Egyptian agriculture in its present state cannot feed the nation, there are few Egyptians who do not dream of owning some land. This ruinous myth has only begun to slacken its hold since the agrarian reform which was begun in 1952.

Rome's granary and Lancashire's cotton-warehouse, Egypt is entirely given over to agriculture, a permanent struggle between man, land, river and climate. Down the centuries the *fellah* (farmer), with the help of the great river, has reclaimed the soil and made himself so much a part of it that the field itself, his house and face, tools and livestock, all shaped out of the same mud, look more or less alike. But the climate is less helpful. For seven months of the year the fellah toils in the open fields at a temperature of from 85° to 105° F., or even more in Upper Egypt. For three months the night-temperature drops to below 40° F. and hardly a day passes without a change of 25 to 40 degrees gripping a rural population clad in nothing but a thin cotton smock. Undernourishment and the endemic parasitic diseases which have undermined the *fellahin* ever since they settled on the fringes of the Nile marshes aggravate the effects of a climate which is two-thirds Saharan and one-third tropical, on human beings who are enslaved to their job and for whom the seasons afford no rhythm of alternating work and semi-idleness, but only different forms of exhaustion.

It is not surprising that a people thus conditioned by nature, yoked to ceaseless toil (under a sky beneath which others are free to dream or pray or move their tents in search of fresh pastures for their flocks), should have suffered long periods of eclipse. Anyone who has lived in Egypt and known its long summers is not surprised at the state of prostration into which these people can fall, or the slowness of their recovery. The effects of the debilitating climate was soon felt by invaders, and the diaries kept by Napoleon's entourage wax eloquent on this subject.

It is certainly easier to enter Egypt than to remain strong once one is there. Easy to enter, as there is no natural frontier to stop the aggressor. Before El Alamein there was hardly any record of a frontier battle. From Avaris to Mansurah, from Ridanya to the

Pyramids, Egypt's destiny has always been defended in the heart of the country or at the walls of its capital cities.

This openness to invasion has left its mark on Egypt, its people and its soil. It has stressed the tendency to passiveness and fatalism which also has other origins—for instance the almost supernatural role played by the overflowing of the Nile in the life of the peasantry —a role which in this connexion is more important than that of religion. But Islam is adaptable and multiple enough for every nation to find its own expression, or rather, the sublimation of its own vital tendencies, within it—whether it be Persian mysticism, the Ottoman Turks' will to power, the Bengali thirst for sacrifice. Here the prolonged weariness of the nation which invented History, the physical exhaustion and resignation inseparable from its agricultural background, have tinged Islam with a greater surrender to the Invisible than orthodoxy allows. Its wide-open frontiers and the river's inevitable movement could only serve to encourage inertia.

To take another characteristic, perhaps the Egyptian landscape which, in the Delta, stretches into the distance and is only bounded in Upper Egypt by the steep banks on each side of the Nile might suggest another line of interpretation. Here nothing escapes the master's eye. There are neither woods for rebels to hide in, nor escarpments for guerrillas. The physical lie of the land commands obedience. There is no outlet or *maquis*, but the nearby desert where life is impossible. A local leader defying the tax-collecter, or an ambitious provincial governor, might certainly stage a rising, only to fall under the gunboat's fire or at the hands of a punitive expedition sent at all speed down the Nile, which can easily ferret them out.

The defeated can sometimes fold back into Upper Egypt and hold out for a while, as the Mamelukes did after the Battle of the Pyramids or after the Citadel Massacre of 1811. But the Cairo wolfhounds always catch up with them. The nationalistic journalist Abdullah Nadim managed to wage guerrilla warfare for years against the English after the 1882 rising, playing the part of a Delta Robin Hood. Strange types known as hermits have been known to flee into the desert rather than yield to Diocletian's police, or to escape the decrees of the Council of Chalcedon condemning the Monophysites. No one could pursue them into their desperate hide-outs, whether on the Red Sea or at Wadi-Natrun. But a hermit is not as other men.

Taking these exceptions into account, and the peasant risings often caused by agrarian feudalism, or the upheavals marking the second phase of Arab settlement in the eighth century, it is obvious that in the Delta and the Nile Valley, whoever controls Cairo, the police, the army and the dams has every chance of holding on to power, for the shape of the land forbids revolt.

Another fundamental factor in the strengthening of central power is the remarkable *de facto* control exercised by the master of Cairo over the country's economic life, conditioned as it is by the canal-system which is neither more nor less than Egypt's bloodstream. Many observers have pointed out that nowhere in the world except in Holland does the common lot depend so much on the technical skill and authority of a handful of men. Even before the development of all-the-year-round irrigation, the authority in control of the rise and fall of the Nile already directed the whole life of the nation. It alone could foresee the extent of flooding and issue the necessary orders for building dykes, distributing water, and so on. That is why Napoleon, the keenest centralizer in history, noted almost with enthusiasm that 'In no country in the world have the government and administration so much influence on public prosperity'. From the Vizier Joseph down to Mohamed Ali and Gamal Abdel Nasser State-control has flourished in Egypt in its most absolute form, with common exploitation of the waterways, collective storing of harvests and distribution of seed. Egypt has been an ideal field for experiment in directed economy. The Saint-Simonists chose it for the inauguration of State-socialism, not without some promise of success. More of this later.

Everything thus seems to help towards a dictatorship over a long-suffering, enfeebled populace, so to speak crucified on the land, obsessed by the idea of owning snippets of a country which it cultivates all the more frenziedly as it gives insufficient support: a dictatorship over a populace concentrated, as it were, into a camp—and indeed the term concentration-camp admirably applies to Egypt—under the eye of countless overseers watching them from a look-out post and closely dependent on a master who rations out water. Such was the state of Egypt in the century when some of its masters reached their highest fame, such as Qait Bey or Mohamed Ali. It was a feudal fief, a pawn in the hands of its master and king, a profitable bit of real estate.

The characteristics of that subjected Egypt have not all been effaced. We shall notice some of them again when we come to inquire

19

in what way living Egypt, the Arabic-speaking *Misr*, feverish and almost proletarian, which is now taking shape under our eyes, is heir to the great granitic empires which have been so long forgotten by the people of the Nile themselves.

Men destroy only what they replace. Alexander's Macedonian hellenism, then a Christianity so cruelly divided between the Alexandrians and Byzantines, could do no more than crack the old edifice. How could the rough conquering Arabs with their dogmatic Book and lush language supplant the Nile civilization to the point of burying it under the sands? However disturbing the idea of the death of civilizations may be, the problem of their succession is even more so. There are grounds for astonishment that out of the ten peoples, the six or seven languages, the three or four religions which could hope, thanks to their quality or proximity, to inherit the dying Empire of the seventh century, a few tribes from the Arab peninsula should succeed in imposing their language and faith on Egypt. Not that the Arabs have failed to prove their vitality and greatness, from Damascus to Cordoba. Not that Islam is any less stirring or less inspired than Christianity or Judaism. But in the year 640 Omar's soldiers were nothing but a Yemenite legion, hastily levied by the *bourgeois* of Mecca and Medina to ensure the flow of provisions for the growing new empire. The Egyptian peasantry, worshipping its rustic deities, seemed ill prepared to adopt a 'faceless' God, or a Prophet who said of the plough, 'It will not enter a family's dwelling without God bringing degradation with it at the same time.' (A *Hadith*—or recital from the oral tradition of the Prophet.)

If we try to explain the arabization and islamization of Egypt, there are positive reasons to be found, such as the strength and simplicity of Islam and the proposal of more modern forms of organization for the new society. There are also negative reasons such as the dullness of Egyptian Christianity, the Byzantine administration's unpopularity, and the spiritual, technical and political apathy of a country which was at the point of nausea. Gobineau stressed how the disorder of the Persian and Byzantine empires helped on the Arab conquest of Mesopotamia, the Iran plateau, Syria and the Nile Valley. But whereas in Persia a national dynasty did try to resist the encroaching Arabs, some Copts in Egypt saw the invaders as an instrument of liberation, so strongly had the Byzantine officials and clergy exasperated their urge for independence.

But the Arab and Moslem triumph had other positive causes.

20

The force that had just crushed the Sassanian empire and seized Mesopotamia and Syria was by no means negligible. God-intoxicated, no people was ever more thoroughly roused to enthusiasm than this, even before the Meccan notables gave their complete support to the faith of Medina, when the struggle for control of the Caliphate was at its height. Such a dynamism was based on prolonged hunger, immense pride and the certainty, however ill founded, of possessing a right and Law. It was also based on exceptional military resources for that period: an overwhelming use of cavalry, extreme simplification of supply-lines, the use of mobile camps which was familiar to the Bedouin, and fluid manœuvre: in a word, it was blitzkrieg.

An army can drive everything before it so long as it is stronger and more self-confident than its opponents. But for it to endure and renew itself other factors are needed. These are to be found in a more modern, more collective, more grouped conception of the city and polity brought by these international-minded, trade-minded, tireless travellers whose caravans and ships linked the Indian Ocean with the Near East.

We must not forget that the Prophet Mohamed was a great traveller, and was at one time a leader of caravans, or that Arabism and Islam were slow in establishing themselves. While the Umayyads were strengthening their political and military hold on Egypt, with an impressive display of tolerance, at the same time they were turning Damascus into a centre of commerce, craftsmanship and culture that had no rival in the East. It was this brand of Islam and Arabism, refined and improved on at Damascus, which managed to penetrate and saturate Egypt. The pattern becomes obvious, once this is clear. In the eighth century A.D. it was only natural that the most advanced civilization of the age should triumph, enriched as it was by all that the many branches of the new enormous Moslem world had to offer. It would perhaps be going too far to see this as the victory of a middle class over feudalism, but it can be regarded as a progress over decay. The Moslem city, with its firm cohesion, its self-confidence and totalitarian 'paternalism', had much the same reasons for imposing itself on the East as the Western Empire itself had in the same century.

If for a moment we isolate the purely religious side of what is really an indivisible Islamic civilization, then it is clear that the new faith, for all its abstractness—for it had relatively little naturalism

21

in its make-up—had something positive to offer the Egyptian peoples, if only its simplicity, its formalism, a certain pride which it instilled into its followers. No people is riper for pride than one which is burdened by its past glories and is tired of being humiliated. Islam's simplicity was bound to appeal to those to whom the local form of Christianity had nothing to offer but endless quarrels over points of doctrine. As for the formalism or even literalism of Islam, its eager trust in anything that is written down for good and all, perhaps it was this very element which most readily attracted a race whose ancestors had carved the laws of religious hygiene in unchangeable hieroglyphs on the granite of Philae.

Thus an irresistible fusion came about between a trading middle class eager for discovery, and at that time technically and socially progressive, a practical religion whose priesthood cunningly practised an easy-going tolerance, and an army inspired with fanatical energy, everywhere victorious and superior to its rivals in the arts of war. If the invaders took root to such an extent that modern Egypt has forgotten all that went before (even thinking in terms of 'Arab Egypt'), blind even to its own ancient and brilliant civilization, it is because Islam brought with it a decent style of life, profound spiritual calm, and a national unity which spread far beyond its own frontiers to embrace a people that had been martyred by a thousand years of fruitless invasions.

But we must also remember that when Islam burst into an officially Christian Egypt in the seventh century, it did not cause the violent split which the two modes of thought and civilization of today might lead us to expect. The invaders benefited tactically from the wranglings of rival Christian groups. For many Egyptians the religion of the Hedjaz seemed little more than another Christian deviation, no doubt to be held in suspicion but more acceptable than the spiritual dictatorship of Rome or Byzantium.

So external appearances were on the invaders' side. Their pure monotheism attracted those Christians who had lost their bearings or lost face, torn by dissensions in which national pride was at grips with bogus dogmatism. Weary of being scolded by a swarming, greedy clergy, sick of a surfeit of ignorant prelates and unbelieving bishops and legions of crowns, mitres and crosiers, it is hardly surprising that the faithful welcomed a religion without clergy, which allows a man to speak directly to God, with no intercessor holding out his hand for payment.

Islam also attracted the Christians by its optimism, its serene acceptance of this world as it is. If the various forms of the old religion of the Pharaohs had any basic assumption in common, it lay precisely in the belief that the world is a harmony, that it is well made, that it always has been and always will be so, and that it is both foolish and criminal to try and change it. What is most noticeably lacking in that spiritual outlook is the idea of sin and redemption. Man must look forward only to starting his earthly life afresh after his death, savouring the beauty of his days.

In reality, Islam is not based at all on such a beatitude of the group and the individual. The notion of sin is not absent from the Prophet's teaching, since according to a *hadith* he declared that 'every creature is stung by Satan, at birth'. But it is certainly nearer to Pharaonic satisfaction than it is to Judaism, based on a nexus of terror between a pitiless Jehovah and his defenceless creature, or to Christianity with its notion of sin and its redemption through sorrow. The God of Islam is hailed as 'The all-forgiving and benevolent' and the believer can find rest in him with a calmness which, in Egypt, is not unlike the believers' sense of trust towards the benevolent Horus. Both Jew and Christian are doomed to play the part of the accused, with God as their permanent judge. They are burdened with a constant supposition of error, in a sin-infested world. A lawyer would say that they are expected to prove their innocence. But this constant desire for renewal, the anguish and will to redemption, seem to give both the Jewish and Christian worlds their sense of effort, dynamism, creative unbalance.

No doubt the Egyptian Pantheon included the murderer of Osiris, the evil Seth and the cruel, lion-headed Sekhmet. But these were outnumbered by such friendly, reassuring gods as Hathor, the good heifer; the wise Toth, the tender Isis, Anubis the embalmer, the resurrected Osiris the Just, while the aggressive virility of Min is a form of virtue. The Egyptian religion formed a system of confidence, certainty of life and the after-life, alliance between man, the creatures and Nature. It was designed for preservation, with a host of satisfied deities watching over the good river-folk for all time.

The Egyptian Moslem is the spiritual heir to his ancestors in the sense that he is not doomed through original sin to an unavoidable struggle with God. For him sin is only a deviation, an accident, the forgetting of some rule. By following the precepts of the Book he finds his proper place in the universal harmony, his conscience

23

finding a definite understanding with the Almighty. He is the Just Man in a world that has become good, and he can enjoy his days as others did before him. Napoleon liked Islam and in his *Memorial* contrasted the 'religion of threats based on fear' as he saw Christianity, to the Islamic 'religion made up of promises, a religion of rewards'.

It should be evident that we have not set out to show Islam as the direct heir to Pharaonism, nor as the successor and prolongation of Egyptian Christianity. We have only sought to explain why the transition went so smoothly, and why the understanding between the Egyptian nation and the Moslem city has lasted so long. The Nile Valley has lived precariously under Islam's banner for thirteen hundred years. Syrians, Turks, Berbers, Circassians and Albanians —her masters have come from every quarter of the Islamic world, whether to build, to make war, to philosophize, to persecute or to make peace. Egyptian Islam has failed to flower like Persian Shi'ism, or to achieve the masculine pride of the Almoravid and Almohad empires or the delicacy of Andalusian civilization. But the superb city of Cairo, the city of five hundred mosques, has survived every conflict and assassination and the swarming and mingling of all the races of Islam.

Despite Egypt's former greatness it was not a sign of decadence that she should be ruled by Saladin, who was no more than a Kurdish chief, or by Baibars, Qala'un or Qait-Bey. Whatever their origins, they proved their worth in the Nile Valley. Yet they achieved greatness when they were most faithful to the teaching of the old dynasties, treating with the landowners, fighting no more in Asia than was necessary for gaining breathing-space in Syria and keeping stable frontiers there, or keeping faith with the feudal lords. This meant that they must not turn home-loving Egypt into a springboard for distant adventures, or rouse her too abruptly from her bed in the Nile Valley, while leaving her open to every influence from outside.

Though Egypt appears to have been split by the overthrow of the great dynasties, the growth and flowering of alien religions, the invasion and rule of foreign powers, yet there is strong and adaptable continuity in its history. Although there were fundamental revolutions in the nineteenth and twentieth centuries they spared basic features which will only be swept away by industrialization and the growth of a proletariat.

Rural custom is the most obvious and most threatened element of stability. Gestures, habitat, implements, family ways and customs, relations between peasant and landowner, whether it be the overlord or the State—little or nothing of all this seems to have changed since king Scorpion, the prehistoric unifier whose existence is known to us only from a club head in limestone dating from before 3000 B.C. He is shown with a hoe in his hand, apparently digging a canal and putting the soil into a little wicker basket—exactly the same hoe and the same basket as the fellah still uses to this day.

After so much has been written on the subject there is no point in stressing such things as the similarity between the modern Egyptian's gestures and those portrayed on the tombs of Saqqara and Deir-el-Medineh; or on the permanence of a setting in which the modern peasant seems to imitate the models in the Cairo museum; the unchanged tradition by which the son is completely subjected to the father; the fixed relationship between master and servant, collector and payer, overseer and executive, of which until recently the like was only to be seen in China. The same agricultural pattern of behaviour, seemingly spontaneous but dictated by the past, is being repeated daily in a rural society which has remained so static that it was able to absorb Islam itself. The very houses and their inhabitants seem to grow from the Nile mud.

There is, then, the same original landscape, brought to life by ceaseless movement. But we must not be taken in by such signs of stability. Evidence of a break can be seen, however unobtrusive— here a pump, there a tractor or mechanical thresher. After the revolution brought about a hundred years ago when permanent irrigation took the place of the 'basin' system that relied on river drainage alone, a second revolution is going on at present in the form of mechanization. But in the latter case adaptation is harder and the returns less certain. Only the setting up of the collective farms laid down in the agrarian reform scheme, and a re-survey and distribution of land, can enable the machine to play its part to the full.

Ought we to see further signs of Egyptian continuity in the monotheism of which Islam is the most perfected type, but which in Egypt's case is a survival from earlier times? It is tempting to credit the discovery of monotheism to the unorthodox Pharaoh Amenophis IV (Akhnaton) and to consider Moses as his disciple, as Freud did. This would complete the chain of the monotheistic tradition running through Judaism and Christianity down to the Prophet. It would thus run from and back to the Nile Valley, passing through Akhnaton, Moses, Jesus and Mohamed. But on the other hand Akhnatonian monotheism is hardly representative of the spirit of the dynasties or of the indigenous population. The attempt to set up Aton as the one god failed miserably, and the solar disc and its inventor have been cursed down the centuries. The Egyptian outlook is, rather, henotheistic, having a pyramid of gods in strict hierarchy, surmounted by a supreme deity, Ptah, otherwise known as Amon-Ra or Osiris. Under this great spiritualized god there flourished a kind of parliament of animal or vegetable deities, from the cow Hathor to the Nile-God, Hapi. It was neither animalism nor spiritualism but a kind of code or cipher to the understanding of the world, striving to bind both minor phenomena and the most abstract ideals into a coherent whole—a whole which reconciled the flower with violence, the stone with the god it enclosed, the sex of Min and the wisdom of Toth, the bull Aphis and the goddess Nut, the goddess of the sky stretched out across the temple vault. It was a serene vitalism, or in the strongest sense of the word a 'realism' which takes things as they are and tries to find some basic coherence in them, so as to draw out all their underlying meaning. Extremely vague tendencies towards the supremacy of a spiritualized deity cannot be taken for the origin of Islam's bold assertion 'There is no other god but God'.

But the fact remains that the Egyptians are piously inclined. A Sun-worshipper (as Nerval believed), or a worshipper of the Ineffable who goes by a hundred names and whose only manifestation is that immense presence in the East, the man of the Nile Valley voluntarily falls to his knees, burning with faith. Is it faith in the flood, in a god of toil, in a god of revenge or of birth? Or is it a simple longing for a present help in trouble?

Whatever the object, magic is not looked down on. Frantic appeals are made to the supernatural powers. When Cagliostro came to Paris the first thing he did was to seek out the Egyptian 'initiates'. In *The Magic Flute* the Queen of the Night's trills are directed against the evil Witch of the Nile. The humblest traveller, entering the Valley of the Kings or a pyramid, is struck at once by the display of magic in the mural decorations, the mathematical lay-out of the chambers and other building devices. The hypogeum of Seti I is a 'Seer's' *salon*, a magician's parlour. Magic is one of the arts that has least declined in Egypt, where astrologers do better than psychiatrists. What with formularies, amulets, fortunes, possession and exorcism, talismans and the evil eye, a census of wizards in modern Egypt would reveal a people living in fear, superstition and greed, as in primitive times.

They show the same humility towards their earthly masters as towards the psychic powers. However cynical the landowners' treatment of the *fellahin* has always been, massacres and risings are infrequent. The fellah is never allowed to raise his head, thanks to the urgent work that lies in front of him, the tight feudalism in which he is a cog, the authorities' methods of supervision, ever watchful over the fields and ditches, and the hierarchical religious system. His behaviour has been conditioned by the long habit of slavery, open or concealed. '*Hādir, ya bay*'—'At your service, Sir'—such is his cry. It is not easy to throw off the password of humiliation, or to make men stand on their own feet when they have been prostrate so long. Egyptian slavery has no legal basis. It is a permanent, almost indestructible expression of economical and physical forces in which the whip, taxation, water and prayer all take their turn. Breaking this down is not a job for the legislator alone, but for the serf himself.

Another aspect of Egyptian deference, perhaps less tragic but more deeply rooted, is the religion of officialdom. This is not just a certain relationship between authority and the citizen, between administrator and administered. The Egyptian's awe for the scribe is not only a matter of fear: it partakes of admiration and a vague kind of hope. The cringing respect shown by the peasant and workman for anyone with the slightest knowledge or power is tinged with envy. Their dream is to become the *ustaz* or master themselves, to be one who knows, writes, administers, who can grasp a technique, however slight, who has his hand on some fragment of power and actually figures in the State budget.

All this implies a thirst for knowledge, a disgust with being whipped, a longing for security, for a fixed wage, an income, or to be able to dole out State moneys. The Egyptian parents' dream is to see their sons clad in the postal-worker's or railwayman's blue overall, sure of a fixed if miserable wage, though it be only a quarter of what they could earn in the meanest business of their own, but at any rate fixed and paid and guaranteed by the Government, by Cairo, by the unseen Powers that rule from a distance, fixing the price of cotton, opening and closing sluices, collecting taxes, conscripting men for forced labour or military service, filling and emptying prisons as they think fit.

It is not surprising that the masterpiece of Egyptian sculpture is not at all some goddess rising from the sea, not a national leader holding the tablets of the law or proudly pointing to the extended frontiers, nor an athlete throwing the discus. No: it is a sturdy, masterful civil servant, with his round head and piercing eye and the firm tread of a man who knows how to make his word felt. This servant of a fourth-dynasty Pharaoh was spontaneously named *sheikh el balad* (The Village Headman) by the Moslem workmen who unearthed his effigy forty-three centuries after his death. A model civil servant, just like the one they obey now. Here Egyptian continuity found its full expression: the scribe is Egypt's common denominator.

Reverence, humiliation and exploitation—however true this is, the fact remains that the Egyptian is a cheerful person. Unlike the peoples that live in the gloom of a terrorist religion or who are haunted by the sense of sin, the man of the Nile Valley tends to put the best light on things, reconciling them as well as he can with his own interests, hastening to laugh for fear that he might weep. The Nile fellah's gaiety is impressive and enduring. However opaque and earthy it might be, there is an Egyptian sense of humour, a sense of the comic satirical story which he calls the *nukta*. We know the part played in the lives of this long-suffering people by the expression *mā lish* ('no matter'), and we also know that one of the three heroes of popular mythology, together with the brave knights Antar and Abu Zaid, is Goha the jester, half Candide and half Panurge, always sure to raise a laugh. *Ihr erou nefer*—'have a good time' or 'take it easy'—is the motto of the average citizen of the Colonels' Republic today, as it was under the Pharaohs. However busy they are kept by the fresh jobs thrust upon them, their endless toil on the irrigation scheme and the rules of Islamic modesty, the fellahs make the slightest respite an excuse for singing and dancing, when with staff in hand they perform the sham-tourney which is the Nile Valley national dance. The village seizes on the slightest pretext for a slapstick entertainment worthy of Naples or Burgundy, with a taste for coarse farce which struck Flaubert more than anything else. Even genuine disputes (except for those merciless ones over

28

family claims to a strip of land or a ditch or a girl's honour) are veneered with an irony that reminds you of Marseilles.

Feast-days are costly, interminable and lively. On such occasions the poor gorge themselves as if to put themselves off food for the rest of their lives. The Egyptian is certainly fond of life, however poorly he lives it. He is both sentimental and mocking. He always prefers a leader who can mix a joke, however broad, into his flow of Arab eloquence, as in the case of Sa'd Zaghlul, Mustafa Nahas or Mohamed Neguib. Nasser might have spared both blood and trouble by being less austere and a bit more jovial. Good fellowship is the key to this nation of Robin Goodfellows.

The desire for well-being is, alas, a tendency rather than a reality. That is why the conditions of his daily life are not enough to explain the Egyptian's deep attachment to the soil. In the east the Arabs have not long outgrown nomadism. In the north the Palestinians, Syrians and Lebanese have fanned out all over the world in search of what their own overpopulated or invaded countries could not offer them. But here the desire for roots is turning an already over-burdened land into something like Balzac's wild asses' skin. However tragic and absurd it appears, this attachment to the native soil is one of the unchanging factors in Egyptian life, not only now but in times of prosperity and power. In the pageant of history the far-flung military expeditions of Sesostris, Thotmes III and the Rameses, even the peaceful missions of Amenemhat and Hatshepsut count for little or nothing. In view of the great human, military and financial resources at the disposal of the great dynasties, it is surprising that they went in so little for conquest. Thotmes III had the means and perhaps the genius of an Alexander. Yet he was content with gaining for Egypt the Syrian 'marches', the control of the spice-routes and tribute from the tribes of the Taurus and Tigris. In the same way Mohamed Ali kept his eager son Ibrahim in check.

There have been no great Egyptian travellers. The world has come to the Nile, but no Egyptian returned the visits of Herodotus, Ibn Batuta or Chateaubriand. Apart from a few merchants prospecting in Crete or Phoenicia, Rifa'al-Tahtawi discovering the Paris of Balzac, or Mustafa Kamil seeking French support, Taha Husain visiting France in search of an intellectual discipline, the Egyptian has lived to himself, content to bask in the shade of the Sultan Hasan mosque. He hardly ventures over his own doorstep, unless we take recent visits to Monte Carlo into account . . . It is often said that the

French are stay-at-homes, but compared with the Egyptians they are globe-trotters. Nothing short of flood or famine can drive them out of their cramped villages, to which they are quick to return.

It is true that the Nubians could be brought or lured into the northern cities long before the Aswan Dam buried their lovely river-side villages. The Sa'idis of Upper Egypt, stifled and starved in the narrow valley, gradually moved to the industrial centres on the Delta, to become masons and turners in the suburbs of Cairo and Alexandria. But such internal movement has nothing to do with emigration. As under Kephren and Baibars the Egyptian is imprisoned in his magic valley. As they say in the bull-ring, he chooses to face his hard lot 'on his own ground', with his back turned to a forgotten history.

This introversion colours all modern Egypt's problems, whether it be the standard of living, distribution of population, the Sudan, the dams or national culture. Such an obstinate attachment to the soil becomes inertia, such stability becomes paralysis: this clinging to the valley reminds one of a mummy asleep in its sarcophagus. The Egyptian might well meet the fate of the royal mummies unless he undoes his own winding-sheet and ventures abroad—or else others will do it for him.

Anyone trying to look beyond these signs of unrest and diversity thus finds Egypt to be agricultural, pious, optimistic, submissive, superstitious, stay at home, impoverished and yet hedonistic. Nerval was being too clever when he called them 'a race of peasants who worship the sun': he could as well have said the Nile. It is a memoryless people, bogged down in the river ooze, tied to the Nile, cut off from the world by four deserts, ill equipped for escaping by way of the sea. Has it found the secret of its own renewal? To tame the Nile and exploit it properly, diverting its course into fresh land and using it to develop dormant energies, would be an unparalleled act of liberation, more important than the passage of Bonaparte, the works of Mohamed Ali, the building of the Suez Canal or the introduction of cotton. It would mean throwing off the age-old resignation, wresting its secrets from the tyrannical but life-giving river. The Nile on which Egypt's existence has always depended, mysteriously rising every summer on the same day, the 20th of July, was the very image of fate, the source of superstitions, resignation and proverbs. The Nile-God, Hapi, with its hanging dugs, could be unmasked and domesticated. Perhaps then we could expect a fresh start, a new outflow of energy, from a people suddenly aware of the basic mystery of its existence.

But in what direction could Egypt most profitably develop? If we look at a map of the country, its history and potential, nothing is more striking than the variety—or fluidity—of its possible methods of development. According to the map, or the Nile, or the native face, Egypt is African. Yet her best minds and her best friends abroad regard Egypt as a Mediterranean country. The fact that Egypt is Moslem does not mean adding some different concept, some fourth dimension. The Moslem polity is such that belonging to Islam creates a political, cultural and diplomatic community, a conscious sense of difference, the sense of a common destiny shared by all members of the *umma* or 'community of the faithful'. However badly placed twentieth-century Islam might be as regards thought, apologetics, the quality of its teachers, or however disappointing the reforms begun by El Afghani and Mohamed Abduh in the nineteenth century, spiritual apathy goes hand in hand with an impressive political awakening. Islam came into being through military conquest and can be recognized more through its men of action than through its philosophers—witness Jinnah, Musaddiq, Mohamed Ali and Nasser. The teaching of the Koran dictated by the archangel Gabriel to a Meccan merchant has become a password to revolution in much the same way as Lenin's pamphlets did. Of course Islam is not such a strongly hierarchized church as Communism. Yet we must not forget the responsibilities and prestige that Egypt has gained through its control of the University of El-Azhar, which is the Sorbonne and cathedral of Moslems all over the world.

Thus we must add Islam to the three other cardinal points of the Egyptian compass. It certainly explains Cairo's awareness of Asia, by way of Indian, Indonesian and even Chinese Islam. But African Islam also makes itself felt with its sixty million faithful, looking to Cairo for subsidies and teachers. Egypt faces serious problems in Africa, which could well lure her out of the Nile Valley and make her betray her ancient precepts which were once the basis of her greatness. After such a long period of humiliation that it is bound to dream of asserting power, Egypt must beware of confusing a natural Moslem proselytism with the idea of political expansion under the banner of Islam.

Is Egypt really Arabic? People often forget to examine what are no more than debatable theories. The Arab is an Asiatic, a white Semite, bound to a desert civilization or to towns which are but desert ports, a civilization of tent and horse. Proud, unproductive, changeable, with almond eyes, often blue, fond of war and movement, thin even when he is rich; or else grossly fat and delighting in grilled meats . . . No description could be more unlike the actual Egyptian, a bronzed African with black and often fuzzy hair, thick-set and on the heavy side, with protruding eyes, thick lips; peace-loving and every inch a peasant, thriving on the defeat of sand by the river slime, a rider of asses, eater of stews and green vegetables, a scraping and hoarding peasant whose only desire is to stay at home. It could be argued that the Nile peasant was naturalized Arab when he accepted the language and religion of his Arab neighbours, much as the Frenchman or Gaul was latinized by Caesar's legions. Arab influences came as a flame licking over a pool, changing its colour, if not its nature.

But Omar's warriors did not change the Egyptian into his very opposite, the Arab. A language, a religion, a way of life, monuments, writing, may upset a civilization but do not entirely replace it. The peasants have remained peasants, their mules have not become horses any more than their stews have turned into grilled steaks, nor have their wattle huts become leather tents. They have learnt Arabic but also throw in gobbets of Italian, Greek and Turkish. They have imbibed the Koran's lesson of detachment and above all the keen awareness of the vanity of things, the absurdity that goes with talent. Hence the *mā lish*, the 'God's will be done' which imposes such a steady rhythm on Egyptian life. If God does not will, then no fuss is made.

The present moment—a mere ripple on the face of history—demands that Nahas Pasha's and Nasser's Egypt should be 'Arab Egypt', indeed the supreme Arab state. Diplomats, journalists and onlookers hear nothing but the word *Arab* and think of nothing but Cairo.

Geography, ethnography, culture, would properly assign that part to Damascus, Baghdad, Jerusalem or Riyad. Only its reputation and political whim speak up for Cairo. It is true that the Nile Valley cuts the Arab world in half: it is Levantine from Israel to the Emirships of the Persian Gulf, and Maghrib on the other side in the direction of Fez. It cannot be denied that Cairo is the headquarters of the Arab League (or perhaps the divan on which it is languishing),

1. The four colossi of Abu Simbel watch over the Nile on the Sudan border

2a. Hatshepsut's soldiers return from the wars

2b. Rameses II exterminates the barbarians. From the Rames-
seum at Thebes

and the only great capital of the 'intermediary continent'. Egypt's promotion to the rank of Arab leader is none the less ironic, much the same as if England became leader of the Latin Bloc.

However ironic, it is a political fact which cannot be overlooked. Like Chaplin in 'Modern Times' being pushed to the front by a mob of strikers, after casually picking up a red flag, for the past ten or twelve years Egypt has been waving the Arab flag which fell into its hands after the turmoil of the recent war, whereas the Pan-Arab reformers had never dreamt of setting up their standard in such a place as Cairo. There is no point in raising eyebrows at the idea of an Arab Cairo. Being the refuge of so many political exiles, it was gradually soaked with dissatisfied and thus all the more efficient Arabism. The key or clue to Egyptian 'arabness' is therefore to be found in a common claim against the world, a similar sense of revolt. Cairo is far less Arab than Marrakesh, but their common bitterness is Arabic. Believers who find that they are strangers in their own city, they feel the same humiliation and share the same grievance. Cairo has not become the capital of Arabism because it is an Arab city, but because it is the centre of many protests of which Arabism is the most vocal.

Cairo stands at the meeting-point of two continents which have been exploited by an energetic and industrialized Europe. It is the obvious capital for Arab demands, being as it is an enormous, heavily populated metropolis, the melting-pot in which undying anger has slowly come to the boil. It is worth noting in passing that this so-called capital of Arab civilization did not produce a single literary magazine worthy of the name before 1956; that the greatest poets since Ibn al-Farid were conventional second-raters, and that its greatest living writer, Taha Husain, has done his best to link his work with the Mediterranean cultural tradition.

Can Egypt be regarded as Mediterranean rather than Arabic? Is she in any way the daughter of that great sea with its living cultures, Greek, Italian, Tunisian, its olive-trees and teachers? The answer is that there was nothing in Egypt on which the wisdom of the Cretan adventurers, the bold logic of Sicily, Phoenician ingenuity or Roman law could take a lasting grip. From Alexandria to El Arish there is nothing but a dreary stretch of sand, an ocean beach, the back shop of the desert rather than a landing-ground for Aristotle or the Commedia dell'Arte. Egypt faces inwards and not outwards, like those blind statues which are the failing of decadent

Graeco-Roman art. Alexander, Caesar and Napoleon came in from the sea, no doubt. But the Macedonian conqueror had to make at Alexandria the first outlet of any size to link Egypt with the Mediterranean, when she already had three thousand years of greatness behind her. Rome did not manage to graft Latin logic on to Egypt, but to find the germs of her own death, in an Oriental madness of despotism. Napoleon's expedition of 1798 was no Mediterranean holiday. It began with solemn homage or lip-service to the Asiatic Koran and petered out miserably on the beaches of Abukir Bay, Acre and Canopus.

Egypt's Mediterranean frontier is best seen in the spring, when one leaves Cairo for the sea. At about 12 miles from Alexandria the desert suddenly bristles with a bit of greenness, struggling with sterility. The line of green can be seen as plainly as a beach. On the west there is a straggle of vine, with some rice eastwards and fig-trees on each side. An occasional shower. The grocers are all Greek, while the hotel-keepers all go by the name of Xenophon or Achilles. Real masons are building real houses of real white stone. But this is only flotsam from the sea. It is true that Greek shop-keepers are to be found everywhere, down to the Sudan of which they are the real colonizers, while there is also something Neapolitan or Marseillais in the Egyptian peasant's broad laughter. Greek philosophy certainly underlies certain efforts towards spiritual revival, while Roman law has helped towards the structure of modern Egyptian life through the medium of the Napoleonic Civil Code. Thus the Mediterranean does not bathe Egypt to no purpose. Yet its influence is relatively feeble when compared with that of the Red Sea on the east, that Arab lake which is the path to Asia, or when compared with the influences drifting from the desert. Not to mention the Nile itself, *el Bahr, the sea*, as the peasants call it, that Nile which has the whole of Africa behind it.

Egypt is African. Geographers are less often wrong than historians and philosophers. Almost all the latter—Hegel, Renan for instance —try to explain away Egypt and all it stands for through some mysterious Aryan strain which mingles with the Hamitic, Semitic and negroid strains. The plea for a black Egypt made by Sheikh Anta Diop in his book *Negro Nations and Culture* is more convincing and confirms Herodotus and Volney. An analysis of physical types based on early statuary, and of the social and political structure of the great dynasties, does not entirely bear out this hypothesis. The idea that the kings of the fourth, twelfth or nineteenth dynasties were negroid cannot be proved by the Kephren effigies. These are short-headed, with a long straight nose and square chin. Thotmes III looks like one of Donatello's pages, while Rameses II is shown with almond eyes and a Semitic profile. As against a few negroid mummies, a few statues of Viziers and notables with long skulls and pronounced fore-arms, we can point to many square faces with harshly defined features, the heads of tropical Celts. We are forced to return to the very essence of Egyptian manners and Egyptian folk, based on a unique situation, that of a river-shaped oasis which links up tropical forest with an enclosed sea. Egypt does not conform to ordinary standards. The mould of the Nile Valley has produced a people 'unlike any other, yet in which everyone looks the same, as was the case with the Scythians', as Hippocrates remarked (quoted by Volney).

It cannot be denied, however, that the great river has never ceased carrying through that self-contained world all the smell and passions and imagination of the negro, something that is black, limitless, naturistic, furious, and which raises Egyptian art above all its imitators. The art of the Nile speaks of the forest, of the forces of nature, animal gods, hymns to the sun, the perennial lotus, water and fire, and man calling on them to be still. However disciplined he was and in spite of his layer of pre-Hellenic reason, the artist of dynastic times had a creative imagination that was often negro. Whence that monstrous and sublime forest of stone, the hypostyle chamber of Karnak, or the tombs of the nobles transformed by a bold decorator into picnic clearings for dancing to jazz; or that mountain turned into a temple, Abu-Simbel, guarded by four colossi in quiet conversation with the Sun-King. At the gateway to the Sudan, on the banks of the Nile, Egyptian optimism mingles with the virility of Ham.

The enormous artery that carries along its stream of black blood after passing for nearly two thousand miles through a forest full of naked giants daubed with ashes and grey mud, must be regarded as Egypt's life-force. Before long, the Nile will be the only river in the world that does not flow into the sea. Once the Aswan dam is completed, not a drop of water from Lake Tana or Lake Victoria will reach Rosetta or Damietta, where the sea will push back into the river. The Nile waters, entirely canalized, redistributed, employed, passed through turbines and filtered through dams, will be entirely absorbed into Egyptian soil. Thus the country will definitely turn its back on the Mediterranean, folding in on its river and towards Africa.

Egypt was Mediterranean from Alexander's invasion till the Chalcedon Council, and then again in the nineteenth century. It remains Arab in so much as Arabism is a valid form of protest for a colonized people. It is Asiatic in its mind and heart, it turns eastwards to pray. Thanks to Western clumsiness it is through India and China that it receives the few sparks of renewal that appear to be free from any taint of imperialism. It has been increasingly African since the revival of the black continent began.

The Khedive Isma'il, eighty years ago, wanted Egypt to be a part of Europe. At a time when Europe was everything there was some sense in trying to attach his country to it in spite of everything. But today, when the balance of world power has been heavily displaced, we must not take the Khedive's pretensions lightly. For the Egyptian revolution was set off by Europe in the nineteenth century. The history of modern Egypt begins in the West, with the progressive awakening to a sense of State, increased production, free thought, and the capacities of man. All this made its impact on a society that had been worn down by Ottoman colonization, which was no more than a system of economic exploitation, and which till then had learnt nothing of Islamic teaching but a few negative precepts, a few illusions and a certain amount of spiritual comfort.

Part One

THE AWAKENING OF EGYPT

I

The Advent of Bonaparte

What is happening here is of the utmost interest, and will have immense
effects on trade and civilization. Great revolutions will date from this
epoch. *Letter from Bonaparte to Kléber, 22. 8. 1798*

Such was the state of decline and torpor into which Egypt had fallen
at the end of the eighteenth century that even Bonaparte was unable
to rouse it. Sixty years later the appearance of Commodore Perry's
ship off Nagasaki was enough to set all Japan to work. But the
Egyptians of Murad Bey's time were less alive to possibilities. The
intervention of a *condottiere* from the Balkans was needed for the
lessons of the expedition to bear fruit.

Yet it is no exaggeration to see the landing at Alexandria as the
first act in the long Egyptian revolution. It would be more exact to
speak of a 'reawakening' or reanimation, for the way this ancient
country was treated by her last foreign masters—from Mohamed
Ali to Lord Cromer—was little short of artificial respiration. However little they interested the Egyptians and however harmful they
first appeared, Bonaparte with his troops and scientists left Egypt
the seeds of restlessness, uncertainty and uneasiness in which all the
later upheavals had their origin. They broke down the structure of
military feudalism which was stifling Egypt and thus made the way
clear for future uprisings.

But whether we use the term revolution or revival, we must note
that the great movement which has taken a century and a half to
raise Egypt from her humiliating position as mere Turkish farmland
to that of a responsible modern State, owes its slowness and the
relative meagreness of its results to the fact that Egypt was not
only kept waiting on the doorstep of the modern world, but was
also, unlike Japan and Morocco, completely stripped of her national
character.

The revolution thus took place in two stages or, more exactly, at
two levels:

39

The first stage was to bring a listless and leaderless people back into the cycle of modern life, with its diplomacy, techniques, culture and science.

The second stage tended towards returning to the Egyptian people —or rather to its ruling groups, which were first an oligarchy, then a slowly emerging nationalistic bourgeoisie—the power which had been seized by a dynasty whom their services in the way of modernization made none the less alien, and which was again seized by 'protectors' with little concern for national feelings.

It is not enough to assert that, contrary to what happens in most cases of national emancipation, the two stages remained distinct in Egypt. As the modernization of Egypt was done by foreign hands, first by the Albanian dynasty and then by British technicians, progress appeared less attractive to the Egyptians than it might otherwise have been. If Mohamed Ali had been an Egyptian fellah, things would probably have moved faster. Then the second phase of the revolution, Egyptianization, would not have taken the form of resisting modernization or of hostility to the most constructive undertakings achieved by foreign countries. The two terms, liberation and progress, might have supplemented each other instead of appearing contradictory.

Modernization and self-rule are the two movements or impulses which, either alternately or sometimes together, made for the renewal of an Egypt which had only too long suffered from the separation of these two ideals. Finally the Wafd, just after the first World War, and after them the rebel officers in July 1952, each in turn managed to reconcile Egypt's will to play its part in the modern world and the exercise of power by the Egyptians themselves.

Thus a century and a half of haphazard efforts, forced measures and abortive risings, find their meaning today. A revolution has come into being and taken shape, the effects of which will go on accumulating even though its leaders might be changed by foreign interference. And a century and a half is not so long, once we take stock of the state Egypt was in before the French 'army of Italy' appeared on the scene.

'Political anarchy, social degradation and intellectual inertia made the last quarter of the eighteenth century the unhappiest period in the whole history of Egypt.' We are the more ready to believe Volney as his remarks confirm those of neutral travellers who cannot be suspected of trying to justify a colonial adventure by giving pessimistic accounts of what they saw, for instance Norden, Browne and Pocock. They were unanimous that 'Egypt is dying: Egypt is dead'.

They all saw the state of Egypt as the effect of a casual abandonment, and blamed it on the Mamelukes. But how are we to explain how those Circassian slaves, the Mamelukes, who were 'imported' from the Caucasus by the Fatimid Caliphs, were responsible for a kind of political and artistic renaissance in Egypt, from the fourteenth to the sixteenth centuries? The reigns of Qala'un and Qait Bey were no less remarkable than those of the great Nile Valley kings. Admiring their monuments which rise sharply all over Cairo, Gabriel Hanotaux had to admit that they were 'half-civilized'. We regard the builders of the mosques dedicated to those princes as certainly civilized, no less than their Italian contemporaries with their machiavellian politics, wringing money out of Popes and patronizing poets.

It was the Turkish conquest which turned these fine princes into a gang of robbers. While they were the free founders of dynasties they behaved much as native rulers would have done. Once beaten, they became greedy middlemen, insatiable landowners, 'reigning as kings with the souls of slaves' as Volney so splendidly put it.

No sooner had the Ottoman sultans made themselves masters of Egypt, early in the sixteenth century—just when the discovery of the Cape of Good Hope was ruining Egypt as the old route to Asia— than they spread anarchy in order to keep the country in a passive state. In order to secure their rule the Porte divided authority between its representative the Pasha, the Divan of Notables and 24 Mameluke beys. The latters' sole task was to offset the Pasha's authority and collect taxes. As soon as a representative of the Porte showed a little authority or fair play, they would league against him, depose him with a cry of 'Inzil' (resign) and, if he was lucky, ship him off to Constantinople. This was the case with Ahmed Kemal Pasha in 1750, for trying to improve his knowledge of the colony's finance.

In all this amazing system of organized impotence there was one positive institution, the *ruznameh*, which imposed and collected taxes. This alone enjoyed the Porte's attention and was given an aura of sanctity and clothed in the greatest mystery. The financial records—which make special mention of the *iltizams* or farming-out of taxes, and their *multazims* or buyers of the right to extort, who were nearly all Mamelukes—were drawn up in a secret code which all the civil servants handling money were forbidden to reveal, under pain of frightful punishment, except to their own son who inherited the office, or to their adopted slave. Thus the exploitation of Egyptian farmlands by the Turks and their agents was very thorough and went unpunished at all levels. The only official crime in fiscal matters was an indiscretion on the accountants' part.

Clever though the system of taxation might have been, it gradually lost its effectiveness as the exhausted and desperate country became less productive. Volney could find nothing but

'ruined villages, revolting nakedness, hideous rags, smoke-blackened shacks where the talk is of nothing but extortion, beatings and murders . . . a government indifferent to everybody's property or safety, a coarse and licentious soldiery which leaves the peasants just enough to prevent them from dying'.

A French traveller of the same period, J.-B. Trécourt, a merchant, observed with insight, 'The people are tormented with impunity. But what is the result? Greed defeats its own object. The worker who knows that the fruit of his labours will be seized by exorbitant levies would rather let part of his land lie idle than farm it.' As Volney concluded, 'Under the barbarous rule of ignorant despotism, there can be no tomorrow.'

No tomorrow? And yet it was the same observer who said of the fellahs that 'the riots that occur when their patience is exhausted shows that there is a smouldering fire which will burst into flame as soon as a man appears who knows how to poke it'. Referring to some future 'peasants' league' which in his opinion would alone be able to drive out the Mamelukes, he had to admit that there was one obstacle to 'any successful revolution: the population's total ignorance'.

But it was not only the neglected peasantry that was ignorant. The pashas, the beys, the administrative and military leaders and the ruling oligarchies did not even know the country's native language. The oldest university in Islam, El Azhar, was sunk in a leaden sleep. The few remaining rudiments of science were smothered by the Koran, and even its teaching was overgrown with superstition, simple-mindedness and fantasies which survived the lectures of Monge. Half a century later Sheikh Tatawi, who boldly brought French culture into Egypt, was outraged at the idea of gravitation, although it was the Arabian astronomer El-Biruni (Abu-Rihan) who laid the foundations of the theory in the eleventh century. The whole culture of Egypt was in a state of decadence.

'If it were controlled by a nation that protects the arts, this beautiful country could once again be the centre of the world's trade. It could be the bridge connecting Europe and Asia. This happy land would once more be the home of the sciences and the most delightful place on earth. These ideas, Sir, are not mere fancy.'

That is what Bonaparte's companions found in Savary's *Letters from Egypt*, which was their favourite reading. The expedition began with high hopes, thanks to the optimistic views of this amiable traveller from the south of France. After their return home they read the sober-minded Volney more carefully.

We are not much concerned at the moment with knowing why the Egyptian expedition was undertaken, and how much it owed to Leibniz's advice to Louis XIV, Choiseul's to Louis XV, or Talleyrand's to the Directory. Did they hope to set up a colony, take the English from the rear, get rid of the awkward Bonaparte in favour of Pichegru, avenge and recoup the French merchants who had fallen victims to the Turks, and graft revolutionary deism on to anti-clerical Islam? We are only interested, here, in the Egyptian campaign's effects, which were both modest and important.

'The year 1213 marked the beginning of epic battles, tremendous events, disastrous deeds, frightful calamities, total confusion, the overthrow of the natural order of things, revolutions, continual terror, social disorders, political discord, general devastation.' Such are the terms in which the Egyptian chronicler Gabarti began his record of the 1798 expedition. It does not tell us all the reactions that it caused in Egypt itself. But at least it shows how the French troops were at first received—as infidel invaders, descendants of the Crusaders of Damietta.

However impoverished the Egyptian people were, both materially and culturally, they still had one certainty, one sign of life, which was their attachment to Islam. They were perhaps still more stunned and bullied than at the time of Byzantine rule on the eve of the Arab invasion. But this time they were not inclined to welcome the foreign troops as liberators, since everything suggested that they came not only for plunder but as enemies of their religion. Their awareness of belonging to the Moslem community was nevertheless quite negative, little more than a sense of difference, which stiffened in the foreigner's presence.

The reasons why the enterprise failed can be traced from the very beginning. These lay in a total and permanent lack of understanding, based on the difference between two civilizations, the one dynamic and expanding and looking to the future; the other indrawn, locked in its poverty, armed with nothing but mistrust.

However much the Mameluke beys and Turkish civil servants were detested, they at least had the same religious faith as the masses. The French conqueror, unlike his Arab predecessors of the seventh century, was unable to exploit a hatred of authority that was even stronger than community of religion.

Bonaparte tackled the problem boldly and sincerely. Being aware that religion was all that held the social fabric together, he tried to use it to strengthen his position. The most curious thing about his Egyptian policy was its strictly Moslem character. We have seen all kinds of 'Moslem policies' at the hands of the British, Spanish, Italians and Russians. But apart from local specialists like Lawrence, probably nobody has gone further than Bonaparte towards the victor's spiritual immersion in his conquest. Even before going to Egypt, Bonaparte loved Islam. He kept and was obsessed by this attachment all his life. He spent most of his conversation with Goethe in discussing Mohamed, while Islam occupied his thoughts and gave him an endless subject of conversation on Saint Helena to the last hours of his life.

An anti-Trinitarian, anti-clerical Deist, he admired a religion which was so monotheistic and without its clergy or Vatican. Assuming the role of Caesar towards the Pope, even to the point of summoning the sovereign pontiff to Paris for the sole purpose of having him bless the unusual coronation on the 2nd of December, what he liked about Islam was its identification of religion and politics. He remarked to Gourgaud that 'it is ridiculous for a head of State not to be head of its religion'. He liked the apparently sensual aspects of the Koran's teaching. The great Caliphs embodied a conception of the State that was his own; a need for order tempered by some regard for counsel, ceremony, the concern to exercise strength with justice, a taste for speech-making, the application of warlike principles to all aspects of life and government. The profound submission to the chief of state which he sensed everywhere in Islam was not likely to displease him.

In offering his hand to Islam, Bonaparte was not only being 'clever', as Thiers suggested. He pushed certain gestures beyond mere plausible sincerity. It is not well enough known that the first Decree issued in Alexandria, the day after a fairly difficult landing in which Kléber and Menou were wounded, bore in the Arabic translation the words 'The French are real Moslems', and not merely the words 'the sincere friends of the Moslems' as in the original text. Writing to Menou, who was converted to Islam in order to marry an Egyptian, he spoke of 'Our Prophet'. One of the historians of the expedition reports that in the course of one of the long meetings he had with the four Mufti of Cairo, there was talk of the expeditionary force making a mass conversion to Islam. The negotiations broke down on two points: there might have been a compromise on the matter of circumcision, but it was impossible to reach agreement on the use of wine.

Bonaparte's outstretched hand was not taken. Cairo rose in arms at the call of the Imams. Of course Egyptian Islam would have had much to gain by more prolonged exchanges with these 'Men of the Revolution'. It might have taken courage and made the effort of elementary self-criticism and exegesis which Sheikh Mohamed Abduh began nearly a century later. Indeed, the optimistic naturalism and somewhat simple-minded scientism of the Egyptian reformer's teaching has much in common with the state of mind of Bonaparte's companions. But Bonaparte met nobody of Abduh's stature. In studying the relations between the expeditionary force and the Egyptian people we often come across the gulf which has been forthrightly described by the Egyptian historian, Anwar Luqa.[1] Egypt was not ripe for what the expedition had to teach. It was not ready to profit from it, it had no idea how to accept the opportunity for progress which was offered.

This rift, this lack of understanding, showed itself especially in the technical and scientific fields. The importance Bonaparte attached to the Institute of Egypt's work is well known. He was anxious for its meetings to be open to all eminent Egyptians. An echo of those strange discussions is to be found in the chronicles of Gabarti, son of a well-known astronomer, and himself regarded as one of the most representative Egyptian intellectuals of the day. Asked for his opinion on some problem of ornithology, the good Gabarti found it enough to answer 'The Prophet said that there are 10,000 species of birds in the sky and 30,000 species of fish in the sea.' One should read the

[1] *Cahiers d'histoire égyptienne, 1955,* Cairo.

reflections prompted in the good man by an unsuccessful attempt to release a balloon over Cairo. At the same time he was not a little surprised when the French authorities assembled a genuine court for the correct legal trial of Kléber's assassin, one Sulaiman of Aleppo: 'This trial gives an idea of what the French regard to be justice, belonging to a nation without religion, but who follow the dictates of reason.'

In fact, all contact was purely formal. The French worked 'in' Egypt but not, as they would have liked, 'upon' Egypt. To be sure, some surprising technical and even industrial achievements by the engineer Conté were noted: 'they constructed hydraulic machines, and made steel, arms and cloth as well as mathematical and optical instruments', according to the *Description of Egypt*. 'The Egyptians were not slow in sharing the benefits brought by these projects . . . they carefully examined the products of French industry and tried to imitate them.' But such attempts at 'imitation' do not seem to have outlasted the occupation. At the most these hints at industrialization prepared a handful of Egyptian artisans for the efforts demanded of them by Mohamed Ali twenty years later. 'Soon we were making hats, boots and belts; the Turks imitated our embroidery to perfection and were clever at making things which were completely foreign to their way of life.' Here the stress falls in the right place, for there were so few points of contact between the two civilizations or ways of life that the lessons of the one could hardly profit the other. Bonaparte's followers were offering Egypt a currency which had no circulation there, which might have come from another planet or another age. The expedition is often credited with setting up Egyptian newspapers, but the *Décade Egyptienne* was little more than the bulletin of the Institute's meetings, while the *Courrier d'Égypte* was addressed entirely to the expeditionary corps. Both of these publications were printed in French.

Perhaps one aspect of the Frenchmen's presence ought to have struck the population and given it some urge to learn the invaders' secrets: that is to say the art of war as 'invented'—according to his rival Moreau—by Bonaparte with the help of European technology. It cannot be denied that the crushing of the Mamelukes struck their imagination. But the Egyptians had already seen many a brilliant general, hurling thunder . . . Nor must we forget that the successful Battle of the Pyramids was quickly followed by defeat at Abukir and the bitter retreat from Acre. We can only say that the Mamelukes' defeat by Bonaparte deepened the discredit into which they had already fallen, and prepared their overthrow by Mohamed Ali.

Yet we must look elsewhere for the fruitful and revolutionary aspects of the expedition's influence. First was the founding and work of the Egyptian Institute. This was short-lived (1798–1801) and the tasks Bonaparte assigned to it rose from the needs of the moment, the first requirement being to provide for the army, notably by finding some way of making leavened bread. The troops had declared Egyptian unleavened bread to be uneatable. However, the hospitals founded by Desgenettes and Larrey were not reserved for the troops, and outlasted the occupation. Braut's work on ophthalmia was the basis for an attack on the commonest and perhaps the most painful of diseases that afflict the Egyptian fellah. The Institute library where, according to Gabarti, 'those Moslems who took some interest in science were gladly helped', must have been the starting-point for many a scholarly career.

But perhaps it was the fiscal system worked out by Poussielgue and Estève, based on the Ottoman *Ruznameh's* accounts (which were divulged under threat of punishment by an official who had compromised himself in the Cairo rising), which made the most direct impact on Egyptians and most contributed to creating a new relationship between the administration and the law. Though taxation remained very heavy it ceased to depend merely on the collectors' requirements and began to be adjusted to the taxpayer's needs, the size of his property and the size of his crops. The taxpayer found that the new system made for stability and efficiency. Another politically effective change was that the French authorities insisted that the top officials dealing with taxation should be made up of eight Egyptian Moslems. Thus the Mamelukes no longer held the higher offices while Copts took over the collecting. Consciously or not, Bonaparte thus ended one of the most bitter causes of strife between Moslem and Christian, the latter being regarded until then as the greedy middleman, an agent of financial tyranny in the interests of alien rulers.

There was yet another positive thing about the expedition. Despite the two Cairo risings, a campaign that was 'worse than that of the Vendée' according to a letter from Dumas to Kléber, and the licentiousness of the troops whose 'approach to the women set the people against them'; despite the malpractices and looting that always go with such undertakings, yet certain human relationships or what we now call 'coexistence' came into being between the soldiers and people, and sometimes between officers and local notables. Gabarti, who cannot be accused of being indulgent to the occupying forces, noted that 'the French soldiers walked unarmed through the Cairo streets and molested no-one. They joked with the people and paid good prices for what they bought. This encouraged the people to make contact with them.'

Almost all those who wrote about the expedition later, such as Miot, Galland, Rigault and Richardot, often stressed the 'high spirits and affableness' of the Egyptian peasant, his 'gentle and peaceful nature, by no means cold or fanatical'. One of them wrote, 'by knowing the country's language . . . the French could have identified themselves, so to speak, with the inhabitants . . . they could have imbued those half-savage minds with the sweet dew of a sound philosophy'. Perhaps this warm contact between the two peoples was the best justification the expedition could have had: perhaps it was this which partly 'opened' an Egypt which had been morosely closed to the outside world for three hundred years, and prepared it for becoming the most hospitable land on earth. Most overseas ventures give a poor impression of their country of origin; the quality of the men concerned, the methods which are used and the immorality of the situation as a whole make the native see the colonizer as something uglier than he really is.

Such was not the case with this extraordinary undertaking, which was a military expedition, a scientific investigation and a cultural mission all in one. Its young leader, only 29, still full of generous illusions but already excelling in the handling of men, thirsting for knowledge and sympathy and who was beginning to bring his lucid and penetrating intellect to bear on the world at large, was accompanied by some of the wisest and bravest citizens of a country which was then the most active and fruitful in Europe—men such as Monge, Desaix, Cafarelli, Desgenettes, Berthollet, Larrey, Geoffroy Saint-Hilaire, Kléber, or the remarkable Vivant-Denon, draughtsman, writer, explorer and archaeologist who made notes of low-reliefs while under enemy fire—a kind of learned Fragonard who shared all the fatigues and dangers of the troops. These men's achievement has lost none of its impressiveness. But it is hard to assess what Egypt got from it.

France's brief encounter with Egypt planted a few seeds, however transient and devoid of political consequences it was. The ideas Bonaparte advanced in his meetings with the Ulama; the library into

48

which Gabarti sometimes wandered; the example of Desaix—the 'just Sultan'—who forgot to crush Murad Bey's Mamelukes because he was so intent on admiring the temple of Denderah; the introduction of the French language into middle-class merchants' families; the setting up of an administration which, for the time being, catered for the needs of the majority; Conté's busy workshops; the beginnings of town planning and some attempts at draining sewage; a few examples of the meaning of justice (such as Bonaparte's clemency towards the Cairo rebels); and finally the proof that 'infidels' could enter an Islamic country without being bent on religious constraint or extermination—all this was enough to make the Egyptians think, enough to make them question many of the taboos on which the closed community of Egyptian Islam was based. It is worth remembering that in 1846 Ampère was accosted by a Suez beggar who addressed him as 'Citizen'.

Through the breach Bonaparte made in the Egyptian citadel were to flow adventurers, new ideas, invaders, reforms, civil-engineers, canals, dykes, schools, a public debt, a pack of troubles—in brief, the world. The undeniable result of the expedition was to fling Egypt into the whirlpool of international politics. Bonaparte had been unable to modify its internal structure or even interest the nation's *élite* in making some effort toward sounder intellectual discipline and more modern organization. He left a legacy of unrest, an unbalance which was to rouse Egypt from its sleep.

After Bonaparte nothing could be quite as it had been before. His stay in the country marks the essential break with the past, the beginning of the first phase of the Egyptian revolution and the bringing of a listless old country into the cycle of modern life.

II

Mohamed Ali Creates a State

Mohamed Ali was a natural consequence of Bonaparte. Without the Corsican artilleryman the Macedonian tobacco-merchant would perhaps have come to seek his fortune in Egypt, being already informed about Europe and the importance of international trade by his associate, the Marseilles business-man, Lion. He might have become rich, but he would probably not have created a state.

We need not linger over the manner of his rise to power, which was constantly favoured by the Expedition and its aftermath. He arrived in Egypt with a force of Albanians sent by the Sublime Porte in order to drive out the French, then acted as arbiter between the two great Mamelukes Alfi and Bardisi, who would never have allowed him to play such a part without the humiliating defeat of 1798. The newcomer found his path clear because the driving power of the Circassian 'samurai' was broken. Neither London nor Constantinople would have allowed Mohamed Ali's power to grow so rapidly had not Napoleon drawn to himself the entire attention of governments, armies and fleets.

But the following of Mohamed Ali on Bonaparte was not just a matter of circumstances. It can be traced also in the means by which the Albanian seized power, and in his methods such as an excess of centralization, state-capitalism, the conduct of war, his adventurous but realistic view of history, his imported but fervent patriotism.

At first glance the Viceroy's conquests and diplomatic activity seem to have little to do with Egypt. They appeared less inspired by national than by family considerations, tending particularly to bring pressure to bear on Sultan Mahmud in order to grasp the hereditary throne of Cairo. But the arrival of Egyptian ships in Navarino Harbour and Ibrahim's appearance on the Taurus none the less had a deep significance; they showed that Egypt, scarcely emerged from its ghetto, could suddenly play a preponderant role in the deliberations of the great Powers. We were speaking a few moments ago of an awakening, a revival, yet here is Egypt acting on an equal footing with England, Russia and the Porte less than forty years after Bonaparte . . .

We will dwell particularly on four aspects of Mohamed Ali's career because they form important stages in the Egyptian revolution: these are his 'election' as Pasha of Cairo by the representatives of the people; the confiscation of land that he apparently carried out for his own benefit; the mobilization of the fellahs, and his treatment of ethnic minorities. Each of these steps was to leave a deep mark on Egypt's later development.

As early as 1803 the French Consul-General, Mathieu de Lesseps, made it known in Paris that 'the *bikbashi* Mohamed Ali, of all the leaders in the field, is the best equipped for raising Egypt from anarchy'. Two years later his successor Drovetti remarked, in greater detail, that in the midst of intrigues which opposed Mamelukes, Kurdish *delis*, Arna'uts (Albanians) and the Turkish Pasha one against the other, 'Mohamed Ali, courting both the sheikhs and their subjects, convinces them that poor administration is the root of all evil . . . he directs the most important citizens' opinions while aspiring to be carried to supreme power by popular vote.' This interest in the popular will is unusual in a man from the Ottoman world where so little concern is shown for the 'people' or for that matter for the 'most important citizens'. Is there a Western influence to be seen here? It appears more likely that Mohamed Ali's insight sensed the rise of a new force grouped round the *suqs* and the mosques, a kind of half-trading and half-religious class, certainly very active, which was already the kernel of the nationalist *bourgeoisie* which had worried Bonaparte, and which was to bring Arabi, then Zaghlul and finally Nasser to power.

While the French diplomats were watching the rising star of Mohamed Ali, the *condottiere* himself was keeping his eye on a certain Sheikh Umar Makram, the oracle and leader of the people. He saw him to be earnest, energetic, respected, and decided to act only with his agreement. Thus it was the people, following a Sheikh Umar, who proclaimed Mohamed Ali Pasha of Cairo on the 12th of May 1805. While the Turkish Pasha, Khurshid, was refusing to resign and hiding in the Citadel, Drovetti sent the following despatch to Paris: 'Everywhere the same enthusiasm reigns as there was in France during the Revolution . . . Mohamed Ali has thrown in his lot with the people who are his strength.' And Drovetti was already scoffing at 'this nation which has never heard the fable about the frogs who asked for a king'.

But the important point is not the way in which the Pasha used his new rank, which he had obtained with popular support, but that such a promotion should have occurred at all, and that a native Egyptian movement, while unable to exercise power of its own, could at least delegate it to the least unjust of the available tyrants. The new master was not long in seizing complete control of all possible sources of power; the land, trade—through a system of monopolies—and the nation's whole military strength after the massacre of the Mamelukes. The *bourgeoisie* stood by and watched, subdued and perhaps fascinated by their chosen master's tremendous adventure, at the same time as he clearly cut himself off from his old allies by leaving Cairo, making Alexandria his capital, with its outlook on the sea, the Porte and Europe.

But the Egyptian people's fate and opinion did not leave the Pasha as indifferent as historians have suggested. Witness the strange pronouncement he made to the French Consul, Drovetti, when the latter proposed to him on Polignac's behalf that he might join the French expedition against Algiers: 'If I did so I would be dishonoured in my people's eyes. I am not reasoning thus for religious motives, for I am no more Moslem than Christian in my politics. But I am something, if at all, thanks to my national reputation and the opinion in which my people hold me.' His remark about being no more Moslem than Christian in his politics goes all the farther as it is the expression of a truth and marks a revolution—Egypt's transition from the status of a canton of Islam to that of a national state; from the notion of the *umma* or community of believers, to that of *watan*, the fatherland. Thus it was from a Balkan pasha, of Albanian origin and Turkish responses, that a new Egyptian unity emerged which was based no longer on religion but on politics. Except for the Greek campaign all his wars were waged against Moslem countries—Arabia, Syria and Turkey—and with the more or less open help of Christian powers.

It is also to be noted that he made constant use of Christians in his domestic policy. His main strength lay in the Armenian Boghos while his advisers were European experts and his immediate entourage was made up of Greeks and Copts. This calm neutrality in religion and politics was to become one of the basic characteristics of Egyptian

52

nationalism. We meet it mainly at the time of the 1919 revolution and throughout the history of the Wafd, during which a political synthesis was effected between Christianity and Islam. It must not, therefore, be forgotten that Mohamed Ali helped to form this Egyptian virtue, whatever might have been his intentions.

But the general confiscation of land cannot be judged so favourably. Before Mohamed Ali, to be sure, Egyptian nationals owned very little property. The Sultan Selim had seized most of the land in the 16th century, so that it was to all intents and purposes leased out by the Porte. In his turn his lieutenant, the Pasha, distributed whatever the Mamelukes had not seized, among his favourites or higher civil servants. Those of them who were not landowners were given a share in the farming of taxes (the *iltizam*) in one of the provinces. There were few land-owning fellahs whose property was not burdened with life-long payments of ground-rent. What with confiscations, usurpation of rights and the agrarian debt (for where ownership survived at all it was offset by a crippling taxation), the Egyptians were as strangers in their own land. But Mohamed Ali's appropriation of the land was so harsh and clumsy that it managed to shock and grieve people who thought it had already seen the worst.

Not that the principle was bad in itself. If there is any country where state-control is justified, in the form of either socialism or state-capitalism, it is Egypt, where the Nile and the need for distributing water make for a lasting and fundamental community of interests. The Pasha of Alexandria was really only returning to the state structure of the ancient dynasties, in which the Pharaoh owned everything and was the sole distributor of all the means of life. The undertaking could be justified so long as it did not result in new economic pressure on the fellahs.[1]

Mohamed Ali set himself up as the only proprietor, manufacturer and business-man in all Egypt. Each year, according to the European market, he decided what acreage had to be sown with a given crop, whether grain, cotton, mulberry or indigo. The harvest, of which part was held for taxation, was placed in public warehouses, valued and paid for at low rates by the fiscal agents. Such radical planning looks well enough on the surface. It guaranteed immense resources

[1] Before the end of his reign failure had to be admitted and the system collapsed. The Viceroy's second heir, Mohamed Said, undertook a vast redistribution of land which was the basis for the large estates. This remained extraordinarily stable, covering one-third of the land in 1880 and the same amount in 1945.

for the Treasury, making it possible to reconstruct the state and finance Ibrahim's campaigns. But closer investigation reveals a system of forced labour which was as inhuman as any ever known to Egypt. Mr Edward Lane's description of the manners and customs of the modern Egyptians describes every form of oppression of the peasantry, with fellahs constantly being hanged, buried alive, beaten and loaded with chains, never mind the way the poor wretches were fleeced at every turn. Another historian of that reign reports that different weights were used for measuring the harvest and the goods in kind that were given in exchange.

However loathsome they always were, these attempts to change things are instructive. They show one of the extreme solutions to the problems set by Egypt's agricultural production. Perhaps, stripped of its oppressive machinery of exploitation, and applied by a carefully selected civil service, the Viceroy's experiment in estate-management might yet prove indispensable. Its revolutionary value lay in the fact that it allowed a total rationalization of agriculture and was entirely systematic, adjusting Egypt's production to the needs of the world market. It was yet another step towards the internationalization of Egypt. From then on the fellah was working for the French industrialist or the British consumer. The old Chinese wall was cracking.

None the less, for the wall to come down it needed to be pushed from the inside. Necessity forced Mohamed Ali to use a measure which, strange as it may seem, was to do much to revive Egypt. This was national conscription. This was the most unpopular of his innovations. For more than two thousand years the Egyptians had endured everything, but had never been asked to fight. The fellah hates war. This pacifist outlook was one of the causes of the misfortunes under which he had to labour, for in order to defend the country the Caliphs had been forced to 'buy' soldiers from the Caspian, and this was the origin of the Mamelukes' military oligarchy. Rid of these and having little confidence in his Albanian compatriots, Mohamed Ali first tried setting up a Sudanese legion with the herd of slaves captured during his second son Isma'il's campaigns. However, 20,000 of these poor men let themselves die of grief in the huge Aswan barracks into which they were crowded. Only the fellahs remained.

Their resistance to conscription has become notorious, and the self-inflicted wounds they invented to escape it reminds one of the tortures inflicted by the tax-officers: 'Peasant women would destroy one of their son's eyes by smearing it with rat-poison. As the Copts who paid poll-tax were exempt, young Moslems had a cross tattooed on their wrists. Other fellahs had their teeth drawn, knowing that soldiers needed all their teeth for opening cartridges . . .' so writes a contemporary Egyptian author, Ibrahim al-Mu'ilhi. And at about the same time Lady Hester Stanhope observed that 'those who were conscripted never came back: whoever had been a soldier in Ibrahim's army ceased to be one only at his death'.

Between 1820 and 1830 Mohamed Ali succeeded in raising a national army of over 200,000 men, who conducted themselves admirably under fire throughout the Greek and Syrian campaigns, and who were to distinguish themselves for some twenty years. Owing to a foreign sovereign's ambition the Egyptian fellah was thus in a sense reborn. These peasant regiments formed the first leaders of Egyptian nationalism, Arabi and Ali Fahmi. Born of a movement supported by the common people, Mohamed Ali's tyranny thus prepared the way for other future risings. Alien in origins and outlook, it helped to lay the basis of a genuine nationalism.

Despite the excesses of its cosmopolitanism, Mohamed Ali's reign was to prove fruitful for the nation as a whole, if not for the individual Egyptian. In less than half a century this debased province of the Turkish Empire suddenly rose to the rank of a Mediterranean Power, easily dominating the Moslem world of Africa and the Near East. The country had been turned into an enormous galley, but it was a galley that could sail. The Viceroy had created a superb national army, laid the foundations of industry, reorganized agriculture, forced Egyptian products into the European market, and encouraged the production of cotton, a crop which was to become Egypt's greatest source of wealth. But here we must digress for a moment.

III

The Cotton Boom

There was cotton in Egypt before Mohamed Ali came. Grown in India from 3000 B.C., it was probably brought to the Nile Valley during the period of Assyrian rule. Except for brief references in Herodotus and Pliny to the 'wool-tree', little is known about how important the crop was until the tenth century, when the Arab chronicler Ibn el Awam was the first to mention its success. We have no idea of the amount of production and export before the eighteenth century. The Marseilles Chamber of Commerce noted in its archives the arrival of 200,000 pounds of spun cotton from Alexandria in 1711. But at the end of the century Volney said that Egyptian cotton was 'far less highly thought of than that of Syria and Armenia'. His contemporary, Browne, mentioned that the Damietta weavers and spinners bought their raw material in Syria. Finally, some of the investigators who came with the 1798 expedition described an active and fairly prosperous artisan cotton industry at Beni-Suef, Rosetta, Damietta and Mahalla-al-Kubra, while saying that it was hindered by the inadequate local harvests and their relatively poor quality.

The whole situation changed from 1820 onwards. A French engineer named Jumel, one of the many European technicians who were attracted by the Viceroy's keenness for modernization, found in his friend Maho Bey's garden, near Cairo, a cotton-plant with fibres of a length and softness hitherto unknown. He at once told the Pasha, who imposed this 'Jumel cotton' on the peasant people he held under his sway. It is still not known whether this plant came from India, the Sudan or Ethiopia. Here the monopoly of agricultural purchase was a boon, for the Viceroy paid twice as much for 'Jumel' as for the old kind of cotton, which quickly disappeared. Between 1820 and 1835 cotton production rose from 1,000 *cantars* (a *cantar* being a little under half a hundredweight) to 243,000. After 1835—the period of great military activity—there was a fall in output due to the lowering of the price paid to the fellahs. Mohamed Ali's greed threatened him with ruin. The upward trend was not resumed until after 1840, when the system of state control declined and broke down.

After at first encouraging the growing of cotton, the Pasha who had his hands on the monopoly became an obstacle to its further development. This became clear when his second successor Mohamed Said gave up the monopoly of land and purchase and gradually shared out the land among the large farmers. The new freedom on the market, particularly for sale to foreign countries, quickly tripled the fellah's income and the output quadrupled between 1845 and 1861. But the real boom in Egyptian cotton was due to events overseas. The war between the northern and southern States abruptly held up American exports which had dominated the world market, and in four years Egypt's cotton exports rose from half a million pounds in 1861 to fourteen million in 1864.

Thus in less than half a century, thanks to Jumel's discovery, the Pasha's bold way of developing new ideas, the Viceroy Said's liberalism and finally the war for the emancipation of the American negro, cotton took over a third of the land and half the working life of the Nile Valley people, and made Egypt the source of the finest fibres in the world. This expansion of cotton plays a prominent part in the Egyptian revolution, of which it is one of the steps or stages. There are four reasons for this:

More than any of Mohamed Ali's innovations it tended to bring the country into the current of international trade. With regard to wheat, hemp or indigo, the Pasha decided on the acreage to be planted, the percentage to be put aside for overseas, and the fixing of prices, all with a view to foreign export. But the cotton trade got out of hand and Egyptian ouput was harnessed to the needs of modern industry. It was no longer Alexandria, but Liverpool and New York which set the price and even the amount of production. Mohamed Ali wanted to open Egypt to the outside world: he left it gaping and exploited. The nation itself, from 1919 onwards, had to insist on its right to its own wealth.

The growth of the cotton crop, moreover, has been the basis of the industrialization of Egypt. Before Mohamed Ali and Jumel there were already spinning-mills and the weavers were prosperous. But only after 1822 did the processing of the cotton-fibre pass from the craft to the industrial stage which produced a new proletariat— there were 30,000 industrial workers by the end of the reign. At first most of the hands were foreigners: the first large spinning-mill, at Bulaq in Cairo, was called 'Malta' because the employees mostly came from there. But Mohamed Ali pushed ahead with bringing Egyptian personnel and even technicians into the industry. As in the case of army recruitment, it was circumstances which forced him to do this, though in 1835 or thereabouts he remarked to Bowring, an English M.P., 'I am operating factories not so much for the sake of profit as to get the people used to industrial work.' The material profit was, in fact, negligible. As soon as the Egyptian workers were reasonably skilled an attempt was made to substitute them for foreign labour, but with little success. Nevertheless, modernization, the emergence of a proletariat and 'Egyptianization' are all related and go forward together. This fact has not been sufficiently noticed. What is usually emphasized is the rise in output and the cosmopolitan aspect of Mohamed Ali's reign.

The development of cotton-growing, between the redistribution of land and the opening of the market by Sa'id to the end of the century, also resulted in a decided improvement in the fellahs' standard of living. It is estimated that the fellah's income was tripled between 1834 and 1890. The Khedive Ismail, writing to M. Schefer in 1863, drew the following moral: 'There is a new situation in Egypt. Since the freeing of trade and especially since the American Civil War, the fellah has become rich. He has found himself in contact with European consumers and this has changed his ideas. I can no longer do what my grandfather did, with impunity.'

The final and perhaps main result of the increase in cotton production was a marked rise in the population. Unfortunately there are no statistics for the development of the population in the nineteenth century, as we have for cotton output. But in 1821 there were 3,200,000 inhabitants, and by 1892 there were 6,800,000. This rise could be attributed to many causes. But we must not forget, either, the heavy losses during Ibrahim's campaigns, nor the terrible loss of life through the economic disasters, epidemics and floods which tragically marked the close of Mohamed Ali's reign. In any case, no cause for the increase of population seems to be as clear as the dominant role played by the cotton crop in agriculture.

No form of outdoor labour demands more time. It needs an enormous, patient and cheap labour force, yet relatively little physical exertion, whether for the preparation of the soil, dressing and replanting, hoeing, picking, or keeping down pests. The fellahs were quick to see that children were best adapted for the last two operations on a small, frail plant which was well within their reach. Hence the link between cotton and the family as a whole, between the number of children and cotton output. This factor is the basis of the demographic problem which governs Egyptian life today.[1]

[1] 'Cotton is a gift made to Egypt by its population of children' (A. Lambert).

IV

A Revolution in Irrigation

Of all the radical changes that came over Egypt in the nineteenth century, none had or is likely to have such a profound effect on national life as the total replanning of the irrigation system. The ordering and domestication of the Nile have made half the country—in the space of a few decades—advance from a miracle agriculture presided over by an unreliable river-god, to a scientific agriculture that works according to man's own will. Egypt was formerly mastered by the Nile, that great male entity which covered it from July to October. But now her concern is to tame the river. The androgynous god Hapi, whose temple was at Phylae, now serves the Egyptian citizen. Anyone can see that this has more than an agricultural significance.

Here again, unless we go back to Bonaparte's engineers, Mohamed Ali was an innovator. He understood that however high-flown his ambitions might be, his and Egypt's fortunes were bound up with the waters of the Nile, and that their use, distribution and storage could double or treble the country's output. Even if he had not realized it, the French experts around him, such as Lambert, Fournel and Linant, could have told him, especially since the development of cotton after 1830 meant that new land was called for. There was not far to seek. Egyptian farming was half dead in winter, when Shitawi cultivation was practised. Leaving land fallow in summer was not without its advantages, as the mud left by the receding waters was exposed to the sun, aired and rested. But this almost always meant some loss to production. The Egyptian summer would have to be used in order to have a second harvest from the soil.

In 1834 the Viceroy called his technical advisers together. Some of them who were disciples of Saint-Simon argued the case for making the 'two-seas canal' that Bonaparte had dreamed of. But Mohamed Ali preferred to give priority to building a dam (it is to be noted that the two questions have been linked before our own time). The task was entrusted to the French engineers Mougel and Linant de Bellefonds, and preparatory work for a great undertaking at the southern end of the Delta was started at once. But it was not until 1847, when the old ruler was dying, that the dam's foundations were laid, and it was 1882 before the project was completed by English engineers.

Thus the transition from flooding to permanent irrigation was carried out in three stages. Under Mohamed Ali came the beginning of the permanent irrigation network in Lower Egypt, starting at the Delta dike. During Ismail's reign they dug the great irrigation artery of Middle Egypt, the Ibrahimieh Canal, which was to double the sugar crop. Finally, under British Administration Mohamed Ali's dike was completed, the three great canals of Lower Egypt were cut, while the storage dam at Aswan was built between 1890 and 1903.

At first, the change from irrigation by flooding the basins to the so-called perennial or permanent irrigation, was only made in order to ensure the full utilization of the land. The idea of an overall scheme did not occur till much later, with the catchment dams, which amounted to an absolute transformation of methods of farming.[1]

By setting up a network or grid of canals all over Lower, Middle, and finally Upper Egypt (remarkably like the circulatory system of the body), permanent irrigation feeds the soil a constant supply of water and allows all-the-year-round farming. Egyptian agriculture is in a kind of perpetual motion. Beside the land's increased yield it is not hard to imagine the social upheaval brought into rural life by this technical revolution.

The first effect, naturally, was to lengthen and intensify the peasant's work. Having been half-marmot he now became more like a beaver. Whether busy preparing the soil for crops that follow one after the other without interruption, or planting or harvesting, tending his cotton plants, bringing water from the canal up to his field, the Egyptian fellah works twelve hours a day for twelve months of the year. The rural areas have an incredible population. Caught up in a merciless round of almost industrial activity, the fellah wears himself out like some performing animal.

The second result was that the agricultural map was radically re-drawn. The 'good land' had changed its place. It is no longer prized on account of its closeness to the Nile or the basins, but according to the position of the canal—whether the land is cut or bordered by it or is on a lower level. A new kind of competition arises as the

[1] Cf. Part III, Chapter I.

canal network is developed, an agrarian touchiness for which there is no cure.

Another result is that the new farming techniques mean that the fellahs have a kind of professional training. Agriculture had hardly changed for five thousand years. But now the Nile farmer must know about the rotation of difficult crops, the upkeep of canals and drainage, and even the repair and service of farming machinery. It might be inferred from this that his judgement, humanity and mental fitness have all benefited.

But the introducing of permanent irrigation has also had one bad effect, the spreading of a parasite living in canal slime which causes an extremely painful disease, *bilharzia*, which affects more than 80 per cent of the population on the land.

V

The Adventurous Khedive

The Suez Canal, which was the work of foreigners and for a long time both alien and loathsome in Egyptian eyes, came to complete Egypt's introduction to world strategy, commerce, diplomacy and thought. From 1869 onwards, even more than during the tense hours when Thiers was threatening Europe with a war to preserve the rights of the Pasha of Cairo, Egypt has been right in the centre of the struggle. This was not always to her advantage. The subsequent steps in her 'internationalization'—the debt fund, the British occupation, the protectorate and the secession of the Sudan—were too bitter for Egypt to resist the temptation of turning against everything that lay at the origin of her troubles. First of these was the Canal, which made Egyptian territory the object of fierce rivalries by opening it to the world.

We have seen that in 1834 Mohamed Ali, consulting his brainstrust of foreign engineers, was against Fournel's and Lambert's proposal to cut the 'two-seas canal'. He was afraid of creating a new Egyptian question by inventing a 'second Bosphorus'. He seemed to be reacting more like a suspicious Turk than a modern innovator. His son Sa'id and his grandson Isma'il were less prudent, seeing the canal as a means of slicing Egypt off the Ottoman Empire, a kind of furrow in which progress could be sown.

Egypt has reaped many benefits from the operation: a great increase in economic, diplomatic and strategic bargaining-power; the birth of two large cities and a province in the open desert; the receipt of large sums in the form of taxation. But the enterprise affected the Egyptian people still more directly. Less than perennial irrigation but nevertheless important, it made up a phase of the technical and spiritual revolution.

We have little evidence of the effect on the Egyptian mind, especially that of the younger generation of the late nineteenth century, which was produced by the success of de Lesseps and his engineers. But, as with the domestication of the Nile, this change in the map of

63

the world could hardly leave those responsible for Egyptian regeneration indifferent. The work of de Lesseps might be regarded as giving a lesson in race-hatred and distrustful provincialism as in the case of Arabi and his followers. But it can also be seen as a demonstration of what energy and enterprise can do. It could be taken as a final answer to fatalism, and it might not be going too far to find in it the reason for that sudden thirst for knowledge which seized young people in the 1880's, and the success of purely scientific explanations of the world which were to be found even in the teaching of Sheikh Mohamed Abduh. The completion of the Canal proved what man was capable of and how modern science could be made to serve him. Its very existence was bound to make a strong impact on a nation which seventy-five years before had been a mere island of mediaevalism. The cutting of the Canal was an object-lesson for the country's youth.

The piercing of the isthmus was to provoke another revolution— the abolition of forced labour. But this fundamental reform was not brought about by humanitarian motives. When the British Government prevailed on Constantinople to ask the Viceroy of Egypt to abolish forced labour, it was primarily in the hope of stopping de Lesseps's work. How were the 20,000 labourers promised to the company by Sa'id Pasha to be found, except if they were requisitioned? The London *Standard* wrote jubilantly, 'It will be impossible to get the work done except at enormous cost.' De Lesseps and his technical assistant, the engineer Voisin, were bold enough to make use of the most up-to-date excavators and dredges to replace the labour force. But though it was outwitted, the Anglo-Turkish device had the advantage of abolishing, at least in theory, one of the curses of rural society. The terror it caused among the fellahs, like their dread of conscription, had resulted in actual movements of population, the abandonment of many villages and the breaking up of social groups. Thus it came about, for instance, that Mohamed Abduh was born on the roadside while his father was fleeing the press-gangs.

Though it was abolished in theory, forced labour lasted until recent years, governments losing interest in the fellahs as soon as they could no longer be used for bargaining in some political manœuvre.

Khedive Ismaïl's reign was, in spite of everything, an essential phase in Egypt's revolutionary attempts to modernize itself. The fact that he went bankrupt does not completely condemn the sovereign who wanted to identify Egypt's fate with Europe. Such a project

3. The Pasha Bonaparte and the Pasha of Cairo

4a. Fellahs cutting sugar cane at the foot of the Valley of Kings

4b. Simonne Lacouture on a *nurag* goes threshing

was and still is out of the question. But in allowing Egypt to pursue this ruinous fancy, Isma'il effectively carried on the work of Mohamed Ali, however seriously he miscalculated, however blameworthy his taste for speculation, his gullibility, or however ridiculous his vanity and extravagance.

The failure of this royal adventurer, intent on modernization at any price, was inevitable. The Khedive had the support of no national group, and only the *bourgeoisie*, still in its infancy, could have given any energy or permanence to his plans. The European Powers may also be blamed for his fall. They were often represented by intriguers, cynically tolerating the plundering of the treasury of a ruler who, by throwing his country open to their initiative and the influx of modern ideas, gave it over in practice to the swindling of adventurers, to all kinds of jobbery disguised as normal practice, and to the greed of the banks.

Yet circumstances appeared to favour this undertaking. The benign Mohamed Saïd, who had tried to draw the dynasty closer to the people and who had bravely gambled on the insertion, between Asia and Africa, of a canal invented by his friend de Lesseps, was succeeded by the son of the great Ibrahim Pasha. The Austrian consul reported to his minister, on the subject of this cheery gentleman-farmer who was said to be a good administrator, 'He has only one fault that I know of: avarice.' Diplomats are fallible, but there are limits . . . Three years were enough to make it clear that this miser was an unbridled gambler. But in fairness it must be added that Isma'il became the trusting prey of a handful of European diplomatic and financial sharpers, because he came to power at a moment of such optimism that everything seemed possible. There seemed to be no daring that failed to pay off. The American Civil War, by cutting off the western supply of cotton, seemed to open an unlimited horizon to the Nile Valley.

How could anyone avoid being carried away? Offers were flowing in from everywhere, credits, visitors, flatterers. The Egyptian legend was never so brightly painted. The godfather of the Canal, the Maecenas of Aida, the magnificent sovereign of Cairo, was compared with Louis XIV. But 'in this court-life after the manner of Versailles, the nobles were notorious foreign adventurers', observed the Egyptian historian Mohamed Sabri. While capitalism in the Paris of the Second Empire was triumphing without having fought a battle, and swelling with its conquests in the naïve trust in unlimited expansion in the name of Peel's doctrine of liberalism, the Egypt of Ismaïl flung itself wide open to foreign credits and schemes. For her own part she also tried to find new markets such as the Sudan, Ethiopia and the upper regions of the Nile. But the Viceroy ought to have grasped that his own imperialism could be no more than the pilot-scheme or agent of that of the foreign powers who were intent on becoming Egypt's masters.

Whether actively or passively, Isma'il Pasha was at the centre of the great capitalist adventure, the game of unlimited exchange, open markets, free trade. It is not just by chance that the opening of the Suez Canal in 1869 marks the highlight of a reign in which he allowed his country to be treated like an open thoroughfare. But it should be admitted that in treating Egypt like a great and expanding business concern, the Khedive gave the country a wealth that no bankruptcy could wipe out. His reign saw the beginning of public education (when 60,000 pupils were taught in 4,600 schools); a rapid development of public works (the port installations at Alexandria, creation of a water-supply, railroads, city lighting); the setting up of a Council of State and above all the ingenious institution, the 'Mixed Courts'. Half a century later the suppression of these tribunals was one of the demands of advancing nationalism, but in 1870 those courts (composed half of Westerners and half of Egyptians in order to try cases in which aliens were involved) marked a great progress over the old Turkish system of 'Capitulations'.

Established in the sixteenth century to protect European traders living in the Ottoman Empire from a legal system far removed from Roman Law, the Capitulations had fallen into abuse, first because the modernization of the Egyptian civil service no longer justified the foreign litigant's appeal to his own consulate; secondly because the enormous development of the European colony of settlers had made the capitulary system a kind of super-law which practically guaranteed immunity for foreigners, that is to say, in fact, for most important business-men. Mr. Sabri observes that 'The capitulary system tended to make Egypt a court of appeal for all the dubious characters thrown out of Europe.' The creation of mixed tribunals put an end to this miscarriage of justice. It cannot be said that Egyptians then began to enjoy equal treatment; but European delinquents were no longer able to rely on a shameful immunity.

We can dismiss the caricature of a parliament invented by the Prime Minister Nubar to impress European moneylenders, but we must credit the Khedive for the freedom given to a Press which was then in its infancy, for the diplomatic campaign with the Porte in order to give Egyptian autonomy a legal basis, and the formation of a half-commercial, half-administrative nucleus of a middle class which still retained some veneer of Oriental methods. But however interesting it was in this and in the field of education, legislation and technical progress, Isma'il's reign is an outstanding example of how bold and generous ideas can be misapplied, a sorry masterpiece of what one might call 'financial imperialism'.

Perhaps Lord Milner, who cannot be accused of systematic anti-imperialism, has best described this looting of Egypt, fallen a prey to the Khedive's frenzy for modernization:

'It is hard to imagine the complete unscrupulousness with which diplomatic agents used their influence to make a weak Egypt yield to their most extravagant demands. At the time, the purpose behind obtaining a concession was not to carry out some project, but to invent some complaint which would allow the contract to be broken and then turn to the government for compensation.'

A French observer summed all this up with 'the most profitable industry was the exploitation of compensation from the Khedive'.

The shower of loans in which Isma'il, who was a wild speculator, became involved—such as the bogus operation of 1866 in which the Khedive sold shares at 69·5 per cent which the initial buyers had taken at 85·5 per cent and offered to the public at 92 per cent; huge contracts thrust on him by his agents and consuls who were scheming together in ways which have not been fully revealed; the part played at Isma'il's court by Europeans who had grounds for thinking that in some way they were representing their governments, such as Herr Oppenheim; the methods used by the founders of the Azizieh,[1] or 'Egyptian Trading' or the 'Agricole'—this whirl of intrigues, this solemn ballet of tricksters, this auctioning of Egypt by a Europe whose thieves were disguised as diplomats, and the diplomats as thieves, such are episodes that must not be forgotten when we speak of Egyptian xenophobia, for they lie at the root of the bitterness and vengefulness of their nationalism.

A generation of young middle-class Egyptians, which was to become the governing class in the twentieth century, came into public life in this poisoned atmosphere of an Egypt open or rather

[1] *Histoire financière de l'Égypte (Financial History of Egypt)*, by M. Claudy.

offered on a plate to Europe; attached to the old continent by the Khedive's will, forced by him to imitate the West in all it did, a country reduced by foreigners to the state of a farm or fair, sucked dry by a horde of untouchable cheats, its provinces in pawn to repay foreign moneylenders. We finally reach the point where Isma'il was flouted, ruined and abandoned by his European 'friends' to the vengeance of the Porte, as soon as he gave any sign of trying to save himself and defend—rather late in the day—Egypt's independence against the public debt fund and a couple of British and French ministers he had had forced on him. Even before Isma'il's fall the dispossessed Egyptian people had found spokesmen to voice the country's indignation.

VI

The Arabi Revolt

The 1882 movement appears to contradict Isma'il's policies in every way. But from the point of view of welding Egypt into a unity, it completes it. It marks the bitter awakening of the national consciousness, but on the other hand it resulted in a transition from a tacit to an open colonization.

Under the Khedive the worst possible rift had shown itself between the two movements of the Egyptian revolution: modernization and nationalization; Egypt must become modern even at the price of ceasing to be Egypt. It was natural for the balance to swing sharply to the other extreme, for the unwary Isma'il to give rise to a strong counter-shock as a result of having tried to turn the Nile Valley into a European province. The wild enthusiasm for the foreigner was to be answered by a wave of hatred which could more accurately be called an attempt to retrieve the nation. No people would have passively watched the country being turned over to foreign money-grabbers just when it was becoming a nation, even if the foreigners' presence spelt considerable enrichment for the country, even though the nationalist reaction might well serve as a pretext for foreign intervention and the setting up of colonial tyrannies.

Thus there emerged Arabi, Colonel Ahmed Arabi Pasha, 'El Wahid' (the Unique). We are too often misled by the picturesque and trivial appearance of the first 'colonels' revolution'. French historians in particular write with spiteful ill humour about an undertaking in which they see no more than a stupid invitation to the English to come and interfere. The ups and downs of the affair are of no great importance, but may be resumed briefly.

Stung by the favoured treatment given to Turkish and Circassian army staff-officers, and by the heavy dismissals they had to suffer at the hands of the European debt controllers, Arabi and the 'fellah' officers rose against the Khedive Tewfik, who was supported by the British. Between February 1879 and July 1882 they forced him to dismiss the Prime Minister, Nubar, who was Armenian, then to exile the War Minister, Osman Rifqi, who was Turkish, and to form a nationalist government under their friend Mahmud Sami el Barudi, who naturally appointed Arabi as War Minister. Other measures were the granting of a liberal Constitution, the calling of a National Assembly (which, composed mainly of 'notables', gave signs of a praiseworthy interest in the well-being of the masses and showed a certain insight), and finally the rejection of the two British ultimatums of May and July 1882, which brought about a military intervention which the panic-stricken Khedive had appealed for.

Arabi was unable to prevent the landing of a British expeditionary force which, concentrating on Ismaïlia and turning the Egyptian positions south of Alexandria, beat him decisively at Tel El Kebir. The route was so complete that the fellah-Colonel was taken prisoner, tried, condemned to death, immediately reprieved and banished to Ceylon, from whence he returned to Cairo in 1904 to find himself completely forgotten.

Ahmed Arabi was a leader of little standing and mediocre ability. His own autobiography shows his lack of culture and his conceit. Historians insist on his incompetence, and only the later advent of a military government, of which his adventure was a brief but striking forerunner, made it possible for him to be regarded suddenly as a kind of African Garibaldi (as the Sudanese Mahdi was soon to prove himself). He was bold enough in dealing with such feeble opponents as the Khedive; he was eloquent and had a certain gift for swaying the mob, a patriotic and indeed democratic fervour, the virtues of an earnest agitator who is sure he is serving a just cause. What cannot be taken away from him is the fact that for several months, from 1881 to 1882, he was the spokesman and even the symbol of an Egypt that was hungering for justice and dignity.

There is no reliable document or evidence that can allow us to paint him as the fanatic and venal bandit so dear to French historians, or to denounce him—as did his successor as head of the nationalist movement, Mustafa Kamil—as 'a traitor concerned with nothing but his own material gain'. But the movement for independence none the less deserved another leader. Mahmud Sami el Barudi was of a different metal; but the revolt had to come from the army, from the officer-corps of fellahs whose condition was a perfect replica of Egypt's, based on racism, alienation and poverty.

This apparently idle and negative episode is actually full of significance. It throws into relief three characteristics of Eygptian and Eastern public life which henceforth were to prove essential. First, the political importance of the native army as a link between the masses and the government, as well as a means of popular action; second, the emergence of a national and social consciousness even in the rural areas; third, the compromise between Islam and certain aspects of the modern world, which patriotic resistance begins through the intellectuals taking part in the struggle, such as reformist sheikhs like Abduh, or relatively liberal politicians like Sharij Pasha, or 'revivalist' writers like Ibrahim and al-Mu'ilhi.

The army that was founded by Mohamed Ali and led to victory by Ibrahim was formed by a system of conscription which worked no more fairly than did the French system in those days. Any citizen of means did his best to spare his son the ordeal of bearing arms. Thus it was not so much a people's army as the army of the poor, and the financial crisis severely affected life in the ranks, with pay falling more and more into arrears as the national debt grew heavier. There was also growing tension between officers of local origin who were kept in ranks below the Turkish Circassians who were the Mamelukes in a more modern form.

Sai'd Pasha had encouraged the promotion to high ranks of a number of peasants' sons such as Arabi. But this development stopped under Isma'il. Rank, responsibility, garrisons, pay, ministerial favouritism, all this made the native Egyptian feel he was being cheated. The storm broke when in order to reduce the level of internal expenditure the 'European Ministry' abruptly dismissed 2,500 officers, almost all of them fellahs, while a firman from the Porte cut the army's strength from 30,000 to 18,000. If we remember that the embittered army had just returned from the disastrous Abyssinian campaign (1876) full of contempt for its leaders (some of whom were American officers . . .) and resentment against the government, then it is not so surprising that between 1879 and 1882 the mounting insubordination should have led Arabi, Ali Fahmi and Abdel Al to lead the national revolt. Only a spark was needed for an army which was poor, defeated and split by racial conflict. As we know, the explosions have not yet come to an end.

We must not allow ourselves to be misled. The army's action was neither a pronunciamento nor the interference of a caste in the country's public affairs: it was evidence of widespread national unrest, the expression of which tacitly lay with the army part of the nation, because it felt the country's frustration and bitterness with more than usual intensity. In a sense, Arabi and Ali Fahmi worked in closer touch with the masses than either Neguib or Nasser seventy years later. With the former the army more genuinely seemed to be a weapon in the people's hands. The meaning of the precedent thus created was at once understood by the British who at once intervened. Through the uniformed fellahs the country had found a way of making itself heard against local and foreign feudalism. Arabi's attempt came to nothing because the leaders of the revolt were little more than agitators who lacked character and political background. But they opened a way for the masses and offered them some outlet. As they trained under the eyes of foreign instructors, the fellahs' sons began to learn something more than how to present arms.

The 'seed' was widely scattered. The most striking feature of the 1882 affair was not so much that the army had emerged as a revolutionary force, but that it was only the spearhead of a collective movement, and that the apparently resigned people lifted its head to share in the struggle. Historians disagree on this point, but eye-witnesses and diplomatic observers all confirmed that the mob's bloodthirsty hatred of the foreigner gave way, early in 1882, to the beginning of a mass recruitment to defend the country. Columns of peasants moved towards Arabi's camp near Alexandria, then to Tel El Kebir; but the army was too hastily improvised to avoid collapsing before Wolseley's expeditionary force.

At the same time a sort of *jacquerie* or gang-revolt broke out with the help of plebeian agitators such as the remarkable Abdullah Nadim, the 'army orator', a talented journalist who, keeping to the bush for several years after the revolt was quelled, invented the propaganda 'leaflet' tattooed on the fellahs' arms or chest. The archives of the provincial courts, especially at Minufiya, have records of the cases brought by landowners against fellahs who tried to profit from the general breakdown of law and order by seizing land. Milner refers to 'the complete dissolution of Egyptian society during the summer of 1882', while more explicitly still Lord Cromer writes in his *Modern Egypt*, 'the majority of the peasants are in sympathy with Arabi. They look to him to deliver them from the usurer and the Pasha.' For the first time Egypt had become a seething cauldron.

To be sure, groups of irregulars fought bravely against Bonaparte's army, and Cairo rose at the Ulamas' appeal. But no movement since the beginning of the century had taken on such proportions, nor, above all, had such a social character. However confusedly, the fellahs had already begun to see the connexion between feudalism and foreign rule. Throwing themselves on the latter, they ran foul of the other, for no land is better defended than one's own.

Decidedly, then, the Arabi incident lifts several corners of the veil. However abortive, it nevertheless brought in question the Nile Valley's 'European destiny', the notion of the fellah's age-old resignation in both civil and military matters; the parliamentary incompetence of which Orientals are often accused, and finally the relationship between the Islamic outlook and modern life. This foiled revolution had the value of a preface, an overture. It brought out three tendencies in Egypt nationalism: with Arabi, that of a strongly anti-European 'National Party'; with Sharif Pasha, that of modernism and constitutional liberalism; with Mohamed Abduh himself, a harbinger of the Wafdist spirit.

VII

The Reformers

A small, bold group of the faithful seized on Arabi's revolt as a signal and impulse for a still more daring enterprise than the political and spiritual liberation of Egypt—the revival of a positively Moslem civilization which would incorporate modern developments without submitting to them in the realm of politics. Anyone who has seen the half-hearted and mediocre attempts that are being made today to renew and re-adapt Islam, is struck by the energy and courage of the men of 1880.

It would be absurd to try to compress the efforts of Jamal ud-Din al-Afghani or Mohamed Abduh and their companions, into the narrow framework of the Arabi rising. They preceded that rising and survived it long after, both in their breadth of vision and the consequences of their work. It is significant that the fellah-Colonel's movement, to all appearances attached to the past, should have cut across the relatively modern programme of the Afghan sheikh and his Egyptian disciple. The reformers' teaching needed a political platform and a field of action. Islam is such that its ideas have no form until they are applied concretely through the community.

Arabi's anti-European behaviour seemed to contradict the teachings of Jamal ud-Din, who had met Renan in Paris, and of Mohamed Abduh, who was a great reader of Herbert Spencer. But neither Renan nor Spencer enabled these pious and proud men to forget that the Moslem community was humiliated and held in thrall. The support given to the anti-European rising went side by side in their minds with a hunger for Western science and the spirit of free inquiry, In both cases it was a matter of working for the revival of Islam through spiritual progress—inspired by Europe's example—as well as by political regeneration, provisionally directed against the foreigner, and by rooting out the people's superstitions which were an obvious instrument of oppression. Nearer to our own times we find the same triple outlook in the Maghrib.

This blend of spiritual reformism and Moslem patriotism had,

74

incidentally, already emerged before the Colonels' movement. It was during the Russo-Turkish war of 1877 that Egyptian Islam and its guiding spirits became strongly aware of their destiny by identifying it with that of the ruling nation with which it had nothing but religious faith in common. Politically, technically and—with the cutting of the Suez Canal—even geographically, Egypt was moving away from Turkey. But a strong spiritual current still attached her to the capital of the Commander of the Faithful, a current which the anti-British movement prolonged until the Caliphate was abolished by Atakurk. Thus we find Mustafa Kamil, an intellectual educated in Paris, tirelessly defending the 'Red Sultan' in Cairo, and even going so far as to reproach Mohamed Ali for warring on Mahmud.

Though they were thus pro-Turkish because of the need for support against a Great Power in their efforts to revive Islam, Jamal ud-Din and Mohamed Abduh none the less used every means, however strange, which might help on intellectual progress, political liberation and the careful exegesis of the holy books. These doctors of Islam became Freemasons, founding the Great Orient of Alexandria in 1878 and affiliating themselves in the following year to the English lodge, where they came into contact with their brother-mason the Prince of Wales. But the experiment proved disappointing.

The part played by Freemasonry in the revival of Egyptian Islam is an interesting example of its empiricism or, better, its pragmatism (is it not natural for a religion which is at the same time a political programme to be politically opportunist?). Thus we see the reformers turning to Arabi the xenophobe for support, as well as to a typically Western and rationalist organization which appears to be essentially opposed to the liberalism of traditional Islam. This subtle flirtation between Islam and Freemasonry is something like what Bonaparte wanted to establish with the Ulamas of El Azhar, a communion between an anti-clerical deism and a clergyless monotheism.

From both within and without Islam, voices were of course raised against the reformers for 'straying' far from the teachings of the Book. Lord Cromer, who had a high regard for it, wrote, 'I suspect my friend Mohamed Abduh of really being an agnostic, and his associates also looked askance at him as a *filosouf*.' It is a fact that the few surviving fragments of Abduh's teachings that have been translated smack of heresy, for instance, 'If reason and tradition clash, then one must choose reason'; or 'The Koran is not precise on all points and leaves the business of deciding the rest to reason, the handmaid of religion.' And again, 'The seeker who is misled is closer to the truth than the sheep-like mentality that stays on the straight path.' Looking at the first two statements in the light of the third, it is clear where Sheikh Abduh's teaching leads: to a rationalism as adventurous as that of some of our Western renaissance thinkers, not all of whom escaped the stake.

With Mohamed Abduh, the spirit of inquiry broke into the closed world of Moslem thought. However shapeless his doctrine may seem, oddly reactionary sometimes and full of an optimistic naturalism which now looks old-fashioned, and however disconcerting his mixture of conformity with a boldness that threatened to undermine the faith itself, yet he offers the elements of the most important spiritual revolution to affect Islam for four hundred years. Far though it is from the lofty humanism of Averroes or the energetic method of Ibn Khaldun, Mohamed Abduh's thought none the less broke the worst of shackles, that of the *taqlid*, the principle of authority and blind resignation to tradition, and so made it possible to exercise intelligence in religious matters.

It is disappointing to have to admit that the Moslems could still go on thinking as they had before, when he was gone. Very few of the faithful have passed through the door Abduh opened to them. It was a quarter of a century before Taha Husain tried to perform another operation on the sleeping body in the form of historical criticism, or for Mustafa and Ali Abd ur-Raziq to begin inquiring into the possibility of separating religion from political power.

The work of Jamal ud-Din al-Afghani and Mohamed Abduh (the politician plus the Doctor of Theology) has nevertheless borne fruit. It is certainly disappointing not to have seen a school of young and bold philosophers springing up in the wake of the 'Eastern Luther' (to quote the heavy comparison with which Mohamed Sabri effaces Sheikh Abduh). The Moslem Reformation did not take the form of Protestantism. But on several points the reformers' teachings have had a good effect on Islamic society—because they taught that man, endowed with a will and free to determine himself, must reject fatalism and begin to act within the *umma* or community of the faithful, and outside this community they made the whole of Islam ashamed of its sleep.

Because they taught that the spirit of inquiry is inseparable from true faith, and that free criticism is a fundamental of Islamic 'democracy', they helped towards the setting up of a Press which at first, however, was the work of a Jew (the popular and brilliant James Sanua, known as Abu Nadara), and a group of Syrians, Adib Ishaq, Selim Naqqash, Selim and Bishara Taqla. The birth of the Egyptian Press dates from 1877–80 and was a capital event in the shaping of the country's nationalism. There then appeared the newspapers *El Misr, El Watan* and *El Ahram* (still the best Egyptian daily). The few numbers of those pioneer news-sheets that have survived are surprising in their outspokenness and brilliance of tone. Incidentally, it is interesting to note that if there was some connexion between Abduh's teachings and the emergence of a Press, there were also great differences: the first was Moslem, the second, Arab.

Because like Arabi, Abduh came from the small-landowner class and linked his struggle for spiritual freedom with political action and a deep concern for reforming the structure of society, we see the gradual emerging of a movement at once nationalist and lower middle class, the slow advance of the Egyptian Third Estate which forty years later was to be embodied in the Wafd. Although his direct spiritual heirs such as Mustafa Abd ur-Raziq associated themselves with the liberal or constitutionalist movement, Mohamed Abduh, thanks to his origins, his religious tolerance and the democratic nature of his programme of reform, appears to be the ancestor of Sa'd Zaghlul's great party.

It must be admitted that the reformers of 1880 made no deep intellectual or spiritual mark on the masses. Mohamed Abduh's attempted reforms at El Azhar were thrust aside. The scholastic mentality remained firmly entrenched and there was no development of the critical spirit. 'Although Abduh's influence is still alive . . . the clearest result of his activities was the emergence of a new fundamentalist school, the *Salafya*, the purpose of which was to protect tradition,' observes Professor Gibb in his *Modern Trends in Islam*.

But on the political level, the message of Jamal ud-Din and Abduh was tremendously effective. Intervening at the time of the Russo-Turkish war, then as part of the Arabi revolt, and finally in reaction against English imperial rule, it gave intellectual cohesion to the Pan-Islamism which was springing up everywhere and made Egyptian nationalism more aware of itself (it is no accident that the word *watan* (Fatherland) was used at that time as the title of a newspaper). Though outwardly antagonistic, the ideas of an Islamic community and an Egyptian nation were brought together by the challenge of colonialism, and both found strength in facing the common enemy.

VIII

British Technocracy

The British administration of Egypt is not very highly regarded abroad. At a first glance it is hard to see it as making a positive stage in the revolution. French historians, most of them hostile, are not alone in providing ammunition for nationalist propaganda, by decrying the relative barrenness and shortcomings of a task begun under police rule, carried on in an atmosphere of bitterness and ended, like all colonial undertakings, in recriminations from both sides. Compared with what was done next door, by Italy in Libya and by France in Tunisia, English colonization in Egypt cuts a poor figure. The school system, communications, hygiene, institutions—with a single exception which we shall discuss later, not one of these fields in which a colonizer usually tries to justify his presence or which he uses as an alibi, showed any marked improvement due to the reforming genius of the West, in the period 1882-1922.

But this was not the view of the artisans and advocates of British policy towards the Nile, such as Lord Cromer, Alfred Milner and Lord Lloyd. It must be admitted that the balance-sheet drawn up by Lord Cromer—who had been practically a Pharaoh for over twenty years, 1883-1906—in his *Modern Egypt* shows less trifling assets than are generally acknowledged. The British occupation of Egypt came about through the danger to foreigners and minorities as a result of the 1882 revolution, and because of the disastrous state to which Egypt was reduced by the intrigues of European adventurers and the disasters of the Arabi period. It took less than ten years to restore order, organize an efficient administration and clear up the financial chaos. The last item was carried out with particular skill, 'the Cromer government having some interest in confusing the Egyptian problem with the financial problem', as a French observer acidly remarks. The English historian George Young honestly admits that this recovery was 'the convalescence of a hard-working people after an imported sickness'.

The noble pro-consul none the less claimed for his administration that it had suppressed forced labour and corruption (rather an optimistic view?); that it had freed the judiciary, developed and improved public education (in 1905 this was still a department of the Ministry of Public Works, but to Cromer's credit, after making education the privilege of a small class, he suddenly had the courage to appoint as head of the newly-created Department of Education the one man who was capable of giving it a good start, as well as the least likely to let it serve British interests, namely Sa'd Zaghlul); that it had reshaped the army (which Khedive Tewfik's laconic and astonishing decree of 1882 had declared 'disbanded because of the rebellion'); and naturally, that an extensive system of irrigation had been installed by teams of engineers under Sir Colin Scott-Moncrieff, Colonel Ross and Mr. Wilcox.

It was the radical change in the distribution of the Nile waters that gave a revolutionary value to the British occupation. Making an intelligent and imaginative use of their experience in India, the British agronomists and engineers carried on and extended the work of Mohamed Ali's technicians, Mougel and Linant de Bellefont. In less than twenty years (1884–1902) they had completed the Delta barrage begun by the Pasha in 1836, dug the three great canals in Lower Egypt and built the first Aswan Dam. But we have to note the Egyptian sociologist Sulaiman Huzayyin's opinion that, however rewarding it was, permanent irrigation 'destroyed the Egyptian village'. For 'with basin-irrigation the village was grouped on high ground and everyone co-operated in the upkeep of the dikes and general work. Now the houses are separate and everybody works for himself. The village is dying.'

The severity of this judgement gives some idea of the state of mind in which even the most intelligent Egyptian approaches any study of British initiative in their country. The British irrigation schemes were certainly not disinterested and aimed at little more than producing better and more cotton for the Lancashire mills. But it should not be forgotten that the administration under Cromer—and even more under Kitchener—showed more concern for the fate of the fellah than any rulers before or after them. This, to be sure, was part of an attempt to pacify the rural poor in order to offset the influence of the city intellectuals, and especially with a view to increasing output. But it is quite true that the Egyptian peasantry are indebted to the occupation for many measures which attacked serfdom and multiplied the small-holdings. Small owners had always lived under the constant threat of the neighbouring pasha, forced labour, the seizure of all they owned at the hands of moneylenders, any underhand trick played on them by the *ma'mur* in the pay of some local politician, banditry, arbitrary requisitioning, an insufficient or too violent flooding of the Nile. British legislation and administration could not put an end to all these plagues, but managed to set a limit to most of them.

Within fifteen years permanent irrigation doubled the output of cotton, a well-paying crop, easy to dispose of, which at last enabled the small farmer to lay by some capital. The setting up of a local administration with legal powers began to rescue the country-folk from the infamous arbitrary power they had been struggling against for centuries. The creation of the Agricultural Bank in 1902 at last made it possible for farmers, whatever their means, to borrow at fair rates of interest. Finally, and above all, the Five Feddan Law of 1912 made it illegal to seize any parcel of land less than this size (about four and a half acres). The total effect of these various measures brought a profound change to the agrarian system and the beginning of a class of small landed proprietors who were henceforth to play an increasingly important part in Egyptian public life.

Thanks to the increasing output, small properties were springing up which might have served as a basis for developing a proper landed middle class, were it not for the Moslem laws of inheritance which tend to share out property as fast as it is acquired. This is one reason why the British 'peasant' policies were unable to give themselves any social foundation, and one of the causes of what a French observer called 'the best example of the failure of the famous "full stomach" colonial policy'.

By the outbreak of the first World War, Egypt appeared appeased and subdued and, if not altogether satisfied with the way the State was working—with its balanced budgets, the high quality of its cotton, the Legislative Assembly newly created by Kitchener and which Wavell thought to have 'stimulated national consciousness'— was at least resigned to being the most 'reasonable' of the Near-East nations and the best inn on the road to India. Since 1904 France had stopped challenging Britain's 'privileged situation' in Egypt. Sir Eldon Gorst, who succeeded Cromer, succeeded in dividing the opposition and setting it against its best ally, the Khedive Abbas. Mustafa Kamil, the herald of nationalism, had died in 1908 at the age of 33, before finishing his task of reconciling the Moslems and

Copts and regrouping the anti-British opposition. Finally, the conquest of the Sudan by united Anglo-Egyptian forces in 1899 had created the Condominium which gave Britain absolute control over the upper reaches of the Nile. And yet . . .

And yet, in his book which is a summary of the situation and which dates from 1908, Lord Cromer came to a melancholy conclusion in applying to Egypt the following remarks which had been made by Sir Herbert Edwards about the Punjab: 'We were popular as long as we bandaged wounds. Nothing can prevail against the fact that we are not Moslems, and that we neither eat, nor drink, nor marry as they do.' It was not simply a matter of marriage or of eating habits. Three hotbeds of revolution had already begun smouldering —the educated *bourgeoisie*, the students and the workers. Since the Dinshawai incident, after which four fellahs were solemnly hanged and twenty others whipped (1906), the peasants could no longer be regarded as friendly to the régime.

Finally, however slight the impression it made on Egypt, the war of 1914 was about to act as a mother—or midwife—of revolutions, as war often does.

IX

The 1919 Revolution

For Egypt the 1914 war at first meant the setting up of the British Protectorate. This broke the last official links with the Caliphate and the Porte, which had been declared enemies, and also swept away the last traces of a national state. This was followed by a mass requisitioning of labour, the presence of large armed forces from overseas, the sudden growth of industry, giving rise to a still under-nourished proletariat, and the tightening of an already very irritating censorship. Then came a sudden jump in cotton prices, resulting in a rapid redistribution of wealth and a rise in the cost of living. Finally there was the proclamation of Wilson's 'Fourteen Points' and the Anglo-French statement of November 1918 promising the freeing of the Ottoman Empire's former vassals. In other words, all the possible elements of strain, uncertainty and hope to which a dormant people can be submitted, were present in this period. It is not surprising that it awakened in 1919 to find itself behind barricades.

It cannot be said that the proclamation of the British Protectorate in December 1914, any more than the replacement of the Khedive Abbas Hilmi by Sultan Husain (and soon after, his brother Fuad), excited Egyptian indignation, apart from a few small groups. Thirty years of dictatorship under Cromer and Kitchener had prepared their minds for any interference with their rights or feelings. Moreover, Sa'd Zaghlul, who from now on became the leading figure in Egyptian nationalism, gave excellent proof of his political wisdom in urging patience so long as the state of war lasted. But the British handling of national sovereignty tended to increase the friction between the two countries and, now that the Ottoman and Khedival factions were cut out, to result in a form of dialogue that was made the more tense by the situation that had arisen owing to the war.

The first source of disgruntlement was the requisition of men and material. We must not forget that beginning in 1914 a Labour Corps of 117,000 was raised, and that part of this unarmed 'army' had to follow the British armies to the Somme and Flanders, while the

Camel Corps played an active part in Allenby's campaigns against the Turks. Furthermore, the requisition of grain, cotton and especially livestock made things very hard for the people since, according to an official British publication, 'the military authorities paid well, but the money was often kept by unscrupulous local civil-servants and never reached the fellahs'. If we also bear in mind that the British Empire's forces amounted, according to other official records, to a million men, one can imagine the shock given to Egyptian society by the presence of such a horde of buyers, turbulent young men, thirsty soldiers on leave and hunting for women: it was no doubt good for trade, but gave rise to a wave of hatred for the foreigner.

Perhaps the most deep-seated cause for disorder was the sudden redistribution of wealth which took place in the country as well as in the towns. George Young, the most penetrating of the historians of the period, wrote,

'The country's wealth doubled during the war, the cotton boom producing an income of £1,000 per feddan ... British gold suddenly flooded and enriched an irresponsible class ... The distinctions between the ruling class of Turco-Circassians, the Copto-Syrian middle-class and the Arab-Nubian peasantry, now gave way to a reclassification of the Western type—wealthy, well-to-do, and workers.'

No social revolution could be better described.

Let us come to another result of the war, which in the long run was just as important. To satisfy the needs created by the Occupation, and because of the difficulty of continuing the practices of colonial trade in time of war and the interruption of trade between Egypt and some of the enemy countries where she had markets, such as Austria (cloth, tarbooshes, etc.), a local industry, spinning-mills, tobacco, and sugar refineries, suddenly came into being. The needs of transport and lading multiplied the number of railroad workers and dockers by four. The time had gone when any scheme for industrializing Egypt would give rise to such a British reaction as that of a *Times* correspondent in 1899, 'One could not expect a representative of the Queen to support a project beneficial to the Egyptian consumer and which threatened to ruin British manufacturers.'

As early as 1899 a strike had broken out in a cigarette factory in Cairo. Two others followed in 1905 and 1908. Although the martial law imposed in 1914 put an end to all forms of protest from the workers, the proletariat, attracted to industry by the relatively high wages paid in the war period, but doomed to suffer the reconversions that came after it, was already appearing as one of the explosive forces of the nation, as was to be clear enough in 1919.

It was also clear after 1915 that the students were going to form the spearhead of national aspirations. Wide unrest in the universities began to show in demonstrations at the Law School where students refused to attend the reception of Sultan Husain Kamil who was regarded as a catspaw of the foreigners. They then boycotted lectures, saying 'it is impossible to study law in a country where all the laws are flouted'. A few months later it was again students who tried to assassinate the Sultan, then his Prime Minister. We can already appreciate the relevance of George Young's statement, 'In the East, the adolescents are quicker in taking political action than the men.'

Exasperation reached its height in intellectual circles because of the severe censorship which in the heavy hand of Kitchener and his successors became 'more inept and intolerable than in any other country under British control except Mesopotamia', if we can believe another English observer. This censorship not only destroyed such systematically anti-British and extremist papers like the *Liwa* (Standard) of Mustafa Kemal, but such moderate and helpful publications as the *Garida* (Journal) of Lufti as-Sayed, whose share in the forming of an *élite* cannot be over-estimated. There was thus no outlet for nationalism except through terrorism or an appeal to some foreign power.

On three occasions there still seemed every reason for hope. First there came the Sherif Husain of Mecca's call for an 'Arab revolt', which everyone knew to be of British inspiration. Second, an announcement of President Wilson's 'Fourteen Points', ideal fodder for those who were hungering after justice. Finally there was the joint Anglo-French declaration of 1918 in favour of freeing the old provinces of the Sublime Porte.

The mistake or even folly of the British (surprising for anybody but the French, who are well versed in this kind of error) was to allow the contradiction between these heady promises and the real state of the nation to worsen to the point of absurdity. Inside the country, police interference and the different restrictions on freedom were aggravated by heavier taxation, non-payment of requisitions, the high percentage of dead and wounded in the Labour and Camel Corps, and the beginning of serious unemployment in industry.

A new source of irritation now appeared. The British administration in the Sudan decided late in 1917 to start a system of irrigation in Sudanese Gazira, a rich cotton-growing area between the White and Blue Niles. This plan struck all Egyptians, from the intelligent Isma'il Sidqi to the simplest fellah, as an unbearable threat to Egypt's water-supply: 'They are turning the course of the Nile!' No English decision could do more to set the whole country against them, causing Cromer's successors to lose that peasant support which they prided themselves on having gained. The 'policy of the full stomach' was over. In four years the British had fallen from the status of brave organizers of a bewildered populace down to that of clumsy exploiters, myopic policemen of a nation now thirsting for its rights.

But in any case, 'War or no war, there would have been a revolution sooner or later because it was the normal end-product of all the nationalist movements of the last century', remarks George Young. The organization of imperial government which the war had strained to its limits had now had its day. The 1919 revolution merely gave it the death-blow by revealing the depth and intensity of the nationalist movement begun in 1882. The Egypt of the twenties could no longer be bowed under imperialist disciplines, first because its rising industry set it against colonial trade agreements; further, because the schools started by Mohamed Ali and Isma'il and the cultural missions sent to Europe had formed a middle class of civil servants, doctors and barristers capable of taking the state-machine into their own hands, and finally because her geographical position at the crossroads of the world made Egypt more open than any other nation to Wilson's ideas and to the first echoes of the great revolt of the East begun by the Japanese in 1904 and the Turkish reformers of 1908.

X

The Wafd

In every explosive situation there is always a man such as Mirabeau or Kerensky who is prepared to press the button for revolt and to become its victim or its master. Fortunately for Egypt, her wrath in 1919 was interpreted not by a lout like Arabi nor a romantic intellectual like Mustafa Kamil, but a genuine statesman, Sa'd Zaghlul, whose popularity was well deserved.

Sa'd was the typical Egyptian peasant with his broad face, bony frame, the powerful build of the manual worker, natural eloquence, determination and good humour. The son of a well-to-do fellah of Lower Egypt, he imbibed the traditional Koranic culture at El Azhar before learning French at the age of forty. As a young magistrate he had taken part in the Arabi revolt of 1882 alongside his master Mohamed Abduh. He then collaborated with the British as Minister of Education, for which service he received the compromising praise of Lord Cromer. He was anything but a fanatic: he advised the Egyptians to show restraint towards the British while the war was on. But the man who refused to profit from British difficulties in order to secure national freedom thought he had the right to demand that the Allies' victory should be shared by the 'protected' nations.

As early as the 13th of November 1918, together with two colleagues, Ali Sha'rawi and Abdul Aziz Fahmi, he appeared before the British High Commissioner, General Sir Reginald Wingate, to ask for Egypt's independence. There is no doubt whatever that he was speaking for the whole of his people, as was shown by the almost mythical value assumed by this delegation or *wafd* in their eyes, it becoming the germ of a party which for thirty years was to be the embodiment of Egypt's struggle for independence. His request was naturally based on the temporary nature of the Protectorate, which had been confirmed (for example) in a letter sent by George V to the Sultan Husain Kamil in 1915.

Zaghlul said to Wingate, 'England is the strongest and most liberal of the great Powers. In the name of those principles of freedom which guide her, we ask to be her friends.' Taken off his guard, the British High Commissioner played for time, but advised the Foreign Office to start conversations and, as a means of exploring some of the political problems, to allow the delegation to state its case at the Peace Conference which was about to open in Paris. London answered sharply, ordering 'firmness'. Sa'd protested, organized meetings, telegraphed to Paris. On the 8th of March 1919 the head of the delegation and three of his followers, Mohamed Mahmud, Isma'il Sidqi and Hamid el Bassal, were deported to Malta. England had learnt that the Egyptian nation was born.

On the morning of the 9th of March, from Alexandria to Luxor, strikes, riots and acts of sabotage broke out all over the country. Three thousand students marched across Cairo shouting their indignation. In Saiyid Zainab Square, five of them fell before Russell Pasha's machine-guns. The outbreaks spread to the provinces with lightning speed, and it was clear that all classes of the population were everywhere caught up in the struggle. The spring of 1919 was a larger-scale repetition of the summer of 1882. But except at Deirut, where seven British soldiers were tortured and killed, there were few atrocities. Almost everywhere the insurgents concentrated on transport and communications, with the insight of true revolutionaries—at Tantah where the station was the scene of a pitched battle, Damanhur, Mellawi, Assiut, Zagazig. This gave the British a pretext for seeing the hand of the Bolsheviks behind the revolt and branding the revolutionary committee, which had dared seize power at Minieh and hold it for three weeks, as a 'soviet'.

The armed revolt ended on the 7th of April as soon as Zaghlul and his colleagues were freed and allowed to attend the Paris Conference. Trouble broke out again at Alexandria in particular in October 1919, then again in 1921 when Sa'd Zaghlul was deported for a second time—to the Seychelles. But it was in other forms and by other methods that the Egyptian revolution was to prove its originality and ensure its success: boycott and overseas propaganda.

No doubt suggested by Gandhi's example, passive resistance, so perfectly suited to the Egyptian temperament, now proved surprisingly effective. It was as though the whole country was brought to a standstill. The British administration was most affected by the strike of civil servants organized in March 1919 by Ali Mahir, who was to become something like the Thiers of modern Egypt. But the most striking form of non-co-operation was in the 'welcome' offered to the British Inquiry Commission headed by Lord Milner, a former colleague of Cromer's and Secretary of State for the Colonies. Its purpose was to seek some basis for an agreement more suited to Egyptian conditions, but which the British intended to be nothing more than camouflaging the Protectorate in more agreeable colours.

The extraordinary muteness which the inquirers met everywhere for almost six months in 1919–20 is one of the most remarkable instances of patient, patriotic unity ever shown by a colonial people. The seven British experts were met everywhere by blank faces, prominent men who refused to talk, tight-lipped politicians, fellahs who turned tail as soon as they approached. Foreign journalists and diplomats give accounts of the situation which were corroborated when Lord Milner, lost in that sea of silence, advised his government to give up the Protectorate. He suggested replacing it by a 'perpetual alliance' which took two years (1920–2) to reach its final form. In the meantime nationalism made excellent use of its third weapon, propaganda abroad.

Sa'd Zaghlul and his delegation were among the pioneers of these 'public relations' tactics which are now, along with terrorism, basic features in the strategy of impatient colonial peoples. They had understood what could be gained by intelligently playing on Wilson's proposals at the peace conference. In this respect their work in London and Paris was a model of its kind. The old Pasha, with his Gallic moustache and Mongol eyes, managed to make himself really popular, after which he 'internationalized' the problem with a skill which the British were hard put to counteract.

Through the use of the Press, publicity, banquets, and diplomatic contacts, the Egyptian problem which had already been fully aired by Mustafa Kamil in the Paris *salons*, had definitely stopped being a preserve of British Imperialism. In order to continue the unilateral talks which for the British seemed to be the only profitable approach to the problem, and to revive output which had been paralysed by the boycott and put an end to the rioting which broke out again in autumn 1921, Lloyd George's government published the Declaration of 22 February 1922, at the suggestion of Field-Marshal Allenby, who was then High Commissioner in Cairo. This statement at last recognized Egypt's independence and sovereignty, but with four reservations which seriously limited the document's value. These were: Empire communications; the 'defence of Egypt against any aggression or interference, direct or indirect'; the 'protection of foreign interests and those of the minorities', and the status of the Sudan which was 'left to his Britannic Majesty's discretion until the conclusion of an agreement'.

This 'independence BUT', which today we would be more inclined to call interdependence, none the less brought the 1919 revolution to an end. Though limited, the extent of Egypt's victory can be measured by the drastic changes London had been obliged to make in her various plans, from the note of the 1st of December 1918 to the Milner Report of 1920, and from the Curzon memorandum of 1921 to the Declaration of the 28th of February. On the 1st of March 1922 Egypt was proclaimed an independent kingdom. Sultan Ahmed Fuad became King Fuad I, and work was started on a constitution which, modelled on that of Belgium, was to be promulgated in April 1923. In January 1924 the people exercised its new sovereignty by electing a chamber in which Sa'd Zaghlul and the Wafd were returned with an overwhelming majority of 191 seats out of 211.

The movement of 1919–22 appears as a national revolution in the energy it released, the breaches it opened and the fruits it continues to bear. It brought about the first withdrawal to which an expansionist Europe had had to agree for a century, the first victory that any people had won over nineteenth-century imperialism. Because of the national character of the two countries concerned, the declaration of the 28th of February 'constituted . . . in the life of people under western domination, a decision whose consequences are not yet exhausted', according to an anonymous historian of *L'Egypte Indé-pendante* in 1936. It was not only a nationalist but a social revolution. A kind of national *bourgeoisie* replaced cosmopolitan and foreign feudalism in the Egyptian state and society which emerged from the war and the revolt.

The Egypt of 1923 to which the fellah's son Sa'd Zaghlul returned in triumph from exile was firmly in the hands of the middle-class which took the lead in resisting the British, not out of Garibaldian romanticism or xenophobia, but for good middle-class reasons. These were, the desire to make use of university training and administrative experience in the running of the State (with all that involves for a *bourgeois* in the way of placing and recovering investments), the natural demand on the part of Egyptians that they should have property rights in their own land; the hope of developing national output so as to escape gradually from the economic brake of colonial trade-agreements and the single-crop farming of cotton. As the driving-power and victor in the 1919 revolution, the *bourgeoisie* rose above verbal and sentimental nationalism by creating what an Egyptian historian calls an 'economic nationalism'. Between 1920 and 1923 a group of industrial undertakings of which the most important and significant was the 'Misr group of spinning and weaving mills' grew up round the Misr Bank, one of the largest native credit-houses in the country. Egyptian independence dates as much from the setting up of the Misr group as from the Declaration of the 28th of February.

The effects of the 1919 revolution are still more noticeable in two other fields: the relations between Moslem majority and Christian minority, and the status of women. The Copts played a particularly active part in the national rising and the common struggle welded the two societies as never before. Sa'd Zaghlul, who fought religious fanaticism as ardently as his master Mohamed Abduh, had much to do with this achievement. He made coexistence one of the golden rules of the Wafd (his Cabinet containing two Copts and one Jew), and after him the President of the Chamber was a Christian, Wisa Wasif. Thanks to the revolution, the Wafd appears to have solved the religious problem and achieved national unity.

Ever since the beginning of the century Qasim Amin had loudly denounced the degradation of women. During the 1919 ferment women, led by Huda Sha'rawi, the wife of an important member of the Wafd, entered into public life to an extent which astonished observers and showed the degree to which the old traditional society was breaking down. The women's demonstrations of 1919 and 1920 should be taken as a hint of the size of the upheaval rather than as a victory for feminism. The abolition of the veil was for many tradition-alists the most startling result of the national rising.

Egypt, which had seemed to be no more than a heap of lifeless matter, a sublime necropolis for archaeologists and a cotton-plan-tation for the benefit of the textile trade, had cast off its British policemen and the traditional structure of its society, to assert itself as a nation. All classes of the population played their part in this awakening. But one of them, the most recently formed, the *bour-geoisie*, wanted to take over the whole movement for its own benefit.

It would have succeeded if the Wafd had been its own organ of political expression.

The Wafd was the expression of the entire people, of which in the fullest sense it was the *delegate*. Any attempt at defining it would involve a complete description of Egypt. It contained all the generosity, intellectual muddle, good nature, contradictions and mythomania of its millions of supporters. It united the unlimited poverty of some and the insultingly bloated fortunes of others, the demand for change and the demand for conservatism, reaction and movement. There was something spongy, lax and warm about it which is typical of Egypt.

The Wafd seemed to bring all the possible Egypts together: that of the lords and that of the fellahs, intellectuals and agitators, anglophobes and anglomaniacs, democrats who were on the side of the Allies while Rommel was approaching Alexandria, and 'blue-shirt' fascists, pious Moslems, Christians and laymen: on the one side black morning and evening dress, well-rounded stomachs and tarbooshes, and on the other the *galabiya* of the poverty-stricken. Few men who have played an important part in modern Egypt have not spent at least a short time in the Wafd.

The great political struggles in Egypt took place between those who once belonged to the Wafd and those who still did, Zaghlul and Mohamed Mahmud, Nahas and Ahmed Mahir, Sabri Abu Alam and Makram Ubaid . . . There is hardly a branch of Egyptian politics which did not grow out of the Wafd, with the exception of the old nationalist party of Mustafa Kamil and the small group of Constitutional Liberals.

The Wafd owes this pluralism to its origin (a Delegation voicing the unanimous demands of a nation and supported by patriots, careerists and profiteers), its structure (an H.Q. composed of *bourgeois* and lawyers, typically Third Estate, economically related to the large landlords thinking only of their own political interests, while stemming from the lower classes), and its total absence of doctrine, indeed of a programme as such. The Wafd cannot be understood without bearing in mind that behind its democratic façade lies the feudal household of the Badrawi, commanding a huge expanse of decaying huts which house the 20,000 serfs of the lords of Mansurah.

But we will understand it even less if we fail to remember its

91

enormous and indestructible popularity, the fact that for thirty years it was the only open and accepted champion of the national cause, even though it only held power for ninety months. The word Delegation kept its full meaning in spite of the damage to its prestige on account of its seizing power with British help in 1942, or the scandals which dishonoured the administration in 1950–2, its servility to the king and its collapse among the burning ruins of Cairo on the 26th of January 1952. An anonymous English observer remarks that 'The corruption of the Wafd was more widespread but less ingrained than that of the minority parties, because it had a larger clientèle to satisfy and one that had gone hungry longer.'

Nothing can change the fact that for thirty years the Egyptian people saw themselves clearly reflected in the Wafd, the size of whose majority in the government was at the same time the size of public freedom. Everyone knew it to be more virtuous in opposition than in power, quicker to accuse its opponents than to clean up its own corruption, and that the more absolute the power invested in it by public confidence, the less it would be inclined to take action. But the masses remained faithful to it.

But is that enough to explain the Wafd's immunity, the way it survived the periodic splits caused by its leaders' rivalries and the cunning hatred that oozed from the royal palace? Can it explain how it alone lived through the three-cornered struggle between the British Resident, the Palace and itself which sums up the contemporary political history of Egypt down to Faruk's abdication? The people's attachment to the Wafd could be seen as a kind of mass narcissism. Its most significant manifestation is the astonishing popularity which Mustafa el Nahas has never ceased to enjoy. What pleases the Egyptians about this booming gentleman with the quaintly pointed skull? foreigners wonder. What delighted them was to find themselves reproduced in him, his moods, enthusiasms, resentments and quirks. A 'sounding echo' if ever there was one. Nahas either gave Egyptians the feeling that they themselves were exercising power, or, if not, that they were being excluded for personal reasons.

But other more material reasons are needed to explain the permanence of that great shapeless political machine. The Wafd's opponents suggest two which carry some weight. They point out that very few of the feudal lords—apart from the King—were bitterly opposed to it. By getting the majority of their fellahs to vote for it, they took out a kind of political insurance, obtaining a kind of option on the business that would come along as soon as the popular party was in power. But above all, in this way they prevented any genuine Left party from coming into being, and it is true that pluralism was the Wafd's weakness as a revolutionary force. Rather than a socialist or communist party threatening the social structure, the swollen, ambiguous bulk of the Wafd absorbed the Leftist youth and held it prisoner to the charm of Sa'd and Nahas. (This resembles the reasoning followed by the American Democrats and the Indian Congress party.)

The second reason for the Wafd's immunity, it is argued, depended on the British. They were quick to grasp that apart from their verbal exaggerations, the Wafd leaders were too Egyptian and rural not to have plenty of that peasant common sense which smoothes the way for compromise, and that only their enormous popularity could persuade the masses to accept treaties which did not contain an unconditional surrender. This is what happened in 1936. Only Nahas could have stood as guarantor of an agreement which would have ruined Adli or Sidqi. Moreover, the British regarded the Wafd as a conservative force because it drew most of its strength from the land. Nahas found his support on the cotton plantations and the careful build-up of the party in the villages, rather than in the streets of Cairo. It is said that this led the British to think that the Wafd would hold back the industrialization of Egypt, and thus prolong the colonial system of economy. Also, its reformist demagogy, directed entirely towards the industrial proletariat so as not to alarm the feudal landlords, would perhaps lead it to overload industry with the expense of social welfare and thus prevent its development. It would be unfair not to add that the British had another reason for backing the Wafd after 1942; no Western democracy can forget that Nahas's government helped the enemies of the Axis with admirable loyalty and effectiveness.

The fact that the Wafd was long tolerated by local feudalism as well as by foreign imperialism, and that it was often no more than the easy-going mirror of the nation, does not rob it of its revolutionary value. Nahas and his colleagues were more than mere agents carrying out measures which, more than any others, have played their part in reshaping Egypt: the achievement of normal relations between the Egyptian people and colonies or settlements of foreigners, thanks to the Montreux Convention; the spiritual reunification of the nation through the political collaboration between Copt and Moslem, and the working out of a scheme of legislation for labour.

We have noted that the 1922 Declaration contained four provisos setting limits to independence. The 1936 Treaty further enlarged Egyptian sovereignty, and this was the work of the Wafd. What makes this treaty something of an innovation was not so much the withdrawal of the British troops (except from the Canal Zone) as Britain's giving up the right to protect 'foreigners and minorities', and the condemnation of the principle of Capitulations which resulted, a year later, in their being abolished at the Montreux conference.

No clause more deeply humiliated the Egyptian Moslems, so proud of the tolerance enjoined by their Book and that their princes have always observed, than that concerning the protection of foreigners and religious minorities by others than themselves, all of which amounted to treating them as fanatics who could not be trusted to maintain law and order. In persuading the twelve nations represented at the Montreux conference to bring this hated system to an end, the Egyptian delegates felt as though they had passed a kind of examination in 'modernism' and maturity, before those whom they could now regard as equals.

Now that the guardianship of the 'capitulary' nations was removed the Egyptian judge and legislator now had the right to control and protect the great privileged body of people who made up the colonies of foreigners in the country, except that the Mixed Courts carried on their activities for twelve more years. This meant the end of the colonial era, by giving the Egyptian person and nation a title to equality in national and international law. The foreigner ceased being above the law. One can imagine the wave of relief that swept over Egypt at this.

Had the Christians in Egypt any right to feel alarm, now that the foreign protection was removed along with the Capitulations? Certainly for the past twenty years the Copts have not always felt happy at being isolated in the midst of a religious majority. But the Wafd was particularly innocent of abuses in this direction, its most constant feature being to give Christians a proper place in the country's political life: in 1926 the key Ministries of Foreign Affairs and Finance were held by two Christians, Wasif Butrus Ghali and Makram Ubaid. This led the Wafd's enemies to accuse 'this delegation of fanatical Copts' of trying to 'establish their supremacy over the Moslems'. The Wafd showed both skill and dignity in ignoring religious differences: perhaps even more than what he had learnt from Mohamed Abduh and Sa'd Zaghlul, it was Mustafa Nahas's political flair which led him to adopt this attitude. It had been enough for him to note how the British, as in India, had fostered religious resentments, for example by exempting Christians from punishments meted out to Moslems. The influence of the Christians in the Wafd, which was a party of lawyers and landowners, can also be explained by their professional gifts and the greater stability of agrarian wealth among the Christians.

As a movement for religious conciliation, could the Wafd become a class-party? We have seen that everything conspired to prevent it. Though it was almost constantly defending feudal interests (except for the co-operative movement which it launched in 1950 in the rural areas, and its prudent plan for an agrarian reform adjusted to regional requirements which the Minister of Economic Affairs, Hamid Zaki, drew up in 1951), Nahas Pasha's party tried from 1945 onwards, under pressure from below, to represent itself as a 'socialist' movement. The Wafd's labour laws were not without a certain vote-catching element. But is the 'spirit' of the law more important than the weapons it provides? To argue that this welfare machinery was a generation in advance of the development of local industry and its ability to stand up to foreign competition (the protectionist tariffs of 1930 seem to have been aimed for the most part at protecting British against Japanese goods), would mean accepting too readily the theory of an 'anti-industrialist' Wafd which was advanced by British-trained economists.

The Egyptian proletariat credited the Wafd with a social policy beginning with the 'Bureau of Intellectual Unemployment' of 1936, which was followed in 1942 by the legal recognition of trade unions, and in May 1944 by the regulation of individual working-agreements. As for the accusation that it crushed Egyptian industry with premature expenditure, while the landowners were still able to exploit the peasants as much as they liked, certain members of the Wafd with whom we have spoken reply that, at the time, Egyptian industry was in foreign hands, whereas the agrarian fortunes were purely national.

A strange mixture of nationalist fervour, agrarian conservatism, social progressiveness and cynical corruption, the Wafd has left a lasting mark on the Egyptian nation. It is hard to see its various phases as a whole, from Zaghlul to Mme Nahas, from Serag ud-Din to Aziz Fahmi. The oversized tarbooshes, insolent paunches and decorations for servility cannot wipe out the services it rendered—its substitution of the idea of nationhood for that of the religious community; spiritual reunification; the great boost given to public education; the proving to the world that a public opinion can come into being and make itself felt in an Eastern country, and the shaking of the Egyptian people out of their long apathy. The Wafd's historical record shows the balance to be in its favour.

XI

Making the Best of War—1939

On the lines of Pascal's thoughts on 'the best use of sickness', some Egyptian writer might well write a treatise on the best use of war. The first World War turned Egypt into a nation: the second of 1939–45 made her something of a world power.

The recipe for this success seems to be a kind of mercantile neutrality, combined with a show of friendship for the victor at the last moment. Egypt followed this with the more merit, during the struggle between the democracies and the Axis, in that very many of its industrialists and political leaders were openly favourable towards Rome and Berlin. A well-timed declaration of war against the losing side crowned an operation which had done much to enrich the country, bringing a marked advance in industrialization, a tenfold increase in bargaining power, Cairo's promotion to a high status in world diplomacy and strategy as the new capital of the Arab world, and, for better or worse, a revolutionary potential based as much on the growth of an Egyptian proletariat as on Soviet victories.

As for the conflict which at first hardly affected her, then brought one of its decisive battles—El Alamein—on to her soil, the Egyptian government held three different attitudes one after another. From September 1939 to June 1940 under Ali Mahir's government Egypt followed a non-belligerent policy which was as favourable to the Axis as the alliance with Britain could allow. Then from June 1940 to February 1942 Hasan Sabri's and Husain Sirri's cabinets tried to help the Allies in spite of majority opinion and that of the country's leaders. From 1942 to October 1944 the Wafd government finally offered the democracies firm support which its successor, Ahmed Mahir's government, took further by declaring war on the Axis—a gesture which cost the Prime Minister his life.

There is no point in being scandalized at the sympathy enjoyed by the dictators in Egypt, from the king and the richer classes down to a good part of the young student body and of the common people.

The Italians and Germans had the merit of being against the British Empire, the detested occupying power. They had the advantage of an ideology which reassured the wealthy and exercised a certain fascination over the masses. Finally and above all, Rommel and Graziani appeared as likely victors to those who had witnessed the fall of Warsaw, Paris, Athens, Kharkov, then Benghazi, Tobruk, Sollum and Mersa-Matruh. Many Egyptians approved of the former Prime Minister Ismail Sidqi who asserted in *El Ahram* on the 19th of September 1940 that 'the Italian offensive is not an aggression against Egypt, but against another belligerent on the territory of a third and occupied power'.

Others had a more acute form of neutralism. Field-Marshal Maitland Wilson tells in his *Memoirs* how at the end of 1940 he found, among the papers in the Italian H.Q., the plans for the defence of the Western Desert which he himself had communicated some time earlier to General Aziz al-Misri, then chief of the Egyptian Army H.Q. Such examples would not be given, were it not that the tendencies they reveal took on more importance later.

The fact that the British were unable to obtain an Egyptian government openly supporting the democracies—that of Nahas Pasha—without besieging the royal palace and threatening to depose Faruk on the 4th of February 1942, is at first sight a political and military episode affecting little more than people's interest in the royal dynasty. But it had deep political repercussions. First it cut Faruk off from the masses who had once been strongly attracted by the ambitious young ruler's display of piety and his imposing presence, while it alienated part of the army which never forgave him for capitulating to Sir Miles Lampson. A number of officers resigned on the 4th of February 1942, among them Mohamed Neguib.

Moreover, the affair struck the Wafd a blow from which it never fully recovered. The great party in the national struggle—that is to say, in the people's mind, the struggle against the British—suddenly allowed the king and country to be 'imposed on by British bayonets', as Ahmad Mahir put it. The credit enjoyed by Nahas must have been immense, for him to have survived such a dangerous operation. But the fierce accusation levied against the Wafd in the 'black books' of Makram Ubaid (the general secretary of the party who was dropped from office later in 1942), that of having 'neglected the nation's interest for the benefit of the British', was one that will never be forgotten. As M. Colombe remarks, from now on 'doubt had slipped into people's minds. The Wafd was no longer the Delegation representing the unanimous will of the nation. It was now nothing more than a political party.'[1] A European observer might find it surprising that Nahas should have suffered for the most logical political stand that, on the historical level, he had ever taken. No Egyptian observer finds this surprising.

But it was on the country's wealth and social life, rather than on its outlook or the political situation, that the war made the deepest mark. War profits were high. Between 1940 and 1943 Bank deposits rose from 45 million pounds to 120 million. Companies like Egyptian Hotels tripled their shareholders' dividends between 1940 and 1944. The number of millionaires (in sterling) rose in the same period from 50 to 400. As during the first World War, the interruption of imports from Europe gave a sharp impetus to local industry, in spite of competition from Palestine. The Misr Spinning and Weaving Co., which paid 11 per cent dividends in 1938, was paying twice that in 1942. If we believe the pamphlet by the Left-wing journalist T. Cliff, in 1943 the sugar-refineries reaped profits in the region of £1,350,000. In March 1942 Ali Shamsi mentioned in his report to the National Bank of which he was president, 'the prosperity arising from an influx of foreign capital as a result of Britain's cotton-purchases and the spending of the allied armies'. He noted that 'the profits of industrial companies have doubled since the war began'. Finally, at the end of the war Egypt found herself Britain's creditor to the extent of £300,000,000 for supplies, compensation and war-damages.

Thus the state and its more privileged citizens grew richer. But following the classic curve of economic trends in wartime, this was accompanied by an impoverishment of the masses as a result of inflation, and an increase in social inequality. The price-index rose from 131 in 1939 to 353 in 1944. Neither wages nor prices kept pace with each other for the peasantry, who suffered from the reduced cotton acreage brought about by the grain-shortage. In 1942 the Wafd had to exempt 1,200,000 small farmers from taxation. At the same time certain essential goods had practically disappeared from the market—one of them being paraffin, which the Egyptian housewife cannot do without for her Primus stove. At a session of the House, Isma'il Sidqi accused the allied troops of 'starving the people'. In January 1942 a Wafd M.P. declared to a reporter of

[1] *L'Évolution de l'Égypte de 1924 à 1930.*

El Misr, 'On the eve of the French Revolution the people of Paris shouted "We want bread." The people of Cairo have just done the same thing, attacking the wheat shipments. The situation in this country can be described as revolutionary.'

Three factors appeared to confirm this. The 'boom' in Egyptian industry had increased the industrial proletariat by 35 or 40 per cent, and at the same time led to an urbanization which was to prove one of the most important social phenomena in modern Egypt. As soon as the war was over the resumption of trade with Europe showed that some of the new undertakings could not stand up against competition. Also the number of workers employed directly or otherwise by the British Army during the war has been put at over a quarter of a million. Thus the closing of non-competitive firms and the dismissal of war-workers in 1945 threw over 300,000 unemployed and semi-unemployed on to the streets.

The horde drawn to the city and to industry by the war found itself, when peace came, thrown out of industry but not out of the city. There could have been no better instrument at hand for the political and social agitation which—aggravated by nationalistic fervour—was to come to a head during the revolutionary days of February 1946. The smouldering unrest among the workers, which had affected the poor and the surburban population ever since the end of the first World War, was fed by the victories of the U.S.S.R. In the eyes of the masses the prestige of the victorious Westerners was tarnished by the continued and increasingly unbearable presence of the British. The Russians had the advantage of being far away. It is worth noting that of the foreign units stationed in Egypt, the most popular were the Greek battalions, with their numerous and active communists. Is it surprising that the Egyptians were more impressed by Stalingrad than by El Alamein?

Egypt emerged from the war richer but unsettled. Local capitalism tended to be monopolistic, while proletarianization was accompanied by the threat of unemployment. The king, humiliated by British diplomacy and cut off from his people, now looked like an unlucky gambler trying to win his stakes back, while the Wafd, no longer identified with the nation, was resigning itself to being hardly more than the strongest of the political parties. But the country where one of the greatest battles of the war took place, where decisive conferences were held and whose strategic value had been confirmed, suddenly assumed an importance that was out of proportion with human and economic realities. This was the moment chosen by Britain for solving the essential problem of her food supply, her reconstruction and oil supplies, by staking more boldly on Arabism and founding the Arab League. Thus Cairo became the capital of a world, which added its own unrest to that of African and peasant Egypt. In this sense the Palestinian war appears as the natural sequel to the 1939-45 war.

European observers tend to regard Egypt's hostilities against Israel on the 15th of May 1948 as an artificial diversion made by a ruler and a government with their backs to the wall, little more than a form of suicide through carelessness. This is an interesting point of view. We are shown a Faruk upset after being jeered at for the first time as he left a cinema in February 1948, and shaken by the police strike in the following April, desperately trying to win back a little prestige by playing double or quits, and deciding that a declaration of war would at least allow him to rule with an iron hand and silence the insolent crowds. Also, the king's Lebanese advisers, including Karim Thabit, are accused of pushing him into the Arab adventure because Pan-Arabism is the only link with their adopted country for these non-Egyptians.

It is also argued that the Nuqrashi government, already weakened by the rejection of its motion against England at the United Nations, was thrown off its balance by the rising influence and boldness of the Moslem Brotherhood, and wanted to anticipate the Brotherhood over the Palestine question, while thinking that to throw a whole army into action would overshadow the Brothers' 'commandos'. But none of this is very convincing.

As a matter of fact it is doubtful whether any Egyptian government could have resisted the drift towards war. Not one of them would have refused being promoted to the rank of leader of the Arab world. Arab policies as well as the Zionist question so developed between 1945 and 1948 that recourse to arms was inevitable. The most intelligent Egyptians such as Azzam Pasha had understood and said as much late in 1947. Fierce exchanges between the Mufti of Jerusalem and the heads of different Arab governments; terrorism on the part of the Irgun; rivalry between Egypt and Iraq; the conclusions of the Anglo-American committee in favour of another 100,000 Jews being allowed to immigrate into Palestine; the secretary-general of U.N.O.'s undisguised sympathy for Zionism; the last-minute change in the demarcation of frontiers to the detriment of the Arabs—everything seemed to encourage the Arabs in the direction of violence, especially as events were being directed by cleverer men than themselves.

Nothing is so monotous or irritating as the constant search, in Middle East affairs, for the 'hand of Britain'. But in this case everything falls into place with remarkable ease . . . It was the British government which, from the 1917 Balfour Declaration down to the hasty evacuation in May 1948, ensured the birth of Israel in spite of pro-Arab sympathies in the Foreign Office. It is the same government which in 1943 entrusted Nahas Pasha's Cabinet with founding the Arab League, in spite of suggestions put forward earlier by the very devoted and intelligent Nuri Sa'id. Finally, it was the same government which fixed the hour and day of the intervention, pressing on with the evacuation so urgently that neither the Arabs who favoured compromise—such as Abdullah of Jordan —nor the British experts such as General Spears who favoured the Arabs, were listened to while they advised caution and stressed the risks of the undertaking. Everything happened as though in order to distract Egypt from the Suez problem, to give Israel a more solid position than was provided for by the partition, and to create a running sore in the heart of the Near East, British diplomacy had deliberately chosen to set the Egyptian bull against the Israeli 'muleta'.

Whether we accept the thesis of a British plot or that of Faruk's poker-game, whether we blame Egyptian industrial circles which were anxious to neutralize Jewish competition which had already proved itself dangerous between 1939 and 1945, the war was declared, fought and lost in a way known to all. Whether the upshot of a foreign intrigue or an act of initiative on the part of the king, or an ordeal that Egypt had to pass through in order to become one with the Arab world, its consequences went far beyond the size of the operations or the material damage they inflicted. We can leave aside for the moment the Palestinian war's most important effect, the rupture between the army and the king which, far more serious than the incident of February 1942, lay at the very root of the *coup d'état* of 1952. There will be ample opportunity for coming back to this.

It has to be noted, however, that as it was conducted as wildly on the financial as on the military plane, the war against Israel worsened the economic crisis, which was the harder to bear as it was accompanied by the army's collapse before the little Jewish state. The borrowing of £15 million at the end of 1948 increased inflation, while there were again shortages of wheat and paraffin. The conflict earned Egypt a new enemy, the Jew, who could be blamed for every public misfortune. However, the wave of feeling that passed over Egypt at that time should not be compared with European anti-Semitism. It can even be said that the Egyptians again showed a certain tolerance by not making the Jewish minority more cruelly aware of the repercussions of the Palestinian wars. However, the poison of race-hatred had entered a land where, only twenty years before, eminent Jews held positions as Ministers and university Professors. For the first time in the streets of Cairo you could hear the word 'Jew' uttered as a threat or an insult.

This state of mind enabled the police to start—under pretext of the struggle against Zionism—a terror for which there had been no precedent under Mohamed Mahmud or Isma'il Sidqi. The Palestinian war saw the beginning of Egyptian concentration-camps, torture used as a means of oppression or to extort information, and encouragement of informers—an Egyptian vice at any time, but then becoming an obsession. Police brutality was followed by racism and sadism, as though for a time the hunted community was at the mercy of both Egyptian police and Nazis together. The strangest result of this development was that the frenzy of bullying turned against the Moslem Brotherhood which was the most determined enemy of Zionism. Having found the war an opportunity for greatly increased activity, towards the end of 1948 the Brotherhood tried to turn the defeat to its own advantage and fell a prey to the fiercest reprisals.

The police terror also turned against the Leftist movements, as the police systematically lumped communism and Zionism together. This looks surprisingly clumsy, but we have to remember that as most of the communist factions supported the partition-plan for which the Soviet Union as well as the U.S. and France had voted, they laid themselves open to a charge of treason from the fanatical Arab groups. In any case, in 1949 the police seized the opportunity to crush the Egyptian communist movement, which was already divided and partly cut off from the masses. But as we shall see, the eclipse of the Left was not to last long.

The most immediate and radical result of the defeat was the disintegration and collapse of the state, with all its organization, taboos, its structure, its most elementary dignity. It was not enough for the army to be beaten in open country by the hardly-trained forces of a state with a population fifteen times smaller than that of Egypt. The people still had to learn, from a few outspoken journalists, that the king and his clique had betrayed them by arming the soldiers with reduced-price weapons and taken their rake-off. All this is unsavoury, but a re-examination of the real state of things, out of hearing of army men who were naturally concerned to prove that the army had been stabbed in the back, reveals more mismanagement than treason, more 'wangling' than deeply-laid plots. Incidentally the trial of one of those who were responsible for the purchases, Colonel Abdul Ghaffar, had to be abandoned in 1954.

The names of whoever were responsible are not the important thing. It was that a criminal trial had been opened between the palace and the army, and that the alliance between them was at an end. Whether the army had been partly or wholly betrayed, whether the crime was committed at the front or behind the lines, the entire régime was sullied and humiliated, and the nation's pride deeply wounded. The state born at the hands of Mohamed Ali and Cromer's reforms and the 1919 revolution had begun to crumble. It only remained to break down the internal framework of the old régime for revolution to break through. It came less than three years after the Rhodes armistice, one Saturday in January.

XII

The Burning of Cairo

The 26th of January 1952 was the first day of the Egyptian Revolution. The tragic, smoking ruins were all that was left that evening of the centre of Cairo, all that was left of a régime and a society, all that was left of the relationship between the people and authority. The fire was the perverted result of a long-felt revolutionary tension. The last days of January were spent in an atmosphere of anger and anguish, in which mob-rule had supplanted legal power.

On the 8th of October 1951, Mustafa Nahas, with his colleagues' approval, submitted to the House a project for abrogating the Anglo-Egyptian Treaty which he himself had signed and had approved by a plebiscite fifteen years earlier. However demagogical and imprudent this gesture might appear, public opinion was excitedly waiting for it. It was enough to bring back to the Wafd government's support the masses of people who had been disappointed by its handling of public affairs, and to raise feeling all over the country to a fever-pitch, whether out of patriotism or xenophobia. Even when it took the stupid form of hatred we must not forget the deep-rooted nature of Egyptian demands. The national question existed for all, like some collective suffering. However restricted it was, the occupation of territory by a foreign force was humiliating and a permanent source of indignation.

In the closing months of 1951, feeling thus gave a dramatic character to the three-cornered struggle that had been going on between the king, the English and the Wafd. It had become clear that the first two of these, who had each in turn tried to win the support of the third, had brutally joined forces against it. The stakes were now high. Since the Treaty's abrogation Britain considered the Wafd unacceptable as a go-between and had made up its mind to destroy it at any cost. In Faruk's eyes, Nahas and his friends appeared, wrongly or rightly, to be threatening his throne. Most observers were now asking the same question, what means Britain and Faruk would take to get rid of the Wafd government and stem the tide of popular approval that was sweeping it forward.

Straight after the abrogation of the Treaty, about the 15th of October, Egyptian partisans started guerrilla tactics against the British forces in the Canal Zone. These were usually limited to grenade attacks, kidnapping and thefts of lorries and material, but cost the British about thirty soldiers. The free-lances were made up of Moslem Brothers, particularly active and well-organized in the Ismaïlia area where Hasan al-Banna had first founded the Brotherhood; the Wafd youth; some communists; representatives of the 'Socialist Party' (more accurately 'National-Socialist') under Ahmed Husain; students attached to no party, little more than adolescents; and a handful of young officers of whom it was rumoured that they belonged to the secret society of 'Free Officers' (whose pamphlets were being more and more widely distributed). The British command also noted that the auxiliary police or 'Buluq Nizam' were joining in the struggle in a way that was hardly in keeping with their profession.

This 'Battle of the Canal', which the Cairo newspapers with their usual bombast called an 'Egyptian Stalingrad', came to its height on the 19th of January 1952. On that day, for the first time the Egyptian commandos made bold to attack—in broad daylight and almost in battle formation—the garrison at Tel El Kebir, the largest depot for materials and munitions in the Middle East. The British Commander-in-Chief, General Erskine, gave up his policy of restraint and resorted to vigorous counter-measures. He decided to attack the Buluq Nizam, the only section of his enemies that he could easily locate. On the 25th of January, at 7 a.m., he sent an ultimatum to the commander of the auxiliary police, giving him two hours in which to lay down arms. At the same time tanks were massed round the two Buluq Nizam barracks in the heart of Ismaïlia.

Colonel Ra'if, commanding the Buluq, at once telephoned to Cairo, asking whether his 800 auxiliaries armed with nothing but rifles should fight against such odds. Fuad Sirag ud-Din, Minister for the Interior, gave orders to resist at any cost. For this man, who had become master of the Wafd and the government thanks to his own cleverness and Nahas Pasha's age, here was a chance to create an irreparable situation at the price of a few dozen lives. He saw that he could force the British into repressive measures which would enable Egypt to reopen—under favourable conditions and at an international level—a case which she would be in a position to win. It must be noted however that the Egyptian minister could not allow a mere surrender, which would have amounted to abandoning national sovereignty, ending the symbolic struggle for the Canal and causing the government to lose face in the eyes of the public. Sirag ud-Din needed an incident of some kind, and the British General offered him a massacre, with apparently no aim except to set off national feeling in order to have an excuse for radical repression, ending, perhaps, in larger occupation forces than before.

When the Buluq Nizam barracks hoisted the white flag at 11 a.m. on the 25th of January there were about 50 dead and 100 wounded.[1]

When the news reached Cairo late in the afternoon there was furious indignation. The Wafd Youth assembled at seven in the evening and called on the government to organize a monster demonstration against the British for the following day. Sirag ud-Din accepted 'on condition that it should not become a demonstration against the King'. (For several months already the Palace had been regularly and openly insulted, especially on the preceding 16th of January which was the birthday of the heir to the throne, Ahmed Fuad.) An extraordinary Council of Ministers, meeting during the night, took decisions of the utmost gravity, to break off diplomatic relations with Britain, appeal to the Security Council and arrest, as hostages, some eighty people belonging to the British colony in Cairo. On the Friday evening the British Consulate advised British subjects to act with the greatest prudence, while many Egyptian servants advised their European masters to stay at home the next day. Cairo went to sleep with the uneasy feeling that great events were in store.

Excitement began rising before daybreak. It was learnt first that workers' unions had decided to boycott British businesses. The airport employees refused to work for B.O.A.C. A little later it was said that the Buluq Nizam in Cairo had decided to go on strike 'in protest against the Ismaïlia massacre'. At 7 a.m. three hundred of them left their barracks at Abbassieh and marched towards the University at Gizeh, where Wafdist students, Moslem Brothers and communists were holding a joint meeting. Such a meeting would have been nothing out of the ordinary—for it was at the University

---

[1] We have been unable to obtain more accurate figures. These figures are an average between the British (36) and Egyptian totals (80).

that the demonstrations of 1928, 1935 and 1946 had originated—were it not that, for perhaps the first time in the country's history, the police sent to watch the students fraternized with them. When, marching at the smart pace of people bent on urgent business and with none of the slackness of strikers, the Buluq of Abbassieh joined the students demonstrating at Gizeh, at about 8 a.m., such an unusual procession was formed that the passers-by (who in that part of Cairo are used to that sort of thing) gazed at them in astonishment. With cries of 'We want arms to fight for the Canal' and 'Down with the traitor Haydar',[1] students and police marched side by side to the residence of the President of the Council, headed by two officers, Captain Abdul Hadi Nagm ud-Din and Lieutenant Raf'at Bahgat.

In front of the Cabinet offices, which was the rose-and-grey baroque mansion of Princess Shivekyar, the 2000 demonstrators from Gizeh were soon joined by a column of students from El Azhar, who had crossed the city in procession and were also demanding arms for the Canal. The thick crowd, which did not express any particular hatred for the foreigner, and which indeed contained more men dressed in trousers than in the *galabiya*, began shouting for the 'Zaim'[2] of the nation, Mustafa el Nahas. It was Abdul Fattah Hasan, Minister for Social Affairs, who came to the balcony. He was Sirag ud-Din's right-hand man. It was he who three months earlier had organized the strike and return to Cairo of the workers employed by the British in the Canal Zone. (This was a bold and effective measure, but one which raised serious security problems and the re-employment of the patriotic workers.)

Thick-set and dark, with a glint in his eyes and his tarboosh at a jaunty angle, Abdul Fattah Hasan addressed the demonstrators: 'This is your day! You will be avenged! And we will expose ourselves to the enemy's fire, in the front rank!' But as a professional lawyer he was quick to grasp that he had no control over this mass of people, he, the party's speech-maker. The crowd, in which police and soldiers with unbuttoned tunics were standing with their arms round students' shoulders, shouted at him with unusual familiarity. All round the microphone into which he was speaking young officers with their caps aslant on the backs of their heads, and even a sailor (evoking the October Revolution), were sitting with their feet

---

[1] Haydar Pasha, the former director for prison administration, was Commander-in-Chief of the army.　　　　　[2] Chief.

dangling from the balcony railing, watching him with sardonic expressions on their faces. Then, borne on by the crowd, still more police advanced towards the building, shouting. When, referring to the Canal battle, Abdul Fattah Hasan cried, 'But must we ask the Russians for arms?' he was stupefied to hear the crowd answer 'Yes, yes.' It was surely not by chance that the mass of listeners, unsatisfied by the Minister's long and brilliant denunciation of the British, the purpose of which was clearly to gain time and calm the mob, produced a list of the 'People's demands'. They called for an absolute boycott of the British; the despatch of armed forces to the Canal, and a treaty of friendship with the Soviet Union. Thus, like some Popular Front meeting, the dialogue between the minister and the crowd went on for almost three hours. Were these the opening scenes of a 'red' revolution? Meanwhile other scenes were being enacted elsewhere, not in the atmosphere of a peaceful demonstration but of murderous frenzy.

For some time a number of demonstrators, moving from the El Azhar quarter and the city centre, had been passing through Lazoghli Square towards the royal Abdin Palace, reviling both the British and Faruk's entourage. Arriving at the large grey palace, they hesitated as if overawed, then turned off towards the Opera House. There they found restless groups of people among which it is said there were members of the Socialists and the Moslem Brotherhood. What were they waiting for? Suddenly, at 11.30 a.m. one of the groups noticed, outside the Badia cabaret, a police-officer who was drinking whisky with one of the establishment's dancers. They asked him, furiously, whether he was not ashamed to be drinking while his brothers were being butchered at Ismaïlia. He answered back, the woman sneered, and suddenly the enraged mob invaded the café and the first-floor balcony, soaked the tables and chairs with paraffin and started a bonfire. In less than fifteen minutes the fire had spread to the café. Delirium broke out among the throng, who had discovered an exciting new game. The 'Badia' flames were to spread far and wide.

The firemen, who bravely did what they could for the rest of the day, were quickly on the scene. But no sooner were the streams of water directed on the target than some hotheads came up and slashed the hoses. A knot of policemen stood by watching, without raising a finger. It appears that either a general strike had paralysed the police or they must have had orders not to interfere. Orders from whom? Half an hour later a detachment of police charged the crowd, went after it and even fired as they fled like a flock of partridges across the square and along Ibrahim Street. There was nothing left of the Badia but a heap of smouldering ruins, but the Rivoli cinema three hundred yards farther along was already burning. A '14th of July' tolerated by the Wafd was being turned into a 'September Massacre' which was to ruin the Wafd and discredit the mass movement. From midday onwards the phases of the plot became evident.

The first fire, which appeared unpolitical and no more than an outbreak of puritanical rage (so that it has been attributed to the Moslem Brotherhood and a similar organization called the 'Young Men of Mohamed'), came as a revelation to the onlookers. But these people were not the ones who fired the Rivoli cinema. Two dozen men carrying bottles and incendiaries had gone on foot or in jeeps along Fuad Street and started the second fire (if not the first?). They were to be seen constantly during that day, always the same men and always where the flames were most fierce. There was now fire everywhere, travelling at an incredible speed. No sooner was the Rivoli in flames than it was the turn of the Metro cinema, then the Turf Club farther on. In it were gathered several influential members of the British colony, along with the Canadian chargé d'affaires, discussing the measures the government was planning to take against them. The fire took them by surprise and most of them tried to escape. But the crowd pushed the poor wretches back into the burning building and then pulled the bodies, blackened and swollen with the heat, into the street. Among them was the body of Mr James Ireland Craig, the government adviser on Customs and Excise and well known as an Arabic scholar.

With their 'work-schedule' in hand the fire-raisers passed from cinema to café and from shop to cabaret. The first squad would thrust a pick under the iron curtain which every shopkeeper kept lowered on that day, or cut through it with an acetylene burner. Another squad would squeeze through the opening, throw their incendiary bottles or explosives and leap out again. In less than a minute another fire was set going. Sometimes they were in too much of a hurry and forgot some friend who was busy inside, throwing their light under the door before he had time to get out. Several of the incendiaries were roasted in this way by their companions. Malika Farida, Sulaiman Pasha, Kasr el Nil and Fuad Streets were soon a mass of flames. The flames belching from Groppi's, where the Cairo *bourgeoisie* used to meet for tea, did not reach Sulaiman Pasha's statue, close by. At the foot of the statue stood one of the heads of the political police, apparently unmoved. When a journalist asked him whether nothing could be done he answered calmly, 'Let them play a bit.'

In Tewfikieh Place, Alfi Street and Adli-Pasha Street the fires gave off a peculiar smell. In front of each bar the rioters had broken bottles of whisky, brandy and rum against the piled-up furniture, so that the smell of the fires would have gone to the head of an old sailor. Now the passer-by found himself in familiar territory, caught up and swept along in a human wave chanting the famous cry, *Allahu akbar!* (There is none greater than God): the Moslem Brotherhood were going past.

Three times already columns of incendiaries had passed by Shepheard's without stopping, past that old Ezbekieh hotel so closely linked with Egypt's historic moments, great or small. From its terrace Théophile Gautier, with his leg broken on the boat that was taking him to the celebration of the opening of the Suez Canal, had watched, fascinated, the street-life of Cairo. At 2.30 p.m. Shepheard's turn came. The fire-raisers rushed in. The staff and travellers were pushed back, frightened, while some twenty invaders, using their well-tried technique, seized the furniture and carpets which they threw in a huge pile in the centre of the majestic hall. Drawn up in the high column of air the flames climbed at a terrible speed, licking the dome which crashed in less than twenty minutes. Two singers from the Italian Opera Company fled in their underclothes, clutching boxes of jewels in their hands, while one unfortunate girl threw herself in a panic from the fourth floor into the street below.

Barclay's was on fire, The Twentieth Century French Art gallery was on fire, and so was Chrysler's. In Kasr el Nil Street the fire-raisers entered a gunsmith's and made fireworks of his cartridges. The display was remarkable but left a dozen casualties. The streets were littered with charred motor-cars lying on their sides. Everywhere were the same blackened faces, streaming with sweat, disfigured by hatred and hysteria. Towards four o'clock two new phenomena were to be seen. The crowd, which since the burning of Badia had been little more than a bewildered witness or an accomplice made drunk by such strange sights, now began to plunder. The fire-raisers

111

turned them away from British or European firms and directed them to Jewish shops and in some cases synagogues.

Increasing numbers of poor folk could be seen slipping into the still smoking department stores—Cicurel, Robert Hugues, Adès. In the doorway of a large Greek grocery shop the salesmen cunningly gave out handfuls of piastres and turned away the mob. In the same way, when later in the afternoon squads of incendiaries crossed the bridges and set out in lorries towards the Pyramids to set fire to some of Faruk's favourite night-clubs, the manager of the Mena House Hotel saved the establishment by confronting the attackers with a motley crowd of guides, camel-drivers and bedouins who would have been ruined if the hotel had been destroyed. Looting was to be the only officially recognized crime committed on that terrible day. Proof was not hard to come by in the following weeks, and several hundred were sentenced to hard labour.

The whole city was given over to a diabolical plot, a reign of madness and terror. Since their intervention at about noon near the Opera, the police had done nothing except bar the road at about 3 p.m. to a few groups of demonstrators marching towards the British Embassy at Kasr el Doubara, forcing them back with gunfire. Was this due to the helplessness of the Minister for the Interior, sabotage or deliberate orders from some other source? Nothing could be expected from the police, but what was the army doing? It was not until after five o'clock that the first detachments appeared in the Ezbekieh Gardens, though it is obvious that a single platoon with machine-guns would have been enough to quieten the centre of the city, as soon as it was realized (at about noon) that a plot was in progress and that the police were not doing their job. They could easily have put the incendiaries to flight and brought the mob to its senses.

Why was there no intervention? An answer has been given to this key question, which forms one of the few reliable documents about that incredible day. This is an article which Fuad Sirag ud-Din himself—who as Minister for the Interior was responsible for order —published on the 10th of February 1952 in his party's newspaper *El Misr*, in an attempt to refute the repeated assertion that he had allowed the burning of Cairo. It is a speech for the defence and is not very impartial. But it rings true, and the fact that so much of it can be checked allows us to have confidence in it, and to quote from it at length:

'At 12.30 the Chief of Police informed me that the demonstrators had set fire to the Opera Casino (The Badia) and were preventing the firemen from putting the flames out. I ordered him to fire on the incendiaries, but he answered that the police were siding with the demonstrators. I at once phoned Haydar Pasha, Commander-in-Chief of the army, asking for his troops to intervene. He replied that it would be unwise to send the army out against the people, as it would become unpopular. I pointed out that the situation was extremely serious and that not only were the police scattered from Heliopolis to Gizeh, but were fraternizing with the rioters. Haydar Pasha then said that his recruits were untrained, that a number of the officers were very young and that there was a danger of their joining forces with the demonstrators. I insisted, saying, "Are you sure?" He answered, "I am not sure, but it's possible." He added that since only the king could order the army to intervene, he would suggest that course to him.

'Shortly after,' Sirag ud-Din continues, 'the Chief of Police phoned me to say that the police had fired on demonstrators in front of the Opera, and that they were dispersed[1] and the situation now seemed under control. As a result the army's intervention could be postponed. I wanted to inform Haydar of this at once, but being told that he was at the Palace[2] I phoned there. I was able to speak to Hafiz Afifi, head of the royal Cabinet, telling him that there was no longer an urgent need for the army to intervene, but that it should be held in readiness for future action. This was at 1 p.m.

'At 1.30 the Chief of Police informed me that the Rivoli was on fire and that the police were doing nothing. I then decided that the affair must have been planned and organized and that the army's help was absolutely necessary. I telephoned Haydar Pasha at the Palace. I was told that he was with the king. I pointed out that the matter was very serious and that I urgently needed to speak to him. I waited for five minutes. A palace official, Wahid Shawki, then told me that His Majesty had ordered him to inquire into the reasons for my call to Haydar Pasha. I said that the army's intervention was called for owing to the gravity of the situation. He hung up, saying that I would be called back.

'But Haydar did not telephone. Many shops and cinemas had by now been set on fire. Towards 2.30 I went to the royal palace. I was taken to see the head of the royal Cabinet and was asking him

---

[1] See above.   [2] Present at a 'gala lunch'. See below.

why the army had not been called in, when Haydar Pasha arrived. After listening to me, the Commander-in-Chief went with Hafiz Afifi to see the king, to inform him of the reason for my visit. A few minutes later he told me that the king was going to order the army into action. It was then 2.45. Haydar Pasha telephoned to General Osman el Mahdi, chief of operations, who reminded him that the army could not be turned out without some delay, but who said that the army would be in the city at 3.30, and that officers would be warned to avoid streets where there were disturbances.

'I then let the Chief of Police know that the army would be in action at 3.30. By 4 o'clock the troops had not yet appeared, and I informed Haydar. At 5 o'clock a detachment of 150 troops arrived at the Ezbekieh Gardens. At 5.30 the army began coming down from Abbassieh, in small groups which had not received orders to fire despite our written and verbal requests to that effect. I telephoned General Osman el Mahdi, reproaching him for the delay in sending his troops and making him responsible for the consequences. He replied that he was about to issue the required orders.

'At 6.50 I went to a Council of Ministers which had been summoned to discuss the situation, then I telephoned at 8 p.m. to the Chief of Police who said the situation was getting worse and that detachments of troops under General Ali Neguib[1] were refusing to shoot in spite of the fires and looting, which went on until 11 o'clock, the worst incidents being after 6 o'clock.'[2]

We can easily understand why such an explanation as this resulted in the confiscation of *El Misr* at dawn on the 10th of February. It was impossible to be more outspoken in accusing the king and the army of allowing the burning of Cairo, if not of having started it. The next day the army H.Q. issued a strongly-worded memorandum denouncing these 'libels against the Egyptian army'.

We now come to the question of responsibility. Who burned Cairo? It is clear that someone had wilfully brought about the systematic and well-directed firing of about a hundred premises in the city between noon and 4 p.m. on the 26th of January 1952. It is quite likely that the rioting before and after that four-hour period was spontaneous. But in the middle of the day there was some carefully prepared and well-executed plot. To understand its meaning

[1] The future President's brother.
[2] This last sentence is highly debatable, as the worst fires came before 4 p.m.

and effect, even if we cannot find its origin, we must first mark off the stages in the events of that tragic Saturday and then look for the consequences. Then some case can be drawn up.

'Black Saturday' falls neatly into four phases. The first runs from dawn till 10 a.m. It covers the strike of the 'Buluq', their march on the University, the meeting at Gizeh, and the united demonstration which moved off towards the Cabinet offices. The authorities were already alarmed, feeling their powers of resistance undermined. But neither the streets nor the population at large sensed disaster.

The second phase is made up, essentially, of the meeting at the residence, the exchanges between Abdul Fattah Hasan and the crowd, while processions composed mainly of students of El Azhar and the Moslem Brotherhood were crossing the city. Excitement was rising everywhere, but it was the kind of excitement that goes with a political demonstration as at the Cabinet offices. Communists seemed to be playing an important part in it, while the tone of the speeches was one of traditional anti-British eloquence, fostered on that particular day by the Ismaïlia 'massacre'.

The third period began at noon. This was the turning-point of the day, but came less with the first fire (the Badia) than with the burning of the Rivoli cinema, where the incendiary squads which were masters of the city for four hours now entered openly into action. The first and second phases were periods of Wafdist imprudence, but the third was a plot by the Wafd's enemies.

The fourth phase, from 4 p.m. till after dark, was for the most part the work of wild mobs, perhaps egged on by trouble-makers, but which took over where the professional fire-raisers had left off, just as the latter had taken advantage of the political demonstrations. This was a period of looting, anti-Jewish attacks and a kind of symptomatic demonstration. At about 5 p.m. a column of demonstrators left Bulaq and went in the direction of the Russian Embassy, 'to submit the Egyptian people's demands to the Soviet Union representatives'. Here a detachment of police posted on the Fuad Bridge greeted the crowd with a burst of machine-gun fire which brought down a few dozen marchers. It was also during this period that the army gradually took possession of the city while avoiding 'streets where there were disturbances', while the Wafd government sat in council, already beaten or, so to speak, burnt alive.

As for the cost in life and property: the loss of life has never been assessed, except for the Canadian chargé d'affaires and the nine

British citizens at the Turf Club. There was talk of the disappearance of sixty of the demonstrators. But this estimate looks wide of the mark if we bear in mind the three actions in which the police were engaged (in front of the Opera, and near the British and Russian embassies), or the incendiaries who fell victims to the risks of their trade. As for the material damage, it has been put at £23 million, without counting the incalculable harm done to commercial credit, the currency-exchange and the tourist trade. Almost 400 buildings were destroyed or badly damaged and as a result 12,000 families were deprived of shelter or their livelihood. Egypt's reputation dropped in every way, but fair compensation was paid to all who had suffered loss.

On the political level the Wafd was the main loser. As early as 4 p.m. Nahas Pasha, warned by Sirag ud-Din that they were evidently dealing with a carefully laid plot, offered the king his resignation, which was refused. It was obviously the Palace's intention to make the government bear the brunt and make it responsible for the unpopular measures that would have to be taken: martial law, censorship and the curfew. It was not until 11 p.m. the following day (when Ali Mahir announced the formation of a new Cabinet after a day of consultations which had taken place in a white ambulance driving through the smoking and deserted streets of Cairo), that Nahas received notice of his dismissal 'in view of the cabinet's inadequate efforts towards suppressing the disturbances'.

The king emerged victorious over the party which he believed to be threatening his throne, and which was on the point of making his British protectors withdraw. Ali Mahir's initial measures—and during those stormy days he showed a shrewdness and sureness of judgement which was appreciated neither by the king nor by the British—served to neutralize the Wafd by making a kind of pact with it. In exchange for the parliamentary support of the majority party, the Prime Minister undertook to protect it against attacks from its numerous enemies who were again becoming active. In particular he was to protect it against the minority parties' demand for an inquiry into the Wafd administration. Ali Mahir's second step was to end the battle over the Canal. This freed the British from their apprehensions, as well as from a painful burden, and ended a situation which they were finding untenable. Of course there was no longer any question of breaking off diplomatic relations with London, or a *rapprochement* with Moscow or an appeal to the Security Council against Britain.

116

Can these results offer any explanation, and do they allow us to reveal who was responsible by simply asking who benefited by the crime? As for the king, the temporary victor, it is hardly an exaggeration to say that he was at least responsible for wilfully allowing the riots to turn into a disaster, by systematically refusing intervention on the part of the army. While Faruk was keeping Sirag ud-Din waiting, he was giving a banquet for 600 officers at the Abdin Palace in honour of the birth of the Heir Apparent. Some have regarded this luncheon, which kept in the palace those forces which might have intervened, as proof of deliberate malice on Faruk's part. His great-grandfather Mohamed Ali had secured his power by inviting several hundred Mamelukes to lunch, in order to have them massacred at dessert . . .

We have a right to ask whether Faruk would have sent in the army had there not been two events, after four o'clock, which forced his hand. It was then that he heard a rumour that the British forces on the Canal were moving towards Cairo and had reached the Suez highroad, about 30 miles from the capital. It was then recalled that the Arabi disorders of 1882 had resulted in the occupation of Egypt. The king's advisers grasped that the best way of preventing such an operation occurring again would be to plant the army in Cairo, for the British could not run the political risk of a clash with the Egyptian army. At about the same time the American ambassador is said to have let it be known that he would not hesitate much longer before taking steps to protect American citizens, and it was known that a small contingent of marines in civilian clothes, on guard duty at the Embassy, might at any moment take action.

The army was not Faruk's only weapon. It was under his direct control that the political police under Ibrahim Iman acted, or rather refused to act. Now it is notorious that Ibrahim Iman played—throughout the day, or for that matter since the Wafd ministry was first formed—a part that was noticeably unhelpful to the Minister for the Interior, confusing messages, sabotaging information and discouraging offers of help. But more proof is needed here, and in view of the attitude of the military régime to this matter, such proof would be hard to come by.

Every Egyptian who is asked who burned Cairo automatically blames the British or the king. But there is almost nothing in the first of these assertions. By what means? Through accomplices? The only answer that we have seen to these questions points to an odd organization called 'The Brothers of Liberty' (Ikhwan el Hurriya) set up by the British in the second World War to incite Egyptians against the Axis and afterwards against communism. The association had already been dissolved by the government some days before, but there are witnesses who assert that the leader of this organization, Mr Robert Faye, suddenly disappeared from Cairo on the same evening, and that members of this group were seen taking part in several of the criminal acts that took place on that day and especially in the afternoon during attacks on Jewish stores and synagogues. There is only a step between this and thinking that the British were seeking to make the minorities swallow the medicine that was intended for themselves, and trying to discredit the movement by tainting it with racism or hatred for foreigners, whereas in the beginning it had been a political and anti-British movement. But again, more proof would be needed. It can be said, however, that the British gained enormous political and military advantages from the day's events.

Sirag ud-Din's and the government's responsibility cannot be overlooked. They may be accused, first, of having allowed the country to develop an atmosphere which was not only one of political fervour, but one in which for the past year no foreigner or member of a minority had felt safe, in a 'peaceful and tolerant' Egypt. Secondly, however provocative the British ultimatum of the 25th of January, they did nothing to stop the Ismaïlia massacre which was the immediate cause of the rising. Finally, they failed to see the danger growing throughout the morning of the 26th, and if some plot against them began to operate at noon, they had done little or nothing to avoid falling victim to it. On the other hand, we can understand that Fuad Sirag ud-Din might have wanted or authorized a full-scale anti-British row as a safety-valve for the masses' anger, or to frighten the Palace and persuade the British that their policy was bringing about the worst—a social as well as a political revolution.

Leaving aside the speech of defence in *El Misr* (quoted above), and which puts Fuad Pasha in the light of a staunch supporter of law and order, an inquiry into the workings of the Ministry for the Interior shows that the Minister was reduced to impotence on that day and fell victim one after the other to the Buluq Nizam strike, civil-service sabotage, and the tricks of the police, quite as much as of the lightning action of the incendiary squads and the inaction of the Palace. Nobody denies that for months past the officials in the Ministry for the Interior had been slyly undermining Sirag ud-Din's programme, and that on that particular morning four-fifths of the responsible officials were absent from the Ministry, while a strange 'conference' brought forty of them together in an office from noon till 7 p.m. As matters stood, the minister's only forces for maintaining order were the Buluq, since the political police came under the Palace and the troops depended partly on the Governor and partly on Army H.Q. But as we know, the Buluq went over to the rioters early in the day and this was the penalty Sirag ud-Din had to pay for allowing or ordering their comrades to be butchered at Ismaïlia. In other words, Fuad Pasha had no means of keeping order in Cairo on the 26th of January, a day on which the demagogue's cunning proved itself a feeble weapon indeed.

It is generally agreed that only three political groups could have had the means, audacity and perhaps interest necessary for loosing the incendiary squads on Cairo. These are the Moslem Brotherhood, the 'Socialists' and the communists.

It seems hard to assign much of the responsibility to the communists. Not that they are backward or have any scruples about their choice of weapons, or that they lacked such means on account of being outlawed. Much has been said of the role supposedly played on that day by the Polish Legation, the head of which at the time was a diplomat skilled in revolutionary tactics. But it is hard to imagine a legation which was closely watched by the political police, supplying a local party with such things as jeeps and bombs. If the unorthodox Leftist weekly *El Gumhur el Misri* (Egyptian Masses) was one of those responsible for the wave of xenophobia, it is not clear what interest the communists would have had in turning public indignation into a hideous disaster, and in brutally ending a situation which had been developing in their favour throughout 1951. The rise of anti-Western feeling and social unrest in the cities as well as in the country was certainly preparing an atmosphere ripe for revolution. Yet it is worth noting that in an interview with the *Observer* (March 1956), Colonel Nasser accused the communists of having instigated the disturbances and burnt Cairo in 1952.

The Moslem Brothers did not try to hide the fact that at various moments during the day they were giving a hand. They were often noticed in the course of Black Saturday, their slogans were heard and their 'signature' was seen in the burning of bars and other places of entertainment, Moreover, more than two years after the affair there was new evidence that suggests their responsibility should be re-examined. It is now possible to maintain that this vast terrorist organization, hidden under the name of a harmless association, this 'secret army' several members of which tried to assassinate Gamal Abdel Nasser in Alexandria on the 26th of October 1954, and which the military government mercilessly pursued—already in January 1952 had the arsenal of explosives and incendiary apparatus which came to light in November 1954. Was not that the moment for using their material?

In spite of its puritanical fanaticism, the Brotherhood's newspaper was relatively moderate in tone during the days which preceded or immediately followed the event. Was this not a deliberate attempt at misleading the public or the government? The paper of a similar organization, *Shabab Mohamed* (Youth of Mohamed), had published, the week before, a furious attack on the cinemas 'where one sees pictures of lewd women', while approving of a crowd which had burnt and ransacked a cinema at Tantah. The next week it printed a veritable hymn of delight over the destruction of cinemas and bars, 'At last we are getting rid of this depravity!'

But none went so far in that direction as the Nazi 'socialists' of Ahmed Husain, founder of the 'Green Shirts', whose reputation was such that he had to disguise them under the title 'Misr el Fatat' or 'Young Egypt', then under 'Hizb el Ishtirakiya' (Socialist Party). His newspaper *El Ishtirakiya* surpassed all others in its maniacal attacks on foreigners, openly appealing to the masses to destroy Jewish or foreign premises. In particular he had denounced the Rivoli cinema, then the property of the British Rank Organization and which turned out to be the first target of the incendiary squads.

As soon as people began wondering who was responsible for the fires, the name of this hysterical and reputedly venal agitator came to mind. Yet he was not arrested till three months later and his trial by a military tribunal was interrupted by the *coup d'état* of the 23rd of July. The judges made no secret of the fact that they intended to acquit him. What was there against him? His articles? Shaking with anger behind the grill which in Egypt separates the accused from the court, the little man could not be kept still. He brandished the writings of some of his colleagues, numbers of *El Gumhur el Misri* and *Shabab Mohamed* and some of the Wafdist papers, to show that others in Egypt had a share in the excesses. 'We are all assassins,' he cried. As to any active part in the outrages, he succeeded in ridiculing the only two witnesses who could be found, one of them the hypnotist Muhibb.

But this trouble-maker's presence in a black Citroen flying an Egyptian pennon, in Sulaiman Pasha Street at a particularly critical moment, has been attested by two perfectly reliable witnesses since the trial. Today men can be found, even among members of his own circle at that time, to assert that he was receiving subsidies from the Palace for spreading such slogans as 'The worst enemy in our midst is the Wafd'. Also, several days after the fires, his colleague at the Bar, Abdul Fattah Hasan whose role on the morning of the 26th is already known, denounced Ahmed Husain in an interview for *El Misr* as being one of those responsible for the burning of the capital.

Had the 'Socialists' the means of doing it? Were these means put into the hands of the maddest and boldest of all? Their active participation as accomplices or executors can hardly be denied. Once accepted, their guilt would enable us to find at least the beginning of an answer to the most intriguing mystery of the day; why the military régime, so insistent about order and dignity and so anxious to wash all the dirty linen in public, never investigated the affair of the 26th of January? Did it not spare former or present contacts— just as it never passed judgement on Haydar Pasha, a king's fool if ever there was one—because of their close connexion with one of the new leaders? Ahmed Husain had been the first instructor of some of the rebel officers, among them Gamal Abdel Nasser, a member of the Green Shirts in 1935. The agitator had kept up relations with several of them, while the same officer whom we saw inciting the Buluq Nizam early on the 26th, Abdul Hadi Nagm ud-Din, was to be the liaison-officer between the 'Socialists' and the 'Free Officers'.[1]

Finally, we cannot altogether ignore the part played by the mob, or rather the poor of Cairo. It is obvious that they did not start it, but a hungry and idle mass of people are ripe for any adventure. As they followed in the wake of the 'incendiary squads', drunk with violence and with no one to hold them in check, the mob simply wallowed in a collective crime. In a curious article published in the following June in *La Bourse Egyptienne*, Ibrahim Farhi ingeniously compared the madness of January with the Potlatch, a destructive rite practised by the Kwatyuls, a tribe of American Indians.

[1]In 1956 he was still occupying some quite important posts.

'It is their own wealth that the Kwakiutl are intent on destroying . . . The more they destroy, the greater their prestige. They disfigure themselves, burn themselves, set fire to their houses. After the ritual they place themselves in the care of a doctor, who treats their wounds.'

Without looking so far afield, most foreign reporters at that time attributed the fires to an explosion of vengeful spite on the part of a people whose unendurable poverty was flouted by the luxury of the Court and the foreigner. The most striking evidence of collective guilt is a decision given out by the Cairo court on the 6th of May 1954. In order to give a legal basis to an amnesty for someone sentenced for looting on the 26th of January, it was placed on the statute-book that 'the accused had only given material expression to the general feeling . . .' In an article published on the 18th of June 1956 in *El Ahram*, Hamada an-Nahl, a lawyer of repute, asserted that the January fires were an act of collective suicide by a population 'driven to despair by its defaulting leaders'.

'The main lesson of the 26th of January,' one of the instigators of the military revolution told us, 'was that the Egyptian people lacked a truly national revolutionary party to guide it. The Wafd had shown itself no longer capable of taking the lead in patriotic movements. The void which appeared on that day hastened our decision.' More than a political crime, a strategic operation or an outburst of collective madness, the 26th of January may indeed be analysed as the revelation of a glaring emptiness. With the exception of a few hired assassins, everyone on that day showed nothing but impotence or cunningly retreated. The state which allowed that was dead. The country's leaders had emerged discredited and divided from the war with Israel. The entire structure of the state was smashed on the 26th of January. Three of the most capable statesman in political circles, Ali Maher, Neguib el Hilali and Husain Sirri, vainly tried for six months to replaster the tottering building. The first came to an agreement with the Wafd, the second held a 'purge', the third wanted to negotiate with the army. It was a waste of time, for if there had been the faintest chance of success, the king, who was tirelessly in pursuit of his own private *potlach*, would have destroyed it. 'There is a risk that the young officers will join the demonstrators,' Haydar Pasha had said to Sirag ud-Din on the 26th of January: and he added, 'Let us not make the people hostile to them.' Was he already conscious of the full meaning of those words?

Part Two

THE OFFICERS' REPUBLIC

I

A Short History of the 'Free Officers' Movement

Two generations of young men, whom we do not know, are now growing up.
They will change the face of Egypt.

SHEIKH MUSTAFA ABDEL RAZEK, April 1946

Early in the summer of 1952 Egypt was oozing revolution from every pore. A parallel with July 1789 would not take us far: in Egypt's case the Third Estate was in uniform and held the bayonets that Mirabeau braved.

The king vanquished the Wafd on the afternoon of January 26th. But this was at the price of his crown. He lost the halo of invulnerability which surrounded the palace; he had shaken the pillars of power represented by the army, the police, the royal Cabinet, and the unity of action between the sovereign and the Fayed occupation forces. The colossus was feared no longer. Defamatory rumours were spread about him. The censorship was hard put to stop the Press from openly defying him, but the whole country knew that if the police seized the issue of *El Misr* which appeared on the 10th of February, it was because it had published Fuad Sirag ud-Din's violent denunciation of the king and the high command. Also, a few days earlier the *Rose el Yusuf* had passed a cartoon showing the train, marked 'revolution', in front of which the station-master Mustafa el Nahas was hesitating to signal its departure.

There were much more serious signs of trouble. While in the course of 1951 forty-nine strikes had shown the extent of social unrest, the patient Egyptian peasantry had in turn become restive. Four risings had broken out in one year on several of the largest estates, those of Badrawi Ashur, near Mansurah; Mohamed Ali, heir to the throne; Prince Yusuf Kamal, in Upper Egypt; and especially at Inshas on the king's own domains. The risings were only ended after bloodshed, and it was rumoured that the last of these peasant risings had cost the lives of fourteen fellahs.

125

Even in Faruk's immediate circle, princes and dignitaries openly criticized everything he did, his divorce, his remarriage with a middle-class woman who was engaged to a diplomat. Even the birth of an heir did not melt this ill will. Faruk's once-amusing escapades now only gave rise to disgust. His trips to Europe where he spent most of his time in one casino after another, and where he became a favourite target for the mockery of the Press, now exasperated the Egyptians. In the palace a seedy clique of Levantine procurers and Nubian valets organized the king's entertainment, brought down governments and made army appointments. It was notorious that ministerial portfolios and the title of Pasha were bought at huge prices, and that no important deal went through without the king taking his share. There was no longer a man in Cairo who, if he had a handsome wife, was not afraid to take her anywhere where she might meet Faruk: it might prove fatal to oppose the whims of a crowned Gargantua, who seemed to thrive on scandals, trying to kill himself with excesses, a man who had lost every illusion he ever held. One day in July he sent a note to a woman-friend, a singer, which was signed 'F.F.'—'Farouk foutu'.

On the 22nd of June he dismissed the Hilali Cabinet which was guilty of wanting to apply its timid programme of reform. The Court had taken its summer quarters at Alexandria. Egypt's life now became a fantastic and absurd parade, a stupid coming and going of a queue of luxurious cars wandering along the coast-road from the San Stefano casino to the Cecil Hotel, from the villas of political leaders to the homes of former and future presidents. In front was the Cadillac of Hafiz Afifi Pasha, chief of the royal Cabinet, on the look-out for a new man to govern the country. Then came the attachés of the royal Cabinet, representatives hungering for a portfolio, journalists, a few ladies of doubtful virtue. From Montazah to Ras el Tin the Egyptian caravan of Pashas, procurers, politicians and eavesdroppers wandered about aimlessly. It was obviously the end, a golden death-agony on the beach.

It was the 1st of July. Summoned in his turn to the state's deathbed, Husain Sirri let himself be saddled with the most criticized of the king's favourites, Karim Thabit, as Minister of State. In exchange he tried to persuade the king to appoint Mohamed Neguib as Minister of War, a general who was reputed to be the leader of the army malcontents, as yet unknown to the public, but worshipped by the troops and respected by the officers. Faruk gave an emphatic 'No' to this and proposed giving the portfolio to General Sirri Amir, who was seriously compromised in the Palestine arms affair and disliked by the young officers. On the 20th of July Husain Sirri warned the sovereign that such a step would endanger the régime; that he had angered the army, and that groups of plotters had been formed with the aim of assassinating him. The one known as the 'Free Officers' was in contact with General Neguib. Faruk knew all this in any case and had just had the officers' club closed down because Neguib had been elected its President. Husain Sirri urged that there were only two solutions: either to appease the widespread discontent by giving him the War Ministry, or arrest him and his friends. The king merely shrugged his shoulders and swore. Husain Sirri resigned.

On the 21st of July the sovereign again summoned Neguib el Hilali. Faruk must have felt himself cornered, for he knew that the former Prime Minister would return only if he was allowed to apply his programme of reforms, to dismiss Karim Thabit from the Cabinet and oppose Sirri Amir's appointment as Minister for War. It was indeed with all this in mind that on the afternoon of the 21st the Prime Minister began his consultations, hastening from the Montazah Palace where the pines shimmer softly by the clear water, to the San Stefano hotel, where Generalissimo Haydar Pasha, keeper of the royal secrets, strutted up and down with a satisfied air, surrounded by reporters whom he laughingly tapped on the shoulder with his ex-prison-officer's cane.

Lounging on the lovely Montazah beach which he had ruined with flashy pavilions, Faruk stared gloomily out to sea. He had given in to almost all the Prime Minister's demands, but was calculating how to foist his brother-in-law Colonel Shirin on to the War Ministry. The Colonel was in charge of Palestine affairs and lacked neither talent nor prestige. But the king was well aware that his appointment would be taken as a challenge by the malcontents. At first he made a pretence of wanting Murtada Maraghi, Minister for the Interior, to carry on the Defence Ministry in the interim. At 4.30 p.m. on the 22nd the members of the Hilali Cabinet came to the Ras el Tin Palace to be sworn in by the king. Then the fifteen gentlemen in grey morning-dress suddenly realized that there was a black coat among them, that of Colonel Shirin. Hilali asked the king what Colonel Shirin was doing there. 'He will be your War Minister,' Faruk answered with a chuckle. That was Faruk's way of ruling. When the Ministers left twenty minutes later, thoughtful and all talking about 'critical hours' and 'tense situations' ahead, they were none the less convinced that they were governing Egypt. They were not to learn till the next morning that not only power, but the very sources of power, had changed hands.

Towards the middle of that same afternoon, the axis of Egyptian politics had suddenly passed from the Alexandria *corniche* to the suburbs of Cairo. While the fat king in his admiral's uniform was sarcastically amusing himself making and unmaking ministries at the sea-side, and while six dozen politicians were fighting for ministerial portfolios in the Palace halls and in tents on the Sidi Bishr beach, a small group of officers were quietly at work near the gates of Cairo, while the city was grilling in the heat.

That 22nd of July 1952 is full of fascinating parallels. At five o'clock, having dismissed the Ministers, Faruk took his late afternoon bath. Two hundred kilometres away, in a little house at Manshiyat el Bakri, a suburb on the east of Cairo, were eight young men in their shirt-sleeves. One of them haltingly read a note of six typewritten pages, bristling with technical terms, erasures and annotations. This was the plan for the military rising which was to take place on the night of the 1st to the 2nd of August, but which the latest developments in Alexandria had caused to be advanced to the night of 22–23 July. At six o'clock Neguib el Hilali assembled his Ministers in his pleasant villa near Montazah, with its soothing view of the sea. Near Cairo the eight men separated. At 10 p.m. all Alexandria was idly chatting on the terraces, enjoying the evening breeze. Meanwhile the plotters were beginning to act, as three cavalry officers drove a number of armoured vehicles out of their garages. At midnight Princess Faïza, the loveliest of the king's sisters, went into the Romance night-club with Mr Simpson, the American Ambassador's secretary. At the same time two leaders of the plot entered the Chief of Staff's office and after a short struggle disarmed him and took possession of Army Headquarters. At 1.30 a.m. the princess was dancing, watched by a circle of deeply interested journalists, while in Cairo seven men were taking over the broadcasting studios. At four o'clock Princess Faïza and her escort left the cabaret. Mohamed Neguib arrived triumphant at what was to be 'his' headquarters, his first council of war now consisting of the officers who had just placed full authority in his hands. Dawn was breaking over the sea in front of the 'Romance' where the reporters watched the princess leave with the diplomat. No one could

5a. The site of the future High Dam upstream from Aswan

5b. The Aswan Dam built by British engineers in 1905

6a. Feluccas on the Nile

6b. Nile mud drying in the sun

make up his mind to go home. Restless groups of people were walking along the coast-road. A strange tension seemed to keep everyone from their beds. Then from a car wireless-set there suddenly came a voice saying, 'People of Egypt! The country has just passed through the most troubled period of its history, degraded by corruption and weakened by instability . . .' The expected event had happened, but what men had brought it about?

The Anglo-Egyptian Treaty of 1936, which gave the Egyptians political independence at the price of legalizing and indefinitely extending the British military occupation, firmly entrenched in the Canal Zone, had left many of the younger generation deeply dissatified, particularly those who were both poor and poorly equipped for understanding the niceties of political realism, while being worked on by the propaganda of such political-religious bodies as the Moslem Brotherhood and the Green Shirts. This propaganda was all the more effective, the more those who listened to it were tired of the dictatorial methods of Isma'il Sidqi or Mohamed Mahmud, and more directly by the economic crisis which was an indirect result of abolishing the Capitulations.

Arising from the 1936 Treaty, a Wafd government decree had opened the Military Academy to young men regardless of class or wealth. This apparently unimportant decision was to play a capital part in the history of modern Egypt by increasing the lower-class recruitment of an army in its early stages of formation, when it had no military tradition and practically no 'caste' attitudes. With a few exceptions the Egyptian armed forces were to become simply that part of the population whose only difference was that it was in uniform. The cadets graduating in 1938, the first class to emerge after the Treaty and the decree, were destined to alter the face of Egypt. This was because, in the first place, most of the young men had chosen the profession of arms as a way of obtaining revenge on the foreign occupants whose stay in the country looked as if it would never end. They were also influenced by economic reasons. Most of them came from the lower landed *bourgeoisie*, some being the sons of fellahs who had managed to some extent to improve their lot, who had become civil servants (in the lower grades) and saw the army, however low the esteem in which it was held, as the path to a career—the wearing of the 'red' as in Stendhal. We can well imagine that these patriotic Julien Sorels were not likely to make orthodox officers.

The army which absorbed the young wolves of 1938 was a mediocre hotch-potch of parade units, forces used as police for hunting smugglers, cavalry squadrons for the sons of Pashas intent on playing polo. At that time, rank depended on physical appearance. A skinny general was either a fool, a sick man or an eccentric. The best formations still consisted of former Turkish officers who despised the 'natives', while the most efficient units such as the frontier corps made up mostly of Nubians and Sudanese, were often compromised in illicit arms-traffic. In some ways the situation recalled that against which Arabi had revolted. 'Our army was not particularly good: it was the British who had organized it and it was in their interest that it should not become a genuine force.' This remark was made to us by Marshal Aziz el Masri, who was head of the army in 1940.

In 1938 three cadets left the Military College at Abbassieh with the rank of Second-Lieutenant and were posted to the hard and remote garrison at Mankabad, situated on a great rock in Upper Egypt, near Assiut. It sounds like the beginning of a song, but was the beginning of a long story. The cadets were Gamal Abdel Nasser Hussein, Zakaria Abdel Magid Muhi ud-Din and Mohamed Anwar el Sadat. They were still full of illusions about soldiering, But their superior 'officers whose one idea was to humiliate them' and the general in command of the district 'who imagines he's the Red Sultan'[1] were not long in teaching them the truth about the quality of the army staff. 'The whole trouble is the work of the English,' Nasser constantly repeated to his comrades. Some of them resigned in disgust, but these three, one night on the Jabal Sharif, a hill near Mankabad, exchanged vows to do everything in their power to rid the country of foreign troops, reform the army and purge the State. These oath-takers, the outraged lieutenants who were now 'beginning to recruit supporters' and 'form groups of other dissidents',[1] will be met along with a few others at every stage of the story.

This was not Lieutenant Nasser's first attempt at forming embryonic revolutionary groups. Three years earlier while he was a pupil at the Nahdat el Misria secondary school in Alexandria, with the aid of a friend whom we shall also meet again, he had turned a students' committee, of which he was president, into a hotbed of political agitation. The young Gamal Abdel Nasser, son of an Upper Egypt fellah who had become a post-office employee, used to drag his companions to Mohamed Ali Square to revile the occupation forces and

[1] Anwar El Sadat: *Revolt on the Nile* (Wingate, 1957).

demand the return of the Constitution. He was wounded in the shoulder while taking part in a demonstration of fascist Green Shirts of which he was a member for a time. This tall, thin young man with a curved nose, olive face and sparkling eyes, sometimes overcame his shyness enough to ask an audience of some political leader, asking them in turn to 'unite to free the country'. Invariably shown out and seething with nationalist fury, he entered the cadet school. He chose the 'red' while his friend Bakuri preferred the 'black' and entered El Azhar, the Koranic university. The rebel schoolboy was changed into an officer but remained a rebel, as his behaviour was not long in proving.

In 1939 Gamal Abdel Nasser was separated from his companions, who were thought to be too 'enterprising', and transferred to Alexandria. There he met the confidant without whom no great plan can be laid, a lieutenant even thinner and shyer than himself, Abdul Hakim Ali Amer, who was also from Upper Egypt. He went with Gamal to the Moslem Brotherhood into which they were introduced by a young airman with slanting Asiatic eyes and refined manners, Abdel Moneim Abdel Ra'uf. Sometimes they went over to Cairo to listen to the 'Supreme Guide' Hasan el Banna, the orator and creator of the Brotherhood. Was this the man, they wondered, to drive out the foreigners and put Egypt back on to its feet by stirring its angry pride?

Nasser and Amer were then suddenly transferred to the Sudan, where they spent almost two years at Jabal Awlia, far removed from politics, working, hunting, dreaming and reading, and strengthening their friendship. They were separated in 1940. War had broken out and Egyptian 'neutrality' none the less found it expedient to hold the Nile army in readiness. Lieutenant Nasser was posted to a camp just behind the lines, near El Alamein. Here, however, cautiously for the moment, he resumed his revolutionary activities, urging his comrades to oppose a plan which the British command was supposed to be considering, to disband the greater part of the Egyptian army because of its openly pro-Axis sympathies. At this point a leader, Major Wagih Khalil, made his appearance among the objectors: he was to have considerable influence over Nasser until the Palestine war, in which he was killed. In May 1941 General Aziz el Masri, a former Ottoman officer who had been Chief of Staff of the Egyptian army and was removed at the request of the British, took a plane to join the pro-Nazi Iraqi rebels of Rashid Ali

Kilani, at a time when Goering's paratroops were occupying Crete. Almost all the Egyptian officers supported him and the two who piloted him were to play important parts: these were Abdel Ra'uf, a Moslem Brother who already knew Nasser, and Husain Zulficar Sabri. However, the plane had to make a forced landing and the three men were arrested, tried and condemned.

This episode, nevertheless, served to crystallize a state of mind, and brought together a number of men who will be constantly reappearing in our story and who no longer needed to seek one another out. Together with the men in the plane there was arrested a captain who, with Abdel Ra'uf, had formed a romantic revolutionary movement two years before, made up of five sections (economics, politics, intimidation, propaganda and security). He was now planning to start guerrilla warfare behind the British lines as they steadily retreated. He was Anwar el Sadat, one of the three who had taken the oath at Mankabad. This bold officer took one of the floating houses moored on the Nile and used it as a snare in the form of a cabaret. While the English officers were dancing on the bridge, thirty Egyptian officers were hidden in the hold below, taking down their conversation. His dream was to take the British Empire from the rear with twelve chosen companions and Molotov cocktails. At about the same time another Air Force officer, Hasan Ibrahim, vainly tried to reach the German lines. The weaving of the pattern began with such patriotic officers as Wagih Khalil, who were unattached to any party, the pro-German airmen, the groups led by Aziz el Masri and Sadat, and the Moslem Brother Abdel Ra'uf. Only the master organizer and the right moment were needed for it to take shape.

The first possible 'moment' seemed to come with the 4th of February. Surrounded by British tanks in his Abdin Palace, and threatened with deposition by the British Ambassador Sir Miles Lampson, Faruk invested the Nahas Cabinet which was firmly on the side of the democracies. The army took the news as a slap in the face. The next day a staff-officer, Lieutenant-Colonel Mohamed Neguib, sent in his resignation from an army which was 'unable to protect its king', but this was refused. But the gesture drew the young officers' admiration and attention: it was on account of his devotion to Faruk that Neguib was called on to oust him ten years later . . . Younger officers were also reacting. Two lieutenants, Salah Salim and Abdel Latif Boghdadi, asked to be received by the Chief of the

Royal Cabinet, Ahmed Hasanain, who unknown to them, was one of those who did most towards the success of the operation. 'What can we do for the king? We cannot allow him to be humiliated in this way.' 'Thank you, my friends,' Hasanain replied smoothly: 'in case of need, we shall call on you.' Another apparently useless gesture; but two more names in the future plot have emerged.

As for Gamal Abdel Nasser, he held himself in reserve. But his feelings were none the less acute and, from El Alamein where he had just been sent as a captain, he wrote to a friend, 'What is to be done after this unhappy event, which we have accepted with a resignation made up of submission and degradation? The fact is that imperialism has only one card with which to bully us; but the day when it realizes that Egyptians are ready to sacrifice themselves, it will retreat like a cowardly boaster.' This letter (quoted by Nasser in his *Philosophy of the Revolution*) was followed twelve years later by the comment

'As for us, as for the army, the events of the 4th of February put new feelings into our hearts. Officers who formerly talked about nothing but corruption and vice were now full of the spirit of sacrifice and abnegation. They were tormented by remorse because they felt impotent to save their country's prestige and wash away the insult it had received . . . In fact the 4th of February shook several people out of their apathy and taught them that there is a dignity which deserves to be defended at any price.'

The affair should therefore be remembered as a crucial date in the rise of revolutionary feeling in the army. At the same time, as we have seen, it marks the beginning of the decline of the Wafd, which so far had been the only party offering any hope for many officers as well as for the masses.

A few weeks later Captain Nasser was appointed Instructor at the Military Academy at Abassieh, and there prepared himself for entrance to the Staff College which he left four years later as a staff-officer. This is not uninteresting, since Nasser's subversive ideas could be far more effective in the tense atmosphere of the military school at Abassieh than in a garrison. The closing phases of the war were followed there with the deepest interest, and the thin captain with the stern look had a strong influence on young officers from the various services. Tomorrow these were to be the new leaders of an army which, while it still had to prove its fighting qualities, reminds one of some Greek 'gymnasium' or of one of those 'staff schools' which at about that time were so popular in the south of France, where revenge was being prepared under the guidance of officers and university teachers.

During those years of 'cold' war the young officers' aims became less romantic and more political. This was, first, because their revolt was given an economic and social basis by the growing difficulties of civilian life; their families, peasants and low-ranking civil servants, had been hit by the reduced cotton-acreage and, in the cities, there was the shortage of grain and paraffin. Also, their study of the military situation led them to discover, from Stalingrad to Pearl Harbour and from Anzio to Hiroshima, a world which would have remained all but closed to them at the normal level of studies at the Military Academy. Finally, the mobilization of reservist officers brought them into contact with intellectuals, university people, doctors and lawyers who had been recalled into the service. It was thus that in 1944 Captain Nasser met Ahmed Fuad, a lieutenant in the reserve and a young lawyer with some knowledge of Marxism, who had some influence on Nasser's intellectual development.

For them, the year 1945 was not that of the armistice, and perhaps even less that of 'victory', but rather the year in which the five men who seven years later were to carry out the July *coup d'état* came together. It was then that Captain Nasser grouped round him the small 'staff' which was the first stable core of the Free Officers. These were Zakaria Muhi ud-Din, his former companion at Mankabad; Abdel Hakim Amir, his intimate confidant; Salah Salim, whose bubbling eloquence enlivened their meetings; the mournful-looking Sarwat Okasha who contributed a political dimension to the group by being closely related to the young Wafd leader Ahmed Abu'l-Fath who was sometimes invited to the meetings. The little kernel or cell of staff-officers had already its ramifications. It was in contact with the Moslem Brotherhood through the aviator Abdel Ra'uf, already twice mentioned, and the sturdy gunner Lieutenant Kamal ud-Din Husain. The latter soon left the fringe of the Brotherhood to link himself more closely with Nasser's group. It had also attracted a young red-faced cavalry officer, Khaled Muhi ud-Din, a cousin of Zakaria's, who had studied political economy at the university and read Engels on the quiet. Captain Abdel Latif Boghdadi, a school friend of Salah Salim's with whom, as we have seen, he protested against the events of the 4th of February, now showed his sympathy for the movement. The indefatigable Anwar el Sadat, who was lorry-driver, terrorist and journalist in turn, a man never out of touch with events, held out his hand both to Nasser and to Hasan el Banna.

The years from 1945 to the Palestine war were years of fruitful apprenticeship. Meetings were sometimes held in the office of Gamal Abdel Nasser, instructor in tactics; sometimes at the homes of Sarwat Okasha or Khaled Muhi ud-Din, or at that of the deputy-judge Ahmed Fuad who lived opposite the Staff College in the same building as Kamal ud-Din Husain, and who used to lend his officer friends books by Laski and Nehru or pamphlets by Bevan. According to Sarwat Okasha, 'Gamal was a veritable dynamo, always working, reading or discussing'. In 1946 the group and its close sympathizers went through a crisis which sprang not so much from a clash of personalities as from a political problem. The Moslem Brotherhood had just affected one of the about-turns peculiar to those 'mystics'. They had broken away from the 'national front' which had grouped together the whole opposition, via the Wafd, from themselves to the 'workers' and students' committees' and given their support to Isma'il Sidqi's government which was trying to push through a plan for an Anglo-Egyptian 'mutual defence' pact which the officers found intolerable. Kamal ud-Din Husain left the Brotherhood. Abdel Ra'uf, on the other hand, quarrelled with his officer comrades, and this was not to be the last of their disputes. But on this occasion the Palestine war held them together for a while.

Even before the 15th of May 1948 the Palestine crisis had roused the officers, who were eager to realize their dreams of heroism and achievement, and who longed to assert themselves and take a spectacular revenge for the humiliations of 1942. Colonel Ahmed Abdel Aziz, the officer who enjoyed the highest prestige in the Egyptian army, set the example by joining up as a volunteer. Excitement was at fever-pitch among the little group who were already, somewhat prematurely, known as the 'Free Officers'. Gamal Abdel Nasser offered his group's services to the Grand Mufti of Jerusalem, Haj Amin al-Husaini, who had taken refuge at Heliopolis: 'You need instructors—will you have us as volunteers?' The Mufti prudently objected that they must do nothing without permission from the Egyptian government, and several days later he refused Nasser's offer. Nasser then tried to resign from the army so as to be able to join the corps of volunteers that was being formed at Damascus, but his resignation was refused.

Some of his comrades succeeded in being freed from the services for a time. This was the case of the artillery officer, Kamal ud-Din Husain, who, under the command of Ahmed Abdel Aziz, took charge of the Arab batteries facing the Zionists' 'Kibboutzim' to the south of Jerusalem, as well as the aviators Hasan Ibrahim and Abdel Latif Boghdadi who joined the H.Q. of Fawzi Qawuqji in northern Galilee, working out a scheme for air-support which had only one defect, that the volunteers had no planes . . . The Egyptian air force, however, was working out plans for an intervention. In his *Philosophy of the Revolution* Gamal Abdel Nasser tells that 'planes and pilots were waiting for a secret message from Syria to take an active part in the decisive battle for the Holy Land, then to land at an airstrip near Damascus in order to watch over events in Egypt . . . Most probably all the aviators taking part in the operation would have been condemned . . . But the order to put the plan into effect was delayed, and in the meantime Egypt entered the war.'

For six months the little group of Free Officers had been watched by the police and the army's security service. Its contacts with the Moslem Brotherhood, its meetings with Aziz el Masri and Anwar el Sadat were not unnoticed by the political police, and together with the first tracts written in 1946 by Khaled Muhi ud-Din had made them suspect. Now they seldom met together, but when their friend Kamal ud-Din Husain left for Palestine, Captain Nasser published a fervent article on the volunteers in *El Misr*, thanks to his friendship with the director's brother, Ahmed Abu'l-Fath. Three weeks later he heard of his promotion to the rank of Major, at the same time as the Arab States' declaration of war on Israel.

'On the 16th of May,' he wrote, 'I left home to start for the front, and as I ran down the stairs I repeated to myself, "We're going to war, we're going to war".' Nasser published in the weekly paper *Akhir Sa'a*[1] (March 1955) a lively, colourful and revealing account of his experience in Palestine. In it he appears full of burning enthusiasm yet suddenly suspicious, naïve, sometimes clear-sighted, intellectually immature, mistrustful, highly romantic, a man with an eye for detail, anxious to spare human lives and constantly angry at the way operations were conducted. We must quote a few passages from this account in which the veiled irony of Stendhal's Fabrice at Waterloo sometimes adds piquancy to a typically nineteenth-

[1] *Stop Press.*

century romanticism and the typical inflated eloquence of the true Egyptian.

'We grew even more apprehensive on arriving at El Arish which, being the main base behind the lines was plunged in darkness. We did not even know the location of the unit we were to join, and there was no one to guide us. We made for Headquarters, expecting to find a hive of activity, only to find it deserted. It looked like an abandoned house in an abandoned area. Finally we met a staff-officer who seemed very preoccupied—he was worried about getting his dinner. We invited him to share what we had left, and soon we were laughing together. But the sound of our voices resounding through the vaulted rooms awakened strange echoes within me.'

As chief of staff of the 6th infantry regiment, on the following day he came across 'a soldier who for the second time that day was striking his tent according to orders and counter-orders and singing at the top of his voice, "It's a damn shame," modulating his dialect in the most touching way and naïvely expressing what was in all our minds.' He was indignant at receiving orders to march on Falluja and Beit Jibrin, since 'the Cairo newspapers had published the itinerary before we set off'. Annoyed at everyone's talk of a 'political war', he none the less observed that the high command's only concern was to occupy as much territory as it could, so as to impress the public and international observers, without realizing that such spreading of forces rapidly worsens the position of each unit. 'I resented these beardless individuals, those chairborne soldiers who had no idea of what a battlefield is or the sufferings the combatants have to put up with, and who think that all they have to do is to put their finger on some position on the map and order it to be taken.'

Three months after the beginning of hostilities he was wounded by a bullet that passed close to the heart. Such a narrow escape from death awakened vague notions of predestination in him, the sense of a high calling, which he was to express with some solemnity when, after he became the sole master of Egypt, he wrote his memoirs for the *Akhir Sa'a*. Had 'the finger of God' pointed out Major Abdel Nasser as unequivocally as the President was to assert seven years later? What is more important is that he felt a growing indignation with the high command ('on the 10th of July I protested for the first time against an extravagant order . . .' 'Covering troops had been withdrawn without our even being warned, I therefore ignored my

chief's orders . . .' 'Nothing less than revolt was brewing inside me:
I was furious with those who, on the eve of the attack, had not even
taken the trouble to show us the air photographs which showed up
all the hazards.')

Soon there came the double siege of Falluja and Iraq al-Manshiya,
in which Israeli forces surrounded the units to which almost all the
Free Officers belonged—Nasser, Amir, Muhi ud-Din, Salah Salim
and Okasha. Not without a certain rhetoric, Nasser made Falluja the
centre of the Egyptian drama. 'Our hearts remained with our dear
fatherland left to the mercy of savage beasts . . . How often I said
to myself: "Here we are in the trenches, surrounded by the enemy,
engaged in a battle for which we were in no way prepared. The irony
of fate! We were enduring the outcome of ambitions, plots and passions, here under fire and without ammunition." But my thoughts
turned towards Egypt. Then I said to myself, "Is not our country
another Falluja, a much greater Falluja? What we are suffering here
is only the reflection of what is going on over there in Egypt. Is not
our country also being besieged by the enemy, a prey to the climbers
and traitors and greedy? Is she not without arms to defend herself
from the enemy?' [1]

If Nasser made a symbol of Falluja, Falluja made Nasser a
military leader whose reputation began to spread beyond his circle
of disciples. His comrades in arms have told how, in order to stop
the Israeli advance-guard from seeping into the Iraq al-Manshiya
pocket, he phoned to Muhi ud-Din, staff-officer on a neighbouring
regiment, asking that his own sector be bombarded, though he
risked being among the first victims of the Egyptian fire. After the
operation succeeded Nasser counter-attacked, and several days
later Muhi ud-Din and Salah Salim managed to remake contact with
the two redoubts. Thus two Egyptain regiments were able to await
the armistice and their deliverance.

The war did more for Nasser than offer him an opportunity to
strengthen his friendship and sharpen his indignation. During the
June truce he met some Israeli officers. One of them, Captain
Yeruham Cohen, later told in the *Jewish Chronicle* how Major Nasser
had eagerly questioned him about the way the Zionists had organized
the underground movement against the British in Palestine and
mobilized world opinion in its favour. The conflict also taught

[1] *The Philosophy of the Revolution.*

138

the young staff-officer that one should not rely too much on one's allies, witness this odd observation on the Jordan army written by the man who was to revive Pan-Arabism: 'Before leaving Gaza we received some strange instructions: we were told to march to the relief of the Jordan army which was in trouble near Bab el Wad . . . We thought it was strange to be shorn of a quarter of our fighting troops by throwing them into the hornets'-nest at Bab el Wad.'

The Palestine war had other effects. It brought fame to Mohamed Neguib. He was thrice wounded, the third time so seriously that he was left for dead on the battlefield. This general who was now famous throughout the army, if not the country, was from now on in contact with Nasser's little group by the intermediary of one of his staff-officers, Major Abdel Hakim Amir, Gamal's most intimate confidant. Moreover, the same fate that Nasser thanked for lowering an Israeli bullet a fraction of an inch below his heart, put an end to two men who till then had a higher claim than he to rouse the Egyptian army against its incompetent leaders and against the British. One was Colonel Wagih Khalil who in 1940, as we have seen, inspired his comrades to resist British plans for disbanding the Egyptian armed forces. The other was Colonel Ahmed Abdel Aziz, leader of the volunteers, who died of wounds while trying to go personally for ammunition which H.Q. had refused him. He died saying to his adjutant, Kamal ud-Din Husain, these words, which probably inspired Nasser to his lyrical outburst on Falluja: 'Remember that the real battle is in Egypt.'

The exasperated officers brought a beaten army back to Egypt. Were they cheated by the United Nations? Betrayed by their leaders? Abandoned by all and sent to fight with second-rate or unusable weapons? Maybe that was the case. But the young men were filled with rage and shame. A defeat is a defeat, and the Egyptian army suffered theirs at the hands of troops which were only just formed into an army, until then going under the name of Haganah or Irgun, the militia of a people twenty times smaller and not previously highly thought of for its fighting qualities. There were certainly some extenuating circumstances. The truce came at a moment when Egyptian advance-guards were approaching Tel Aviv; Czech arms were delivered to the Jews during the cease-fire; the Arab Legion had behaved strangely; Iraqi forces had remained inactive. The Egyptian and Sudanese had behaved well under fire; one officer in

139

four had been wounded and acts of heroism had been accomplished by such fine leaders as Neguib, Shawki, Taha, Nasser and Amir. But a man in revolt like Gamal Abdel Nasser could never be satisfied with such excuses. A handful of men had saved the honour of the army, but the whole edifice of Egypt had cracked. The Palace, the high command, the political parties—not one of them had fought. He was even obliged to note that such bodies as the Moslem Brotherhood were exploiting events with the object of seizing power. As Major Nasser returned from the war he had no more illusions about anyone. At the time of the Canal battle in 1951 he again set his hopes on the Wafd for a time. He thought of rallying this or that person to his cause. But by now he had decided that his own group and himself 'would work for nobody' and go their way alone.

In 1949 after the return from the war the first Committee of Free Officers was set up. At that time it consisted of Nasser, Amir, Khaled Muhi ud-Din, Kamal ud-Din Husain, Hassan Ibrahim and Abdel Moneim Abdel Ra'uf, though the last-named, who was always closer to the Moslem Brotherhood than to the Free Officers, was finally to be expelled in 1951. Within the orbit of this first Committee there were already some officers who were morally part of it and who were provisionally kept at a distance only through force of circumstances: Zakaria Muhi ud-Din, Salah Salim, Abdel Latif Boghdadi, Anwar el Sadat. The group was soon to be strengthened by two more powerful personalities who occasionally offset Nasser: Wing-Commander Gamal Salim, Salah's brother, who had been kept out of the Palestine war by a serious injury due to a plane crash, but who, during his treatment in an American hospital, had read widely and picked up a knowledge of economics and politics which was to make him one of the driving forces behind the Agrarian Reform. The other was Lieutenant-Colonel Yusuf Sadiq, who knew how to give forceful expression to Left-wing opinions and had a real Marxist culture which came from no one knew where. Colonel Okasha was to write later, 'We were really men of the people in uniform.'

The nucleus of an organization was there as well as the need to act. But how? Terrorism is always a temptation for small groups of rebels. Anwar el Sadat, who was at one time compromised in the assassination of Amin Osman, the Wafd Minister, suggested they should blow up the British Embassy. Salah Salim suggested that picked men should each strike down one of the most 'harmful' of the régime's leaders, naming the king, Hafez Afifi, Haydar Pasha, General Sirri Amir, Fuad Sirag ud-Din, etc. Nasser pointed out that if the undertaking was not to be suicidal, each gunman would have to be covered by five of his comrades, and the group was not big enough for that. The Free Officers none the less tried to do away with the most heartily-detested of the military chiefs, General Sirri Amir, who had been compromised in the arms-traffic during the war. Nasser has told the story of this attempt in his *Philosophy of the Revolution*:

'The sound of our shots, immediately followed by the harrowing cries of a woman and a child's screams of fear, pursued me to my bed and kept me awake all night. A kind of remorse weighed upon my heart. I stammered, "If only he doesn't die." By dawn I was hoping that the man I had tried to kill was out of danger and, feverishly scanning the morning paper, I was glad to find he had not died of his wounds.'

Underground propaganda was more attractive to Nasser than terrorism. Late in 1950 he founded *The Voice of the Free Officers*, the movement's paper, which was full of threats against the government. The little group had already composed a few pamphlets before the Palestinian war. But it was not until 1950 that the 'pamphlet battle' assumed any importance. The tracts were written by Khaled Muhi ud-Din under Nasser's direction, and distributed by the Officers themselves, who slipped sheaves of them into letter-boxes or boldly gave them out to their units. The first was called 'The Army gives a warning'. It dealt with the defective weapons issued for the Palestine campaign. Among those guilty of engaging in the traffic it named men in the king's circle. But it has to be admitted that this did not call for unusual courage, for at about the same time an M.P., Mustafa Mara'i, rose in the Senate to accuse certain people close to Faruk of corruption, notably Karim Thabit. Also the weekly paper *Rose el Yusuf* disclosed some of the war-scandals almost as frankly as did the Officers' tracts. This naturally resulted in the editor, Ihsan Abdul Qudus, being thrown into prison.

Incidentally it was officers in Nasser's group or very close to it, such as Anwar el Sadat—who had been expelled from the army and was now a journalist—and Abdel Moneim Amin, who were to be called on to play some of the most important roles. Another was Mustafa Shukri, who gave *Rose el Yusuf* its information on the

141

arms-traffic. Occasionally, even, the paper featured short, bitter articles signed 'The Unknown Soldier': only Abdel Qudus knew that they were written by General Mohamed Neguib. Thus the Free Officers' action was not confined to secrecy and overflowed into the Press. *Rose el Yusuf* was not the only organ open to the rebels. As we have seen, since 1946 Nasser had been friendly with the editor-in-chief of *El Misr*, Ahmed Abul Fath, who was soon to represent, in Parliament, those Left-wing tendencies in the Wafd which were led by the very popular and brilliant Aziz Fahmi. *El Misr* was thus bold enough to print, with pointed evidence, the news of the assassination of a friend of the Free Officers, Abdel Kader Taha, who according to public rumour had been done to death by General Sirri Amir.

It is a fact that Abdel Kader Taha, a member of Faruk's 'Iron Guard', was connected with one of the secret societies of rebels which, along with Nasser's, were being formed on all sides at that time. This one's leader was the handsome Captain Mustafa Kamil Sidqi, whom we will meet under the next régime involved in a trial of communists. He was the fourth husband of the most famous Egyptian danseuse, Tahia Carioca. These conspirators were in contact with Nasser's band of rebels through Anwar el Sadat, a friend of Faruk's private physician Yusuf Rashad, who was himself in touch, via some women, with the rebels in the Iron Guard. All this brings back the atmosphere of some fifteenth-century Florentine chronicle, complete with *condottiere*, courtesans, hired assassins, corrupt princes and masked conspirators.

But now a new field of action was offered to the Egyptian officers—the battle or more exactly the guerrilla-campaign for the Canal. In an article in *El Tahrir*, Colonel Okasha described the Officers' excitement at that time: 'We had become a seething hive, busy forming commandos helping the partisans and supplying arms.' In his house at Manshiyat el Bakri, Nasser had a small-arms depot, and there he used to lay his plans with his comrades. Of all the Free Officers Khaled Muhi ud-Din seems to have played the most active part in planning the attacks; but it is natural for us to be surprised that the army should take no more direct part in a battle in which all Egypt considered itself—rightly or wrongly—involved. At Fuad Sirag ud-Din's trial, Major Boghdadi, chairman of the court, criticized the accused for having 'undertaken the battle without preparation'. To this the former Minister for the Interior had only to reply that such preparation might well have been made by the army, and that in any case the Free Officers (among them he, Boghdadi) had done their share in making the fight possible. Captain Kamal Rifat seems to have been delegated by Nasser to take charge of certain commando operations, while other groups such as that of Mustafa Kamal Sidqi were engaged in actual combat. However that may be, at that time the Free Officers' tracts supported the Wafd, and without shutting their eyes to the domestic administration of Nahas's government, Nasser and his friends backed what— along with the masses—they called the patriotic struggle.

They reacted as Wafdist sympathizers to the burning of Cairo and the Ministry's dismissal, as can be seen from a tract they put out early in March 1952. In it the Officers denounced Neguib el Hilali's talk of 'purging' the country before freeing it of the occupier. This was exactly the same as the Wafd's attitude. Sarwat Okasha wrote in an article in *El Tahrir* in 1953, 'The people had just received a stab in the back, out of the dark.' Also on the next day Nasser went to see Ahmed Abul Fath, editor-in-chief of the daily *El Misr* and a Wafd representative, to inform him that he and his group were preparing to take action, and offering to co-ordinate their activities with the Wafd's. But as a good democrat, full of respect for normal procedure, Abul Fath replied that he was against any form of violence.

Gamal Abdel Nasser then announced to his comrades that he was going to resign, but all of them hastened to dissuade him and put themselves at his service. The plans which the Free Officers had been considering so far provided for action to be taken in 1954 or 1955. But the régime's tottering state, as revealed by the disaster of the 26th of January, together with a revival of action on the part of the police, which, under the energetic Murtada Maraghi, appeared to be threatening the Officers, made them advance the date of their attempt to seize power. Khaled Muhi ud-Din pointed out that as the Wafd had challenged the government to hold elections in November, it would be to their advantage to act then and profit from the general excitement.

The next stage was to recruit support. First a flag-bearer, a 'boss', was wanted to give the movement prestige and respectability. Three names came up: Aziz el Masri, Fuad Sadiq and Mohamed Neguib. For ten years Aziz el Masri had been the godfather or spiritual father of the movement. The cadets used to climb over the wall into the old chief's villa at Heliopolis to have talks with him. This former

Ottoman officer used to tell them stories about battles against the Italians in 1911, the Greeks in 1919 and the Bulgarians or Serbs. He was a non-conformist, a man who hated the British and never gave way. But this whimsical old man was unwilling to accept any political responsibility, and Nasser was too shrewd to stake everything on this leather-trousered Bernard Shaw. General Fuad Sadiq was reputed for his honesty and genuine military ability, as well as having been the only officer from the General Staff to have seriously tried to fight in Palestine. He was known to the public and enjoyed the army's respect. But the Officers had no sooner sounded him out than the king appointed him Chief of the General Staff. He found it hard to resist success of this kind. The General let the plotters know that promotion to the top of the hierarchy is hardly an inducement to engage in revolutionary activities.

This left Mohamed Neguib. Indeed, since the Palestine war he had been in almost constant contact with the Free Officers, especially since Major Abdel Hakim Amer became his aide-de-camp early in 1951. His anonymous contributions to the *Rose el Yusuf* brought him into touch with other groups of plotters and with Anwar el Sadat. In November 1951 Nasser and Salah Salim went with Amer to put the proposition to him. Neguib at once agreed to be put at the head of the list by the Free Officers in the elections for the administrative committee of the Officers' Club. These posts were much sought after and military observers regarded the outcome of these elections as very significant. Nasser set out to make the election a test of the Free Officers' popularity and influence. At the doors of the military cinemas at Heliopolis he had his comrades distribute copies of 'his' list, on which Neguib was nominated for the Presidency and Zakaria Muhi ud-Din and Hasan Ibrahim for membership of the council. The election proved a great success for the Nasser group, which at once exploited it by going outside the confines of the army and letting the public know about the movement. It was again Ahmed Abul Fath who published the news, noisily enough, in *El Misr*. The rebuff to the monarch was such that he soon had the election annulled, organizing a poll in the interest of his favourite Sirri Amir, the Free Officers' chief enemy. The conflict between the Palace and the conspirators had thus been brought into the open. It is a curious fact, and one which shows Nasser's extraordinary deftness and genius for intrigue, that his name should have remained unknown to the police till the very last day. He had strictly applied the basic principles of any secret society—that only one man must know everything and hold all the threads of the plot in his own hands. The group metaphorically speaking was star-shaped, Nasser being the only one with a knowledge of its ramifications, with the possible exception of his friend Abdel Hakim Amir. Salim had not the same information as Khaled while Okasha was ignorant of Sadat's activities. Such a man as Ihsan Abdul Qudus, who had the well-developed curiosity of all newspaper-men and was so closely involved in every public dispute, was to remain unaware of Nasser's existence until after the *coup d'état*. The secrecy in which Nasser shrouded himself enabled him to evade the dragnet which the political police had been preparing for a year and which Husain Sirri was to propose using again on the 20th of July 1952.

But the master of the plot nevertheless felt the screw tightening. Nobody can play for long with police officers of the stature of Ibrahim Iman. It was impossible to delay action until November: they would have to strike during the summer. The great problem was, with what could they strike? Except for the aviators (Gamal Salam, Boghdadi and Ibrahim) all the plotters were staff-officers. That meant they had no troops at their disposal. They would have to find accomplices among the fighting units. Three names at once suggested themselves: a colonel of cavalry, Husain el Shafi; an infantry colonel, Ahmed Shawki; and an artillery colonel, Rashid Mehanna. The first of these was already a close friend of Okasha and Khaled Muhi ud-Din. He was absolutely loyal to them. On 'J-day' his tanks were to be in the forefront of the fighting. The infantry-man, Shawki, was a friend of Neguib's and succeeded him as head of the best regiment in the Egyptian army, the 13th Infantry. Shawki was a courageous fighter, as he had proved in Palestine. The son of a pasha, a club-man and with little sympathy for various H.Q.s, fond of life and drink and intimate parties, he was altogether unlike the puritanical plotters. But he was impressed by the quiet Gamal and was disgusted with Faruk after the Palestine affair. He could be counted on.

As for the artillery officer, Mehanna, he had perhaps more prestige than any officer in the army, and was held up as a model by instructors. Brave, pious, tall, dignified before his superiors, skilled in the profession of arms, everything seemed to destine him to play a major part in the rising. But he was alarmed at the young officers' plans. Mutiny appeared to him out of the question. To be sure the king was doing damage, the General Staff was hopeless and the country was in danger. He thought it would be enough to wait for the younger classes of officers to mature, when the army's outlook would be completely changed, then the king would have to change his way of life, his politics and his politicians. When the young men insisted he grew angry and reminded them that the Arabi revolt had thrown Egypt into slavery. 'It would be mad,' he said, 'to begin a revolt under the eyes of the English and with the Israeli threat still there.' He was not content with showing the door to the young men who had called on him. Appointed to El Arish, he acted to such purpose that a report from the Information Service noted towards the beginning of July 1952 that 'thanks to Colonel Mehanna, the unrest once widespread throughout the units has disappeared'. (Quoted by Salah Salim in an article in *El Tahrir*.) Thus they could not count on the chief gunner. But the movement already had enough artillery officers—Kamal ud-Din Husain, Salah Salim, Abdel Moneim Amin—to ensure at least the neutrality of those units, while in any case their active participation was not essential: infantry tanks and mobile machine-guns would be enough.

The Court had left for Alexandria. The public was exasperated by endless ministerial changes. The police were sniffing a conspiracy. When would the blow fall?

'On the 10th of July [wrote Colonel Okasha in an article in *El Tahrir*] Gamal and Khaled (Muhi ud-Din) came to my house and, as they often did, asked me to play Rimsky-Korsakov's *Scheherazade*. Gamal listened with dreamy eyes and attentive ear to the charming symphony. With the final note he rose, lifted the needle from the record and suddenly announced "We will strike at the beginning of next month." '

The 5th of August was chosen, for two reasons: the Officers preferred to wait a few days after the first of the month in order to collect their pay, while the return from Palestine of the basic unit (the 13th Infantry) for carrying out the bid for power, was still awaited. But, continued Okasha,

'On the 20th of July I was lunching at my home with Husain el Shafi when the telephone rang with the sound peculiar to long-distance calls. It was Ahmed Abul Fath[1] who, phoning from Alex-

---

[1] The narrator's brother-in-law.

146

andria, told me that Husain Sirri was going to resign; that the king was going to impose General Sirri Amir on the next Cabinet as Minister for War, and that this appointment would be followed at once by the arrest of fourteen of us. I immediately went to see Gamal whose house, as usual, was full of officers, and I let him know what had happened.'

It was then decided that they should act within forty-eight hours.

Several witnesses have described how Nasser remained quietly in his office at the Staff College, the next day, correcting cadets' examination-papers, while Abdel Hakim Amir and Zakaria Muhi ud-Din put the finishing touches to the plan of action and several others passed their time drawing up lists of suspects, working out appointments, promotions, measures to be taken . . . On the 22nd, 'J-Day', everyone was calm. The last of so many meetings which had brought together ten, twelve, twenty comrades according to what crisis was to be discussed or changes of police supervision of personnel, took place at four o'clock at the house of Khaled Muhi ud-Din, at Manshiyat el Bakri. Those present were Gamal Abdel Nasser, Khaled and Zakaria Muhi ud-Din, Abdel Moneim Amin, Kamal ud-Din Husain, Abdel Latif Boghdadi, Hassan Ibrahim and Abdel Hakim Amer, who read the plans he had drawn up in accordance with Nasser's general instructions. Anwar el Sadat was urgently summoned from Rafah where he was garrisoned, and returned by train to join the group in the evening. The brothers Salim (Salah and Gamal), who were stationed at El Arish, the main Egyptian base facing Israel, were made responsible for operations there.

At six o'clock the plotters separated, to be ready for action at midnight. But an hour later Captain Sa'd Tawfiq informed Nasser that the Chief of Staff, General Husain Farid, whose arrest was provided for in one of the items of the plan, had called an urgent meeting of the General Staff for ten o'clock. He appeared to know that some plot was in progress. Also, it emanated from the Ministry for the Interior that 'something big' was going to happen. Reporters had been told of it. 'Good,' said Nasser: 'we'll start an hour sooner and take them all in the same net.' He set off in his small Morris to warn his comrades one by one that the plot was to be put into effect an hour early. He managed to catch Anwar el Sadat just as he was leaving for the cinema with his children to wait for midnight. 'Towards 9.30,' writes Sarwat Okasha, 'I saw a tall young man in a sports shirt and trousers approaching: it was Gamal. He was perfectly calm. He told me that the opening of operations had been put forward, and said in English "Sarwat, don't let your feelings get the better of you . . . Don't think you are at the cinema. Our chances of success are 99 out of 100." '

Since then the leader of the plot has told, not without humour, of how, with the plan in their pockets, Amir and he had barely left the office to begin their task, shortly after eleven o'clock, when they met a strong column of armoured vehicles advancing threateningly with all their lights out. They imagined they were discovered and lost, and were about to open fire in despair when a familiar voice called out of the night, 'Greetings, brothers. I've already taken a few prisoners.' It was Lieutenant-Colonel Yusuf Sadiq, who was in charge of the mobile force and was a little ahead of schedule. Apart from this, things went off more or less according to plan. Commanded by Colonel Ahmed Shawki, the 13th Infantry Regiment occupied the H.Q. attacked by the first motorized battalion under Yusuf Sadiq. Together with Abdel Hakim Amir, revolver in hand, this officer entered the office of the Chief of Staff, Husain Farid, who refused to surrender and fired three bullets from behind a screen. Three, but no more . . . Meanwhile, Khalad Muhi ud-Din's armoured cars surrounded the military area containing Abbassieh, Koubbeh, Manshiyat el Bakri and Heliopolis. Husain el Shafi's tanks entered the city where they occupied strategic points, especially the broadcasting buildings (at about 1.30), the telephone-exchange, the airports and the station. Apart from a short struggle outside the G.H.Q. where two soldiers were killed—the only victims of the *coup d'état* —the army and the city passed from Faruk's hands into those of the Free Officers with hardly a shot being fired.

At three o'clock, seven of the twenty officers in the plot met together, triumphant, in the brilliantly lit H.Q. building. Twelve Generals and other high-ranking officers (among them Ali Neguib, brother of General Mohamed Neguib) had been taken and interned at the Military Academy. There had been one hitch: the conspirators' chief enemy, General Sirri Amir, had managed to escape and was fleeing towards Libya. However, he was captured the next day when he arrived at Sollum on the frontier. Two officers in a jeep went to find General Mohamed Neguib, whom the Minister for the Interior, Mortada Maraghi, had awakened half an hour earlier, telephoning from Alexandria saying, 'Look here, Neguib, what are your men up to? Calm them down.' The General had pretended to be surprised, but a moment later he was ready to answer the call of the victors who had just made him Commander-in-Chief of the Army. Striding into his new office where they were waiting for him, he cried out joyfully, 'Boys, I congratulate you.' The second measure to be taken was to neutralize the Great Powers. At four o'clock Major Ali Sabri telephoned to the assistant naval attaché at the American Embassy, David Evans, saying that the Free Officers had taken control of the army and put General Neguib in command, and that if the foreign powers did not intervene the take-over would be made peacefully, order would be maintained and the lives and belongings of aliens safeguarded. Two hours later Lieutenant-Colonel Abdel Moneim Amin went to awaken the counsellor and chargé d'affaires at the British Embassy, Mr Hamilton, to tell him much the same thing.

But Alexandria had already received the alert from Heliopolis, where the few shots fired at the entrance to the H.Q. and the movement of armed cars had attracted attention, as well as from Cairo where the presence of a number of tanks had surprised people still in the streets. A little after four o'clock the telephone rang at H.Q. This time it was the Prime Minister, El Hilali, who was phoning General Neguib from Alexandria. 'Now look here, General, what are you trying to do? What is the aim of this rising? Kindly enlighten me.' Surrounded by officers, the General simply replied, 'To purge the army and set up a clean government.' El Hilali and Maraghi now knew what it was all about: the Minister for the Interior jumped into a car and made for Cairo. When the king, suddenly sobered, asked him for news, Haydar Pasha, now no more than an ex-generalissimo, answered, 'Your Majesty, it is merely a storm in a tea-cup.'[1]

On the second floor of a plain, yellow-coloured building on the road to Heliopolis, housing the G.H.Q. offices, the calm summer morning now broke amid joyful excitement. It had just been learned that the brothers Salah and Gamal Salim had taken possession of the G.H.Q. at El Arish and were in control of the large garrison. Two reporters who were their friends had already arrived: Ihsan Abdul Qudus and Ahmed Abul Fath, who from time to time had made *Rose el Yusuf* and *El Misr* a sniper's post for the Free

---

[1] It is obvious that the former prison-chief promoted to Field-Marshal, and now cleverly outwitted by the young officers, was deceiving his chief.

Officers. The first photographs were taken, showing Neguib, a little over-dressed under his splendid cap, surrounded at his table by Gamal Abdel Nasser and Ahmed Shawki—on each side—with Zakaria Muhi ud-Din, Yusuf Sadiq and Abdel Latif Boghdadi seated opposite him, and Abdel Hakim Amir, Kamal ud-Din Husain, Gamal Hammad, Ali Sabri, Abdel Moneim Amin, Anwar el Sadat standing. For the public most of these were new faces. Abdul Qudus, who remarked that it looked like a family gathering, got down to business at once and familiarly addressed Neguib, who had collaborated with him in *Rose el Yusuf*: 'Well, Neguib Bey, what do you intend to do?'—'Respect the constitution and reform the army and the State.'—'Will you take power into your own hands?'—'No. The constitution would not allow that.'—'What will your first measure be?' —'I think we will have to recall the previous parliament, to make sure that proceedings are constitutional.'—'Whom are you considering for Prime Minister?'—'Ali Mahir, perhaps. What's your opinion?' —'Fine. He's just the man for an emergency. And the king?'—'He will have to go.' Such was the first of many interviews given by Neguib, then by the Officers.[1] A number of the characteristics of the change-over *in its early stages* are already evident: legalism, a regard for democracy, a concern for continuity and even a certain timidness on the part of men who felt the full weight of responsibility on their own shoulders . . .

While Neguib was expounding his views, Abdel Hakim Amir, sitting in a corner, was scribbling a message under Nasser's direction, which at about six o'clock Anwar el Sadat carried with him in a jeep for broadcasting to the country. It was an account of what had happened.

The former reporter-terrorist's fine voice, resonant and warm, as it spoke in Neguib's name into Egyptian households at 7 a.m., brought the night's events into history.

'To the Egyptian people. Egypt has just passed through the darkest period of her history, degraded by corruption and on the point of collapse owing to instability. These destructive factors affected even the army, and were one of the causes of our defeat in Palestine. Led by ignorant, incapable and treacherous men, the army was no longer able to defend Egypt. That is why it has been purged. It is now under the control of men in whose ability, integrity and pat-

---

[1] Ihsan Abdul Qudus's Preface to Ahmed Baha ud-Din's book, *King Faruk*.

riotism you can have complete confidence. Egypt will welcome our movement wholeheartedly. The army will safeguard national interests. Those former leaders whom we found it prudent to arrest will be set free as soon as circumstances allow.

'I am taking this opportunity to warn the people against its enemies and to ask it not to tolerate any act of violence or destruction, for such acts can only harm Egypt. They will be considered acts of treason and will be punished with the utmost severity. Together with the police, the army will ensure that the law is respected.

'I wish, in particular, to reassure our foreign friends, to affirm that the army holds itself fully responsible for the security of their persons, their property and their interests. I beg my fellow-citizens not to listen to malicious rumours, for there is calm everywhere. May the almighty God be with us.'

Here we can pick out a few more of the Officers' favourite themes: the régime caused the Palestine defeat; violence is a mistake; disorder is a crime; xenophobia is folly.

While, as they shaved in the early morning sunlight, the Egyptians heard the name of Mohamed Neguib and the end of an era, excitement was still rising in the small H.Q. offices near the Koubbeh bridge. The place was bubbling with congratulations, full of messengers at their wits' end, orders and counter-orders, embraces between those who had been on the spot all the time and those who were coming in from action, visits, phone-calls, in a word, a wonderfully Egyptian uproar. In the midst of this jovial outpouring, the watchful journalist Ihsan Qudus noticed a tall, swarthy officer, unusually calm, who after reading the text of the public proclamation, was talking to Neguib in an undertone. The Commander-in-Chief called the journalist over: 'Ihsan, we want to contact Ali Mahir Pasha, but don't know where to find him. Could you take one of my officers to his house?'

The journalist accepted with pleasure, and at once turned to the tall Lieutenant-Colonel with the dark skin and calm bearing, whose name as he had just learnt was Gamal Abdel Nasser, to suggest that he be led to the former Prime Minister's home. Anwar el Sadat at once intervened: 'No, not him. Leave him alone.' The journalist then realized that, silent in the midst of the tumult, cool at the height of the fever, this strange officer was the key-figure in the whole operation. Anwar el Sadat and Kamal ud-Din Husain went with

Abdul Qudus, towards noon, to the former Prime Minister's large, green-shuttered villa at Gizeh.

Ali Mahir was just getting out of his bath. Edgar Gallad, owner of the *Journal d'Egypte* and an intimate adviser of Faruk's, had already brought him the news. Mahir at once understood that one did not keep visitors of this kind waiting, at a time when tanks were nosing round the street-corners. None the less, he suggested that Gallad should be present at the interview. Sadat dryly refused, and began by telling Ali Mahir that the army, now master of the situation, offered him the Presidency of the Council. He then made a furious outburst against the king, the Palace and various government circles—in short, against the whole social world of which Ali Mahir was one of the outstanding ornaments. Abdul Qudus tried to calm the seething Colonel. 'No!' said Sadat. 'He has to realize that a revolution has taken place!' Both disturbed and sceptical, Ali Mahir asked time to think it over. 'For the moment I can only take the matter to the king, and I can only decide after speaking with General Neguib.'

Meanwhile the city had awakened in a mood of surprise and joy. It would be an understatement to say that the army's action was popular from the start: it was welcomed with immense relief, as though some decaying whitlow had been removed. Surprise and delight struck the early-risers, and then the crowd, at the sight of tanks stationed at important crossings and in the central squares from Sulaiman-Pasha to Sayeda-Zeinab. The fruit-juice vendors, shrewdly patriotic but with an eye to business, offered a few free drinks 'In the name of the Revolution'. But as yet people had little to go on. Neguib's broadcast was far from precise as to the movement's aims, and said nothing about Faruk. They would have to be patient for a time and live in hope. But how would Alexandria react?

As though in answer to that question, the government's man of action, Mortada Maraghi, arrived from Alexandria. Installed in his office at the Ministry of the Interior, he at once telephoned General Neguib to tell him to come over. He was politely told that the Commander-in-Chief would wait for him at General Headquarters. Maraghi was astute enough not to wait for this instruction to be repeated. He took no steps before weighing up his opponents and judging the extent of their power. He found that all strategic points had been occupied and that, technically at least, the capital was in the insurgents' hands. The meeting at G.H.Q. would not take place.

Maraghi was certainly on his guard, understanding that there was nothing to be done and that the Officers had control of the situation. He made this clear to Ali Mahir, who, when he received Ihsan Abdul Qudus again in the afternoon, showed less scepticism than before and began admitting to his visitor that they were dealing with something more important than a struggle between two army factions. But when the journalist began talking of a clean-up and the abolition of the political police, the old statesman raised his hand: 'Young man, do you realize what a remarkable instrument of government that is?' None the less, they came to an agreement, and General Neguib's visit to Ali Mahir Pasha late in the afternoon became an investiture. In any case, that is how the newspapers put it the following day, under huge headlines announcing 'Unexpected military *coup d'état*'.[1] The same editions mentioned the arrest of several military personalities, among them General Ali Neguib, brother of the new Commander-in-Chief. Was it because they were related that at the last minute the censor blacked out their photographs, except for Husain Sirri Amir's? They also published the first pictures of the victorious officers, a snapshot showing them tired and perspiring as they stood round Neguib early in the morning. No names were given except the Commander-in-Chief's. This rule was relaxed next day for Ahmed Shawki, photographed beside Neguib, and the day after for Anwar el Sadat, arriving from Alexandria next to his 'chief'. That is why these two officers were at first thought to be grey eminences and the real authors of the *coup d'état*.

On that Wednesday morning the embassies were in a state of panic. Who were these people who dared disturb the Egyptian summer, when the temperature is over 90 degrees in the shade? The various ambassadors were either in Alexandria or in Europe. The military attachés, hastily summoned, looked through their files feverishly. 'Yes, we were aware that a crisis was developing in the army. Refer, sir, to my telegrams of such and such a date. It's something to do with the Officers' Club, something about appointing Mohamed Neguib as Minister of War.'—'But who is this Neguib?' —'Fought brilliantly in the Palestine war, brother of General Ali Neguib, commanding the troops in Cairo; his mother was Sudanese. He has a reputation for integrity and for getting on the wrong side of the king. He is said to have republican views and to be in touch

[1] *El Misr*, 24 July 1952.

153

with the Moslem Brotherhood. He has apparently written two or three books on military tactics. He speaks English, French, German and Italian. He is very anti-British . . .'—'And what about the other officers?'—'We are told that Anwar el Sadat was among them. There are three red marks against his name on the English black-list. A terrorist, detests Britain, arrested several times, once for taking part in the assassination of Amin Osman, the Wafd Finance Minister. A staunch pro-German, connected with the Moslem Brotherhood and with Ahmed Husain's National Socialists, now thought to be responsible for the burning of Cairo. Not very re-assuring! Others are Colonel Shawki, son of Shawki Pasha and Ali Mahir's nephew—a hothead; Zakaria Muhi ud-Din, Ali Sabri, good intelligence-officers. It all looks a bit improvised, the work of young men.'—'Is it serious?'—'Well . . .' The British 'experts' whom everyone consulted made no secret of their displeasure at being duped, led by the nose—they who in theory knew the Egyptian army's secrets better than its own Chief of Staff. They muttered that the Moslem Brotherhood seemed to have had a finger in the pie, and that it would be a mistake to think that Neguib would emerge unscathed. Among the Americans, on the other hand, there was a certain open satisfaction. They had been thinking for some time of substituting an authoritarian and reformist régime for Faruk, and since a cocktail-party given by their naval attaché in Alexandria on the preceding Saturday they had not been completely ignorant of the affair. One or two Egyptian officers had taken their American colleague aside to ask him what the reaction might be should the army make a bid for power. Besides, the Americans had one or two people on the inside . . .

The first phase of the operation was now over, with the conquest of the military command and the arrest of those army and police officers who presented any immediate danger. The second—setting up a sound government—was in progress. The third, Faruk's elimina-tion, was to prove more delicate. The cautious skill with which this affair was carried out reveals—even more than the commando operations of the 22nd–23rd of July—Nasser's tactical genius. Why, for instance, choose Ali Mahir? To be sure, his forcefulness, his ability to manœuvre in tight corners, his anglophobia and political imagination were appreciated and most useful in a novel situation. But Nasser, who was trying to avoid a stir over the Faruk issue, was mainly aware that the former head of the royal Cabinet was perhaps the only man with enough sway over the king to force that violent man to abdicate. The young Lieutenant-Colonel intended using the old statesman as a kind of lubricant.

On the 24th of July, finally convinced of the Officers' strength, Ali Mahir left for Alexandria. There he was received by the king, late in the morning. He has never described the reception given him by his former pupil, but Faruk's anguish at that time is well enough known for us to understand that he preferred the sight of the little dark-haired, pouchy-eyed man with his jaunty tarboosh, to that of three Captains armed to the teeth. In any case, when three hours later Ali Mahir entered Bulkeley—where the Alexandria Cabinet offices were situated—he was wearing a Prime Minister's morning suit and carrying in his pocket a list of Ministers which had been read and approved. After a first Council of Ministers presided over by Faruk that afternoon at Ras el Tin, the new President drove quickly back to Cairo. Arriving at nine o'clock he was about to tell Neguib and his officers that 'His Majesty has deigned to approve such of the army's requests as it has so far been possible to submit to him'. That is to say, the change of government, General Neguib's appointment as head of the armed forces, in place of Haydar Pasha who had resigned along with Hilali early on the same day, and the dropping of most of the royal favourites, Hafiz Afifi, Karim Thabit, Elias Andraos, Antoine Pulli and Yusuf Rashad.

This is what the Prime Minister announced at his first Press conference the next morning, adding with a smile that 'everything was going very well' and that 'the greatest calm reigned everywhere'. But on the evening of the 24th General Neguib had sent out a second message to the nation, protesting against 'the ill-disposed rumours that certain quarters were spreading against the movement', and asserting that 'its only goal was the reform and purging of the army while respecting the constitution'; that 'it had only succeeded because it emanated from the people' and, in conclusion, that 'the situation was well in hand'. At the same time the new leaders were arresting several leaders among the political police, including Ibrahim Iman and Mohamed el Ghazzar, while freeing their friend Fathi Radwan, who had been imprisoned after the events of the 26th of January.

At noon on the 25th of July, after receiving the British and American attachés to inform them of the military *coup*'s objectives—which were at that very moment being set out in a new public proclamation[1]—General Neguib and Anwar el Sadat took a plane to Alexandria. The third act of the drama, which was to end with eliminating Faruk, was now opening. In Cairo, the Officers had already tasted the people's tremendous enthusiasm, but their welcome in Alexandria was overwhelming. The 'saviour of the country' was engulfed in a happy, roaring tide of humanity, madly exhilarated.

Nasser knew they would have to act quickly, and for that matter had already sent Zakaria Muhi ud-Din ahead to Alexandria the previous night, to direct operations there. There were three dangers to guard against. First, there were the negotiations between Faruk and the commander of the coast-guards, Wahid Shawki. Was the king preparing a counter-stroke? Secondly, there was the entrance on the scene of Colonel Rashid Mehanna, who after refusing to share in the conspiracy had just returned from El Arish to Cairo, where he was acclaimed by artillery units and then left at once for Alexandria. Was he going to try and save Faruk, so as to play the king-maker? No: he took the side of the victors, but obviously with personal aims in mind. The third danger was much graver. It is said that, evoking a secret clause in the 1936 Anglo-Egyptian Treaty which was said to guarantee British protection to the king and his family, Faruk had appealed to the occupying forces in the Canal Zone. The British Ambassador later gave an emphatic denial to these rumours, and Faruk has never confirmed them. None the less, the officers had every reason for expecting the worst: it would be safer to present the foreigner with an accomplished fact, especially if it were not one that might give cause for horror.

This was one of the arguments which enabled Nasser to save Faruk's head, which was being demanded by a number of officers, in the forefront of whom was Gamal Salim, the victor of El Arish, who had come back to Cairo on the 25th and was at once sent on to Alexandria. In the course of the night of the 25th–26th a strange

---

[1] 'The movement within the army has its programme, which has existed from the start. Its aims are to clean up the government, within the framework of the constitution, and to restore the freedom of the individual . . . It was essential that a group of loyal and devoted men, whom their struggles, their experience and their youth had prepared for such a destiny, should take on themselves the responsibility for putting public affairs in order . . . These men have worked out the measures to be taken to ensure the cleansing and reform of the State. All these measures are of a provisional nature. All those who find themselves in positions of leadership in this *blessed* movement, will return to their normal posts as soon as they are satisfied that the country is in good hands.'

and dramatic trial took place between the two capitals. It was the trial of Faruk. On being consulted, old Aziz el Masri gave a terse answer that was worthy of a Marat: 'A head only interests me after it has fallen!'[1] Gamal Salim quickly made the return journey from Cairo to Alexandria, and on the 26th at 7 a.m. he brought back the Free Officers' majority verdict, which was that the king would be exiled.

Having left the night before, an armoured column had also gone to Alexandria. By eight o'clock it had surrounded the Ras el Tin and Montazah palaces, though not without a sharp exchange of fire resulting in seven wounded. In a panic Faruk sent a messenger to Mr Jefferson Caffery, the American Ambassador, who after a conversation with Ali Mahir informed the king that he had obtained a sort of guarantee that his life and that of his family would be safeguarded.

On the 26th, at 9 a.m., General Neguib and Lieutenant-Colonel Sadat handed the Prime Minister the text of an ultimatum which the army had issued to the king.

'In view of your . . . misrule, your violations of the Constitution, your contempt for the will of the nation, which has gone so far that no citizen can any longer feel his life, property or dignity to be safe . . . and because under your protection traitors and swindlers are allowed to amass scandalous fortunes by wasting public monies while the people are dying of privation and hunger; and since these abuses were aggravated during the war in Palestine which gave rise to an abominable traffic in arms and munitions . . . the army, which represents the strength of the people, has ordered me to demand that Your Majesty abdicate in favour of the heir to the throne, His Highness Ahmed Fuad, on this day, Saturday, the 26th of July 1952, and that he quit the country on the same day before six o'clock. In the event of a rejection of this ultimatum, you will be held responsible for the consequences.'

This document was signed: Mohamed Neguib.

Anwar el Sadat relates that while reading this declaration Ali Mahir 'was as pale as death'. Had he hoped to restrict the affair to a change of Cabinet and the quiet liquidation of the 'king's jesters'? The old statesman murmured with a voice weakened with emotion, 'He never listened to me: he is getting what he deserves.' He left for Ras el Tin.

[1] Anwar el Sadat: from an account published in *Action*, Tunis, 23 July 1955.

The interview was a long one. Faruk did not try to resist. The tanks round the palace and the firing that morning had already convinced him. He tried only to obtain certain concessions such as the protection of his wealth, his departure on the royal yacht, the *Mahrusa*. He asked to be allowed to take with him his companions Pulli and Hilmi, and inquired whether he could return to Egypt as a private person. 'The Duke of Windsor sometimes returns to England,' suggested Ali Mahir Pasha at a venture. The king signed and waited for the act of abdication to which Abdel Razek Sanhuri and Sulaiman Hafiz—President and Vice-President of the Supreme Court—were putting the finishing touches. They were 'helped' in this, and even corrected, by the officers, who insisted that the text must contain the reference to 'the will of the people'.

Sulaiman Hafiz, who was to deliver this final blow to Faruk, has narrated the scene as follows:

'He cast a brief glance over the text and asked me what the Act was based on. I replied that provision had been made for it in the preamble to the Constitution. He appeared calm, but judging from his slight coughs and the shuffling of his feet he was terribly nervous and trying to control himself. He read the document twice, then begged me to add to the phrase 'the will of the people', a reference to 'Our will'. I pointed out to him that the text was drafted in the form of a royal rescript. He asked whether that meant that the royal will was understood? I said that it was. He signed and said: 'I hope that in view of the circumstances you will excuse this signature. I had better sign it again. He did.'[1]

Towards the middle of the afternoon it was announced in a broadcast from Cairo that 'some very important news would be given at six o'clock'. Everybody understood and prepared to listen.

All round the Ras el Tin palace and along the coast-road of Alexandria an enormous crowd had gathered, tense with expectation and with mixed feelings of anguish and joy. Then came the prodigious sight: the royal exit in the rays of the setting sun, on to the sea which a hundred and fifty years earlier had brought, to the Egyptian shore, the Albanian soldier of fortune Mohamed Ali, the great-great-grandfather of the sovereign who was now taking his leave.

[1] From a letter addressed to President Ali Mahir on the 11th of August 1952. quoted by R. Badrawi in *The Military Coup*.

At ten minutes to six, after saying farewell to his sisters and other relatives in the hall of Ras el Tin, Faruk, in his splendid white uniform of Admiral of the Fleet, came slowly down the palace steps towards the sea. He was followed by Queen Narriman, carrying the new king, six months old. At the deposed sovereign's request, Mr Jefferson Caffery's presence assured him of a kind of diplomatic guarantee against any last-minute violence. While the royal flag was being fetched from the palace, a cruiser in the bay fired a twenty-one-gun salute.

Faruk went aboard. He appeared to be waiting for someone and looked impatiently at his watch while the royal yacht began to heave in its mooring tackle. This last visitor who was risking missing the traveller, was General Neguib, who had let the king know—against his comrades' wishes—that he would come aboard to pay his respects. The new Commander-in-Chief's jeep at last managed to pass through the crowd which was clinging to it and had delayed it until after six o'clock.

General Neguib went aboard, followed by three of the leaders of the conspiracy, Ahmed Shawki, the infantryman, Husain el Shafi, the cavalryman, and Gamal Salim, the aviator. Deferentially advancing towards Faruk, who was leaning against the rail, the General reminded him that when the British had used force against the Crown in February 1942 he had resigned his commission in order to prove his fidelity to the throne. Faruk appeared to be touched, behind the screen of his dark glasses. 'Take care of the army,' he said. 'It is now in good hands, sire,' Neguib replied. The answer did not please Faruk, who said in a hard voice, 'What you have done to me, I was getting ready to have done to you.' Then, turning on his heel, he took leave of the conquerors.

II

Power—to what Purpose?

'Ours is a bloodless revolution,' the Egyptians proudly told Robespierre's fellow-countrymen in the month of August 1952. It was a white revolution in that there was neither a Terror nor the guillotine; but it was a khaki revolution.

Now and then, as he had to thrust his way through a throng of people, you could see a stocky man, his military shirt half-open on his hairy chest, his big dark face always breaking into the smile of some favourite uncle, his eyes glinting like anthracite under his bushy black brows. 'Yaish Mohamed Neguib!' the crowd shouted, as women held out their children towards the new prophet. Idlers and poor, galvanized wretches would be torn from their jeering indifference as he passed. 'Yaish, Yaish.' [1] The man in khaki waved his cap, kissed a baby, slipped his cane under his arm and disappeared laughing into his car with one or two of his silent Captains.

He was coming from the rococo palace which housed the Ministry of Foreign Affairs where Ali Mahir, Prime Minister and at the same time War Minister, Minister for the Navy, Foreign Affairs and the Interior, all in one, was 'presiding' over the government. He was on his way to the paltry H.Q. buildings where, squeezed into four offices, a dozen Lieutenant-Colonels ('Bikbashis') and Majors ('Saghs') had already begun being Egypt's real rulers. Even the most obtuse foreign correspondents did not need a week to realize that Mahir, chosen to carry the 'Faruk Operation' through with as little trouble as possible, and to reassure foreign governments for the time being, was no more than a passing instrument.

What, then, lay behind Mohamed Neguib's broad smile? Who were these bronzed fellows in sand-coloured shirts; what were they after, for whom were they working fifteen hours a day in the H.Q. offices, occasionally breaking off to hold a parade, enigmatic behind their

[1] 'Long Live!'

160

7a. Christian Egypt. The monastery of St Antony on the Red
Sea, scene of the Temptation

7b. Moslem Egypt. The mosque of Ibn Tulun in Cairo against
the background of Mohamed Ali's Citadel

8. Agrarian Reform—the first harvest. A fellah handles £E.100 for the first time in his life

large peaked caps, behind the pipe-smoking General? Who was inspiring them, who was the real chief of these shirt-sleeved Bikbashis who, in the course of one night, had brought down a century-old monarchy? 'The *coup d'état* began like one of Stendhal's Italian Chronicles' wrote Roger Vailland.[1] Yes, except that in this case the 'traitor' did not get his throat cut like old Cenci. The Gargantua robbed of his cardboard crown was not turned into an embarrassing martyr. He was simply sent back to his true spiritual home, the casinos. A mixture of good nature and peasant cunning, the 'chronicle' here is in true Egyptian style. But it is none the less ambiguous.

It is easy to see who was beaten: the king and the feudal lords. But who were the victors? As on the day after elections in long-established countries, everybody claimed victory. On the 27th of July, Mustafa Nahas and Fuad Sirag ud-Din, who were at a water-ing-place in France, took a plane to come and congratulate Neguib, loudly proclaiming that the king's dismissal could only spell the triumph of his greatest rival, the Wafd. Nahas climbed the H.Q. stairs to pose proudly on the second landing beside the obscure General to whom a few days earlier he would not even have offered his hand to kiss, he, Nahas, the Pasha. Also, it was soon common knowledge that Ahmed Abul Fath, Editor-in-chief of *El Misr*, the Wafd's large daily, was not only the brother-in-law of one of the most influential of the Officers, Major Sarwat Okasha, but that he was a friend of Lieutenant-Colonel Gamal Abdel Nasser, the tall thin fellow with constantly lowered eyes, who was said to be one of the all-powerful 'Committee of Nine'. A timid man, this Nasser, the Wafd leaders thought with satisfaction, of whom we shall easily make a docile ally. They would soon be going to the polls and expected to be back in power shortly after. Nahas would be President of the Republic, Sirag ud-Din Prime Minister, and Neguib Chief of Staff. Fine chaps, these officers!

In the Moslem Brotherhood verses of the Book were recited in thanksgiving. On the morning of the 23rd of July one of their young leaders, Hasan Ashmawi, had been called to G.H.Q. and had car-ried the Officers' invitation to the Brotherhood's Supreme Guide, Hasan el Hodeibi, who, being on vacation in Alexandria, kindly answered that he would consider honouring those young men by a visit. This he did a week later. No one in the Brotherhood had

---

[1] *Choses vues en Égypte* (Things seen in Egypt), August 1952.

forgotten the contacts established six years earlier between the late Hasan el Banna, the venerable founder who was assassinated by the king's men in 1949, and Anwar el Sadat, one of the authors of the *coup d'état*. Everybody knew that several of the Free Officers such as Kamal ud-Din Husain had made common cause with the Brotherhood, and that Abdel Moneim Abd el Ra'uf, leader of the movement in the army, had been one of the first members of the officers' group. On the 3rd of August the Brotherhood published a 'White Book' which set out its programme in a tone suitable to an official political party: 'The Koran is our only constitution . . .' Hodeibi's staff drew up a list of five or six Ministries to which they considered they had every right. Ah, they are pious men, these Bikbashis: Allah preserve them for our greater good!

On the Left, rejoicing was almost as unqualified. On the 2nd of August Radio-Bucharest broadcast its warm praise of 'the people's movement which has just struck down Egyptian feudalism and overcome the war-mongers'. Already the chairman of the *Hadeto* committee (National Liberation Movement), one of the seven or eight communist-inspired groups among which Egyptian Left-wing militants were shared, chose to give 'conditional support' to the military movement. This decision was based on the presence of one of its members on the military committee, Lieutenant-Colonel Yusuf Sadiq, the principal actor in the putsch of the 23rd, and that of Major Khaled Muhi ud-Din, known for his progressive views. Besides, other influential officers were reputed to be 'Leftist': Colonel Ahmed Shawki, Major Lufti Wahid, Captain Ahmed el Masri. Also, progressive circles thought they could count on the active sympathy of Nasser, Hakim Amir and Okasha, all more or less familiar to the revolutionary bodies in Cairo and Alexandria. Several of them made contact with the communists immediately after the Palestine war, in order to study Russian views on the Israel question. Others collaborated in the Marxist review *El Gamahir* (The Masses), and it is said that one of them sent his men in an army lorry to manhandle some Moslem Brothers who were trying to prevent the paper's sale. At the time of the disturbances of the 26th of January there were fresh exchanges between the Free Officers and groups of the extreme Left, and these had not stopped since.

In addition, a Marxist analysis of the situation led some of the Egyptian progressive leaders to have a certain confidence in the rebels, who were sons of small middle-class landed proprietors or minor civil servants. In so far as they were sons of fellahs and oppressed by the big landowners, as well as by the 'imperialists' in their capacity as officers, they could change themselves or be changed into genuine revolutionaries.

On the American side, people regarded these tendencies with a certain degree of mistrust. But the ambassador Jefferson Caffery pretended to ignore them and posed as godfather of the movement. 'These young men can save Egypt from the red tide that Faruk's and the Pashas' abuses could not have failed to let loose over the country. They are going to carry out reforms (you can take my word for it) and raise the people's standard of living. We shall encourage them.' The British were more doubtful. Having recovered from the first moment of surprise—and thus of an unprecedented 'technical' humiliation—the local agents, the commander of the Canal forces and the Foreign Office agreed that there should be no intervention, as the Officers: (*a*) were going to rid Britain of the nuisance of the 'crown of Egypt and the Sudan', which was Cairo's best legal argument when directing its ambitions towards the upper valley of the Nile; (*b*) were sufficiently aware of the inequality of forces to avoid renewing guerrilla activity in the Canal Zone; (*c*) should be reliable people who would understand arguments of strategy in any negotiation over the Canal Zone. *The Times* thought it was sufficient to say that this was simply a matter of domestic politics.

These reactions were no more than bets. For no one highly placed in politics, in the embassies, or indeed even among the journalists had yet examined the thews and heart of this khaki sphinx made up of a 'military committee' of nine,[1] then later of twelve. No one, except the intimates of these men, had been able to follow the heated debates which, from the 27th of July to the 9th of August, had violently opposed, on the second floor of G.H.Q., and for nights on end, the 'Westerners' and 'Progressives', the 'authoritarians' and 'parliamentarians'. The first debate took place with the return from Alexandria on the 27th; should they mention the Wafd parliament elected in 1950 and suddenly dissolved by Faruk in May 1952? Nasser, who was chairman of the committee although nobody knew that except its members (his resignation handed in on the 26th in favour of Neguib had been rejected), was the most determined one in favour of recalling

---

[1] Then made up of Nasser, President; Abdel Hakim Amir, Abdel Latif Boghdadi, Salah Salim, Khaled Muhi ud-Din, Hasan Ibrahim, Anwar el Sadat, Kamal ud-Din Husain, Gamal Salim. However, Yusuf Sadiq and Ahmed Shawki seem to have taken part in most of the discussions.

the nation's elected representatives. But in the absence of the pro-
moter of this idea, Khaled Muhi ud-Din, who was detained in Alexandria, he was heavily out-voted. Nasser at once telephoned to
Khaled saying, 'Come back at once, we must not let ourselves be led
into a dictatorship.' (This was almost the appeal of Brutus to
Cassius.) On Khaled's return the discussion was resumed in the
presence of new members: Mohamed Neguib, Zakaria Muhi ud-Din,
Husain el Suafi and Abdel Moneim Amin. Meanwhile four officers
held a meeting with Fuad Sirag ud-Din at the house of a militant
Wafdist. Gamal had the impression that the stout Fuad was not
taking his young interviewers very seriously, refusing all control and
refusing to commit himself to a political clean-up. The Twelve
decided against recalling the former Parliament: they were in favour
of a return to constitutional liberties and a general election in
six months' time, but against the principle of 'single party'
government.

Between the 4th and the 9th there were more discussions of foreign
policy. Here it was easier to be unanimous again, in spite of differing
tendencies. Any offer of military co-operation with the West before
the British evacuated the Canal Zone would be refused, and this in
spite of tempting offers. On the 10th of August the *Sunday Dispatch*
had suggested that General Neguib be made Commander-in-Chief
of the forces in the Middle East. Of all this the public knew little
or nothing.

But this strange movement, whose only colour seems to be khaki,
whose real leader went about furtively with bent head, shut lips and
lowered eyes in the wake of the popular General, can only be judged
on its acts. The only definition that can be given is phenomenological.
Was it Leftist? We must consider its attitude to the masses. Was it
slyly counter-revolutionary? The big landed capitalists[1] will be the
judges. Was it fascist? The parties and trade unions can answer that.
Was it religious in inspiration? The fate it had in store for traditional
institutions will make this clear. Was it a puppet of the Americans?
Its attitude to the Middle East Defence Pact will decide. We must
watch them at work, those whom the preachers in the mosques
saluted as members of a 'Blessed Movement'; those whom Faruk,
in his Capri villa, called 'Communists', and whom the international
Press referred to as a Junta.

---

[1] We prefer this term to 'feudal lords', as will be explained in our chapter on the
peasantry.

A PHENOMENOLOGICAL DEFINITION OF THE MOVEMENT

A blow against the Left. On the 12th of August 1952, towards seven o'clock in the evening, a group of union workers at the big spinning mill at Kafr el Dawar[1] belonging to the main Egyptian trust, the Misr Company, assembled in front of the office block asking for an increase in wages and the dismissal of the company's secretary and the head of the employment office, 'in the name of Mohamed Neguib and the revolution'. An effort was at once made to disperse them. The workers then began to shout slogans against the manager. The factory's trouble-shooters got out their clubs, and the workers, apparently led by two men, Mustafa Khamis and Ahmed el Bakhri, went and occupied the premises. The police opened fire on them. The enraged workers burnt down two of the buildings, shouting 'Long live the army's revolution, the people's revolution!' Early on the morning of the 13th that same army, sent in haste from Alexandria, clashed with the workers who were leaving the factory in an imposing procession. The military reoccupied the buildings, opening fire on 500 demonstrators who had locked themselves in. There were eight dead and more than 20 wounded. Two hundred workers were arrested. The next day, the 14th of August, a court-martial, hastily convened at the end of a meeting of the ministerial council and told to make an example of the agitators, was already in session at Kafr el Dawar, presided over by one of the members of the military committee, Colonel Abdel Moneim Amin.

It was a strange trial. Five days were enough in which to sentence Khamis and Bakhri to death. It is said that as he rose, the Public Prosecutor quoted a classic of Arab eloquence, 'I can see heads ripe to fall. I demand them, they are mine.' The tribunal had the strange idea of having the sentence read out in the factory, to the workers who were drawn up in ranks. Loud-speakers were shouting out the death-sentence while the two condemned men ceaselessly repeated, 'We followed Mohamed Neguib: long live the Revolution!' Were they as simple-minded as all that? With an odd mixture of blindness and cynicism, General Neguib himself has related[2] that he wanted to see Khamis before his execution, and that he offered him his life if he would give the names of those who had put him up to it. The condemned man was taken to Cairo, to the General's office. Khamis

[1] About 12 miles from Alexandria.
[2] In his autobiography, *Egypt's Destiny.*

refused to talk. Was he only the ignorant instrument of provocation, or a political militant who knew full well what he was doing? In any case the officers found themselves forced to make a hard decision. Were the workers to be the first victims of a 'revolution' which prided itself on being bloodless? Once again the Twelve of the military committee argued all night long. Nasser, Khaled Muhi ud-Din and Abdel Hakim Amir, who favoured clemency, had to yield. The next morning Mustafa Khamis and Ahmed el Bakhri were hanged in the prison courtyard at Alexandria. Some say that Khamis murmured, 'I will not die!'

Colonel Nasser was discovering, after Saint-Just, that 'one cannot govern innocently'. At the end of August, *Hadeto*, the only communist group which had shown confidence in the Officers, withdrew Left support from the 'people's movement' and in their pamphlets, without referring to Kronstadt, denounced the 'military dictatorship which, after sparing Faruk, the feudal lords, traitors and embezzlers, spilled only the workers' blood'.

In the formation of the plot, agrarian reform did not play the doctrinal part that was later attributed to it. To be sure, Gamal Salim, the most brilliant of the Free Officers, had studied the question during his long convalescence. But for the most part it was only after seizing power that 'in order to give the movement a social and economic foundation' as one of its promoters told us, the Nine made Agrarian Reform one of the pillars of their programme. Under Gamal Salim's supervision, two Left-wing economists, Ahmed Fuad, a former Deputy Judge and an old friend of Nasser, and Professor Rashid Barawi, the translator of Marx into Arabic, drew up a scheme which, after six weeks of brief but feverish composition, on the 8th of September became the most symbolic of the new régime's laws. There were to be no more than 200 feddans (rather more than 200 acres) per proprietor; no more than 300 feddans per family. The king owned 55,000, Prince Yusuf Kamal 16,000, the Badrawi 9,000. It is well to remark in passing that a feddan of good land in the Delta or Middle Egypt, bearing two harvests a year, can be worth as much as £700. Was this, then, to be the 'revolution'?

A blow against the Right. Adli Lamlum, the eldest son of a rich and powerful family of Bedouin at Maghagha, a great hunter of animals and girls, a sort of provincial Robert le Diable, refused to admit this kind of change. He fired his carbine and set his dogs on the surveyors who had come to measure how much land the Lamlums would have to hand out to their fellahs. He was surrounded by two squads, and after a veritable siege the young bey, who on his own domain was a kind of demi-god, and whose father was the only completely illiterate M.P., was trussed up like a calf. On the next day he was taken into Cairo in handcuffs and chains.

No appearance of Neguib's ever caused more rejoicing than the sight of this fat youth on the steps of Cairo station, with his dashing moustache, open collar and dwindling arrogance, chained to one of his own stewards. This was the real celebration of the 'revolution', a living symbol of it. The Cairenes had not seen Capet die, but they could gloat as the feudal baron went past, caught in the net of the law. Adli Bey was not hanged, and the communist pamphlets were able to contrast the Khamis and Lamlum cases, the man with the carbine and the man with empty hands. Sentenced to forced labour for life, Lamlum somehow managed to finish his education and pass his school-leaving examination . . .

Thus there was a blow to the Left and a blow to the Right. The 'Blessed Movement' remained an enigma. Would it show its hand towards the political parties or in religious matters? Throughout August relations between Ali Mahir and the Junta continued to worsen. The Prime Minister and the military committee were opposed in every respect. In deciding on a foreign policy, Mahir made no secret of intending to bring Egypt into a Western coalition in exchange for the evacuation and important financial advantages. As for the agrarian reform, the President, warmly encouraged by Colonel Mehanna, the Regent, who gave himself the airs of a sovereign, would have liked to see the minimum acreage increased to 500 feddans. As for relations between the government and the various parties, after forty years of political life Ali Mahir did not understand the word *purge* in the same sense as the Officers did. On the 1st of September a paragraph in the aggressive weekly *Rose el Yusuf* brought on the crisis. 'Who is governing?' it asked. 'Mahir or the army?' This exasperated the Prime Minister, who offered his resignation, then withdrew it to avoid giving the impression that he had 'fallen on the agrarian reform issue'. Politicians of the Right dread being brought down for opposing liberal policies. He gave up the Premiership to Neguib four days later, on the 7th of September, several hours before military police arrested forty-three worthies of the old régime. Two of these were former Presidents of the Council, Neguib el Hilali and Ibrahim Abdel Hadi, friends or colleagues of the retiring Prime Minister.

A blow against the Left. With the army's effective seizure of power which occurred with the formation of Neguib's Cabinet, the struggle between the political parties came to its height and brought out the Officers' disturbing bent towards authoritarian methods. Of course all they did was directed against corruption, in the name of the catchword *tahtir* (purge), which seemed to become as sacred as the word *tahrir* (liberation). But in cleaning the Augaean stables, were Neguib and his group going to fall into the dictatorship which on the 27th of July Nasser had claimed must be avoided at any price? Could the kind of purity they were seeking only be obtained through harshness? Had six weeks in power been enough to change so completely the outlook of those young men in shirt-sleeves who before the bid for power had not, after all, been so innocent of the political jungle, and of whom several, at the end of July, had thought of nothing but recalling Parliament? Brutus was already giving way to Mark Antony.

The affair began on the 8th of August. That day, General Neguib said to an American journalist, 'If the parties prove unable to weed themselves out, we shall have to step in.' The warning was the more brutal as all the parties, without exception, had applauded the *coup d'état*. They had lost no time in publishing in the Press, between the 28th of July and the 5th of August, their respective programmes, the first article of which in every case was 'total support for the military movement'. Also, on the 4th of August the Wafd, the main party concerned, had undertaken to exclude twelve members of its parliamentary group, one of whom was the influential ex-Minister for Agriculture, Abdel Latif Mahmud. But on the 10th of August Ali Mahir himself—to whom the Officers had been cunning enough to leave the major indictments—uttered these surprising words: 'The parties in their present form must disappear. They have the choice between reorganization and destruction.'

While the small parties, in a panic, were busy changing their names[1]

[1] The Sa'dist party, the furthest to the Right of them all, chose to call itself 'social-democratic'.

the Wafd, the powerful Wafd, tried to change its tone. At the annual ceremony at the grave of Sa'd Zaghlul, the party's founder, on the 28th of August, Nahas tried to close the breach. 'The army's aims are those of the Wafd,' he said. 'The Wafd has nothing to fear from a purge, so long as it is justly conducted. The army is acting for the country's good, in the limits of the Constitution.' All this was labour lost. On the 7th of September the new Prime Minister, Mohamed Neguib, chose his Deputy Premier and Minister for the Interior. This was a sworn enemy of the Wafd, Sulaiman Hafiz, who as Vice-President of the Supreme Court had access to documents deeply compromising to Nahas and his friends. On the 8th of September the 'Law on political parties' was announced, forcing them to what amounted to self-condemnation. It was child's play for Hafiz, Nasser and Zakaria Muhi ud-Din (Chief of Army Intelligence) to break up the old party, to set its various tendencies one against the other by cunning 'revelations', then to have two groups led by Nahas and Sirag ud-Din on the one hand and Abdel Salem Gum'a on the other, to denounce one another. Humiliated and unbalanced, the Wafd had to yield and accept the conditions imposed on political parties by the 8th of September law as well as the 'resignation' of Mustafa el Nahas, which came as a bitter pill. When the Minister for the Interior asked him on the 21st of September to 'abstain from all political activity', Nahas replied with some dignity in *El Misr*, 'I remain in the hands of a faithful people, who alone are qualified to decide what has to be done with me.'

The old Pasha's resignation was not enough to save the party. Because it tried to retain Nahas as an *Honorary* President the Wafd was 'not authorized to reconstitute itself'. At the same time the Green Shirt fascists were allowed to become the 'Socialist Party' and to take back their President, Ahmed Husain, whose share in the burning of Cairo had not been determined by his judges. On the 16th of January 1953 the Officers completed sweeping the board by announcing the dissolution of all political parties and the confiscation of their assets 'for the benefit of the People'. Then on the 23rd of January Neguib announced the creation of the 'National Liberation Rally', an organization which seemed to herald a single-party system. This was done in terms that had a decidedly fascist ring. Finally, on the 10th of February came the promulgation of a 'Provisional Constitution'. This was of a clearly authoritarian type, placing total sovereignty in the hands of 'the leader of the revolution and the members of the Military Committee', in other words the twelve conspirators of July.

A blow against the Right. Neguib, Nasser and their followers did not intend to use these powers against the politicians alone. The same severity was to be shown towards all who might try to question the legality of the régime, which was just getting to its feet but was none the less energetic, like Gargantua. Colonel Rashid Mehanna, who had been Regent for two months, soon came to understand this. Although he had had absolutely nothing to do with the *coup d'état*, this famous officer had none the less succeeded, from the 25th of July, in making a strong impression on the victors. Furious at having to do so, but in order to placate the artillery over which Mehanna claimed to have control, Nasser and the Committee had made this imposing aristocrat the army's representative on the Regency Council. There Mehanna soon showed himself to be a stubborn reactionary and an aspiring climber, as Nasser had suspected. Giving himself, at the Abdin Palace, all the airs of a blue-blooded prince, openly scoffing at the agrarian law and making (in the large daily *El Ahram*, 2nd of October) declarations smacking of the Moslem Brotherhood, Colonel Mehanna (to whom the European Press were still attributing the part of Grey Eminence which was in fact held by Nasser) was obviously hoping to supplant the military committee. Compromise was obviously no longer possible between him and Nasser. The imposing Colonel-Regent was none the less astonished, on the 14th of October, to learn that he had been removed from the Regency Council, the reasons offered being expressed with a particularly humiliating coarseness and sarcasm.

Expelled from the Abdin Palace, Mehanna could not rest until, with the help of fellow-officers, he had regained access to it. But the army's intelligence service did not allow him time to make the necessary contacts. On the 16th of January 1953 he was arrested together with Lieutenant-Colonel El Damanhuri 'for having tried, on or about the 14th of January 1953, and with the complicity of other persons, to foment a mutiny in the army'. Lieutenant-Colonel Nasser himself presided over the court-martial which tried Mehanna, Damanhuri and twenty-three subalterns. Only Damanhuri was condemned to death, but the next day the sentence was commuted to hard labour. The former Regent was sentenced to imprisonment for life, and it is noticeable that not one of the collective reprieves which in the past three years have marked various stages in the régime, has included this man who, in Nasser's eyes, is the perfect type of counter-revolutionary officer.

The February 'Provisional Constitution' had pointed out that laws and decrees from now on would be promulgated not in the king's name but in that of the nation. Coming after the dissolving of the Regency Council, this boded no good for the future of the little king whom Faruk was trailing with him from Italian beaches to Swiss watering-places. Thus the proclamation of the Republic on the 18th of June came as no great surprise. It had been thought that the Officers would wait for the anniversary of the *putsch* in order to do this. Several reasons may be given for their haste. For one thing, there was a discreet royalist campaign being conducted in England by the former seventy-year-old 'Dauphin', Prince Mohamed Ali, who went about saying that if Faruk was distasteful, not all the members of his family were without merit. Secondly, in their eagerness to find a successful conclusion to their talks with the British over the evacuation of the Canal base, the Officers felt the need to 'normalize' or establish their position. In Cairo a remark by the British minister, Selwyn Lloyd, was quietly being passed round: 'Negotiate? But with whom? What does this nondescript régime represent?' A first attempt at negotiation had already failed in 1953. Moreover, Nasser and his followers realized the size of the task they had taken on, and how slow recovery would be, and thought they might be able to lay the blame on 'sabotage' by their civilian collaborators, though these had been well chosen. They wanted to be able to take all powers into their own hands, and make themselves directly responsible. But they also wanted to cloak what they were doing behind a sensational change of government.

Finally, they tried to 'whip up' the enthusiasm of the first few weeks of the revolution, which had waned somewhat. It was at this time that Mohamed Neguib declared to a working-class gathering, 'one social class has stood aside; another has taken refuge in a policy of wait and see; a third is asking itself: What have we got out of it?' At the same time Nasser remarked in his notebooks which were to become *The Philosophy of the Revolution*, 'We opened the breach, but nobody followed us through.'

To what classes was the General-President alluding? The one which had stood aside was obviously that of the large estate-owners, those who in fact had been pushed aside. Not, to be sure, that the Egyptian feudal lords had tried to foment against the new régime any resistance of the type of Coblenz or Denikin's cossacks. It was as though they had all overheard what Neguib said to an Egyptian diplomat: 'My dear ambassador, just explain to your friends that if we had not seized power, others would have overthrown the monarchy and by other means.' Certain things would have to be given up. Adli Lamlum had been almost the only one to reach for his gun. They were half resigned, not without some hope that the Officers would prove ephemeral or usable. Each had hastened to discover a cousin in the army, hastening to honour the lowly *yusbashi* (Captain) whose marriage with Aliya had been such a scandal the year before. 'My dear, he is attached to Salah Salim's office. I'll introduce you!' Then, as time went on, the boys in khaki were found rather irritating—they continued to block the roads to power, and to hatch 'reforms' against the old order of things. The *yusbashi* cousin had said how much he appreciated their invitations, but shown a complete lack of understanding as soon as it came to rendering the family a few political services. The Agrarian Reform was pressing on, and the confiscation of the royal family's wealth made it feared that others might follow, while the arbitrary reduction of rents was quite simply calculated to ruin decent people. 'How long are they going to last? When are they going back to their barracks?'

The middle-class, that of half a million civil servants, business-men, small landed proprietors, the one from which the new masters had emerged, also began to murmur. Why? It should be noted first of all that the civil servants, for thirty years, had voted for the Wafd, which had never failed, when it was returned to power, to increase their numbers and meagre salaries. Also, quite a number of minor civil servants and small business people were only able to live thanks to rents from some little strip of land in the country—five or six feddans inherited from their fathers which, rented to fellahs, brought in the hundred a year which enabled them to balance their budget. The Agrarian Reform did not stop at dividing up the large estates. What was even more crucial for the peasant masses was a 70 per cent lowering of rents. Thus the class of urban civil servants saw their extra source of money drying up. When towards the end of June 1953 a decree lowered the state employees' cost-of-living bonus by 11 per cent, disillusionment was replaced by disgruntlement.

'What have we got out of the revolution?' the lower classes were

172

asking, if we can believe General Neguib. On the other hand, the fellahs were beginning to see the surveyors of the Agrarian Reform, who showed them the boundaries of the bit of land of which they were to become the 'owners'. The word 'owners' sounded unreal to them. In theory, no word can have more meaning for those poor devils toiling fifteen hours a day on the *shaduf* along the canal, for no more than ten piastres, and, if they are tenants, the privilege of still being alive at the end of the year. But was it possible that these 'city men' were offering them land—these men from whom they had so far received nothing but taxes, requisitions, levies of men, law-suits and hunting-parties? As they sat round the little enamelled tea-pot, in front of the village 'baqqal's' display of goods, they refused to believe it, and still did not believe it when the distribution began. Yet everywhere Neguib's portrait, pinned up even in the most desolate hovels of Upper Egypt, seemed to spell a certain hope. Because of his origins in ancient Egypt, because of the practices of the Caliphs, or simply because of a poverty too heavy to be borne on his own shoulders, the Nile peasant feels a strong need for a ruler, an intercessor, a father-in-chief, a protecting priest. Neguib was all this, at that time, in the eyes of the *fellahin*, a person of inestimable value. Anyone who moved about the country in the wake of the General-President cannot deny this.

The proletariat, also, was divided between mistrust and sympathy. Sympathy for those who had brought down Faruk; for the authors of the law of the 7th of December 1952 on the arbitration of disputes between workers and management and the individual work-contract (which made a worker's dismissal a costly business for an employer), and sympathy for a government which was honestly trying to end the rise in prices. Mistrust for those who had opened fire at Kafr el Dawar; of the creators of a treacherously Falangist type of unionism, completely controlled by the officers of the National Liberation Rally; distrust of those who had started repression of the communists in an outstandingly brutal manner, with three major trials in one year. Moreover, we must not forget that fickle mass of people, neither proletarian nor engaged in business, which makes up three-quarters of the Cairo population—poor peasants come to town, domestics, semi-tramps living on trivial odd-jobs, minding cars, carrying parcels, shining shoes, managing on whatever happens to turn up—the public and author of triumphs, demonstrations, merciless city fights, the bedizened spectators of the burning of Cairo. They had applauded Faruk's conquerors, only to realize very soon that millionaires were the source of their own meagre profits, and that it was the crumbs of their shameless luxury that enabled them to pick a living from tips, cleaning, gardening and carrying. Thus they gradually cooled towards the men in khaki, except for that man with the pipe, the smiling ra'is[1] with a common accent, the baladi[2] President who had refused to leave his shabby little house in Zeitoun to live in Faruk's palace.

The Egyptian Republic—the republic of the Bikbashis, as the Cairo idlers ironically called it—was born on a June evening in 1953, in an atmosphere of anxiety. One felt the presence of birds of ill-omen over the enormous crowds lost in the shadow of Abdin Square, while the bronze voice of Gamal Abdel Nasser slowly vibrated, dictating the 'Republican oath' to the crowd, which repeated it slowly and raggedly. Many of us that evening felt it was not the change of régime that mattered, so much as the 'introduction to the people' and the open accession to power—as Deputy Prime Minister and Minister for the Interior—of this tall bikbashi with the greenish complexion, the over-long nose and reserved yet burning eyes. Many of us knew this, for the Egyptians are sensitive, quick to smell out the truth. The man speaking in such passionate tones was not the same as the decent Neguib. He was obviously a changer of history, a revolutionary. He was not liked. They felt misgivings as they saw him grow in stature, or rather come out from behind the curtain behind which he had hidden his influence. Egyptian good nature was not much in evidence, in this taciturn individual who got rid of Faruk.

The Republic's baptism did not amount to much, as an entertainment and a political revival. But the army had more success with the anniversary of the July coup. Military parades, banquets, distributions of land, the bestowing of honours by the hundred—foreign visitors were struck full in the face by a feverish Egypt, an Egypt which seemed to be seething with inhuman hope. All this passed like a hot breath over the glaring poverty. Over it all emerged Neguib's hearty laughter and sallies, his self-confident robustness, his naïve slyness, his quick retorts to journalists, his fatherly advice to the peasants—all he did seemed worthy of Goha the Simple, the legendary, simple-minded jester of the Nile Valley. The anniversary of the coup d'état, in which he had taken part only at the last moment, turned into a celebration of Neguib himself, rather than of any political event.

[1] President. [2] Meaning local, 'one of us'.

Neguib's triumph did not please everyone. It annoyed his young companions who had intended making him a symbol and not a chief, and who felt that his popularity was going to the 'boss's' head. He irritated the political leaders who, watching the public's disappointment growing daily more bitter, were making ready to re-enter the arena. They were losing patience with this barricade of applause which Neguib's popularity set up between them and the resumption of political action. Thus we see the development of the stresses of a period which was to end in the régime's supreme test, that of February–March 1954. It may be summed up as the progressive estrangement between the General-President and the young men of the Revolutionary Council: constant plotting by the men of the old régime to draw Neguib into their own orbit; incoherent acts of repression which brought out the differences between Neguib and Nasser; the consolidation and redoubling of the United Front's opposition, made up of the communists (all of whose groups had broken with the régime), the Wafdists and a growing proportion of the Moslem Brotherhood. More and more pamphlets signed jointly by members of all three groups appeared in the year 1952.

The summer of 1953 was a season of plots; the autumn, a season of judges. But neither of them recalls the dealings of Mirabeau and the royal Court, nor the lawyer's gown of Robespierre. Events were marked by that all-pervading irony, that sense of the ridiculous which is to be found all over Egypt, which means that even the most grave actions are given a dash of a comic provincial accent, or for instance Nasser's famous mocking laugh—a genuine laugh none the less—at the crucial moment of his career when he braved the West and Capitalism in the Alexandrian dusk. But what, then, were these plots?

They almost all amount to attempts on the part of the politicians of the former government to persuade the foreigner—especially the British and Americans—that the Officers were no good, that they were on the verge of bankruptcy, and that it was no use lending them money which was thrown away in advance; that they would be unreliable partners in any negotiation, and that, since they represented nobody but themselves, any treaty signed with them would not be recognized by the nation; that they were 'communists' (according to some), or Moslem Brothers (according to others); that they were divided, that they were becoming corrupt, and that their cupboards were full of Faruk's jewellery! Against this smear-campaign—this characteristically Egyptian form of calumny on which Rossini might have composed a wonderful aria—the Officers reacted like a bull stung by hornets: they struck out blindly in the summer heat.

On the 11th of September Major Salah Salim, Minister for 'National Orientation' (Propaganda), solemnly assured the Press that military security agents had found proof that 'a certain number of professional politicians are in constant touch with the British Embassy'. On the 15th he treated a huge gathering to an indictment of the old parties, and, so that nobody could mistake his meaning, he gave a music-hall imitation of an interview between Faruk and Nahas. Then, sharply switching to other matters, the man in smoked spectacles announced in cutting tones the setting up of a 'Revolution-ary tribunal' composed of three members of the Revolutionary Council. These were Major Boghdadi, then Minister for War, Lieutenant-Colonel Anwar el Sadat, and Major Hasan Ibrahim. On the 20th, about fifteen prominent men of the old régime were arrested, among them Ibrahim Abdel Hadi.[1]

There were only two moving incidents in the trials which took place, too often in camera and with an extraordinarily arbitrary procedure, in a little room on the second floor at G.H.Q., overlooking the Nile. When Ibrahim Abdel Hadi was being led away after being sentenced to death for 'high treason and corruption' the police stopped him in the courtyard, in front of the photographers. Beneath the flashing lights, the foppish face of the irresponsible man-about-town quivered and reddened. Then he drew himself up, calmly placed a cigarette in his mouth and lighted it. Then, when during the next trial the President ordered the accused, Ibrahim Farag, former assistant secretary-general of the Wafd, and Nahas Pasha's favourite collaborator, to stand and hear his sentence (he also had been accused of high treason and had not yet heard that Abdel Hadi's sentence had been commuted), a waxy pallor like the shadow of death passed over his sharp face; the little man in black suddenly looked like the hunted Charlie Chaplin of the early films. He was condemned to imprisonment for life.

But the most interesting of the trials was undoubtedly that of Fuad Sirag ud-Din, because of the historical revelations it brought out and the personality of the accused, who had been master of Egypt under Faruk, in the closing years of the dying régime. He looked unrecog-nizable. Where was that flabby personage, that caricature of the

[1] A former Prime Minister and head of the royal Cabinet, president of the Sa'dist party, the typical 'king's man'.

Egyptian pasha who was easy bait for the Left-wing reviews? After seven months in prison, where he had suffered cruelly from diabetes, he was twenty-five pounds thinner, younger-looking and almost elegant. On his wasted face there hung pockets of empty skin. The enormous wart, made much of by caricaturists, still adorned his right cheek. But there was now only a single ring on his fingers. His vanished paunch still seemed to inconvenience him, while the amputated leg still appeared to give pain. His gestures were not yet adapted to his new waist-line, his hands always moving at some distance from his body. But for a marked man he showed enormous authority, and a self-confidence unusual in a prisoner. He faced his adversaries without meekness yet without arrogance, in a parliamentary manner, sure of his facts and figures. The man was obviously of a different stature from those who had been in the dock before him. He remained on a level with the great political warriors, good-humoured, sarcastic, disconcertingly supple, abruptly harsh. Born for demagogy and great enterprises, forceful policies, a man fit perhaps, even, for public service. But like others he had perhaps been softened by the prevailing political habits of the decadence.

Naturally, it was the Wafd rather than this man which was on trial. The prosecution had stopped looking into Fuad Pasha's responsibility for the burning of Cairo. Not that it mattered much. On the other hand, if those investigations were broken off it was perhaps because they were leading nowhere, argued Sirag ud-Din and his counsel, Abdel Fattah Hasan, former Defence Minister and the orator of the 26th of January. Let us look at it more closely, they argued. Thus the trial which was intended to prove to the world and especially to Egypt that the former leader of the Wafd was no more than a base intriguer, a cynical exploiter, turned into a fierce debate on two themes. The first was, who had less interest than the Wafd in setting fire to Cairo on the 26th of January 1952? The second, whether in declaring the 1936 Treaty to be void, and provoking guerrilla warfare in the Canal Zone in autumn 1951, the Wafd had placed the British in an impossible position and advanced the date of the evacuation? This being the case, and in spite of the penetrating skill of the president (Major Boghdadi, whose real talent came out in the course of some exchanges with the accused), the sentence of fifteen years' imprisonment appeared arbitrary. But the former general secretary of the Wafd had not wasted his time: his bearing in the presence of his judges won back the esteem of a section of the militant Wafdists, and the possibility of a political future for him is not to be under-estimated.

The revolutionary tribunal was unable to complete its work. While all Egypt was wondering whether the Officers would have the nerve to make the next accused, Zeinab el Wakil—'Zouzou', the beloved spouse of Mustafa el Nahas—appear personally before the slimily insinuating judges, and whether the brief of this opulent Egeria would be as much as looked into, the storm broke over the régime. During the night of the 25th–26th of February 1954 it was learnt that General Neguib had resigned.

III

Neguib's Fall

Cairo was thoroughly crestfallen on the morning of the 26th of February. Neguib's portraits were still smiling in the shop-windows, but the newspaper-sellers and their customers were not in a mood for joking.

From 7 p.m. till midnight a dramatic meeting of the Revolutionary Council had been held in the chief office of the Gazira Palace. Reporters, napping in an office on the ground floor, had been awakened by the sound of loud voices, which at times were raised to the point of bawling. It has been said that Colonel Anwar el Sadat placed his pistol on the council table. Majors and Colonels came and went, slamming the doors. Towards eleven o'clock, officers who seldom came to this place were seen arriving in jeeps, men on active service, from the artillery and cavalry. Shortly after midnight General Neguib left the building, alone, in his big car with the green flag, his face a blank, his jaw set hard. Major Salah Salim said in a jerky voice to a pack of reporters who ran towards him, 'Neguib has offered his resignation. We have accepted it. Gamal Nasser has been made Prime Minister.'

Why?

For about six months relations between the General and his 'inventors' had been turning sour. A month earlier there had even been rumours that the President had been arrested and that Nasser had taken his place. Neguib's reappearance side by side with Salah Salim, said to be his most violent opponent, had put an end to these reports. But something was expected to happen, especially as a number of foreign diplomats who had been received by the President of the Republic were echoing the grievances expressed by Neguib himself—'These young men are imprudent . . . They no longer listen to me. They are piling up stupid mistakes and heading for disaster.' This was the talk of the town.

Their differences had both remote and immediate causes. It should be noted first of all that the General and the Colonels belonged to

179

different generations, the former being 53 years old, the *bikbashis* between 32 and 37. Of course it was not by chance that the young men had chosen a man of years, for they aimed at giving the movement some appearance of respectability. But this need had become a source of disagreement because of their different reactions and judgements in moments of crisis. Nor should we forget that Neguib was already a General and entitled to be called Bey under the old régime, to which he belonged whether he liked it or not. If he resigned on the day in February 1942 when the British forced the king to change his Cabinet, it was not to protest against Faruk's surrender but to prove his faithfulness to the humiliated monarchy. His eldest son was called Faruk.

To put it briefly, Neguib was a man of the old régime, shocked by its abuses, whereas Nasser and his group had no truck with the monarchical system. The red cap of a *lewa* (General) had lifted Neguib from the semi-proletariat of the Egyptian army in which the others remained involved. A bloody, radical and terrorist revolution on the French or Russian models would have inevitably attracted him to the young—or else caused him to have his head chopped off. But the bloodless transition from autocracy to regency, and from a regency to an authoritarian republic, allowed all sorts of relationships to continue or be set up: the revival of old friendships could be brought about easily with a little Egyptian good fellowship, especially that of Mohamed Neguib. That was how he appeared to the common people. But to the men of the old régime he was still Neguib Bey. How could the young revolutionary wolves, the Nasser who had tried to assassinate Sirri Amir, or the dynamite-throwing Sa'dat, fall in line with that outlook?

It should also be remembered that Neguib came in at the last minute, and that only a phone-call at dawn linked him with the victory over Faruk. The 'publicity-man' of the revolution subsequently gave great service by his smile, his good nature, charm and cunning; but the other eleven Officers could not allow the law to be handed down by the twelfth, nor even that he should appear to be the real master to anyone but the common people and tourists. This was suddenly raised into an issue after Neguib's personal triumph at the July 1953 celebrations.

Early in August, Neguib decided to make the pilgrimage to Mecca, a gesture which could only increase his prestige in the eyes of a large part of the masses, and delight the Moslem Brotherhood with whom

Nasser was having a kind of flirtation at the time. The Vice-President had him accompanied by two reliable members of the Revolutionary Council, but Neguib was also taking along his friend, Colonel Ahmed Shawki, who had quarrelled with Nasser and was such a free-thinker that his trip could only have political motives. Were they working towards some collusion between liberal elements in the army and the Moslem Brotherhood? Nasser noticed that Neguib's conversations with King Sa'ud had been particularly cordial, and that the President-pilgrim's prayer on Mount Arafat, thanks to its pan-Islamic violence, had the air of a political programme, a programme that was trying to go one better than Nasser's.

Neguib returned to a Cairo full of plots and rumours. It is true that he attended the great meeting of denunciation on the 15th of September. But every day one heard how, at the Groppi Café or on the terrace of the Semiramis, he expressed his disapproval of the arrest of this or that former minister, or the sentencing of some other. He confided to a European envoy that Fuad Sirag ud-Din's sentence was 'a blunder and an injustice'. Furthermore the Sudan, which had been given self-determination as a result of the Anglo-Egyptian agreement of February 1953, in the November elected a parliament with a strong pro-Egyptian majority. This was an unhoped-for triumph for Cairo and the régime, but it also resulted in a new cause for disagreement, for both Neguib, who was the idol of the Sudanese thanks to his mother who was born there and to the friends he had made at Khartum early in his career, and Salah Salim, the Minister for Sudanese Affairs, wanted to take all the credit for the success.

Another of Neguib's grievances was the dismissal of his friend Shawki shortly after their return from Mecca. The commander of the Cairo garrison, who made no secret of his views and openly said that the army should 'get back to its barracks' and give parliament a chance (Nasser's own thesis a year earlier), had been dropped at the beginning of September, in spite of some lively opposition from the infantry units.

Finally, the affair which brought on the crisis was the outlawing of the Moslem Brotherhood. On the 11th of January 1954, in the quad of the University of Cairo, students of the Brotherhood held a meeting in the course of which Nasser was cursed as a 'dictator' and accused of being an Anglo-American pawn. Several students who were members of the National Liberation Rally were horse-whipped by the young 'brothers', who then dared to set fire to a jeep belonging to the police who tried to intervene. Nasser acted at once. Without even consulting the double president—of the council and the republic —he had the powerful Brotherhood forbidden and closed all its premises, which he knew had been used for several months as centres of agitation, as confirmed by certain statements by the Supreme Guide Hasan el Hodeibi, as well as for mounting terrorist activities the extent of which was revealed by the accidental blowing up of an explosives dump at Heliopolis, in the house of an engineer, Faiz, who was a member of the Brotherhood. The break between the régime and those who had long appeared to be its firmest supporters was complete. It is certain that Neguib was in contact with the Brotherhood at that time, through his aide-de-camp Mohamed Riad. How far did the relationship go? It does not seem to have been very political and was probably limited to declarations of friendship by both sides, just in case. . . .

Neguib reacted vigorously to the suppression of the Brotherhood.[1] He reminded his young companions that Faruk had dissolved the Brotherhood long before them. He strongly criticized the régime's repressive measures and, suddenly showing his hand, demanded a 'right of veto' over the Revolutionary Council's decisions, without which he would resign. Nasser and his friends were astonished: 'But you are asking for nothing less than dictatorship,' they said. At all events the General was trying to carry off a genuine *coup d'état*. Until then his twelfth share of sovereign power had not weighed very heavily against the block of eleven—apart from one or two occasional abstentions—who were manipulated by Nasser. It was now the 23rd of February. Neguib's ultimatum had been well timed: he was to leave a week later to inaugurate the new parliament and the trip was to be a symbolic celebration of Egyptian-Sudanese union. To deprive Egypt of a friend of the Sudanese at such a moment meant throwing a trump card away.

The Revolutionary Council was called for the 25th. We know what happened. We have seen how Neguib came out of it beaten, if not resigned, and how his adversary Salah Salim announced the result of the struggle to the Press. The next day, Salim declared to the foreign journalists who hastily assembled at G.H.Q. which was still

[1] It was said in Cairo at the time that the crisis came about as follows: After a violent dispute with Nasser, Salah Salim had gone to 'open his heart' to Neguib who, off his guard, confided to him that in agreement with the opposition United Front and especially the Moslem Brotherhood, he was making ready for a return to parliamentary government. Salah Salim at once reported this to Nasser.

echoing with the disputes of the previous night, 'In spite of the shock that the news will give to public opinion, we have had to break with Neguib who aimed at dictatorship, criticized in public and to foreigners decisions that had been made by a majority, and with no thought but his own popularity, played a double game by coming to an understanding with the opposition.' This happened on Friday, the 26th. Two days later, on the Sunday towards noon, Neguib, Salim and Nasser, all smiling and arm in arm, emerged from the President of the Council's residence. On the Monday morning the General and Salah Salim cheerfully entered a plane together, for Khartum. What had happened?

The news of Neguib's departure—he was at once isolated in his small house in the suburbs, which was surrounded by a guard—not only grieved the public, disturbed the foreign residents and minorities, alarmed the embassies and so upset the Sudanese government that it at once sent an official delegation to Cairo: what was more serious was that it had divided the army. Mehanna's condemnation a year before had caused some stir among his friends in the artillery, but none of them had done anything about it. Three months earlier, Shawki's dismissal had irritated a number of infantry officers and displeased the 'liberals'. But they had done no more than give him a party on the day of his leave-taking.

The Neguib affair, on the 'professional' as well as on the national and international levels, was on an entirely different scale. The smiling General was a symbol of the unity between the different tendencies in the army, between the army and the country and between Egypt and the Sudan. But it now became obvious that it was the liberal and progressive factions in the army which regarded themselves as closest to him. Not that Neguib was a man of the Left: it was simply that his friends in the former government tried to prevail on him to make the Junta restore the parliamentary system. Officers of Shawki's inclinations did the same thing out of concern lest the army be too involved in politics, and in the hope of being able to devote more energy to building it up again. The Moslem Brotherhood itself, in so far as it had any freedom left, sought to persuade the President of the need for civil liberties. This was also the leftist officers' programme. Their spokesman was Khaled Muhi ud-Din, a member of the Council of the Revolution, who had been one of Nasser's comrades from the very first, a confirmed 'progressive' and commander of the corps of motorized cavalry.

Thus it was from the cavalrymen that the protests came on the Friday evening. Nasser first sent Salah Salim, the Junta's orator, to explain to his comrades that Neguib, the standard-bearer of the 'liberals', was in fact aiming at becoming dictator. Salah strained his voice in vain: he was met with shrugged shoulders and blank faces. Meanwhile the cavalrymen had increased their numbers by several dozen officers from other branches of the service and were demanding Nasser. 'Only he will be able to explain such a decision.' Nasser, called to the telephone towards midnight by Husain el Shafi, who was Colonel in an armoured division, and therefore a cavalryman, jumped into a car and set off to face the first audience hostile to the man of the 23rd of July. 'You haven't the right . . . You prefer power to the army . . . authority has gone to your head. This is not what we were promised. Where is the liberation? You have replaced Faruk's autocracy by ours. Only Neguib can reassure the people.' Nasser fought every inch of the way. Someone came to tell him that the building was surrounded with mounted machine-guns—just as on the 23rd of July, except that this time he was inside the trap. He was also told that his friend Khaled had taken this step, and that he had chosen to support Neguib against him, Gamal. He tried reasoning again, to warn the officers that to yield today would mean abandoning the revolution and inviting Sirag ud-Din to return to power tomorrow. Then, suddenly, perhaps when he was on the point of shaking his opponents, he gave up: 'Call back Neguib. I'm going. I resign.' He got back into his car like a broken man, and only with difficulty drove past the posts of mounted machine-guns which Khaled had positioned. He did not know the pass-word.

It was three o'clock in the morning. In the course of the night some of Nasser's units, hearing that the Colonel has been 'apprehended' by rebels, carried out a counter-stroke against Khaled Muhi ud-Din, then against Neguib who, held in a jeep between three threatening officers, made a strange trip from which, as he has since told, he never expected to return. Khaled was taken to H.Q., expecting to be put to trial. But there he found Nasser broken and resigned, overcome by the opposition he had heard so harshly expressed the evening before—he, Nasser, who had imagined he could carry, if not the country, at least the army in one spontaneous impulse. He kept the promise he had made the cavalrymen, to re-call Neguib. The astounding rumour began to spread round Cairo the next morning: 'Neguib is back! Neguib is again President!'

People could hardly believe it; they went up to each other in the streets, incredulous, with joy in their eyes. The shoe-blacks and thousands of destitutes were already shouting 'Yaish Mohamed Neguib', so that uninformed passers-by turned round in astonishment. A broadcast at four o'clock in the afternoon put these doubts to an end and roused Cairo in a wave of enthusiasm such as Faruk's departure had not evoked, and equalled, they say, only by Zaghlul's return from the Seychelles.

Was the evening of the 27th of March—with bands of people marching arm in arm, the singing and stick-dances, the cries and shouts, the common joy of an entire population in the streets—was it only an expression of devotion for a particular man? In that ardent atmosphere we thought so, at first. But it soon became apparent that the manifestation was not as spontaneous as all that: and that behind the hymn of public thanksgiving there was a chief of staff, an organizer at work, and that the crowd was doing no more than obey a signal. The next day showed things in their true light. Then we heard a shrewd observer of the Egyptian scene call it 'Koran Sunday', while others were saying 'Parliament Sunday'.

At dawn an immense crowd began assembling round the Abdin Palace. It was known that Neguib was to appear on the balcony. They greeted his arrival with enormous applause. But together with the 'Yaish Mohamed Neguib', the cry of 'Allahu Akbar', the famous Moslem Brotherhood slogan, was heard more and more often and insistently. Sure enough, all round us we saw many short beards, yellow rosaries, turbans and grey caftans. What did this mean?

Neguib left the inner courtyard balcony and moved to the terrace directly overlooking the square. The clamour was redoubled. But suddenly a brawny man with a black beard and fiery eye broke through the crowd. In his hand he was holding a blood-stained handkerchief, and began crying out, 'This belongs to one of our brothers!' Pushing aside the guards at the palace entrance, he raced up the staircase and appeared at Neguib's side, to be greeted in his turn with a load roar: it was Abdul Qadir Awda, the deputy of the Moslem Brotherhood's Supreme Guide. As he stood next to the President he dramatically waved the blood-stained cloth. Among the crowd it was learnt that Awda had received it from a student who had been fatally wounded by the police only a few minutes ago, in Liberation Square, when a column from the University was marching towards the Cabinet offices. Was this the meaning of it all? Was 'Neguib's triumph' first and foremost a formidable anti-Nasser demonstration on the part of the Moslem Brotherhood? It was so, technically. Such a turn-out, such warmth, such punctuality at appointed places implied a careful organization, and everything in this case pointed neither to the Wafd nor to the communists.

Triggered by the Brotherhood, the demonstration took on some character of its own when Neguib, managing to dominate the uproar, spoke the magic words '. . . and we are going to call upon the people to elect a Parliament!' If ever a man was acclaimed by a crowd it was Neguib at that moment. It seemed as though the shouting would never die down. He left for the great reconciliation-scene with the other eleven officers which was to take place at the President of the Council's residency. The smiles and handshakes that were photographed by the dozen masked the wrath of Nasser and his followers, as we afterwards learnt. Neguib had not been authorized to announce elections. Nasser, having regained his coolness and energy, was now wondering anxiously what sort of man he had just recalled to power, whether he was just a decent chap of the Junta which had built him up, or a popular leader and idol, imposed on him and supported by the masses. He would count for little against such a rival . . . But the struggle had hardly begun.

It was going to last a whole month and bring out Nasser's amazing tactical genius. It soon became clear that the man who had beaten Faruk, once he recovered his balance after the lapse of the 26th of February, was made of sterner stuff than his Egyptian rivals. At the outset everything was against him. The masses were attached to Neguib and passionately impatient to win back constitutional liberties. Most of the army was against him and had forced him to recall the General. The foreign powers, with the exception of the American intelligence services, were disturbed at the possible growth of the Left in the wake of Nasser, were reckoning none the less on the smiling President's success. All the political bodies were against Nasser, the Wafd, the Brotherhood and the communists, and of course the wealthy people who were comforted by the sight of the man with the pipe. And yet Nasser was to triumph. His tactics may be summed up in three points: make concessions to the mob; win back the army; force Neguib and his friends to make mistakes which would split them up and rob them of their outside support.

Neguib returned badly shaken from his journey to the Sudan where the anti-Egyptian party, El Umma, had greeted him with a demonstration which had caused thirty deaths. He had to leave in a hurry, only twelve hours after his arrival. Nasser had to yield twice to the General, to whom he had only restored the Presidency of the Republic while retaining the Premiership for himself. The first surrender was on the 5th of March, by yielding to Neguib's demands to elect a parliament without further delay, and by lifting the censorship and freeing numerous political prisoners. The second defeat was by declaring the Revolutionary Council dissolved and announcing 'the end of the revolutionary phase' on the 25th of March. As we were able to approach him closely on each occasion, we can assert that if the first decision showed that he wished to avoid a civil war and to give in to the majority, the second was purely technical, and nothing more than a trick played on Neguib in order to draw him out of his defences, while provoking a carefully-staged anti-Neguib reaction from the people by confusing this 'return to freedom' with a 'return to the old régime'. He proved himself a master of the political game. On the evening of the 5th of March we saw him come out of Ali Mahir's villa on the heels of the cheerful Neguib and the President of the Supreme Court, Abdel Razek Sanhuri, whose face reminded one of some subtle hippo. He must have just yielded to the General and his two Liberal friends. The exultant Mahir announced that the elections were not far off. Nasser strode away with that heavy tread that he has when things are difficult.

Later that night we joined him on the stone steps outside his villa at Heliopolis. Symbolically, he was in civilian clothes. His smile did little to hide his anxiety. 'Do you think that the army has finished its political task?'—'Yes, after putting the finishing touches to what we have already achieved.'—'Do you really think this is a wise decision?' —'Yes.'—'Not a bit too hurried?'—'You must be aware that we have spent forty-five days working out a system for electoral representation and taking stock of public opinion.'—'But you had not intended to act so quickly?'—'That is true.'—'Do you think the return of Parliament will make it easier to solve the Anglo-Egyptian problem?'—'I know at any rate that Mr Churchill and certain English M.P.s will no longer be able to dub us nazis and fascists. Anything that makes for stability is in Egypt's interest.'—'Do you and your comrades intend to follow a political career within the framework of parliamentary government?' Nasser laughed. 'Some of us will return to barracks; others will enter the political arena.' However brief, in our opinion this conversation does not point to any deep scheming. At that moment Nasser was sincere, or three-quarters sincere.

But he was already in the process of contriving a kind of filter through which the transition to a democratic system and other political developments could be effected without too much danger to the July rebels, that filter being the army. The whole history of this month—the Ides of March, so dangerous to Caesar—may be summed up as follows: Neguib, taken up with the idea of democratizing Egypt, drew closer to the politicians day by day, to the point of being caught in every possible trap; while Nasser thought only in terms of the army, of his control over the officers which, though it had failed on the 26th of February, was again complete from the 15th of March onwards. Meanwhile he transferred two colonels of cavalry, promoted about fifteen generals, and dismissed three of Neguib's shock-troops. He played very cleverly on the army's class-consciousness, reminding it of all it owed to the régime and stressing that it—like Sieyès's Third Estate—which had been nothing had now become everything. 'Are we going to fall back into the old rut, despised and badly armed, badly led and badly paid?'

Then he turned his attention to the trade unions. He put the situation to them in this way: 'Either a military revolution or the return of the pashas.' He told them that Neguib had phoned Nahas calling him 'Ya habibi' (My very dear friend). Was it only in order to fall back on an old Pasha and politician that we got rid of Faruk at the risk of our lives? (The Brutus of July is now almost forgotten: this is Mark Antony pleading with the mob for a dictatorship—'Brutus and Cassius are honourable men . . .')[1]

All was ready for the scene which was to be enacted at the end of the month. Democratic liberties had ripened and intoxicated public opinion. Things which apparently could not be changed again had happened: prisoners had been released, the University was rejoicing and talking heatedly about purges; the Press shook itself into activity, daring to make a few thrusts at the army and demanding a full return to parliamentary government, while the two best Egyptian journalists, Ahmed Abul Fath, editor of *El Misr*, and Ihsan Abdul Qudus, chief editor of *Rose el Yusuf*, made a cruelly lucid analysis of the régime of which they had been the first supporters. But

---

[1] By an amusing coincidence, the main Cairo cinema was then showing Manckiewicz's adaptation of *Julius Caesar*, and it was whispered that all the military leaders had unobtrusively gone to see it.

Nasser let the squall pass, limiting himself to a few sharp little blows at vital points. He had the Egyptian Catiline, Ahmed Husain, leader of the Green Shirts, thrown into prison, as well as Abdul Qadir Awda, the man who waved the bloody handkerchief on the 'Koran Sunday'. Thus the Moslem Brotherhood was warned. Nasser needed the streets, and anyone who might hold them against his own men must be thrust aside.

Everything was ready by the 25th of March. Called together in a very tense atmosphere, the Council of the Revolution suddenly decided, towards the end of the afternoon, to dissolve itself. The revolution was over. Had Gamal Nasser given in again? Was it Robespierre yielding to the men of Thermidor? But he still had some cards up his sleeve. Hastening to the little Gazira Palace where the Eleven were still in session, we passed columns of demonstrators, many of whom wore the National Guard uniform (a militia controlled by Nasser's men). They were shouting slogans 'for carrying on the revolution'. When they reached the H.Q. these young men, who were several hundred strong, began to shout 'Maglis el Thawra' (Council of the Revolution), until Salah Salim came out with a stony face and asked for a bit of discipline on their part. But at the same time one of his closest collaborators whispered into our ear, 'You'll see big things happen shortly.'

It took no more than three days. On the Saturday evening, the 27th of March, Major Amin Shakir, the head of Nasser's office, summoned the foreign journalists to tell them that Neguib was no more than a tool in the hands of those who had burned Cairo. The main counter-attack came on Sunday, the 28th. In the morning the mob, after being 'worked on' for a week, besieged the Cabinet offices shouting its support of the Council of the Revolution. Nasser then arrived and, borne on the crest of a wave of heads and arms, reached his office with his uniform torn, while Neguib had to use a side-entrance in order to reach the council chamber where the decisive meeting was to be held. 'The people will choose between them,' one of Nasser's officers had told us the night before, his eyes glinting as he talked. But was it really the 'people' that was making the choice? When General Neguib was seen leaving the council session to receive the Commander-in-Chief, General Amir, Nasser as he followed him looked like a culprit awaiting his sentence. But he had not yet given in, and what Nasser really wanted was a completer victory than a noisy siege of the Cabinet offices. He needed a plebiscite of the whole capital, and it was learned in the course of the evening that the unions had decided on a general strike for the next day, so as to demonstrate the people's attachment to 'the leader of the revolution'.

It was a crazy day, with a general strike organized by the government, an entire city given over to political passions by enforced idleness, deprived of transport by the Minister of Works, with streams of demonstrators rushing through the streets shouting its hatred of civil liberties (!), groups forming everywhere in feverish excitement, rickety old vans with loud-speakers and overloaded with hired orators, pouring out their hymns of praise for the army at every street corner. At nine o'clock the tone of the drama improved a bit. Neguib, Nasser and some members of the Council of the Revolution (that almighty body which had committed *felo de se*) went to the airport with King Sa'ud of Arabia, who had spent four days as Cairo's frightened guest, the city being like a seething cauldron in which he was never sure whether the person he was talking to would be the hanged or the hangman. When the sovereign was about to enter his plane, some of Nasser's officers had the impression that Neguib, who was shaking hands with him affectionately, was going to board the plane with him and try to escape to Riyad. They ran forward, tore the General from the King's embrace, manhandled him and brought him brutally (it is even said that Colonel Sadat slapped his face) back to the hangar, where the President suddenly collapsed in a state of nervous depression. He was carried off to his house at Helmieh where, all day long, cut off from the city by the transport-workers' and petrol-distributors' strike, we had to wait for the sick man to yield, and promise the young men who had once made him the idol of the people, that the democratic measures which had been taken in the last month as a result of his personal influence, would be abandoned.

Then, shortly after midday the situation managed to grow even more tense. It was heard from officers who had come out from the city that the Supreme Court was besieged by the mob, and that its President, Abdel Razek Sanhuri, one of Neguib's closest collaborators and regarded as the likely head of the future civil government, had been attacked in his office and beaten by toughs, and that he had taken his revolver and shot down three of them. Salah Salim was seen hurriedly leaving Neguib's house, making for Cairo in a jeep to stop the outrage. Were the Officers to have the blood of Egypt's greatest lawyer on their hands? Was such a clumsy mistake to bring dishonour to the new régime? Slightly wounded in the head, Sanhuri had already been brought back to his home at Heliopolis, not far from where Neguib was about to capitulate. Meanwhile, to avoid the risk of a fresh outburst when the news of the assault on Neguib began to spread abroad, an armoured column drove into the city and quietly occupied a few strategic points.

It was five o'clock when one of the Officers read us the official communiqué, signed by Neguib, which brought an end to the Ides of March. Neguib remained President of the Republic. Nasser was Prime Minister. The elections were postponed; the censorship was re-established and a vague 'national consultative council' was to be created. After a month of intrigue Nasser had won. The authoritarian revolution, 'big-stick' reformism and police-rule had managed to stem the rising flood of freedom. Dictatorship had prevailed. For those who had lived through the hopes of the younger generation—the students, the free journalists, progressives of all colours—for those who had sat up at night with the democrats of *El Misr*, or welcomed a score of political prisoners turned loose at the prison gates, or who had heard the crowd's immense applause as they greeted Neguib's promise of elections as he stood on the balcony of the Abdin Palace, or for those who in secret had read the left-wing pamphlets or discussed the future with the chubby, cheerful progressive Major Khaled Muhi ud-Din—it was impossible not to feel disappointed. But apart from matters of sentiment, what can one think of all that now, except that at that moment the Wafd ought to have won, for the Wafd stood for the electoral bosses, the big landowners, the cunning ones—in a word, Sirag ud-Din rather than Saleh Eddin, and certainly more likely than Ahmed Abdul Fath's left-wing friends? For sincere friends of Egypt the choice between Sirag ud-Din and Nasser was not easy then, and it is not much easier now.

What, indeed, is 'Nasserism'—if it is permissible to define in any theoretical or abstract terms, or to enclose in a doctrinaire 'ism', a political force which has created itself under our very eyes, which has formed and modelled itself in 'the school of hard knocks', and since the night of the 23rd of July has passionately sought its own identity, scarcely veiled by Neguib's smiles, and which, entirely empirical and pragmatic, as we have seen, can be defined only by its actions, from Kafr el Dawar to the Agrarian Reform?

IV

The Structure of Nasser's State

To the extent to which it may be said that this régime exists only according to what it has accomplished and not according to any pre-established doctrine, before attempting even the most sketchy political portrait it would seem desirable to examine its main acts, such as the Treaty of Evacuation with London, the liquidation of the Sudan question, the trip to Bandung, the purchase of Soviet arms, and the nationalization of the Suez Company. Only then can one try to define it as seen by its allies and opponents and those who are interested in it, and to draw up some temporary balance-sheet.

All we can do now is to describe the state's structure as seen by Nasser. The Egyptian republic is first of all an army, an army in the shape of a pyramid. At the top, Nasser rests on the revolutionary Junta, a Council of ten officers. This rests on a larger base, the 'Society of Free Officers' (Zubat el Ahrar), with about 250 members, which was the instrument for bringing about the *coup d'état*. The base of the pyramid is the army itself, with 2,000 officers and 100,000 men who, parading twice a year through the Republic Square in January and July, show on each occasion what progress is supposed to have been achieved.

Gamal Abdel Nasser is at the top, yet has absolute control neither of the Council of the Revolution nor of the Free Officers. A number of strong personalities were to appear at his side. Salah Salim was the first of these, a Samurai in sun-glasses, the 'slogger' of the régime who was driven out in 1955, brought back in 1956 and imprisoned in 1957. Then there was his brother Gamal Salim, the leader of the radicals, a Deputy Prime Minister whose only ambition was to eliminate the word 'vice' from his title, before being dropped in his turn in June 1956. There was also Zakaria Muhi ud-Din, a Fouché[1] with a seminarist's face, the unobtrusive chief of police whose powers never stopped increasing; and the solid Boghdadi whose successes as a town-planner brought some personal popularity.[2] Finally there was

[1] Fouché, Napoleon's chief of police.
[2] Boghdadi, President of the 'National Assembly' of July 1957.

9a. Ibn Saud being received by Neguib in 1954 in front of the Officers' Club fresco portraying Faruk's departure two years before. On Neguib's left are Husain el Shafi, General Amir and Nasser

9b. Agrarian Reform. Gamal Salim, who was responsible for putting the law into effect, hands out title deeds

10a. Peasant women at work

10b. Peasant women at home

General Abdel Hakim Amir, a friend from the start, Nasser's closest adviser, known to his intimates as 'the Fox', and whose long poker-face hid a diplomat's temperament. More thoughtful and more firm, and more experienced than any of his comrades, Nasser was clearly the strongest. With such a Number One, no Number Two was needed or possible.

There are stresses and strains within the Junta, but it is hard to translate them into political terms, to make out any Left or Right wing, a Western or neutral wing, a lay or religious. One might well be progressive as regards social legislation, yet conservative in religion and at the same time pro-American. Another might be a neutralist, little disposed to making social concessions, yet liberal in matters of religion . . . Those who have tried to subdivide the Council of the Revolution into camps in this way have merely been wasting their time. They could only study lists for each of the problems concerned. The most that can be said is that the three airmen, Gamal Salim, Boghdadi and Ibrahim, were most strongly against a return to parliamentary government; while as regards foreign policy, Anwar el Sadat, Abdel Hakim Amir and (of course) Khaled Muhi ud-Din were regarded by the British and Americans as their most dangerous enemies.

Up to 1954 the Junta very intelligently managed to preserve the 'fraternity' of fellows-in-arms of the early days. The Neguib affair revealed certain splits and the Junta was no longer a solid block after that. None the less, its members realized that any violent break would be fatal to the régime. This gave an almost friendly appearance to the eviction of several of Nasser's lieutenants. Thus in January 1956 the Prime Minister was able to dissolve the cumbersome Council of the Revolution and establish his personal authority, based on a plebiscite, within the framework of a Napoleonic constitution.

But the problems were not confined to the upper layers of the pyramid. The Society of Free Officers was constantly being excited by violent currents of opinion. Of course the left-wing factions which had reinstated Neguib in February 1954 had lost their leader owing to the exile of Khaled Muhi ud-Din and the severe sentences passed on sixteen young officers in April of that year. But Liberal tendencies (by left-wingers and partisans of the constitution) remained unabated among the more or less recognized representatives of various political extremes. This became clear during the Moslem Brotherhood affair. Several of the Free Officers (among them Neguib's aide-de-camp Captain Mohamed Riad) were seriously compromised in this conspiracy.

The army is the régime's foundation, the alpha and omega. The army has penetrated everywhere, into the banks and into the reformatory schools, into the 'higher committee for cultural development', into the sports clubs, the day-nurseries, unions, casinos, the frontiers. In a sense, it plays the same role as a party in any popularly-elected democracy. But it would be unwise to push the comparisons too far. Nasser issues and derives his power from the army, its fate and his are inseparable. A grey suit and coloured tie change nothing: the word *bikbashi* (lieutenant-colonel) means 'leader of a thousand' and is a military rank.

The army is indebted to the régime. Before the 23rd of July 1952 it was the last of the social 'orders', falling between those of the tradesman and the navvy. It was somewhat less than in China before Mao—and the defeat in Palestine had not improved matters. A respectable *bourgeois* would not allow his daughter to marry an officer, unless he belonged to the cavalry, which played polo and was made up of pashas' sons. The pay was low and so was prestige, and at a time when everything British was loathed, nothing seemed to be more British than the Egyptian army. After the 23rd of July the despised men were regarded as heroes. They said that they merely wished to 'clean out the stables and make room for decent politicians', yet they established themselves in power and clung to it like limpets. The tramps had become the masters, and then—according to an ancient Egyptian saying, 'scribes and Masters of the Secrets'.

From now on the army was a kind of governing class. As of Prussia, though with certain reservations, it might be said that Egypt is not a state with an army, but an army with a state. At one time the army was not an isolated caste, but it is tending to become one. It is still an army drawn direct from the nation, from the families of civil servants or well-to-do fellahs or the minor *bourgeoisie*, which constitute the backbone of the nation. But the army has come 'unstuck' from its humble origins, to the extent to which it has become the ruling order. It rules, but from a distance, envied and uncertain. The officers are far from being as incompetent as people say. There is no reason why the new army should fail to become what Napoleon's technical colleges became for France at the beginning of the nineteenth century. The army may be considered in this way as a training school. These soldiers might be unpleasant, but they work hard. They are clumsy and pretentious, but they do try to improve themselves. Half their efforts are wasted in fighting the sabotage of disgraced civil servants, but the other half is worth quite as much as their predecessors' permanent 'couldn't care less' attitude. Between four and five hundred officers working ten hours a day carry out Egypt's administration, ponderously but effectively.

Their zeal is rewarded in the form of promotion, increases of salary, expenses, clubs, social services, goods in kind, sitting on various Boards. In Nasser's Egypt it has become 'a good thing' to be an army officer, and fathers now seek them as sons-in-law. Even the common soldier benefits from the glory of the military order. New uniforms, ample food, clean barracks, sports grounds, cinemas and— until the Sinai campaign—the shy admiration of children and nannies, all of which is more than tempting to the sons of fellahs.

How could the army not be faithful to the man who had done so much for it? It trusted him until the Sinai campaign of 1956, which did much to shake the military's confidence in itself and its leader. But before that, such things as the following could be noticed. A thirty-four-year-old colonel had been able to turn out Faruk, seize power and become the master of Egypt. 'Then why not me?' dozens of officers must have said to themselves, and especially those generals who were supplanted by colonels and chafed at the bit, losing patience with this 'dictatorship of children'. Some foreign power, interested in bringing about some change, is all that is needed for making a further putsch possible. But in domestic politics the Colonel has several good cards in his hand. First, the fact that the Society of Free Officers, of which he is the unquestioned master, is a secret society except for about thirty officers at the top. Thus anyone wanting to stage a plot risks approaching someone in favour of Nasser, without knowing it. Also the young head of the army, General Amir, is not only the Prime Minister's best friend, but a clever tactician playing on group rivalries within the officer corps. Finally, the political police and intelligence service are ever on the alert, so that it is much harder to do to Nasser what he did to Faruk.

Outside the army there are a Council of Ministers which, apart from its military members, is rather a committee of secretaries of State; the Assembly elected in July 1957; a few special advisers; two or three small groups of economics or law experts—such as those who prepared the Suez nationalization—and lastly the vague, unidentified mass listening to the wireless. But it is a mass which, as we shall see, plays much more than the part of a mere echo.

V

The 'Diplomacy' of Small Nations

'First we must end our disputes with Britain.' Such were more or less the terms used by the first of many officers who used to expound to us tirelessly 'the tasks of the revolution' during the régime's early days. The disputes with London were, first, the most important of all questions for Egypt, in other words its relations with the Sudan; and, second, the problem which most irked nationalist feelings, the occupation of the Canal Zone, which for Egyptians was a kind of Alsace-Lorraine.

Well, before the Israelis (who were one of the remoter causes of the military revolt) it was the British whom the Egyptians regarded as needing the most immediate attention, and this was especially so for the officers, with their attention naturally focused on military problems and being much more familiar with what concerned the Sudan than were their predecessors. It must be noted here, to avoid repeating it, that if the Egyptian people as a whole harbour a deep-rooted rancour against the British, for the stiff Tel el Kebir staff-officers, for the cold impersonal administration of former times, yet it is unusual for an Egyptian not to feel a vague, indefinable respect when he is in the presence of an Englishman. It is not a matter of memories, which would most likely be unpleasant. Complexes? They hardly know what complexes are, except for those connected with sex. 'It isn't the Egyptians who detest the British, but the British who detest the Egyptians,' Azzam Pasha remarked to us one day, with his melancholy air. What is worth remembering is, briefly, that the Egyptians are capable of approaching an English negotiator without too many preconceived ideas, without harbouring too many blind resentments, and this is especially true of the officers who were formed on the British model, for whom the language they used at work was English, and who, being fiercely pro-German during the war, must have felt some respect for those who beat Rommel.

In August 1952 the British, well disposed towards the Officers' régime—Mr Churchill had said he 'followed its efforts with sympathy'—had mentioned resuming the talks which had begun half-heartedly with Ali Mahir, then with Hilali earlier that year. They were agreeably surprised when Neguib pointed out that the new régime would prefer to subdivide Anglo-Egyptian problems and consider the Sudan question separately. This was a tactical error on the Officers' part, for which they were at once criticized by Ali Mahir. It was playing into London's hands to separate the Sudan question from that of Suez, for the British could thus avoid discussing principles and reduce them both to technicalities, their arguments thus gaining weight. But fortified by their links with the Sudan—Neguib's mother was born there, so were the Salim brothers, while Nasser, Amir, Muhi ud-Din and a number of their comrades had served there —the young revolutionaries had convinced themselves that they were cut out for handling this Sudan affair. They did not feel ready for going into the problem of the Suez evacuation, not wishing to discuss it with London until the army was reorganized and strengthened, while they hoped to bring Washington in on their side. Thus they looked to the south first, without taking enough stock of the difficulties they were facing, without having sufficiently understood that it was a really vital question, a royal road to the Egyptian revival, and that failure in this would compromise everything else.

THE SUDANESE MIRAGE

The sovereigns of Thebes and Memphis had thrice extended their empire as far as the fourth or fifth cataract, well beyond Nubia. It was from the Sudan that the kings of Meroe came to be Pharaohs of Egypt. They shared the same valley, and the dream was always to reunite it into one. The scribes of the Delta, looking southwards, spoke of it as the 'contemptible land of Kush'. It was down there, nevertheless, in the land of the two Niles, that the god Hapi with hanging dugs had come into being and every year overflowed the lower valley.

But Egyptian claims on the Sudan cannot clearly be traced farther back than the Albanian adventurer Mohamed Ali, who is now frowned on by his most skilful imitators. In 1820 he sent his son Isma'il to bring back slaves and gold. The conqueror was burnt alive while sleeping in a straw hut, for having insulted a tribal chief, while the slaves all died near Aswan before being turned into soldiers for Ibrahim; the Viceroy was not enriched by gold so much as by the cotton from the Delta. But from then on, Egypt levied taxes in the Sudan, and Bosnian soldiers were garrisoned in the country of the 'pelican-men'.

It was a poor administration, to say the least, made up of slave-parties, looting and official corruption. When the Khedive Isma'il, the modernizing sovereign, sent Gordon—the hero of the campaigns in China—to the Sudan he returned enraged. A whole nation was being disgustingly exploited by those whom it called the 'Turks', and were looking for mercy and justice. A few reforms and a ruthless pursuit of the slave-traders by the English general were not enough. In 1881 a man appeared who claimed to be the Mahdi. He stirred up the whole people against the foreigner and the infidel (in his eyes the 'bad Moslems' of the north were worse than infidels). He moulded them into the army of Dervishes who were ready to die at any moment so that they could come more quickly into the presence of their god. By 1885 all the Egyptian garrisons, even those commanded by British or Austrian officers, had fallen, and Gordon was calling for help from besieged Khartum. The relief party arrived too late: Gordon's headless body lay at his command-post and the Dervishes were masters of the Sudan.

It took thirteen years to prepare for the re-conquest. Kitchener led an army which was three-quarters Egyptian and nine-tenths financed by Cairo. The victory over the Dervishes at Omdurman was two-headed, and so was the treaty of 1899, establishing over the Sudan—which had been lost by Egypt alone and reconquered by both—an Anglo-Egyptian condominium, a formula which is as risky as the indivisibility of an estate in private law. London interpreted its powers in such a way that the Sudanese soon had little contact with those Egyptian officials whose fathers had left such a loathsome memory . . . The new administration was mean but wise, and a prudent realization of the country's resources might have justified this one-sided view of the 'condominium', had the British not cynically taken the assassination of Sir Lee Stack in 1924, the 'Sirdar' or General in Chief of the Egyptian army and governor of the Sudan, as a pretext for literally confiscating Egypt's share, and expelling its few representatives from the Sudan.

Egypt not only had the Sudan taken from her, but soon learned that the British had started a large-scale growing of cotton in the Sudanese Gazira, between the White and Blue Niles. Cairo felt this to be a double threat, both to its water-supply and to its cotton exports. London had to compromise, and signed with Cairo the Convention of 1929, most advantageous to Egypt, which was given the right to nineteen-twentieths of the river's water. Despite this handsome 'tip', the Sudanese question remained in the forefront of Egypt's demands. The 1936 Treaty had merely provided for a return to pre-1924 arrangements (the *status quo ante*).

While London was cunningly doing its best to develop Sudanese autonomy, which would have certainly evolved into independence on the Jordan model, in October 1951 the Wafd government took a bold decision by declaring the 1899 Treaty invalid as well as that of 1936, and proclaiming Faruk 'King of Egypt and of the Sudan'. This formula was beginning to become a commonplace in diplomatic practice and to be accepted as a *fait accompli*. As we have seen, this was one of the reasons why the English were not too ill disposed to those who had expelled Faruk. However, the Egyptian delegation to the United Nations Assembly, meeting in Paris in November 1951, had made it understood that Egypt was not against the principle of Sudanese self-determination.

This is how the matter stood when Neguib and his followers boldly undertook to settle it. As a basis for their plan they took up their predecessors' idea—the free choice of the Sudanese people who were to be appealed to—for here they felt themselves to be on safe ground. And Neguib, with his solid common sense, suggested to his comrades that 'Since everything is to depend on the Sudanese people's opinion, let us give them our attention and try to enlarge the circle of our friends in Khartum.'

Sudanese problems are complex. First of all, there are two Sudans: that of the North, with a vast grassy savannah in the west, a desert plateau in the east, is inhabited by a Hamitic population, vaguely Arab, in any case speaking Arabic, and ardently Moslem. The South, on the contrary, wet and almost equatorial, covered with swamps and forests, is peopled by fetish-loving negroes who speak various nilotic dialects. These two countries are as unlike each other as Algeria and Ghana. The 'frontier' passes near to Fashoda. London had completely isolated the Southern Sudan with the possible intention of attaching it, at some future date, to Uganda. In addition to this there were two main nationalist parties, the 'Umma' who were resolute enemies of the Egyptians, and not without contacts with the British administration; and the 'Ashigga', which was connected with Egypt.

But above all there were two great Moslem sects, that of the Ansar, heirs to the Dervishes, venerating their 'Pope', Sayed Abdel Rahman el Mahdi, the rebel's posthumous son; and the Khatmia, whose 'Pope' is Sayed Ali el Mirghani, whose one thought was to withstand the power of the Mahdists, whose rule from 1881 to 1899 had left some bitter memories. Since the Mahdi and the Ansar sponsor the Umma party, the Mirghani and the Khatmia are naturally forced to support the Ashigga. Since the former are not hostile to London, the latter do not fail to look to Cairo. But Egypt's partisans were divided, round the Ashigga, into some eight parties or movements.

The Officers thus had three problems to solve. First, they must avoid the secession of the Southern Sudan which is a source of wealth, and break through the British ring with Egyptian propaganda. Next, they must smooth out the hostility of the Mahdi and his followers towards Cairo. Finally, they must gather all their potential friends as closely as possible round the Ashigga.

In the first stages of their efforts they succeeded brilliantly. Invited in October by Neguib, the son of the Mahdi, the high-priest of the Ansar, showed himself touched by the gesture, deigned to find some merit in the young Officers, and talked business—being the largest cotton-producer in the Upper Valley. He did not drop his English friends in favour of these new connexions, but the Officers could have some hope of transforming an implacable enemy into an eventual neutral. Then, descending on Khartum, Major Salah Salim, to whom the task had fallen since he was a son of Port Sudan, worked to such effect that he managed to set up a 'Front' of the partisans of Egypt, under the title 'National Unionist Party'. He had its Presidency given to Isma'il el Azhari, who was known to be Egypt's most reliable agent in Khartum, and as such had been imprisoned by the British several times. More enterprising still, Salim managed to reach the southern tribes and the dance he performed, naked among the unclothed natives, was evidently not the only argument he employed.

With this done the Officers confidently started the negotiations with London which ended, to everyone's satisfaction, with the agreements of February 1953. The 'Sudanization' of the administration was to begin in three years' time. The following November the Sudanese people were to elect a Legislative Assembly, before choosing by referendum, in 1956, either their independence or 'a form of union with Egypt'.

The Sudanese appeared to have won on all counts. Neguib and his men had, in the eyes of the world, won their stripes as 'reasonable negotiators' and wise rulers. As to the British, they considered they had won the match. The mirage of the word 'independence' opened up cheerful horizons.

In the following November it was none other than the National Unionist Party created by Salah Salim which—after a delightfully picturesque manner of voting which was not entirely regular—entered the Sudanese parliament with a comfortable majority. One evening in November, at Omdurman, an officer of Salim's circle was already talking to us, in Ali el Mirghani's ante-room, of what he called 'Egyptianization'. Cairo was jubilant. But those who had followed the election campaign from Atbara to El Obeid, who, like us, had been able to talk quietly with the 'pro-Egyptian' leaders, were much more cautious. One question constantly came up in conversations, that of the Nile waters. 'We will effect a close union between the Sudan and our sister, Egypt,' Isma'il el Azhari told us with hypocritical sweetness, spreading his broad glistening face in a large smile. 'But the waters of the Nile?'—the smile grew wider still, till his ears disappeared: 'We have a proverb which says that he who has a doorstep by which the waters flow, will never want for water' —Well: it would be in Egypt's interest to establish good relations, federal or otherwise, with the people in front of whose doorstep there flows far more than the twentieth part of the Nile to which they then had the right.

The Egyptian-Sudanese honeymoon lasted less than a year. We have already seen how only three months after the elections, Neguib's visit to Khartum on the 1st of March 1953 was the occasion of a bloody sabotage on the part of the Umma party. Ten thousand Ansar, armed with spears and standards bearing the Mahdi's arms, came up against British troops. 'There were thirty killed, but we forced Neguib to get out,' the Mahdi said the following day. Although the affair was no more than the work of a faction, it showed that the Sudanese have a long memory.

Five reasons may be found for the break between the two countries: British policy had done its best to hasten the divorce, neglecting neither cash nor promises, nor the reception of Azhari at the Court of Saint James, nor 'local incidents'. Next, Neguib's dismissal shocked and outraged the Sudanese who, as we know, regarded the General as one of their own, and who were most annoyed that their intervention on his behalf failed to cause the brother-government to unbend—a government which the Khartum Press always called 'totalitarian'. The third reason was the cumulative effect of Salah Salim and his team's blunders. They had been well inspired and brilliant in 1952-3, only to become heavy-handed afterwards, making one stormy interference after another, playing the pro-consul, cynically dishing out 'gifts' while all Khartum was made aware of who had received them and who had not, and in whose interest they were made. The fourth reason was naturally the question of sharing the Nile waters, together with that of the Aswan Dam which would result in flooding more than 300 square miles of Sudanese Nubia. On this issue Khartum felt it had not been correctly consulted, nor sufficiently favoured as to the sharing of surplus water (38,000,000,000 cubic metres annually) which would be saved thanks to this feat of engineering.[1] The fifth, last and fundamental reason for the quarrel is simply that all the Sudanese, whether they looked to London or to Cairo during the 'incubation' period, wanted neither more nor less than their independence . . . While Abdullah Khalil and the Umma relied on London to stop the Egyptians from taking over their country, Isma'il el Azhari and his followers were only making use of Egypt to 'kick' Britain out of the condominium (he was saying as much, with admirable frankness, in the corridors of the Cairo parliament as early as 1951). These men had the same thought in their minds, and this could be seen in 1956 when Abdullah Khalil as Prime Minister was almost as reticent towards London—though he was a former British army Brigadier—as Azhari once was towards his Cairo 'protectors'.

Nasser and Salah Salim, realizing late in 1954 that the wind was turning, after a ridiculous attempt to get the South to rise against Khartum, tried to propose a makeshift solution which would exclude the idea of Cairo's domination over Khartum and replace the vague protectorate by an association (which is much the same as what Mendès-France was doing with Tunisia at that time). In an article published in his paper in *El Sha'b* on the 30th of June 1956, Salah Salim disclosed this 'federation plan' which provided for each of the two republics to have its own president, parliament, government and army. A 'federal parliament' was to be set up and the

[1] Cairo offered Khartum 50 per cent of the water after allowance for evaporation, that is to say about 14,000,000,000 cubic metres. The Sudanese demand at least 18,000,000,000. Some even demand a third of the gross output, viz. about 28,000,000,000 cubic metres.

federation would have 'a supreme head, Sudanese in the first instance, Egyptian in the second . . .' This was conceding a great deal
and was said to have stirred up a certain amount of opposition in
Cairo. The 'dancing Major' has ever since reproached the Sudanese
politicians, especially three of the Ministers in Azhari's Cabinet, for
rejecting such a novel scheme.

In the end Cairo had to resign itself and Salah Salim had to give
up his functions. Nasser was among the first to congratulate Azhari
over the proclamation of Sudanese independence in January 1956.
He was even the first to send him an ambassador. But smiles change
nothing. The brilliant and ingenious Sudanese policy invented by
the Colonels' régime ended in failure. Faced by two adversaries such
as London, and the word 'independence', success was probably out
of the question. It is none the less true that this bitter separation from
that great land to the south was the most costly defeat that Egypt
could bear. It turns her from her true destiny, which is African, to
throw her back into the pan-Arab adventure.

Her future is heavily mortgaged, whether over the Dam, the sharing of the waters, the eventual exploitation of the enormous surplus
of Egyptian labour, or the strategic and economic independence
of Cairo. Reconciliation is not impossible. The Sudan, once its thirst
for independence has been slaked, might consider the advantages
of a closer union. But this would most likely be as part of a group of
River States making use of the Nile waters—Ethiopia, Uganda, the
Sudan and Egypt.

THE PRICE OF THE EVACUATION

But more so than its military leaders, the Egyptian people remained
obsessed by the occupation of the Canal. This was what the Press
called 'the national problem'. An alibi for bad governments and a
stumbling-block for the best. In the autumn of 1953 we witnessed a
significant scene. When Neguib, Nasser and Salim came to open
the university term in the great lecture-hall of Cairo University, they
were welcomed with sustained shouting, so that not a word of their
speeches was heard.

When, astounded at such a display, we asked our military guide
about it, he translated, quite unabashed, saying 'the students are
demanding arms with which to go and fight on the canal . . . they
want to enlist to defend their country'.

For their part, the Officers knew that as in 1951 such a battle could only lead to disaster. Stripping this old problem of the Mediterranean and Semitic tendency to dramatize, which only made matters worse, they approached it with a perfect professional realism which caused the highest-ranking British negotiators to say, 'These men are the first serious people we have had to deal with.' And certainly neither London, nor particularly Washington, could have wanted a better preface to the debate offered by the Junta after November 1952, than the 'Note on Strategy' published by the Egyptian staff on the 10th of February 1953. Arguing that Egypt was 'perfectly capable of defending the Canal', the author of this document limited the question to its technical aspects, situating the problem from a purely Western angle and viewing the affair only in the light of a possible Soviet aggression. The Egyptian note—which observers attributed to Gamal Salim—remarked that 'the strategic importance of the Canal depends on the security of navigation in the Mediterranean', and that 'the security of the eastern Mediterranean, should it be threatened', would depend on '(a) the evacuation of Russian submarine bases in Albania; (b) the success of Turkish forces in defending the Straits; (c) the defence of Greece and Crete; (d) the destruction of Russian air-bases in the Balkans; (e) the resistance put up by the countries in the east and north-east Mediterranean'. And, wondering 'what traffic would be apt to use the Canal in time of war', and 'whether it would be intelligent to defend the base at any price', the Egyptian officer concluded, 'The presence of British troops in this zone is definitely useless.' This is a reflection to which the events of 1956 lend an unconscious humour. But people reasoned no differently in Washington. Nasser and his companions had thus won the support of American diplomacy and of the Pentagon, a support which remained solid until the conclusion of the Treaty.

In March 1953, a month after the signature of the Sudan agreement, and the publication of this 'Note on Strategy', London suggested that talks about the base be reopened. Nasser, who had just defined the Egyptian position in three successive speeches, thus openly taking the responsibility for Egyptian diplomacy, laid down a condition on the reopening of discussions, although he devoutly hoped for them: Great Britain should abandon any intention of making Egypt pay for the evacuation by adhering to the 'Middle East Pact', something which the British had tried to force on the preceding governments. After a brief stay in Cairo Mr Selwyn Lloyd, then Minister of State, informed London that the Officers would be adamant on this point. He had, however, reached agreement with them on the following principles: 'Negotiations would bear on two points only: how the evacuation would be carried out, and the maintenance of the base.'

In very general terms the problem was as follows: between Port Said, Suez and Tel el Kebir, in a triangle about 87 miles from north to south and 30 miles from east to west, some 40,000 British soldiers had been stationed since the war, while the 1937 Treaty authorized a garrison of no more than 14,000 fighting men. The British government wanted to reduce this 'extremely costly base' (Churchill) as much as possible, since it was hardly compatible with the requirements of nuclear strategy. It wanted to keep as cheaply as possible a base that might be useful in war-time, while keeping on friendly terms with Cairo so as to be able to pursue an effective Arab policy. As for the Egyptians, they wanted as complete an evacuation as possible, well publicized and involving as little commitment to the West as could be managed.

Beginning on the 27th of April 1953, with General Neguib leading the Egyptian delegation and General Sir Brian Robertson and Sir Ralph Stevenson, H.M. Ambassador, at the head of the British team, the negotiations were broken off on the 6th of May. In the House of Commons Mr Selwyn Lloyd gave the following reasons for the failure of the talks: 'The Egyptian government sought to have direct and technical control of the base evacuated by the British; to have the absolute right to dismiss the technicians, who would be its employees; to exercise a right of veto on the utilization of equipment and installations, and to substitute its own agents for the British experts in as short a time as possible ... If Britain had yielded to these demands, the base would quickly have fallen into ruins. Anyone with any common sense will realize that it was out of the question to do so.' The breaking-off of the talks set a match to the fuse at both ends. In the Commons, Churchill gave vent to a flamboyant demonstration of his usual rhetoric in which, as a well-versed reader of Plutarch and Carlyle, he made a cruel thrust at Neguib: 'The trouble with dictators is that they dictate nothing, and that others dictate their conduct.' The General, losing his smile, answered in the manner of his Wafdist predecessors: 'Independence is not won by a scrap of paper or a pact, but by the shedding of warm blood ... We are on the eve of a great battle, for which we must make ready.'

During the last days of June, one wondered whether this verbal fierceness—which no one took quite seriously—was going to degenerate into hostilities. Egyptian agents kidnapped an English corporal called Rigden, in Ismaïlia, and the officer commanding the base sent Cairo the following ultimatum: if the soldier was not returned to his unit in twenty-four hours, he would not answer for the consequences of retaliatory measures that would have to be taken. 'Blood is going to flow!' Salah Salim said, breathlessly, to journalists who were called to H.Q. in the middle of the night. But on the following day the British Embassy made it clear that the Note was not an ultimatum but a 'fair warning'. There the affair ended, the kidnapped soldier (who, incidentally, had not been entirely unco-operative with the Egyptians) being returned to his family after a 'good time' in Paris at the expense of the Egyptian high command. Very soon there was talk of resuming negotiations, which, more cautiously, were this time to be known as 'informal talks'. There were frequent meetings from the end of July until a day in October when, leaving the final one, Nasser, who had taken over the leadership of the Egyptian delegation, said with a glowering look on his face as he got into his car—'Impossible!'

A month later, however, when he received reporters on the day of the Egyptian electoral success at Khartum, General Neguib, all smiles, said with his pipe in his mouth, 'The moment has come to resume talks on the Canal.' When one of us asked him whether Egypt could now accept the base's being 're-activated' in the event of an attack on Turkey, the General let slip, 'We all know that in case of war, if Turkey were attacked it would not be long before our turn.' Had Egypt compromised on the essential point? Nasser did not say so in the course of a conversation which took place several weeks later, just before his great battle against Neguib. At that time he told us that the main obstacle to an agreement was the British insistence that the experts who would look after the upkeep of the base after the evacuation, should be in uniform. 'We cannot admit this,' said the Colonel, 'for in the eyes of the Egyptian people that would be a symbol of the permanence of foreign occupation. We cannot ask them to accept that.'

The Colonel wanted an agreement so badly—for he regarded this as an essential requisite before any radical attempt at remoulding the country—that as soon as he became master of Egypt in April 1954 he decided to take the risk of a compromise. On the 27th of July, following the anniversary celebrations over Faruk's abdication, and after several days on which short meetings were held, with Mr Antony Head, British Secretary for War, who had hastily come over from London, he signed a preliminary agreement to the treaty of evacuation. This text was in accordance with most of what had been foreseen by all those who since 1950 had followed the ins and outs of the Anglo-Egyptian conversations. The three fundamental questions were the time taken over the evacuation (one year, two years?), the number and status of the technicians (1,000, 5,000?—civilians or soldiers?), and the conditions under which the base could be placed on a warlike footing (in case of an attack against an Arab country—against Turkey?—Iraq?). It appeared that in all cases the British and Egyptians had wisely followed the line of making concessions.

As to the duration of the evacuation, it was the Egyptian spokesmen who had given the most ground. Twenty months was a lot, not for soldiers depending on limited transport, but for public opinion which would want to know the reasons for such a delay. As for the technicians appointed to maintain the base, Nasser had come off best: first because it had been stipulated that they should be civilian contractors; second because the Company had the right to hire no more than 1,200 British experts. On the third and last point, Nasser had had to capitulate since Egypt admitted herself to be 'committed to grant the United Kingdom every facility needed for placing the base on a warlike footing and operating it effectively', and to do so 'in the event of an armed attack by a power outside the Middle East, against any country which, at the date of the present agreement, is a signatory of the treaty of mutual defence between the Arab states, signed in Cairo in 1950, or against Turkey'. Nasser had therefore given in on the Turkish clause, accepting that the Egyptians should consider that any attack on Turkey involved themselves. This was indirectly linking Egyptian defence with the Atlantic coalition. In exchange the Egyptian negotiations had obtained that the British be unable to take advantage of an Israeli-Arab dispute in order to return to the base, by stipulating that the attack invoking the application of the treaty would have to come from 'a power outside the zone of the Middle East'.

In the Cabinet offices, where this document, putting an end to seventy-two years of British occupation, had just been signed, only one serious face was to be seen in the typically Egyptian uproar of rejoicing. It was not that of any of the British signatories, which were perfectly relaxed, but that of the morose dictator. As we drew near to ask him 'What now . . . ?' he looked at us without a smile. 'Now we must start reconstructing our country.' Affectation? He was perfectly aware that the task had barely begun, that it was easier to wring a treaty of evacuation from the British than to give fifty calories more a day to every Egyptian fellah, to reinvigorate that mass which for three thousand years had been humiliated by foreign occupation and feudal oppression. He also knew that the document he had so painfully extracted from the tenacious British would give rise to no enthusiasm in Egypt, because the concessions were too obvious. Compared with the eternal nationalist slogan 'unconditional evacuation', Nasser's treaty looked a bit too 'reasonable', and smelled too strongly of 'mutual defence' with the West.[1]

Nasser's aim was clear: liquidate the British occupation as cheaply as possible and redirect Egyptian energies away from the hereditary enemy to the real problem—poverty and social stagnation, the problem of modernizing and industrializing the country by attracting capital from the erstwhile enemy. A dangerous game, to be sure, but the only one open to a régime which was then cut off from the masses, unable to rely on them to defend a total national independence, and for that reason led to seek its sole justification in material and technical successes. In the collusion which was constantly offered by the British and Americans and which Nasser accepted, there was certainly an element of ideological understanding, a common determination to block the passage to a violent social revolution by offsetting it with technical reform (the idea being less to bar the road to an imaginary Soviet invasion, than to nip in the bud some Mao of the Nile Valley). But there was also, in the thirty-six-year-old dictator, a clear determination to lift the masses from their humiliating poverty, to deliver the country from the obsession of hunger, from its resignation to squalor, its abandonment to ignorance.

But the statesman's bold choice was not founded on any widespread national commitment. Nasser had steered Westwards: the Egyptian ship was slow to respond and resisted until the day when the pilot, leaving for Bandung, began to steer a middle course. The remarkable phenomenon which he had foreseen in signing the treaty, had materialized: public opinion set itself, with surprising firmness, against this agreement which to all appearances was so fruitful.

[1] Nothing was stipulated as to the régime of the Suez Canal, except that Egypt was to exercise full sovereignty there. In thus neglecting this all-important question, London assumed an overwhelming responsibility for the crisis which came to a head two years later.

The gagged Press could certainly not react: but nobody familiar with Egyptian street-life could be mistaken: these 'people's parades', these mass demonstrations hastily organized by the police, this 'march' of the people on the Cabinet offices—none of that could mislead anybody. 'Cheap labour, cheers at two piastres apiece,' said a man of insight as he stood at his shop doorway in Kasr el Nil Street, from which he had watched these triumphant processions go by. 'And they are not even fanatics!'

It is common to be contemptuous of public opinion in Egypt, whereas in fact it is very much alive, sensitive and demanding. From the university lecturer to the student and down to the Nubian door-man, and from the café terraces down to the seething pavements of the El Azhar district, one finds nothing but passionate arguments and denunciations. It was this enormous murmur from the people that had forced King Fuad to accept the national leader Sa'd Zaghlul; it had compelled Faruk to recall the Wafd; it had kept the same Wafd in 1951 from signing a more 'Western' agreement than that of 1954. Such is the public opinion which was believed to be partly silenced and in part won over, in part drugged or cowed by the régime. Here we see it returning to life, more prosperous than ever. The fact is that rarely in the course of Egyptian history have the confused rumours from the city so markedly offset the will of one man or weighed so heavily on his ultimate decisions. Even if this refusal on the people's part had not taken the degenerate form of an attack by one of the Moslem Brothers on the Prime Minister a week after the signing of the final agreement on the 19th of October 1954, it would have to be credited with an essential part in the political and psychological development which led Colonel Nasser to go to Bandung, or to bargaining with the East and the nationalization of the Canal. We come back to Churchill's words, 'The trouble with dictators is that others dictate their conduct.'

None the less, Anglo-Egyptian relations looked healthier during the autumn of 1954. Economic missions, cultural exchanges, the welcome given to the 'contractors' when they came to the base—it recalled the palmy days of 1937. The reconciliation extended to the entire West and resulted in smiles for Washington and France, praise of M. Mendès-France and even of Turkey, the offering of cordial hospitality to a 'delegation of journalists' made up of a General, the Governor of Ankara and personal friends of M. Menderes. Major Ali Sabri, the Prime Minister's closest collaborator, said to us at the time, 'Have we not turned towards the West rather than towards the East? So much the worse if our relations with the U.S.S.R. become less good than they were.'

This honeymoon was harshly interrupted by the signing of the Baghdad Pact. The Turks came to the conclusion during their December talks with Nasser in Cairo, that in spite of the 'Turkish Clause' (or perhaps because of it and the reactions that had followed in Egypt, Syria and Jordan), Egypt could not be enlisted in the anti-communist coalition which was being worked out in Ankara with American help. It was they who, catching the British off their guard and even surprising the State Department—if not the local American agents—landed at Baghdad with the Pact in their pockets. It was quickly signed. *Le Monde* called it a 'Bashi-Buzuq operation'— meaning no doubt that it was a sly and Oriental piece of work—and Nasser and his Officers had the same reaction. But they showed their feelings so plainly that they appeared in the light of losers. Had they been forewarned, had they been offered a place as one of the founder-members? It seems that between Nasser and his Anglo-Saxon inter-mediaries the idea of Egypt taking part in the Eastern anti-communist coalition had not been definitely set aside; but the Egyptian dictator had warned that such a move would need a long preparation of public and army opinion. He had also insisted on the fact that he did not intend allowing himself to be treated as a 'rear-guard force' when the arms-distribution began, or to be content with light machine-guns while Iraq was receiving heavy tanks.

The Baghdad Pact upset all these plans, to the great regret of certain American diplomats. As for the British, they lost no time crying over spilt milk in Cairo and turned to more urgent matters, the exploitation for their own ends of a scheme laid by others. Since they had not invented it, they wanted at least to ride on the band-wagon in the hope of having some hand in its progress. They had no illusions as to the effect such a policy would have on Cairo, and were satisfied that they would gain at least as far as Iraq was concerned. Since then, Anglo-Egyptian relations never ceased to deteriorate, to be capped by the arrival of warships at Cyprus and the bombing of Cairo in 1956.

And yet sincere efforts had been made on each side, especially by the British, who carried out the 1954 agreement in an exemplary manner. Whatever the political situation, the rate of the evacuation, which was completed on the 18th of June 1956, was always in advance of the Treaty schedule, by at least a month. The embarking troops never provoked the slightest incident. No trace of sabotage robbed the Egyptians of a jot of their inheritance, and above all the British 'experts' made themselves so inconspicuous that the casual visitor, such as ourselves and probably many Egyptians, had the impression ten months later that the base had been completely emptied. Thus, in spite of the embittering of relations, and the ridiculous anti-British demonstrations which, at the time when the evacuation was being celebrated, were enough to make one imagine that Egyptian combatants had 'thrown the British off Egyptian soil', the Colonel-President, on the 20th of June 1956, in the presence of his former partner in the negotiations, General Sir Brian Robertson, paid a tribute to the good faith of the British—only a month before his speech at Alexandria, and five months before the invasion.

WICKED UNCLE SAM?

'Mr Dulles, we hate you!' Such was the unusual greeting which the cleverest framer of public opinion—Mahmud Abul Fath, head of the great popular daily *El Misr*—set out right across the page on the day when the new leader of American diplomacy arrived in Cairo in May 1953. Why? First, and perhaps simply, because this master of the Press knew that these words were what his readers wanted. He offered the crowd what it expected, and the Egyptians are delighted whenever the American giant is criticized.

United States responsibility in the creation and development of the new State of Israel is not enough to explain this obsession, for the good reason that until the attack by Israeli commandos on Gaza on the 28th of February 1955, the Israeli question remained, whether one likes it or not, well in the background. Of course the matter was constantly thrown up in anti-American talk, but more as a stylistic device than as an expression of deep feeling. In the litany of curses that fell on Mr Dulles's broad shoulders, the word 'Israel' appeared several times, but certainly not so often as the words 'Imperialism', 'military pact' and 'war-policies'. Indeed, in the political life of contemporary Egypt the United States are not really judged by their acts—which are often positive, except for the abrupt withdrawal of their offer of financial aid for building the Upper Dam (on the 17th of July 1956). They are merely a target which enables us to measure, by the number and force of blows received and by the marksman's style, the powerful influence of communist propaganda, an influence which is out of all proportion to the meagre resources of local Marxist movements.

But if the slogans and themes of extreme Left propaganda are so rich and have such strong echoes, it is not only because they are sent out by talented men and dropped almost everywhere in the Press and at all the strategic points of public opinion and business: it is because such seed falls on ground which is ready for it. The Egyptians like Americans but have an *a priori* hatred of America. Between the folk of the Mississippi and those of the Nile there are certain affinities, the same good-fellowship, healthy good humour, a taste for the earth and the family. The Egyptians are more than keen on American films and—when they have read them—place Steinbeck well above Malraux. Their Press tries to imitate that of Mr Luce, and some of their journalists ape New York reporters. They enjoy drinking Pepsi-cola or Coca-cola, and if they can afford it they wear those American shirts which seem to derive from some mad painter's nightmare. Thus there is a veneer of Americanism, but in politics this is compensated by an instinctive hostility, a kind of reflex. Can it be taken as a sign of an inborn political insight if the Egyptian automatically sees Washington's hand when natives are hanged in Cyprus, rebels crushed in Kabylia or Kikuyus burnt to death in their huts? There are few countries in which the Rosenberg affair excited so much anger and feeling as in Egypt, though it was at 'war' with Israel. Thus, in a country heavily occupied by the British for seventy-two years, and where only a short while ago nothing could be done without going through the British Embassy, any shabby event was attributed at once to Washington, not to London. This was the case even in 1957, even after the tremendous services rendered to Egypt by Washington early in November 1956, when without Eisenhower and Dulles, neither Russian threats nor warnings from the Commonwealth, nor the Labour Party's indignation, would have sufficed to stop General Keightley's and Admiral Barjot's paratroops. Cairo radio was never more violently anti-American than in early September 1957.

During the first two years of the régime, when it was unpopular with the politically-minded masses, that is from Kafr-el-Dawar (August 1952) to the trip to Bandung (April 1955), public opinion was sure that there were close connexions between the military dictatorship and the Americans. This was not altogether wrong, and the connexion dated from the very first minutes of the life of the new régime. The deputy naval attaché of the United States, Mr David Evans, was probably the first foreigner to learn that the Officers had seized power, and sound observers take it for granted that American secret services had been taken into the confidence of one of their Egyptian colleagues involved in the plot two or three days before the event. Friendly relations were at once established between the young Officers and such American diplomats as Mr Lakeland. They often met and exchanged ideas about the future. Mr Jefferson Caffery, slightly bending his tall frame and narrowing his grey eyes, gave a dignified blessing to these beginnings of reform, and deigned to chat for whole hours with the Bikbashi, Gamal Nasser, 'a very capable boy, very gifted . . .' It was the time when the Cairo students were calling Nasser 'Colonel Jimmy'. The time, also, when during a great anti-communist trial, a lawyer said to the military judges, 'These men are being brought before you in order to please the Americans.'

The American approval came from the highest quarters. On the 3rd of September 1952, six weeks after the seizure of power, the Secretary of State, Dean Acheson, solemnly promised the new Egypt 'the active friendship of the United States'. All kinds of agreements were then signed: economic, within the framework of Point IV, and cultural under the Fulbright programme, and then there were promises of technical help. American experts of every kind, specialists in developing desert regions, in the war against flies, in the feeding of cattle or the organization of personnel, began landing at Cairo, while Washington raised Egypt's development credits from six to forty million dollars. All this to end with the notorious article in *El Misr* in which Abul Fath bawled at the frightened pilgrim, John Foster Dulles, 'You counted on buying us with your Point IV programme: but it is you who need a moral Point IV.' Mr Dulles's trip was none the less to result in a diplomatic success for Egypt. As he left Cairo the Secretary of State declared to the Press and the chancelleries that the West must realize that 'a Middle-East command is not an immediate possibility', which amounted to an honest acknowledgement of the lesson to be learnt from the preceding week's fruitless conversations between Britain and Egypt. On returning to Washington Mr Dulles affirmed, with his mournful air, that 'Egypt is now on the threshold of a great future'.

American policy towards Egypt may be summed up under two heads: the effort to integrate Egypt in a Middle-East pact in exchange for diplomatic support over the Canal issue and for the sale of arms to the Egyptian forces; and secondly, an attempt to control Egyptian economy by means of a loan for financing the High Dam at Aswan. We know that the help of American diplomacy did make a practical contribution to settling the Suez affair (no one could believe that it was purely by chance that journalists learnt of the imminent signing of the draft agreement, on the 27th of July 1954, at a cocktail party at Mr Caffery's residence. He stood jubilantly at the entrance to the garden . . . everyone put down their drinks and sandwiches to hasten to the Cabinet offices, near by, where the photographers were already taking pictures).

As for the arms urgently requested by the Egyptians—in July 1952, confronted by six modern Israeli divisions, Cairo could only muster three old-fashioned ones—thanks to its clumsiness or its particularly short-sighted legislation, the American administration brought about the disaster of September 1955: the purchase of Soviet arms by Colonel Nasser. This was not because the Officers had not done their best to get what they wanted from Washington. Already in the autumn of 1952 Major Sabri had been sent to the United States to negotiate for the purchase of planes. He came back dazzled but empty-handed. It was already clear that the Pentagon would deliver nothing unless Egypt joined a strategical network controlled by America.

In December of the same year an agreement in principle was reached. Egypt would be given equipment on condition that 'she would undertake no act of aggression' and that 'such armament would be used only for interior defence'. In other words only light arms were being offered, whose purpose would be to defend the régime against Communism. This was not at all what the Junta wanted, concerned as they were to build up an army, and pressed as they were by the whole officer corps to give them modern weapons at last.

In the spring of 1953 there was a fresh Egyptian attempt made, a further mission to the United States. This time Washington answered that it could not deliver arms which might be used against its British allies in the Canal Zone, and that consequently all deliveries would be suspended until the Suez problem was solved. But on the 2nd of August 1954, a few days after the signing of the Anglo-Egyptian

214

draft agreement, the talks were resumed. Three weeks later Colonel Nasser, sick at heart, once more had to face the fact that he would obtain nothing from Washington unless he bound himself to the Pentagon staff, and without accepting the setting-up of an American military mission in Cairo. A final attempt was made in the month of October. It was then that the Prime Minister's closest collaborator said to us, 'We have had to renounce the hoped-for American military aid, the conditions imposed being incompatible with respect for our national sovereignty.' For his part, Salah Salim told a group of Syrian reporters, 'We have refused a million dollars' worth of American military aid because it was offered in exchange for our adhesion to a military pact.'

A note published by the United States Embassy in Cairo shortly after the Egyptian purchase of Soviet arms read, in part, as follows: 'Although Egypt did not wish to conclude military-aid agreements such as those which were signed by nations all over the free world, including the Middle East, the United States . . . up till June 1955 answered Egypt's requests in respect of the purchase of small and medium arms.' But by having tried to catch Egypt in the net of an arms deal, Washington had lost the game for the time being. The Pentagon zealots, the most short-sighted of the Senators, and the Israeli Lobby, had won the struggle, and much the same happened over the issue of the High Dam. But that is another story . . .

BETWEEN EGYPT AND FRANCE—THE MAGHRIB

So long as the Maghrib question remains an open wound and relations between France and Algeria remain abnormal, there can be no healthy understanding between France and Egypt. Indignant over Cairo's interference in the Algerian question, French public opinion in general approved of the expedition of November 1956. We shall return to this, but note in passing that acts of this kind cannot end a situation which depends not on the deeds of one man, but on the relations between two societies.

It is overlooking an essential factor in the Moslem world, its sense of unity, if we show surprise that Eastern peoples, themselves only semi-independent or still colonized—with living and intellectual standards and public institutions fifty years or more behind what is to be found in North Africa—think they have the right to intervene in Tunis or Algiers. What unites the Arabs of Islam is a very keen and deep awareness of an oppression shared by them all—even when it has come to an end—a uniform sensitiveness to every kind of domination and, in the oldest and most vital sense of the word, a 'sympathy'. It is this which is constantly and strongly reviving the cohesion of the Umma, the great community of believers which the Koran enjoins to remain united 'like the stones of the same wall'. The primordial cement of this spontaneous interdependence is, of course, the common faith, whether one prays by bowing down towards the East as in the Maghrib, or towards the North as in Yemen (Maghrib means 'setting sun' and Yemen 'right hand'). But there is also a sharing of the same humiliation and situation, and in Arab or 'arabized' countries there is the powerful link of language. Arabic is not only the language of a race, a nation or a people; it is a tongue springing fully armed from an 'uncreated' or inspired masterpiece, and spoken among people who, all taken by surprise in an age-long sleep, were 'chained and exploited' together.

Thus, all those who speak Arabic and have had to put up with some form of European domination, feel that they are sharing in the same drama, and are aware that they have the same means of communication, like prisoners who tap messages in code from one cell to another. Language is an all-powerful weapon in the East. It is not by chance that the founders of the State of Israel made the people's first task the revival and common use of the sacred tongue. The bond is all the stronger for being known only to the initiated. So it is with Arabic, whose mysterious script makes it difficult for the foreigner, or at least for those who are neither Orientalists nor in search of some religious revelation. Like the wall of some enormous ghetto, the language of the Prophet encloses, isolates and protects the peoples of the Crescent in their wounded pride.

Egypt is now the hearth and natural leader of this unsatisfied and protesting community, thanks to its political influence, Cairo's historical role, the efficiency of its press and radio, and its size. Here neither the nature of the government nor uniform have much to do with the matter. Royalist Egypt welcomed or kidnapped Abdel Karim, 'invented' the bombing of Fez, badgered the United Nations with unfounded complaints, and formed a commando-group of Maghribi students. The end of the Colonels' Republic will not spell the end of intervention, even though the Officers have gone a little farther than hitherto by inventing 'The voice of the Arabs', which was due to General Neguib's personal intervention, and makes the fullest possible use of the negative hysteria with which we are all familiar. For those in a position to grasp the importance of speech in Islam, of the magic, sacred nature of words uttered in the language in which the Archangel addressed the Prophet, and consequently the effect that can be obtained by using it on crowds who are extremely sensitive, this verbal armoury appears as a very weighty item in a heavy dossier.

Other items are well known: financing the purchase of arms, training commandos, strategical advice, the somewhat meagre hospitality offered to political refugees from the Maghrib, and above all such direct provision of equipment as there was in the case of the ship *Athos II*.[1] This aid can be compared with what the French Popular Front government sent to Republican Spain during the period of 'non-intervention', or by Belgrade to the Greek communists up to March 1948. But it should also be noted that the Egyptian government, Press and public are not well informed about North African problems, which merely come sharply to the surface from time to time without the stimulus of some immediate event, like a volcanic eruption. One recalls Gambetta's remark about Alsace-Lorraine, 'Let it never be absent from our minds, never present on our tongues.' As regards North Africa, Cairo's injunction would be more like 'Let it never be absent from our tongues, never present in our minds.'

One could imagine Cairo with some government capable of setting a brake on this movement or playing it down—for instance a government under some dictator emerging from the owning classes and with some measure of French culture, such as Sidqi Pasha, or emerging from a truly revolutionary Left and thus aware of the progressive aspects of French action in the Maghrib in spite of its political blindness and police brutality. But this cannot be expected of a man like Nasser who represents the Nationalist and Islamic *petite bourgeoisie*. Such a man is interested in North Africa—as in Iraq, Palestine or the Yemen—first of all because he is a member of the frustrated Umma; also because from Tunis to Agadir he can see the clients and allies of tomorrow, of whom he would like to be the master or at the least the political sponsor; finally he is afraid lest the West should turn them into another Iraq, a springboard for strategic power. For this African Moslem—and that is what in future all rulers of Cairo

---

[1] A freighter chartered by an Egypto-Sudanese, which was intercepted off Oran on the 15th of September 1956, carrying arms to Algeria.

are likely to be, now that the era of pashas of Turkish origin, laymen and clients of the Ritz, is finished—no frontier can really prevail against the common pool of complexes, interests and the hope of a common future, which appear to lie ahead for an Islam scarcely liberated from imperialism.

However coldly realistic he appears to be at times, Nasser is first of all a non-white who was for too long humiliated by the European occupation and by a mismanaged monarchy of foreign origin, not to identify himself automatically with the Algerian *fellaghas*. If you mention North Africa to him he has a tendency to answer 'we', and to pass at once to imperialism, exploitation and all the old humiliations. Is this just a trick? Perhaps, to some extent. But it is also a firm and unshakable conviction. Is this pan-Islamism the same as 'Arab Nazism'? We must face the fact that apart from the leaders educated in Oxford or Paris, and whose hour seems to be over, all the members of the Arab-Moslem world are in the same position, and that Pan-Islamism cannot be separated from Islam any more than pan-communism can be divorced from communism. The West itself once tried desperately to form a Christian state, and even undertook the Crusades to crush Islam. Seven centuries behind-hand, as Nasser says in his little pamphlet *The Philosophy of the Revolution*, the Arab-Moslem world is only now reaching the eighteenth century, which in the West saw the emergence of the nationalist principle by which the notion of the fatherland was substituted for that of a religious community. Inter-Arab solidarity is bound to decline in the same proportion as Arab frustration. Morocco was more distant from Cairo and Baghdad when it was an independent state than when it was a dependency—until the day when sympathy was awakened for Egypt's misfortunes.

Let us look forward a little. Cairo runs a serious risk of losing most of its influence once it ceases being a place of appeal for unsatisfied protests, a kind of unreachable promised land for Arab independence. The Egyptian capital glitters in the eyes of the Maghrib people merely on account of the Algerian tragedy. As soon as a settlement is reached between the north and south of the Mediterranean, Cairo will be no more than the Arab East's most imposing and fascinating cultural and religious centre. It is not out of the question to suppose that in the eyes of North Africans it might become what Paris is to French Canadians. The Catholic and Francophile French Canadians cherish Notre-Dame and the Sorbonne, if

218

not the French way of life. But neither religion, language nor the Great Lakes can turn them away from the world of modern America. All considered, New York is closer to them than Paris. Neither language nor religion nor the Mediterranean should prevent the people of the Maghrib from being quite prepared to look north-wards, and, freely moving into the modern world, regarding Paris as closer than Cairo.

It might be asked whether the November 1956 expedition destroyed the many links between France and Egypt of which, two months before the furious onslaught of the summer of 1956, M. Pineau painted such a vivid picture in the French Chamber. There were £400,000,000 of French investments in Egypt; 150,000 pupils in French schools, of whom 40,000 were Moslems for whom French was the first foreign language. There were fifteen large companies at work, to the benefit of both countries, to give Egypt an industrial equipment comparable with that of Morocco. Two-thirds of our cotton industry drew its raw material from the Nile Valley. Add to this the building of sugar-refineries, the sale of locomotives, the success of small French cars, and it can be said that no nation in the world had a better economic footing in Egypt than France. It was better balanced than that of Germany or Britain, who exported too much, and better adapted to the local buyer than the products of the United States or of Eastern Europe.

If the cultural importance of the French language, which was that of the upper caste, of 'high society' as well as of national minorities, tends to lose ground with the decline in luxurious living and in the very existence of these groups, at the same time French is finding its way into less-favoured Moslem circles, such as the minor civil servants and middle-class people to whom it was hitherto unknown. From now on French will be spoken less in Egypt. Soon it will no longer be the accepted language of the modern part of Cairo, the night-clubs, tea-parties of elegant ladies. But as it declines among the cosmopolitan class, it will have some future among the rising classes.

In Egypt, France is very much represented by the Paris of the couturiers, cabarets, boulevard theatres. All this is threatened, even if a less puritanical and peasant government came to power. But France is also Michelet, Jaurès and Sartre. France is a profound revolutionary or at least progressive influence, making for freedom

219

of thought, analysis, political change and dispassionate inquiry. No left-wing circles are to be found in Egypt without such works as *A l'échelle humaine* or the works of Aragon, side by side with Lenin and Laski. After being the language of the rich, is French to become that of the poor? No, not in the same proportion, but it will remain a language for intellectuals, who are themselves more and more from poorer classes and turning left-wards. If this is so, then how are we to sum up France's political action on Egypt, in the past, present or future? In the period before the table-thumping at Alexandria, French diplomacy on the Nile showed boldness, realism and patience, and made the best use of its cultural and economic levers. Whether the French ambassador was fearless and cold, or the essence of charm and warmth, the team on the spot knew how to control the resentment stirred up by Paris in the local Press and parliament, how to obtain the handsomest contracts (an electric power-station in Cairo at the height of the Moroccan crisis, or a scheme for the electrification of the whole country in the midst of the Tunisian disputes, the building of a fertilizer-factory when the Algerian war was at its height); or to keep the movement of the stock market in France's favour, and to keep highly qualified French teachers in Egypt. As to the delivery of arms (heavy arms which were not to be handed over to the Algerians), in fairness to the French it must be pointed out that the suspension of one of these contracts—made almost inevitable by Cairo's attitude in the summer of 1955—was one of the immediate causes of the great crisis:—Nasser's purchase of Soviet arms in September of that year.

In addition to this, French diplomacy did not hesitate to co-operate openly with Cairo in resisting the unfortunate Baghdad Pact. The French, to be sure, made many reservations when the Egyptians began to set up a barrage of red propaganda. But the *rapprochement* which began to be achieved between February and September 1955 seemed full of promise. At the same time, those who were mainly responsible for the High Dam project at Aswan—such as the Deputy Prime Minister Gamal Salim, and Mohamed Ahmed Selim—tried to base the scheme financially and technically on the 'European consortium' in which France and Germany played a major part. In exchange for this service, it was then possible to expect Cairo to leave France more or less a free hand in Algeria. Nasser the dam-builder might have submerged or overcome his feeling of Arab frustration. After the 27th of July 1956, Paris gave up this hope, as though looking back to the mediaeval Crusades. The new Saladin had to be destroyed . . . But let there be no mistake—in the East nationalism is never embodied in one man, and the fall of Musaddiq no more affected the nationalization of oil in Iran than the exile of Zaghlul delayed the creating of an Egyptian nation. People like to imagine that without the Egyptian 'big brother' the Algerian rebels would lay down their arms. This is a striking instance of the silly attitude which for years consisted in 'building up' Nasser, making him into a giant, a terror, inflating him in such terms that he could not help thinking it was his due, so that he used the same terms in talking with those Arabs, the Egyptians, who were least taken in by his charm. All this while our diplomatic agents in Egypt were devoting themselves intelligently to the only things that were at all profitable: trying to link the two countries more closely by means of services rendered to one another, and trying to encourage Nasser the builder rather than Nasser the fanatic.

A TRIP TO BANDUNG

Ask a hundred Egyptians what Egypt should do in the event of world war, and what camp she should side with. Unless your inquiry is limited to some society club made up of ex-presidents of the Sa'dist party, or to the lounge of the Automobile Club, you will not find five who will want to side with the West. Nor are you likely to find six who will want to side with the East. The Egyptians are neutralists. They were neutral in 1914, 1939, then at the time of the Korean war in 1950, when they thought the abstention of their delegates was not enough: they ought to have voted against intervention.

In Europe and perhaps in India, neutrality is a kind of doctrine, or at least a political attitude, the outcome of a calmly-thought-over choice. In Egypt neutralism is a reflex. Egyptians don't regard themselves as involved in the great debate between East and West, having no reasons—with a few thousand exceptions among them—for feeling that the capitalist system is in any way superior to the communist one. The people of the Nile cannot help sneering at the expression 'the free world'. The Egyptian citizen, the Misri Efendi, feels neutral as a matter of course, just as he knows that it is hot in July, or that life is hard, or that it is better to own an estate than be a labourer, or that Faruk was not a good king.

If he ever had any doubts about this, if his neutralist faith should momentarily be shaken by some American blandishment, it would be enough for him to open one of the newspapers in order to return to his middle course. The Egyptian Press is like an anthology of neutralism. Even those sections of it which are thought to be committed to American interests never cease their praise of non-commitment. Neutralism is preached everywhere, sentimentally by Ihsan Abdel Qudus in *Rose el Yusuf*, hypocritically by Fikri Abaza in *Musawwar*, blatantly by Husain Fahmi in *Sha'b*, dogmatically by Ahmed Baha ud-Din in *Sabah el Khair*.

Perhaps this attitude took longest to make its mark on the Prime Minister. And yet for a long time his interviews with Nehru had been making a strong impression on the Colonel. But in the minds of the Officers, and especially of Nasser, the neutrality at issue in the early years of the régime was essentially a refusal to be committed to the West so long as the British had not evacuated their base, and even a refusal to make this eventual commitment the object of bargaining as it had been in the first Anglo-American plan— evacuation bartered against adhesion to the Western military bloc. After the treaty with the British, Colonel Nasser no longer excluded the possibility of a later adhesion to Western organizations, by way of an inter-Arab military pact. Cairo then thought of leading westwards an Arab world under its own aegis, but this was to be done between free powers with neither held hostage to the other. It was to avoid this arrangement, which would have made Iraq merely one of a crowd, that Baghdad played the Turkish game and agreed to upset American plans for a Turko-Arab pact, which the Egyptian Prime Minister had vaguely allowed the West to hope for in a preface to a book on Turkey in which he spoke of the traditional friendship and common interests between the two countries. When he heard the news from Baghdad, Nasser thought he had been tricked by the British and Americans and reacted with a burst of adolescent spitefulness. Then, recovering his calm, he took the opportunity of Tito's passage through the Suez Canal, when returning from a trip to India, to talk for several hours near Suez with the head of the Yugoslav state. Could the Colonel still be won back by the West? Six weeks later came the outburst at Gaza, with forty-three Egyptian soldiers killed by Israeli commandos on Arab territory, and with no chance of striking back. No Egyptian will ever believe that Israel can take the slightest initiative without reference to London, or, according to the circumstances, to Washington.

The West seemed to have its finger everywhere ... It was then that Colonel Nasser, receiving the ambassador of a Western Power which had never shown him anything but active sympathy, said to him, 'As you know, until last month I was a sincere friend of the West: from now on, don't count on me.' A month later the Colonel left for Bandung. That does not mean that, in any case, he would not have attended the Afro-Asian Conference in Indonesia, where Egypt obviously had a part to play and interests to defend. Nor does it mean that with Nehru, Chou En Lai, Soekarno and U-Nu, Nasser played a role that was particularly harmful to the West. Several days after his return Mr Byroade told us with every appearance of sincerity, 'We are very satisfied with Nasser's conduct at Bandung. He did not allow Chou En Lai to cast a spell over him. He agreed to sign a resolution favouring "a peaceful solution to the Palestine problem" and he contributed towards defining an independent stand to both communism and colonialism.' But, seen from Egypt, the trip to Bandung none the less took on a style and appearance which the American diplomat's nice words could in no way change: the appearance of a liberation and the style of a revenge, which Nasser at that time took with a serenity which he has since lost.

For Egypt, Bandung was the Suez of 1955. But it was at no one's expense, and above all not against Egypt's interests. It was none the less a choice which shrewd observers regarded as vital, first because of the contacts made by the Egyptian dictator in Indonesia: Chou En Lai is not a man to be met without risk or without profit. These contacts were the basis for important trips to China by several Egyptian ministers, who did not waste their time there. The choice was also conditioned by the attitude of left-wing parties all over the East, who suddenly decided to support the Egyptian régime, only a few of them raising the question of concentration-camps and civil liberties; there were also many communists who undertook a campaign in favour of the régime even while they were still imprisoned in such camps. It was also at this time that regular contacts were made between Nasser and the Soviet Ambassador, Daniel Solod, resulting six months later in the signing of a contract for the purchase of Czech arms. In signing the evacuation agreement with London in July 1954, Nasser had steered sharply to the Right, and was followed by his officials. On his return from Bandung, with his portrait alongside those of Chou En Lai and Nehru on banners of welcome and on the front pages of the newspapers, Nasser had turned sharply to the

Left and had a great part of the masses behind him. Bandung was a decisive turning-point.

Since then, Egyptian neutralism has taken the most varied forms, one of which consists of holding out a hand to the East or West on alternate days, using methods which the Western Press describe as blackmail. Until July 1956 when he was abruptly 'dropped' by Washington and London, with nothing better in hand than Moscow's hearty encouragement, the President had been cynically playing a kind of pendulum-game. 'We have invented positive neutralism,' exclaimed Mohamed Hasanain Haykal, who often acts as Nasser's spokesman, the day after Moscow offered to build an atomic power-station on the Nile, in answer to the West's first offer to finance the Aswan Dam. It looked so easy, how could they keep sober? The development of the Suez affair, which brought the 'triangle game' into the diplomatic and military spheres, has turned out to be much too dangerous for Egypt.

Colonel Nasser's diplomatic principles are simple, and, in the absence of the most elementary ideological basis, remind one of Physics as taught to small children. Means: a lever. Objective: to smash one by one the shackles on Egyptian independence. He made excellent use of the American lever against the British. The operation was a success. Against the Americans he used the Soviet lever, and the experiment was at first crowned with unhoped-for success— arms, industrial equipment, diplomatic support. But he had always been careful to bring pressure to bear on only one point at a time. In throwing himself at the Canal problem he brought together forces which had been almost constantly divided, and which decided in the end that they would stop at nothing.

The weakness of Nasser's neutralist policy, contrasted with that of Nehru and Tito, is that it rests neither on a doctrine nor on military strength, nor on any desire to bring about a peaceful settlement of international disagreements. It consists merely of speculating on the antagonisms between Great Powers. This attitude was profitable for a time, but it was negative and resulted in various resentments piling up. Indeed, Nasser's neutralism has served him best in domestic politics, by rallying the Left and reconciling public opinion.

THE ALTERNATIVE: ENTER WORLD-COMMUNISM

A tall fellow with his hair on end, looking like one of Tolstoy's peasants, came and sat down in front of the press dais. He was almost

11a. Cairo: street scene

11b. Cairo: café scene

12. A street in old Cairo

alone in the huge square where Nasser and Soekarno, his guest, were about to give long speeches on the occasion of the anniversary of the *coup d'état*. 'Who's that big chap?'—'A special correspondent from *Pravda*, called Shepilov.'—'He certainly doesn't mean to miss anything.'

Miss anything, indeed ... Since that day in July 1955 Dmitri Trofimovitch Shepilov always arrives on time, but he has now quit the ranks of the spectators. Eleven months later he was the U.S.S.R. Minister for Foreign Affairs and one of the stars in the 'evacuation festival'. In the unchanged Republic Square, but now installed in a place of honour, he could watch a parade of the Stalin tanks whose sale, as a 'journalist', he had negotiated with the Egyptian Colonels. On the 18th of June 1956 the Soviet Union, through his eyes, could almost see at the same time the last British soldier leaving the Canal base and the first Russian tank driving down the streets of Cairo. A good year, beyond doubt ...

The U.S.S.R.'s appearance on the Arab scene was not due to the initiative, good or bad humour or resentment of Colonel Nasser. Should it be traced back to the Nahas-Maisky correspondence of 1943, or the commercial agreements of 1952, or the flirtation with U.N.O. from 1951 to 1953? More recently, it was through Syria that Moscow began to take an active part in the Middle East. Already in 1954 an arms contract had been signed between Damascus and Moscow, and several dozen German Mark 4's modified by the Skoda works had been delivered to the Syrian staff. Washington was not unmoved by this and began to take every precaution to avoid the 'contamination' of Egypt. On the 18th of August, however, a Russo-Egyptian barter agreement opened the way for an exchange of cotton for wheat, machinery and chemical products. The door, already thrust ajar by agreements of the same kind with East Germany and China, was going to keep on opening still further. The State Department might well try to stop Egypt from convening a new Istanbul conference for the purpose of defining the right of passage and international status of the Suez Canal. This conference would have had the disadvantage, for Washington, of hastening the appearance of the U.S.S.R. on Arab soil. But at the same time Washington could not fail to realize that for Moscow the Baghdad Pact would be an excuse for breaking into Middle East affairs under the pretext of protecting those nations who needed some court of appeal from the edicts of the West.

Everything did not start from, but everything took on a definite shape with the Baghdad Pact. What until then had been mere soundings on the part of Moscow, and short-term risks on the part of Nasser, became a matter of common interest and a common struggle. The Pact dates from January. Not later than February, the Soviet ambassador Daniel Solod, a former teacher of French who had entered the diplomatic service via the Lebanon and was thus a past master of Oriental bargaining, was seen to visit Nasser. They spoke of industrial co-operation and the sending of technicians. Then came the Gaza attack. There were fresh visits, and this time there were rumours of the delivery of armaments. Western diplomats shrugged their shoulders: 'Nasser, Russian arms? He is too anti-communist, he wouldn't dare . . .'

On the very eve of the opening of the Bandung Conference, on the 16th of April 1955, the Soviet government published a Note which marked its formal entry into Middle East politics. It was a document of capital importance, not only because of its violent criticism of the Baghdad Pact and of 'the pressure exerted by the United States and Great Britain to draw the Arab States into a military organization which would be an extension of the Atlantic pact', but because it clearly arrogated the right to intervene in that part of the world. It was said, for example, that Moscow 'would bring the matter before the United Nations if London and Washington persisted in this attitude', and that 'the Soviet government would not remain indifferent [i.e. to this situation] since the setting up of military bases in this region directly affects the security of the U.S.S.R.' The Egyptian Press gave a great welcome to this document, which announced that from now on, in the Middle East, the Three had become Four—and that the fourth intended pushing with all its strength in the direction in which Egyptian diplomacy was already pointing. London and Washington, thinking in terms of support only in exchange for submission, had preferred Baghdad to Cairo. As a result, Cairo had found an ally to be reckoned with.

'At a diplomatic reception which took place in May 1955,' Nasser wrote recently in an Egyptian weekly, 'I was approached by Mr Daniel Solod, the Russian ambassador, who took me into a corner and asked me point-blank whether my government would be interested in the purchase of arms from the Soviet Union. In the event of an affirmative answer he would inform Moscow . . . I answered in the same tone, that the suggestion appeared to me to be of the greatest interest, and that I was ready to begin talks with that end in view.' When Mr Shepilov, *Pravda's* 'special envoy', landed in Cairo two months later, the foundations of the transaction were already laid. But Nasser was still hesitating. He wanted to be sure, by discreetly sounding the English and Americans, whether the West would give him the means of catching up with Israel, whose military superiority had been dramatically displayed in the Battle of Gaza. He had turned towards France. In August 1955, for serious enough political reasons, when a contract which had been signed six months before with a French armaments firm was broken, the Egyptian staff lost patience and Nasser and General Amir were no longer in doubt as to what must be done. On the 10th of September the head of the Prime Minister's office told us 'If, in the course of the coming week, the Americans do not agree to give what we are asking yet again, we shall have to buy our armaments from the communist countries.'

On the 28th of September, towards dusk, when he opened the 'Army Fair' in Cairo's exhibition park, Colonel Nasser spoke harshly. He, the severe mentor whom the people usually listened to in polite silence, for perhaps the first time drew rounds of applause from them. 'The West refuses us the means of defending our existence: we have just signed a contract for the purchase of arms from Czechoslovakia.' Ninety-nine per cent of the Colonel's audience had no idea where Prague was, or the political ideas of Antonin Zapotoky. But whether it be that the left-wing movements had already been at work on the audience, or whether the rumour about 'red' arms had already swayed their minds, Nasser now carried the crowd with him. He had touched a deep chord in the Egyptian masses, in their dislike of the West, as well as the hope that there might be some alternative, some freedom of choice, apart from the West's perpetual habit of attaching 'strings' and conditions to everything. We must not forget that the Colonel did not invent this solution, but was only carrying out what the Wafd had already thought of doing in 1951, and that two days before the burning of Cairo, on the 24th of January 1952, the newspaper *Ahram* announced that Egypt was going to try to buy arms from Moscow.

The West's reaction to this gesture—a far more serious one than those that followed, since it upset the balance of power in the Middle East—was pitiable. Though it was obvious that the agreements between Moscow and Cairo would mean that communist instructors would come to work in Egypt and that their presence was hardly compatible with the evacuation treaty, or with the activities of the British technicians at the Canal base, London merely showed the bitterness of a deceived husband. Washington went one better, hastily sending Mr George Allen, deputy secretary of state for Middle East questions, to Cairo. Nasser has since told—between two roars of laughter during his famous Alexandria speech—how he agreed to see Mr Allen only on condition that he did not hand over the indignant Note which had been composed by the State Department, and how Allen left with the abashed look of someone who had put his foot in it. The Colonel was a shrewd judge of the weaknesses in those he was dealing with: Moscow and all its freshly opened perspectives; the Egyptian people, and the confusion of the West.

This buying of arms was certainly the most sensational episode in the Soviet penetration into Egypt. But it had been preceded and was followed by considerable economic inroads. From the barter agreement of August 1954 to the agreement between China and Egypt in April 1956, the tightening of economic links did not cease. First there was a series of industrial exhibitions from East Germany, Rumania, Hungary and China, with their inevitable outcome. The metal bridges required for the canal-system come from Hungary. The cranes in the port of Alexandria come from Bulgaria. Poland supplies the most rolling-stock. The U.S.S.R. is providing Egypt with its first nuclear-physics laboratory. Between July 1955 and July 1956 China suddenly became the largest buyer of Egyptian cotton. We might add to this the Russian offer to finance the High Dam, which Mr Solod was said to have made in February 1956, by means of a loan at two per cent to be repaid over a period of thirty years, and partly payable in cotton.

By the middle of 1956 trade with the communist countries still represented only 35 per cent of Egyptian commerce, while there was some disappointment over some of the products from the East, especially Russian petrol. But the prices asked by exporters in the Russian bloc are very favourable. In tendering, it is enough for a German or French firm to ask 100, for the Hungarian steel-foundries or Czech spinners to quote 70. The golden rule is to ask about a third less than the Western price, and these methods have every chance of success.

The cultural invasion is almost as striking. Since the close of 1955 the windows of Cairo bookshops have been crammed with cardboard-bound books selling at a quarter of the price of those imported from the West: Gorki, Lenin, Ehrenburg translated into English or sometimes into French, and even such French novelists as Zola and Hugo. There are also beautiful Chinese editions at ridiculously low prices. There is a Soviet Information Bureau which shows films and exhibitions of paintings. During the past year Cairo has seen the first Russian films to be shown in Egypt: *The Fall of Berlin* had a success far out of proportion to its real merit. The embassy has an inexhaustible stock of the 'classics' of Russian film, which are very popular in the private film-clubs. Though an occasional troupe from Paris or the Milan Opera can still be seen in Cairo theatres, they cut a very modest figure beside the picturesque folklore performers from the East. What with Rumanian, Czech, Polish and Russian ballets, the Egyptian public might well wonder how the communist countries find any time for work, between two bouts of dancing . . . There is immense applause at the end of these performances, which are delightful yet not very ambitious. The audience itself is a sight worth seeing, swept away into unrestrained sympathy. The Egyptians now feel a kind of glow radiating from the north-east.

But the Egyptian masses have even more interest and sympathy for China than for Russia. Communist thinkers, particularly Stalin, often compared the two countries, especially the two peasantries. Before his talks with Shepilov, Nasser had met Chou En Lai no less than three times in Asia, and since then there have been constant exchanges of economic and cultural missions. In the summer of 1955 the Egyptian public were very interested in statements made on his return from a long journey in China by Sheikh Hasan el Baquri, Minister for the Awqaf (i.e. religious properties) and the government's spokesman on matters of public worship. The Sheikh came out in enthusiastic support for the Chinese revolution and gave special praise to Chinese Islam, stressing its modernism: 'Because they have understood the Koran, they have abandoned polygamy,' said Baquri, with an emphasis that caused a stir in some circles. Also, when a young left-wing publisher, Lutfullah Sulaiman, began to bring out a series of popular works, he began with a pamphlet on the Chinese revolution and not a study of Russia. The edition was sold out in a week.

Armaments, books, machines, dancers—the communist world has reached the Nile. It has made tremendous progress in the past two years and has had far greater success than was expected in Moscow. This is in marked contrast to the prudence shown under Stalin, which was shown in Iran when, Musaddiq having prepared the way to power for the Tudeh communist-party, the slightest encouragement from Moscow could have set up a red republic in Teheran, or at least for the northern part of the country. Moscow did not take its chance, but now, three years later, it is sending arms to the banks of the Nile, an operation both remoter and more adventurous than support for the Tudeh would have been.

Was there a 'Shepilov line' cutting across the 'Molotov line'? It is obvious from remarks made here and there in official Russian quarters that one school of Soviet diplomats thought the present break-through too rash and the arms-contract too great a danger to the international situation. They were disturbed at seeing Russian foreign policy too strongly committed to the Arab cause and regretted the days when Moscow, more cautious, was content to cash in on the West's mistakes by appearing to the East as the ideal, almost abstract alternative to British 'imperialism'. The present role entails more risks and responsibilities.

The Soviet penetration has not given Colonel Nasser unmitigated pleasure. What, in his own mind, was at first intended to be no more than a scarecrow for the British, then a means of blackmailing the Americans, then an alternative to Western pressure and a policy to be used only in emergencies, has tended to become the only course left, a refuge which the former friend of Jefferson Caffery, the strategist of the 'defence of the eastern Mediterranean', obviously feared being trapped in. The Suez affair overshadowed the sensational change of policy that Nasser had just made: this paragon of 'neutralism's' acceptance of help from the International Bank for building the High Dam—a loan which could only result in bringing the Egyptian economy under American control. The fact that out of the Soviet offer, however vague and half-hearted, and the dictation of Anglo-Saxon financiers, the Colonel should have chosen the second (which he was to pay for dearly), proves beyond all doubt how little an alliance with the Eastern powers appealed to him. The Suez affair, which was to strengthen the Cairo-Moscow axis, will be dealt with later. What is important to bear in mind at this point, is the psychological effect made on the masses in the East, by our idea of the relationship between the Western nations and recently emancipated small powers. It is this outlook which makes the Soviet Union increasingly attractive in the eyes of Eastern races as being their only and lasting recourse.

THE BLUE LINE OF SINAI

Although it is not Arabic, if we look at this populace of African peasants, cut off from the Semitic peoples by uncompromising deserts, and the shape of this oasis which opens at its two ends into the Grecian Mediterranean and into the black Sudan, was Egypt inevitably destined to become the standard-bearer and soldier of the Arab world? She was certainly conquered by the warriors of the Hijaz thirteen hundred years ago, and brought into Islam at the same time. But since the fourteenth century she has been ruled for the most part by Circassians, Turks, Albanians and a few great Armenian administrators. The miracle in all this is that, carried along by the sacred Book, the Arabic language should have survived in Egypt, that it should have reshaped the Egyptian mind and created profound affinities with other Arabic-speaking peoples.

But the 'arabness' of Egypt was still not completely evident at the beginning of the present century. Even Mustafa Kamil, the creator of the nationalist movement, looked on Arabism as a delusion, and preferred to turn towards Istambul or Paris. The best minds in modern Egypt—Taha Husain, Isma'il Sidqi, Mahmud Azmi—thought of Egypt's future as exclusively Mediterranean. Up to the end of the second World War the matter was still being debated. It is tempting to suggest that it was the Oriental scholars, English information-officers and Syrian politicians established in Egypt, who pushed the country on to the magic carpet of Pan-Arabism which it is very unlikely to give up. But it would be wiser to acknowledge that at the time of the great Arab awakening which quickened at the end of the first World War and has continued after the second, Cairo happened to be the natural capital of this shifting world: Cairo, that immense urban melting-pot, with its mobs which may be used to serve any form of indignation, El Azhar and its turbans, and the great mass of 23 millions of the river-folk of the Nile.

No other country, not even a more Arab one such as Syria, would have had the authority necessary for placing itself at the head of militant Arabism. This was clear enough in the years of trial, 1948 and 1956, when only Egypt fought, however badly, for the integrity of the Arab world. Since 1945, among the scattered fragments of an Arab League which looked like fading out as soon as it was created, the various Cairo governments ran after the same chimera. They failed to see that while it was certainly spontaneous, permanent and

231

alive, Pan-Arabism is incapable of any movement except opposition; that one can set it aflame and be consumed in its fire, but it cannot be tamed or used for purposes of peaceful diplomacy, while in a word the Arab neighbours to the east and north, and even to the west, might be exacting clients for Egypt, but not reliable allies. Egypt is carrying a burden rather than reaping a harvest.

On the other hand, of course, by trying to find support in Damascus and Amman, to control the Syrian stronghold or lay down the law in Mesopotamia, Faruk's and then Nasser's Egypt was merely following one of the golden rules of a long tradition, that of Tothmes III, Saladin and Mohamed Ali. The Pharaohs of the eighteenth dynasty had the same endless disputes with the kings of Mitanni as there are now between Egypt and Iraq. But should a young republic, hardly on its feet, undertake what was once the task of an empire at the height of its power? To sum up, well before autumn 1956, the grouping of the Yemenites, then the Maghribis, under its aegis appeared to foreign observers to be too costly a task for a reviving Egypt. It looked infinitely less profitable or urgent than twenty other ventures such as the Sudan, water-power, industry . . .

In other words, Egypt has embarked on an adventure. But because British diplomacy chose the years following the first World War to transform the Arab countries from colonies into allies, while at the same time Mr Balfour opened the gates of Palestine to Zionism; and because the Levantine politicians who made up Faruk's entourage did their best to 'arabize' Egyptian foreign policy, so as to establish more solidly their right to rule—and also, quite simply, that every country has to think of protecting its frontiers—Egypt found herself alone against Palestine.

The men who seized power in Cairo on the 23rd of July 1952 were certainly full of resentment towards Israel. But there was a kind of admiration mingled with this ill feeling. The defenders of Falluja had some respect for the technical and moral calibre of the Israeli officers and men who had paid homage to Nasser and his troops by letting food and despatches through when they were besieged. After the defeat, the Egyptian Free Officers tried to re-examine the Palestine question in the light of the facts, and with this in mind some of them made contacts with extreme left-wing groups which had supported the partition plan and had paid for their attitude through large-scale arrests. A number of Left sympathizers among the officers saw at the time that twin states, economically linked, would have been the wisest solution and would have given the Arab world something worth aspiring to, by introducing the virus of 'modern' life.

But the facts could not be changed. The partition plan of 1947 had had its day. A million refugees were huddled in reception camps. Even if the more realistic officers had wanted to settle the question by some sort of compromise, the Arab countries—of which Egypt is a prisoner rather than the master—would not have allowed it. Moreover, for the Egyptians the problem of the evacuation of the Canal Zone pushed that of Palestine into second place. And in any case, the first two years of the military government were years of relaxation in the relations between Egypt and Israel. The Americans then thought that Neguib and Nasser were men capable of keeping the Arabs at peace, and more or less discreetly, in 1953 and early in 1954, tried to extract promises to this effect, in exchange for diplomatic support over the Canal issue. At that time indirect but generally encouraging contacts were made between Nasser and Sharett through various intercessors, usually British, such as the Labour M.P.s Richard Crossman and Maurice Orbach. To the latter, Nasser spoke of his 'hopes' and 'his lively sympathy for Mr Sharett'.

But Israel was both irritated and worried by the evacuation agreement, as it removed the buffer of the British forces and left her face to face with Egypt. A state of nervous tension on both sides followed two years of relative oblivion of each other. On the 28th of September 1954, before daybreak, an Israeli cargo-boat, the *Bat-Galim*, appeared flying the Blue Peter in the roadstead of Suez. This was obviously a political and military test-case aimed at bringing into the open the illegality of Egypt's barring of the Canal not only to Israeli vessels but even to neutral shipping with goods for Haifa or Elath. Egypt's attitude had been twice condemned by the U.N.O. Security Council. The *Bat-Galim* was at once hailed by Egyptian launches whose officers swore that the Israeli crew then opened fire on a coastal battery and on fishing-boats. The next day, when Israel was lodging a fresh complaint with U.N.O., Major Amin Shanir, chief of the Prime Minister's staff, summoned foreign reporters to tell them about the 'unjustifiable armed aggression by this Israeli vessel' whose fire was alleged to have caused 'the death of two Egyptian sailors'. As a matter of fact we were able to obtain no more than the victims' names, but we could not investigate the matter further. It seems that two fishermen were drowned on that day, but by natural causes.

The Jerusalem government had hoped to demonstrate the urgency of the problem of free passage through the Canal, at a time when London was preparing to hand it over unreservedly to Colonel Nasser without any new international guarantee. If Western diplomacy ever lost an opportunity to prevent a great international crisis, two years in advance, by honestly facing a problem when it held the means of solving it, it was certainly that day.

The situation grew worse. On the 1st of October a 'Zionist conspiracy' was disclosed in Cairo, organized by the 'John Darling network', of which twelve of the fourteen members were arrested. The trial of the twelve accused went on serenely in the presence of foreign observers and of M. Descamps, the French consul, who insisted on attending each hearing at the side of Dr Marzuq, the main defendant, who was a Tunisian under French protection. But then it was learnt that one of the more important of the accused men, the Hungarian Max Beneth, had committed suicide in prison. Then, in spite of formal promises made by Nasser to Mr Baldwin, President of the International League of the Rights of Man, to the effect that there was no fear of a death-sentence, the military tribunal, which was presided over by General Digwi, on the 27th of January 1955 sentenced Dr Musa Marzuq and Samuel Azar to death by hanging. Were the unhappy Marzuq's smile and gesture of the hand as he looked at us, signs that there was still some hope? The embassies went into action, the Chief Rabbi redoubled his efforts up till the last moment, but four days later Marzuq and his comrade were legally assassinated in a Cairo gaol. The shame of the Egyptian authorities must have been such that no reporters were allowed to witness the death of these unfortunate men.

Why inflict such an odious penalty, when it was clear to all that the 'plot', foolishly financed by Tel Aviv, was little more than a college prank, capable of little more than burning a few books in the American library and broadcasting some news intended for Israel? It was a schoolboyish kind of espionage with no danger to the State. But it was said that the Colonel, who six weeks earlier had six Moslem Brothers hanged in order to put down a genuine and dangerous terrorist plot, had been under pressure and was constantly harassed by some of the men about him. 'Are we going to hang the faithful and spare Zionist spies?' In some parts of the Arab world where the execution of the Moslem Brothers was badly received, the hanging of these two Jews was awaited as a kind of reparation, and the Iraq which had signed the Baghdad Pact was sarcastically preparing to denounce Nasser's bogus Arabism and pro-Zionism. . . . Marzuq and his companion thus had to pay the price in all this cruel bargaining: but others were to pay also.

On the 28th of February 1955, at five o'clock in the morning, an Israeli commando unit, made up of the boldest shock-troops in an army which has no lack of them, went about three miles into Egyptian territory near Gaza. They blew up the town's water-tower and machine-gunned the station, protecting themselves with a curtain of flame. An officer and 14 Egyptian troops, surprised in their sleep, and 9 terrified Arab civilians, were killed. Their mission completed, the Israelis withdrew, only to meet the first Egyptian reinforcements which came up by lorry. Before they could get out, their vehicles were riddled with bullets and 22 soldiers were killed. Thus there were 43 killed altogether, in an act of flagrant aggression. Less than five hours after the incident General Burns, head of the United Nations observers, cabled that 'The Israeli army had attacked Gaza . . .' However favourable to Israel it usually was, the International Press was roused. Egypt submitted the matter to the Security Council which,

'noting that the Arab-Israeli mixed armistice commission on the 6th of March 1955 established that a premeditated and organized attack on regular forces of the Egyptian army at Gaza had been carried out on the order of the Israeli authorities . . . condemns that attack . . . and once again calls on Israel to take whatever measures are necessary to prevent such aggressions'.

Here, again, we must ask why this government ('adult' in this case) had dared permit the massacre of several dozen men without even taking the trouble to invent an alibi. We were answered a few days later, in Paris, by an Israeli diplomat: 'We had to do it to prevent war, which the Arabs' endless provocations were leading us into. Now they'll leave us alone . . .' There were to be other occasions for appreciating the effectiveness of this type of 'preventive action'. The next month we were in Gaza, trying to get at the origins of the affair. With documents in hand (a list of complaints made to the mixed commission and the minutes of the commission's debates) it appeared that, in the three months preceding the attack on Gaza, responsibility for the incidents was about equally shared: there were 53 Arab and 47 Israeli violations. But it should be noted that more than a third of the Arab violations were 'infiltrations' on the part of destitute refugees, packed in the Gaza camps, trying to harvest something from 'their' nearby land, now in enemy territory. One of the best-informed local neutral observers said 'The Israeli attack on the 28th of February cannot be compared with the previous acts committed on both sides, and it opens a new phase—that of sizable military operations in a zone which has long been living in a state of insecurity.'

Egypt did not strike back at first. Nasser and General Amir realized that they did not have the means to do so. This gave rise to the feverish arms-race which resulted, six months later, in the contract with Prague. At the beginning of April, however, the Egyptians began raising young volunteers from among the Palestine refugees into 'sacrifice battalions' (the *fida'iyin*) to worry the Israel frontier-posts. There were ten or twelve victims in the next three months. Then General Burns was given authority to convene and preside over an Egypto-Israeli military conference, to 'take measures to prevent frontier incidents'. Colonel Nasser suddenly decided to be represented, while issuing on the 5th of June a suggestion whose acceptance by Tel Aviv would have pacified the area. This allowed for the simultaneous withdrawal of the two armed forces to within about half a kilometre on each side of the demarcation-line, thus creating a corridor one kilometre in width. Evidently the Egyptian Prime Minister had reasons of his own for doing this; since they had built their first *kibboutzim* or fortified farms immediately adjacent to this line, it was the Israelis who would have to demilitarize.

In any case the Colonel's offer was turned down and the talks in Gaza, which began in June, broke off in August, while a battle— for which the Egyptian responsibility this time was very heavy—was raging at Khan Yunis in the Gaza strip. Once again the Arab combatants left over forty dead on the field, impotently watching Israeli tanks machine-gunning an Egyptian command-post at point-blank range. It was a bitter lesson. Headquarters in Cairo answered by letting its *fida'iyin* loose on Israeli territory, where they massacred 11 civilians. The infernal round had started again. On the 1st of September Israeli artillery bombarded Gaza, killing more than 46 civilians. On the 28th of September, three weeks after accepting the suspension of hostilities at General Burns's request, the Israelis re-occupied the 'demilitarized' zone of El Auja, into which in any case there had been some infiltration by forces of both sides. Finally, on the 3rd of November there came the Sabha affair.

This small fortified position about two miles south of the demilitarized triangle of El Auja, and therefore in Egyptian territory, was attacked by an Israeli battalion which took the post after two hours' fighting, killing about 35 of the defenders and taking the rest prisoner—about 40 in all. The Egyptian command at once prepared a counter-attack. But the force, hastily assembled, had no difficulty in retaking the place as the Israelis had left it as soon as they had achieved their ends. The Cairo Press and radio none the less announced that 'the lightning counter-attack had resulted in enormous losses for the enemy, more than 200 dead'. This technique of 'phoney casualties' might appear contemptible, but it is better than if there had been real ones.

Tension only grew after that. It came to a head again in April 1956, resulting in Mr Hammarskjöld's worried visit to the Middle East. He found in the course of long parleys with the heads of the two governments, particularly Ben-Gurion and Nasser, that neither of them wanted war in spite of the clamour for revenge which was always coming from Damascus and Amman, and the agitation for a preventive war which was willingly echoed by General Moshe Dayan. In August and November 1955 Mr Dulles and Mr Eden had presented plans for a settlement which had something to offer to both sides. The trouble was that the Dulles plan seemed more in line with the Israeli point of view—mere 'adjustments' of the territorial *status quo*—while the latter came very close to Arab aspirations— going back to the 1947 partition plan as a basis of discussion. As anyone could have foreseen, Jerusalem declared the first plan to be 'constructive' and the second 'totally unrealizable and unacceptable', while the Arabs described the American suggestion as 'stupid' and the British as 'realistic'.

Incidentally, it would be more exact to say that it was Colonel Nasser who, 'speaking for himself', as he pointed out, praised the Eden plan, 'the first serious approach to the Israeli problem made by a Westerner'. For more than two years, however, the Egypt governed by the military had set itself in the forefront of the Arab states in pressing for a return to the partition plan of 1947–8. Nasser and his followers knew perfectly well that the rejection of the plan at that time did not leave the Arabs in a very good position for demanding its revival after defeat. They also knew that no Israeli in public life would dare suggest that his country should accept such an amputation. On this subject it is to be noted that Nasser had made several declarations to the Press[1] in view of a peaceful settlement. But he often assumed quite a different one . . .

There were two problems which looked like insurmountable obstacles to any solution, as things stood in 1956: the fate of the refugees, and the frontier question. What was to be done with the million refugees forced out of Palestine since the 15th of May 1948, either by the terrorist Irgun or the Arab League's absurd cries of 'every man for himself', its incitements to panic? Israel would only take back ten thousand or so. Egypt talks of 'repatriating or indemnifying' them. As to the refugees themselves, they stone anyone who suggests anything but the return of their land, though some of them sold it at good prices to Zionist organizations between 1930 and 1948. Even supposing that the Johnson plan for irrigating the Jordan Valley (which Egypt tried to get Syria and Jordan to accept) should be carried out, the arable land thus created would not be enough to absorb the surplus population five years hence—that is to say, about 150,000. As to the frontier problem, 'Israel does not intend to give back an inch of the land for which she shed her blood,' an official spokesman said in speaking of the Eden proposal. The most moderate of the Arabs—the Egyptians—talk only of the Bernadotte plan of 1948, the application of which would deprive the new Israeli state of over a third of its territory!

The official theses were separated by the gulf of warfare; but what can be said of the unofficial ones? It is common knowledge that Israeli theorists, though not all of them make maps of their country extending 'from the Euphrates to the Nile', think that their new state will not be strategically, politically and economically sound until it is firmly planted in the Middle East, and until the day when it has a population of four to five million. All of which, of course, involves the conquest of new territory in eastern Palestine or Transjordan, and Sinai. As for the Arabs, few of them frankly accept the idea of the permanent existence of such a state as Israel.[2] Only the more hysterical ones talk about 'throwing the Zionists into the sea'. Others would accept a 'static' Israel which gave up all thought of further immigration. But those who hope for the transformation of Israel into a 'Jewish home' are still more numerous. This would be a large, non-

---

[1] *Newsweek*, May 1955; *France-Soir*, November 1955.

[2] Several of the left-wing movements agitated for peace with Israel. Witness the line taken by Yusuf Hilmi, leader of the Egyptian Left, at the Helsinki Peace Congress, and in an article which appeared in *France-Observateur*.

state collectivity, with a special status, no more than a province or protected minority in an Arab state, either of greater Syria, if one looks northwards, or an enlarged Palestine if one looks southwards. Azzam once spoke to us in favour of a 'Jewish Vatican'. But the Vatican has only 5,000 citizens . . .

But we must not imagine the problem of Israel to be the permanent obsession or national passion of the Egyptian people. Palestine, for the Egyptians, is not Alsace-Lorraine, which the occupied Canal Zone perhaps was. Only an urgent military danger could deeply move the Egyptian masses, as at the time of the aggression of the 29th of October 1956. The Sinai line was not the 'blue line of the Vosges'. But even if, as an Egyptian, Nasser or any other head of state could approach the Palestine problem coolly in his capacity of leader of the Arab community, he would at once be drawn into a whirlpool of emotionalism and forced to take extreme measures. The Palestine problem cannot be solved peacefully unless Cairo and Egypt can control Arabism itself.[1]

[1] See the last chapter.

VI

The Political Parties

Whenever we asked a military leader—Nasser, Salim or Sadat—
whether a return to parliamentary government through a general
election was being considered, the answer was 'No. The country is
not yet ripe for that. It would purely and simply amount to the
return of the Wafd and undo the work of the revolution.'

THE WAFD—A STATE OF MIND

The Wafd? Would the Wafd still be returned after so many ups and
downs, trials, the disclosure of its corruption, its open failures? To
have any doubts would mean forgetting that the Wafd was and
unquestionably is still a party, an electoral and administrative
'mafia', indeed a financial one also; but that it is also a state of
mind, an expression of an important period in Egypt's history.
Perhaps that period is over, but there are few in the country who
realize it yet. The Wafd stands for a certain mob appeal, a certain
dynamic and nationalist view of the State: it stands also for parliamentarians, and free thought. It is everything that the military
leaders are not, Neguib excepted. It is an Egypt of café terraces,
where eloquence is more important than results, where principles
count for more than effectiveness, and where there is a fairly sincere
and generous basis of respect for the will of the people.

It also stands for the freedom of the Press, questions in the House,
student gatherings, congresses and back-slappings. It is a kind of
meeting-point for the rising class at the beginning of the century, the
lower *bourgeoisie* greedy for freedom and power, the landed Third
Estate gradually being urbanized via the University; the legal and
administrative professions, and those of the big landowners who
chose to cut their losses by financing the 'popular' party after electing
it, and thus keeping their hold on it. It is also a form of liberalism, a
typically Egyptian tolerance in the approach to religious and racial
problems.

240

In brief, this all made for a progressive force within a middle-class framework. But in 1952 when Zaghlul's great party was deprived of power by Faruk while Cairo was still burning, this force was at a low ebb. It called to its rescue those masses which it had already begun to fear, and which, losing faith in the Wafdists, had by now given themselves other aims. The Wafd then tried to save itself by tearing up the 1936 Treaty, which had been its own work, yielding to the pressure of popular opinion, but it then fell a victim to the relentless provocation of 26th of January 1952. Could it still have prolonged its own life by exiling Faruk and setting up a republic? The Wafd no doubt thought of this but without daring to do it. When others carried it out, the Wafd saw this as the execution of their own plans. Nahas Pasha hastened home from France to take the credit.

As we have already seen to some extent, the issue was decided in the following eight days. The Wafd came very near to taking control. On the morning of the 23rd of July, Nasser, on the advice of his Wafdist friend Ahmed Abul Fath, editor of *El Misr*, had no other thought than to recall the 1950 parliament, entirely devoted to the old party. But he was not the only one. A strong faction in the Junta, the Salim brothers, Anwar el Sadat and Boghdadi, was strongly opposed to bringing back the 'corrupt politicians'. On the 3rd of August a meeting was arranged at the house of a friend of all those concerned, for Nasser, Gamal Salim and Khaled Muhi ud-Din to meet Fuad Sirag ud-Din. The meeting was a complete failure, and the idea of a Regency prevailed over that of government through an Assembly. With that, the Wafd was lost. Called on to reform itself or disappear, it played for time, threw out some ballast, dropped a few of its own men, and avoided neither splits nor vendettas nor the dreary settling of accounts inside its own ranks. But the Officers, who had discovered exactly how to make it fall to pieces, then rendered it a service by arresting some of its leaders: the Wafd was half-saved by a half-martyrdom, when it was on the point of collapse in the eyes of the public.

The trials of Fuad Sirag ud-Din, Sulaiman Ghannam and Ibrahim Farag ended, on the whole, in what might be called a draw. Accusers and accused exchanged their blows without undue ferocity, and the Wafd reappeared, first as a sizeable target, then as a voice capable of making itself heard. And while the military government became more and more harsh towards its own citizens and more accommodating to British spokesmen, people began to talk once more of such political leaders as Nahas, Salah ud-Din, Abdel Fattah el Tawil, Zaki el Arabi, Abdel Fattah Hasan. The Wafd once more became increasingly a symbol of suspended freedom, while the peasants looked back regretfully to the high cotton prices of 1951, forgetting that the Korean war was the cause.

The crisis of March 1954 in which Neguib, the instrument of the reviving parties, and Nasser, the defender of revolutionary dictatorship, fought it out together, certainly looked like a chance of restoring the old Wafd. Everywhere, in Cairo and the provinces the 'electoral committees' started meeting. The chemist of Mansura, the station-master of Maghagha, the vet of Luxor were again chairmen of private meetings. Already Nahas's house, a big, light-coloured villa, and Fuad Sirag ud-Din's big grey house opposite, were filling with an eager horde of guests. A few hundred yards away the great daily, El Misr, became a sort of embryo Parliament. In its offices and corridors, in the presence of the charming Ahmed Abul Fath, its editor and leader of the party's Left wing, journalists, teachers, politicians and idlers were rebuilding the republic. Politics, the national sport, came to life again with 'our Wafd'. Mohamed Salah ud-Din—spared by the military government, and still in touch with public affairs by means of journalism—became very active, and all Cairo was talking of a transition cabinet, whose main figures would have been Abdel Rahman Azzam, Abdel Razek Sanhuri and Salah ud-Din, while awaiting the 'real' Wafd government, that of the Pasha, the Pasha being Nahas.

Suddenly Nasser took action. 'The revolution is being continued.' Yelling crowds reviled 'the pashas, politicians, civil liberties'. The old Wafd, inclined to caution, quickly drew back into its shell. El Misr, when it was stoned one night by a crowd of 'unionists', still tried to fight back. Ahmed sent Gamal Nasser a number of warnings, especially against dictatorship. Three weeks later a squad of military police entered the newspaper's premises, politely asked everyone to leave and closed the offices. El Misr which, thanks to Ahmed Abul Fath, Nasser had used as a weapon against Faruk, in its turn suffered the fate of those who try to reconcile revolution with freedom.

Since then, the Wafd has been no more than the throbbing of the city's inner life, the great elusive murmur which serves as a barometer if not a guide to the ups and downs of public opinion. It was against the Anglo-Egyptian agreement of 1954; favoured the buying of arms from Czechoslovakia; was against the January 1956 constitution; and in favour of the nationalization of the Canal—and all this was true of the mass of the population. To be sure, one might well say that in these events the communists and the Moslem Brotherhood—or the flair of the people—were more important than the 'grand old party'. But the strange thing is that the Wafd, though it rarely blazes the trail for public opinion, is always in line with it.

Two remarks before leaving this party, whose existence is inseparable from Egyptian parliamentary government. The first concerns its electoral structure. There is no doubt that thanks to its network of provincial committees it remains the strongest electoral force in Egypt. Nor is there any doubt that the new régime on one hand and the communists on the other have dealt it blows from which it will never recover. Its strength lay in the overlapping of the large landowners' interests—who made their village vote in its favour—and those of the *petite bourgeoisie* of the towns. Now, however disappointing it might be, the Agrarian Reform shook the fellahs' cowed fidelity towards their landlords. The latter, with their estates split up, lost much of their ascendancy, their aura of omnipotence and much of their effective hold.

As for the Egyptian 'Third Estate' or lower orders, we have seen it pass from the era of *bourgeois* reformism—its ideal of twenty years ago—to revolutionary aspirations. Nationalism is no longer a cure-all in its eyes. Economic freedom, the freedom to have enough to eat and to keep one's family decently, is what it now regards as most important. It will not accept independence in any disguised form. It is hard to see what the Wafd could do about such problems as the Third Estate raises at present. But two out of every three of its electors would still vote for it.

Here again a problem arises—which Wafd? Unity was never the party's strong-point and this is more and more threatened: it would be enough for the Wafd to come within reach of power for the basic differences between its factions to break out again. Its Left wing is drawn closer to the communists every day by its 'Wafd advance-guard', which contains such brilliant leaders as Abu Bakr Seif el Nasr, followed at some distance by the group created by Aziz Fahmi, who died tragically in 1952, and of which the best brains are Ahmed Abul Fath, Ibrahim Tal'at and Hanafi Sharif. Then there is the conservative 'old guard' of which Fuad Sirag ud-Din is the unchallenged leader. The magic name of Nahas still has its supporters, and despite his eighty years the old Pasha takes a sprightly walk every day along the Nile banks, with his charming wife. Of course such men as Salah ud-Din and Ibrahim Farag can play at patching up differences and at giving guarantees to the Left, especially in the domain of foreign policy. But this line looks like being weakened in the eyes of public opinion owing to the trial of Mohamed Salah ud-Din, Abdel Fattah Hasan and about ten of their friends, in August 1957. They were accused of 'Treason', 'Attempts to assassinate the President', all of which sounds very unlike the pleasant Salah ud-Din. The man in the street is quite aware of this. But it does not alter the fact that these men were denounced as traitors by Nasser at a time when Nasser was a symbol of the nation itself. The mud is likely to stick. As for the Left wing, it is already a progressive party which would be better studied together with Egyptian communism, rather than in any estimate of the forces within the Wafdist movement which shaped modern Egypt.

THE MOSLEM BROTHERHOOD—CRUSHED BUT NOT ANNIHILATED

On the 8th of December 1954, between 8 and 10 a.m., six men clothed in red caps and loose-fitting black shirts, barefooted and in handcuffs, were hanged one after the other in a corner of Cairo gaol, after thanking Allah for granting them a good death. When the hangman covered their heads with a brown hood, their eyes, which had been so evasive and uncertain in front of their judges, now expressed only a serene faith which was beyond any hesitations.

Ibrahim el Tayyib, chief of the Cairo region terrorist commandos, came towards us with a smile of scorn on his face and shouted, 'We were judged by our enemies!' and added, 'I am happy to die as a martyr.' However he murmured to the executioner, 'Don't pull too tight—they have broken my arms.' And his naked feet were gashed all over. Abdel Qadir Awda, the Supreme Guide's deputy, the Brotherhood's theorist and who had been Neguib's friend, walked firmly in spite of his shackles, holding his head high and reciting, in a loud voice, some verses from the Koran. He stopped for a moment, glanced over at our group of shame-faced reporters and policemen, and cried, 'My blood will bring a curse on this revolution!' His face showed an astonishing spiritual strength, and it was he, stumbling because he was bound, who dragged his executioners into the darkened room. A black flag flew over the prison which echoed cruelly with the sounds of the awakening city.

The tragic ceremony of the 8th of December made a deep impression on the public, however carefully Nasser had prepared against it after the attempt on his life seven weeks earlier, at Alexandria, by a Moslem Brother. 'Better a bloody revolution than none at all . . .' Despite the tales that are told, the Egyptians have little liking for cruelty or any absence of mercy. They can be violent at times but they are not often without pity. They delight in flamboyant indictments in which the heads of pashas and traitors are lopped off verbally; but at the same time they dream of being the generous Caliph who, at the end of the play, stays the executioner's axe. Most of them did not like the Brothers, neither for their gloomy outlook, their puritanism nor their bloody conspiracies. They found them troublesome and a bit sinister. But they had no love, either, for the brutal repression which at least theoretically ground the Brotherhood into the dust, so that a kind of sympathy grew over its ruins and smouldering centres of revenge were left alight. Even more than in Corsica the vendetta is a permanent feature of Egyptian rural society, and on the evening of the execution the families of the hanged men let it be known that they would not claim the bodies until they had been avenged.

It was at Ismaïlia, where the Canal Company and British occupation forces imposed such a powerful image of the technological and capitalist West, that in 1929 an obscure teacher of the Koran founded 'The Association of Moslem Brothers' (*El Ikhwan el Muslimin*). Sickly, short, with a pale snub-nosed face and ragged black beard, he was not a handsome man, not the kind who would attract attention at first sight. But as soon as he spoke, Sheikh Hasan el Banna became fascinating. One needs to have heard him address a crowd of ordinary people—with his fiery eyes and resonant voice, the head held high on his dwarfish body as he declaimed in a loud voice verses from the Koran, which he accompanied with a lyrical commentary to emphasize their urgent relevance to modern events—in order to appreciate what an inspired orator can be, and to understand the fascination and influence wielded by the prophets over the masses of the East.

His doctrine was simple. 'The Koran is our constitution.' He never worked out the details in a complete treatise, but two years after his

245

death one of his helpers, Abdel Qadir Awda (one of those executed in December 1954), answered this need by publishing *Islam and our Political Institutions*. This charter of the Association is a synthesis of the basic texts of Islam, the Koran and the Sunna, and of a few of their great modern commentators, especially Rashid Rida. Awda, who was a judge, versed in French law and a talented barrister, outlined in his book the main characteristics of 'Islamic government': a Caliph, elected by the *shura* or consultative council of wise men representing the community (*umma*), holds executive power and the essential right to formulate laws which are implicit in the sacred text. A Caliph unworthy of his post can be deposed at any time, and like the *shura*, comes under the control of the *Ulama* or Doctors of the Faith, who are ultimately the only interpreters of the Koran. The Moslem Brothers lay great stress on the 'democratic' nature of their doctrine, which according to them is incapable of being reduced to autocracy or theocracy.

Was it this doctrine, which to our eyes looks oddly mediaeval—which gave the Brotherhood its electrifying success, or was it rather its bitter denunciation of 'colonialism' which was held responsible for the humiliation of Islam and which was given a prominent place in Awda's book as in all the Brotherhood's public pronouncements? There are two other possible causes for its success. First, the organizing genius of the first *murshid* or Supreme Guide. A prodigious preacher, El Banna, was also the creator of a network of surprising ingenuity and ardour. He managed to build up his Association in the form of cells, and to superimpose on the relatively harmless Brotherhood groups of agitators and commandos who were little less than terrorists and whose existence was unknown to the royal police until one or two flagrant attacks made it known. But it should also be noted that when the authorities turned their attention to the Brotherhood in earnest, in 1949 and 1954, it did not hold out for more than a few weeks.

The second cause of its success was the striking appropriateness of its propaganda and organization to the state of Egyptian urban society from the 1940's onward. At that time a kind of half-agricultural, half-artisan proletariat was forming round the cities, trying to eke out its existence in districts that were close to industrial centres swollen by war. The end of the Capitulations in 1937 had shown the wretched masses that the European was no longer all-powerful. During the war, the traffic in supplies and the heavy

246

occupation of the country by the allied forces brought about a profound demoralization which struck at the roots of the traditions of a people who were now faced by unconcealed alcoholism and forms of prostitution which disgust the Oriental. For these poverty-stricken masses, under-fed, demoralized and irritated by the foreign soldiery, El Banna and his men brought a message of revenge and hope, vague enough to unite the most opposed groups, lyrical enough to act as a drug, faithful enough to religious teachings to look like a buoy to which the drifting mass could cling, and, finally, with enough social egalitarianism to attract all kinds of disinherited.

The Brotherhood also recruited many supporters among small business people or artisans who were feeling new economic pressures as a result of the relative modernization of Egyptian trade and production. This phenomenon is not unlike the 'poujadism' which came into being in 1953. It would be too much to state that the Brotherhood of Hasan el Banna gave the impression of being a 'union for the defence of the artisans and small tradesmen', and as far as we know it never preached any revolt against taxation. But it often took on the appearance of a kind of league of provincial shopkeepers and an instrument of revolt for the scattered mass of artisans. The Brotherhood was less solidly entrenched, as an organization, in rural areas. The large landowners and the administration made common cause against these 'fanatics—who, in the name of the Koran, sometimes went as far as talking of a share-out of wealth and the duty of disinterestedness. But the Brothers, representing themselves simply as 'good Moslems' to the rural masses who were still deeply religious, excited the fellahs' sympathy and had their support when the military government prosecuted them in 1954.

The University was another stronghold of the Brotherhood, though as Roger Vailland has stressed[1] this was not the old Koranic university, El Azhar, where the Association had only a few supporters among the young sheikhs. The latter instinctively distrust anything resembling a brotherhood, a kind of organization that is not encouraged by Sunnism and which has never been so popular in Egypt as in North Africa. On the contrary, it was the lay or modern University of Cairo which had a strong contingent of Moslem Brothers. Before the repression they were said to make up 30 per cent of the student body. In 1953 they were led by an extraordinary leader and orator, Hasan Durr, who was very active, always

[1] *Choses vues en Égypte* (Things seen in Egypt), August 1952.

drawing up petitions, organizing meetings, censuring student behaviour and ready for any form of violence. Oddly enough, their
position was strongest in the Law faculty. But while among the
masses the Association sometimes looked like a proletarian movement, in the University it was frankly reactionary, not unlike the
royalist movement in France.

The Brotherhood's leadership consisted mainly of lawyers,
magistrates, and lecturers in law, some of them French-trained. The
Association's upper stratum thus resembled that of the Wafd, though
on an inferior level. The Western visitor who ventured into the huge
baroque building which served as the Brotherhood's headquarters,
could not help feeling uncomfortable, and the seedy look of the
people there and the unkempt surroundings were as much to blame
as the excesses of their propaganda. Since the tragic death of El
Banna in 1949, no Brotherhood leader had been able to impose himself on a national scale and achieve anything like the stature of a
people's spokesman, that is to say neither Hodeibi nor Ashmawi,
and Abdin, the general secretary, least of all. Abdel Qadir Awda
was the only one who came anywhere near it.

Not that the Brotherhood despised power. They were capable of
strange recantations, for a group which tended so much towards
mysticism, capable of tactical manœuvres, advances to the Palace,
even contacts with the British. But they also neglected to seize power
at a time—in 1947—when Hasan el Banna appeared to have a firm
grip on the Egyptian towns and, without fear of ridicule, could
claim to have over a million supporters. He was then head of a state
within the State, so that the U.N. Special Committee on Palestine
went so far as to consult him. But the Palestine conflict turned out
to be a fatal trap for him, though it gave him the opportunity for
his finest successes as an orator, and a pretext for training and arming
his commandos who soon appeared to be a genuine threat to the
State.

He could not resist the temptation of giving the court a striking
lesson in nationalism, and a demonstration of his strength. At the
head of his groups of volunteers he set his best fighters, who for
the most part were killed. Those who returned were arrested by the
royal police on the excuse that they would become terrorists. The
defeat had come about in the interim. All-powerful at the opening
of hostilities during the winter of 1947–8, ten months later Sheikh
Hasan was a semi-outlaw, cut off from his troops. He fell back on

terrorism and one after the other the public heard of the death of a district Judge who was said to have been hard on the Brothers, Judge Khazindar, then the violent death of General Salim Zaki—who prided himself on having been trained in the Tzarist Okhrana—and then, after the government announced that the Brotherhood was liquidated, the assassination of the Prime Minister himself, Mahmud Fahmi el Nuqrashi Pasha, who was struck down with astonishing daring by men disguised as policemen, in a lift in the Ministry for the Interior.

Several weeks later, Sheikh Hasan el Banna was murdered in the open street by men of the political police acting on the orders of Colonel Abdel Magid. The all-powerful Brotherhood, thus decapitated and broken in less than three weeks by government action, then spent about two years in a kind of coma, from which Faruk roused it in 1950 in order to create a rival to the Wafd, to whose recall to power he had had to resign himself. But the king wanted to take precautions by placing the Association in the hands of someone he could count on. A judge of sanctimonious appearance was found, whose friendship with El Banna would make him acceptable to the Brotherhood. This was Hasan el Hodeibi, who made all the promises required of him by the Palace. Perhaps he kept them, and everything suggests that the Brothers who took part in anti-British guerrilla-warfare on the Canal at the end of 1951, then in the burning of Cairo on the 26th of January 1952, were severely reprimanded by the new Supreme Guide. But these events showed Hodeibi that he was not the real master of the Association, cut off as he was from the clandestine 'action-groups' set up by El Banna and which were directed in the Canal Zone by Sheikh Farghali and Yusuf Tal'at (both hanged in 1954), and in Cairo by Abdel Rahman el Sanadi. From then on his whole policy was to draw closer to these secret groups.

Then came the *coup d'état* on the 23rd of July 1952. Flags were put out at the Brotherhood's premises, especially as the victorious Officers at once had a visit from a Brotherhood delegate, Hasan Ashmawi. In a state of great excitement the Association office went through its files and decided that at least a third of the Free Officers were fairly closely attached to the Brotherhood. Invited to a meeting with the Military Committee, the Supreme Guide kept it waiting for four days. The Brotherhood then hastily drafted a White Paper in which it expounded its programme, which in their opinion could not fail to be accepted as the only possible one by the Officers in power. They over-estimated their influence. No doubt the Regent, Colonel Mehanna, was very close to them, while Major Kamal ud-Din Husain (the present Minister for Education), a member of the Committee, had worked for them. Nasser, Hakim Amir and Boghdadi had often been in touch with them and had not refused their help in Palestine or on the Canal. Moreover, Anwar el Sadat was one of El Banna's intimates and had formed a link between the Brotherhood and one of the groups of rebel officers between 1942 and 1947.

But if there was anything the Officers particularly disliked (Nasser especially), it was any attempt on the part of any governing group to turn to their own profit the revolutionary victory for which they knew they were alone responsible. They made this clear to Sirag ud-Din. Now they were going to make it clear to the Brotherhood. In September, with the fall of the Mahir Cabinet, the Brothers asked for two ministerial portfolios, for Munir el Dalla and Hasan Ashmawi. The Officers answered that they could have one Minister, to be chosen by the Military Committee, and named Hasan el Baquri, who was the leader of the Brotherhood's Left wing and was an old class-mate of Nasser's. The Brotherhood tried to prevent Baquri from taking up the appointment, threatening him with dismissal from the Association. But this did not deter him and he became Minister for the Awqaf (Religious Properties). To suppose that this meant a break would be to misunderstand the Brothers, who were masters of opportunism. They expelled Baquri but redoubled their advances towards the régime. When the law on political parties appeared, Hodeibi persuaded his colleagues to pass themselves off as being members of a 'religious association', and thus sent the Brotherhood into retirement for a while.

But he had a twofold plan. He patiently went on bringing control of the secret terrorist groups into his own hands, and set out to insert them into the militias created by the new régime in the Liberation Rally and National Guard. Meanwhile he ran a cunning campaign of opposition to the régime, which he was careful not to attack openly or directly, and towards which he affected an attitude of saddened disdain. Twice, in August 1953 and early in January 1954, he told us of his regret that the government had not restored civil liberties, and repeatedly reminded us that Islam could only accept leaders who were elected by the whole population.

It was only a matter of time for the Brotherhood and the government to break off relations. The crisis, which Nasser clearly encouraged, first showed inside the Association itself. For many months factions and splits in its ranks could easily be distinguished. Round the Supreme Guide, Hodeibi, were grouped the moderates, apparently against the use of force, hostile to the régime and apparently in favour of democratic methods. The hotheads, though they seemed unwilling to attack those in power, aligned themselves with Salah Ashmawi, Banna's former deputy, an anaemic puritan worthy of El Greco, and director of the weekly paper *El Da'wa*. Finally, Abdel Qadir Awda and Sheikh Farghali showed a considerable liking for the régime, but would have preferred to see the Association take more initiative and have more voice in state policy. The struggle broke out between Hodeibi's supporters and those of Ashmawi, over the Guide's dismissal of four Brothers belonging to the group of hotheads, and who had once been compromised in a terrorist escapade.

One evening in November 1953 came an incredible event. A commando attached to Ashmawi entered the Association's premises, ran to the Supreme Guide's room, manhandled him, then led him to an office where they tried to force him to resign and reinstate the four dismissed Brothers. The rumour at once got about that Hodeibi had 'abdicated' in favour of one of the plotters, Sheikh Sayed Sabiq. This was not true. Hodeibi held out, refused to sign anything and was freed early in the morning by some of his followers who had been warned of what was happening. The same evening, in great excitement, the assembled staff pronounced the exclusion of the rebels who had dared raise their hands against the Supreme Guide—an unheard-of event when one remembers that the Association is primarily religious and that its leader is endowed with a kind of sacred dignity.

Another surprising matter was the unusual indifference of the police towards this disturbance, which was calculated to threaten the peace. With the Brotherhood, everyone knows where things begin, but not where they will end. Were the Officers supporting that madman Ashmawi? It seems that they were not against having Hodeibi shaken up a little: they were not blind to his hostility to the régime. The next day, Nasser convened representatives of all three tendencies in his office, to try to arbitrate between them. The Brotherhood pretended to submit. But they had not yet sufficiently realized that

Nasser and his followers were more dangerous opponents than the Palace had been, for the Officers knew them better than the secret police had done, since they had carried out attacks and commando sorties side by side.

It was then that the Brotherhood made the blunder for which the Colonel had been waiting a long time. On the 11th of January 1954, disturbances were created in the University grounds by students belonging to the Brotherhood. They had been over-excited by a speech given by Nawab Safavi,[1] chief of the Persian 'Islam Fida'iyin', in his personal, epileptic style. This gave the Officers the pretext they had been looking for, to dissolve the Association, by proving that the Brotherhood possessed arms of which it would not hesitate to make use. Several days later, commenting on this step, Nasser declared, 'The Moslem Brotherhood's crime was to have tried to introduce itself into the police and the army, with the object of gaining control of them in order to seize power by force. They were trying to start a kind of holy war against us.'

The proscription in January 1954, as we have seen, cost the Officers more than the Brotherhood, since it brought about the great show-down between Nasser and Neguib, for whom the Brotherhood fought so effectively that it managed to come to life again once the disagreement was settled. Many observers then saw it as having profited from the operation, and as arbiter of the situation. Once again, this amounted to attaching too much importance to the Brotherhood, which was about to enter into a conflict with the Colonel-President which ended in disaster.

With the signing of the draft agreement of 1954, the Brotherhood started a violent opposition campaign. On the 2nd of August Hodeibi addressed Nasser an 'open letter' which was distributed as a pamphlet, calling on him to renounce a 'treasonable agreement' (with the British). At the same time there were more signs of co-operation between the Brotherhood and the communists who, loosely grouped into a United Front with a faction of the Wafd, signed numerous tracts in common with the Brotherhood against the treaty. The Officers began to lose patience and published the minutes of their conversations with the leaders of the Association, from which it appeared that the Brothers had advised co-operation with the West 'so as to be able to fight communist atheism'. In September, the Brotherhood's pamphlets became more threatening: 'Gamal, if

[1] A terrorist executed at Teheran in 1955 after organizing a number of outrages.

you dare make any attack on the unity of the Brotherhood, your days are numbered. The Anglo-Egyptian treaty which sells Egypt to the West will not be ratified: the military dictatorship will crumble away.'

An atmosphere of civil war gradually spread through the capital. Here and there supplies of arms were discovered, which gave an impressive idea of the Brotherhood's strength. Hodeibi was arrested early in October, but signed a tract which was published six days later. In the face of constant defiance and threats, the Officers, who until then had had no trouble in breaking their enemies, maintained a reserve which seemed to be full of apprehension. People wondered whether they were afraid to strike at such a formidable enemy. Then, eight shots fired at Nasser by a mad terrorist[1] in Alexandria, on the 26th of October 1954, sealed the Brotherhood's fate. This attack rid the Officers of their inhibitions regarding the Brotherhood, which, by organizing such a clumsy attack and multiplying the risk of failure by increasing the risk of arrest, showed themselves to be far weaker than was generally supposed. It then came out that Colonel Muhi ud-Din, Minister for the Interior, had been holding all the cards in his hand for some time, and that only considerations of foreign policy (i.e. Egypt's Moslem policy) had held his hand. Now the terrible machinery of suppression was set in motion.

In the little room at the Gazira H.Q. where the People's Tribunal held its sessions, under the chairmanship of the sarcastic Gamal Salim (like some eighteenth-century 'philosopher' in spurs, sitting in judgement on a religious order), we watched the leaders of this huge Islamic Ku-Klux-Klan, these Sinn Feiners of the Faith, haloed with such a legend, enter the box one by one. With shaven heads and bent backs, they almost all humbled themselves before the court, except Awda, who challenged his judges with the ringing voice of a Danton, and Yusuf Tal'at, head of the terrorist commandos, who tried to joke with the president of the court. These humble men, who also humbled us a little, were vastly different from the militant Egyptian communists whom we had often seen defying the military tribunals and loudly proclaiming their beliefs: but in the present case

---

[1] Many observers argue that the assault was a put-up job in order to afford an excuse for repression. In our view this thesis is weakened by Nasser's behaviour. At the moment of the attack he was badly shaken and found it hard to regain his composure. It is also weakened by the conduct of the accused and the condemned in the days that followed. Not one of them, either before the judge or at their place of execution, maintained that he was the victim of a police conspiracy—all of which seems to us to exclude the theory of an attack arranged by the Officers themselves.

we had little idea of the tortures they had undergone, and which had reduced them to repentant wrecks.

That short man who had just entered the court-room, with his lips pinched together (his dentures had been broken by blows), with shifty eyes behind his steel-rimmed spectacles, and a colourless face, is the Supreme Guide, Hasan el Hodeibi, who used to wear the assured look of a high priest. Now he has the half-anxious, half-ironic mien of a professional watching amateurs at work, for this head of a terrorist organization was once a district judge. He was asked what he did when he had to sit in judgement on a question of usury, since the Koran forbids all profits from moneylending. The accused gave the significant reply, 'I performed two separate operations. First I reminded the suitor of the rules laid down in the Koran. Then, having fulfilled my duties as a good Moslem, I passed judgement according to the civil law.' This is a revealing remark, which sums up the attitude of those men who hoped to bring back the seventh-century community without giving up the advantages of thirteen centuries of material progress. The only way out was an opportunism which led them from collaborating with the British secret service during the war, to the abandonment of the National Front and to rallying to the Palace in 1946, and passing from the racist terrorism of 1948 to the fanaticism of 1954, ending in a repentance without pride.

As a matter of fact the Brotherhood's fanaticism was always tinged with a kind of mournful lucidity. Witness another scene at the tribunal. Before the ill-tempered President, the witness did his best to look as stupid as possible. This was Dr Khamis Hemeida, Deputy to the Supreme Guide, a man whom under other conditions we had seen to be alert and cunning. With a half-open mouth and glassy eye, he resisted Major Salim's point-blank questions with a passiveness which neither entreaties nor insults could change: 'But why did you refuse to co-operate with the government, you idiots?' —'Because we did not want to create uneasiness among foreign nationals.'—'Uneasiness? What kind of uneasiness?'—'Why, they would have been afraid to see the Brotherhood come into power. Foreigners are afraid of us, I am not sure why.' The rest was lost in a confused stammering. But this time, the tongue-tied Khamis had said a good deal, showing the extent to which he and his companions were aware of their race-hatred.

But as their ideological emptiness and lamentable opportunism were none the less prompted by an unshakable faith, the companions of these men who gave away their own underground organizations, and weakly confessed their guilt before the brutal military 'judge', were to die as heroically as can be imagined. Is it right to say that the Moslems, who can be the bravest of men, make a poor show once they are beaten, except when they come face to face with their God?

Where do the Brotherhood stand now, after their defeat and torture and mock trial, after their sinister humiliation of the 8th of December 1954?

It must be noted that as against the 'western' Nasser of 1954 and the 'realistic' military government as it thought it then was, the Moslem Brotherhood had all the prestige that comes from extremism and radicalism. Together with the communists they stood for neutrality and unconditional independence. They raised the most revolutionary problems and signed inflammatory pamphlets together with the Marxists. They stood for Egypt as well as for Islam, they stood for resistance to imperialism and were thus in line with the masses. How do they stand now in relation to the Nasser of the Suez venture? What can they oppose to the man who defied the West just as the masses hoped? The Colonel-President stands for both Egypt and Islam in 1957. Even if the Brotherhood's Egyptian leaders, still stricken by the events of 1954, are unwilling to come out in open support of Nasser (though negotiations to that effect took place in September 1956), the Nile Valley rank and file together with 'Brethren' from the whole Moslem world—in Syria, Jordan and the Sudan—will sooner or later oblige them to support Nasserism in one form or another.

All the available evidence on their secret activities suggests that the Brotherhood, who lack neither arms nor men to use them, remain a force to be reckoned with.[1] But this rather brainless force, as we have tried to show, can only be effective in so far as it contains men capable of thinking and agrees to listen to them. Strong links were forged between the Brothers and the Marxists while they were in prison. The Brothers were the worse treated, while the Marxists found plenty of opportunity for helping them. Since news travels fast in Egyptian prisons, such incidents and relationships did much

[1] Lieutenant-Colonel Abdel Ra'f, one of Nasser's early associates, has disappeared and become a dangerous opponent, well versed in terrorist tactics. There is also an active group of Brothers in Damascus, under the leadership of the Association's general secretary, Abdel Hakim Abdin.

for the communists' prestige in the minds of the Brotherhood. The communists seem to have made good use of their instrument for instructing the Brothers. 'When we approach them the right way or suggest some plan of action or an acceptable subject for a campaign, they go all the way with us, without the slightest reservation,' an Egyptian communist leader told us recently.

As its ideological basis is so ill-defined, while it recruits its members from the lower classes, the Association looks as though it is bound to be gradually absorbed by the Egyptian Left. Shortly after the execution of the Brothers an American diplomat made much the same remark to us, although he was in close touch with the military government: 'The trouble is that the crushing of the Brotherhood is now freeing the Egyptian masses and leaves them unprotected against the attractions of communism.' Who, then, will come forward to replace the Brotherhood? Though it has not yet, so to speak, made its will, what it stood for is already being passed on.

EGYPTIAN COMMUNISM: AN ENIGMA, YET A POWER IN THE LAND

The history of Egyptian communism will be seen by political schools in the future as a striking example of a movement whose disintegration merely released more energy. It will also show how a movement can play an essentially nationalist role although its followers and sympathizers associate it with foreign Powers, except in the 'line' it takes and the sources of means at its disposal. The observer might be intrigued by so many paradoxes, but he should avoid being absorbed by them. The essential thing to notice is how the masses are increasingly gripped by a movement which until recently was inspired and led by foreigners, a movement mainly composed of intellectuals whose links with the masses are generally superficial, and which has little or no genuine roots in the rural community. In spite of its small numbers, its lack of hold on such Labour organizations as there are, its absurd inside bickering, the Egyptian communist movement played a decisive part between 1945 and 1947, then in 1951 and 1952, and has brought increasing weight to bear on Egypt's development since April 1955.

But are there any real communists in Egypt? This question is so often asked that it cannot be avoided. We have sometimes tended to confuse the terms 'left' and 'communism', though they are not necessarily the same even in Egypt. We must stress that if the move-

13a. Neguib planting a tree—not digging his own grave

13b. Abdel Qadir Awda of the Moslem Brotherhood on his way to the gallows

14a. Peasant child in the cotton fields

14b. Peasant girl in Cairo

ment contains some very serious militant Marxists, it is quite true that most of the 'communists' mentioned in this chapter are no more than revolutionists who believe that the answer to Egyptian problems is to be found in Moscow, or better still in Peking. It must be added that the Soviet Union is admired not only on account of its victories in 1942–5 or the success of its socialist system, but because Moscow has never interfered in Egypt as an imperialist power.

'Just as the October victories created Chinese communism, so Stalingrad gave birth to Egyptian communism.' The anonymous author of an Egyptian communist party bulletin formulated the essential data of the development of Marxism in Egypt in those terms. In many countries the communists do their best to give the impression that they have nothing but ideological ties with Moscow, and are constantly insisting on their independence, calling themselves 'patriotic progressives' or making their most of the term fellow-traveller. This is not the case in Egypt. There, nobody hesitates to urge on the communists by pointing to the Russian or Chinese revolution, the victories of the Red Army or Mao. Communist or not, the Egyptians like to feel they have solid values, and that is why they have more sympathy for the friends of a victorious Stalin than for the sufferings of Lenin, while Trotskyism has never found a hearing. This is not just a matter of opportunism, but rather a realistic outlook, a great simplicity of mind. They cling to Moscow or Peking because they can be leaned on and relied on, because communism has been successful there and is still strong. They approve and encourage communism because it is prospering, and not out of romantic fervour; because it offers recipes for success, powerful allies and certainties. The first attempts to establish communism in Egypt date from the time of the Bolshevik triumph in 1918, and communist action began immediately after Stalingrad in 1943.

The Egyptian communists often call the party's first years (1919–24) the prehistoric period, and few of them are anxious to talk about it. Right from the beginning it showed signs of splintering, and today it is hard to distinguish between the Alexandrian Workers' Party, apparently led then by Husni el-Arabi, a Marxist group founded by J. Rosenthal and Antoun Maroun, and the socialist party which was inspired by the writer Salama Musa. But these little groups which seem to have had about 3,000 members seem to have played an important part in the workers' agitation during the

E.T.—9   257

1920's. Neither Husni el-Arabi's trip to Moscow for the third International, nor the Comintern's recognition of the party in Egypt, proved enough for the movement to obtain a proper footing. It was already too fragmented, was exceedingly weak on the side of political theory and was mainly composed of members drawn from the minorities, such as Jews, Christians and foreigners.

The movement—from which Rosenthal was soon dismissed as a 'right-wing deviationist'—lasted for five or six years, during which it was harassed by the British political police. It still looked dangerous in 1924, in which year the first nationalist Egyptian government under Sa'd Zaghlul—oddly enough—dealt it its death-blow. The communist party collapsed in 1925, after which a strange thing happened: it became impossible to find the slightest link between the 'prehistoric party' and its successors. They had nothing in common except the label. The first groups literally vanished.

It was thus the 'guns of Stalingrad' which rewakened Egyptian communism. A few men of foreign origin, who were working without any apparent real connexion with each other, had just founded a 'Marxist study-group'. One of them was Jacot Descombes, while the others were Hillel Schwartz and Henri Curiel. The last-named was the most brilliant and the most listened-to. In the 'Cross-roads' bookshop he owned in Cairo he attracted a number of young men who were eager for instruction and information. Events and circumstances favoured the emergence of an extreme left-wing group. Fascism, which had appealed to many Egyptian intellectuals, had just collapsed. Egyptian independence as achieved by the Wafd, which had raised such hopes, had turned out to be a mere blind as soon as the British brought pressure to bear on the Palace in February 1942. Meanwhile the Soviet Union was in the ascendant, so that the war helped to bring the revolution into being.

Thus towards the end of 1942 Henri Curiel founded the 'Egyptian Movement for National Liberation' (E.M.N.L.) while Hillel Schwartz set up the *Iskra* (The Spark). A third group appeared shortly after, with Marcel Israel beginning his 'Libération du Peuple' (Free the People). They were separated not only by personal rivalry but by differences in their tactics and organization. The E.M.N.L. reproached *Iskra* with giving in to 'intellectualism' and being too concerned with theoretical matters of doctrine, while *Iskra* accused its rival of 'activism' or 'action at any price' because it was concentrating all its strength on 'preparing for the struggle'. As for 'Free the People', it criticized both its rivals for the way they recruited from all kinds of nationals and stressed the need for 'egyptianizing' the movement.

The first (anonymous) historians of Egyptian communism call the 1942–5 phase 'uterine'. This phase saw the birth of various other groups, one led by Anwar Kamil (this had a Trotskyite bias: the surrealist poet Georges Hinein was its brilliant but sceptical mentor[1]) and another under the syndicalist leader Mudarak. To call it 'uterine' gives a good enough idea of its growing-pains and its lack of direction. However at that time Curiel and the E.M.N.L. began to outstrip their rivals, who have not caught up with them since. Henri Curiel is a frail-looking intellectual who would seem more at home in the Bodleian than in the factories in the Cairo suburbs, but he knew how to attract and inspire small groups of workers. His mind was adaptable enough to offer satisfactory answers to the most grudging questioners, and his complete devotion to his cause disarmed the most sceptical. The E.M.N.L. came out of the 'uterine' phase as the most dynamic branch of the Left, and then counted about a thousand trained followers.

It was this group, then, which threw the communists into the great workers' struggle in February 1946 when workers' and students' committees were set up and for the first time Egypt felt the hot breath of revolution. After the tragic 9th of February—when in order to quell an anti-British demonstration, the police-chief Selim Zaki had the Guizeh bridge opened while students were on it, so that over twenty of them were drowned—the communist leaders and trade-union chiefs came together and prepared for the huge mass-demonstration which took place twelve days later.

Thus the 21st of February was a gesture of defiance on the part of the Egyptian Left, aimed at Isma'il Sidqi Pasha's dictatorial government which was backed by the British. While the whole city went on strike as arranged, columns of people marching into the Ismaïlia Place came up against detachments of British troops, while machine-guns behind the railings of the British barracks mowed down the demonstrators, leaving 3 dead and 120 wounded. On the 4th of March the left-wing groups organized an impressive 'day of mourning' in Alexandria. On the 8th of March Mr Attlee

---

[1] They published a short-lived newspaper, *El Tatawwur* (Evolution), which had Albert Cossery among its contributors.

announced in the Commons that the British occupation troops were to evacuate the Cairo and Delta zones to take stations along the Canal. Rightly or wrongly, the Egyptian Left then claimed that it had won an 'outstanding victory over imperialism'. In any case it had showed its strength or rather its influence, and had suddenly emerged as the most effective opposition party in the country. The Prime Minister, Isma'il Sidqi, was too intelligent to fail to take the communist threat seriously. He used every possible device to split it up and had no great difficulty in stirring up trouble within it. He succeeded, particularly, in smashing the 'workers' and students' committees' whose action marked the height of communist influence in Egypt. Egyptian 'militants' still look back to the time of February 1946 with a certain emotion.

The E.M.N.L. was to enjoy yet another success. After endless discussion it managed to bring *Iskra* round to its support, and from this collaboration there emerged the D.M.N.L. (Democratic Movement for National Liberation—in Arabic, the initial letters forming the word 'Hadeto', *Haraka Dimuqratiya el Taharrur el Watani*). But trouble was coming: the Palestine conflict was setting a painful problem for the Egyptian communists. Russia had voted in favour of the plan for partitioning Palestine, which meant recognizing the Jewish State. Many Moslem militants were bitterly opposed to this solution, which was obstinately defended by Curiel and most of the leaders of the extreme Left wing. However, this was not the only reason for new splits during 1948 which resulted in fresh offshoots such as the O.R. and the N.H.S.M. On the 15th of May 1948, the day when war was declared on Israel, 150 outstanding communist leaders and fighters, particularly among the D.M.N.L., were arrested and sent to concentration-camps at Hukstep (near Cairo) and Aboukir. So long as the war with Palestine lasted, martial law failed to keep the communists entirely quiet. They distributed leaflets debunking the military victories which were announced from the Palace. Meanwhile the prisoners who were freed at the end of 1949, had taken the opportunity, together with detainees belonging to other parties (Wafdists, socialists and Moslem Brothers), of working out plans for the 1951 United Front, thanks to which the communists were to recoup the power they had in 1946.

Henri Curiel had hardly been free for six months when he was again arrested by the Wafdist government and deported to Italy in August 1950. Thus he had little share in the creation, at that time, of the local movement of 'Peace-Partisans' which, with the United Front, became the Egyptian communists' main vehicle for action. He was unable, also, to take any part in contacting groups of revolutionist officers who were attracted by communism. In 1950 a new grouping emerged which went under the name 'Egyptian Communist Party'. It was superior to its rivals on the intellectual level, but fell short of them in contacts with the workers as well as size of membership.

The later months of 1951, which covered the Wafdists' breaking-off of talks with the British, under pressure from public opinion, then the repudiation of the 1936 Treaty, guerrilla action in the Canal Zone, and mass demonstrations in November and December, followed by the demonstration on the morning of 26th January 1952, showed the mounting influence of Egyptian communism which was now strengthened by an understanding with the Wafdist left-wing and that of the Moslem Brotherhood, and the appearance of the Soviet Union in the Press and the Egyptian Parliament. Many M.P.s were demanding a non-aggression pact with Moscow in order to bargain with London. The Press made the most, on the 25th of January, of the reception given by Egyptians in the Canal Zone to some Soviet ships that were passing through. The 26th of January 1952 almost turned into another 21st of February 1946, except for an outbreak of hatred against foreigners which appears to have been deliberately engineered.[1]

On the eve of the *coup d'état* of the 23rd of July 1952 which resulted in a shuffle of political power throughout the country, the position and future outlook of the Egyptian Marxist movement was not hard to assess. Twice (in February 1946 and late in 1951) it had managed to place itself at the head of the wave of nationalism sweeping the country, and with extraordinary cleverness turn it into revolutionary channels. On two occasions, even when the Wafd and the Moslem Brotherhood were numerically more powerful and better equipped, the militant communists had succeeded in making them fall into step with the 'party line'. They turned disorganized crowds, who wanted nothing better than to shout their hatred at the British or the Palace clique, into organized marchers and groups demanding peace, friendship with the Soviet Union, and 'down with war-agreements'. The disgruntlement of the lower levels of society was canalized into revolutionary action: the very opposite manœuvre

[1] See *The Burning of Cairo.*

was organized by other experts on the 26th of January, when the communists were given some of their own medicine.

One thing working in the Marxist leaders' favour was a kind of natural harmony between their own aims—to prevent Egypt joining the Western bloc, undermine feudalism, raise the standard of proletarian life—and the spontaneous aims of the masses, and the demagogy of the two great parties, the Wafd and the M.B.[1] In the latter connexion the communists' enormous influence can be measured, at that time, by the fact that they had forced the others to come over to their own kind of demagogy, so that a good Wafdist's or Brother's speechifying had to be peppered with Marxist slogans. Active members of the D.M.N.L. or the Egyptian Communist Party also had the advantage of a definite superiority over their rivals in their technique of 'agitation', as well as political background. They were further served by the sympathizers they found in some of the extreme Left elements of the two bigger parties, such as Sayed Qutb's group within the Brotherhood and Abu Bakr's in the Wafd. Finally, they drew strength from the increasing world influence of the U.S.S.R., the victory of the revolution in China, and the blunders made by Western diplomats in their prolonged discussions on 'common defence'.

It might be asked whether they suffered on the doctrinal side, for instance through the contradictions between Marxism and Islam. It did happen occasionally, and still does, that the Moslem Brotherhood made hard going for communist orators, for instance by quoting an official Soviet pamphlet on 'The origins and social foundations of Islam'. The author of it asserted that the Prophet Mohamed never existed, and that the Koran was a collective work, consisting of Oriental legends written down in quite different historical periods. But the whole game of the communist leaders lay in avoiding any discussion of religious questions, as well as of the right to own property (which is formally recognized in the Koran), or of civic equality, since Islam is definitely hierarchical. But apart from the rural audiences, which have hardly been tapped, arguments of this kind rarely arise, particularly in the city.

No: the great weakness of Egyptian communism on the eve of the *coup d'état* lay not so much in its numerical weakness, the preponderance of intellectuals over proletarians—who were few—or its disagreement with Islam. The real weakness was the way it was

[1] Moslem Brotherhood.

broken up into splinter-groups. There were at least ten movements, fractions or tendencies, each of which claimed to represent the Lenin–Stalin party-line in Egypt. For instance, in 1952 any young Egyptian attracted to communism would have to choose between the D.M.N.L. or *Hadeto*; or the *Nawat* or so-called 'kernel' of the Communist Party; or the N.H.S.M. or 'Towards an Egyptian Communist Party'; or the *Dalshin* or 'Workers' Advance-Guard' which was closely linked with the *Fagr el Gadid* (New Dawn); or the *Negm el Ahmar* or Red Star; or, finally, the 'Communist Unity'. Even then, two or three new groups were formed in the following months.

It was hard to find any reason for this dispersal of effort and forces, once the serious problem of the attitude to be taken towards Israel had passed into the background.[1] The *Dalshin*, which was the only serious rival of the D.M.N.L. in workers' circles, was reproached for its 'economism' or tendency to set trade-union action and questions of industrial output higher than the need for revolutionary action. But it looks as though the worst disagreements arose over personalities. Many of the differences centred on Henri Curiel (known as Yunis) whom rival pamphleteers, in that tough style common to extreme left-wing propagandists, denounced as 'a scruffy criminal sold to the police'. But apart from the classic branding of a man as a stool-pigeon, it appears that the main accusations levelled at Curiel were: his contacts with Marty (see the report published in *L'Humanité*, 22 November 1952, in which the former leader was reproached for his relationship with a 'suspect Egyptian couple'); the D.M.N.L.'s translation of a book by Tito; and finally his tendency towards 'popular front' tactics. Perhaps in the light of more recent events these complaints would be revised.

The military *coup d'état*, thanks to its nature and its action, was bound to result in the debates between the Egyptian Marxist groups becoming more objective.

Only the D.M.N.L. hailed the seizure of power by the Officers as a 'popular victory'. They based their enthusiasm for it on the fact that 'at least two of the Military Committee officers belong to the Movement'. These were Lieutenant-Colonel Yusuf Sadiq, who was openly known to be a member and never hid his views, and

---

[1] Though it still remains a cause of disagreement between the D.M.N.L. which favours peace with Israel, and the E.C.P. which continues to denounce Israel as a 'permanent imperialist plot', while acknowledging the need for a peaceful solution.

whose wife was a keen 'peace-movement' propagandist; and Major Khaled Muhi ud-Din, who was no more than a communist-sympath-izer. The D.M.N.L. leaders also claimed the 'support and sympathy' of a third 'democratic officer' who was none other than Gamal Abdel Nasser. It is a fact that the leader of the Officers' Plot had made previous contacts, years before, with representatives of the D.M.N.L. and that one of his closest advisers and friends, the magistrate Ahmed Fuad, was at that time a member of the Movement. In short, with the help of information given by the D.M.N.L.'s London delegation, the *Daily Worker* wrote the day after the *coup d'état* that this was a 'popular movement', the leadership of which was shared between communist officers, pro-Americans, Moslem Brothers and liberals. But a few days later it had to withdraw the word 'popular'. The different communist parties were far from all having the same standpoint. Radio-Bucharest hailed the 'liberation of the Egyptian people by its democratic army'. The French, then the British parties (the latter with some days' delay owing to the 'unfortunate' article in the *Daily Worker*) passed from extreme reserve to open hostility against the 'Cairo fascist movement'. The Italian party, as usual, had a more subtle approach altogether.[1]

In Egypt itself the D.M.N.L. remained alone in its support of the Officers' movement, while the other groups were struggling futilely with one another to decide whether it was a 'military dictatorship' or plain Fascism. For three weeks Curiel's friends vented their enthusiasm for the new régime which had overthrown Faruk, and which allowed 'people's committees' to be set up everywhere. Then came the Kafr el Dawar affair, the hanging of Khamis and Bakhri. D.M.N.L. publications reacted immediately and almost as violently as the other movements, though efforts were made to pursue a policy of supporting the régime in view of the need for using force in order to protect 'the revolution' against trouble-makers. To this end they produced plenty of examples taken from the French and Russian revolutions.

The real break between the D.M.N.L. and the Officers came early in 1953. Colonel Sadiq broke with the military Junta and left for

[1] The relations between the Egyptian communists and the great 'brother-parties' of the East and West have always been rather intermittent, even in the case of groups in other Moslem countries such as Syria and Iran. Little progress could be made between them because of internal strife within the party.

Paris,[1] while anti-communist repression, which had already affected
the Egyptian Communist Party and the *Nawat*, fell on the D.M.N.L.
All the para-communist organizations and publications which had
been exerted in support of a 'non-aggression pact' with the Junta
—such as the National Liberation group led by the 'Red Pasha'
Kamil el Bindari, former Egyptian ambassador to Moscow, and
the Peace Movement led by Yusuf Hilmi and Sa'd Kamil, the
newspapers *El Muarda* (The Opposition) and *El Katib* (The Scribe)
—were dissolved, hunted down or kept under firm control, while a
few score of militants were arrested.

The first great anti-communist trial held under the new régime
took place in July 1953 under the chairmanship of a high-ranking
officer with a reputation for advanced views, Colonel Ahmed
Shawki. During it there were some extraordinary scenes which
apparently were not exactly frowned on by the chairman, who did
not appear to enjoy the role of head-hunter. One day Colonel
Shawki ordered the court to be held in camera while an 'explanation
of communist doctrine' was expounded by a professor of public
law. The next day he held a cordial discussion with a lawyer who
maintained that the trial was merely staged in order to please the
Americans who were backing the government. Everything went off
so smoothly that they had to look round for a sterner judge, while
the President of the Court went on a pilgrimage to Mecca after
declaring, 'Communism, in my opinion, is only an offence if it is
accompanied by conspiracy with a foreign power.'[2] The other
judges did not hold the same opinion. Every six months or so
about fifty communists were sent for trial (the police selecting them
carefully from the different groups, in the right proportions) before
a military court and given harsh sentences to hard labour. These
tribunals in their 'objective' tactics managed to impose some measure
of unity on the E.C.P., D.M.N.L. and Nawat by treating them all
with the same brutality.

In the past three years or so the Egyptian communists have set
themselves three essential tasks, with surprising results. The first,
going up to April 1955, was a struggle against Egypt's adhesion to
the 'bloc of warmongers' and the grouping together of all the

[1] After returning to Egypt in 1954 he was apprehended and placed under house-
arrest.
[2] Colonel Shawki was arrested a few weeks after the Neguib–Nasser crisis, during
which he was one of General Neguib's most trusted advisers. He was tried and condemned to fifteen years imprisonment, and is living under house-arrest.

'democratic' forces including the Moslem Brotherhood against the military government. The second, from April 1955 onwards, was in support of Nasserist 'neutralism' and of a policy in favour of economic exchanges with the East. For some this meant unconditional support of the military régime, and for others, trying to set up an opposition with a view to liberalizing the system, freeing political prisoners and a radical change in foreign policy. The third task was to re-unite all left tendencies and concentrate the Left's resources in support of the military régime.

As is well known, the first of these was successful. Whether the communists helped or not—the way in which they filtered into the government Press suggests that they had something to do with the political decisions that were made—Egypt made a sensational change of policy between the 25th of January 1955, when the Baghdad pact was signed, and June 1956 when Shepilov, the Soviet Foreign Minister, paid an official visit to Cairo. It was not exactly a transfer from one bloc to the other, but it was different from the attitude of 'Westernism but . . .' which had followed the signing of the Anglo-Egyptian treaty. It was different, also, from the 'non-co-operation, until . . .' which had preceded it, and different from the verbal neutrality which irresponsible elements had often demanded. Taking into account the point that was started off from in 1954, it was clearly a policy of resistance to the West and of closer contact with the East, and especially one of a free play between the two blocs to see which would go farthest towards satisfying Egyptian requirements. The head of the military State seemed to have taken for his motto 'to each according to *our* needs' without caring whether it should commit him to one or the other.

After the trip to Bandung which was the first demonstration of the new policy of independence, two-thirds of the extreme left-wing movements came warmly round in support of the régime. Nasser stopped being called the 'American fascist Gamal, a torturer and traitor', and in the Nawat and Dalshin leaflets became the 'brave defender of the nation's peace and independence'. But a strange situation now arose. On the very day of the Colonel's departure for Asia (15 April 1955) an enormous police-raid was put in hand against the communists, and the very men who had spent the night writing copy in Nasser's praise were captured at dawn and flung into camps in the Cairo region where they were brutally manhandled. This did not stop them from holding meetings, almost at once, to proclaim their 'support of the government that stood for independence', and during the long months of captivity they never withdrew that support. The victim was indeed paying his respects to his executioner. The imprisoned communists maintained that they were victims of police provocation, and that forces were at work in the government to try to separate them from the Prime Minister so that he would not come under their influence . . . Shortly after the January 1956 Constitution was given out, that is to say in the May of the same year, most of the political prisoners, and especially the communists, were set free and were able to give vent to their enthusiasm for the Bikbashi in their own newspapers.[1]

Since then almost all Nasser's measures—buying arms from the Soviets, the recognition of China, the nationalization of the Suez Canal Company—have only served to bind the different communist groups closer to him. However the D.M.N.L.—which was the first extreme-left movement to have maintained that the military government was not merely the result of a 'plot by imperialist Americans'; that Nasser and his men were not mere 'lackeys of Wall Street' and that the nationalist movement could be made 'progressive'—hesitated a long time before coming round again, after having burnt its fingers late in 1952 by collaborating with the Junta, then been cruelly hounded by its former allies and the object of furious attacks by its rivals. At the end of 1956 it still appeared to be on its guard, criticizing the Nasser régime's remaining fascist tendencies, while thoroughly supporting its foreign policy, particularly the recognition of China, trade with the East and the nationalization of the Canal Company.

On the other hand, the E.C.P. (Egyptian Communist Party) was slow in coming back to the fold. Even when the government had begun its 'left-turn' the movement was pitilessly attacked, culminating in a great trial which opened on the 9th of June 1956, six days before Shepilov's arrival in Cairo. The trial was discreetly 'suspended' while the Soviet visitors were being entertained, reopened and concluded on the 28th of June. The principal defendant, Isma'il Abdullah Sabri, a brilliant professor of political economy in Cairo University, and who was accused by the police of being the notorious Khaled, secretary-general of the E.C.P. whose tracts he signed, was acquitted

---

[1] The ones freed were those who had been held without trial. About a thousand of those who were sentenced for political offences have not benefited from the measure. These include from two to three hundred communists, most of them trade unionists.

in the absence of sufficient evidence against him. During the trial he displayed scars from the tortures that had been inflicted on him. Only a few weeks before the leaders of the E.C.P. had in any case, while in prison, given proof of their support of Nasser by sending him a telegram congratulating him on the recognition of communist China (April 1956). There could be no more striking example of the political evolution of the most radical branch of Egyptian communism than a summary of two numbers of *Rayet ash-Sha'b* (The People's Flag), the secret newspaper of the E.C.P., which were signed by the famous Khaled, one dated January 1956 and the other March of the same year.

In the number published on 6 January 1956 the anonymous editors demanded the liberation of Hodeibi, the 'Supreme Guide' of the Moslem Brotherhood. In another article they celebrated the party's sixth anniversary. In a third they attacked the 'treasonable agreements' made by Nasser with the International Bank (and which were broken by Washington six months later). In a fourth article they asserted that 'there is no democracy without liberties', and that the struggle for the people did not consist in 'building dams, but in raising wages, abolishing agrarian indebtedness, ensuring work for all, especially students, and tightening relations with the U.S.S.R.' On the 8th of March 1956 the change of line was plain. 'Gamal's foreign policy deserves support', wrote 'Khaled' in the same paper as before. 'Against the threats of Israel, that agent of American imperialism, and of the Baghdad Pact, the British weapon against Russia, Nasser's active neutrality is the best stand for defending peace.' The E.C.P. went on to demand that everyone should enter the struggle in support of a government 'which needs the masses' support'. But the editors of the *Rayet ash-Sha'b* went on to remark that the required closing of the ranks could only be complete if the persecution of patriots were stopped, and if haste were made to free 'all those who are fighting to create a powerful national front'.

We note that they talked of closing the ranks to support Nasser —but what exactly was dividing the Egyptian communists into so many groups? For a year serious efforts had been going on to link them up. Secret meetings held in September 1954 and early in 1955 had resulted in a considerable regrouping. In November 1955 the D.M.N.L. journal (published in France) proudly announced the reunification of six branches or tendencies of Egyptian communism: the D.M.N.L.; the pro-revolutionary wing of the D.M.N.L.; the

N.H.S.M.; the Nawat; the Red Star and the Communist Unity. The new organization took the name *Unified Egyptian Communist Party* (U.E.C.P.), but two groups remained outside still: the Egyptian Communist Party (E.C.P.) which seemed absolutely against working more closely with Curiel and his friends, even in a larger organization; and the Dalshin with its offshoot Fagr el Gadid which wanted to remain independent. To understand the violence and gravity of the differences which still poison Egyptian communism, one has only to read the pamphlets commenting on Curiel's (Yunis's) suggestions as to how unity could be achieved.

How is its real strength to be estimated now? It is not enough, in order to do so, to recall a few external signs, such as the March 1954 demonstration during the Nasser–Neguib crisis, or that of April 1955 when Nasser returned from Bandung, or that of July 1956 in favour of the Canal nationalization. It is better to summarize its influence in the various fields in which it has been active: among the working classes, the university, the Press, intellectual and artistic circles.

In 1955 one of its best analysts wrote, 'Egyptian communism has not quite been "proletarized", but it has certainly become Egyptianized.' [1] This is true as regards making itself Egyptian. There is no better test than to look at the list of sentenced communists. In 1924 and 1944 most of them had Armenian, Greek, Jewish or European names. In the last few years they have nearly all been called Mustafa or Ahmed. As for proletarianization, the extreme left-wing trades-union movement is very divided. It was enough for Mudarak to lead an Egyptian delegation to Paris for the World Congress of Trades Unions in 1945, for another group to send representatives, on the pretext that Mudarak had no right to say he could speak for 80,000 syndicalists. Such inner dissension made them easy prey for employers' attacks in 1946 and 1951, and enabled the military to 'domesticate' Egyptian trades unions after 1953.

Major Abdullah Tu'aima, leader of the workers' section of the government's Liberation Rally, exercised a *de facto* dictatorship over the movement, working through such weak men as Sawi Mohamed and Abdel Aziz el Sayed. This enabled the government to organize whenever it liked, for its own political ends, so-called general strikes which enabled it to lay claim to working-class support even when it was at the height of its unpopularity. Inside the unions

---

[1] W. Laqueur: *Communism and Nationalism in the Middle East.*

it appears as if the D.M.N.L., which was well established in 1946, has lost ground to the Dalshin, which its rivals accuse of 'economism'. This explains why the unions held by the communists kept outside the great crisis of March 1954 and allowed themselves to be swayed by government orders of the day, whereas they could well have played a decisive role. Militant communists have expressed bitter reactions on this subject. Egyptian communism, which is already half made up of workers, could be quickly proletarianized. But this is not the direction in which it has most success, nor will its future progress necessarily originate there.

On the other hand, it has had tremendous success among the intellectuals. It is said to have a hold on at least a third of the university students. Its slogans are so clever and appropriate that it can easily rally most of the student body in moments of crisis, especially, as we have noted, since its main rivals contain many communist infiltrators and are inclined to put unity first. Almost all the 'study groups' that have been set up in the university are directly led and inspired by the communists. They have penetrated even more strikingly into the Press, considering the military government's hostility to communism and the ease with which a journalist's work can be censored, traced or interrupted. Apart from the very conservative *Ahram* it might be said that 'progressive' teams have been brought into all the editorial offices since early in 1955. Apart from this, after a few sharp eclipses which usually took the form of mass arrests, men who might be described as more or less Leftish[1] from 1954 onwards had practically taken control of the cultural sections of the Cairo papers. Thus Egyptian readers were more or less at the mercy of social realism in literature and the arts, much as in Warsaw or Belgrade.

As we shall see when we come to examine cultural activities in Egypt, Marxism and its derivatives have acquired a surprising hold on the thinking part of the community. Articles, books, interpretations, all combine to make up an intellectual climate which in most cases tends to move leftwards, towards socialist unity. All this has been fed by an enormous resentment against the West, whose culture has never been well absorbed by Egypt and whose politics have given only too much cause for indignation. This hatred of the

---

[1] The left-wing men are, of course, not all communists. But unlike the West, there are hardly any anti-communist left-wingers in Egypt, and a genuine 'unity of action' has been achieved through a 'spontaneous popular front'. The same kind of unity is to be found in France where the question of colonialism is concerned.

Anglo-American world and all it stands for is one of the fruits of an insidious and effective Soviet propaganda, which can exploit the worst forms of xenophobia as well as the most idealistic and noble ideas of progress. The net result is that the gulf between the West and Egypt naturally tends to draw the people of the Nile Valley closer to the way of thinking, hopes and resentments which are those of the Soviet-controlled part of the world. Even some realms of society which have a religious background or formation are open to communist thought: an instance of this is Sheikh Khaled Mohamed Khaled, whose book (translated into English under the title *From Where We Start*) lays down the main lines of Moslem progress in a way which gives more room to *Das Kapital* than to the Koran.

In a word, in spite of its relatively small numbers,[1] Egyptian communism seems to have an impressive future. Is this a result of the international situation, or of the Bikbashi's policy? Whatever its internal dissensions, we believe this to spring from the activities of the local Marxist movement, which, never afraid of the boldest reversals of policy or the most realistic, nor flinching before any risk to itself, has been almost constantly successful in its effort to canalize, for its own profit, the great feverish upsurge of Egyptian nationalism and the proletariat's anger. Communism has been the one party to profit from the ageing and senility of the Wafd, the scattering of the Moslem Brotherhood, the lack of a firm ideology on the part of the military government, who were in such need of advisers, the almost total lack of understanding between East and West, and above all the Franco-British expedition of November 1956.

THE FAILURE OF FASCIST ORGANIZATIONS

Compared with the above movements and political parties which never lost their vitality in the face of repression, the government's attempts to give itself some popular basis through brownshirts, fascio, phalanges and militias are almost laughable. Perhaps this provides some proof that whether we like it or not the military régime cannot be described as fascist. They have neither the 'mysticism' of leadership, however much the Bikbashi-President is praised and flattered, nor is there any race or blood theory, pan-Arabism being rather, as we have pointed out, a vague and loud-mouthed

---

[1] In an interview with a *Times* representative, Nasser put them at 5,000 in 1955. Whether they are 10,000 or 15,000 is not the important question.

'sympathy' with a linguistic rather than racial background. Nor is there any monstrous discipline or uniformed parades, for the plans for modernizing dress and suppressing the *galabiya* and tarboosh as relics of the past cannot be interpreted as a step in that direction. The military government have not even a social and political basis in the *petite bourgeoisie*, who form the traditional and fundamental market for Fascism. As for propaganda, which is Fascism's nervous-system, Nasser has never given it much thought, even in the days of the ebullient Major Salim. Apart from a few huge images of the President which are set up in public places on the 18th of June (the anniversary of founding the Republic) or on the 23rd of July (anniversary of the seizure of power) and countless photographs of him in the newspapers, there is little of this nature worth mentioning.

Military in its origins, the nationalist and socialist dictatorship of Nasser and his men has remained military, and has not managed to strike very deep roots outside army circles. Though it can fire the masses to enthusiasm as at the time of the Suez affair, or introduce vital reforms and raise the masses' standard of living, the dictatorship has never managed to 'civilianize' itself. The Junta, the Committee, then the Revolutionary Council have all in turn remained in the hands of army men. The *Misri effendi*, the well-meaning Cairo citizen, the elector of the Wafd, the source of public opinion, has been left outside the centre of things and is nothing but an onlooker.

This is why the Nasserist attempts at creating some political and popular basis for itself have constantly failed, and particularly the Liberation Rally set up in 1953 under Nasser's own personal leadership (indeed he made his first public appearance on that occasion) which was already in a moribund state two years later. It certainly had a large membership. It was known to be the 'government's party' and of course everybody joined it, especially in the provinces. According to official figures which were perhaps correct, it had about two million members. But membership of it was sought merely in order to obtain support or protection. We took the opportunity of following one of the 'caravans', led by a Minister, which the Rally sent out now and again to tour the provinces. First came the speeches, which were listened to with respect, and then a kind of forum was held during which citizens could voice their complaints or suggestions. They did so, and were allowed to say as much as they liked about drains and schools. But as soon as the discussion turned towards political questions they were cut short; that was the end.

The caravans were not entirely useless and performed such services as the 'Winter Help'. But they soon petered out, and after 1955 the headquarters of the Rally were abandoned.

As for the efforts at creating a militia, which disturbed us when on the 23rd of January 1954 we watched, on the 'Square of the Republic', an endless procession of youths wearing symbolic brown shirts and caps, these also fell through for another reason. The 'national guard' was infiltrated by the Moslem Brotherhood, who at the very beginning had laid claim to its staffing and command. When in March 1954 Nasser thought of playing the card of the National Guard he was quick to realize that it would be wiser to keep it out of action, since it was dominated by the Brotherhood from within and would inevitably have turned against him in favour of Neguib.[1]

In January 1956 Nasser offered the people a new Constitution. Democratic ideals were not its strong point. Was he openly turning towards Fascism? A French lawyer with whom we discussed it and whose objectivity cannot be questioned, answered, no, and gave the definition of it as 'a technical caesarism'. The text of his Constitution, set four-square like the Colonel's own broad shoulders, spoke of creating a 'National Union' which would have the role not so much of a single political party as of a censor of political activity, a kind of crucible in which the whole public life of Egypt would be re-moulded. This 'National Union' successfully controlled the July 1957 elections, excluding 55 per cent of the candidates and backing the majority of those who were elected. It gives the new Cairo Assembly an atmosphere which certainly makes one think of single-party government, even though the election as President of the House of Abdel Latif Boghdadi, one of the President's three or four closest collaborators, was not managed without there being some opposition. It has also been noticed that as he passed from the National Rally to the National Union, President Nasser excluded two of the Rally's leaders from the Union, namely Major Tahawi and Major Tu'aima, who are often considered as fascists.

All this, one might say, reminds one of totalitarianism and dictatorship. There is much truth in that. At the same time we have to remember, first, that Egypt has always been ruled from above. Power as held and wielded by the only democratic force that ever

---

[1] Operations in the north of the Canal in November 1956 involved the use of popular militia forces containing communist elements. These were dissolved a month later.

273

had any authority—the Wafd—bore a strong resemblance to dictatorship by Assembly, the only counterbalance lying in royal caprice or the interference of a foreign occupying power. Second, that in spite of manifestations in the towns and cities, Egyptian democracy was no more than a mandate given by feudal landlords (the agrarian electorate amounting to 75 per cent, 10 per cent of whom were serfs) and with the king's permission, to a well-regulated electoral machine. Finally, that the very structure of the country—which depends entirely on the control of its irrigation for its economic life, and on whoever rules Cairo, whose power can make itself felt automatically and absolutely throughout the most centralized country in the world—is bound to lead to an authoritarian form of government, whether it be socialist or not.

The overthrow of the monarchy, the ending of the military occupation, and Nasser's popularity at the beginning of 1957 might well have allowed an honest attempt at a more democratic form of government. The creation of the National Assembly in July 1957, however carefully controlled or contrived it might have been, gave rise to too many electoral surprises for Nasser to avoid running into serious difficulties. There is some likelihood that it will not run its full term of office.

VII

Revolutionary Tendencies, 1952–57

The deplorable state in which Egypt was foundering in 1952 was not of the kind which a popular revolution can cure in the space of four years, and least of all a hybrid government created by a chance and short-lived collaboration between a military junta and the masses. In Egypt the top political and administrative levels are often quite out of touch with reality and have no idea how to impress and influence the lower levels. The real problems are skated over and never solved. Just as in India the reformer finds his path strewn with hundreds of jobs all waiting to be done, heaping up and rapidly growing larger, religion interfering in social tasks, economics treading on political reform, diplomacy and foreign policy laying a heavy hand on everything. We are reminded of an Indian civil servant, a few years ago, telling Tibor Mende[1] about his anguish and despair over this, saying that they are no sooner attacked than the vices of an old civilization multiply like weeds or like people: no sooner are abuses touched than they breed others sometimes more horrible than themselves. Claudel said, 'You cannot count on anything being the worst'—the kind of slogan that is meat and drink to the revolutionary.

Revolutionary governments always find the moment of stocktaking a bitter pill to swallow. The more enthusiasm there was at the outset, the higher their expectations. The cynics who closed one eye to the abuses of the defeated régime, saying 'Such is life', will never allow an inch of rope to the victors. What virtue they have, if it remains uncorrupted, is mocked at, but if they allow the slightest departure from it they are branded as hypocrites. Then their predecessors' police-measures are held up as models of wisdom, and the word is passed round that the 'people' have been betrayed and that dictators have taken over. Such is the logic of those who sit in judgement on revolutions, who as often as not are the official historians of the former government. All the more so, since governments set up

---

[1] *India before the Storm.*

275

out of indignation do not know how to grow old gracefully. The worst phase they have to pass through is their teething period, so to speak, between their first and fifth anniversaries: this was the case with the Convention in 1794, the Spanish Republic in 1936 and the Bolsheviks in 1921.

In July 1952 a few dozen young officers boldly took the initiative from the tyrant, Faruk, who was about to crush their plot, overthrew a detested dynasty in less than two hours during the summer night, seized power and suddenly found themselves responsible for the fate of 22 million people, of whom some 20 million were living in distress. These daring young soldiers no doubt hoped to replace Byzantium by Sparta (or in some cases Petrograd by Moscow). But if the issue was clear to one or two of them, not even the sad-faced *Bikbashi* who led them had any idea of what means to use for bringing it about. The great Egyptian lawyer Wahid Rafat has written, 'The unfortunate thing about revolutionaries is that as soon as they are in power they have to go through their apprenticeship.' Rafat showed great courage in daring to write this during one of the short periods when the liberty of the Press was restored. But, in this case, are they revolutionaries?

The word revolution is easily bandied about in Cairo. The word (*Thawra*) is the delight of the newspapers, it gives orators some of their best effects while diplomats are often reminded that it is the answer to themselves. The only other words which enjoy such public favour are *tahrir* (liberation), *sha'b* (the people) and *istiqlal* (independence). But even when all its implications are borne in mind, was the Egyptian Revolution in any way comparable with the upheavals felt in Britain, France and Russia in 1648, 1789, and 1917? Does it really amount to a radical change in the political and social structure, to a genuine redistribution of wealth, or the transfer of power from one order or class to another? Has there been any profound change in the way of life and behaviour of people in their relation to each other, or to groups or to foreign nationals, or the substitution of one set of beliefs for another? Has the internal balance of the country, or the international situation and the outlook on Egypt's future been transformed? Is it a revolution or not?

None of these things occurred at the outset. There was neither a triumphant rising of the masses, nor the seizure of power by the downtrodden, nor the setting up of a new order by a revolutionary party. It is true that the Officers could never have seized power or have kept it for more than a few days had a prolonged tension, originating from below, not already been cracking the Faruk system, and if four organized risings had not already, since early in 1951, profoundly shaken the feudal régime. The Officers' Plot could never have succeeded if the whole of Egypt had not been in a state of conspiracy for the preceding two years. However, the 'people' certainly did not overthrow the Bastille or install themselves in the Winter Palace. The small group of plotters who seized power could say they had seized it in the people's name; but they could not pretend they were the people. That is why they were still faced with a choice afterwards whether to adopt liberalism or totalitarianism, democracy or militarism. Their intervention did not arise from the determinist cycle of 'class' history, but rather from the capricious, pathetic ups and downs of minority groups. They had an almost individualistic idea of liberty. It was a revolt rather than a revolution. But this kernel of 'liberties' was soon to feel the pressure of demands for vengeance, pressure from the exploited, from the semi-colonial position of the country, pressure from the rising population.

None the less, in under three years this 'putsch', having set things in motion and begun to germinate, blossomed into a stubborn attempt to renew the State and nation from end to end. The adventurous but scarcely popular night of 23 July did open the way to something like a revolution, something similar to those stages which had awakened Egypt under Bonaparte, Mohamed Ali, Arabi and Zaghlul. But the founder of the Wafd had none of the weapons of his foreign precursors in his hands, and his brief taste of power ended by looking like little more than an oversight on the Court's part. The same can be said of Nahas Pasha and his group when they came to the surface for a while. And however strange this might appear to the foreign observer, perhaps the military government's most fundamental claim to be *revolutionary* is that at last, through them, Egypt was governed by Egyptians.

Of course there is no comparison between 23 July and October 1917. But the Egyptian upheaval was more than a South American shuffle. It was no mere exchange of Colonel X for General Y, of the Army H.Q. for the Palace, or the Republic for the Monarchy. What really began to happen was that the fate of Egypt was taken into genuinely Egyptian hands. The leaders were local men, indeed men from the land, simple and even naïve people, with families and money worries, men who believed in God, who distrusted foreigners but did not refuse them the traditional hospitality. More will be said later of the class from which these officers are drawn. It is enough to remark for the moment that they are all 'natives' of the Nile banks.

In order to grasp the revolutionary importance of the change-over we have to remember that the old régime was led by a dynasty originating in Albania, with Turkish customs, French caprices, English interests, a Levantine notion of public morality, and an Italian background. They would have been no different had they governed Rumanians, Montenegrins or been princes of Monte Carlo. At court Arabic was only spoken to insult someone, and the Egyptian people who were the source of their revenue were only thought of as an excuse for holding lavish 'charity balls' at which the fat Caligula, always looking for trouble, openly sold titles, jobs, ministries and embassies. It was a court of croupiers, touts, panders, in which decent people (and there were some in the royal family itself, even among those most closely related to the king) had a lonely time of it. It was a foreign court, a court even more alien to Egypt than that of George II was to England.

From the time when (4th of February 1942) Faruk gave in to the British ultimatum the gap steadily widened between the king and the nation. While in the course of 1951 the masses tried to force the Wafdist government to break the 1936 Treaty and obtain an unconditional withdrawal of British troops, Faruk was preparing his grossly provocative measures of January 1952 and dismissed all the Cabinets that tried to obtain a negotiated evacuation. All that he was worried about was to avoid being abandoned by the British. That is why Ali Mahir and Hilali were dismissed. The Maraghi ministry which ought to have succeeded them was to be no more than a ministry of harem mutes.

A few months later men of an entirely different stamp were to be seen in the Abdin Palace. Broad-shouldered, heavy of gait, deeply bronzed, they trod gingerly across the carpets and knocked on the door before entering their own offices. At night they returned to their modest houses or their barracks at Helmieh or Manshiyat el Bakri. Thick-necked, in their khaki shirts, they spoke in ringing tones, and brought bean sandwiches with them which they ate in between their reading of the files, and which they kept hidden in the drawers of their Empire desks. They were Egyptians who for the first time since the Assyrian invasion, that is to say for twenty-seven centuries, were the real masters of the lower Nile Valley.

They were natives twice over. Not only did most of them come from Sa'id, from that Upper Egypt from which the forces of revival have always emerged (and in this sense we could see the military revolution as the Thebans' revenge on the Memphites who were perverted by foreign masters, as at the beginning of the seventeenth dynasty), but they were almost all of modest country origin. Almost all of them came from small or medium landowning peasant families, or the families of provincial administrators. One might almost use the term rural proletariat, were it not for the fact that Egyptian farmland has been so broken up that anyone with three hectares (about seven acres) is regarded as an average or medium landowner. Nasser and his friends were by no means the first Egyptians to have left a dried-mud village to reach the heights, for before them such 'great' contemporaries as Mohamed Abduh, Zaghlul, Nahas, Taha Husain and Mahmud Azmi had done the same. But in this case it was a whole stratum, almost a class, that came to power. It was the rising class made up of farming families whose grandfather was a fellah, the father a deputy stationmaster or postmaster, and whose gifted son is sent to the city to try his luck at the University or in some technical college or the Military Academy. Owing to a certain Egyptian vulgarity, the triumph of the newly-rich is not a pleasant sight.

Faced by these 'men of the land' the outgoing ruling classes made a feeble showing. In a series of brilliant articles in *Le Monde*[1] Edouard Sablier spoke of the 'Twilight of the Pashas'. It was more than any twilight: it looks rather as if the feudalists[2] suddenly vanished into the night. The battle for the Agrarian Reform which the Junta hastily improvised, and in which the large landowners had won the Prime Minister Ali Mahir to their side, the 'Supreme Guide' of the Moslem Brotherhood, Hasan el Hodeibi, and the Colonel-Regent Rashid Mehanna, ended in less than a month with the complete collapse of the feudalists, who had to stand by and watch, without raising the

---

[1] August 1952.
[2] The word is only used here for convenience: it is not strictly applicable, as we shall see, to the local or national situation.

slightest protest, the symbolic pillorying of the boldest among them, Adli Lamlum.

The Egyptian youth—no doubt one of the Ministry secretaries—who showed us round the former royal palace, the Abdin, as he took us through a maze of corridors to a princesses' drawing-room which had been turned into an office, stopped suddenly. Forgetting his duty as a propagandist for a moment, he exclaimed, 'Ah, that's the revolution, if you like—I've just realized it for the first time. How else could I have ever dreamed of entering the royal palace and walking through it like a pasha!' The officers have certainly freed the Egyptians from having to bend the knee and observe social taboos. There's no king, no pasha nor master any more—though the formula has never been publicly announced in 'revolutionary' circles, since the idea 'no more master' would already have raised a smile, less than three months after the chance of power. But the odd efforts that were made after 1952 towards replacing abolished titles by new ones such as *sayed*, or the new forms of humility, the common use of such forms of address as *pasha* and *bey* or the new dignity given to vaguely scientific titles of the type of *ustaz* (master) or *duktur* (Doctor), cannot obscure the fact that some genuine levelling has taken place.

The 'great' before whom people had to make way even in places of public recreation, those powerful few without whose backing and participation it was impossible to get any business done, that regular audience for the sport of kings, the massacre of the poor, have now become a mere laughing-stock. However, the poor are not blind, and fully understand that the disappearance of a privileged caste was a bitter blow to the way things used to be done, especially in the interim before a new system has come into being. Their own miserable share in the circulation of money and goods is even less than before. The collapse of the capitalists, inasmuch as for a long time there was no positive alternative to them, did not bring the poor unmitigated rejoicing. They were not slow to see a still cautious but greedy horde of new profiteers rising in the shadow of the army. The down-and-out on the Cairo pavement, the suit-presser who works long after midnight to complete an important customer's order, the unskilled labourer toiling till dawn on a scaffolding in Kasr el Nil Street, see just as many gaudy saloon cars running all night through the city, between the cabarets and the 'roof-gardens', and the chauffeurs and often the owners are the same people as before. Maybe Madame has put on weight and wears a shade less jewellery, and her husband looks slightly worried about something or other. The Nubian chauffeur shows no sign of emotion. The car is a 1955 model: Madame tells you with a sigh that they would never have dreamed of having anything but the latest model, before the abdication. The 'great evening' of the revolution seems to have passed Cairo by.

But although the economic and social eclipse of the former masters of Egypt has been incomplete, they are certainly finished where politics is concerned. The military government has neither ruined nor persecuted the moneyed class of yesterday, and never intended to even at the worst moments of bitterness and emergency, but has succeeded in stripping their economic power of its former political influence. The characteristic of Egyptian wealth was that without being a genuine feudalism related to either land or locality[1] it was a form of capitalism based on the land but also closely related to the exercise of public powers. Every pasha was 'worth' so many million pounds, so many acres, so many villages, so many votes in elections. The same ex-pasha has been allowed to cling on to most of his millions, and has even added to them if he had the courage to invest them in industry; but he has lost the large part of his acres, villages and political influence in the country.

The merits and weaknesses of the Agrarian Reform will be discussed later, but a few remarks are called for at this stage. It was intended to have four eminently revolutionary virtues, the first of which was to destroy political feudalism, that is to say the bond between capital and voters. This can be considered as having been achieved. The second was to restore the fellah's right to own property, and through it a certain dignity and initiative, and a sense of responsibility. This will take longer. The third was for the State to take over all the feudalist's activities, outgoings and investments which cannot be charged to the small farmer, and thus to bring about, from the top, a modernizing of agriculture on model lines which was intended to spread gradually to those regions which had not immediately benefited from the Agrarian Reform: thus the State co-operatives or collectives were intended to serve as pilot experiments. This operation is still under way and is being carried out slowly, timidly yet effectively. But, fourthly, perhaps the essential aim was to force the landowners to divert into industry whatever capital was

[1] See the chapter 'Forgotten Men'.

'freed' by the reform scheme (we recall that it was not a matter of confiscation but of forced sale), and that the relative smallness of holdings will in future prevent investment in the land of the former large-estate holders. Here there has been a definite set-back, as will be seen later.

It could thus be said that the Reform of September 1952, in so far as it has failed in a space of four years to achieve its economic aim, can hardly be described as genuinely revolutionary. It has proved effective on the political plane, thanks to a redistribution of power, and also on the social plane by opening a new future for the peasantry, in the process raising the standard of living for two sections of the rural community (the smallholders and tenants) though not for the first, the agricultural labourers. The 'Reform' was reformist, at the most, rather than revolutionary, though it is permitted to hope that it will end in a reinvestment of Egyptian capital into industry, by freeing the Egyptian mentality of its mania for acquiring land, and by favouring the emergence or rather consolidation of an agrarian *bourgeoisie*. Such a middle class would need to be freed from the last remnants of slavery by ridding it of debt. Egypt has need of such a class, from which its best men must be recruited, and which can finance its internal loans and stabilize public life.

The nation has a peculiar structure, with its two forms of public life existing side by side without contact with each other. On the one hand is the life of the town and city with its upheavals and slogans, its half-baked ideologies and mass organizations. On the other is the country life with its local intrigues, its narrow outlook, its restrictive influence, the all-powerful *umda*, both mayor and government official. The private Egyptian citizen moves from the one world to the other, especially from country to town. But so far as public interests go they are completely shut off from each other. One of the leaders of the military government said to us one day, 'You say that Egypt doesn't like us. You mustn't speak of Egypt, but of the two Egypts: the city Egypt will never like us because we have taken over the politics they made their living out of, or thought they did. The rural Egypt does not even know us. If it knew what we are doing on its behalf, it would approve of us.' The petty and middle *bourgeoisie* of the country districts which has just been freed from a kind of slavery, forms the ideal following and client for a new régime which is anxious to build and to last. However, it still remains to be

282

created, in the sense of being a class conscious of certain common interests that go beyond the mere village level. This is another job that is only in the course of being seen to.

Meanwhile Nasser and his friends have been obliged to appeal to the urban Egypt. His victorious secret society has had to face and cajole the masses. These staff-officers were obliged to mount platforms and play the demagogue and clothe their nationalism, which, as Von Salomon put it, was only 'smouldering in their minds', into that full, direct, wordy speechifying for which the Egyptian masses are always agog. We have already told of the only mild success they enjoyed in this sphere until the purchase of arms from the Soviet Union in September 1955. But it is not the degree of their success at speechmaking that is important. What is important is that the Bikbashi and his team, whose natural tendencies and professional training would—in spite of the left-wing formation of some of them—have inclined them towards a kind of administrative oligarchy without consulting the common people, did in fact make contact with the masses. They did actually take a kind of census of opinion, a kind of democratic referendum, while this 'appeal to the people' which circumstances constantly demanded, ended, not by bending the people towards the régime, but bending the régime towards the people.

Thus in order to win, keep or win back the masses' support, this reformist oligarchy was increasingly tinged with radicalism, or some might say extremism. Themes and slogans like 'liberation and nationalization', 'independence and socialism' or 'revolution and neutrality' cannot be played with lightly. Even in Egypt people are easily committed to their own terms, attitudes and promises. Nasser no doubt intended to attach Egypt to the West through 'honourable' means in 1954. But he had said so much and so loudly about independence, neutrality and imperialism that he had to begin listening to himself and be faithful to his own words. Thus, from being a mere audience and echo, the Egyptian people ended by reflecting or refracting themselves into the governmental system. The words and promises that had been uttered only to win them over were thrown back to the source of power and made themselves strongly felt. Even more than the setting up of a genuine parliament, the great monologue, with its popular echo, had a powerful influence in inclining the Colonels' régime both towards the left and towards uncompromising neutrality, and to bring some elements of Egyptian progressiveness to the top. Even more than the government by Assembly, this government by means of public forum, microphone and plebiscites was buttressed by public opinion, the weight of which was felt and resulted in popular slogans being introduced into councils of state.

Indeed this authoritarian régime, this government of law and order which caused strikers to be hanged, this khaki H.Q. has probably done more than the Wafdist demagogues to give a permanent and from now on inevitable ear to the clamours of Egyptian nationalism. It has sometimes cheated the masses, using them as a blind instrument at the time of the 'General Strike' which was engineered on the 30th of March 1954 in order to frighten Neguib and bring him to terms. But even that trick gave the working class, which was then misled, certain claims on the government and a means of bringing pressure to bear on Nasser. The Colonel-President did not fall hostage to the 'descamisados' because he had the army behind him. But on the one hand he owes them an obligation, and has also gained their applause, for he was seeking the support of the masses. He has been able to regain this support on several occasions, but at the price of giving them a certain unformulated, confused but none the less decisive share in the exercise of power. One of Nasser's most significant contributions to the great national revival is the way in which he opened the Pandora's box of revolutionary themes.

In spite of the system's fascist and militarist appearance, from July 1952 onwards there were Egyptian progressives who thought it could be influenced and grafted upon, because of its lack of ideology, its lack of technicians, its inexperience in almost every field. 'The Junta?' 'It's a force on the move . . . Where to? It has no idea: we'll give it a sense of direction.' Such, more or less, were the words used by a left-wing Egyptian journalist speaking to his colleagues early in 1953. It was in this way, by skilfully suggesting lines of action or thought, points for the programme, propaganda slogans for a tongue-tied government which was looking for recipes—and which was able to dispose rapidly of the ideological emptiness of the Moslem Brotherhood and show the incompatibility of its aims with those of the Wafd—that progressive intellectuals played their part in the system and pushed it towards the Left. They often took their cue from Western experts (generally American or German) who between 1952 and 1954 were trying to crystallize the régime and direct it towards a cautious reformism on the Stolypin model. This effort was abandoned early in 1955.

On the 21st of September 1955 the Egyptian Republican Government suddenly issued a law which was very revolutionary in appearance. At a blow it suppressed the Egyptian religious tribunals or courts, that is to say the Islamic *sharia* courts at which the *qadis* passed judgement on matters of personal status according to Koranic law. At the same time it suppressed the Christian and Jewish courts which also applied religious laws to differences between members of the same religious minority. It was clear that the aim of this act was to rid modern Egypt of the deplorable malpractices affecting the exercise of this 'religious' form of justice, and to restore to the State, in accordance with international usage, the entire judiciary power which is an integral part of sovereignty. At first sight it was thus a welcome, bold, modest and beneficent reform. 'We are at last emerging from the Middle Ages,' a Cairo lawyer said to us that day.

Moslem opinion, which had no illusions regarding the quality of *sharia* justice, for the most part welcomed the measure as brave and sensible, and this prevented the traditionalists, particularly the great Azhar University, from intervening publicly against the reform. But after the initial enthusiasm, the Christians examined the law more closely and two days after its publication in the official Gazette a delegation from the religious minorities went to the Ministry of Justice to ask for some amendments to be made to the text.

The text contained two items, 6 and 7, according to which a Christian who was converted to Islam, during the course of legal proceedings, would automatically benefit from all the advantages of the Moslem law with regard to his spouse: the husband would be entitled to divorce, custody of children, polygamy and the rest. Thus a Christian had only to become a Moslem during his divorce case in order to solve the problem to his own satisfaction. On the other hand, in the case of a married Christian couple belonging to different confessions (Greek Orthodox and Maronite, for instance), they would be dealt with according to Moslem law.

After several fruitless approaches to the Prime Minister and the Minister for Justice, the bishops and other religious heads in Egypt decided to publish abroad a 'scandal' on the 17th of December. An episcopal letter was sent round which sharply denounced the 'law running counter to all the laws and rulings in force in all countries of the East and West', and put the faithful on their guard against what 'as Christians' they must 'refuse'. As a gesture of protest the Christmas solemnities were cancelled and the churches remained closed on Christmas Eve. An hour later, two bishops were arrested. One of them spent eight days in prison.

A serious crisis had arisen, since it raised the whole problem of the coexistence of religions, which can only be maintained so long as they show each other respect. The essential point is whether Islam can allow, not merely religions living side by side with it—it is well known that in principle Islam is very tolerant and is careful to protect minorities—but the very distinction between the civil and the religious? The Prophet never made any such distinction, and the Moslem city is marked by a complete confusion between faith and law, preacher and administrator.

It is not hard to see how the problem that is being raised today in Egypt can be solved. First there must be a single judiciary to administer the law, based on a single legislation, which would naturally be civil. The answer is not to unify personal status by means of the Koran, but to unify it according to a system of rules in keeping with the needs and outlook of the layman. It is not unlikely that this is what the Egyptian dictator intended. But it was not easy to follow Ataturk in this field. Egyptian Islam has fallen into a state of lethargy, which might lead people to think it is becoming more adaptable. But it is likely to have a rude awakening if there is any interference with the general principle of a close unity between religion and politics.

The confusion that has arisen is serious enough. Did the legislators aim at secularization, or a step in that direction? What is made clear from a study of the text of the new law is, thanks to a Moslem confusion between civil and religious matters, an obvious islamization of Egyptian justice so far as personal status is concerned. They suppressed, indeed, the Koranic courts (whose corruption was often imitated by the Christian courts) of which true believers were rightly ashamed. They suppressed their legal powers. But the law remains and now covers new cases. A sly encroachment has been turned into a legal victory. It is not the Koranic rule that has been defeated, but on the contrary it has penetrated into the civil courts, better armed than before, cleansed of its faults and comic side, given the dignity of national law, in the hands of judges who yesterday were no more than rather moth-eaten specialists and who are now promoted to State civil servants.

Robespierre's contemporaries made much of the idea of 'virtue'. Since 1952 Nasser's associates have tried to practise it. They have plenty of examples to follow, beginning with Neguib leaving the palatial Abdin Palace to rejoin his family in a little villa in the suburbs, and Nasser whose only time off in a harassing day was when he played chess with his friend Abdel Hakim Amir, or those drinkers of soda without whisky who preferred the bungalows in barrack square to the pleasant villas of Zamalek, and ate beans rather than caviar.

Plenty has been said about the military caste's risen standard of living, or their wives' increasing assertiveness, indeed of a new privileged class. A woman was to be observed making a scene in a large store in the city centre because she was refused discount ('And I, a Captain's wife at that!'). It has been noticed that the turnover of certain *de luxe* shops and tea-rooms has not gone down in spite of the relative disappearance of their former important customers. Why? Because they were more and more patronized by officers and their families. The story went round of the wife of one of the Junta, who took her son away to Switzerland for medical treatment, and who, in order to pay for it, sold a Genevese jeweller a gem which could not possibly have been a family heirloom. Many such stories have circulated, and it has been remarked, for instance, that at least two of the officer-ministers repudiated the wives who shared their former poverty, in order to marry the daughters of rich *bourgeois*.

Everyone knows that certain commercial undertakings bolstered by the new régime, such as the El Nil company, dabbled in underhand practices and faded out in disgrace. It is an open secret that certain officers who were somehow fitted by Nasser into government offices, either in order to reduce the commissioned ranks or to set up dubious enterprises, or because they had ceased to please, behaved like rough-neck bosses in the same way as the profiteers of the old government. After two or three scandals—in public transport and public works—certain higher-grade officers were dismissed who were on the fringe of the most select government circles. When we recently asked an Egyptian industrialist who was engaged in a life-and-death struggle over a vital contract, whether bribery was still the rule in such matters, he said, 'Today you have to go higher and it costs more. For the simple reason that it's more dangerous now.' He added, calmly enough, 'In any case, I find it quite normal to reward a civil servant for his common sense and insight, when he offers me a contract, since I am exactly the man for it. The public benefits in the long run.'

But all this, however bad it smells, is nothing compared with the corruption that has been cleaned up. 'Higher and it costs more, because it's more dangerous,' said our tycoon. It has to be pointed out that what was once common practice—such as slipping a fat banknote in order to have a visa for your passport or a seat in a 'full' train, or permission to visit some site closed to visitors, or even the most ordinary permit for staying in the country, or an interview with a civil servant whose duty it was to see you, or to have a telephone installed or to meet a minister—all this has now become exceptional. It used to be the custom and nobody minded. But now it is risky, and few take the risk. You can still see the horrid sight of poor folk handing over their month's savings to a pot-bellied janitor in order to speak to a minor court clerk. But now the janitor does his best to hide the transaction.

In actual fact, this 'virtue' is to be found only at the very top of the pyramid of government. Lower down one can only speak of tendencies in that direction. But when we think of former palace practices and the hair-raising stories that came out when the royal servants were put on trial—for instance the Nubian valet, Mohamed Hasan, who had a man appointed governor of Cairo in exchange for a 'good reward' after meeting him by arrangement at a poulterer's, that 'economic adviser' to the king who went on a tour of large business firms offering 'His Majesty's sympathy' in exchange for a wad of shares—or if we look at the 'Black Book', the indictment drawn up against the later Wafdist governments by the former Finance Minister and Secretary-General of the party, Makram Ubaid, there is every cause for thinking that the atmosphere of Cairo has become healthier. The purge was not too much for political justice, though notorious blackguards went unscathed while many who were merely imprudent or weak were punished. The cause of morality has not entirely been upheld, but Egypt's face is a bit cleaner than before, and her voice is no longer that of Pecksniff.

Egypt went through the 'moment of truth' of the Spanish bullfight during the first two years of the military government, and for

15a. The house of a fellah who has been to Mecca

15b. Infant snake-charmer

15c. Sugar-cane shop near the Citadel

16a. Tapestry designed and woven by pupils of Wisa
Wasif

16b. Father Ayrout, director of free schools in Upper
Egypt, enrols a class

some it was long and painful. Since then, totalitarian logic has created new legends and new taboos to replace the old. Let us consider for a moment the process of 'de-mystification', pulling the wool off people's eyes, which the revolutionary system amounted to when it began. Until the 23rd of July 1952 Egypt was an enormous theatre in which false values and illusions held the stage, without anyone being taken in or pretending to look the other way. The *coup d'état* knocked down this cardboard theatre, if only by showing that a handful of uninfluential officers could knock down not only the royal colossus, but all the Palace clique and those who pulled the strings of Parliament and the cotton-trade, and indeed the Army clique itself. (Of course another cardboard theatre has been built since, but that's another question.) It was a dangerous game to play. Demagogy could flourish in the climate of trickery and illusion which their predecessors created around themselves. The common people knew they were being lied to, but such lies were their opium and surrounded their poverty-stricken existence with clouds of hope. Everything took place in a sort of dimly-lit opium den, in a sort of floating universe. But now pitiless arc-lamps show up the limitations of people's acts, the exact value of men, the proper shape of things, the real nature of whatever is being done.

Far more dangerous was the new attempt at mystification that was made, based on Arab rhetoric, the ardent Egyptian imagination and favourable currents in the international situation and the immense dreams which suddenly appeared on the Egyptian horizon. It had to be fed with deeds. The injection of truth which was given at the beginning of the régime, when Egypt was in a permanent state of public confession, has produced its effects.

The people sit in judgement. The time has gone for dreaming aloud.

The military government have never hesitated to act. One of the most serious reproaches that can be made against their experiment is, on the contrary, that they tried to do too much all at once, whether the time was ripe or not. They were led on by a feverish desire for action which often did no more than create disorder whereas more would have been gained by a cautious approach. Take, for example, September 1952. The 'Twelve' tackled six big problems at the same time. On the 9th of that month they issued plans for the Agrarian Reform. Only the day before they had decided to seize effective power through Neguib, who was suddenly put in place of Ali

Mahir. The simultaneous arrest of twenty-five political leaders or personalities was a prelude to a great struggle with the various political parties. Two days later the military cabinet decided to abolish *waqf-ahli* or property in mortmain (viz. held by some impersonal corporation or society). During the following week they either decreed or set afoot a lowering of rents and forced reduction of the price of foodstuffs, together with plans for the control of labour and the cleaning-up of the administration. No one would be surprised at such activity on the part of some well-controlled state machine, but we have to remember that Egypt at that time was being run by about seventy officers and a few trusted civilians, a khaki club. Such a display of energy was natural enough, given the dimensions of the jobs waiting to be done, and it was well-directed and often fruitful. But it was hardly avoidable for so many hastily-conceived undertakings to run foul now and again.

This spate of activity none the less did much to change the Egyptian outlook. The people of such a hard-worked, impoverished country tend to be only too resigned to their lot. They have seen so many foreign rulers come and go, and put up with so much evil. So they tended to say, 'What's the use?' The Officers set out to show them what a bit of initiative could do. They built a new Cairo, a Cairo worthy of Haussmann and the engineer Speer. They built social centres and schools near and in the villages, they laid down concrete pipes to bring tap-water to the fellahs, they built factories, they demolished condemned houses and threw metal bridges across the Nile canals. Fascist Italy and Nazi Germany saw the same miracles performed, but such initiative was no lesson for the Berliner or the Milanese, who had no need of a strong man's whip to set them building and planning. Egypt was still sleep-walking when all this was put in hand. It acted as an inspiration. The people realized that things can be changed, that the slope can be mounted, that resignation is not the only form of wisdom. The most valuable thing the Officers' régime had to offer Egypt is not merely the stiffening of the individual and the nation against local exploitation or foreign rule, but this fresh impulse to creation, this denial of fatalism, which perhaps will outlive the present government.

In this respect it is permissible to speak of a revolution, that is to say, in the last resort, the transformation of man. Such things are not obvious to all. It is not at all obvious that the Egyptian citizen has risen from his knees, confident in his own future and determined to change his lot. It is not to be deduced from a stroll through Cairo, where one is struck most by the beggars and swarms of odd-jobbers who still survive, or the downcast look on some faces, the aggressiveness on others. The idler in Cairo would not hesitate to sum it up as 'aggressive nationalism doing its best to camouflage poverty and outwit despair'. But that would not be true. The truth is that certain indefinable evidence shows that the Egyptian appears less resigned to his misfortune, more conscious of his own responsibilities, less passive and more alert. He is less of an onlooker and takes a more active part in his own drama.

It might be answered that this was not the army's doing, but the outcome of twelve years of change. No matter whether it comes of the Junta's determination to get things done, progressive propaganda or an awakening due to the workings of history. The fact is that the citizens of Egypt have slowly opened their minds to a life which is something better than a hunt for the next meal, huddling on prayer-rugs or shouting slogans they do not understand. The men that 'God forgot' now walk along the marvellous promenade that has been built along the Nile banks, enjoying the cool of the evening with their wives and children. As they look into the great river they have something more to think about than idle dreams of escape.

VIII

Not a Real Revolution

Must a real revolution be physically visible, follow and be founded on a definite ideology, demand the favouring of one class and the suppression of another, and bring about a radical change in methods of production? If revolution is defined in those terms, then the changes which began in the Nile Valley in July 1952 were not of a revolutionary nature.

The reshaping of Egyptian society is but faintly visible. There is nothing here comparable with what happened in China when 600 million people were put into overalls, or with the way the untouchables were cleansed of every trace of indignity, in India. Nor, as in France, do you see the outgoing ruling class take to wearing trousers, or the *sans-culottes* wearing the red cap. Apart from one or two good instances of town-planning Cairo is still an enormous 'village' reeking of poverty, while in the country the villages are still little mud-islands full of dirt and rubbish. One has to see those regions where the Agrarian Reform has been thoroughly applied, before coming across healthier-looking faces, children who no longer have their eyes covered with flies, and women with new dresses. One has to go to the 'Liberation Province' to see the beginning of some idea of a rural community, and there it is artificial but a pattern. You have to travel over a good stretch of country to see here and there little blocks of new buildings, schools and social centres. All that is far away and scattered. The government, unlike Peking or Ataturk, has done nothing about modern dress. 'The *galabiya* is on the way out,' Jacques Audiberti remarked as we walked through Cairo; but it is still the main form of dress in the towns and has nothing to compete with in the country. The tarboosh is on its way out and is no longer the emblem of the Wafdist right-wing. But the lower proletariat in the city still wears untidy and dirty little turbans which look like clumsy bandages. The small-income group is perhaps encroaching on the more select districts, officers of unexalted rank are made welcome in former palaces, the poorer shops are

292

beginning to sell nylon, while the flabby heavyweights no longer run the ministries. But such changes amount to very little.

No, the switch of power has very little to show in the way of visible results, and even less in the way of ideology. The word 'fascism' hardly comes into it, and while we have mentioned it already and will do so again, it is not really applicable. All the *isms* have to be rejected in this context. A few days before his dismissal on the 23rd January 1954, Mohamed Neguib gave an important policy-speech, outlining a programme which—since it was not his own work— could well have survived his disgrace. In it he said or was made to say, somewhat labouredly, that the Egyptian State could be 'neither fascist, communist, nazi, nor socialist, nor capitalist', so that the only possibility left was *opportunist*, indeed the Opportunist State we have seen developing under our very eyes.

No doubt the Nasserite Constitution of January 1956 laid more stress on the socialist aspect of their programme, and as a basis for the new State put forward not the Mussolini-type 'Corporatism' but 'Co-operativism', a term which in Egypt is still somewhat ambiguous. But how seriously has all this to be taken? There is no more sign of an ideology in the new Egypt than under the previous régime. The Wafd itself was no more than a network of opportunisms, based on the two themes 'democracy' and 'independence', which none the less agreed to allow the party (in 1942) to become a tool in the hands of the British and (in 1950) the king's puppet. The new rulers were perhaps not all agreed that they had to get rid of Faruk, or of the monarchy, and marked time for ten months before doing so. On the same day they thought of bringing back the Wafdist parliament, after having spent months in trying to crush Nahas Pasha's party. In 1954 their one desire was to come to terms with the West, yet in 1956 they became its fanatical enemies. They denounced economic imperialism while at the same time accepting money from the International Bank. They hanged the Moslem Brothers a few months before making Koranic teaching compulsory in Christian schools. It is clear that these men had neither a doctrine nor a plan nor any coherent conception of what the State should be. They have been empiricists from start to finish.

It cannot even be said that, in all these ups and downs of policy, they were guided by some awareness of the interests of the particular class to whom they have given a new political status. For, after all, is it really a *class* which took power, or merely a *caste*? Is it a definite social group or category, or what one might call a clientèle? It is tempting to define the July government as being the rise to power of a class of rural smallholders and people with moderately-sized farms; but that would be both hasty and incorrect. The reason against such an assessment is that such a class does not yet exist as such, but is only just coming into being. In 'deproletarianizing' the small farmers and tenants, cancelling the land-debt and stabilizing small properties, the Agrarian Reform is vital to the very formation of such a class. But from July 1952 to the present time it has been nothing but a floating, imprecise social category, torn between ambition and despair, looking more and more towards careers in the civil service, which is a poor palliative, to say the least, to all the problems of domestic economy. But what reserves of energy it had, led it to push its sons upwards into the higher layers of society, into the army, teaching or technical jobs.

It would also be wrong to define the régime's bases of power and relations with the rest of society, as a caste dealing with a certain group of customers, or patrons. We have already drawn attention to the differences between the Egyptian army, which springs directly from the people as a whole, and any caste army such as the Prussian or the Japanese. It is true that the scions of important families are to be found even among the successful conspirators—for instance the Husain brothers, Ali Sabri, Ahmed Shawki, even the Muhi ud-Dins—but the army they came from thrust its roots right down into the peasantry and, socially, it was drawn from a more democratic source than the outgoing Parliament.

But as it is inexact to speak of a 'caste', it is more so to think in terms of an open professional structure. Even if the French Third Republic was a professors' régime, yet lawyers could do well in it; Vichy was an admirals' régime but trade-unionists were given their opportunity. In Cairo the military—and noticeably, those of the military who were trained at the Academy and the Staff College—have refused to share their power with any other professional group. They looked at first like a group of 'resistance' troops united in a common determination and unduly suspicious of those who had not fought side by side with them, rather like the Free French group in London during the recent war. But after a spell of collaboration with some of the best experts in modern Egypt, such as Emari, Qiritli, Abbas Ammar, Bahgat Badawi, Hasan Boghdadi, Nasser and his colleagues closed their ranks, then filled the ministries with other military men—oddly enough, officers from the former régime, whom they seemed to dislike more than anyone else. However, they had to reshape the army without creating any strong feeling against themselves. Even those who had already been generals under Faruk were taken on, the government no doubt feeling more at home with military people like themselves.

In order to avoid the idea of class which they resent for its Marxist flavour, American sociologists speak in terms of 'social groups', such as the 'white collars' (or collareds?) who make up the clerical grades. The American sociologist could apply their idea of the social group, in Egypt, by speaking of the 'khaki-shirted' group. These form something less than a class but more of a profession. They are closely related to the rising middle-class or *bourgeoisie* and share much of their outlook. They do not give any particular political colour to the system since they include almost as many left-wingers as reactionaries, while their nationalism is often more hostile to the West than it is to Moscow.

But the way they have taken over power, much as one occupies a piece of territory, cannot, for all that, be compared with the complete, collective promotion of a whole class, as in the case of the *tiers état* during the French Revolution, or the Russian proletariat with its stiffening of intellectuals. This 'class', if any, is just emerging. Its rise was begun by the Wafd and is being continued by the middle-class officers. A further stage—whatever it might be—is required before it is established.

The transfer of the means of production has already begun, though the 'socialism' so often shouted about by official speechmakers has to be taken with a grain of salt. But if we put industry aside for the moment and take only the agricultural producer, then it can be said that something is going on which, on a long view, might be termed a revolution.

Whether we like it or not, agrarian capitalism has suffered some severe attacks. For the moment, many of the large-estate owners who are renting all or part of their requisitioned land from the Agrarian Reform service, can soften the transition by this means, in such a way that for them business appears to be much as usual. But in the furious discussion which the law of September 1952 (Agrarian Reform) started between the 300 biggest landowning families and the farming administration, the latter came off best. The big problem is that of the co-operatives. If the State allows the reform to go so far as to raise the number of satisfactorily working co-operatives from two hundred to two thousand, agrarian capitalism is bound to shrink rapidly and give way to the State, both in planning and production. As for the future, one of the permanent features of Egyptian society, which is the obsession for acquiring land, has been practically destroyed. Grasping more and more acres is no longer the only solution. Egyptian capital is being less and less bound up with land-investment.

In the industrial field the situation is at present much more confused and harder to assess. What was Egyptian industry before the change of régime? In most cases it was a foreign enterprise, or at least it was a minority activity, with no permanent relationship to the land and population. One of modern Egypt's basic weaknesses, responsible for the slowness of the national awakening and desire for change, was the lack of an industrial middle-class. This is still wanting. Certainly the activities of the 'Misr Group' covering banks, holdings and industrial undertakings have been expanding ever since 1920. Ahmed Abbud, for his part, had built up a kind of economic empire based on both sugar and cotton, petrol refineries and a shipping company. There were also groups like Henry Rabbat's 'Delta Trading', 'Delta Steel', 'Behera', the latter being an example of an enterprise relating land, commercial exchange and industrial production.

Since 1952 there should have been signs of other Abbud empires, other Rabbat groups and syndicates; firstly because of the land-requisition and secondly because of the government's efforts to encourage industry, even to the point of encouraging Moslems to go into it; and finally, because of the urge to competition which must have been stimulated by foreign investment. But these groups have been slow in coming forward in spite of the appeals, blandishments and incitements such as tax-reduction on the part of the new government. Also, foreign enterprise—such as Schneider's new generating-station, the Demag syndicate's steel-works, the Italians' laying of a pipe-line, Krupp's bridge over the Nile, the 'Grands Travaux' (of Marseilles) converting the old Aswan dam for electric power—all these should have aroused Egyptian initiative and resulted in a spontaneous nationalization of industry. In actual fact Nasser has only succeeded in breaking up Abbud's—the Egyptian Thyssen's—monopolies, but he has not succeeded in making new Abbuds spring up in the Nile Valley, though its need is so great.

In the case of industry it was not intended, at first, to transfer the means of industrial production from local capital—still in its infancy —to the State and nation. The so-called 'nationalization' meant, at first, linking the great undertakings already set up in the country, more closely to Egypt itself, even if it only amounted to the bulk of their profits being locally reinvested. That was at the beginning— and the happiest period—of Nasser's dealings with the Suez Company, which have since gone adrift. The second stage was meant to be the investment of as much Egyptian capital as possible in industry —even private capital—and to follow this by starting national undertakings side by side with the foreign pilot-enterprises. Nobody was against these national undertakings being capitalistic. In a word, the aim was not to 'nationalize' in the technical sense of the term, but to egyptianize, to 'patriotize' capitalist wealth. As for directly restoring such wealth to the nation, that could only be a remote theoretical aim in the eyes of any Egyptian leader or administrator in the period 1950–5.

The very first of these operations (egyptianizing foreign undertakings) was already running into trouble when Nasser and his colleagues embarked on the Suez adventure. Having failed to egyptianize industry by peaceful means, the tide of events led them to use strong-arm methods and in 1957 start confiscating, sequestrating, nationalizing foreign companies either temporarily or permanently.

The stupid Franco-British spree against Port Said certainly gave the Egyptian government an excellent pretext, but it could not make the operation any more profitable, economically, than it was before. The whole scheme has more to do with the law of property and demagogy than with actual production and long-term national interests.

What is regrettable is not so much the relatively socialistic and revolutionary nature of these measures as their emotional and negative aspects. Egyptianization can only benefit the country if it goes together with a rise in output and a modernizing of the country's economic structure and outlook. Has this been the case?

It is well known that from Saint-Just to Lenin, revolution is to be identified with authority rather than with liberty. But in both Paris and Moscow, revolutionary order—terror or not—never lost a dynamic principle working for liberty, which went as unquestioned as the divine right of kings in former times. In Cairo, the setting up of the new régime and four years of rule by the military, on analysis, amount to a closed dictatorship.

Anyone who has worked as a journalist in Egypt during the past few years is not likely to be biased in favour of the new government. We are not speaking, at this point, of foreign correspondents, who enjoy special benevolent treatment, the reason being that since they write for a public outside Egypt they cannot possibly 'corrupt' the innocent Egyptian people. Thus a genuine freedom of speech was limited only by each journalist's own temperament. Recent expulsions and arrests on the grounds of spying are only symptoms of the emotional state that any nation, especially if it is weak, goes through before being actually or hypothetically invaded . . . But our Egyptian colleagues and friends have had to suffer every kind of humiliation.

Any censorship is hateful. But when it is exercised as in Egypt, irrationally and irresolutely, floundering at one moment, then absolutely merciless as soon as its mind is made up, it makes the Press one of the worst forms of slavery. The total suppression of the newspaper *El Misr* which, from the 15th of March to the 10th of April 1954, made so bold as to remind Nasser of the promises he had made to get out of a corner, is perhaps the least distressing element in the unequal struggle between the new government and the papers, which has ended in a radical form of dragooning. Even then, the slave-drivers watching over the Press have not had wit enough to notice the strengthening opposition, which has been organized by the extreme left-wing through its grip on Egyptian culture. The Left have been able to do this under a mask of absolute respect for the 'official line'. Here the policeman's stupidity and lack of political education help to offset his brutality.

The dictatorship is its own prisoner. It would like to be revolutionary and some of its acts would give it a claim to being so. But its own nature defeats its own boldest and most novel innovations. On the very day of Nasser's departure for Bandung an enormous raid was made on the very people who had demanded that he should go and who were ready to support the step. On the 1st of August 1956, a few days after the nationalization of the Canal, a communist partyworker who was distributing tracts in praise of the government's action was arrested for 'trying to disturb the peace and upset the government by force'. Nasser tried to attract foreign capital at the same time as he hanged two Jews for espionage, and when he was throwing the Jews out of the banks. Hoping to expand the tourist trade and setting up a Casino for an Italian company, he chose the very day of its opening to forbid Egyptians to gamble.

Nobody would want to plead blindly in favour of the bizarre way of life followed by the Egyptian University years before the *coup d'état*. In his work *Communism and Nationalism in the Middle East*, which we have already quoted, Walter Laqueur goes into the 'political diary' of the University of Cairo in October 1951: on the 9th of October there was a general strike as a demonstration against the British; the 10th of October, a mass-demonstration of Sudanese students; the 11th of October, a public meeting to secure the boy-cotting of imperialist goods; the 16th of October, a symbolic cutting of lectures as a gesture of sympathy for the brave students of Ismaïlia; and so it goes on. It is obvious that whether there was a state of revolution going on or not, this behaviour could not continue with-out a breakdown in higher education. It was estimated that a law-student in the University of Cairo, at that time, was attending about a quarter of the lectures on the programme. Knowing the extreme servility with which young Egyptian students are spoon-fed by their tutors, without any effort of their own towards completing or making up for such teaching, it was not hard to prophesy that the country was falling into a frightful cultural inertia.

However convinced we are about such truths as these, we must none the less openly condemn the state into which the University was reduced over a period of three years by one of the Ministers, Major Kamal ud-Din Husain, whose field-rank does not hide the fact that he has a sergeant-major's mentality. Military and police coercion reached such a state of perfection between 1954 and 1956 that the Minister was able to withdraw almost all the guard-pickets which had been installed permanently at strategic points on the University premises. The admission of stool-pigeons enables the authorities to supervise the undergraduate mind from within and stamp out the slightest sign of agitation. It has to be added that the communists' adhesion to the government has robbed the University of its stiffen-ing of opposition. The University is now disturbingly quiet, sunk into silence, bowing to authority and apparently beaten into submission. A questionnaire put recently to some of the professors tended to show that the military whip has no more cultural value than national-ist frenzy had a few years ago.

For its blunders and harshness to be overlooked, a revolution ought to be able to open up new horizons, and in exchange for the corpse of the past offer some pattern or image, however rudimentary, of the man of the future. But it is hard to see this happening in Egypt, behind the wounds inflicted on those who are 'questioned' by the military police, or behind the gibbet on which they hanged the Moslem Brothers, or behind the newspaper Censor, the University overseer, the factory inspector who asks an employee whether he is an 'Egyptian', meaning a Moslem. Is it possible to have revolution through dictatorship? Or is this a dictatorship camouflaging itself as a revolution?

The 'new man' whose emergence would have certainly justified the asperities of Nasserism could only arise out of the suppression of the social taboos which make the status of Egyptian women a shocking anachronism; and from a radical reform of the whole system of teaching and education; above all from the abolition of child-labour; from the abolition of the anonymity which results in three out of four Egyptians being thrown into the common grave while they are still alive; in an active resistance to the disease of the civil-service mentality which strangles all initiative, and an energetic campaign against that servility which results in Nasser, the Bikbashi, and the hundred Bikbashis who are now ruling Egypt, being bowed down to and kowtowed to as only the pashas used to be. The khaki revolutionists have hardly begun to tackle these fundamental causes of social stagnation.

The status of women is none the less being closely examined, and the law is being changed in their favour. She now has a political vote (which was granted under the 1956 Constitution, but under the later electoral law was limited to those women who formally apply for voting rights, and thus, presumably, educated). As for private questions, a bill which was given out through the Press but has not yet been passed, will aim at ending one-sided repudiation of the marriage-partner, and the limitation of polygamy to certain cases. There are now women acting as magistrates, some who are bus-conductresses, quite a few women doctors, very many in the legal profession, while some of the university faculties have more women than men undergraduates. But what has hardly changed at all is the prevailing idea of woman's role and nature. In Egypt the so-called 'second sex' is almost automatically regarded as an object rather than a person, and often sees herself in the same light, but far less than formerly. More and more young women revolt against being married off to old men or to men they have never met, the revolt taking such forms as escape, suicide or sometimes horrible murders (as in the case of a fifteen-year-old girl who recently drenched her octogenarian husband with petrol while he was asleep, and burnt him to death). But such cases are still too uncommon for them to make the menfolk revise their attitude beyond keeping to the letter of the written law.

The President of the Republic gave women the right to vote, but his own wife has never been seen with him in public. The universities are full of women, but how many of them, once married, are ever introduced to their husband's closest friends? Even if they are, they have to watch their dress and refrain from expressing an opinion, especially if it is different from their husband's. And even then, we are speaking only of the *bourgeois* class of people. It could be replied that such notions are not confined to Egypt but are widespread among the Mediterranean peoples, advanced peoples at that, and can be found in Sicily, Greece and Andalusia. But the fact that such evils are widespread makes them no less harmful.

On the other hand, once she becomes a mother the Egyptian woman, as is common in anti-feminist societies, seems to become another person. She then rules the household and is given proper respect. But the lack of education given to the children can largely be attributed to the humiliations the woman has received earlier on in life, humiliations which arise from the country itself, the peasant outlook and the way Islam is interpreted in Egypt. What can such a long-humiliated person have to offer? Education is surely one of the fundamental problems of any revolution. The teaching itself needs to be completely overhauled, purged of its scholasticism, its learning by rote and literalism. The Egyptian schoolboy is like an uncomfortably fattened-up goose. The same approach is made, from reciting the Koran to working out quadratic equations, although the little Egyptians are so alert and quick and attentive. The spark in them is killed by sheer repetition of laws, figures and set phrases.

But the problem is not just teaching but education, or the complete lack of it. It is painful to watch a child growing up in a Moslem family in Egypt (the case is different with Jews and Christians, who lead a more active family life). Such a child certainly has to submit to a kind of formal law, but it consists mainly of a series of *don'ts*. There is nothing in the way of moral formation, no spiritual

301

intimacy or struggle between father and son, no exchange of confidences, or lessons of any kind between mother and children. There is nothing in France to compare with the isolated existences of the members of an Egyptian family, whose daily lives appear like a surprising collision between people completely unadapted to and ignorant of each other. They merely live in the same place, like pieces of furniture.

However disturbing it might seem, the totalitarian solution of taking the child from its family and bringing it up in a State collectivity, would on the whole be an advance on the cell-like process that goes on in Egyptian families.

Another sign of the weakness of family ties is one of the most peculiar defects of Egyptian life, that is to say the lack of a family-name. A man might be called (like some thirty thousand others) Ahmed Abdel Aziz. His brother (like twenty thousand others) will be called Abdel Latif Mahmud. The British empire has not fallen through having too many George Smiths; but at least George and Donald Smith know they are both sons of Edward Smith, they are brothers, members of a group yet still individuals. The European family has a basic structure, which thinks of itself as a structure and goes under a certain name. The piling-up of names, in honour of Allah or the Prophet (Abdel Aziz means 'slave of the Magnificent'), buries all the men in a destructive kind of anonymity. No doubt a name does not make a man a man or a monk, any more than his dress does, but Egyptian anonymity is a form of impoverishment which diminishes a man. There are some families which preserve a name of their own, but these are frequently of Coptic or Turkish origin. Against one or two people of well-defined name, like Heykal or Zaghlul, there are thousands of Salah ud-Din (meaning 'the pious one') or Gamal Abdel Nasser ('Beauty, the slave of He who brings victory').

The Nasser 'brains-trust' went into this problem and drew up a scheme for legislation to make a choice of family-name compulsory. This would become the condition for renewing the whole system of civil status, registry offices and the like. But this was still no more than a hazy project by the end of 1956.

We have already mentioned the way in which the civil-service mentality is firmly rooted in Egyptian society. It will be impossible for anyone to give Egypt a more creative outlook, until it can abolish or canalize this feverish desire for public employment merely because it provides a steady income and a pension. One of the Wafd's gravest mistakes was to have encouraged this weakness, encouraging it in fire-eating speeches and basing its electoral campaign on civil-service pay and conditions of employment. In 1951 the Egyptian budget carried 550,000 civil servants, of whom 200,000 had no clearly defined duties.

The military government, which was supported by another great State organization, the army, behaved less tenderly towards post-office workers and overseers. In 1953 it reduced their cost of living bonus, which was restored as an 'increase' two years later. The immediate effect of this and such measures was to discourage young Egyptians from going into routine administrative jobs, in favour of some kind of private enterprise. However, it looks very much as though the net result was for the young to set their minds on any army career which offers another 'safe job'. The day for enterprise is postponed a little longer.

'Lift up your head, comrade, for the days of oppression are over!' This slogan, signed by Gamal Abdel Nasser, used to be displayed on large posters in the main streets of Cairo. 'Lift up your head!' The Egyptian citizen has begun to act on this advice and has lost some of the nauseating bowing and scraping that came of centuries of serf-dom. It was always 'Yes, Bey . . . Very good, Bey . . . At your service, Bey' (*Hadir, ya bey*). The fall of the first 'bey' in the land, and so many other overlords with him, was bound to make them lift their heads and even start thinking with them. In the summer of 1952 and for a few months thereafter, the 'comrades' went about with their noses in the air, completely freed.

But they were not long in noticing, with that insight characteristic of the weak and the frail, that the Bey's disappearance was made up for by the arrival of an even more powerful gentleman whom it was better to keep at arm's length. In Turkish the word Pasha or Basha means a chief or leader. The Bikbasha or Bikbashi (pronounced '*Bim*bashi') means the leader of a thousand. The new man with his peaked cap or in khaki uniform was certainly less arrogant than the Bey or Pasha, and certainly not so easy to get money out of, but still more powerful. It was more difficult to manage to see him, though the process was quicker than before. During the first few months of power, perhaps out of shyness, the Officers failed to establish that contact between themselves and the lower classes which would have given the new régime a dash of realism and made for a better understanding with the masses. It was they who failed to be 'comrades', so that they became another set of Beys.

It is hard to refrain from laughing when one looks at the Cairo papers of a few years ago, in which the king was never mentioned without his porpentine majesty being described as 'deigning to see a film' or 'deigning to call on such and such a lady'. The Colonel-President had not yet reached the point of 'deigning' to review his cadets or to preside over his Cabinet. But the fulsome praise he had to take for about a year was one of the causes of his 'going off the rails' in July 1956. '*Hadir, ya ra'is*' ('As you wish, President') was the order of the day. Nasser fell back into the whole vicious circle of servility. The 'comrades' have bowed their heads once more. And that was at the very time when another revolutionary country had just noticed, after a period of thirty years, that the personality-cult is one of the forces of reaction.

A Pharaoh is not only the man before whom all heads must be bowed. He holds all the reins of government and public affairs in his own hands, and the whole nervous and circulatory system of the body politic must pass through his person. When Pharaoh has the toothache the whole of Egypt must go to bed. When he sleeps, Egypt must not breathe aloud. When he dies, it must wait for another Pharaoh to bring it to life. After 1952 the word Bikbashi was substituted for Pharaoh. The idea of dictatorship is of no account, compared with the fantastic and inhuman way in which so many forms of power are vested in and necessarily weigh down on whoever is master of Egypt. Nasser could easily have divided the various elements of power and shared them at least outwardly with an Assembly or a genuine Cabinet. But could he have broken up the Cairo myth, and made other sources of life than the great city flow through the great body of Egypt? Yes: but that would have amounted to a genuine revolution.

This is not only a matter of the classic problems of decentralization or devolution, of the type discussed in books on constitutional law. It is a matter of creating life at local, regional level. However absolute Pharaoh's authority was in ancient Egypt, yet the country was then divided up into *nomes*, provinces which were more administered than governed by the monarchy and which had some life of their own. There were close bonds between Thebes and Memphis or Sais, but not such as to stifle all local initiative. Nothing is more striking in Egypt today than the futility and lifelessness of collective bodies at local level. There is no sign of any communal life. Since Alexandria is now merely Egypt's cotton-market and most important health-resort, and since various foreign settlements have withdrawn from such small or average-sized towns as Minia, Damanhur and Assiut, Cairo sucks up and centralizes all the country's vitality, seizing on every power and right for itself. The masses call the capital and the country by the same name, 'Masr'. A civil servant cannot bear to be appointed to any place but Cairo, and a doctor cannot see his way to making a career anywhere else. What would a provincial *mudir* or a district *mamur* do if the telephone to Cairo were cut? Everyone appreciates the joke about the Englishman who, on hearing there was a storm in the Channel, remarked, 'The Continent is cut off.' But if communications with Cairo were broken it would be quite true to say that Egypt would be cut off.

A high British official who gave us his views about certain aspects of Egypt remarked, 'We are largely responsible. We were unable to organize any community life at the local, district or provincial level. We succeeded in that in India but have done nothing to-wards it here.' Where Cromer failed, what has Nasser achieved? He had at his disposal an excellent scheme for decentralization which was presented by Ali Mahir in 1953. It was not very original nor sweeping and bold enough, for the need is very pressing, but it offered a rough solution to the problem. The project had got no farther by 1956. There were to be elected *umdas* (both mayor and government representative or officer), local councils and the beginning of local finance, but even that, however inadequate, has gone no farther than being committed to paper. Only when some statesman gives such places as Mansura and Girga some prospect of community life, and restores a sense of responsibility to the village, settlement and small town, and enables them to think and act for themselves instead of being mere passive objects of government, will the Egyptian revolution be a reality.

A careful description of the 'Officers' Republic' leads only to such definitions as operation in progress, a stage of revolution, ruthless drive, a certain re-equipment of the country. There was a credit balance up to the 26th of July 1956, but it must be taken as a step in the right direction rather than an end in itself. It represents a rather tricky stage in a very long voyage which began a hundred and fifty years ago.

Part Three

WORKING LIFE IN THE VALLEY

I

The Land and Its Men

The village stretches out alongside the canal, as grey as the soil in the fields. From a distance there is no sign of it but the minaret of its mosque or sometimes the bell-tower of its church.

Water and problems arising from water make up the whole of Egypt. For the fellahs the Nile is 'the sea' and the fields are 'the banks' or shores. The whole of life is concentrated round the river, canals and drainage. For six or seven hundred miles at a stretch the villages of Upper Egypt and the Delta are all alike, their similarity being conditioned by the unchanging landscape, with its endless plain, together with the Nile, the silt deposited by the river and which is no different in appearance or composition from north to south. The monotonous countryside is grey and sun-baked.

The canal and its banks swarm with activity of every kind. Little naked boys harry and beat the water-buffalo, that sad-eyed creature which spends all its time in the water when it is not at the plough. With their skirts tucked up a group of women will be seen cleaning their kitchen-ware, usually pans of tin or copper. Nearby young girls in gaudy dresses will be washing clothes on the flat stones. A long procession of women in black come to draw the family's drinking-water in beautiful jugs or petrol-tins, no matter if some fellah has relieved himself in the river a little farther along, or if a corpse has floated by. The water is sacred.

The village is humming busily. Between the tall houses winds a narrow alleyway, or just a path, dusty and littered with rubbish, dirty children, lots of children. Through the half-open doors you can see women who squat there, passing flour through a sieve. The men will be in the village square: no sign of a woman here. Round the tiny café-tables they sit listening to the wireless, noisily sipping a glass of sugary black tea which they wash down with great draughts of water. The air itself is grey, full of dust, full of the famous, fertile dust of the Nile which is bad for the eyes and lungs.

There is a heavy smell of frying: the restaurant, as it calls itself,

309

sells piping-hot *tahamias* or little fritters made of beans which are an Egyptian delicacy. Beans are the Egyptians' staple food, whether for soup, stews or dessert. A few feet away a girl of five crumbles up a little ball of beans and feeds it to a few-months-old baby, who munches it greedily. Her older brother of six or seven fills his *baladi* bread with *ful*, the same beans cooked into a stew.

The *baqqal* or grocer sells everything under the sun. His shop-window is a picturesque assortment of little enamelled, flower-painted bowls from which *ful* is eaten, tin pans, baskets, ropes, bags full of uncertain foodstuffs, salted white cheese, cigarettes and brightly coloured sweets. The women come there to buy the dear, powdered black tea which is necessary for even the poorest of fellahs; 'local' printed cottons at two shillings a yard which are bought for holiday-times; sugar, salt and above all the inevitable '*gaz*', the petrol or paraffin for lighting the stoves without which the village would go without cooking. Stuck between the sugar and the spices, the wireless-set blares out army propaganda or the wonderful songs of Umm Kulthum which are enough to make anyone forget all about poverty. The grocer looks happy, oddly enough.

At home he has no eye for the children, who sit or crawl about listlessly without playing. The little fellah has no idea of how to keep himself amused. But what joy there was one day when we brought a ball. The children came to life. The old woman, peaked and dark-skinned, lined and worn like a parchment, was kneading the maize-bread. The mother is head of the house and the daughter-in-law has to obey her. It is she who heats the baked-earth oven and places the moist ball of paste on a wooden tray. As by magic she transforms the ball into lace-like thinness which disappears into the oven and comes out again all golden and crusty. However, the bread is kept for fifteen days or more and becomes horribly rancid. Heating the oven is too expensive, in a woodless country, for them to bake it oftener. Fuel is hard to come by, whether it be cotton-stalks or maize-stalks, according to locality.

The women have noble gestures, and this is the only sign of beauty to be found in all this poverty. The little girls are pretty with their great green eyes, bronze complexions, slim hips and multicoloured headgear. They are entitled to wear bright dresses, which the grey water of the canal soon dims. When the bread is ready the old woman bends over the Primus stove and invites us to take tea. This is the only distraction and luxury in the monotony of this poverty-

310

stricken existence. She takes a tiny pinch of tea-leaves from a screw of paper which she keeps hidden in her bosom, then a pinch of sugar. The drink boils for a long time, then the old woman pours the black brew into a tiny glass—only one—which is first used by us, her guests, then by the family, beginning with the father. This thick black mixture is the fellah's opium. It gives him some kind of energy which enables him to put up with the wearing climate and ceaseless toil. Egypt imports about ten million pounds' worth of tea a year.

The houses are the same as they have been for thousands of years, made of crude bricks as in the days when Moses complained about the slaves mixing their mud and straw. Now it is the fellahs who are the slaves. We catch a glimpse of them through an open door, looking as if they were pressing the wine with their feet: no, as one might make a cake they have made a huge crown-shape of mud from the soil they live on, then they have poured some water into the centre. They tread it down with their naked feet, together with chopped straw which is so valuable that the cattle are allowed it only for food, not for litter. The freshly-made bricks are set out to dry in the sun. It is an ideal material for a country where it hardly ever rains. It keeps out the heat, and indoors the temperature is almost pleasant, although it is over a hundred degrees outside. But should there be a flood when the Nile overflows, then the house melts away and disappears, as the whole city of Kena did in 1954. Then the fellah starts all over again.

The houses usually have one story, but sometimes two. Egypt cannot afford to waste space on mere human beings, as the land must be devoted to cultivation. There are neither gardens nor vegetable-plots. The houses are bunched together and get higher and higher, squeezed round their narrow alleyways. A dubious wooden balcony is all there is for taking the fresh air in the evening. The flat roofs are not used for living purposes, but are covered with stalks of maize or cotton to be used for fuel, and which serve to keep down the heat. This practice makes the houses look untidy and dirty as well as increasing the risk of fire; in addition it helps to spread cotton parasites, the seeds being blown out by the wind and endangering the crops. The flat roofs like the one we climbed on to are often 'decorated' with piles of 'pancakes' which the girls make from manure and straw. When they are well dried they help supplement the costly 'gaz'.

The rooms open on to a courtyard full of children and hens, and here the worthy ass may be resting and all sorts of odds and ends are heaped in the corners. The first room, at our host's, is occupied by the *gamusa* or she-buffalo, and a camel. They have no litter as the straw is too dear. The animals lie on a bed of fresh soil which is removed from time to time to serve as manure. A *gamusa* is worth about eighty pounds, a camel fifty to a hundred pounds according to its age and strength. A wife is 'worth' about twenty to thirty pounds in dowry, which has to be returned to the in-laws in the case of a separation: she is more easily replaced than an ox or a camel. However, the fellah treats his wife well so long as she gives him children, preferably sons—they mean more help in the fields, and the problem of feeding more mouths is hardly thought of.

Awshim is a very large village which would pass for a town in Europe. It has 25,000 inhabitants according to the man who keeps the post-office, who is a 'scholar' because he can read and write and discuss the wireless programmes and sometimes the newspaper. He earns about £7 a month, he is an *efendi*. The word 'agglomeration' would seem to have been invented to describe these Egyptian villages. There isn't an isolated house or a farm in the great flat countryside. They all huddle and stick together to save land.

We go into a so-called rich house. Its owners are comfortably off and send their son to Cairo University to study medicine, to be a real doctor. The student is present and helps us out with his sketchy English. The women are all smiles and attention, bringing us the *tisht* and soap into the courtyard full of poultry and broken pots, for us to freshen ourselves up. They stand round us, laughing. On what they call the 'agricultural' roads through the villages, motorists drive in a cloud of thin dust, even if the peasants throw down a few pailfuls of water from the canal, hardening the mud for a short while.

The two rooms on the ground floor are reserved for the ladies. There are no signs of order: the only furniture is a surprising four-poster bed, in black, lacquered metal patterned with glinting fragments of mirror. There are no sheets on the bed; the cover is in grey cotton, like the mattress. No wardrobe or tables. Chickens and geese come in and out as they please. The men receive their guests on the first floor, in a long room furnished with hard benches running round the walls, which are hung with charming photographs, showing the

312

father dressed as an *efendi*, complete with tarboosh and a Western suit, the elder son looking down proudly in his tight military uniform. All the males in the huge family are shown, cousins, brothers-in-law, grandfathers, but no women.

However, the mistress of the house comes in. She lays a sumptuous meal on the table, which is covered with oil-cloth. Nobody is more generous and hospitable than the Egyptians. As soon as we arrived Miriam killed the fattest goose they had. Now she breaks it up with her fingers and serves enormous helpings to the guests first, then the men of the family. The goose is served with the inevitable *mulukhiya*, a kind of slimy spinach soup which comes as a shock to the European palate but which is a feast in itself for the Egyptians. (It is said that the Caliph Hakim detested this dish and condemned to death all those who ate it. He went mad in the eleventh century—the *mulukhiya* has survived.)

The only dish on the table is the enamelled soup-basin imported from Japan, full of *mulukhiya* into which everyone dips his bread while gnawing at his portion of goose. The bread is very spongy, made of a mixture of maize and flour. It is in the form of two pancakes stuck together at the edges. This unsubstantial bread is delicious just after it leaves the oven, but it is only made once or twice a month in the country. The only drink is water, poured by the housewife into the glass reserved for the guests. The family drink straight out of the jug. In poorer houses the solitary 'glass' is made of tin, usually a fruit-can which is hammered a bit at the smithy and sold for a penny. Manufactured things are expensive, beyond the fellah's means.

A little girl clears the table, the remains of the food being taken into the courtyard, where it will be finished by the women and children. Anything that is left will be given to the poor, following the Koran's rule of charity, the bones being given to the animals. Nothing is wasted. It is unusual to find a reception-room like this one. Only the notables, richer merchants like our hosts, or the mayor himself, have such a room. It is hardly ever used except when there are guests. In all other houses two or three rooms, all of them alike, are used for everything. The floor is of beaten earth, the windows are tiny because of the heat, the walls are not whitewashed. Sometimes a fellah who has made the pilgrimage to Mecca will decorate the outside with simple, humorous drawings which tell the story of his journey—the train, the boat, the Kaaba, palm-trees and blue waves,

313

all are there, together with the whole family set out in rows, like onions. The Christians, on the other hand, used to narrate their pilgrimage to Jerusalem before the frontier was closed. There you see the priest holding the censer, and angels flying round the walls of the Holy City. These Christian drawings of pilgrimages are to be found chiefly in Upper Egypt.

However, even in the neighbourhood of Cairo it is not unusual to see a church-spire next to a mosque's minaret. While Egypt has about three million orthodox Copts (one inhabitant in every eight is a Christian), about 50,000 are Catholic converts. Thus some villages have a small Latin community of about five or ten families. The Copts are generally even poorer and more sober in their ways than the Moslems, and certainly dirtier. The Coptic peasants are only distinguishable from the others by a blue cross tattooed on the inside of the wrist. But they are no different from their Moslem neighbours in physique, customs or dress. They generally get on well together, except when some peasant vendetta, the curse of Egypt, divides the village and gives rise to bloodshed. In one of the Upper Egypt villages the Catholic priest was thrown into the canal. But it was Moslems who avenged his murder, for here the Christians are the 'clients' of the Moslems, who regard themselves as their protectors.

The *umda* or mayor now welcomes us. He is wearing the same cotton *galabiya* as any peasant, for it is the only clothing suitable for the hot climate. He is rich, with 100 feddans of cotton, some wheat, a Cadillac, children who are away being educated by 'The Sisters' and Jesuits, in Cairo. His house is clean but hardly more luxurious than his neighbour's. He has little to say, thinking no doubt of the threshing of his wheat. We understand that he had been a doctor in Cairo and had a good practice. His father, the village mayor, was assassinated. He took the *galabiya* with his father's inheritance and responsibilities, and has spent two years waiting for a chance to avenge his father by killing his murderers. Thus, especially in Upper Egypt, the endless vendettas go on, the law being powerless to end them. The 'crime against honour', whether it be adultery or mere suspicion, is always plunging Egyptian villages into mourning.

The streets are swarming with unwashed children. Men are dozing in the shadow of the walls. The women gossip on the doorsteps. Yet the fields are covered with toilers, like ants, who never stop from morning till night throughout the year. The fellah fears neither

314

rain nor frost nor snow nor cold. The 'ideal' climate condemns him to work the land without respite, from one year's end to the other.

The Egyptian, whom the Old Testament describes as 'he who treads the water with his feet', is in fact the slave of the water which makes for the land's richness and his own body's misery. One of the paradoxes of this strange country is that the most fertile soil in the world supports the poorest peasants in the world, except perhaps the Indians. The fellah who receives us into his house today has no geese. He shares his meal with us, consisting of over-salted white cheese, raw onions, maize-bread and, as an unusual luxury for him, some hard-boiled eggs dipped in melted butter, or *samna*, of which the Egyptians are very fond. The family consists of the fellah and his wife—the second or third—an old grandfather, now past work, and his broken-down wife, then several children who might belong to anybody, six in all, four boys and two girls, the eldest of whom sometimes goes to school. The others work in the fields or hang about the streets when there is nothing else to do.

The family is supported by two feddans, just over two acres. They grow cotton, wheat, *birsim* or lucerne for the ox, and rice, according to the crop-rotation laid down by the village administration. Of course these crops are not enough. Therefore the fellah has to hire himself out as a labourer: in the 1956 harvest he earned about two shillings a day. Two of his children earn about 14 piastres between them. The whole family of ten people thus lives on about five shillings a day at the outside, that is to say in the good months: allowance also has to be made for the months when there is no work, for the agricultural labourer's work is strictly seasonal. Naturally, the fellah has no idea of how to plan ahead. As soon as he has some money, he uses it. His earnings do not allow for saving. All the family can do is to keep the wolf from the door, and buy a bit of tea, but never meat. They cannot nurse a sick child nor pay for medicines, while there is no medical service to provide them.

The fellahs spend most at the 'feasts' for circumcision or marriage, for which they often get themselves years into debt, and for religious anniversaries such as Mouled el Nabi (the Prophet's birthday) and the two *Bairams*. On such occasions they spend all they have, even what they haven't. They borrow at usurers' rates from moneylenders or the village landowner to buy a new art-silk dress, a *galabiya*, a sequined head-scarf decked with little 'pearls', and some meat, which they only have on such occasions.

Contrary to what is often said, the women work little. Only the girls go to the fields with the boys, drudging in the blazing sun, taking the pests from the cotton-plants and gathering the fragile pods or bolls. They are remarkably nimble at this, advancing untiringly in a long line under the supervisor's eye as he stands protected by a big white sunshade. When they are taller they carry off to the *suq* the household's meagre products, a few skinny chickens, some tiny eggs, some badly churned butter. They sort the corn out grain by grain, or wash clothes in the canal. Above all they carry the water, which is their special task.

If the village has no tap-water laid on—which is the case with more than half the villages in Egypt—they go down to the canal in a long procession and carry at least six or seven gallons a day on their heads, pouring it into the *zir* at home, a great pointed jar of the kind they have used down the centuries. Its porous earthenware keeps the water cool. Water for domestic use is taken from this in a tin scoop.

There is not much difference in the two thousand villages where water has been installed before or since 1956. There are pumps or drinking-fountains in the village squares, and a few houses have a pump in the courtyard, which is used by the neighbours. Dressed in their black *melaya* which trails in the dust, the women come and draw really clean water from the pump: nowadays they tend to appreciate this luxury, but were distrustful at first, regarding the 'creamy' canal-water as richer. But the fellahs are very adaptable, more so than we in Europe, and the modernization of the villages is only awaiting government action.

The European visitor, even when he is already familiar with North Africa, is usually surprised at the women's incredible laziness. They appear to be busy but do no useful work. Their houses are filthy and littered with droppings from the cows or chickens. You have to step over the *gamus* to enter a room, the floor of which has never felt a brush. With few exceptions the womenfolk have forgotten any form of artisanal work or craftsmanship. They neither spin nor weave, they cannot embroider or even sew. They have none of the fine dresses you can see in Palestine or Libya. The village tailor has to be called on to machine the black cotton smock worn by the women, the little girls' flowered dress and the men's *galabiya*.

The men take off their *galabiya* while working in the fields, sometimes also their sleeveless shirt, working in nothing but a slack pair of shorts rolled up on the thighs. The women's robes are long, gathered in with a yoke under the bosom: they don't wear a belt, so that they have plenty of liberty and suffer no discomfort from the heat. The children who have a new dress on the annual feast-day are soon in rags. The women don't bother to mend clothes. If one of them happens to have learnt needlework from the nuns, she becomes the village seamstress and is paid two or three shillings for making a dress up. This is a highly envied position. An old sewing-machine represents a little fortune, or a dowry.

The fellah's wife does little or no cooking. Even if she wanted to her income would hardly allow her to use her imagination. Bread is the staple food, which they eat at midday with a little white cheese and raw onions. They also eat turnips and tasty little cucumbers. Only the evening meal, largely vegetarian, shows any pretence at cooking. That evening we were served with a dish composed of lentils and rice. Another evening they will have a stew of beans or marrow. According to the seasons they eat melons or toasted maize, or gnaw sugar-cane stalks. Both children and adults eat plenty of green lettuce, rather like cos lettuce, which is carelessly washed in none-too-clean water.

Bread accounts for 80 per cent of the fellah's food: he eats an average of about a pound a day. It is a wholemeal bread and very nourishing. The women usually have a primitive 'mill' made of two stones, but they generally take their corn to the communal mill, where they watch the operation closely, gossiping and jesting with the miller. With their hands they scoop up anxiously any loose flour and carry it away in their head-basket. All their loads are carried in this way: we once met a woman with her naked baby sitting in a big tin bowl on his mother's head.

Child care is at a most elementary level. The woman suckles her child as long as she can, until of his own accord he lays hold of any food that comes this way. It is frightening to think of what some of those babies eat. Infantile mortality is still high. As soon as the mother is expecting a new baby she pays little attention to the last one.

In theory, school is compulsory. But many of the 14,000 villages in Egypt have no school to go to. In any case, when there is any, work in the fields comes first: an eminent Egyptian who represented his country in U.N.O. said, 'Egypt is kept going by donkeys and children.' The children's small stature makes them particularly useful for looking after the cotton plants. Their nimble hands are gentle with the valuable bushes. Three or four times in the season the leaves have to be examined against the cotton-worm, which lays its eggs on the underside of the leaf. The branch has to be turned up and the diseased leaves taken off. Working in long ranks, the children move forward at a regular pace, working in this manner for eight or ten hours at a stretch, stopping only once in the blazing sun, when they eat their onion and bread just where they stand. According to their age, whether for this work or for harvesting the crop, they are given five or eight piastres a day. This child-labour is not only the cheapest but the best, and only by watching them at work can one have any idea of their marvellous skill.

So the fellah, hard put to feed himself, wants to have more and more children. Physical debility is so widespread that only the adolescents have enough energy to work the land properly. Men are at their best between the ages of 14 and 19, although 80 per cent of them have to be rejected as unfit for military service. Then their health declines so rapidly that they are like old men, very often, by the age of 40. In Egypt the average age is 27, the same as in France before the 1789 revolution. The average wage in the country is about a pound a month, and 80 per cent of the population is suffering from *bilharzia*. But the under-nourished, sickly fellah must go on ploughing, sowing, hoeing and harvesting, whatever he feels like. And his poor body is progressively weakened by the water with which he feeds the soil.

CONCENTRATION CAMPS

From Alexandria to Luxor the Egyptian countryside offers a picture of intense activity, perpetual movement. Where are the host of asses, camels and men and women bound for? What are all these ants toiling at, when the village we have just left seemed full to bursting with people fast asleep? The country districts have such a surplus of labour that half the population can spend its time napping, without affecting the bustling appearance of the fields. That is why the most hard-working people can give the impression of being the idlest. We should pity the fellah. The whole country is in a state of semi-unemployment all the time. It is estimated that two-thirds of the population are 'unoccupied'. Three times as much land would be needed in order to feed the 23 or 24 millions of Egypt's population in 1956. Eighteen millions of them are the fellahs we are now watching. At prayer-time the peasant kneels in the direction of Mecca, on a space set aside for that purpose, surrounded by a little curb a few centimetres high and sometimes spread with a straw mat. He does not leave his field. When harvest-time comes the fellahs make themselves little huts out of maize-stalks and sleep on the spot so as not to waste a minute. When the Nile rises he stays in the field all night, in case of an emergency.

He leaves home at sunrise, clad all the year round in the same cotton *galabiya*, even though in the Delta region the temperature drops to about 40° Fahrenheit, when he wraps his head in a brown cotton scarf. There is no wool, as the land has no pasturage and bears no sheep. On his shoulder he carries his *fas* or short-handled hoe which has been the same for four thousand years, except that the end is now made of steel. He has no spade, barrow or cart. His ass follows in his wake, carrying the primitive plough which is the same as can be seen in the murals of Egyptian tombs, but again the share has now changed to steel. Two thin bull-calves, sometimes even a *gamus* or a camel, which look strange yoked together, will be harnessed to that antediluvian machine which merely scratches the soil without turning it over. But that will be enough. There is no automatic transport or power—wheels are practically unknown on the land.

The fellah's main work is connected with irrigation, beginning with levelling his land. You see a boy of six playing in the mud: actually he is levelling a foot or two of earth. He leaves neither humps nor hollows, knowing the value of his little effort. His father has squared his field up into patches about four yards square, each with a little bank round it. He has no proper instrument for levelling with and trusts to his own eye, which is pretty accurate. Unless the ground is perfectly flat the soil easily loses value. The humps receive no water and grow nothing, the hollows fill with salt, since the Egyptian subsoil, especially in the Delta region, is highly saline. When the ground is well prepared about six or seven inches of water are enough. Later it has to be drained off, so that the muddy soil will not be too soaked and rot the roots.

It hardly ever rains in Egypt. Cairo has drains for taking away rain, but in three years the present writers have experienced only ten showers lasting ten minutes. Only on the Mediterranean coastal belt is there any fall, enough to spread a green coat over the desert in

319

winter and spring. It does not rain in the Nile Valley. But if the life and toils of the *fellahin* have remained unchanged for five thousand years, irrigation has been completely transformed. In the past, between July and October the rising Nile used to spread its mud-laden water over the squared-off fields. They used to sow the seed in the fresh mud, without ploughing, in autumn, then reap the harvest in May or June of the following year. The earth lay fallow all the summer, accumulating oxygen, until the new river flood brought more water and natural manure. So there was only one harvest a year.

It was Mohamed Ali who decided to introduce all-the-year-round irrigation in order to intensify the whole system of agriculture. They dug canals and channels of all kinds which now make up a whole system about 18,000 miles long. Starting from the main canal, down to the ditch feeding the individual field, the water network is extremely complex. The canal-water always has to be raised, somehow, to the field-level. Various kinds of machines, usually archaic, are used for raising the water. In Upper Egypt they use *sakiehs*, like the *norias* of North Africa, consisting of a vertical wheel fitted with pitchers, which creaks all day while an ox, with a sack over its eyes, turns endlessly in a circle, a little boy sitting on its back singing his two-note song. These wheels usually belong to a group of fellahs, since no one of them could own both a wheel and an ox. Often in Lower Egypt the *sakiehs* and their scoops are made of metal, but they are not much more efficient. There are about 16,000 such wheels in the country.

The *shaduf* is still more primitive. Ancient frescoes have familiarized us with the long beam or pole, weighted at one end and with a skin-bag or pitcher at the other. When the fellah has to raise the water more than two or three yards he rigs up a system of *shadufs* at different levels: we have seen four at a time being used in this way to bring the water from the Nile itself into the riverside fields. There are about 50,000 of these *shadufs* in all.

When the water has only to be raised about a yard or a metre, the fellah's favourite device is the Archimedes screw. This is a wooden cylinder about two yards long and eighteen inches wide containing a wooden spiral. The spiral is turned by a handle and makes the water rise in the tube. To do this the fellah has to stand with his legs in the canal, working the tool in front of him. This is a very tiring job, but it gives good results. Such a screw costs about seven pounds, which is dear enough, but of course Egypt is short of wood. The most up-to-date models are protected with a zinc covering. Every village has its craftsman who specializes in making and repairing these screws, which are extensively used, there being about 250,000 in use.

On State lands and large estates you find much more modern machinery, such as pumping-stations, threshers and tractors. There are about 12,000 of the latter in Egypt. Only cotton and rice-growing are not mechanized. There are about 2,500 diesel pumps. These figures give some idea of the balance between traditional and modern methods of agriculture.

After irrigating and sowing the fellah harvests his corn and rice. Bent almost double, he does this with a sickle. As the stalks are cut they are heaped up in the open, since the dryness means that crops do not need to be stored indoors. For treading out the ears, the corn or rice is arranged in a vast crown-shaped heap, over which they drive a *nurag*, consisting of a heavy wooden sledge mounted on sharp discs. Oxen or she-buffalo drag it along, with a child driving them, as it neatly cuts the stalks of straw. There are always two sharp points sticking out from the sledge: these serve no practical purpose, but are one of the few fantasies that liven the fellah's drab existence: they are phallic symbols, emblems of fertility. When they have been cut apart the grain and straw are made into two heaps which the men winnow in the wind. Sometimes in the sweltering midday heat we have seen fellahs sitting on the ground, 'waiting for a breeze', like so many pirates. The grain is finally collected into the *shunas* or barns belonging to landowners or banks: one is astonished to read the words 'Barclay's Bank' or 'Land Bank' written on the notices over heaps of corn in the middle of a field. The fellah is often up to his ears in debt and all his fortune is there, the property of the bank, on the other side of a thin fence or wall, without him being able to touch a penny of it. As we shall see, agrarian indebtedness is one of the greatest evils in Egypt.

SHAM EL NESSIM—THE SPRING FESTIVAL

Sham el Nessim, the Spring Festival, is the most unique and popular festival in Egypt, though it has dozens of others. It is a survival from pagan beliefs and early in Christian times was fixed as the first Sunday after Easter. It is the most authentic symbol of peasant and African Egypt. Celebrating the rebirth of the land in a manner that goes far back before the Koran or the New Testament, it also provides for both the Moslem and the Christian population. In the towns everyone pours into the parks or open spaces. The whole population piles in to wagons or old carriages. Even the most town-loving land-owner has to go and see his *'izba* or country house at this time.

He takes all his friends and acquaintances with him. M . . . with whom we went, followed the usual custom. We had to leave the holiday atmosphere of Cairo very early on the Sunday morning, as one is expected to eat breakfast out in the country as a kind of tribute to the rural gods. We eat *ful* or beans, hard-boiled eggs, little fresh onions and a peculiar kind of fish called *fisir* which is only eaten on that particular day of the year. Thus the divinities of both earth and water are propitiated.

The black servant has gone ahead of us to open the *'izba's* windows, which have been too long closed. The owner only goes there for a few days a year, either to supervise the harvest if he is conscientious enough, or else to spend an occasional week-end. It is a pretty white house, colonial-style, hidden away in the palm-trees. There are flowers—which are rare things in Egypt—geraniums, bougainvillea, delphiniums, all the way down from the verandah to the bathing-pool. The house is comfortable inside, with roomy arm-chairs, bathrooms, a refrigerator. Our hosts were dispossessed of their land, or rather of some of it, by the Agrarian Reform laws, but they are honest enough to admit that their 300 remaining feddans of good land enable them to live comfortably, giving an income of some £500 a month . . . They do not administer their own property, as landowners almost always live in Cairo. The Agrarian Reform has hardly disturbed their way of living, except to curb its lavishness a little. The estate usually consists of the *'izba* and a number of small villages. One of Faruk's former estates at Zafaran, near Mansura, had sixteen villages, each of two hundred families, which are now administered by the Agrarian Reform Committee. Our friend M . . .'s estate has only two villages. They have provided pleasant and clean housing for their fellahs, with baked brick foundations and walls in crude mud-brick as is usual in Egypt. Being not far from Cairo, the property has running water and electricity. The streets are lit up, but any fellah wanting electric light in his home has to lay it on himself from the mains. Most of them prefer to use spirit lamps, which are more economical. There is a pump in the public square but so far none of the fellahs have water in their houses, nor are there drains or gutters. But these houses which belong to the landowner are cleaner and better looked after than those of the normal village *fellahin*.

Most of the peasants rent strips of 1, 2 or 3 feddans, and hire themselves out to work on the rest. Thus they are both tenants and wage-earners, which is usually the case in Egypt. It is unusual to find any direct farming of the great estates by their owners. The absent landowner prefers to let his land for prices going up to as much as £50 per feddan, roughly £50 per acre, or at least until the Agrarian Reform of 1952, which will be described later. Any more direct farming is left to his overseer. His office might employ quite a number of people. All the owner has to do is to collect rents and profits, but all down the scale it is the peasant who has to bear the brunt of the different forms of exploitation.

It has been wrongly said that the agricultural structure of Egypt is feudal. It is a handy formula but does not apply except, perhaps, when it comes to an economic analysis. A feudal lord is one who lives on his land and exploits it directly, governing and literally possessing both the land and the people on it and having his own financial, political and legal system. He lives by barter, paying his serfs and workers in kind. Having little money for his own needs, he can yet live well, while having power over those who live on his land. He feeds them, gives them in marriage, punishes and rewards them. Such was the land-system in Poland or South America before the recent war. It is still to be found on large estates in southern Morocco. Feudalism is a kind of paternalist autarky.

Where Egypt is concerned it would be more accurate to term it land-capitalism. The owner collects rents or lives on the revenues from lands he farms himself, while living in the city and often travelling abroad. With few exceptions the large landowner does not know his fellahs, takes no interest in their welfare and is indifferent to their physical or mental health. His only thought is his income from the land. The more civilized and progressive of them, such as Prince Toussoun, had reached the stage of paternalism. They must have been aware that the better he is fed and treated the better the fellah will work, the more he will bring in. In the above analysis, we have left out of account the owners who live on their land and who are, generally, much less open to reproach.

Socially this form of land-capitalism is less humane than feudalism, since the latter allowed for a certain generosity, depending on the personal quality of those men who wielded such power. By attacking land-capitalism the military government has still not overthrown the country's old land economy nor its political structure, but has none the less tended to restore the peasant's dignity.

MEN THAT MAN HAS FORGOTTEN

Egyptian children are good-looking and intelligent. The little fellah is full of mischief and wit. He is quick to learn, in school. Mechanics and electricians of a good standard are produced by the technical colleges, which are too few. The girls can make excellent child-welfare workers, midwives and doctors. Both the girls and boys tend to aim at the liberal professions, whereas they are genuinely gifted for more practical trades. There are enormous numbers of *noktas*, boy street vendors hawking 'Coke' or delivering dresses and suits for the dry-cleaners. They all have the same round head of the typical fellah, green or black eyes glinting with fun. The young middle-class youths who study at the French Lycée or with the Catholic Brothers or the Jesuits do very well.

How is it, then, that the nation as a whole gives such a depressing appearance of passiveness, slowness, shapelessness, dirt? It is partly through ignorance and partly through physical poverty. Atlas lifting the world on his shoulders had no greater a task than the government in trying to rid this country of its evils.

The Egyptian is poor because he has not enough land. He is sick because he is poor and lives in the water. He is ignorant because for thousands of years he has been held down in a state of mental and physical bondage. The word Egyptian always conjures up a picture of the fellah. That is because the mass of the Egyptian population is not simply a class in the usual sense: the fellah, the *fellahin*, are the whole body of Egypt. Not only because out of 23 million inhabitants 17 or 18 million live on the land, but because the city population itself is often so close to rural conditions that sociologically the townsman is to be identified with the fellah. The *petite bourgeoisie* still has many links with the land, and the poorer districts of Cairo, with over 2 million inhabitants, are more like a village than a town.

A hundred years ago the Egyptian was stronger and healthier than his descendants of today. At the present time it is the southerner, the Saïdian, who is a finer human specimen than the Egyptian of the Delta. Taller, thinner, darker, these men are called on for heavy jobs which are beyond the strength of the northern fellah. It is the all-the-year-round irrigation system which is to blame for this. In Upper Egypt, where the system is not everywhere in force, the fellah lives with the rhythm of the water, waiting for the flood to subside in order to farm his land. But where there is permanent irrigation the same water that feeds the land afflicts the fellah.

He lives all day with his feet and often part of his upper body in water and mud. He cleans out the canals and ditches, standing thigh-deep in the stinking ooze, which he takes out to spread over his field. He turns the Archimedes screw with his feet in the water which covers his field for half the year. Everything he does, planting, dressing the soil, weeding, is carried on in the same unhealthy dampness. Then it becomes so hot that the animals and children throw themselves into the canal to keep cool and to clean off the horrible muddy dust which clings to the pores. And half of them drink the polluted water.

The water in the ditches and canals and even in the Nile shallows is infested with a death-giving parasite, the *bilharzia*. This is a tiny mollusc, the larvae of which enter the body through the skin. This parasite undermines the whole organism, attacking the bladder and the kidneys, causing ulcers and fistulas, completely upsetting the intestines. Contaminated faeces are returned to the canal and the cycle of disease is complete. This frightful, endemic disease has affected 80 per cent of the population, including about 95 per cent of the fellahs, the parasite being less common in the towns. People with this sickness do not feel any acute pain but waste away slowly, so that a boy of fifteen easily looks stronger than his father.

The peasant who remains free of this water-parasite can well fall a victim to the earth-parasite. Anchylosetomiasis is the more terrible disease of the two, though it is less frequent. It spreads from the soil and human offal. The fellah never uses human manure but tends to leave faeces anywhere. If he is already sick the larvae multiply in the wet soil and, making their way into the palms of the fellah's naked feet, attack the intestines. Peasants suffering from these two forms of disease may spend about twenty years in a state of exhaustion and anaemia. Little real effort can be expected of them. Most of the fellahs are attacked by the two diseases at the same time.

Malaria is still common in the Delta rice-fields, in the north-east, and about 90 per cent of the people in that region are a prey to it. The fellah is so vitiated by these different forms of sickness that he accepts them as natural to his lot. He collaborates only half-heartedly with the health service's efforts to stamp them out. He will only take more positive steps himself when he is better educated than at present.

The toll taken by these three diseases is further increased by all kinds of diseases of the eye. The fellah, whether in his village or in the fields, is always enveloped in a sort of powdered dust. The wind blows more dust from the desert, the strong sun burns his eyes, and meanwhile flies are busy at their work of spreading microbes. We did not see a single child with perfectly healthy eyes, in any of the villages we visited between Damietta and the Sudanese frontier. There are countless people who have lost the use of one eye, and many who are completely blind. Statistics put these cases at *half a million*, but that falls short of the truth. Added to this, there is only one doctor to every 4,000 people.

But perhaps the worst affliction of all is under-nourishment and all its attendant evils. If 90 per cent of the population are the victims of parasitic diseases, the entire population suffer from deficiency diseases, the most acute being pellagra and troubles arising from lack of vitamins. The countryfolk lack more than doctors, they merely need more meat and the simple foodstuffs that the earth provides for all but the land-worker.

Seventy-five per cent of Egyptians, that is to say 95 per cent of the fellahs, are illiterate. The concept of the peasant-serf whose only use is to work the land has kept the peasant in a state of total ignorance for centuries. Of course since 1906 there has been a great effort towards basic education. In 1950 the Wafdist Minister of Education, Taha Husain, passed a law for compulsory education. At the same time the building and providing equipment went ahead, so that now a new school is being opened every day. (Against this last figure one has to set an even more impressive one: two children are born every minute in Egypt, that is to say, more than 3,000 every day, of whom two-thirds survive.) But however great the effort in this direction may be, it comes up against an evil which has so far made a mockery of the compulsory-education law, and that is the use of child-labour in the fields.

The fellah children love school, but how is the family to do without their wages? Even when something is done towards sending the boys to school, the girls are kept at home or on the land. The military government has tried to tackle the problem of illiteracy, but nothing will come of this so long as there is no way of controlling the use of child-labour. Whatever happens, the results will only be felt in the next generation.

SPINELESS VILLAGES

The greatest hindrance to modernizing rural life lies in the fact that it is both gregarious and individualistic. We saw evidence of this when going through the enormous villages which were nothing but a heap of houses cut through by straggling lanes. They are neither communities nor social unities of any kind. The Egyptian has no idea of social or civic organization. There is no corporate life, nothing resembling, for instance, the Moroccan *jama'a*. All authority is vested in Cairo and is wielded through the *umda* who represents it. The *umda*, who has to be richer than his fellow-citizens and must own at least 10 feddans of land, is all-powerful. He can administer justice to the first degree, can imprison a person for 24 hours without trial, directs the rotation of crops, helps to gather the taxes, and with the aid of 25 *ghaffirs* or auxiliary police maintains law and order in the village. He is not paid for all this but enjoys many privileges, such as partial exemption from tax, and exemption from *corvée* or public labour, as well as military service for his sons. His functions are often made hereditary. The *umda* is a local dictator, feared by the fellah who humbles himself before him and offers him small presents in the hope of keeping on the right side of him. A bill introduced in 1956 aimed at the appointment of *umda* being made by ballot. The fellah thus has no share in the public life of his own village. Even when he exercised a semblance of power by sending a Member to Parliament, it can hardly be said that he ever voted. The whole procedure used to be a cross between forced labour and a village festival. Until now the fellah has never known the slightest liberty under any form of government, and no sign of initiative has ever been asked of him. Whatever name the régime cares to give itself in Cairo, the Egyptian peasant remains the slave of the soil and a puppet in the hands of the State. Since Mahomed Ali with the introduction of cotton-growing and of permanent irrigation, the countryman has done nothing but decline. The Ministries of Agriculture and Public Works distribute water, determine the annual acreage for cotton according to international supply and demand, of corn according to foreign stock-exchange prices, of rice according

327

to the available water-supply. The administration also fixes the crop-rotation, decides what types of cotton are to be grown, buys it at its own price. The fellah in the hands of the administration makes one think of Chaplin in *Modern Times*, at the mercy of the machine.

A directed economy, political dictatorship and land-capitalism keep the fellah in a state of submission and dependence. One of the most unpleasant facts to be drawn from a study of this agrarian society is that the collective use of labour has never resulted in creating a community existence. The world of the peasant is closed and suspicious, and within it is the equally closed world of each family. Their gregarious life is not a communal one. It is a kind of organic existence ruled by taboos and arbitrary orders, under pressure from the sheikh and the *abuna*, the barber-circumciser and the witch-doctor (for in spite of Islam and Christianity, magic plays a fundamental part in the country). There is, however, a kind of peasant solidarity, but it is almost always 'against' something or other, against some foreign enemy, against thieves or over-inquisitive people. But there is little bond of feeling from family to family, although charity is respected in accordance with the Koran: nobody in a village is ever allowed to die of hunger. But they have no conception of the public good or of collective unity. We happened to pass twice, at an interval of six months, through a village in which there was an enormous hole in the middle of the main thoroughfare. Nobody had thought of filling it in, though it was a general nuisance. But when a new schoolmaster, abashed at such a lack of initiative, decided to form a group of youths to do the job, they turned up without the slightest protest and mended the road free of charge. They were all full of praise for the schoolmaster's cleverness. At harvest-time everybody becomes suspicious, as the crop left in the open air might easily be stolen. At night the whole village sleeps, so to speak, with one eye open, and shots are fired for no apparent reason. Grudges and jealousy set family against family and crimes and punishments carry on from one generation to the next. It is an honour to take revenge, so the police are kept out of it.

The only things which reunite the village are the danger of a flood and the raids made by the police.

If the Egyptian peasant is such a poor citizen so far as his village is concerned, it might be asked whether he is at all conscious of his Egyptian citizenship. When we went visiting country districts, always in the company of some Egyptians from Cairo, the fellahs regarded us all equally as foreigners. It was quite clear to us that the village is a little world of its own and on its own: there was nothing in common in dress, behaviour or even language between the villager and the townsman. The main road rarely passes through the village, which is hidden, about 100 or so yards from the road, behind a clump of trees along the canal. Tourists pass by without looking into the village. It is so unusual to visit a village that when we crossed the Nile at Sohag in order to pass through two or three villages on the other side, on our return in the evening we found a policeman waiting for us at our hotel. During the day he had heard that some 'foreigners', people from Cairo, had come into the district. It has to be added that the Upper Egypt people are easy to take offence. This policeman questioned us very politely:

'What interests you about this uninteresting part of the country? It appears that you bought some peasant shawls. Do you intend to make fun of us in Cairo?'

It was hard for us to persuade him that we were attracted by the beauty of the landscape—the grey villages surmounted by those beautiful pigeon-cotes which are, so to speak, the cathedrals of Egypt—by the picturesque handwork done by the women, which is rare in the country, and wished to see Fr. Ayrout's Christian Schools. Only the last of these items seemed to him at all convincing. This onion-district had never seen a tourist before and perhaps it will never see one again. For a time he was worried over the shawls, until the hotel-keeper soothed his conscience by explaining that the Cairo people were odd folk, called 'Zistantialistes' (Existentialists)... This unknown word, pronounced as it was in Arabic by a travelled man, was regarded as a magic formula. This happened in 1955, in a township of almost 100,000 inhabitants.

SMALL-HOLDINGS, RENTS AND WAGES

Egypt is an oasis between two deserts. Its exploitable area is only 3 per cent of its total surface, 1,200 square yards per consumer. The Egyptian part of the Nile Valley contains 13,000 square miles, which supports 24 million inhabitants. These figures can be set against those of Belgium, where 11,500 square miles support seven million inhabitants, thanks to its mineral, industrial and colonial wealth, of which Egypt has none. Egypt's density of rural population is 1,425 people to the square mile as compared with 190 in France. It reaches 2,200 in more densely populated areas, and 1,950 per square mile is frequent. These are huge figures, once it is realized that we are speaking of an almost entirely agricultural economy.

The land in question stretches for 1,200 kilometres (about 750 miles) along the Nile, which has already covered 3,000 miles before reaching Egypt. The valley is only a kilometre (five-eighths of a mile) wide at the Sudan frontier and gradually broadens to 5 kilometres (three miles) at Idfu, 10 kilometres at Luxor, 25 kilometres at Beni Suef. Then it spreads into the huge delta from Cairo onwards. Between the mouths of the two branches of the Nile at Rosetta and Damietta, it is a distance of 260 kilometres (161 miles). Beside the valley there is only one useful oasis, the Fayum, south-west of Cairo: this province has been fabulously rich ever since ancient times. There the land is quite uniform, with never a stone or a stretch of gravel: the muddy silt of the Nile is 15 metres in depth on the average and has a high mineral value. There is neither rain nor tributary in all this land. The country's very existence is a political problem.

Agriculture depends entirely on the working of the irrigation system. The permanent distribution system covers five-sixths of the land and now permits of four crops in two years. It is one of the most intensive methods of farming in the world. Crops are yielded by 9,500,000 feddans, whereas only 6,000,000 feddans are actually cultivated. However, the soil's fantastic fertility is not enough to make up for the gap between production and over-population: 9 million crop-yielding acres cannot feed 24 million people.

Egypt is a country of small-holders, even, shall we say, very small holders. Two million peasants own less than a feddan and 500,000 have less than one to two feddans, or less than two acres. Against these small-holdings we have to set the large estates. Two and a half million individuals own one-third of the cultivable land, while another third is owned by only 12,500. Ninety-four per cent of owners possess only 35 per cent of the land, whereas in 1950, 61 land-bosses owned 117,000 hectares, that is to say, 4,800 acres apiece. Between these extremes there are 1,300 owners who each have over 100 hectares (240 acres).

Yet another way of defining this curious agrarian structure is by pointing out that 2 per cent of the landowners held half of the entire land before the Agrarian Reform. The 'large' estates are in fact enormous, and there are few of medium size. The breaking up of property finds its explanation in the Koran, by which each male child inherits two parts, each female one part. Children are numerous, so that in two generations a fine property of 50 feddans can be divided beyond recognition.

Recent calculations show that the minimum requirement for a family of 8 persons would be 5 feddans. This shows that the fellah has to supplement his property either by letting part of his land, or as a wage-earner under some richer neighbour, or by working in all three ways together. Rural society is thus divided into nine categories of people: the large landowner; the medium landowner (representing the still small numbers of the *bourgeoisie* who live on the land); the small owner-farmer; the main tenant who sub-lets to the small tenant; the small owner-cum-tenant; the small, wage-earning owner-tenant; the permanent wage-earner; the casual wage-earner.

As the small properties are too small and the large ones too large, letting or renting is the most widespread means of farming in Egypt.

There are two factors which make this system harmful to the country's economy and ruinous for the fellah. First, the lack of land results in a cruel see-saw between supply and demand. Second, the fellah's passion for land together with his improvidence lead him to accept almost any terms of rental, so that he falls in debt for life and becomes to all intents and purposes his creditor's slave. These factors result in shocking abuses, with hordes of profiteers renting land in order to sub-let in little strips, living as parasites and doing no farming themselves. The structure of Egyptian agriculture is one of a declining series of sub-lets. As we shall see later the military government has successfully begun its struggle against this scourge by controlling rents and obliging those who live on the land to farm it themselves. Before 1952 there was anything from rents for tiny strips of land (1 *qirat* or about 200 square yards) going up to as much as £130 per hectare (2·4 acres). Whereas in France rent works out at about three to six hundredweights of corn, in Egypt it is four times as much.

This lack of balance is made worse by a religious factor, which is that Islam does little towards preserving the dignity of labour. The Arabic word *fellah* comes from the verb *felaha*, work. But in spite or because of this the expression 'ya fellah' is used as an insult. The Koran does nothing to glorify farming and it is said that the Prophet exclaimed, on seeing a plough, 'Where such things go, humiliation follows.'

However passionate his attachment to the land the Egyptian thus prefers not to cultivate it. His dearest ambition is to make a poorer man than himself work for him. After the sub-let and the sub-sub-let there comes the wage-earner, who is the most exploited of all. As soon as he has enough for immediate needs the peasant stops work, for he would regard it as absurd to make any further effort. The only bait that will make him work more is the idea of buying land. But there is none to be had.

This is how the letting works. We have a friend who lives in Cairo. The Agrarian Reform left him with 250 feddans. He complains bitterly about this, but it was not enough to make him set to work himself. His *nazir* or overseer directs the farming of 150 feddans. The other 100 are given out for rent to 45 fellahs, of whom 25 have rented 1 feddan each, 23 of them between 1 and 9 feddans and only one of them rents 10 feddans. This gives an average of about 2 acres or 2 feddans per family. Most of them actually possess a small patch of land of their own. Added to this, it is these same tenants who are working as labourers on the 150 feddans managed by the *nazir*.

In that particular region rents have been fixed at £18 per feddan, so that for his rented land the owner has an income of £1,800, and since his 150 farmed feddans bring in about £3 apiece, they yield him £4,500. His total income for these 250 feddans in 1955 was £6,300 per annum. The more adequately supplied tenants have managed to make ends meet, but the 41 tenants of 2 feddans apiece or less have fallen into debt, either towards their landlord or towards the new Agricultural Bank. As for the wage-earners, in spite of the minimum wage fixed by law at 18 piastres per day, the men only earned 12, the women 8 and the children 5.

Before the Agrarian Reform in 1952 almost all the smaller fellahs were in debt. We have been able to see the accounts of the *daira* or estate of Faruk at Zafarana. All the families of his fellahs were in debt, some of them since several generations back. The fellah does not look very far ahead and rents land beyond his means, always gambling on good cotton years without remembering that the market might weaken the following year. As we shall see, the Agrarian Reform has by no means been able to overcome all these evils. The peasant is so poorly off that his earnings are hardly enough to cover his inadequate diet and costly tea. They certainly do not enable him to buy all his land needs, such as fertilizer, seed and insecticides. It means ruin for him if the cotton-worm attacks his plants. The next year he will try to hire some more land in order to recoup his losses, but runs a great risk of getting deeper into trouble.

The tenant has no initiative. He does not even choose the plot he is going to pay rent for. It is the overseer or manager who applies the government's rulings, telling him which areas he has to sow with corn, and what the crop-rotation must be. He also directs the irrigation, looking after canal and ditch maintenance which he charges against the tenant's harvest. The peasant is thus directed by both the State and the local boss. This is why the tenants' yields are much the same, in proportion, as those of the large estates.

The landowner usually houses his tenant, provides him with livestock as well as some of his seed and manure and insecticides. But it is he who arranges the sale of the harvested crop, deducting these various services from the revenue, as well as the rent for the land.

The wage-earner is in an even worse situation. There is no word for it but poverty. We have already mentioned the average wages for 1956: 12 piastres for men, 8 for women and 5 for children, all for a day of 10 to 12 hours' work. But they can fall below that, depending on the harvest or world prices. In 1954 in the onion-growing district of Sohag (onions are the second largest export) the men were paid 4 piastres a day (about $9\frac{1}{2}d$.) for picking. A woman could be seen weeping because her doctor had prescribed penicillin for her baby—at what cost? Those wage-earners who are permanently hired on some large estate are the least desperately off. They are housed, are sometimes allowed to grow a few vegetables for their families and sometimes these dependants are also taken on by the landlord. Though this is rare enough, if the landlord happens to live on his land a vaguely patriarchal relationship is set up, with at least some human touch about it.

Certain wage-earners, the *tamallias*, are given a plot of ground in return for their labour. They are not allowed to grow cotton on it but they can keep poultry from which their wives can sell a few eggs. The system would be more acceptable if the plots allowed them were somehow related to their family needs and not given according to the price of cereals, particularly maize. As the price of maize has increased the landlords had a tendency from 1954 to 1956 to reduce these plots of land, from an average of half a hectare to a quarter of a hectare or three-fifths of an acre.

The *tarhilas* or temporary hands are recruited by agents who take

6 to 8 per cent of their meagre salary. Most of them come from Upper Egypt. Either because permanent irrigation is less widespread in Upper Egypt, so that there is a surplus of labour for a few months, or because they are poorer yet healthier than the people of the North, the Saïdians undertake the hardest forms of labour and give better results. They are used for navvying, building embankments, digging and cleaning out drains and canals, and for harvesting. So small is their pay (10 to 12 piastres a day) that they often bring enough food from home to last them the season, consisting of bread, onions and lentils. Thus they manage to put something aside, sending almost all their earnings back home in the South.

But it is not only the menfolk who are 'imported' in this way. As soon as there is any cause for alarm, such as the advent of the cotton worm, the trains and lorries bring in masses of boys and girls between 10 and 12 years old, who are experts at disinfesting these plants. They are given from 5 to 7 piastres a day, less the 6 per cent taken by the agent, and work and live in indescribable conditions, labouring for 12 hours a day under the taskmaster's pitiless eye. One day on a model farm a little girl gave us a demonstration of her skill, in return for which we gave her 5 piastres. The child was nonplussed and did not dare to close her hand. The overseer remarked, 'That's her day's pay.' At noon she and her companions were each given a tiny flap of bread, thin as a pancake, together with a raw onion and a morsel of white cheese.

It is estimated that at present the average annual income of these two types of fellah (*tamallias* and *tarhilas*) is some £20 *per family*. Their food is almost entirely vegetarian. However, they have to buy '*gaz*' for cooking; sugar (about eightpence a pound), tea (fourteen shillings a pound), rice (sevenpence) and lentils (a shilling). The poorest cottons are nearly two shillings a yard: the simplest *galabiya* for a man costs twelve shillings, a woman's *melaya*, a pound; a pair of men's shoes thirty shillings, and women's shoes a pound. Children going to school have to have a smock or overall and shoes, costing at least fourteen shillings per child. Most of the little ones go to school barefoot.

OVER-POPULATION

However low it is already, the fellah's income is being reduced from year to year. This is caused by the pressure of population in the Nile Valley.

Herodotus, and later the seventeenth-century explorers Thévenot and Vansleb, described Egypt as a rich country. The Hebrew slaves of Moses' time pined for the 'flesh-pots' of Egypt. The fellah has been impoverished because the rise of population is beyond the land's resources. The population is rising at the rate of half a million a year, a man a minute. 1955 beat all records, with 750,000 survivors out of a million births. In spite of every effort since the turn of the century, and especially by the military government recently, over-population is overtaking the relatively modest economic advance of the country. At the present rate of increase Egypt will have 50 million inhabitants in the year 2000. What are they to live on?

In the last fifty years the individual income has decreased by 25 per cent, while the population has increased from 10 to 23 million souls. Whereas the world-population is increasing by 1 per cent per annum, this country in which the land under cultivation can only be extended by superhuman efforts is increasing at $2\frac{1}{2}$ per cent. In the country areas the density of population is 2,200 to the square mile. In the towns the situation is even more remarkable. In Cairo there are more than 31,000 to the square mile, rising to 287,000 in the Bab el Sharia area. In 1914, $12\frac{1}{2}$ million Egyptians shared $3\frac{1}{2}$ million tons of cereals between them, but in 1940 there were only 4 million tons for 17 million people. What is the reason for such an increase?

The first cause for the change in population is the improvement in hygiene. In the nineteenth century, habitual, long-term diseases replaced epidemic diseases. In the twentieth century the former have been attacked and, however gradually, the rate of mortality has been improved. This has affected the young particularly, the infantile mortality-rate having passed from 28 per 1,000 in 1944 to 19 per 1,000 in 1952. At the same time there are far more births, for as half the population is under 21 years of age, there are more and more men and woman capable of producing children.

These causes are to be found in most countries, but there are also local ones. The Koranic law allows a husband to put away his wife, thus there is a succession of wives, each of whom may be several times a mother. (Polygamy need hardly be taken into account, having dropped to $1\frac{1}{2}$ per cent of the total.) A man has only to repeat 'I put you away' three times for his wife and her children to be banned his house. This is more frequent in the towns than in the country, where the family is a more closely-knit unit. We met several 'repudiated' wives in Cairo. Aliya was twenty years old. Her husband put her away with her two children to 'take a younger wife who would earn more'. She sent the children to her mother in the village. Two mouths more for the old mother to feed. Within a few weeks Aliya was remarried and already pregnant. It is regarded as shameful for a married woman to fail to have children. A husband repudiating his wife is, in law, expected to repay her part of her dowry and to make some provision for the children. But the bulk of the population cannot afford to have the law enforced. Aliya was first a mother at 16: at the age of 20 she was expecting her fourth child, from a second husband.

The economic factors on the land are still more important. In view of the use of child-labour, a fellah regards a child as part of his capital. He is quick to reckon what a child will bring in, while forgetting what it will cost to keep him. He is hardly aware that his assets go down from year to year, that his field is more and more split up between the family, or that there is less work to be had. Under-employment means that out of every two fellahs one will be unemployed, or they will both be semi-employed. But he goes on increasing his children: 10 feddans of cotton employ 500 adults and 1,500 children.

If Egypt's agricultural wealth does not enrich the farmer, it is not only because of the shocking distribution of property or the pressure of population. It is also because at present the farming is speculative, rather than being geared to living requirements. Egypt sells cotton and buys wheat. Its two main products, cotton and rice, are almost entirely grown for export. Most of the cotton is exported raw. Rice is regarded as a great luxury in the country where it is grown. Of the abundant crops, only sugar-cane is consumed in the country itself.

The introduction of all-the-year-round irrigation was an enormous technical progress, but failed to raise the peasant's standard of living for any length of time. It brought an improvement only in the speculative crops, while demanding a greater effort on the fellah's part and crippling him with disease. On the other hand, it enriched the big landowners, that is to say some 300 or 400 families, who made colossal fortunes in the course of about fifty years.

Egyptian farming products consist of three food-crops, wheat, maize and sugar-cane; one fodder-crop, *birsim;* one semi-speculative crop, which is rice; one industrial crop, cotton.

In actual fact, everything else is overshadowed by one crop: we might almost speak in terms of monoculture. Cotton brings in £70 million a year, which is a lot for a country whose budget is about £200 million. In the Cairo agricultural museum there is an old seventeenth-century engraving showing the 'wool-tree', in the form of a sheep. But as we have seen, it was only in the nineteenth century that cotton took a firm hold and began to expand. It was encouraged by the land system as well as by the soil and water conditions, climate and labour. Now the yield and quality are the best in the world. Egypt farms only 2 per cent of the total area but manages to produce 6 per cent of the world's cotton. In relation to area, Egypt produces three times more than might be expected. The Egyptian yields are twice those obtained in America, while the length of the fibre ensures it first place in the international market.

A third of the land is given over to cotton, which is as much as is devoted to cereals. As crop-rotation is half-yearly—as in the Delta —or thrice yearly, three or four crops are obtained in two years, or four crops in three years. On a particular field the crops are grown as follows: April to October, cotton; November to April, wheat or barley; May to November, rice or maize; December to March, *birsim* for fodder. That is to say, so as not to overtax the soil the crops are alternated in three main categories: winter crops from October to April, cereals, vegetables and *birsim*. Summer crops from April to October, cotton, sugar-cane and rice. Then between July and November there is the Nile harvest which is maize. The sugar-cane has to remain two years in the soil. After the first harvest, especially round Luxor, you see enormous fires round the ruins of Thebes, flaring throughout the night, when the fellahs are busy burning the leaves and stubble from the cane. The ashes make a good natural manure.

Cotton-growing is practically gardening, more like horticulture than agriculture. It demands daily attention and plenty of labour. Even when the farming is highly developed machinery is of little use except for the initial ploughings. It is by hand, working with a dibble, that the peasant digs little holes about eight inches apart, into which he drops the little seeds. On a Lower Egypt farm we saw them drop a pinch of 'new' soil into the hole before and after the seed. Fifteen days after the first sowing a check is made and the seeds which have failed to sprout are replaced. The field has to be watered every 15 days, making sure that every row is properly saturated, while the children go along taking out the weeds. After six weeks the thinning-out is done, leaving only two plants to each hole. Pruning is carried out in such a way as to favour the boll and decrease the wood. After that a careful watch has to be kept on every plant, branch by branch and leaf by leaf, for the worm can destroy a whole field of cotton. In 1954 we saw several acres destroyed in a single night, with nothing but the empty stalks left. Few owners can afford insecticides, which are expensive, and are also regarded as unsatisfactory, so that handling still has to be continued.

The cotton flowers early in July, with its pale-yellow bloom. The boll ripens and bursts and the fibre is ready for picking. However, the bolls ripen at different times between the end of August and the beginning of October. The whole village turns out, and in rows of twenty or thirty the children advance under the eye of the *ra'is* while a woman sings to keep their work in rhythm. The little girls are incredibly deft with their fingers. The bolls are laid in heaps at the end of the fields, after which they are put into *Shunas* and taken to the workshop for ginning or stripping. These are rough-and-ready places, where children again provide the labour, sorting out the bolls and stripping the seeds which are used for making oil, and detaching the long white fibres. All this is done in unhygienic conditions. After watching all the different operations required for cotton-producing, about a third of them done by adults and two-thirds by children, it is understandable why the Southern States of North America fought in order to keep slave-gangs on their plantations.

The life of a fellah, little better than a slave, is so hard that his every action is as utilitarian as the soil he works. Tourists would be wasting their time if they hoped to find a square yard of grass on which to picnic. The most they can look forward to is to find themselves with their feet in a ditch, or sitting on the little mud-bank dividing two fields, with a couple of dozen jeering fellah children looking on. The Egyptian fellah does not grow flowers. He lives in dirt and squalor without seeming to notice his surroundings. He has not only lost all aesthetic sense, but seems to have lost the desire to create anything. This race, which for thousands of years excelled at building, sculpting, painting, pottery, weaving and embroidery, seems to have forgotten how to make the simplest pot. Tin and enamelled dishes have spread the same ugliness from end to end of every village. The fellah has forgotten everything except how to use a hoe and irrigate the land. Only in distant Nubia, which so few appreciate, do the craftsmen still practise their baroque art.

The Egyptian people are not dead, however, but sleeping. Even the most ignorant and backward Egyptian peasant is extraordinarily adaptable and perfectible. In less than a hundred years he has learnt the new methods of irrigation which came to replace an age-old tradition. He has modified his crops, planting cotton and eating rice. Neither his customs nor behaviour have been much affected in the process, but much is to be expected of this purely material revolution. Some people blame the fellah for having always put up with his conditions instead of rising up in revolt, but they are forgetting a number of movements and risings which are all the more impressive in view of the way in which Egypt's whole geographical structure favours repression or tyranny.[1]

Even in Europe, farming and rural areas as a whole tend to be painfully conservative. However strange it might sound, the Egyptian peasant is less opposed to progress than our own. Obeying the *nazir*, the *umda* and even the reforming *khawaga* without raising a murmur, he accepts and carries out all sorts of experiments without ever grasping them imaginatively, or understanding their significance. He is not, as some have suggested, the best farmer in the world, but he is the most perfectible, the most capable of being educated.

[1] Egypt has known a number of risings due to poverty. The most famous of these was at the end of the Old Kingdom in about 2250 B.C., when the poorer classes in the townships of Lower Egypt turned on the rich, burnt offices and administrative centres, 'squatted' in palaces after turning their occupants out and seizing their possessions. Such episodes amounted to revolutions, both because they were widespread and because of their social consequences, and at the same time *jacqueries* inasmuch as they were local risings in which old scores were paid off. The effects of such risings are known from three later texts in which it is recorded 'They took goods from one and gave them to another from without', and 'The lowly was exalted', and 'The poor ate according to his hunger, but the great was cast down'. (Note from Serge Sauneron.)

II

The Agrarian Reform

This lethargic society, this servile and swollen population, and its
speculative, one-crop system, give a typically colonial appearance to
the Egyptian economy.

The revolutionaries had to react against this state of affairs in
1952. They had to extend the cultivable acreage, redistribute
agricultural wealth, reconvert agriculture, open new markets and
industrialize the country. But they also had to teach, tend and
modernize the Egyptian himself, and adapt law and custom to the
needs of the modern world. It needed many measures to be taken
together, or each in its proper turn, to offset the effects of over-
population. But the Officers were so little prepared for taking or
rather using power, that this enormous programme could only be
gradually worked out in the four years or so of the régime's existence.
That is why it is still in its first stages.

But after the first few weeks of government, the Officers tackled
the problem they knew most about and which appeared most urgent:
this was the sharing-out of the country's agricultural resources. On
the 9th of September 1952 they announced the law known as the
Agrarian Reform. Neguib and his men were not the first to have
tried redistributing landed property. Pharaoh, the sole owner of
the land, often modified its distribution by means of gifts or trans-
fers between the religious and military orders. But there is no document pointing to a new, overall system of property-ownership. By
proclaiming himself the sole master and exploiter of the Egyptian
soil, at the beginning of the nineteenth century, Mohamed Ali,
as we have seen, was achieving what amounted to an agrarian
reformation.

That harsh reversion to state ownership was far from being
socialistic, and was closer to the old serf system. This cynical exploitation worked very well for about twenty-five years. But Mohamed
Ali's second son, Sa'id Pasha, had to redistribute the land, which
had been neglected by the thwarted peasantry. The most powerful

or cunning quickly grabbed the freed lands and created a capitalist system which was still in force in 1952. The Wafd and certain other governments had drafted plans, and in 1948 some state properties were shared out among about a thousand fellahs, in lots of five feddans. But capitalistic tenure was in no way affected by this. On the contrary, the 1952 Act was revolutionary, in that it both limited and redistributed property and tended to end the abuse of ground-rents.

The essential lines of this law, which was drafted on the initiative of Major Gamal Salim by the economists Ahmed Fuad and Rashid el Barawi, are as follows: (a) the limitation of holdings; (b) distribution and sale to the fellahs; (c) an obligation on the owner or leaseholder to farm the land; (d) a collectivization of farming; (e) the setting up of obligatory co-operatives; (f) fixed rents; (g) control of agricultural wages; (h) trade-union rights for agricultural labourers; (i) the bringing of fresh land under cultivation.

The 1952 law limits the possession of land to 200 feddans, though most often 300 are allowed because the first two children give a right to 50 feddans each in addition to the basic upward limit (300 feddans = 315 acres). On the day when the law was enacted, 660,000 feddans thus became available for distribution, apart from 180,000 feddans belonging to Faruk and the 200 members of the royal family, which were simply confiscated. All other lands above the legal limit were bought at requisition-prices and officially sold to the new owners. The administration was elastic enough to go about this gradually so as not to upset the entire farming system at once and avoid any drop in output. The law allowed for a delay of five years for the change-over. In 1956, after four years, a third of the available land remained for distribution.

For about six weeks after the promulgation of the new law, owners had power to sell the requisitionable surplus at prices fixed by the government (seventy times the land-tax), in lots of at least 2 and not more than 5 feddans, to farmers who were already working the said land and either lived on it or in a nearby village. In this way 145,000 feddans were sold privately, and the landowners were able to realize considerable capital. The confiscations, on the other hand, came into force at once and Faruk's lands in particular were the first to be distributed, by Neguib himself, to the small fellahs. The requisitions came about more gradually.

The State could not afford to take over all holdings for fear of disorganizing agricultural production. The landowners were allowed to cultivate their property, for the time being, and had to pay a rent for whatever part was requisitioned. In July 1956, about 100,000 feddans were still being managed by the landowners; 460,000 feddans (about 500,000 acres) having been actually taken over by the State. The compensation to be paid to the previous owner has been fixed at ten times the rateable value of installations, implements and even trees. This is paid in Treasury Bonds redeemable in thirty years and carrying an interest of 3 per cent per annum. In July 1956 the value of the distributed Bonds amounted to £5,000,000 and all interest had been met. But the Bonds were not as yet transferable, not negotiable on the Stock Exchange. A Bill allows their investment in industry; but their exchange is extremely difficult and prevents the Bill from being enforced. This state of economic stagnation is a threat to the country's prosperity.

All the measures involved under the new legislation are carried out by the Agricultural Reform Committee (whose Director, M. Sayed Mara'i, was made State Minister for Agricultural Reform in June 1956). This is an autonomous corporation with its own budget, administration and technicians, which is responsible for requisitioning and distribution. It manages all land-holdings either by exploiting them directly or by giving the new fellah-tenants all the necessary directions for the rotation of crops and acreage and managing their co-operative associations. This organization also selects the engineers and technicians who are appointed.

Such a Board was vital to such a huge undertaking, as the State had become suddenly manager of almost 750,000 acres. Up to 1956, about a third of this surface came under its direct management and the Committee exercised strict control over the running of the remaining two-thirds. By the end of 1955 the Agricultural Reform Committee had collected £15½ million, distributed £3 million in interest to holders of Treasury Bonds and spent £8 million for the administration of properties, modernization of equipment, improvement of irrigation and draining systems and on the problem of housing. The balance was put into a reserve fund.

The transfer of estates involves only 13 per cent of the arable land. In July 1956, 500,000 persons (65,000 families) had taken over 260,000 feddans of requisitioned holdings (250,000 acres). The entire scheme affects a million and a half fellahs out of the 18 millions in Egypt. How were the beneficiaries chosen?

Once sold to the fellah, the land has to be paid for in thirty years.[1] The legislators were guided by two principles: to provide for basic needs while increasing production. Thus, the areas of land were distributed not only according to family circumstances but according to the cost of living in a given region and the yield of the soil. As we have seen, the basic requirement is about 5 feddans for a family of 8 persons—which represents £125 a year. For over 8 persons —which is not unusual—a supplementary portion of not less than 2 feddans is granted per family unit. The beneficiary may be a fellah who already owned less than 5 feddans. He must be an Egyptian subject and a peasant. The land was distributed by priority: (a) to peasants who were 'sitting tenants'; (b) to people living in the village nearest the estate; (c) in the village itself, to the poorest and largest families. The land devolves upon the head of the family who may be a woman: we have seen women receiving their title-deeds from Mohamed Neguib's own hand. One of the most revolutionary and salutary aspects of the law is that holdings cannot be split up by a testator. The descendants must come to an agreement as to the inheritance of the land.

COLLECTIVE FARMING AND CO-OPERATIVE SOCIETIES

The breaking up of the estates into holdings of 3 to 4 acres could ruin productivity if cultivation were not strictly co-ordinated. In the place of the owner's overseer, a government expert responsible for a given area decided the rotation of crops, the acreage under seed, the choice of farming methods, the fertilizers and seeds to be used. The fellah-owners farm it according to a collective plan. One area is reserved for cotton, another for cereals, another for *birsim*. In fact, land-ownership is essentially a right to have one's share of the common harvest in proportion to the acreage. This series of operations can only be carried out through co-operative societies. These societies have been declared compulsory by law in all regions where the new scheme was enforced. All beneficiaries have to become members but neighbouring fellahs who own less than 5 feddans can also join.

In July 1956, 198 agricultural co-operative societies of this type were working in Egypt. They also act as co-operative stores for

[1] Ten times the tax-rate plus 3 per cent interest, plus 15 per cent for the cost of exploitation. The total sum is payable out of the yearly crop.

production and marketing as well as a training-centre for the fellahs. Thanks to them alone, it is possible to keep this advantage of large-scale production drawing on carefully planned groups of holdings. The first aim of these societies is to give the fellahs material means of cultivating their land: fertilizers, seeds, animal or motor power, equipment, maintenance of the irrigation-system and (with the help of the Agricultural Bank) loans of money. Its second function is collecting crops, selling them without the help of middle-men and sharing the profit between the fellah-members after deducting the Committee's dues and service-charges. Two State representatives, one of them an agronomist, are advisers to the Co-operative Society Board composed of peasants elected by members. In the village we are passing through today, the President of the Board is an old, alert-looking sheikh. 'He is rich,' one fellah whispers to us, 'he has two wives.'[1] The social facilities consist of a combined centre for nursing and education under the direction of teachers and doctors. The problem of their recruiting is a difficult one.

THE AGRICULTURAL REFORM PUT TO THE TEST: FARUK'S ESTATE AT ZAFARAN

On the 23rd of August 1953, first anniversary of the 'Blessed Movement', General Neguib himself started the first distribution of lands in the Nile Delta. The ceremony took place at Zafaran, one of Faruk's former estates, under the multi-coloured tent reserved for important occasions—a moving 'prize-giving' to 461 families thus rewarded after so many centuries of slavery and resignation. We had been driven in coaches; at first we were a bit startled, soon after we felt thrilled by this festival of ex-serfs. Since then, we have been able from time to time to follow the progress of these peasants who are now free, if not prosperous, but at any rate no longer hungry —something which is still unusual for Egypt.

This 5,000-feddan estate includes sixteen hamlets. The best agricultural conditions are to be found there: excellent soil, decent housing in five of the villages (built of brick with water laid on),

---

[1] In addition to these 200 Agricultural Reform Co-operative Societies there have existed, since the beginning of the first World War, a number of agricultural co-operative societies (2,000 in June 1956) which are essentially credit-societies, financed by the Agricultural Bank. They make money loans, supply seeds and fertilizers. Technically they have been very helpful, but have not modified the life of the fellah as the Agricultural Reform Co-operatives intend to do.

eight pumping stations, tractors. Not all the estates are so well equipped. But here all the fellahs had run into debt before the Reform. On a maximum output of five *gintars* of cotton per feddan, the king, who owned the land, demanded three. In the best years, two *gintars* only were left for the family to live on, to cover the purchase of seeds, the cost of farming and the payment of their debts. In the best cases the fellah earned £10 per feddan; but rarely did he get more than £2. So eight to ten persons had to live on £20 a year. And if a bad year came? . . .

With a stroke of the pen Faruk was suppressed and his peasants' debts with him. There they are, in front of us on this 23rd day of July, under the blazing summer sun. They have put on their best *galabiya* to receive these impressive title-deeds from the hand of a smiling Neguib. That day, 250 families were given 2 feddans each and 211 others 2½ feddans each. Some women, wrapped in their black *melaya* and now officially land-owners, shed tears as they kissed the President's hand. Then Neguib in peasant speech—which is his own—explains the law, the rights and duties of all concerned: 'And when I come back next year, I don't want to see you with two wives each . . . Better buy a heifer.' The coarseness of this good joke tickles the country people and sets them roaring with delight.

The following year, we find these same fellahs in their villages. 'They are still suspicious,' the young agronomist who is showing us round tells us. 'Who can be sure that what has been given will not be taken back from them? They have been cheated so often by the city-people.' However, after the sale of the first crops and their distribution by the co-operative societies, they gained confidence. The next year, in 1955, we found them better organized and more assured. Living conditions have certainly improved. In the 'streets' —as dusty as ever—the children are decently clothed. They look well fed and the adults who work at the *nurags* harvesting the corn make a good impression. 'It is very simple,' says the doctor of the centre; 'they have eaten. Food works wonders on those under-fed bodies. Their earnings go mainly on food. At last they can drink the milk and eat the eggs they produce. Here the mortality rate is five times less than in the villages . . .'

The co-operative society members are busy deliberating: today their great decision is to buy each family a table. In Europe it is difficult to understand the progress implied by such a purchase in houses which have, for furniture, only one straw-mat and a rope fixed across the room to hang their rags on. A table is a sign of civilization: it means that they are giving up their habit of squatting and at the same time it is bringing a sense of luxury into their life.

The young man fresh from the city makes the old fellah—once resigned to his poverty—aware of new needs, just like the woman we have just seen, near the pump, doing her washing with white soap.

This re-distribution, spectacular though it may be, is not the essential part of the new agricultural scheme. Its significance is more exemplary and social than economic, since it cannot affect more than a million and a half fellahs. More important, in fact, is the compulsory drop in rents which affected the enormous mass of tenants and at least acted as a brake on the abuses we have pointed out, even if it did not entirely stop them.

The agricultural rent cannot exceed seven times the basic rate. The average rent which before the Reform amounted to £40 and £50 per feddan has been reduced to £18 or £21 (the equivalent of £36 per 2½ acres). We have seen that before the Reform the land-owners went so far as to demand 100 per cent of the crops and reckless sub-letting led to absurd and scandalous situations. The new legislation affected several millions of fellahs. Though flouted here and there, in most cases it has been respected and has greatly improved the tenants' position—that is to say the position of about a third of the peasantry. Unfortunately, these results have been partly cramped by the general slump in cotton which mainly affects the Nile Valley grower and by the destruction of part of the 1954 crops by parasites. In the long run, however, the effects of this control will be felt over a very large area.

The limitation of ownership does nothing to improve uncultivated land. This remains the property of private individuals or of estate companies for twenty-five years because the great problem in Egypt today is to 'make' land either by State action or by encouraging private initiative. As we shall see, the administration has undertaken great public works in this direction, but there are people who do not hesitate to buy a 'patch of desert', generally on the fringe of cultivated land or near an arm of the Nile or the branch of a canal. Naturally these speculations are kept under control with regard to the amount of water supplied every year by the Nile to the valley. Nobody has the right to dig a canal or to catch water without the approval of the administration. In fact, Egypt will not be able appreciably to extend its surface of arable land as long as the great waterworks to increase the serviceable flow of the Nile have not been completed.

THE BALANCE-SHEET OF THE AGRICULTURAL REFORM

By 1956, three years had passed since the first re-distribution of land. Two-thirds of it have already been shared between the fellahs. Is it time to take stock?

The agricultural reform is much criticized in Egypt: first of all by those who have been dispossessed; then by those who have not profited by it. Some reproach it with its relative timidity: the limit of 200 feddans is thought inadequate. It is true that in Gamal Salim's original draft, the property limit was fixed at 50 feddans. But it is not only because of political pressure that the reformers have raised the number of feddans. The people responsible for the nation's economy have judged that it would be too dangerous to destroy the property structure so radically or to break up the estates completely, and that, in particular, two of the main crops, cotton and sugar-cane, do not lend themselves easily to cultivation in small holdings. The reformers, anxious to get the maximum output, have been thus inclined to caution. Experience seems to show how right they were.

Major Gamal Salim told us in 1952: 'The principal aim of the agricultural reform is to transfer capital from agriculture to industry. Egypt lives entirely on its agriculture: this throws the economy out of balance and we want to put it right.' The problem, then, was to free the Egyptian economy by enforcing industrialization. More than three years are evidently needed for such a reconversion. At least thirty years will be necessary for Egypt to transform its agriculture and create a proper industry. But in 1956, had the movement really started? We must reply in the negative. In 1955, an excellent year, if ever there was one, the agricultural income amounted to £420 million of a national income of £850 million—neither the capital of the great landowners, nor the profits made by the small farmers, have been directed into industry.

The landowner has no faith in industry. Those who in the past thought only of buying land, now only invest their money in the building trade. In 1955, for instance, £7 million were invested in industry and £49 million in the building trade. And if the reform has not made the capitalists turn towards industrial production, it has equally kept them from reinvesting their capital in land for fear of a a new spate of measures against their property rights. Suspicion is such that there are few who try to increase their agricultural income by modernizing their methods and equipment.

As for the fellah, has his situation generally improved? In the case of those who have benefited by the distribution and of tenants, it certainly has. Two observations are necessary. With regard to production, the upheaval caused by the reform did not bring about a slump; we have seen on the contrary that the agricultural income had reached a particularly high rate in 1955—due largely, it must be admitted, to a rise in the price of cotton. On the other hand, the official statistics show that the income of the small landowners increased by £30 million a year. The fellah has literally eaten them. He has spent them on food and we have seen that, in the villages, he can now afford to consume the poultry, eggs and milk he produces. But he has not yet reached the level where he could afford to consume Egyptian-made goods which would mean creating an internal market, indispensable to the expansion of a national industry.

Thanks to the co-operative societies, on the other hand, most of the new income of the small landowners is usefully reinvested with a view to modernizing agriculture. It used to be said that only the big estate-owners could afford to mechanize agriculture. After a setback in 1953 the import figures for agricultural machinery were, in 1955, as good as the figures obtained by the estate-owners in the best years for cotton (1,000 tractors). It can be noted, on the other hand, that in Egypt it is on the medium-sized estates—about 12 feddans—that the best output is obtained, thanks to the concentration of labour. Now the co-operative system of the Agricultural Reform gets about the same results with grouped holdings. Moreover, the peasant landowner is inclined to keep the soil in better condition than one who is not afraid to exhaust it by aiming at an immediate yield. The problem of keeping the soil in good condition has become urgent in this country of intensive farming, in which reliance on alluvial deposits has disappeared with the new methods of irrigation.

The economic progress is therefore real, but will only be fully felt when the agricultural structure has been completely changed. This will be dealt with later on. From the social point of view there has been a huge success and a complete failure. The aim of the reform in this respect was to lift the peasant masses out of their 'proletarian' condition. It has succeeded to some extent by giving land, a certain amount of dignity and responsibility to a few hundred thousand peasants. On a larger scale, it succeeded in ending their habit of running into debt. But where the failure has been complete, is with real proletariat: the agricultural labourers who form 38 per cent of Egypt's agricultural population. For them the reformers hoped to lay down a basic wage of 18 piastres a day (3s. 9d.) and also to allow the formation of agricultural trade unions to protect their rights. But this has come to nothing. The trade unions were taken over by semi-fascist groups with allegiance to the government and rendered useless. Strikes have been declared illegal. As for the basic allowance of 18 piastres, it was hardly compatible with the economic situation of 1953-4; with the distribution of land, a general slump in cotton, a fall in consumption, the landowners thought only of reducing their labour. The Agrarian Reform, in this field, has been responsible for more unemployment and a drop in wages. We have already mentioned the present wage-rate (12 piastres or less) and said that it could fall—as it did in 1954—to 4 piastres a day.

There is one positive point to conclude with. In the absence of any civic or social structure at the village level, the co-operative and the social centre may become the corner-stone of social progress. However limited the experiment is, the Egyptian peasant, who had never done anything but execute orders, will find himself member of a group studying and discussing village problems and taking decisions. He is in the process of becoming a responsible citizen. This is a great step towards a sense of his human value. From his former gregarious but individualistic outlook, the fellah will rise to a state of genuine 'co-operation'. Instead of being a lonely slave, he will tend to become free within a community.

In this respect the Agricultural Reform is an experiment applicable to the whole of Egypt. Besides, we shall see that this experiment seems to be a point of departure for a whole system of co-operation which the military leaders would gladly make the backbone of the Egyptian economy.

FORMATION OF A MODERN RURAL UNIT

We were driving on the desert road towards Alexandria when our guide turned to the right. An asphalt track cut through the desert and for 18 miles we saw nothing but sand. But soon a huge building yard appeared, surrounded by intense activity. Tractors with clusters of people clinging to them were unloading their cargo in front of a building encased in scaffolding: the mosque, neon-lit, even in broad daylight, into which the workmen went between shifts.

All around the vast square stood low, grey-brick houses, clean, hygienic and dreary. We were in Umm Sabir, the capital of the so-called Liberation Province, Mudiriyat el Tahrir. The men were coming out of the mosque all in green-blue overalls, black and white checked shirts. And where were the women and children? We felt we were far from Egypt as we knew it, swarming with warm humanity.

When we shyly enter a house, the women who welcome us kindly wear the green-blue skirt, like the men's overalls, and the same severe blouse as the young woman showing us round, who is the village social-worker. The Province apparently wears uniform. It is slightly irritating, childish and moving at the same time. Young Nahid shares the life of the fellahs in this desert-village for the princely salary of £20 a month. She boils over with eagerness; she feels that she has a mission in life. You would think Umm Sabir was built by well-behaved children—a bit simple-minded, maybe—with washed-out toy-blocks. Will the trees ever grow here?

In 1953 there was nothing but desert sand. The Officers had the idea of creating a 'model' rural unit by reclaiming the desert, extending the arable land, modernizing equipment and social conditions. One morning, in autumn 1953, the startled Bedouin saw a long column of lorries and tractors leave the Alexandria main road for the desert. Then they stopped and set to work under the command of a sturdy young man, Major Magdi Hasanain. Bulldozers, fertilizers and workmen got to work on the sands. Nothing was spared and the site on the fringe of the western canal had been rather well chosen. Five thousand men have been working hard for over three years with the most up-to-date machinery. The results: 10,000 feddans of 'baby-crops' wrested from the sands, mainly crops which do not exhaust the soil: *birsim*, ground-nuts, marrows, water-melons, with a view to enriching the soil and to getting it ready for the cereals and market-gardening in ten years' time. Two such 'model villages' have risen from the sands; a third one is being built. There are canals and ditches, pumping-stations, roads: the outlook is bright enough, and the *mudiriya*, hoping to be self-supporting, has its own workshops for machinery and carpentry, its own furniture and shoe-factories. A host of brand-new machines go about the streets and fields. One gets the impression of a rather aimless excitement, a comedy that the 'people' are acting for themselves.

But in this artificial rural unit, a thrilling social experiment is being carried out. The outlay on fertilizing the soil by such methods is far beyond its marketable value. When the land agents develop land at the price of £80 a feddan, it costs the *mudiriya* £200 for the same area. But this figure includes the equipment and building of houses, redeemable over a good many years. Moreover, the plan must be judged from a social angle as well as a financial one. We must never forget that in Egypt the problem is twofold: to acquire more land and at the same time improve the living conditions of the fellah. The agronomist who showed us round Umm Sabir said: 'To reform the village is out of the question. We must start at the beginning, build anew, create experimental villages where everything will be new; the way of living, dressing, eating, working.' As a result only the mosque reminds us that we are in Egypt. The houses are set in rows along large thoroughfares; the workshops, stables, poultry-sheds make one think of a farm in a Welfare State.

Indeed, what was 'co-operation' in the villages where the Agricultural Reform applied, here becomes a genuine 'collectivization'. Need we recall the *kolkhoz* or the *kibboutzin*? Here everything is collective: land, cultivation, cattle-breeding, maintenance, dairying, even household chores. The bakery makes bread for everyone. A collective laundry does the washing and ironing for all the village. Here is something to upset the oldest country traditions. The housing accommodation is also revolutionary. Each house has four rooms, a kitchen and a bathroom opening on to the yard. It has electricity and running water, and real furniture. Breaking one of the oldest customs, the cattle have been separated from the houses and herded in stables and paddocks outside the villages. Each village has its 'centre' in which elected representatives meet and discuss their common problems with government officials: the agricultural officer, the doctor, the schoolmaster or social workers who live in houses like the peasants'. There are a school, a small hospital, an assembly-hall with a library and cinema. A co-operative store stocks all essential goods and an agricultural co-operative unit supplies fertilizers, seeds, tools and machines. The village crops are collected and sold through this co-operative unit. Here, everything is ultra-mechanized since the vast desert spaces lend themselves so well to mechanized farming.

Here the land has not been distributed among the peasants, but the reverse process was applied. It has been possible to arrange an ideal distribution of 5 persons to each holding of 5 feddans. The families, chosen and selected like so many seeds, must not exceed a couple and three children. They have been chosen from the neighbouring villages—the Egyptian, as we have seen, is reluctant to uproot himself—the ex-servicemen and the peasants without land were easy to get, but it was hard to find workers who were really healthy.

The constitution of the *mudiriya* forbids polygamy, divorce and mothers-in-law. Just as it is the cowl which makes the monk, the first 227 families to be installed in 1955 were not allowed to take any personal belongings. They came naked, like Adam and Eve, to Umm Sabir. There, they were dressed in the uniform of the future model fellah; we have seen this uniform: green-blue linen skirt or overalls, white and black checked shirt. However, women have been allowed bright-coloured head-scarves. The men wear the little canvas cap of American mechanics. The *galabiya* and *melaya* are banned. New men can be made with new garments, as the Chinese have proved. If the man wants a divorce, he will have to leave the *mudiriya*. If his wife is expecting a fourth baby, 'family-planning' methods will be applied. The three children per family allowed by the law will become peasants, technicians and cattle-breeders.

When they arrive at the *mudiriya*, the families are sorted out in a training-camp where they have to pass a medical examination and where the social workers test them with a view to future occupations. One is chosen for cattle-breeding, another for work in the fields, a third for the workshop. The women undergo the same tests. The children are sent to school. There they will be taught a rural handicraft with a view to training village-technicians who will modernize rural conditions. The training period in the camp lasts six months. Only then do families take over their houses. In 1956, after having been settled for one year, before the harvests, the fellahs were paid by the State the unusual rate of 30 piastres a day (6 shillings). As soon as the first crop is sold, they pay for their land by yearly payments in the same way as the Agricultural Reform farmers.

Foreign visitors are tempted to smile at the childish, toy-soldier side of the experiment. It is easy to see these peasants in uniform in their model houses as a drop of water in the ocean of 18 million fellahs. But with such an adaptable population, the experiment was worth trying and must be carried on. In ten years' time, if its organizers persevere, the *mudiriya* should extend to Alexandria with a population of 30,000 fellahs in ten villages. On the other hand, the experiment has a technical value: the construction of the Aswan Dam will provide irrigation for 1½ to 2 million feddans of desertland. On this reclaimed land the experiments made in the 'Liberation Province' will facilitate the use of new fertilizing methods, choice of crops and transfer of labour. This new land will perhaps create a new kind of man. The Mudiriya el Tahrir—costly and odd as it is —must be considered as a kind of laboratory.

LIFE ON THE LAND IN 1956

The Nile Valley continues to underfeed its inhabitants. But their situation has not remained unchanged since the beginning of the military régime. As we have seen, the condition of the wage-earning fellah—more than a third of the peasant population—has become worse. In spite of official statements and statistics, all prices have risen. The rural proletarian earns less, pays more and has more children. He is becoming poorer and poorer. The small landowner is slightly better off: he eats well and can have loans from the Agricultural Bank. The year 1955 brought him a profit: cotton sold well and the worms had spared the crops. The tenant is in a similar situation. As for the big estate-owner, he is practically 'ruined': 'Just think'—one of those dispossessed people told us between two stays in Paris where he is 'reading for a degree'—'Just think. I have an income of only £10,000 left . . . with all my children, my servants and all the people who live on me . . .'

It is true that rural capital has changed hands because of the Agricultural Reform, but this only affected a minority. In 1951 21 per cent of the rural income went to the big landowners. In 1955 they got only 11 per cent. But a property of 200 feddans still brought in an average income of £5,000 or £6,000 a year to its owner. The agricultural year 1955 marked an improvement on the preceding years, for no serious difficulties arose. That year, the agricultural income increased by 15 per cent and the average income per inhabitant reached the level of the best year, 1951, £27. If we note that the population increased by 1,500,000 inhabitants between 1953 and 1955, we can observe that the demographic increase has not proportionately impoverished the country. But the poorest have become poorer still.

This rural economy is made terribly unstable by the fluctuations of the cotton exchange. This gamble on monoculture is the main weakness of Egyptian economy. The average yearly fluctuation is estimated at 20 per cent.

The food production—cereals, meat and dairy-produce, vegetables, fruit—is inadequate. The responsible minister himself explained this as being due to the inadequate yield per acre of land. 'Egypt is far behind most countries in many agricultural products; the yield of corn is only 50 and 67 per cent of that of the Netherlands and Great Britain; that of rice 76 per cent of what it is in Spain and Italy.' This is a strange remark if one thinks of the famous Nile slime. The cattle situation is more deplorable still. The livestock is plentiful (1,300,000 head of cattle, in addition to sheep, goats and a few pigs), but is used for labour; cows and heifers turn the *saqiya*, bulls draw the plough and the *nurag*. Thus the yield in milk and flesh is mediocre. As for the poultry, they have to seek their own food. Soil, animals and men are insufficiently productive.

The points to be affected by initial improvements are the drainage-system—for the fellah saturates the fields in his fear of being short of water—the use of nitrate fertilizers—for which a factory is being erected in Aswan—the stackage of cereals—the loss caused by parasites is in the region of 10 per cent—and finally a rational and scientific struggle against plant and human diseases. But these are only limited aspects of the general design: a large-scale reconversion of agricultural production.

This gigantic operation is both agricultural and industrial. From an agricultural point of view, the aim is to change the monocultural system, especially by reducing the cotton-growing acreage in favour of a better-quality food-production; by restricting the acreage given to cereals and by lowering the cost of production. Mechanization is not an unfailing answer in an over-populated country where the irrigation-system with its network of canals and ditches hinders the use of machines. On the contrary, pumps are obviously very useful. Machinery will help mainly when new lands are to be fertilized. What does the word 'industrial' mean in this context? The leaders of the Agricultural Reform have asserted since 1953 that the industrialization of agriculture alone can save the anaemic economic system. They had to wait for three years for a ten-year plan to be introduced with the advice of foreign economists—among them Oscar Lange, the Polish economist. This ten-year plan aimed at creating co-operative societies to industrialize farming. The Director of the Plan told us: 'The poor and suspicious fellahs would never invest their small savings in an ordinary industrial concern. But they will bring their milk, eggs and vegetables to a local factory which will transform under their very eyes, so to speak, their produce, sell it and share the profit between them. They will be the first to consume what they have helped to produce and thus will have a share in financing these agricultural-industrial co-operative societies.'

The new slogan in Cairo is: 'agriculture cannot prosper without being geared to an industrial system', or, as Nasser says, 'to a co-operative and rural industrial system'. In a speech in May 1956 he promised the setting up of a national scheme based on co-operation. He asserted that, without national or foreign capital, this was the best way to change from a colonial economy (monoculture and export of raw material) to an independent economy (polyculture and export of finished goods) and to use the vast numbers of unemployed for recreating national capital. The industrialization of the country by means of rural units aims at reabsorbing part of the farming labour force, directing agricultural capital into industry and creating a home market. The instrument of this industrialization is the agricultural-industrial co-operative based on two principles: decentralization and local control. There will be no huge concentration around the main cities but industrial and rural units at district level: local capital, local labour, local markets (without of course excluding arrangements for export). In order to give the necessary impetus, the State makes the first investments and keeps watch over those experiments whose nucleus will be the Agricultural Reform Centres. These industries will be, first and foremost, food industries, and the development of market-gardening is already encouraging. 'Household' industries (furniture, ironmongery, small machines) will be carried on side by side with the former; they have been started already in the rural centre of Wadi Natrun and in the Liberation Province.

This plan is still in its initial stages. At first sight it seems to be a mere utopia. 'It is household economy,' a foreign economist commented in front of us. On the other hand, the success of the plan implies an equipment and, above all, an organization of transport and distribution which are far from ideal in the present state of Egypt. If the experiment is actually given a chance, it should be followed with attention and sympathy; it may well achieve a substantial profit if the foreign market is well sounded. Let it be said now, that those are the kind of results which have ensured the success of the State of Israel.

III

The Problem of Over-Population

The population in Egypt increases by one more human being every minute. The Nile Valley, over-populated like all oases, is so crowded that it can no longer feed its inhabitants. The political and diplomatic history of the country revolves round this problem: there are too many Egyptians in Egypt.

In the days of Ramses II there were 9 million Egyptians. The figure dropped to 5 millions in the Christian era and to $2\frac{1}{2}$ millions in Bonaparte's time. Towards the middle of the nineteenth century Bowring recorded a rise and estimated the population at about 4,750,000. All these figures are obviously rough estimates. The first official census in 1897 gave a figure of 10 millions and the 1947 census 19 millions. In 1956 the population was put at 23 million inhabitants. Thus the population of Egypt has doubled in less than fifty years, making the Nile Valley the most densely populated area in the world.

We have seen that the average density is 1,400 inhabitants per square mile, nearly twice that of Belgium with 730 and seven times that of France (187). A density of 1,800 inhabitants per square mile is not uncommon in rural areas, and we have seen that in Cairo it rose to 290,000.

This increase is constantly accelerating. More disturbing still is the fact that this is a recent phenomenon which has not changed over the past twenty years. The average increase of 1·3 per cent (until 1937) became 2·2 per cent, and even 2·5 per cent by 1955. And this perpetual increase suggests a steadily rising curve. But, in fact, it is due to a lower rate of infantile mortality. As many children are born as ever, but fewer of them die. A great number of adults thus reach the age of marrying and procreating and the number of births will soon be increasing. By 1965 Egypt will have nearly 30 million inhabitants.

We have already said that the main towns attracted the farm workers and that the two biggest towns, Cairo and Alexandria, account for one-sixth of the population. However, this enormous increase weighs far more heavily on the rural areas than in the city districts. This is because the inadequate industrial development cannot absorb all the surplus labour. In the three last years the labour force used by all activities other than agriculture has increased by only 35,000 persons (industry, commerce, transport, mining), against the total of 500,000 persons added every year to the population. During the war years when, as we shall see, industry met with especially favourable conditions, it employed only 30,000 more workmen than in 1938. Thus the rural areas are becoming more and more over-crowded: in 1900, two men lived on one feddan; in 1955, four men. So there is more and more unemployment and the average number of actual working-days in the rural districts was, in 1956, 150 per annum. With its bulging cities and its densely populated fields, Egypt now has twice as many citizens as it can afford. Despite the progress made, agriculture has not been able to keep up with the rising tide of population: while the population doubled, the productive area increased only by 36 per cent and, thereby, the national income fell by 25 per cent in fifty years.

In the course of our survey of town and country, agriculture, industry and the human element, we have seen the causes of this demographic increase. The reasons for it are both economic and social and we shall only sum them up rapidly at this point. From an economic point of view, the extension of cotton-growing requires a large and cheap labour force. The fellahs procreate children in order to employ them on the cotton-fields. Then there is the lack of national capital: this was estimated at 60 to 80 million Egyptian pounds in 1956. Finally, there is a lack of efficiency in agriculture, industry and the use of labour. Egyptian mills need to employ three workmen against one in European mills.

From a social point of view, ignorance, superstition, ill-health and poverty and the Islamic customs themselves (polygamy and divorce) are responsible for this state of affairs. The remedies need to be both economic and social.

In fact, there is a double task to be performed: on the one hand to absorb the surplus population, on the other hand to stop the demographic progression. The 'Planning Committee' created in 1956 has worked out a ten-years' social and economic scheme to co-ordinate the social efforts of 'Public Works' of the 'Production Council' and of the Ministry of Agriculture. The Plan provides for three stages: (1) the reorganization of agriculture (more variety, increased productivity and quality, increased production to satisfy the home market, while at the moment there is no branch of agriculture capable of meeting domestic needs); (2) maximum increase of the potential of existing factories by improving output; (3) to create an industrial structure in the three following phases: (*a*) manufacture of essential consumer-goods; (*b*) production of intermediary goods (agricultural equipment, bicycles, electrical equipment); (*c*) the creation of heavy industry. 'But we must not put the cart before the horse,' the Director of the Plan told us; 'first of all we must try to increase production itself. What is still more pressing is to change the technical structure of our national economy.' The development of agriculture by integrating it into industry can alone save this country.

The fact remains that the Egyptians need new land. Soil and energy can only be provided by the construction of a new dam on the Nile: the High Dam, or Sadd el Ali or any other waterworks able to supply water for irrigation and hydraulic power. But the most optimistic economists think that these measures will hardly be enough to absorb the increase of population even with a maximum output in both agriculture and industry and the building of the dam, and believe that in twenty years' time Egypt will still be facing the same problems.

It is now for the sociologist to say how the demographic expansion is to be restrained. Birth-control has aroused violent controversy in Egypt. On the one hand, the Marxists assert that Egypt is virtually and potentially rich enough to feed a population of 50 million inhabitants by a rational use of its soil and subsoil. On the other hand, the true Moslems are, for religious reasons, against any practice that opposes Allah's will.[1] It was necessary to find a formula which would satisfy religious conservatism without discarding all means of curbing the rising tide of population: this formula goes under the euphemistic name of 'Family Planning'.

Since May 1956 the 'Ways and Customs Committee' has been undertaking a sociological and scientific survey of the Egyptian way of life with a view to finding the safest and quickest way to 'modernize' the Egyptian family. This 'modernization' involves first and foremost some control of the birth-rate. The method of applying this

[1] Some of them, however, have found in the Sunna an 'advice' of the Prophet excusing contraceptive practice in the case of poverty.

control is not uniform: on the one hand, everybody agrees that the progress of education, by restoring women to a sense of their human dignity and men to a sense of their responsibilities, will naturally bring about a noticeable decline in the birth-rate. But not in the near future. For 76 per cent of the Egyptians are still illiterate, and if there is a new school opened every day, there are nearly two Egyptians born every minute. Then a quicker and more efficient way will have to be found. We have seen that an experiment has been attempted in the Liberation Province, where the families must not exceed three children. Family-planning has been applied only in a limited number of cases. It can be applied only in strict proportion to the development of education and a rise in the standard of living. But, as an experiment, the State has opened twelve nursing-homes where legal abortion will be authorized under medical and family conditions.

What must be noted is that some Moslems defend family-planning and birth-control. In 1953, at the International Congress of Demography, Dr Abbas Ammar, former Minister for Education and Social Welfare, came out in support of birth-control. The same year Dr Mohammed Awad, then Chancellor of Alexandria University, said publicly: 'The progress of industry is slow; there is no emigration. There are pseudo-solutions but we cannot apply them. The most practical solution would be a limitation, or rather planning, of the birth-rate in proportion to income. Such planning should take place at the family-level, each family limiting the number of births according to its resources.' Despite the indignant protests by the Rector of El Azhar in the name of the Koran and of the *Sharia*, the Sheikh el Baquri, Minister of the Awqaf and a former Moslem Brother, was to close the debate by expressing the view of the progressive religious leaders and of the government that: 'Nothing in the Koran forbids birth-control.' Moreover, the sacred texts assert that the infant does not really 'exist' before the second month after conception—before that it has no real existence.[1]

The same sheikh, El Baquri, came back from Peking in the summer of 1955 asserting that: 'The Chinese Moslems who know the Koran well have abolished polygamy.' This was another step forward in the revolutionary era. In fact, some months later the draft of a new bill was given great publicity in the Press; it pro-

---

[1] Parts of holy writ seem to imply that the child only 'exists' after the fourth month of gestation.

vided for the suppression of polygamy except in the case where sterility was established ('even after surgical operation'); for the suppression of repudiation, and for new legislation with a view to a divorce system similar to the French one. Thus the basic family unit was protected, the number of successive wives, and thus the number of children, was limited and a more modern social structure was given to a modern economy.

But in 1956 the law had not yet been promulgated. As in the case of the 'Ways and Customs Committee' decisions tending to modernize dress, housing and even the traditional festivities, more 'favourable' circumstances are awaited. These are both economic and political. Only a government at once popular and bold can take such steps.

IV

Economic Growing-Pains

Since 1953 Egypt has been passing through a grave economic crisis. Everyone knows this and the most pessimistic foretell bankruptcy. The crisis is obviously a real one. To be convinced of this one has only to read the daily list of declarations or petitions of bankruptcy. It is true that Egyptian trade is in a state of stagnation. But is the country's economy beyond hope or cure?

Before July 1956 the finances looked sound enough. In 1956 the gold reserves covered 37·3 per cent of the paper money and bills in circulation. There was no inflation and the National Debt was only £E160 million. The finances were carefully managed in spite of resort to government loans up to £150 million with a view to creating a sound money-market. A French banker described this as 'too timid a financial policy—sound, but too much so. A poverty-stricken economy.' Here we see the effects of British financiers' lessons being practised by the Egyptian leaders, and their haunting memory of the Khedive Isma'il's mistakes and imprudence which brought Egypt under alien rule. Their caution is praiseworthy but is hardly compatible with a vast plan for equipment and economic expansion. However, 1955 and 1956 showed a tendency towards a 'controlled inflation' after the systematic deflationary policy of 1953–4, which the 1950–1 inflation had made imperative.

But at the same time the balance of payments in 1955 showed a deficit of £35 million instead of the £33 million surplus of the year before. As for the internal trade balance, it has worsened and Cairo has been the first to suffer. The causes of this economic crisis are both national and international.

The Egyptian economy depends on cotton. For two years—up to the end of 1955—Egypt passed through a serious crisis owing to international conditions in the cotton trade. The declining demand for cotton threatens to continue with the growing use of artificial fibres. After the 1951 boom the awakening was painful. The drop

362

in market prices, worsened by the land requisition, was felt all over Egypt, with a slump and a fall in farming wages and incomes. In 1954 a natural scourge made the situation worse, when the cotton-worm and pink capsule-worm destroyed the crops. The government counter-attacked in two ways, by reducing the cotton acreage and increasing the land under rice, and by opening fresh markets in the East, especially Russia and China, with which agreements were concluded in 1955. Thanks to these agreements the market prices rose again and stocks were eased. The reopening of the Cotton Exchange at Alexandria in autumn 1955 and the resumption of free selling on the Liverpool market were signs that the situation was righted.

But Egypt lives under the threat of American cotton policy, with its long-term credits and large stocks which can flood the market at any moment. This is why Egypt is tending to increase its exchange with the Eastern countries and sets great store on a market serving 600 million Chinese. Before the Peking régime was officially recognized in 1956, important trade agreements had already been reached, amounting to £5 million, in 1955–6. On the other hand, in 1956 Czechoslovakia created a sensation by taking second place among cotton-buyers, coming after India but before France, which had been the best customer in the previous year. However, most of the agreements with the Eastern countries are on a barter basis, for oil and corn in exchange for cotton with Rumania and Russia, cotton in exchange for arms with Czechoslovakia.

This trade with the East, which has been made so much of, did not amount to more than 30 per cent of Egyptian imports in 1956. For Egypt cannot sell all her cotton in the Western world but still continues buying her machinery, chemicals and tools in Europe. This explains why Egyptian trade is out of balance with the Western countries, France, Germany, Britain and Italy. On the other hand, the Eastern countries take Egyptian cotton while being unable to supply Egypt with the products she needs. Their exports are limited to heavy machinery and rolling-stock, carriages from Hungary, metal bridges and cranes. But up to 1956 Egypt still imported most of her machine-tools from Sweden and Britain. The recent conflict has changed this situation, mostly to the detriment of Britain and France and to the benefit of communist or neutral countries.

The aim now is to equip the country, whether by developing its economy or modernizing agriculture or building up industry. But for Egypt equipment means imports. The country has no coal, and its iron ore has not yet been exploited. Its cement production is inadequate and its oil resources meet only two-thirds of its needs. From 1953 onwards the government decided to devote most of its resources to buying equipment, while restricting imports for home consumption. In 1956 this policy became very stringent. Practically no import licences were granted except for public utility goods such as equipment, building schemes, factories and raw materials. Only a very small amount of luxury goods were allowed in, after being prohibitively taxed. The importing of private cars, wireless sets and refrigerators is not allowed. In 1951, 30 per cent of the imports were made up of food, 9 per cent of machinery, and 24 per cent of armaments. In 1955 food represented only 16 per cent, machinery 18, armaments 38. This sudden reversal has contributed to Egypt's crisis.

Egyptian trade used to be based entirely on the import of manu-factured articles. To simplify, Britain bought raw cotton and sold Cairo textiles and other finished products at such rates that Egypt felt no need for a national industry of her own. All this remained on a colonial basis. In 1952 and 1953 the home market shrank. The ousted rural capitalists tightened their purse-strings, they reduced their style of living and bought less. This freeze of upper-class capital was not compensated by the much slower rise of middle- and lower-class capital. The £30 million of income trans-ferred between 1952 and 1955 from the upper to the lower strata did not pass directly into trade but were devoted locally to improving the peasants' lot and reinvested in purely farming needs such as fertilizers or cattle. At best the demand for utility articles has replaced a demand for luxury or semi-luxury goods. But the demand for mass-produced goods is only slowly increasing. This shrinking of the market has caused many commercial failures, especially in Cairo, where many retailers find themselves in the paradoxical position of having lost both their stocks and their customers. Many shops still refuse to replace formerly imported goods by Egyptian products. It is not infrequent to hear an assistant in a Cairo department-store saying to some customer asking for Egyptian cotton materials, 'Sorry, but we don't sell local goods.' It must be admitted that the local product is still inferior, except for poplins. But the quality of most goods (furniture, ready-made clothes, leather and plastic articles) is now improving.

The present crisis is hastening a development which is upsetting the normal structure of commerce. Egyptian trade used to be almost entirely in the hands of foreigners, or of a minority descended from foreign immigrants, Greek, Lebanese, Syrian, Jewish or Armenian. The luxury trade was in the hands of French, Italian or Greek merchants, the last of these being the most successful. The drop in turnover forced many of these dealers to close their shops and leave the country. At the same time the government outlined a policy to protect Moslem trade, in the hope of keeping commercial trans-actions in Egyptian hands, especially where cotton is concerned. By protecting the 'true Egyptians', the political leaders favour the Moslem at the expense of the Jews or Christians, whatever their origin. This protection takes the form of very generous loans or, as in the Cotton Exchange, of preferential treatment. In spite of the dis-appearance of foreigners and thus of dangerous competitors, the Moslem tradesman does not yet seem to be filling the place that has been made for him. Whether for lack of tradition or want of method, or for lack of imagination or initiative, many have gone bankrupt or gone out of business altogether.

Is the situation desperate, for all that? We seem to be witnessing a period of growing-pains, or rather the crisis brought about by the economic conversion. Naturally the world cotton crisis is a permanent threat to the Egyptian economy, but another reason for its running into debt is the outlay on equipment, which is not an unhealthy sign. On the other hand, there are many signs of a re-awakening of economic life. First there is the credit-expansion and the 25 per cent increase in bank deposits between 1954 and 1955. This should give grounds for real optimism, were it not that in the past two years the massive purchases of armaments, which in 1955 represented 38 per cent of the imports, increased in 1956 owing to a 25 per cent rise in the army estimates, thus gravely slowing down the country's economy. This buying of arms has brought about a reduction in output.

But Egypt's real crisis, its endemic disease, is its shortage of capital. Whether we like it or not, Egypt is a poor country. Even if its capitalists invested boldly, the whole national heritage would not be enough to provide the necessary incentive for throwing off a thousand years of apathy. So far the mobilizing of local capital has been a failure. As for foreign capital, even before the nationalization of the Canal Company it was holding back. Only oil-prospecting is likely to attract much investment. The Western capitalists have always been wary of the military government. The Egyptian military leaders made repeated approaches to them. A law of 1953 gives seven years' exemption from tax to all commercial and industrial profits of new concerns, and allows, under certain conditions, the return of profits to the country of origin. But foreign firms nearly always have two objections to invitations to settle in Egypt.

The first objection refers to the 1947 law governing labour, which forces all foreign companies to employ 90 per cent Egyptian workers drawing 80 per cent of wages paid. This law shows a purblind nationalism as the Minister of Production recently remarked. The second objection concerns State intervention in private companies, such as the nationalization of sugar-factories, the expulsion of all men over 60 from administrative Boards, and Egyptianization which is no more than a protection of the Moslem. This State policy has in a sense reached its peak in the sudden nationalizing of the Suez Canal Company. This nationalization is not likely to help the Egyptian economy out of its state of stagnation, since to a large extent it springs from a collapse of confidence.

V

Industrialization and Social Problems

A survey of Egypt's population problems and agricultural development shows that the building up of industry could alone answer all
its economic and human problems and ensure the country's food and
independence. But at the same time it can be seen that neither its
natural resources nor its structure favours Egypt's becoming an
industrial nation.

It is natural that the military government's first care has been to
set up a Production Committee whose main task is to speed industrial development. But it was only at the beginning of 1956 that
Nasser set up the Planning Committee to synchronize agricultural
and industrial policy after experience had shown that, in a country whose structure is essentially agricultural, industry can only
develop in close harmony with the development of the land. This
attempt at planned economy is still cautious, but as much as the
diplomatic situation it has helped to knit Egypt and the Eastern
countries more closely together. In the past two years, in the course
of many journeys and missions to China, Russia, Poland and
Czechoslovakia, Egyptian engineers, businessmen and economists
have become convinced that some planning of the national economy
could and must be achieved.

Of all the advice given to the government between 1954 and 1956,
that of the Polish economist Oscar Lange was given most attention.
But before being able to formulate an overall policy the Egyptian
technicians had to make a systematic survey of agricultural resources,
industrial potential, the population's needs and the demographic
problem. None of all this had been done before. This lack of basic
information partly explains the slowness of government planning,
and we already know that a fifteen-year Plan has been drawn up with
a view to industrializing the country on a co-operative basis.

Of course, Egyptian industry is not an invention of its military
leaders. Arriving in Cairo, one is struck by the huge industrial
districts of Bulaq and Shubra, or in Alexandria by the great

factories with their towering chimneys which are seen from the harbour, or the Kafr el Dawar factory and its housing estate. All these undertakings were prosperous long before the Officers seized power.

It was Mohamed Ali who created what we might call a real industry. But already in the Middle Ages there were thriving mills which were at their best in the Fatimid period. There was a flourishing trade with foreign markets, dealing in wool and linen fabrics, leather goods and arms. As early as the sixteenth century, however, the Ottoman conquest ended this development. Egyptian craftsmen were transferred in their thousands to Constantinople, and the luxury-trade vanished from the country, leaving nothing but some local craftsmanship. It was mainly in order to satisfy the army's needs that Mohamed Ali created large factories. The first of these produced only warlike stores (muskets, sabres, gunpowder), and the new textile industry had the army as its first customer.

The sudden expansion of cotton-growing led the Viceroy to mechanize spinning and weaving on a large scale. The State factories in 1840 employed up to 100,000 hands, not only supplying the home market but exporting all over the Levant. The Viceroy, who was the sole contractor and banker, appealed to foreign engineers, technicians and administrators, mainly French and English, but his plans finally broke down. However, he achieved one of the aims which made him a modern-minded statesman, which was 'to get the population used to factory-work'. His successors drew conclusions from this relative failure, and when the factories were in difficulties Sa'id Pasha gave the finishing blow by abolishing the monopolies, less than ten years after his father's death. In the course of the second half of the nineteenth century it was foreign capital's turn to try to develop Egypt. The boom in cotton brought about by the American Civil War, the cutting of the Suez Canal and the Capitulations system which practically made foreign businessmen immune from the law, attracted both capital and immigrants to Egypt. But they were less interested in industry than in transport companies, public services, building-societies and the like. Trade and commerce remained in Levantine hands. The main aim of the British occupation was to open the Egyptian market to British industries and develop cotton still further. Cromer's and Milner's programme can be summed up as follows: Egypt represents an important market for British industry and a perfect supplier of raw materials for its textiles, and must remain an agricultural country.

Thus the few surviving industries (textiles, sugar, paper, soap, cement, glass) came to a low ebb by the turn of the century.

It was the first World War that revived Egyptian industry. The growing scarcity of European imports was the natural cause of this, but the government encouraged it by setting up a Committee for Commerce and Industry under a young financier, Isma'il Sidqi, who was to play an important part in Egyptian history. Immediately after the war, in 1920, the creation of the Misr Bank gave the necessary impulse. The Bank aimed at setting up new industrial concerns with the help of Egyptian capital, which was called on for the first time. The State also gave its support to the new small industries by opening the Industrial Credit for this purpose, and by guaranteeing the Misr Bank which was enabled to issue industrial loans. By 1936 the credit funds amounted to a million pounds. But government help was no longer enough to face industry's growing needs or encourage its further development.

With the second World War the era of true industrial expansion began. While import tariffs in 1930 already favoured national undertakings, the new conditions brought about by the war increased production by 50 per cent and the number of companies rose from 2,400 to 3,200. At the end of the war the national income had increased by a quarter. The food industry (sugar, spirits, beer, salt, flour, oil), the clothing industry (textiles and shoes) and the tobacco industry benefited most from the presence of thousands of foreign troops on Egyptian soil. The departure of the troops left many firms in a precarious state in the next three years. But the upward trend had started and the large factories modernized their organization and equipment.

The next encouragement came from a war, that in Korea. In 1951 cotton fetched fantastic prices and the industry reaped huge profits. But a year later the government collapsed and, for different reasons, so did the price of cotton. If the military leaders had it in their power to better a corrupt political set-up, they had more trouble in facing disastrous economic conditions. While cotton prices were falling in the world market the British, the traditional buyers of Egyptian raw material, were boycotting the crop in order to force Neguib's hand during the Canal Zone negotiations. New outlets had to be found. The Officers saw for themselves how their country's economy depended on agriculture, and more precisely on cotton which can either make Egypt's fortune or ruin her. So they determined to rescue Egypt, at all costs, from her position as a purely agricultural country.

ENSURING ECONOMIC INDEPENDENCE

The first care of any Egyptian government worthy of the name must be to try to free Egypt from a system of colonial economy and create an independent economy. But such a vast reconversion, involving both agriculture and industry, cannot be achieved in ten years, never mind two.

What, in fact, are Egypt's resources? There is some iron-ore near the Red Sea, but no coal. So far Egypt's oil output, two and a half million tons a year, is not enough for her needs. The electricity output is 50 kilowatts per head, less than half the average consumption in the Lebanon or Greece. On the other hand, the national supply circuit covers only half the production, since the large factories in Cairo and Alexandria produce their own energy. Two new power-stations have been built in Cairo since 1952, but the costs are very high. This is why the electrification of the Aswan Dam is regarded as being so urgent: this would give in 1958 or 1959 enough electric power to achieve the first stage in industrialization: the production of enough nitrate fertilizers to meet the country's needs, and cheap electric current. But the military government's first aim is to produce iron and steel, the two symbols of a strong State. There is already a small iron industry, the recovery of scrap-iron from the surplus left by the armies in the last war, to which some imported iron (especially from France) is added, mainly for making railway-sleepers and building rods. But with a rapidly increasing demand, imports were already doubled by 1947. When the Officers seized power three big concerns were producing 50,000 tons of iron per annum. The fuels used were heavy oil and electricity. Egypt's mineral resources have not yet been exploited: the reserves are thought to be about 200 million tons, half of which contains pure iron.

It was the German firm Demag which in 1954 obtained the much-sought contract for building blast-furnaces where the Red Sea ore will finally be treated. At first there was a plan for building the foundries and factories near the future Aswan Dam so as to use the cheap electrical power for smelting the ore. As the mines are not so far from Aswan there would have been some saving on transport. But, wisely, as events have proved, the Egyptian leaders thought it

370

would be imprudent to count on the dam, when the finances for its construction were still not forthcoming. So the steel-works are being built near Cairo, at Helwan, a spa-town which was fashionable in the nineteenth century. Using imported coke, it should produce 150,000 tons of steel in the first year (1958 or 1959) and 240,000 tons three years later. The present needs being 300,000 tons, and with two other factories producing 50,000 tons, Egypt could be self-supporting by 1962. On this account the subsidiary metallurgical industries (light tools, household equipment, car-bodies) are rapidly expanding.

In order to protect this new industry and save the scarce foreign currency it requires, import licences for luxury and expendable goods were suppressed early in 1956. Only raw materials can be imported, and tariffs on these have been reduced (one per cent *ad valorem* for iron and iron by-products) and sometimes even abolished (on materials for making tyres, cinema equipment and machine tools). The first result of this protectionist policy has been to fill the market with many Egyptian-made goods (household articles, plastic goods, furniture). As there are no more import licences for private cars, some firms import chassis (2 CV Citroen) and the bodies are fitted in Alexandria. Many buses and coaches are thus 'dressed' in Egypt. By the end of 1957 a factory now being built should be producing railway-carriages (now mainly imported from Hungary and Poland); a bicycle factory, 25,000 machines a year. Nor must we overlook the factories for light armaments, munitions and the upkeep of war material, and the two arsenals which Nasser—like Mohamed Ali—is bent on creating. These can supply not only the Egyptian army but also those of the other Arab countries.

Though metallurgy is given most attention by the government, whose ambition—we repeat—is to create heavy industries in Egypt, the most spectacular boom is now in building materials: cement, bricks, tiles and sandstone.[1] But the demand is so large that the three cement factories, though they have lifted their output, cannot meet present needs. This is the more so because the large State public works need 75 per cent of their production for building roads, installing drinking-water in the villages, town-planning, building cheap housing, and harbour installations. The government has had to allow imports in order to fill the gap until a fourth factory starts producing and the existing factories are enlarged.

[1] 1939—369,000 tons; 1953—1,500,000 tons.

The traditional industries are also sharing in this expansion. As far as cotton goods are concerned, the government is trying to increase the output of spun fabrics and improve their quality, so as to export finished goods instead of raw material. These fabrics are already a matter for trade pacts, especially with the new Eastern customers. Their production has gone up by 14·5 per cent between 1954 and 1955. But local consumption is increasing too slowly—by only 2·1 per cent in 1955.

Oil-refining has increased by 80 per cent since the State refinery started up in Suez in 1956. The building of a new refinery in the same year in Alexandria should enable the country to meet its needs. On the other hand, there was disappointment at the drop in extraction owing to the drying-up of the Red Sea wells, in spite of the discovery of new oil reserves in the Sinai Desert. American oil-companies are still prospecting in the western part of this desert. Today Egypt has to import about a third of her oil and this lack of fuel is one of the nation's main problems, especially as there is an increasing demand together with a falling output. Imports necessarily have unfortunate repercussions on the balance of payments. This has been partly offset in 1955 by barter agreements with Russia and Rumania. On the other hand, the completion of the Suez–Cairo pipeline in July 1956 means a drop in the initial cost of fuel.

Despite considerable local resources, the food industries are developing very slowly, and this can be traced to a narrow home-market. Only the sugar industry, the oldest in the country, is prospering. None the less, Egypt has to import 100,000 tons of raw sugar, although she produces 200,000 tons of cane-sugar. At the beginning of 1956 the government nationalized the sugar-factories and invited tenders for the building of a new refinery.

The chemical industries are developing at a normal rate, especially the oil, soap, perfume and soda industries. The production of fertilizers is expanding. Egypt turns its phosphates into super-phosphates at the rate of 200,000 tons a year, which meets its requirements. A very modern factory built in the Suez in 1951—which the government would very much like to nationalize—uses the gas from the oil-refineries and produces 200,000 tons of nitrates. On the other hand, a Franco-German concern has been given a contract for building another nitrates factory at Aswan, which in 1958 or 1959 will be using the existing dam's electric power and produce 300,000 tons of fertilizers per annum.

Finally, we must also mention the prosperous state of some new industries (tyres, tiles and stoneware, wool-carding, ready-made clothes, furniture, aluminium articles, and above all electrical equipment and all materials connected with the building industry).

A STRANGE STRUCTURE—NO 'MEDIUM' INDUSTRY

The striking feature of Egypt's industrial position is the way it resembles the agricultural structure. In both there is no 'middle-class' group. Side by side with a multitude of small concerns bordering on craftsmen's workshops and employing less than ten workers, we find only huge trusts run on 'vertical' lines. There are now about a million industrial workers in Egypt. 25,000 firms employ less than 10 workers each, and 68 per cent have less than 5. Only 65 of the factories employ more than 500 workers. These conditions will be seen to be of the first importance when it comes to enforcing labour-laws or those on social conditions. The spinning mills have the largest concentration of labour: the two large factories of the Misr firm, at Kafr el Dawar and Mehalla el Kubra, alone employ 30,000 workers. At the same time, in Cairo a host of weaving-rooms have a staff of less than five hands.

Indeed, Egypt has not yet reached the industrial stage in the proper sense of the word. The factory-structure is still that of the craftsman stage, while the big concerns still depend on a colonial system of monopolies. Their creation was due to the fact that many large factories had to produce their own energy, repair their own equipment, transport their own products and even sell or export them themselves—some factories have their own shops. The narrowness of the market obliges certain firms to treat their basic products themselves, so as to be able to increase their initial production. Thus some cement factories have to make pipes and tiles, on which they reap larger profits than on the raw material they set out to make.

The most striking instance of multiple production is the firm belonging to Ahmed Abbud, who formerly owned all the sugar-factories and neighbouring distilleries (which are now nationalized), as well as an oil-refinery in Suez with its adjoining fertilizer-factory and, finally, an important shipping-company.

THE STATE AS PUBLIC CONTRACTOR

It is probably in the field of industry that the military leaders' policy is most clearly defined. The policy can be summed up in a few words: direction and strict control of the means of production; war on private monopolies; an effort to set up medium industries and the establishment of a vast system of 'mixed economy'.

The January 1956 constitution lays down the main lines of the national economy: to increase production while taking social justice into account, and to co-ordinate public and private economy. Only the State feels that it is capable of remedying the lack of financial resources and of individual drive. Thus it plays its part in the new industries and banks (The Industrial Bank, Republic Bank) so as to encourage private capital as well as production: in some cases the State owns 51 per cent of the shares. We once asked Mr Ahmed Fuad, said to be Nasser's closest economic adviser, whether this meant the beginning of a development towards Socialism, and he replied, 'No. The Egyptian State only interferes in two ways; to give businesses more initiative or to right abuses which might have been brought about by private enterprise.'

State direction and control are none the less very strict. For instance, nobody is allowed to open or extend a factory without permission from the Production Council, whose task is to synchronize such efforts with national requirements. The State also intervenes in the matter of granting or refusing import licences, and in 1956 only firms working for the government got what they wanted. Another sign of State intervention is the enforcement of the law which protects the Egyptian: employment of foreign labour is practically forbidden, except for such technicians as cannot be found locally, priority being given to what are called 'true Egyptians', in other words, Moslems. On the other hand, since the State controls the two great industrial-credit organizations, it thus controls the distribution of credits. Only in exceptional cases has the struggle against the monopoly system taken the form of nationalization. The two main instances of such steps affected Ahmed Abbud's sugar-factories and distilleries, and the Suez Canal Company. The first case was essentially a repressive measure, and the second a political gesture with international implications.

As for the creation of medium-sized industrial firms based on local Egyptian resources, this is one of the military government's most urgent problems. We have seen how in its first stage this took the form of rural-industrial co-operatives which are the nucleus of small rural industry. But for the moment they are groping in the dark. On the other hand, the government can give decisive support to the few medium-sized national undertakings by becoming their best customer, instead of buying abroad. For the State, which is now local industry's best customer, is in a sense a public contractor.

The present state of Egyptian industry is not bad. But the total invested capital is put at £200 million, which is not much. Existing firms are prosperous and their profits are substantial. In 1955 there was a sensational increase in profits by companies producing building-materials, with a 65 per cent rise in share-values. Industry is characterized by its high profits and stability just as much as foreign trade is marked by its instability. Average monetary returns fluctuate between 13 and 20 per cent, and customs protection is strong.

But though prosperous and reasonably well balanced, industry is only developing very slowly. Companies prefer to distribute large dividends instead of reinvesting in order to increase their production. And the Egyptian capitalists are still loth to invest, while foreign investors are afraid and holding off.

Egyptian industry has to face problems common to all under-developed countries. First there is the absence of a middle-class which alone could supply the savings needed for local investments as well as the human element for a genuine home-market. Only an expansion of the home-market by raising the living-standards of 18 million fellahs, and their promotion to the rank of consumers, can break down the barriers facing industry. Egypt can do nothing about this: without consumers there can be no producers and no capital.

Another handicap is the poor output and quality of the labour-force. A 'fall in the technical level and output of the workers' and a standstill in production[1] have been noticed recently. An industrial revolution cannot be managed without an improvement in the workman's technical training and modernization of equipment. In Egypt, as in most under-developed countries where capital is relatively scarce and labour plentiful, industrial executives tend to prefer men to machines and neglect improvements in technique and production, so reaping illusory profits. The output of the underfed, badly housed and often sick Egyptian workers is very low. For the most

[1] Dr Zaki Badawi: *The Labour Problem.*

part illiterate and without technical skill, they make up a body of underpaid and over-numerous labourers. Two large textile factories admit to employing twice as many hands as would be needed in Europe. As for the managerial staff, they are too numerous, often inefficient and almost always overpaid. In the end the cost in manpower for a given article is sometimes higher than in Europe.

Moreover, basic materials are more costly. The lack of coal and the inadequate water-supply are badly felt. Wood, rubber, silk, tobacco and most wool are imported. This is also true of most agricultural produce. In Cairo, milk costs twice as much as in Europe and most farming products, whether meat or vegetables, are of inferior quality. If the government is to industrialize agriculture it must first of all rationalize and standardize production.

One of the most surprising and disappointing results of this situation is the price of Egyptian cotton fabrics. This is because the raw material is inadequate. Local industry is obliged to use superior-quality cotton of long and medium-length fibres, whereas with its market for the cheapest possible goods it should be using short fibres. Other countries such as India could supply these, but the introduction of new seed of this type would result in a decline in quality of Egyptian cotton. Thus Egypt is in the paradoxical position of having to produce cheap cotton goods, out of cotton that France, Britain and Italy import for their most luxurious textiles.

As we have seen, in Egypt everything is against a rational development of industry. Industry has no real future unless the State gives support and protection, natural and human resources are developed, equipment modernized, and the masses' purchasing power high enough to give industry a proper home-market. In the words of one of the government leaders, 'It will take Egypt more than thirty years to become a truly industrialized country.' Such a vast upheaval of the social and economic structure obviously takes more than a generation.

The ruinous dilemma in which Egypt is placed as regards industry, is that the State, which is its best backer, contractor, customer and protector, frightens the already over-cautious national capitalists as well as the foreign ones, by inopportunely or harshly interfering, and sometimes with racial prejudice. Without foreign investment being attracted, the Egyptian economy is condemned to its vicious circle. It was because Nasser was so painfully conscious of this that his repeated demands on the West strained their relations to the point of bringing about the Suez crisis. But the crisis is likely to result in a further flight of capital, which cannot be attracted by threats.

It is interesting to note that the present development of the Egyptian economy appears to be coming full circle. In the nineteenth century Mohamed Ali set up state-capitalism. At the beginning of the twentieth century this was replaced by private capitalism, both foreign and Egyptian. With Nasser's mixed or compromise system of economy there is a curious return to the original formula.

EGYPTIAN WORKERS ARE NOT A PROLETARIAT

Anyone visiting the housing-estate of the Misr spinning-mills at Mehalla el Kubra, 60 miles north of Cairo, is struck by the difference between the agricultural 'civilization'—whose sad image can be seen in the villages through which one passes—and the appearance of this industrial civilization. The cottages are white, laid out on urban lines, with hospitals, mosques, clubs, sports-grounds and swimming-pools. A large restaurant enables 2,000 unmarried people, housed in hostels, to be decently fed. 500 families live in the relatively comfortable two- or three-roomed houses. The factory's 25,000 workers benefit from a proper system of social services planned according to modern standards, with savings banks, co-operative stores, insurance against accident, sickness and old age. Here the outlay for social facilities amounts to a fifth of total outlay on wages (in France this is two-fifths). But out of 25,000 factories, only 23 have built homes for their workers. Only 37 have a resident medical and nursing staff. Only 125,000 workers, employed in 150 factories, benefit from social and medical services worthy of the name. In spite of strict legislation, social facilities and their running are left to the discretion of the management. The paternalist system dominates industry just as the semi-feudal system dominates the rural areas.

Egypt today employs 1,300,000 workers, of whom 7 per cent are children and 3 per cent women. So far only a small minority enjoy the benefits of labour and social legislation. The Kom Ombo sugar-factories in Upper Egypt, which have just been nationalized, offer their workers none of the 'luxuries' available at Melhalla. They have a club and a swimming-pool, fine cottages are scattered about in a park, but none of this is for the workers. Only the engineers and clerks profit from them. In the sickening and suffocating heat of the sugar-refinery, the workers, bare to the waist, earn their 12 piastres a day—about two shillings. They are seasonal labourers, fellahs who come from round about into the factory, when the sugar-cane harvested in the district is brought in. Work in the sugar-factory lasts only six months, so the worker remains a peasant for half the year and goes back to his *fas* when the factory shuts down.

Undertakings of this kind which employ real fellahs are not numerous. Most factories are in the great industrial areas, 25 per cent of them in Cairo and 22 per cent in Alexandria. There the industrial pioneers—generally foreigners—came to settle, creating a centre of attraction for the labourers, who hope to earn more than their pittance in the country. This explains why the Egyptian worker is still very much a peasant at heart. In most cases he has not lost his attachment to the soil and often lives alone in the city, leaving his family in the village. We shall see later that this attachment to the land is one of the main reasons for the lack of an efficient workers' organization.

Thus there are a million workers but no working-class. This enormous mass of workers contains more than 90 per cent un-skilled labourers, who come into industry because they cannot make a living in the country, and who have no unity of purpose or sense of class. A mere minority consisting of foremen and skilled foreigners are to be called workers in the Western sense of the word. However, it is not absurd to say that the industrial workers are a privileged group as a whole. This can be explained by a rapid survey of the distribution and employment of the population. Out of 23,500,000 inhabitants, 6 million are effectively engaged in agriculture, 1,300,000 in industry, 900,000 in commerce, 450,000 in the liberal professions, 500,000 in the State service, 3 million in domestic service, while 1,500,000 have 'non-productive' occupations and 10 million are 'unemployed'. The laws regulating labour are not applied to civil servants, domestics, peasants, members of the professions, nor, of course, to 'non-productive' and 'unemployed' persons. The huge mass of the workless population (one cannot say 'out of work' because that would mean that they had worked in the past) is left outside State protection. The industrial workers alone are protected.

Most of them, however, do not get the benefit of the law. Laws regulating work are not enforced in the case of smaller undertakings, and we have seen that they form a large majority: 20,000 of them employing 70 per cent of the total number of workmen escape the application of the law. The individual labour-contract introduced in

1944 and modified by an Order in Council of December 1952 does not apply to concerns employing less than five workers or using no machinery, which is frequent. Neither is it applied in the case of seasonal or temporary employment, nor of domestic servants or children under 17 years of age (these are considered as employed 'on trial' and the employer can break the contract without compensation or notice).

Thus, when we say that factory-workers are a privileged group— an undeniable fact if we compare them with the true proletarian— the huge mass of 'non-productive' persons and the peasants—we must add that the laws regulating work and improving the workers' conditions are preferential and flagrantly unjust. The larger undertakings are the only ones which cannot escape the regulations. Mr Zaki Badawi, a competent specialist in all labour problems and a lecturer in Alexandria University, wrote on this subject, 'to extend the laws regulating work to all enterprises, without distinction, is a question of justice because there is no doubt that workers in small enterprises have the same need—if not a greater one—for social protection'. On the other hand, he stresses that 'a large part of the legislation governing working conditions remains a dead letter, either because the directors of small firms avoid enforcing it, or because its application gives rise to different or entirely erroneous interpretations'.

Though they are numerous, the social laws drafted by the military government remain fragmentary and preferential. Only a firm employing 20 workmen is under any obligation to keep a 'medicine-chest' with a supply of first-aid materials in case of accidents (August 1953). Only in factories with over 50 workers is the employer obliged to have resident nurse and a visiting doctor at regular intervals for medical examinations and care. But the doctor himself is only bound to give the 'normal attention' expected of a general practitioner. When a firm employs 500 workers, then only is there any obligation to supply free medical aid and hospital treatment. Now, there are only 64 undertakings in Egypt coming into this category, and the total of workers they employ is about 150,000 out of a working population of 12 million.

WOMEN AND CHILDREN FIRST

The first social law goes back to 1909. It hardly came before time, for it fixed 9 as the minimum age for children to work in industry, 'in order to end abuses'. More surprising still was the new law of 1953, which keeps this age of 9, while restricting the employment of children to 'light, non-mechanical industries', that is to say spinning and weaving, which employ many children. There is no restriction on the employment of children in agriculture, commerce, domestic service and arts and crafts. The young 9-year-old worker, however, will benefit from certain advantages—a 7-hour day, one free day per week, and exclusion from all kinds of dangerous occupations. But at 12 he is regarded as an adult. His day's work goes up to 9 or 10 hours as in the case of adults. It is really startling that a régime which aims at both developing productivity and output, and expanding general education, has not forbidden the employment of children of 14, or at least 12, when there is a redundancy of labour in the cities. Such a step would of course dissatisfy everyone, the parents robbed of extra income, the employers of cheap labour, and perhaps the children themselves. But such considerations are of little weight in view of the fact that the employment of juveniles not only results in illiteracy but also in the poor quality of the Egyptian worker. Entering the factory at the age of 10, a child without primary education or technical training can at best be turned into a specialized labourer. As a consequence, Egypt is suffering from a low rate of production, the worker from a miserable wage and the whole country from illliteracy. What would happen if primary education were not compulsory?

As for women, who make up only 3 per cent of industrial workers, let us note this piquant remark by Professor Zaki Badawi: 'Most Egyptian weaving-mills employ women because of the low rate of their wages and the gentleness of their disposition.' One could hardly put it more plainly.

This piecemeal legislation has some intriguing details. Thus in 1944 the law-maker decreed, 'Considering that under-nourishment is a threat to the health of a great many workers, the owners of industrial and commercial firms with at least 50 workers, and owners of more than 200 feddans of land, will be under obligation to supply a meal on every working-day at a very low price, only half of which will be paid by the worker.' The military legislators in 1953, concerned at the inadequate enforcement of the law, passed a decree to complete it, laying down the menus to be served. Nine menus, as varied as possible, including even three breakfast menus, were offered to unimaginative employers. Here is an example: 'Meal

No. 3: two rolls; 2 ounces of cheese or 1 gill of milk; a dish of 4 ounces of beans or lentils, not to be mashed, with an ounce of cotton-oil, an ounce of tomatoes, 15 grammes of salt, ¼ gramme of pepper, and if possible half a gramme of lemon; and, finally, 5 ounces of greens or salads.' Three meat-meals per week are recommended, consisting of buffalo, goat or young camel meat. There follows a series of instructions and definitions: 'By salads, are meant . . .' and a final, touching recommendation, 'The meals served on two consecutive days must not be identical.' Obviously these 'menus' have served no other purpose than to water the mouth of the poor, painstaking civil servant who so lovingly worked them out: '. . . and if possible half a gramme of lemon.'

This humorous example shows once again how ineffective the law is, because it is badly adapted to conditions in the country. In Europe the laws regulating labour have been the outcome of a human and social progress which kept pace with industrialization. Here, the working masses remain unorganized, helpless and so to speak apathetic to their own fate. Thus legislation has been out of step with the organization of the trades and professions; it is the work of a few lawyers, cut off from the masses and with only the vaguest idea of the country's economic conditions, the capacities of employers or the workers' actual needs. On the other hand, the government's often untimely interference in relations between employers and employed, and in the workers' organizations, is a hindrance to the development of class-consciousness, which remains the principal agent of social progress.

A decree of September 1953 created a High Advisory Council for Labour Questions, responsible for 'giving advice on laws regulating labour, before they are promulgated'. But out of its 26 members there are 14 State representatives (the Minister, as Chairman, 9 Under-Secretaries of State and 4 executives) as against 6 employers and only 6 workers (4 industrial workers, 1 peasant and 1 commercial clerk). Furthermore, these workers are selected by the administration.

This shows how badly the interested parties are represented. In December 1953 the government brought in another law concerning the 'settling and arbitration of labour disputes'. Each committee (for this purpose) is made up of a magistrate, a higher civil servant from the Ministry of Labour, an employer and two trade-union representatives. The latter are entirely helpless, as we shall see.

COMPLIANT TRADES UNIONS

The State's grip on the working classes can only be explained by the inefficiency of the workers' organizations. This inefficiency springs from extreme differences from one factory to another. Two large factories employ 35,000 workers; 66 factories have a total of 110,000 workers, but 25,000 others employ 150,000 between them. It is very difficult for the workers, scattered as they are, without any spontaneous sense of class, and directed by foreign foremen, to group themselves into trades unions.

The old mediaeval guilds had degenerated and collapsed by 1882. Eight years later the first attempts at creating syndicates on the Western model were started by tramway and tobacco workers. Their numbers continued to increase and in 1921 the first trade union was founded. In 1930, the Nabil Abbas Halim, who had political ambitions, founded the General Federation of Egyptian Workers. Roused by this competition to its Left wing, the Wafd tried to turn this new force in its own favour and to attract the working-class vote. With this aim in mind Fuad Sirag ud-Din founded the Free Trades Unions group. In 1942 the Wafdist Nahas Pasha government brought in the first law recognizing trades unions, at least as negotiating bodies.

This first trade-union law was completed and modified by the new régime in December 1952. 'Workers belonging to the same trade . . . may group themselves into trades unions with a view to safeguarding their interests, defending their rights and improving their material and social conditions.' The law became applicable for the first time to agricultural labourers. But 'the worker cannot belong to a trade union if he is under 15'—a clause which excludes a large number of workers. Civil servants and members of the army and police are also excluded. Trades unions within factories and trades are authorized and several unions for the same trade or profession are allowed to merge, but only one Federation is allowed for the country as a whole.

The government, which had not forgotten the 1936 strikes (echoes of the Popular Front movement in France), or those of 1938 and the labour unrest of 1945-6 and 1951, has provided for a strict control of the workers' organizations by the administration. Each union must declare its founding to the Labour Office, which can veto it in case of any breach of regulations. All meetings must be notified at the Labour Office in advance, and the union must declare its balance-

382

sheet to the Office every six months. At all times the Labour Inspectors have the right to inspect the books at the trade-union office or headquarters.

But there is also another kind of pressure, which is not stated in the law. This is pressure brought by the working section of the Liberation Rally, the régime's mass-movement. As might be expected, it is an officer, Major Abdallah Tu'aima, who has supreme control over the trade-union organization and is in charge of the leaders' political education, and the law expressly states that 'it is forbidden to deal with political or religious problems'. Major Tu'aima does not confine himself to education: among the union leaders he has recruited—especially in the transport unions—some picked men who ensure that he has absolute control of the situation. It can be said—without any malice towards him personally—that the employers never knock in vain at this zealous officer's door, and that his interference causes some dissatisfaction among the official labour-administration.

It is also under cover of 'training for union membership' that an expert from the American C.I.O. was attached to the Labour Office in 1954 and ran a course with a view to 'perfecting' union officials. On the other hand, we must note that the union leaders are, if not appointed, at least approved by the administration, and that the running of the unions is practically under the management's control.

But the main restriction on the workers' organizations' independence and activities lies in the fact that the new Constitution, though suppressing martial law, did not give the workers the right to strike. Strikes are illegal, and the working class is thus deprived of its chief weapon. There have been some attempts at striking since the new régime came to power, but these were generally crushed in secret. There is no need to insist on the bloodshed at Kafr el Dawar in August 1952, which only stiffened the army's hostility to the working classes. There is still less need to insist on the peculiar 'General Strike' of April 1954, carefully prepared by the Liberation Rally to give Nasser the appearance of the masses' approval and ensure his defeat of Neguib. The business executives had orders to pay the workers their day's wages and give them transport, so that they could demonstrate in a body in the centre of the city, while public transport had been brought to a standstill by order of the administration . . . But a real strike broke out in Alexandria among the dockers in the spring of 1956. They did not have long to wait for the greater part of the wage-increase they were asking for (2½ piastres a day), but it was

383

impossible to find out whether the ringleaders were arrested. The year before, in the Shubra weaving-mills in Cairo which has the most powerful trade-union organization in Egypt, the workers stopped work to protest against their poor pay and unhealthy premises. But when compared with the extent of Egyptian poverty, such expressions of discontent are mild indeed.

The agricultural unions, numbering 62 and with a membership of 12,000 fellahs, are still less efficient. Even at the local level they have never been able to enforce the minimum wage of 18 piastres a day—as unions they exist only on paper.

The 1,157 trades unions—717 of them representing industry and 438 the professions—nearly all penetrated by the administration and the police, remain weak when confronted by the employers and management and a suspicious, well-armed government. In any case the movement lacks leaders. When one emerges there is dissension over his personality. The very energetic Mudarrak was sent to Paris in 1945 to represent Egypt at the Congress of Workers' Trades Unions, but this mission aroused considerable jealousy and not long after his return to Cairo he was imprisoned as a communist, along with many other leaders. Freed in 1949, he has since taken no part in workers' organizations.

The attitude of the military government towards the unions is two-faced, but can easily be explained; on the one hand by its genuine concern for social reform, on the other by the need to encourage capital investment in industry, its use of demagogic methods and its fear of any mass disorder. It may be remarked that in most labour conflicts the administration decides in favour of the workmen. But there are some heads of firms who, when critical situations arise, have been known to appeal to the Liberation Rally leaders.

The trades unions' weakness is not only due to the action of the military leaders. Long before the *coup d'état* they were used for political purposes, exploited as a shock-weapon against this or that government and especially against the British. A typical instance of 'trade union' activity in Egypt was the part which the workers were made to play in November 1951, after the denunciation of the Anglo-Egyptian treaty by the Wafdist government. The workers employed in the Canal Zone by the occupation forces were summoned back to Cairo by the Ministry for Social Affairs, and in exchange were given financial compensation. This was severely criticized in the Press, which pointed out that 18,000 workers had been called back but that 60,000 salaries had been paid out.

All the trade-union leaders with whom we have been in contact during the last three years regret their inability to create a class of responsible workers with a real trade-union spirit, who would pursue their activities without fear and build up a strong central union. They all regret that they have been unable to obtain the enforcement of the law on collective work-contracts. The protection allowed by this law is illusory, because the so-called work-contract is settled between the firm's union and the employer, both taken individually, while the factory union is in no way independent of the employer. The most elementary rule of equal pay for equal work is not applied: wages are not standardized within a single industry, and the conditions of employment remain geared to the availability of labour in a given region, and to the cost of living.

But considered from the point of view of quantity, it must be said that Egyptian trade-unionism is steadily improving. About 90 per cent of transport workers belong to a union. Textile unions have only 38 per cent of workers' membership, on account of the host of small workshops. Finally, from 1950 to 1952 the number of unions has doubled, and the membership rose to about 300,000 in 1956. After all, Egypt is not the only country where trade-union activity has a strong political bias. Once set in working-order, improvements and efforts towards independence can be expected.

A final word on the relations between the military government and the unions. One is easily tempted to see Nasser as another Peron, and to compare their appeal to the working masses. At that level the comparison would be in Nasser's favour. He has not exploited the unions as cynically as Peron. But the Egyptian proletariat have been far from drawing the same benefits from Nasser's reforming dictatorship as the *descaminados* did from Peron's. Nasser has exploited the poor less than Peron, but has also served them less well.

YET THESE ARE THE PRIVILEGED . . .

Inadequately protected as they are by the laws we have examined, and by their unions and even by the administration, the factory-workers remain—and this is no scandalous assertion—none the less a highly privileged section of the huge, poverty-stricken mass of the

Egyptian proletariat. In actual fact they still have two legal weapons which they can use against foreign industrialists as well as against arbitrary decisions on the part of their employer. The first of these weapons is the clause which obliges all undertakings to employ at least 90 per cent Egyptian labour, which must draw 80 per cent of wages (we have criticized this text elsewhere because it does not encourage immediate industrial expansion). But humanly speaking it is easy to justify this. On the other hand, the factory-worker has the advantage of being well protected against dismissal. Even when a reduction of staff is justified by a fall in output or a shrinking of the market, the employer must apply for a dismissal-permit, which is almost always automatically refused. The same thing happens in most individual cases, whether there has been a professional offence or not. Still, we know of a large concern which, by obtaining support from influential people and paying for it, manages to dismiss a few workers every year. Part of the budget has even been devoted to this operation, for it is important to keep the fear of insecurity constantly in the worker's mind, even if it costs money.

Such legal obligations as there are, even if they can be subject to errors of interpretation, give the factory-workers enormous advantages compared with other trades, because, as we have said, they are the only ones to benefit from legislation.

But it is especially in his wage-rates that the industrial labourer is privileged, compared with the agricultural worker and domestic servant. In 1956 his average wages were 25 to 30 piastres a day (5 to 6 shillings). But in many industries the average is higher. Moreover, they have increased considerably since 1952, while agricultural wages have dropped. In the building trade the average wage rose from 15 to 40 piastres a day between 1953 and 1956. The highest wages are paid in transport, being about 30 shillings a day in 1956. Next come wages in the oil industry at £1 a day; electricity, 12 shillings; mining, 8 shillings. The textile industry, which employs the largest percentage of labour, pays an average of 8 shillings a day because of the number of underpaid women and children. But this is still far from the florin or half-crown a day paid to the agricultural worker. To be sure, the town worker has to give 15 to 20 per cent of his wages for accommodation; but he can live on a few piastres and in any case eats as frugally as his country cousin.

Married workers generally allow their wives to take a job, mainly in domestic service—there are some 2,600,000 domestics!

Ahmed is a telephone engineer in Cairo. He earns 30 piastres a day. He drinks 10 glasses of tea at 1 piastre each, making 10 piastres. He smokes 8 piastres-worth of cigarettes. At noon he has a bean-sandwich for lunch with a piece of cream-cheese and a bean-salad, for 3 piastres. He takes the bus twice, 4 piastres. He is left with 5 piastres with which he can afford a seat in the cinema now and again (1 piastre) or save enough to smoke hashish (25 piastres, which is dear). His wife Suraya has a 'good' job and is paid £6 a month for acting as a general maid from 8 a.m. to 4 p.m., being given her midday meal. She pays the rent of 35 shillings a month for a very poor room. She does the shopping for the evening meal. She 'hides' money for the celebration-cakes (there is always some celebration in the offing in Egypt). From time to time she buys a cotton frock at 8 shillings, a pair of shoes at 12 shillings. The children are left to their own devices and do not thrive. The doctor is expensive. They never save—there is no such thing as saving in Egypt.

Thus the man who is in work is not exactly 'miserable'. But one hardly dares think of the hundreds of thousands of unemployed, the million and a half who figure in the statistics for 'non-productive occupations', that mass of humanity trying to raise one piastre in order to eat or smoke, and who more often than not smoke, or spend their piastre on the black tea which helps them to forget.

In short, the worker would be relatively happy if he had a job. Or rather, the masses would be happy if they could do a real day's work instead of a thousand odd-jobs.

VI

The Aswan Dam Problem

Aswan is first and foremost a masterpiece of negro art. The first Nile cataracts contained by the present dam or barrage since 1902 have polished and carved the purple slabs of rock on the river-bed. You can row among the rapids in a little boat, in a fantastic landscape worthy of Henry Moore. The huge dam (the so-called 'small' one) thrusts a vast sheet of calm water amid this chaos of stone. A group of French and Swedish engineers are now installing the power-stations which in 1958 will supply power for the new industries, especially the fertilizer-factory which is now being erected by Franco-German firms.

After a calm sail on the lake we approach a dark line. Soon the cornice of the temple of Philae emerges, built on an island submerged beneath the waters. In September when the river is in spate and the sluices are open, the island and its temples reappear on the surface. Only during the three months of spate, the hottest months when the temperature rises to 120° Fahrenheit, can one see the thirteen Nubian temples built on the river's edge, as one sails up the river towards the Sudan. Abu-Simbel, the temple-mountain with its four colossi carved out of the rock, alone stands out all the year round amid this strange scenery where the apparently trunkless palms lift their green-plumed heads out of the water. One day there will be nothing left of Nubia ...

Long before approaching the temple of Ramses on the Sudan frontier, and before reaching Kalabsha and Dendur, two white lines on either side of the river mark out the site for this huge building project. Labourers have been at work there since January 1956. A French company has the contract for the first stage of the project, that is to say, preparing a bed for the foundations. Men are at work night and day on two rafts on the river. Their boat-house is moored lower down. The office is a tiny building high on the riverside, commanding a fine view of the Nile. Here, in the awe-inspiring solitude about three miles south of Aswan, there are neither desert, fields nor villages. The granite bank is 35 metres high, and the river about a mile wide at this point. This is the site chosen by some of the best civil-engineers in the world for building the most powerful hydraulic station in existence. In this waste-land the ambitions of two great empires clash. Everyone knows that this is where the Suez crisis originated. Refusing the dearly-paid help so insistently asked for by the Cairo government is not only signing a régime's death-warrant, but in the long run would also mean condemning the 23 million people, crowded into the valley, to the same fate.

We have seen[1] that Egypt is shrinking in proportion to its population. In a century the population has increased fivefold while little land has been added. In two years (1954–5) the population rose by a million and a half. Nothing short of a revolution can save the people. New lands are needed for agriculture, electric power is needed for industry. More water is essential.

The Nile supplies water, but 45 per cent of the river is wasted as it flows into the sea. Then there are fat or lean years, with disastrous floods or low waters. The flow of the river varies with the rains falling into the impetuous Blue Nile that comes down from the Ethiopian plateau and supplies 80 per cent of its waters. The dam project aims at catching the wasted water, and regulating the flow and supply according to requirements. As far back as antiquity the Pharaohs were anxious to control the river waters and to irrigate and extend the arable land. Ammenhemet II, a monarch of the Middle Kingdom, when he surrounded Lake Moeris in the Fayum district with an enormous wall, was a forerunner of the builders of the Upper Dam. Now there are six dams or barrages regulating the water in Upper Egypt: these are situated in the Nile Delta, and at Edfina, Assiut, Nag Hamadi, Esna and Aswan. The latter is the only one for storing water from February to June.

It is obvious that the storing and regulating of water should not be restricted only to the last 1,000 miles of the Nile, where it no longer receives any tributaries, and that the problem to be faced is the utilization of the water-supply in the upper reaches of the river. In actual fact, years ago surveys and plans were drawn up by the British for a Nile Valley development scheme. This was to include a number of very large installations on the equatorial lakes (Lake Victoria, Lake Kioga, Lake Albert, Lake Tana in Ethiopia) and a series of linked canals in the Sadd district (the Sudanese marshes)

[1] See the chapter on Agriculture, p. 335.

in order to provide what has been loosely called a 'hundred years' supply'. But such huge water-works not only imply enormous capital outlay but also an African policy covering all the interested countries, including British possessions, Ethiopia and the Sudan. Such a policy is far from being realized. Spurred on by the problem of its swollen population, the Egyptian government has worked out a purely Egyptian plan, affecting that part of the Nile over which it has control.

As long ago as 1882 a French engineer, M. de la Motte, proposed a plan to include three installations south of the Jabal Silsila gorge, to be completed by a reservoir at Kalabsha, about 30 miles south of Aswan. Thus the idea is not new. But the story of the beginnings of the present High Dam is a strange one. In 1947 the agronomist Adrien Daninos offered the government a scheme for a dam twenty times as big as the present Aswan Dam. South of Aswan he had noticed a large natural basin which would hold thousands of millions of cubic metres of water. The Palestine war held up investigations into this plan. In 1952 the West German government, being under an obligation to give the State of Israel substantial compensation for the sufferings of Jewish minorities in Germany and central Europe, became the object of protests from the Arab States. Germany at once sent an economic mission to Egypt to restore good relations and, so to speak, to make up for those reparations. When the government was asked what could be done to satisfy Egypt, Cairo suggested that Germany should build the High Barrage. Thus it came about that German experts were the first to study the schemes drawn up by Daninos and Galioli (an Italian engineer who undertook the stereoscopic survey for M. Daninos). Later, an international committee consisting of the finest specialists in the world took over and perfected the plan drawn up by the Dortmund *Hochtief* after it had been re-cast and revised by Egyptian engineers, among them President Ahmed Salim. Two technicians, the American Terzaki and the Frenchman Coyne, remained in constant contact with the 'High Barrage Committee'.

In November 1954 Nasser announced the government's decision to build the High Dam. This 'mass-barrage' (working on a weight principle) as opposed to the coffer-type barrage will contain a huge lake-reservoir with a capacity of 130,000,000,000 cubic metres. The natural basin stretches for 250 miles, 120 of which are in Sudanese territory, and covers a surface of 23,000 square miles. Thus all the region from Aswan to Wadi Halfa and far beyond to the Sudan frontier will be submerged. The lake thus formed will be one and a half times as big as the Lake of Annecy and thirty times the present Aswan Dam capacity.

The barrage itself is a kind of artificial mountain, 120 yards high and 5 kilometres (3 miles) long, made up of granite blocks representing, in all, seventeen times the volume of the large Cheops Pyramid. The blocks will be joined by clay pillars—clay in preference to concrete so as to make the huge edifice more pliable and elastic. A slight porosity reduces the pressure at flood-time. This is the best and most economical way of stopping a river over a mile wide and holding back 130,000 cubic metres of water. The barrage has to lie on a sandy bed, and this is why the ground has to be strengthened. By injecting colloidal clay into the soil, the dam's foundations will be made firm but supple. The engineers of a French company which specializes in such matters are already at work.

The preparation of the bed alone will take two years. The building of the dam will take eight years, but after the first five years it will already be possible to begin storing water. The water's level will be at 182 metres above sea-level, the altitude of the site itself being at 85 metres. A further five years will be needed for the electrification of the barrage. Sixteen turbines with a power of 120,000 CV will supply 10,000 million kilowatts an hour at a very low price—at a tenth of a penny in Aswan and three-farthings in Cairo.

The total building-costs will reach £400 million, the first part of the work taking half that amount. But the advantages that Egypt will reap from the barrage are out of all proportion with these already impressive figures. The expansion by 2,000,000 acres will raise the arable surface to nearly 10 million acres, thus increasing farmland by 30 per cent. Moreover, the whole of agricultural production will be steadied. At the moment all Egypt's agriculture is at the mercy of the river. So it would mean not only an increase in output but a change making for a steady cycle of production. The growing of rice, which is essential for Egypt, will extend to an area of 600,000 feddans. Lands now impregnated with salt and unsuitable for farming, as in the Delta area, will be turned into paddy-fields. The barrage will also protect fields and villages from excessive floods, and by reducing the water underground will lower drainage-costs by 24 per cent. As we have seen, the output of Egyptian agriculture suffers much from the inadequate draining-system. Finally, when the flow of the river is tamed and controlled, this will allow untrammelled navigation and the transport of iron-ore from Aswan to the blast-furnaces now being built at Helwan, near Cairo.

The cheap mass-production of electrical energy would completely change the face of Egypt. As at present Egypt consumes only 300,000 kilowatts an hour, supplied by thermal power-stations, one can imagine the economic upheaval that will be produced by 10,000 million kilowatts an hour at a negligible price. Nearly £17 million worth of oil-fuel would be saved per year. The electrification of agriculture will make for a further increase in output, which will already have been improved by the regulating and abundance of water. There will be no further hindrance to industrialization, which has at present reached its limits because of the lack or cost of power. Already a Franco-German firm is building the fertilizer-factory which will supply both old and new land with the nitrates they need.

The increase in Treasury income which the barrage should bring is put at £23 million a year, and at £355 million for the total national revenue. The general expenses of the 15-year plan include building the barrage and power-station, fertilizing the land, modifications in the existing irrigation and drainage systems and the electrification of agriculture. In short, the cost of the total Aswan scheme will be in the region of £1,300 million. All the financial experts consulted, including those of the International Bank, have declared the undertaking to be sound and indispensable. It is the only measure by which economic conversion can be achieved, re-absorbing the surplus population, modernizing agriculture, making it possible to create proper industry, in short, by raising the standard of living and consequently ending the discrepancy between the birth-rate and the country's resources. It is known that French bankers offered Egypt a loan of £20 million, and one of them declared in Cairo, 'The barrage is another Suez Canal.' But at that time people thought only of the Canal's advantages.

Naturally certain objections have been raised, on both technical and political grounds, against the greatest undertaking that has been attempted in this hemisphere. The first relates to the danger of the great reservoir to Egypt in the event of war. The destruction of the dam would send 130,000 million cubic metres crashing down and wipe Egypt off the map. But without even replying that such a disaster would be only one feature in the universal doom of an atomic war, the barrage engineers have provided against such an occurrence.

In case of conflict the water-level can be brought down to mark 150, that is to say, 46 metres from the top of the 'artificial mountain'.

A second objection is that the barrage will deprive Egypt of the fertilizing alluvium and will itself soon be choked with silt. The calculations show that it would take five hundred years to fill up the huge lake with silt. Other solutions will have been found before then. As for the mud, we must recall that the present system of permanent irrigation by means of canals already deprives the soil of alluvial deposit, and that in February every year it has to be dredged from the canals by teams of 'requisitioned' fellahs. On the other hand, the Nile alluvial mud, resulting from the breaking down of Ethiopian basalts, is of essentially mineral composition and contains only 2 per cent organic matter. All its mineral elements, that is to say 40 per cent of it, can be replaced by fertilizers. Egypt already has phosphate reserves, and the nitrate factory under construction can supply all the nitrates required. The quantity needed represents no more than the present cost of dredging the canals.

A third objection is a technical one: the huge lake, situated in a terribly hot and dry climate, would increase the evaporation of water on a disastrous scale. But according to the reckoning of the international commission, the evaporation will be 7 per cent, that is to say, 9 thousand million cubic metres out of a total of 130. The operation will still pay.

The fourth objection is human and sociological—one which has happened in most countries—that is to say, the uprooting of the population in the submerged areas. About 250 miles in Egypt and the Sudan will vanish under the waters—8,000 feddans of semi-desert inhabited by 60,000 people. The town of Wadi-Halfa, with 15,000 inhabitants, on the Sudan frontier will be wiped off the map. But we must remember the poverty of this Nubian desert, where the heads of families are forced to leave their homes for Cairo and Alexandria in order to feed their families. The situation is none the less pathetic when one realizes that these people have twice been driven away from the river-bank where they lived, by the construction of the first Aswan Dam and two successive rises in the water-level. There are a few wretched villages perched on the cliff-edge, and it is only in the three months when the level of the river falls and uncovers a strip of Nile bed 25 metres wide that the Nubians rush to harvest the maize which will enable them to hold out, on the starvation-line, until the next harvest. The Sudanese standard of living is hardly any better. Egypt has set aside £10 million for re-settling these populations, and arrangements have already been made for their reception on good land near Aswan and Kom Ombo.

The fifth objection is the loss of Nubian archaeological treasures. Thirteen temples including the magnificent one of Abu Simbel will be engulfed for ever. Some of them can be saved by modern techniques and dismantled stone by stone, then transported to the Aswan region, but at Abu Simbel the Ramses colossi, 27 metres high and carved out of the solid rock, will be submerged. The porousness and brittleness of the sandstone make it impossible to hew them out and transplant them, as had been thought. But Egypt has chosen to safeguard its people rather than its monuments, and the lives of 25 million people justify such measures. In any case, Philae will be saved and the island will emerge once more, because of the fall in the level of the present lake.

Even with all these objections refuted, there remain political and financial difficulties. First of all there is the Sudan. Parodying Herodotus' words, one might say that Egypt is in the gift of the Sudan. Cut the Nile at Wadi Halfa and Egypt would no longer exist. In 1929 a convention signed by Britain ('Protector of the Sudan') and Egypt fixed the proportion of water to be allotted to each country. Egypt was allowed 48,000 million cubic metres and the Sudan only 4,000 million (viz. a total of 52 thousand million cubic metres from an average flow of 84 thousand million cubic metres, the difference of 32 thousand million flowing into the sea). With regard to the new barrage it will have to be decided how the surplus supply, viz. 32 to 34 thousand million cubic metres, will be apportioned between the two countries. The Sudan, an independent state since 1956, claims half of this surplus (before deducting the amount evaporated), that is to say 16 to 17 thousand million net, whereas Egypt wants to divide the evaporation loss and leave its southern neighbour only 12 to 13 thousand million cubic metres. Several attempts at negotiation have failed over the past two years, and Egypt can do nothing without the Sudan's approval, which will mean a hard bargain.

But the financing of the barrage remains the foremost problem. The 'Point IV' Bureau was entrusted with the topographical survey. French banks had proposed making a loan of £20 million (in the form of equipment and services) and the Germans offered a sum of the same order. The Egyptian budget could stand a supplementary outlay of £10 million a year. But only one international organization

—the International Bank—was in a position to help Egypt on a large scale and provide the foreign currency needed for importing all the power-station equipment. As early as 1953 its experts went to study what general measures were needed, on the spot. Their conclusions being satisfactory, Dr Qaysuni, the Egyptian Finance Minister, twice went to Washington in 1954 and 1955. While diplomatic talks were going on with America, the Russian envoy to Cairo, M. Solod, announced that his government was ready to grant Egypt first 'technical' and then 'economic' aid towards building the High Dam. In the course of 1955 and the first six months of 1956 there developed a race against time, a struggle between the powers to outbid each other as to who was going to pay.

Very soon it looked as though the main object of all this, the building of the barrage, was completely forgotten, and as if the only thing that mattered was a struggle for influence at any price. Nasser was brazenly playing off the rivalry between the two sides, blackmailing Washington with 'Russian proposals', the extent of which was never made clear, while letting his closest friends understand that he was too much afraid of communism in his own country to set the fox to mind the geese. The International Bank's terms were: control of the budget of the borrowing state; the forbidding of any other or further loan and the right to scrutinize accounts. Nasser was unwilling to bring his country under American control in this way. Meanwhile the alarming demographic situation was worsening, Egypt was becoming poorer and poorer and the régime was in danger of collapse. Such were the conditions early in 1956, which was to be a year of crisis.

Part Four

FORGING A SOCIETY

I

Cairo—City of Convulsions

It is impossible to form any idea of Egypt as a whole, or of its function or its difference from the rest of the world, without some view
of the great city that battens on it. Wrapped in its perennial cloud
of dust and ashes, surrounded by the three Cities of the Dead, harsh,
sandy, waterless as the desert, Cairo is an incongruous capital for a
nation of riverside farmers, a small-holding African peasantry whose
feet are never out of the waters of the Nile. Twenty million paupers,
bent double over the cotton-plants and mindlessly enslaved to the
seasons, have as their capital an arrogant city in which the meanest
beggar can gaze out across the roof-tops, holding himself erect and
bowing his head only towards the East, in homage to an abstract
God.

But Cairo evokes too many such images. No one can fail to notice
the Turkish contours of the Mohamed Ali Mosque, in the Citadel.
But somehow the Pyramids have lost nothing of their mystery.
Loti long ago deplored the fact that they could be reached by tram
or carriage, and today the city has crept up to their feet and the
villas sprout like mushrooms in the shade of Cheops.

Between these two poles of ancient and modern stretches an
immense city, all flat and dusty, grey and gold, rich and lice-ridden,
living and dead, a town over which hundreds of kites weave an
ominous net, where haughty skyscrapers are jostled by derelict
hovels. It bears the name of Egypt itself, for in the vernacular there is
only one word, *Misr*, for both country and capital: Cairo is Egypt
yet the contrary of Egypt.

The centre of Cairo is astonishing, dazzling and disappointing. We
hardly expect to find such spacious, well-kept avenues, such enormous
blocks of buildings ten or fifteen stories high, these elegant shop-
fronts and long American cars the colour of strawberry ices or
moonlight. But turning behind some marble and concrete building
you will find a sordid alley, dirty children, overturned dustbins, the
old Cairo in the very heart of a business centre full of banks and

cinemas. You catch a glimpse of a three-year-old child perched on a cart, on top of a heap of rubbish collected by his father. Round the corner you can again breathe the 'civilized' atmosphere of what is still known as the European quarter. The air-conditioned teashop offers some respite from the heat. July is unbearably hot—the Egyptian July, month of revolutions, strikes, sudden nationalizations. All the major events from the Hyksos invasions to Faruk's abdication have happened in July.

July is the time when fever and the Nile rise in Egypt, and especially in Cairo. In olden days at this time they used to offer the city's most beautiful virgin as a sacrifice to the river. The story goes that when General Amr, the Caliph's lieutenant, rode into Cairo, he was horrified at this barbarous custom and carried the girl off on his horse. Since then the citizens of Cairo have contented themselves with throwing a doll—the 'Nile's Bride'—into the river. Feluccas with huge sails festooned with gaudy streamers run between the island of Gazira and the fashionable river-banks, overlooked by two palaces, the old Semiramis Palace and the modern Shepheard's.

What used to be exclusive, upper-class districts now belong, to all appearances, to the masses. This is their only clear gain from the revolution. A magnificent river-side walk has been expropriated and built up for them, though it involved a slice being cut off the British Embassy which used to jut down to the river's edge. This was achieved through one of the additional clauses to the Anglo-Egyptian treaty. This minor 'evacuation' of the Ambassador's bathing-pool has produced nothing more than a long promenade which the crowds invade at holiday-time. Their own hot and stuffy streets with hovels nestling close beside the mosques are more appreciated by tourists in search of the picturesque than by the poor who have to live in them.

The lower-class Egyptian dons his best green-and-white striped *galabiya* and strolls like a *bourgeois* along the river-bank, together with his children in flashy art-silk and his wife invisible in her black *melaya*. He walks as if he owned the street: there's no point in the motorist blowing a horn or losing his temper, for the crowd won't make room for a car. The city policeman is helpless and advises you to turn back and cross the nearest bridge. The one taken over by the gaudy crowd today, still flanked by two bronze British lions, is the one which is zealously guarded on the other side by the statue of the uniformed Zaghlul. On the left the 'people' chews sunflower-seeds and drinks its Coca-cola. It is easily pleased. In the evening the crowd crosses over the bridge and lounges all over the lawns of 'Liberation Square'. The revolution has given it all this grass, and the fountain—in glorious technicolour—which somehow keeps it alive. It was not far from here that the barracks used to stand, symbols of the British occupation. On the very day when the evacuation agreement was being signed—in July, of course—they were attacked with pick and shovel. Now an American cinema is rising on the same site—one occupation following another. The French-built Museum is still standing.

The holiday, like all holidays, ends tonight with a firework display. The taste for this sort of thing was begun by the Germans, when the Democratic Republic gave the city of Cairo a magnificent show. Since then festivities are never concluded without this expensive and impressive trifle which lights up the Nile, much to the joy of the mob.

Next morning it is hard at work again. The snob quarters are full of beggars, porters, car attendants and suit-pressers. Indeed, these particular jobs give a clue to the lay-out of the city. Beggars are disappearing, not because the Cairenes are getting richer but because Major Boghdadi, intent on building new boulevards and demolishing hovels, determined to thrust them out of sight. Now and then you come across a lorry packed with shameless girls, cripples and illegal barrow-boys, who have all been 'nipped'. They are merely returned to their rightful, poverty-stricken suburbs, so as not to shock the sensitive tourist. Some of them refuse to be daunted, however. One of them, particularly obstinate, has clung to his brazier for the last three years, brandishing his stump of an arm under the nose of embarrassed motorists.

Few women are to be seen in the fashionable streets. The chic upper-class women only go about in cars, taking tea at L's or G's, doing a little shopping after which their chauffeurs carry them off to the Club. The 'Gazira Sporting Club' is the heart and soul of the old and new upper-classes. It has about 250 acres of grass, always in good trim, trees, flowers, swimming-pools, a race-course, cricket-pitch, golf-course, restaurants, a 'lido' and even croquet for the more sedate ladies. There are also squash-courts to provide some violent, English exercise. Round the lido you meet diplomats wearing shorts, their methodically sunburnt wives, American babies dressed in frilly clothes that died out in Europe fifty years ago; ravishing slim girls playing the bohemian with youths in blue jeans; ex-princes, pale and disillusioned; foreign journalists on the look-out for scraps of news, and a few tennis-playing officers, friends of Nasser.

It is these officers, or those who were not admitted to the Club, who have nationalized it. The Suez affair was only a matter of international politics, but the Sporting Club did far more damage in the Cairo upper-class. Taking over the Club was proof that everything had changed and that the Bastille had fallen. Alarm and despondency were spread by this attack on privilege, merely to make sports-grounds for poor youths, when there was plenty of waste ground outside Cairo. And thereupon a wall was built across the Club's grounds, so as to remind everyone that privilege has its limits. On the evening when Nasser reached this decision we were dining with some friends, when some well-born golfers took our hands with every sign of distress and exclaimed, 'Have you read the latest? They are taking over our Club! It's not the first time, since the Wafd intended to confiscate it, only then it was saved by the Great Fire . . .' This from a lady who had been forced to give up quantities of land to the State. Her neighbour, Prince M., was chuckling ironically. The Egyptian nobility are the most charming, refined and cultured people you could hope to meet. They have usually studied in Paris or Oxford, which detracts nothing from their snobbery. They give subtle dinners, served on exquisite china or plate. They have taste and education and tend to be radical in politics. The ladies reshape the Republic, dressed in their Dior gowns, while the men dream of a golden age when uniforms will be abolished. They invite Audiberti or Michaux, who are better known here than in Paris. They organize literary and artistic discussions against a Vivaldi back-cloth. Underneath all this they remain rabidly nationalistic and lose all trace of their irony and humour once the 'foreigner' tilts at Egypt or criticizes the nationalist policy. Their opposition ends where Egypt begins. For this left-wing *bourgeoisie* has a brand of sentimentality which can include the liberalism of the previous generation, Marxism which is so exciting from a distance, and the realistic nationalism of the Bikbashi. In their background of opals and Bokhara carpets, one can admire these prudish men who hide their wives and who eat the native *ful*.

At sherry time—without sherry—you might find yourself in one of those bookshops where argument seems to take the place of business. There Arab dialectic flows freely, even in French, with its gross exaggerations, interruptions, violence, hyperbole and angry outbursts. They work themselves up over the latest book—for Cairo has been publishing feverishly in the last year or so—or the latest pamphlet or 'booklet' as they prefer to call it. Young Egyptian writers fresh from China or Russia are wild with enthusiasm. They are penniless, and have most of them been in prison for expressing, about two years ago, ideas for which the official newspapers now pay them about a hundred pounds a month. But they are not all converted. Take for example this former workman, a Nasserite Marxist, son of a fellah, with a heavy, frizzy head, loud, stubborn, intelligent and cunning, who has been in and out of most of the prisons and suffered every indignity. Few intellectuals have his inside knowledge of the working-classes and their outlook. Few real Egyptians have anything like his lucidness and gift for synthesis.

A real Egyptian—there it goes again. It has become a fashionable term since the Colonels came to power. In Cairo it is quite in order to ask what is a real Egyptian. There, they don't ask you what your nationality is, but 'What passport do you hold?' You can be an Egyptian with a French passport, a Jew with an English passport, a Greek with an Italian passport, or a 'foreign foreigner' or an 'Egyptian foreigner'. Every combination is allowed here. As people get married and cling on to their passports, you have to be clever to know who you are in all this. The administration shows a certain grim humour in calling stateless persons 'undecided nationalities'.

With the naked eye it is impossible to distinguish one 'real Egyptian' from another. The poor devil who sells liquorice-water, wearing a *galabiya* and his bottle strapped round his belly, is no doubt a 'real Egyptian'. But what about the *efendi* at the wheel of his Cadillac, or the shopkeeper who boasts he 'speaks all the languages of the land' (meaning Arabic, French, English, Italian and Greek), or that tall dark thin man, that little pale fat man, that straight-haired chap, that curly chap, that one with green eyes, that one with blue? It is easy enough in the country, for the fellah reminds you forcibly of the frescoes painted in the tombs, with his big head, heavy features, long slit eyes remarkably like those of his oxen. So many conquerors have passed through Cairo and so many immigrants have settled and intermixed that there's no means of knowing who or what they are. Officially the 'true Egyptian' is the Moslem Egyptian—but this is a recent, 'revolutionary' (or reactionary!) idea which has little to do with the real state of things.

Some readers might remember Nerval's story of a 'Coptic marriage' in Cairo. The Copts are still there and are to be found at all levels of society. Direct descendants of the ancient Egyptians—for the term Copt was merely a Greek name for them—these former worshippers of Isis and Osiris who became Christian converts number about three millions in Egypt today. In Cairo they are ministers (in one case), writers, teachers (though less than before), doctors, lawyers and small tradesmen. They are so notorious for their simple way of life that one day when a young Egyptian was offered about six Egyptian pounds a month he replied, 'Do you think I'm a Copt?' Christianity gives them a certain cosmopolitanism, an international outlook and open-mindedness which are rarely found in the Moslems. The poorer Copts have nothing to distinguish them from other Egyptians but the blue cross which they have tattooed on their wrists. They live in the oldest part of Cairo, on the edge of Fustat, which was built by the Arab conqueror Amr on the ruins of the Roman Babylon. The walls are still standing but Fustat is no more than a heap of rubble, for the towns or quarters making up Cairo are never built on an old site.

After the Coptic potters, with their jugs shaped in the form of women's heads, Picasso fashion, we go past the Amr Mosque, a severe rectangular building watching over the dust of the razed town. The Christian township, surrounded by walls, thrusts downwards like a kind of basement into a maze of paved alleys, the entrance to which is barred by a heavy gate studded with nails. Nowadays the gate is always left open and nobody interferes with the poor Copts who live round the crypt where, it is said, the Virgin Mary once took refuge and which is half-filled every year by the rising Nile. At the end of an alley-way stands the old synagogue which was once a Christian church. Here there is never any close distinction made between the old Pharaonic temple, which became a church, and the mosque, which made use of both. There is nothing here to draw a line between Christians and Moslems. They have the same poor homes, the same cotton clothes, the same jobs, though among the Christians you can often pick out the fellah-types of Upper Egypt who have never been absorbed by the Arabs. However, it would be a mistake to regard these as 'true Egyptians', any more than the rest.

Let us look farther on, past Fustat and an extraordinary vista of lime-kilns and ruins. It seems a waste city until you suddenly find yourself among an orgy of mosques and minarets and bulbous domes, *mashrabiya* windows, colourful lanes full of people, full of smells and shouts and neon-signs and the strains of the radio. A babel of noisy

404

children, flute-players, with little pans of burning incense outside the butchers' stalls, piles of china painted over with flowers, donkeys, taxis, camels as high as the houses, and houses that look as though they will fall down any minute. On the narrow pavement you pass a little table and two men smoking a hookah. The unwashed women go past, proudly carrying ridiculous things on their head. They are beautiful, like great black statues, and their veils raise the dust as they walk. We are now near Ibn Tulun, the cloistered mosque, which is the finest and oldest in Cairo. The town-planner has not yet reached this part of the city.

The same applies to the district beyond the walls, which are as thick as fortifications and topped by minarets, surrounding the pathetic ruins of the mosque built by the mad Caliph el Hakim. Benches and tables have been set up beneath its wide, gutted vaults, and here the children come to learn their lessons. Still farther out, over miles of tangled alleys and among the thousand mosques of this legendary city, the houses huddle together, crumbling down and propping each other up or disappearing in a cloud of dust. Only Cossery could describe these 'houses of certain death'. They are full of a strange race of proud beggars, madmen and seers, outcasts, beautiful young girls, mothers with a thousand children.

Beyond the Citadel and its fortifications which were overrun by Napoleon are the streets where the famous dancing-girls live, whom Nasser has sworn to suppress and who have more than once inspired our classical ballerinas. The same leprous-looking houses, ready for the pick and shovel. This is where our pretty servant Halima lives, and she introduces us to her bit of Cairo, including her friends and family. She warns us not to reply if we are spoken to. There are no 'ladies' to be seen around here: 'So they'll set out to shock you, just for fun.' Somehow the street reminds you of a village, with the women gossiping at the doors and the children playing among the dirt—do they ever go to school? Halima pushes a high door open. Proudly she announces, 'You see, my house is made of stone.' That is because here, as in the villages, most houses are made of dried mud. We go inside and see a cubby-hole under the stairs: when she opens the door we see that a man could hardly stand upright in it, but would just fit if he lay down. 'It's let for 40 piastres (8 shillings) a month to a "family"—a woman and a fifteen-year-old boy.' We are introduced to the neighbours on the first floor, and shake hands, with exclamations of 'Sa'ida, Sa'ida'. The women are only half-dressed because of the heat, but greet us with smiles. On the third and top floor we come to Halima's home. The neighbour's three youngest children are crawling on the landing. 'She's a bad woman. You see her little boy's arm? To stop him crying, she heated a knife on the fire and hit him with it. I had to look after him.' The boy is horribly thin and ugly. We pass the room on the right and go into Halima's. The two-roomed flat is shared by two families: the neighbour with her husband, the grandmother and three children, and on the other side Halima with her husband and mother-in-law. In the 'No man's land' there is a kitchen with a Primus stove and a shower. Halima's room is clean. She has taken out the traditional married woman's bedspread, to let me see it. There is a fresh newspaper spread on the table. 'You can look round,' she says proudly: 'there aren't any bugs.' The poor girl pays about thirty shillings a month for this single room. 'But it's nice here—I have a window, and half the kitchen.' That was true. We were also to see the most squalid rooms imaginable, let at a pound a month, with no windows, water or drains, in which half a dozen people lived on top of each other. The luxurious flats in Zamalek are relatively cheaper at £50 a month than these poverty-stricken homes.

The lowlier civil servant spares no effort to buy the inevitable gilded sofa and flower-patterned armchairs which adorn the 'hall'. We know someone who works in the Ministry of Welfare. He has a degree, speaks French, though rather poorly, and English well. He has 'advanced' ideas. He is surrounded by friends, cakes and Coca-cola. I am surprised to see neither his wife nor his sister. He takes me to their room and lets me talk to the two women. They are very pleasant, speak French very well, and like most well-brought-up women here have been educated at a convent-school. They have both been to the university, and this year the sister will be taking her B.A. in English. 'But why don't you join us?' I ask.

'We are not allowed to mix with men, and my brother is very strict. Our families are very conservative and religious, and women have to know their place.'

'Yet you have been students. You must be modern, free?'

'Of course. But our husbands and brothers will not allow us to mix with men.'

'Then how will you ever find a husband?'

'My brother and father have chosen me one already. I don't want one; but no doubt I'll have to marry him.'

'You had the vote this year, for the first time?'

'Yes, but the family did their best to stop me from voting.'

'Do you ever go out with your university friends?'

'With girls, but not boys. It would be unthinkable of me to go to the movies with a young man to whom I am not engaged.'

This is no exceptional case. In the lower middle-class, by which I mean those who never travel abroad and who represent the 'real Egyptians' or Moslems, the womenfolk still have to submit to the old taboos. Few Moslem women work, even in Cairo, which is the most advanced Egyptian city. Most of the young women employed as secretaries, typists, saleswomen or waitresses are Christians or belong to one of the minorities—Jewish or Greek, for example. Nasser is never seen with his wife.

In the working-class districts the women still wear the black *melaya* or veil, often held in place over the lower part of the face by a kind of gilt bobbin or stopper inserted above the nose. Servant-girls working in foreigners' homes are not allowed to go without it. When there was talk of forbidding the *melaya* in May 1956 the menfolk were up in arms. The poorly-paid husband does not mind his wife earning six pounds a month, even if he earns less or is out of work, but he would feel insulted if she entered a bus without hiding herself in a kind of sack. So great was the protest against modernizing dress, particularly the women's, that in official terms 'it will only be imposed in more favourable circumstances'. The introduction of modern dress would upset the lower classes' entire way of living. However, the military rulers' one idea is to make Cairo a twentieth-century city complete with skyscrapers, the men in overalls and the women in skirts, as in the 'Liberation Province'. Attempts are being made to coax the students into wearing grey flannel outfits consisting of a pullover, trousers or skirt, by offering them at reduced prices. Children who are lucky enough to be sent to school are usually well clothed, both boys and girls being made to wear a light smock. But thousands of children are to be seen about the streets or working in shops although they are of school age.

We happened to know for about three years a little girl who 'sold' lottery-tickets in the centre of the town, and who had taken up her stand outside the National Bank. She must have been about 8 years old; she was small, weedy, but cleanly dressed in a long flowered cretonne frock. 'Hey, give me a piastre,' she cried.

'But why aren't you at school?'

She found this remark so tickling that every time she saw us she shouted 'School, school' as if it were a wonderful joke. Once at about five in the afternoon I found her squatting on the pavement surrounded by onlookers, while a man counted the day's takings of a number of such beggars, the eldest of whom was no more than ten.

In a street just off Cairo's most impressive boulevard you find boys of about 8 or 12 stripping the paint off car-parts with the help of acid, then hammering and polishing them. The important Ma'ruf quarter, which is like a village cut off in the very heart of Cairo's 'west-end', will soon be demolished. It has an interesting history. In the early thirteenth century, in Sultan Qalaun's time, it was a lake. In due course the lake became a field and the street-names such as 'Bull Street' and 'Goat Street' still recall the time when animals were grazed there. When Napoleon came to Cairo it was a cemetery. He turned it into a port, making Mohamed Allah ud-Din responsible for the dues from ships and warehouses. It was this 'learned man' who knew how to read and write, notorious as 'the well-known one', who gave the name Ma'ruf, meaning 'well-known', to the quarter. Now there are two thousand families or about ten thousand people living there, which means a density of 1,000 inhabitants to the acre. They are living in 3,400 rooms, which is about six to an apartment. Fifteen per cent of the population earn less than £3 a month per family. About half of them—43 per cent—earn between £5 and £10 a month to keep an average of six people.

The 'well-known' Ma'ruf is to go, being an embarrassment to the rich tourists of the Hilton Palace Hotel which will tower over the site. The town council has already built or repaired clean, comfortable and cheap houses on the outskirts which will take about 5,000 of those who are ejected. The others will have to fend for themselves in other old districts near by, such as Bulaq and Maspero. These are even bigger and more thickly populated: their ten thousand mean houses will in turn be demolished and their light industries transferred to the outskirts of Cairo.

The Director of Reconstruction knows exactly what he is in for, and says that two-thirds of Cairo need to be pulled down. Thirty per cent of the buildings are unfit for habitation and already 10,000 have been condemned. But these 'houses of certain death' will only disappear gradually. The frenzy for destruction and building which has come over Cairo in the past year or two and which is turning the city-centre into a vast builder's-yard has hardly touched the working-class quarters. The 1,200 buildings pulled down in 1955 were not shacks and slums. These are being replaced by luxury flats which can be let at exorbitant rents, since there is no rent-restriction, from which investors can recoup their capital in ten years. They are not interested in housing for the masses. The government's ten-year building scheme will cost over £20 million. Meanwhile about two million people are housed in slums and a whole new city would be required to do the job properly.

The rise in population—a million and a half for the years 1954 and 1955—is disturbing enough for the country as a whole, but in Cairo itself it is distressing. There the density is over 19,000 to the square mile, while in the working-class districts it amounts to 36,800 at Abdin, 94,400 in the Muski and 179,600 at Bab el Sharia. Such a density is to be found nowhere in the world, except certain towns in India. The birth-rate is still higher than in the country and the children are rather better looked after. A quarter of the population consists of children under 6 years of age. At the same time the inflow from the country to the capital is increasing all the time. Today Shubra forms a kind of city of its own inside Cairo, having twice the population of the whole Aswan province, whereas fifty years ago it had only a sixth of that number. Those who leave the over-populated areas of Minufiya or Girga and are drawn by the mirage of the great city find themselves without work and driven into unproductive, parasitic labour. Out of every 100 city workers 10 are domestic servants (chiefly Saïdians and Sudanese), while 6 are waiters or porters (Nubians) or else *farrashes* or errand-boys. There are some 16,000 *makwagis* (suit-pressers), shoe-blacks and hair-dressers.

Cairo has thousands of little makeshift jobs. The poor devils who do them are hounded from place to place for fear they spoil the centre and recall the Egypt of the past. There are swarms of mobile cafés or snack-counters, garishly lit, with mounds of rice and maca-roni smothered with tomato-sauce heaped up behind their windows painted with flowers and arabesques. These glittering shrines parade the streets day and night in search of customers, or huddle against the walls of the mosques.

Everything on earth is sold in the streets, from valuables to odds and ends. One man is going about trying to sell a typewriter, an-other hangs on to you singing the praises of a certain make of tyre; this one shows something glittering in the palm of his hand—'a diamond, cheap at the price!' and that one flashes 'a gold watch, duty-free!' An undersized trader has taken his stand on the sidewalk outside the National Bank: his overall is as spotless as a surgeon's, his sandals dazzling white, while he squats on his heels selling laces—three black and three white—which he shows to advantage on a bit of pink paper.

The light is on in the shops long after midnight. Tailors and shirtmakers are at it till dawn, when the eight- or ten-year-old apprentices arrive.

In Cairo, as in Alexandria, there is a social class much less heard of abroad. These are the 'louts'. They find their place in official statistics and state prisons: every month the Press reports, 'This month 873 louts molested ladies.' This strictly urban species only thrives in capital cities and is unheard of in the villages. In Cairo it is busiest in winter: in Alexandria, in the summer season.

These louts are usually dressed in European clothes, to all appearances well-behaved but swift, cunning and furtive in action. They 'molest' the ladies by pawing, nipping and sometimes kissing them, but so smartly that they are hard to catch. 'He' has always somehow melted into the crowd. The lout is not put off by the presence of a husband. He prefers blondes. It only leads to disaster if the woman retaliates, for the whole art of the lout consists in looking innocent and being surrounded by witnesses in his favour. A young platinum-blonde—whose 'horse-tail' was admittedly provocative—had her collar-bone broken because she dared to reply by smacking a man's face. There are severe penalties: these men risk three months' imprisonment if they are caught.

This is one of the darker sides of the two largest Egyptian cities. Such horrible sexual repression arises from economic conditions as much as from the taboos governing relations between men and women. There is nothing like it in the country, where people marry young. Life is hard in Cairo and unemployment prevents many men from marrying. Students have to wait years before they can hope to do so. Prostitution is forbidden, while custom does not allow even the most innocent friendship between girls and youths. The lower middle-class suffer most in this respect. The lower classes make less fuss about marriage. So the louts increase in spite of punishments, press campaigns and furtive prostitution.

The men toil like ants wherever buildings are going up. Few firms have any modern machines for doing the work. So they still build ten-story houses in the way they built the pyramids. There is no lack of human material. There is nothing more startling at night than to see men silhouetted against the sky as they stand on slices of wall twenty or thirty yards high, demolishing them under their own feet, with wooden mallets. The stones crash down, the men shift for themselves. When it comes to driving metal piles into the ground to serve as foundations, they don't always have those heavy steam drills which deafen Cairo. Then some thirty men will be dragging on a rope, driving the cylinder with their combined strength, singing a kind of shanty to its rhythm. It is in the name of Allah, a thousand times repeated, that the State workers, wearing American overalls, are to be seen lifting the heavy lid from the solar ship tomb at Giza.

Chains of men are also used as a cement-mixer. It is common enough in Cairo to see a workman heaping up a pile of cement, sand, gravel and water. Another man steadies the huge spade, which is swung this way and that by a chain-gang pulling in rhythm. The same operation goes on in story after story. There aren't any pulleys, but an inclined plane along which the men pass up and down like ants, carrying on their heads a metal jar full of concrete, or a basket of stones or bricks. In the country the women do the same jobs, singing a kind of dirge at the same time. Seeing women carrying a heavy stone on their head, we expressed our surprise that such drudgery was not left for the asses. 'That would cost more. A woman works alone, picks out the right stone from the heap and works without stopping. An ass needs a man to load it, another to lead it and to unload the stone and carry it to where the mason is working. Then an ass can spoil the fields. So you see, a woman is far cheaper.'

Prayers are said anywhere, in the open air, in the centre of the city, in car-parks or kneeling behind a Cadillac. On Friday mornings at eleven o'clock the traffic is stopped on a section of the Kasr-el-Nil (something like Cairo's Regent Street) and the cars sent round another way. In front of the little Kikhya Mosque the crowd prays on the road, beating their brows against the asphalt. Thus in Cairo the most ancient and most modern are to be seen side by side. Occasionally a zealous policeman will wrest his camera from some collector of folk-lore and drag him off to the *karakol* (a charming word for the police-station). Then you are likely to find an extremely polite and embarrassed police-officer at the other end, saying,

411

'Madam, I am profoundly sorry this has happened. How many strokes of the cane would you like me to give him?'

In a word, the whole Arab world comes together in Cairo, although its heart is in Damascus and its soul in the Hijaz. The whole Moslem world comes to listen to its doctors. The dependent peoples, in particular, come to voice their grievances. Cairo is the capital of malcontents and *sans-culottes*. The awakening African continent, awakening hungry and lost like a traveller, comes here to diagnose its anguish and feed it with arguments, seeking those answers and remedies from Asia which in the past were metaphysical but are now political. Cairo is a microcosm of Egypt, with its best and worst, its ugliest and most splendid, stone and mud, rich and poor, extremes of heat and cold. Like the people who live in it, Cairo knows nothing of half-measures. Cairo is a storm-centre.

II

In Search of a National Culture

Egyptian books and newspapers are eagerly read throughout the Arab world. The voice of her famous singer Umm Kulthum entrances a hundred million Arabs and Moslems. It is surprising, then, that friends of Egypt find such a dearth of material in cultural matters. Is it because the language does not invite translation? Taha Husain, the most outstanding Egyptian writer today, informs us, on the contrary, that Arabic can easily go into French without losing anything in the process, and referred to the success of his own works in translation.[1]

There are at least two reasons for this relatively small output: the neglect of folk-lore and ancient Egyptian works, which ought to be the main and deepest sources of a national art; and inadequate teaching, both in quality and quantity. The Arab-Moslem source of inspiration is still strong, but it is no insult to Islam to say that through poring over one Book and concentrating so much on its sacred text, more encouragement is given to repetition than to creation. Moreover, by forbidding any portrayal of the human body, Islam killed off the Egyptian genius for drawing and painting of which evidence can be seen in the decoration of ancient tombs.

There are few countries in the world where the Egypt of the Pharaohs, the oldest civilization in the world and the creator of art and of statecraft, has left less spiritual imprint than on modern Egypt. Everyone has some claim on the art, science and thought of the pupils of Imhotep or Chephren's ministers, if only by way of their Greek followers. The paintings in the tombs of the Nobles are being acclaimed every day with renewed enthusiasm, while the discovery of any new sarcophagus moves public opinion all over the world. But only three out of a hundred Egyptians who can afford the trip to Luxor ever bother to go there. When the colossal statue of

[1] Not knowing Arabic, perhaps the author should hesitate to raise such a subject. Perhaps he will be forgiven for not mentioning such remarkable writers as Edmund Jabès, who are writing, in Egypt, works that are completely un-Egyptian in their origins and inspiration. As for novelists like Mme Qut el Qulub, who writes her works in French, they are hardly part of the 'national' culture.

Rameses II was being set up in a square in Cairo, an onlooker exclaimed, 'Who is that?' and in all seriousness the man next to him replied, 'A Coptic king.'

The divorce between Egypt and its past showed itself at its worst in the frightful buildings in a so-called 'Pharaoh' style through which Faruk's architects imagined they were taking up the lost tradition. A good instance of this is the incredible 'Rest House' built not so long ago at the foot of the Cheops Pyramid. Even European imitations such as those of General Montriveau are more genuine than these modern efforts in plaster which set up a screen of ugliness between the very source of Egyptian art and those who have as yet no inclination to go back to it. Such a revival would do little better by following the sculptor Moukhtar, who seems to have been trying to recreate the Theban style with a nineteenth-century technique akin to Rude's. Imitation of that kind is just as bad as complete neglect. Occasionally you see something of the old fullness of form in the firm draughtsmanship of some of the young Egyptian painters. Maybe they will rediscover what has been so long lost.

The link with the art of the great old dynasties was certainly hard to keep up or refind. But there is less excuse for letting the popular tradition wither away. Until very recently only a few foreign specialists seemed to take any interest in a folk-lore which must have been unusually rich, according to evidence now coming to light. After a brilliant Italian film, *Carossello napolitano*, was shown in Cairo recently, full of popular tunes and simple rhythms, a group of Egyptians could be heard exclaiming angrily, that it was a disgrace that the Egyptians couldn't produce such a work themselves, with the songs, dances and poetry of their own country. They were indignant at such things being neglected.

It is a fact that the Nile Valley seems to have swallowed up every spontaneous sign of artistic expression. When you think of the wonderful things that can be seen everywhere by a visitor to Fez, Marrakesh or Tunis, in the way of pottery, clothes, wooden articles and carpets which all bear witness to a living tradition of art, it is impossible to avoid disappointment in the small or average Egyptian towns which have nothing to show but a few relics of Coptic art. In the Khan-Khalil in Cairo, a sort of gigantic junk-shop in which you can see all the wonders of the East, Turkish, Persian, Syrian, you will find nothing Egyptian. You have to go as far as Nubia to find a good piece of basket-work, to Qena for good pottery, or into the western oases for well-designed ornaments, while beside the Sidi-Badawi Mosque at Tanta they produce strangely shaped candles.

In Cairo there is still some life in the folk-song and folk-dance, thanks to a few artists who are sensitive to tradition, such as Shu-kuku, while in the country they survive through circumcision or marriage ceremonies. Thus you can still see the horse-dances, musical regattas along the Nile, the stick-ballet, a mock fight whose various movements sometimes emerge suddenly in Cairo, between two workmen who have eaten their fill for once or are welcoming some friend up from the country. Sociologists and ethnologists who have looked into regional folk-art say that it is extraordinarily rich and that it would not take much effort to revive it completely. Every village, indeed each of the four traditional 'quarters' into which the village is divided, has its own songs, its familiar *nuqtas* or jokes, special poems for praise, satire or the offering of gifts. Finally there is a genuinely Egyptian writer, Ahmed Rushdi Salih, who has taken on this essential task of revival. Now that the thread is taken up, much may be expected of the encouragement it will give to the country's art.

We have already touched on the problems of teaching. Weaknesses in this domain are at the root of all the country's other evils. Not that it is so badly provided for. Times have changed since, under Cromer, the head of the 'Board of Education' as it was called had little more than *six thousand* pupils to teach and provide schools for. When he was appointed 'Minister of Instruction' by the same Cromer, Sa'd Zaghlul had to lay the foundations of elementary, primary, secondary and university education which only developed after the Wafd came into power in 1924, and especially under the last Wafdist minister. Taha Husain made the strongest drive against illiteracy and tried to insist on the law requiring compulsory education, which had been ignored for over twenty years.

At the present time the military régime is opening a new school every day. Fifty per cent of children between 6 and 12 years of age, that is to say about two million, are now at school. If the present rate of expansion is kept up, all children should be at school by about 1970, which shows that an impressive effort is being made.

The achievement in further education seems no less admirable. The University of Cairo, founded in 1925 by King Fuad, when it grew out of an Institute for advanced studies set up in 1908 by Zaghlul, now has its counterparts in Alexandria and Heliopolis, to be followed soon by another at Assiut. The three existing University centres had over 40,000 students in 1956, when they were reorganized on more economic lines, which gives the highest ration of students in the world to the potential in the schools. So far as numbers are concerned the results are quite extraordinary, but the quality is another matter.

The students can no longer seek any excuse in the atmosphere of political tension of four years ago, which disrupted most of the courses. The university staffs are of high standard, to judge by the French department with such teachers as Gabriel Bounoure, Étiemble or Jean Grenier, or the Faculty of Law with such professors of international fame as Abdel Hamid Badawi and Abdel Razek Sanhuri. And yet the level of achievement among the students seems to be going down rapidly. The enormous number of failures every June results in furious press campaigns directed either against the professors, the students or their parents, or else the moral background, the syllabus or the useful scapegoat of imperialism. But it would be a mistake to take all this too seriously.

We have met many an Egyptian student whom any faculty elsewhere would be proud to have educated, and who continue their studies just as brilliantly at Oxford, Paris or Princeton. This applies to Law as well as Arts. There is no lack of material, no shortage of brilliant personalities. But to confine ourselves to what falls within our own competence, there is no doubt that in the French departments of the Egyptian universities, the majority of papers handed in for the Licence or B.A. finals would not even scrape through in France. This was not the case even ten years ago. By following a policy based on mistaken notions of prestige the universities and government have merely lowered or destroyed a level of studies which was beyond reproach in 1940, as can be seen from the intellectual attainments of the young teachers at present engaged.

The question remains whether Egypt will be able to produce the leaders and the *élite* without which she cannot possibly take her proper place among the nations, out of the forty thousand students she is producing annually, on present lines.

What about El Azhar, the great Koranic university? It is not easy to speak of it without some preconceived ideas. This extraordinary institution has three faculties (*Usul ud-Din*, or Origins of

Islam, *Shari'a*, or Law, and *Lughat el Arabia*, or Arabic Language).
These contain about twenty thousand young people, ranging from
children under ten years old to men of mature years, and teach the
elements of a religion which has remained in an arrested state for
hundreds of years, as well as of a culture which has some claims to
greatness in both literature and philosophy. This great mosque and
seminary was founded a thousand years ago by the founder of
Cairo itself, the Fatimid Caliph, El Mu'izz. The Azhar, the precious
mosque, the *madrasas* or schools clustering round it, the students'
cells which you can glimpse through their half-open doors, the
surrounding quarter with its shops and stalls, doss-houses, street-
vendors, junk-shops, pedlars of hashish and prosperous *suqs*, is a
fascinating world of its own which has been well described by Taha
Husain, who evokes all its subtle spiritual life, and Albert Cossery,
who dwells more on its sordid poverty.

From the point of view of modern culture the Azhar hardly counts
for anything, except through the efforts of a small group of young
sheikhs led by Khaled Mohamed Khaled, who are trying to make a
bold synthesis of Western revolutionary thought (Marxist and
Fabian-Socialist) with that of Islam. Their leader's book *From
Here We Start* is perhaps the most serious attempt that has been
made to discover in what way Eastern thinkers can lay any claim
to dialectical materialism.

However, the future of the great Koranic university is now being
threatened. Taha Husain, who was educated there, is openly demanding radical reforms which would reduce the old centre of
Islamic thought to the position of an Institute of Advanced Moslem
Studies. Everything relating to primary and secondary education in
the present 'vertical' structure of the Azhar system of education,
will be handed over to the Ministry. This is likely to happen very
shortly, as some of the best of El Azhar's teachers, especially Dr
Mohamed Ghallab, are in favour of the change. Unifying education
in the hands of the State might well be regarded as a step forward,
just as from a technical point of view the co-ordination of the whole
legal system was when it was carried out in 1955. But this does not
mean that standards will be raised, and this fundamental problem
might well remain unsolved.

Let us now turn to the contribution of Cairo, the cultural and
religious capital of the Moslem East, with its potential public of

three million souls. In literature we find three or four writers who have long been famous: Taha Husain, Tewfik el Hakim, Abbas el Aqqad and Mahmud Taymur. These are all over sixty; only the first two have any readers abroad and they are losing the younger generation's support. The first of these, Taha Husain, is a dominant figure with such prestige in the East that everything he does is news. His *Stream of Days*, the poetic autobiography of a blind Azhar student, is a noble and sensitive story which was much appreciated by André Gide. The second, Tewfik's, *Maze of Justice* contains a witty and suggestive satire on the provincial administration, conveyed through an extraordinary detective story, not unlike Gogol's *The Government Inspector*. Mahmud Taymur has frankly rewritten Maupassant in an Oriental setting. As for Aqqad, who always refers to himself as 'The Great Aqqad', he specializes in putting over the most bitter of conservative creeds. Next to this small-scale Maurras, Salama Musa has been for half a century the patient advocate of peaceful evolution and intellectual liberalism.

It would be unfair to the author of *The Stream of Days* to forget for one moment the truly revolutionary and enlightened part he has been playing for thirty years in his outspoken struggle against Islamic taboos, or the way in which he has fought to link Egypt spiritually with the culture of the Mediterranean, forever praising and recommending the Western idea of impartial inquiry. Taha Husain still plays an active part in the political and aesthetic debates going on in contemporary Egypt: he was a Minister of the Wafd and has apparently given his complete support to the military régime. Tewfik el Hakim still publishes highly readable memoirs and lively sketches, full of puppets drawn from his experience as a civil servant or else from his sly, bantering imagination. But in the feverish, earnest Egypt of today these two writers can be no more than brilliant witnesses of an earlier generation. Like the musician Sayed Darwish and the sculptor Mukhtar, they are men of the revolutionary phase of 1919, not that of 1952.

But who is to replace them? Is it not surprising that (in autumn 1956) there is not a single internationally known literary review, whatever might be the merits of *Risalat el Gadida*?[1] Is it not astonishing that the best-known writers only sell about eight or ten thousand

---

[1] The excellent *Revue du Caire*, edited by Alexandre Papadopoulo, is written in French, but it publishes many translations from the Arabic. Our knowledge of contemporary Egyptian writing owes much to this review.

copies? Or that sound dramatic works—such as those of Tewfik el Hakim, for example—cannot be produced in their own country because there is no public for them?

New writers and a new public are slowly emerging, but enormous courage is needed in Egypt for anyone intending to live by his writing or art. A public means book-buyers and spectators who will be prepared to dip their hands into their pockets.

As we have seen, there is some danger that the young Egyptian who wants to write, paint or compose will not have a proper cultural background. But let us suppose that it is satisfactory. In the hope of becoming a novelist a young man sends his short stories to a daily paper, and has one of them accepted. He has some imagination and the life he has led since leaving his village on the Delta is of the kind which shapes experience. What is he to live on? No doubt this problem exists everywhere, even in Socialist societies, where no young writer can expect to be spoon-fed by the State from the very beginning. But it is particularly acute in Egypt, where intellectuals as a whole have a lean time. The Press, whether through local papers or foreign agencies, can provide outlets to some extent. But the young writer is not likely to receive even that pittance from his family which he could hope for as a student, for a writing career is hardly approved of by the provincial small-holder. Radio and cinema, which provide so many openings for young American or European writers, hold out little hope for beginners in Egypt. Writers' societies sometimes give a little assistance or offer opportunities for picking up a few shillings. That is all, and it is not enough.

Another problem which does not arise in Europe is that of the language. Some writers managed to express themselves in a foreign language—for instance, Hinain and Cossery, though it might be said that they did not exactly choose French but had it thrust upon them. What alternative is there? There are, in practice, two forms of Arabic. The first, which is used from the Koran down to the newspapers, is common to the Arabic-speaking peoples everywhere. But each country also has its own national or local dialect existing within or side by side with the international form. Linguistic unity between the provinces has long been established in Egypt, though an Alexandrian and a Saïdian will have different features in their speech. It is also quite obvious that the written language tends to be artificial or 'literary' as in most countries. However, the problem is not easily solved for the dramatist or the novelist or short-story writer who wants to convey the slightest degree of realism. He tries to bring as much of the spoken colloquial language into his writing as he can, which is like putting sparrows into the gilded cage of classicism. This was begun by Taha Husain, who succeeded to some extent in taking the literary language off its stilts, and was taken further by Tewfik el Hakim. The young novelists are now pushing the process so far that it might result in some reform of the system of writing itself, while the Press is also helping to bring the dialect into the written language.

The young novelist's troubles are still not over, once he has made sure of a living and solved the language question. He is still faced with two obstacles, though perhaps he does not realize it, but which are no less formidable on that account.

Plagiarism is a form of temptation to which Egyptian artists are particularly susceptible. This might be a matter of natural indolence. Perhaps they are convinced that Arabic is such an unusual language that there is no harm in taking credit for an Italian story or French play which they have merely copied hastily into their own tongue, and that in doing so they are not borrowing but creating. The copyright law is fairly recent and it holds no fear for them. An Egyptian colleague with a good knowledge of French, and who reads various popular series of historical tales, said that one page out of every three in such publications (which are sold at such cheap rates that the author would never recover his royalties) has been lifted from European literature. He made almost a hobby of discovering such plagiarisms.

The borrowing often takes subtler forms. Sometimes it appears to be nothing more serious than following some highly respected model too closely. About thirty years ago the Egyptian public was very keen on French novels. Among the post-romantic novels they liked, Alphonse Karr's *Sous les tilleuls* was especially popular, though it is hard to see why, unless it is because the book was well translated. For fifteen years Egyptian literature was full of lime-trees (*tilleuls*), each of them sheltering a pair of forlorn lovers. Then about ten years ago they turned to the American novel, especially Hemingway, with the result that in Cairo novels were written full of terse sentences, laced with tough interjections of which there is no lack in Arabic. Now Chekhov and Gorki are in favour, so everyone writes his *Evils of Tobacco* if he has any gift for irony, or *My Universities* if his

genius takes a more serious turn. The models will shortly be Sholo-
khov and Aragon, who are appearing on the horizon.

The second danger facing the young writer is that he will toe the
line and write like everybody else. Not that socialist realism is in
itself a trap or a dead end. It has its greatness, there is something to
be learnt from it, it has produced some excellent results. Even in
Egypt there are already some outstanding books in this manner:
Abdel Rahman Sharqawi's *The Earth*,[1] Neguib Mahfuz's short
stories, or those of Rushdi Salih. It is not realism in itself which is
dangerous for the young writer. On the contrary, there is every sign
that this school corresponds pretty well to the present state of
Egyptian culture and the country's immediate problems, and it
allows some synthesis to be made between the struggle for national
independence, social reform and the needs of art itself.

The real danger lies in being a yes-man, trying to be in the swim.
The young Egyptian writer easily succumbs to this. Being surrounded
by friends who 'write like Gorki' you only have to 'write like the
friends who write like Gorki'. This happens in every country, but in
Egypt the risk from the literary point of view is all the greater as the
local masters of socialist realism have all the power in their hands and
great courage is needed to refuse toeing—or following—the line.
There still remains the sentimental novel, with a bit of eroticism
thrown in, in which the journalist Ihsan Abdel Qudus has excelled. But has an independent writer nothing to choose from but
the fellahs, however moving, of *The Earth* and the neurotic young
ladies of *Lost Youth*? Yusuf Idris is a writer of strong personality
who belongs to the first group. His *Threepenny Nights* certainly
springs from social realism in the best sense of the term. He has
obviously gone his own way without worrying about fashions or 'lines'.
He is a revolutionary writer not only in the matter of form but in his
vengeful tone, generous irony, and intense love for human beings.
We are inclined to set him apart, having been able to read some of his
stories in translation, but perhaps Mahfuz and Khamisi write on
the same high level.

In spite of the foregoing difficulties—income, language, plagiarism
and 'toeing the line'—the young Egyptian school of fiction is not in
such a bad way. Contemporary poetry is also said to be very much
alive. The lack of a literary review is to some extent made up for by

---

[1] A novel which has already been used as a set-book for M. Régis Blachère's
lectures at the Sorbonne.

the daily 'cultural' page in the two main Cairo newspapers. The newspapers which have a literary page rarely fail to have a poem in it. In poetry the Marxist aesthetic is now very strong. The model of this kind of writing is Sharqawi's long poem, *Letter from an Egyptian Father to President Truman*, which as its title suggests has nothing in common with art for art's sake. Some readers might prefer symbolist poetry, but Sharqawi and his followers are capable of sustained writing and generous feeling. As for Kamal Abdel Halim, who was first arrested with Roger Vailland in August 1952 and who was so harshly treated in prison that it is said that his reason was affected, the French translations that have so far appeared of his work apparently give no real idea of his achievement: those who have read him in the original say that he is an Egyptian Mayakowsky.

Egyptian literature is not all left-wing, however. The diplomat Yahya Haqqi, lonely, unassertive and at present fully occupied with his official duties, published a fine story, in a French translation, in the *Revue du Caire*. *The Oil-Lamp*, as it is called, describes a Cairo quarter huddled round its mosque, a boy discovering the world through the haze of vague religious feeling—a sentimental, gossipy little world of its own, marvellously Egyptian in its atmosphere. Following on Taha Husain and Tewfik el Hakim, there are many young short-story writers with a gift for the picturesque and no lack of imagination, who are all helping to reshape the language and the tale itself, liberating them from the old tendency to formalism.

It is a pity that the writers give so little support to making Egyptian films. The film could well play a decisive cultural and educational role in Egypt. Both fellah and townsman are mad on films and the open-air cinemas give shows at rates which are well within reach of the agricultural labourer's pocket: usually a piastre or a piastre and a half. Cinema was a prosperous industry not so long ago. As many as eighty-two films were made in 1954, and Cairene films were in great demand all over the East, from Baghdad to Marrakesh. There is now a crisis in the film industry which has arisen not only on account of the censorship but because the public are turning away from Egyptian in favour of American films. This is no new craze, however, for experienced film-fans in Cairo say that no local reel, however full of Egyptian singers and dancers, ever had a chance next to Tom Mix, who was the hero of two generations of little Egyptian film-goers. Colour and the Cinemascope have been additional attractions. The national product's only strong-point lies in the language. Foreign films are not dubbed but are only given sub-titles, while part of the public cannot read. If American producers could get Marilyn Monroe or Gary Cooper to speak Arabic the Egyptian cinema film industry would collapse.

Is it as bad as all that? The answer is, no. It certainly suffers from having a small market, limited to a public of 50 million Arab-speaking people with little to spend. However, it has an excellent stock of technical equipment, having made good provision for studios and machinery when the going was good, which can bear comparison with the best to be found in Europe. There is also the unusual advantage that in Cairo there are two or three intelligent promoters and producers who are prepared to risk money in turning out ambitious films. The climatic conditions for film-making are ideal, since it never rains and outside filming can be done all the year round, though local producers have not yet made the best of this.

The industry can depend on an impressive team of producers, managers and technicians. It has men of skill and experience such as Badr Khan, Henri Barakat and Izz ud-Din Zulficar, very young directors such as Kamal el Sheikh, author of the poignant *Life and Death*, and whoever it was who made *Ruelle des Idiots*, a film which reminds one of Cossery but which for some reason did not have the success it deserved. There are also Salih Abu-Seif and Yusuf Shahin, two film-makers of entirely different personalities and styles. Their work is complementary and they should be considered as being to cinema what Taha Husain and Tewfik el Hakim are to literature.

Salih Abu-Seif is a burly man of peasant stock, rather slow and thick-set. His work is like himself—popular, a bit rough, genuine and real. He acknowledges his debt to Fritz Lang, but he could be better described as a Duvivier crossed with Germi. His films all turn on some social problem, such as a workman corrupted by the 'high society' among which he has to work (*Ustaz Hasan*), or the struggle against agrarian banditry in upper Egypt (*El Wahsha*), or the trouble caused by the arrival of a shy young man, the son of a fellah, at Cairo University (*Shebab el Mara'a*). A show consisting of Abu-Seif's films would provide an excellent social account of Egypt. He might well produce a masterpiece.

Yusuf Shahin is as spritely as his rival is massive. A pure Medi-terranean type, a Christian of Lebanese origin who speaks French like a Parisian; thin, ironical, sharp as a needle, Shahin had his art at his finger-tips by the age of thirty and has been perfecting it ever since. He has some of the qualities of Christian-Jacques and at the same time of such American virtuosi as Garnett. His *Sira fil Wadi* (*Hell's Sky*) contained some fine shots of Egypt and of popular ceremonies, and showed a mastery of narrative which might well alarm older hands at the game. But his *Sira fil Mina* showed rather less spirit. His craftsmanship was still outstanding, but had nothing behind it. He is a master *metteur en scène*, ably supported by such gifted actors as Fatima Hamama, the cinema's 'Egyptian girl' type, full of delicacy and gentle charm; Omar el Sherif and Ahmed Ramzi, strong and handsome young men who are taking over the screen-lovers' parts from those who acted them for thirty years. To these artists we should add young Magda with her beautiful leonine features; Imam, a ravishing young newcomer to the screen; the resourceful Shukri Sarhan; the excellent all-round actor Abdel Warith Azz, and above all the astonishing Tahia Carioca. Carioca began as one of Egypt's most admired cabaret-dancers, then took the lead in *Partisans de la Paix*, but Salih Abu-Seif's latest film has turned her into a kind of Egyptian Magnani, her voice, style and gesture making her a stormy embodiment of voluptuous Egypt.

There are good producers and some talented actors, but Egyptian cinema is withering for lack of script-writers. Why have the films already mentioned managed to rise out above the pretentious mediocrity or even silliness to which almost all the others fall victim, whether they be comedies of manners or social dramas? It is because their themes gave them life and substance and allowed a Shahin or an Abu-Seif to forge ahead with the narrative, and because real characters inspired the rather green actors who interpreted them. Cases where well-known writers think in terms of cinema are few and far between. More often the scripts are scraped together by hacks who use the paste and scissors on some novel or do their best with some foreign scenario or subject (*Wuthering Heights* or *The Lady with the Camelias*). This is the tragedy of Egyptian cinema. If it calls on Tewfik el Hakim or Yusuf Idris they might produce some better results than their present best. For the time being, the national Egyptian culture can hardly expect much credit for so much hasty and vulgar work, out of which only two or three interesting films appear a year. Cairo is still far behind Mexico and Japan in this field.

Perhaps Egyptian painting is the most hopeful branch of art at the present time.

Is it because they are perhaps the only Egyptian artists who are not held up by some particular difficulty? (For only the Moslem Brotherhood show some signs of being inhibited by the old taboo on representation of the human figure.) The painters are not faced by any linguistic problem, nor are they bothered about markets and censorship like the film-makers, and their relationship with the public is much the same as it is for the European artist. They are usually poor and working in isolation, in very similar conditions to those of their French or Italian counterparts. There are few patrons, while the State is stingy and has little sense of artistic values. The painter rubs along, perhaps giving a few lessons or illustrating for a review, but somehow managing to work.

There are four or five of these young artists who seem to be worth considering as a Cairo School which, though lacking in experience and confidence, has a style of its own—a rather self-conscious but suggestive simplicity which evokes all the poverty and easygoingness of Egypt. The most ambitious and established of these is Hamid Abdullah, whose ability was at once recognized as a result of his one-man show in 1956. It is not only his choice of subjects, all drawn from popular imagery, which merits attention, but also his very direct style, angular drawing, large canvases with a daring use of flat tints of colour, his skilful handling of tones which are far more carefully worked than appears at first sight. Abdullah likes to take his forms from children's drawings, using them for striking effects which are very evocative of an Egypt which is, so to speak, still in a state of infancy. Hamid Abdullah excels in large compositions as well as small and delicate gouaches: it did not take him many years to outgrow the virtuoso stage and he is now approaching the height of his achievement.

His very deliberate, lucid painting is the very opposite of Abdel Hadi el Ghazzar's work, which is instinctive and often awkward. His canvases are full of strange shapes, magical fantasies, esoteric symbols which, in spite of superficial appearances, owe very little to foreign surrealism and serve to remind us that Egypt is haunted, or imagines it is, by evil spirits or djinns. The background for this exorcistic painting is made up of a miserable world of dwarfs, madmen and old crones. Ghazzar is a wonderful draughtsman, but as a painter he seems to be more interested in driving out evil spirits than in harmonizing his colours. Each of his canvases seems to be a kind of *Zar* for his own private use.[1]

Hamid Nada is closer to reality, with his canvases crammed with frightened animals and cheap, humble objects, dingily lit, that suggest something of the terrible living-conditions of the Cairo poor. Since 1955 he seems to have been moving towards a more decorative, intellectualized art. The group's purest 'painter' is Samir Rafi, a subtle colorist with a good sense of composition. He also seems to be haunted by a kind of supernatural atmosphere of poverty, but his feeling for colour gets the better of his pessimism. Kamil Yusuf uses muddy colours for portraying an Egypt peopled by slow-moving beasts and scrawny fellahs. Tahia Halim is sensitive, Hamuda bright and precise, Sida amusing; Gazbia Sirri and Inji Iflatun, two women artists, offer solemn commentaries on the life of peasant and worker. In Alexandria, Seif Wanli opposes to Sa'ad el Khadem's wise and subtle art a baroque, luxuriant painting which has certain affinities to that of Mahmud Sa'id, the leader of the renaissance of Egyptian painting.

These painters are all working side by side with some foreign artists who are so thoroughly at home in Egypt that they should be included in the 'Cairo School', for there is a sense in which nationality ceases to count in art. Michaela Burchardt, the wife of the Egyptian mathematician Jacques Simaika, is a most lyrical painter, lavish and enthusiastic, who has fallen under the spell of the pathos and mystery of peasant life. There are also Enrico Brandani, a rather precious draughtsman and an extraordinarily inventive decorative artist, and Cléa Badaro, Angelo de Riz and Margot Veillon.

At the same time an Egyptian architect, Ramses Wisa Wasif, is trying to revive the weaving of Coptic rugs and tapestries which is an old and highly imaginative branch of the Egyptian tradition. The Egyptians of the first few centuries of the Christian era used to weave tapestries decorated with fanciful designs. These were made in bright colours, rather preciously arranged, and were for the most part used in churches. When the craftsmen were exiled to Constantinople by the Turks, this art died out in Egypt, and the pieces that have survived are now worth their weight in gold. On the fringe of Cairo, not far from the Pyramids, Mr Wisa Wasif has gathered

---

[1] A *Zar* is a ritual for driving out spirits, consisting of a kind of Dervish dance, deriving from voodoo. In spite of government efforts to suppress it, it is still practised in lower-class and country districts.

together in a workshop-cum-school a little group of children and youths, drawn from the villages, who since 1950 have been weaving admirable 'folk' tapestries which show striking inventiveness and imagination. They are all ordinary children of fellahs, both Christian and Moslem. Their spontaneously woven works, which they make without any preliminary drawing—much to specialists' amazement—remind one of the image-makers of our early Middle Ages. Perhaps these little fellah children are paving the way for a genuine renaissance of folk-art in the Nile Valley?

The Press is usually alert and interested in such matters, but it has not given this experiment the publicity it deserves. The newspapers are bound to be the normal medium for the spreading of culture in a country as backward as this. It is natural that we should expect rather a lot of the Press in a country where even a best-seller has a sale of only 10,000 copies, which has hardly a cultural or artistic review to its name, and in which students are as often as not content with being spoon-fed with lectures instead of studying for themselves. The part played by the Cairo papers in the development of Arab nationalism from Selim Taqla to Ahmed Abu Fath is no secret. They never ran short of invective or calls to arms or heroic slogans. Perhaps it is now time that they acted as guide and counsellor to the general public. Interesting efforts are being made in this direction by the 'official' newspapers *El Gumhuriya* and *El Sha'b*. They both carry a daily 'cultural' page containing not only stories and literary news, but which is a battle ground for the partisans and opponents of social realism, the latter having the worst of it. As for *El Masa* (Evening News), which was founded in 1956 and owed much to Khaled Muhi ud-Din, the moral leader of the Egyptian Left, its leading articles (which we have followed for about a year in translation) show it to be very Marxist, but distinctly better than its rivals. Its analyses of the cultural and political situation are both intelligent and serious.

The Egyptian Press has lost none of its dash although it is held in check by the censorship. The sensational weeklies *Akhbar el Yom* and *Akhir Sa'a* are racy and full of bite. *Rose el Yusuf*, which is perhaps the only paper in the world which bears its founder's name, or at any rate a woman's (she was a famous actress before the war and runs the paper herself), is an odd cocktail of progressive ideas and society gossip, mixed by the attractive Ihsan Abdel Qudus, Rose's son and the most popular journalist in the Arab world. There is no lack of talented young men who are well qualified to act as interpreters of culture to the masses, such as Ahmed Baha ud-Din, Kamil el Mallakh, Anwar Abdel Malek, Kamal Zuhairi. There are also the brilliant and popular caricaturists Zuhdi, Georges, Hasan Fuad and Gamal Kamil.

In spite of the foregoing, Egypt still has no sense of proportion, critical spirit and drive in its search for a 'national culture'. It is still at the stage of laying the foundations. This highly stratified society has begun absorbing and dissolving the foreign or cosmopolitan superstructure which perhaps 'stole' two of its most gifted artists by claiming them for French literature, in the case of Hinain and Cossery. It has also begun to draw a few working-class artists from below, making intellectuals of those who hitherto wanted nothing better than to join the *bourgeoisie*. Perhaps such a vertical regrouping was a necessary condition for artistic development.

This Egypt which is now gathering itself together socially while breaking away from an Islam which until recently was its be-all and end-all, is still too self-conscious and self-seeking to produce anything really creative. The new generation has certainly some genuine writers and two or three painters to be reckoned with. There are many signs of talent about to mature. But as yet there is no collective effort that can in any way be compared with that of the Mexican painters, the Japanese film-script writers and producers, or the Greek school of novelists.

The process of 'egyptianization' is still under way. Egypt is in pursuit of a culture to which she had been blinded by alien rule and influence. But this is not a matter of 'liberation', it means, rather, that an old inheritance has to be taken over and absorbed. It is this idea of a national culture remaining open to the past as well as the present, with its need for autonomy as well as universality, that we find formulated in the conclusion to an admirable article written in March 1957, five months after the Port Said incident, by the eminent writer Georges Hinain and published in the French review *Études Méditerranéennes*:

'My opinion of the November crisis is that for many intellectuals it was something like being plunged into an absurd and cruel reality which at the same time sobered us down. Now it looks as though a genuine ideological hunger, a hunt for our source, our roots, has gripped the younger generation and consequently stirred their elders. Translations are being made of Tolstoy's *War and Peace*, the main works of Freud: people are beginning to examine Sartre's position more closely, they are demanding raw material, evidence. These are reassuring signs, in as much as they show that the rising generation is fully aware of the enormous task it will soon have to take over. It is standing on the threshold of that knowledge without which nothing can be done, on the threshold of a science of perspectives which should enable it to dominate the irrational and the mental folklore from which it still derives its energy. The problem now facing it is a problem of intellectual equipment, and we all agree that it cannot be solved except by our re-entering the great orbit of world-culture and putting aside all reservations and idle sectarian motives.'

III

Egypt, Islam and the Modern World

Some five hundred minarets fret the Cairo skyline. Egypt has been Moslem for close on thirteen hundred years, since not long after the death of the Prophet. Ibn Tulun and Saladin were great rulers, and Egypt tasted the glory of the arts, warfare and law just as much under her Islamic masters as under the old dynasties. For almost a thousand years El Azhar has been the shrine of Islam's law, of which Egypt as a whole is the centre and citadel. In spite of this no other part of the Islamic world more invites us to ask the dangerous question, whether the salvation of Moslem man has to be achieved through the revival or by the rejection of Islam?

There can no longer be any doubt that this 'go-between' nation which holds the balance in Islam is now awakening. Fifty years ago it was a mere link in the chain of European imperialism, but now it can alarm the whole world and show us that the trial of the West is only in its first stages. But what part does religion play in this? We must inquire whether this renaissance springs from a spiritual revival within the framework of the Law, or whether it is a break-away from it. Even if it is taken for granted that the believers' sense of dignity is a force to be reckoned with in that outburst of indignation whose effects can be seen everywhere and which it helps to organize, it still remains for us to estimate what the religious contribution is likely to be, towards that reconstruction which may be expected when the present struggle is over. It does seem surprising that the Moslem world should be engaged in a political revival at a time when Islamic studies, apologetics and the exegesis of the Koran are at such a low ebb. On the one hand we see political vitality, and on the other religious sterility.

It can be argued, of course, that Islam is a 'total' religion, and that it is idle and foolish to distinguish between the political and the spiritual, religious behaviour or the act of prayer, whether in the religion or in its followers. But the problem is to know whether this is going to be the case much longer. The question is forced on us by

430

the Egyptian experiment with all its ambiguity, its deficiencies, its brutality and over-simplification. The word 'Islam' means submission. However noble the word might seem in the believer's eyes, we might well ask whether the optimistic, static and formalist view of the world which underlies the Moslem faith can hold out long against any revolutionary undertaking. Once when we were discussing the Egyptian revolution with Sheikh Hasan el Bakhuri, the Minister of Awqaf (religious properties), he intervened quickly and explained at some length that the military had merely carried out a *coup d'état* which opened the way for a reasonable evolution. All very lucid and prudent, but such statements do not explain the facts away. Can the Moslem world's struggle take Islam along with it? Will Islam be a source of strength or a liability? It is tempting to reply that it will result in a split involving a breakdown into rival nations, spiritual detachment and a flight from the religious code.

Such a cross-fire of questions and answers is particularly sharp in the case of Egypt. This is not only because the break with the politics of the past has been so abrupt there, but because Egyptian Islam is far from being well equipped for the community's revival. It might be answered that Egypt is none the less the centre and yardstick of Islam. Yes, but—to take an example—Italian Catholicism in the past fifty years has lagged far behind in all the reforms on which the future of the Roman Church depends. And this comparison is a mild one, for however weak it often appears, the Vatican's formalism is nothing like the apathy of El Azhar. Sartre recently said that French Marxism was in an arrested state: this term applies precisely to Egyptian Islam,[1] which is now a barren religion whose only concern is to carry out religious observances at the correct time of day. Anguish has never had any place in the faith and has never been able to inspire it with energy as in the case of the Christian world. On the contrary, as in the case of the ancient Egyptians, Moslem fervour always relied on a confident serenity, a system of certainties. But this fervour seems to have faded into nothing but a memory, an echo of former certainties, untouched by everyday life and in no way open to question. Yet it was an Egyptian, Sheikh Mohamed Abduh, who wrote, 'The seeker after truth who falls into error, is nearer truth than any sheep-like mind following the beaten

---

[1] Discussion was officially ruled out after the publication of the works of four great theologians, Malik, Hanifa, Shafi'i and Hanbal, who founded the four great schools of law.

track.' It is hardly necessary to add that Abduh has few followers. Egyptian Islam, sluggish and many-sided, shapeless, hanging on to its shibboleths and pedantically confusing Arabic grammar with orthodoxy, seems to be little more than a rather formidable assumption. The masses no doubt pray, fast and give alms, and anyone coming fresh from the empty mosques of Iran is at once struck by the Egyptians' regular practice of their articles of faith. But anyone coming from Morocco and remembering its genuine fervour feels that the Egyptians are only concerned with the outward forms of worship. A young Egyptian philosopher defined the Islam of the masses in Egypt as a 'build-up of the poor's passiveness'.

Of course Egyptian Islam has reasons for survival which cannot be dismissed lightly. The first of these is the way in which it has, rather surprisingly, been able to merge itself into the great pantheistic ritual of the peasantry, to the extent of admitting Pharaonic or Christian elements. It has absorbed certain traditions and practices where necessary, adapted its calendar, taken over such pagan and Christian feast-days as the *Sham el Nasim* and a worship of the dead which perhaps survives from the cult of Osiris. Islam is half a city religion and half Bedouin, but in Egypt it has become peasant. The way in which it has adapted itself might result in its surviving for a long time in the country areas—but as we have suggested, the Egyptian peasant, despite all appearances, is capable of bold experiment and revolution, though so far this has remained at the materialistic level.

Egyptian Islam is also spurred on by the presence of an important Christian minority. This is not likely at any time to result in a fruitful rivalry, especially where research is concerned. The Coptic clergy for the most part have little intellectual appeal to make. Even when they tried to revive its old Monophysite[1] debate in 1955 the Ulema brought forward nothing very deep or new. If Egyptian Christianity has any part to play it is not in the sphere of doctrine but that of a will to power. The existence of this worthy, hard-working community which is well equipped for public office and constantly aspiring towards it appears in Moslem eyes as a direct challenge which cannot be ignored. This thorn in its flesh is one of those circumstances which prevents Egyptian Islam, at least as a social and political entity, from falling asleep.

---

[1] The heresy of Eutyches, condemned at the Chalcedon Council, according to which Christ had not two natures, divine and human, but only one.

Another strong factor at work for the preservation of Islam in Egypt is its diplomatic value. Mustafa Kemal admittedly broke with the Caliphate, but that was when it was at a very low ebb. It is hard to imagine any Egyptian government wilfully depriving itself of the immense political asset of El Azhar and the 'missions'. If Moscow is clever enough to exploit the patriarch Alexis in the Middle East, the ruler of Cairo is unlikely to disdain such a weapon. This is particularly true of Nasser who, on his return from his Asian tour in 1955, told us how amazed he was by the prestige (seen from a distance . . .) of the great Koranic university of Cairo, saying, 'In Indonesia, Pakistan, Egypt, what counts is El Azhar.' For the past ten years in Africa the teaching of the Koran has been making remarkable strides.

This is why the ancient stronghold of scholasticism has resisted the bitter attacks that have been made on it, with open approval on the part of the government through its official newspaper, by Taha Husain, the most powerful personality in the country. Voltaire and Renan struck no harder blows at the Western Church. 'You are ignorant brutes and reactionaries! Any Christian, particularly those in orders with the slightest knowledge of Arabic, is better informed than you about our religion and civilization.' It was in more or less those terms that the author of the *Stream of Days* attacked the Ulema in Egypt in the government daily *El Gumhuriya* early in 1955. Three months earlier the Alexandria Assize Court had passed a sentence of hard labour for life on two *Shari'a* (Koranic Law) judges who were accused of accepting payment 'in kind' from two plaintiffs who were suing their husbands for desertion. A fitting, if severe, example! In 1955 (31 December) a law was passed putting an end to denominational courts, especially affecting Koranic courts. This amounted to a grievous blow to El Azhar, as it closed at least a third of the openings for its students in abolishing the courts of 'personal status' which, even among Moslems, had a scandalous reputation for corruption and incompetence. Its inward collapse, the measures taken and criticism made against it either by or with the approval of those in power, would all combine to reduce El Azhar to the level of the slums that surround it, were it not for the political prestige it still has abroad.

El Azhar still has some outstanding teachers, such as Mohamed Ghallab, who is trying to link Moslem humanism with the Greek tradition. The teaching of Arabic and also of the other Semitic languages still reaches a high standard. But two attempts that have been made to revive the ancient house of learning met with failure. Early in this century Mohamed Abduh tried to introduce a more critical spirit and a technique of free inquiry, but his efforts went adrift into a form of modernism which, in the hope of 'rationalizing' the message of the Koran, resulted only in translating 'djinns' by 'microbes' and trying to justify miracles by pointing to the invention of wireless. Twenty-five years later Mustafa Abdel Raziq also tried to infuse some new life into El Azhar. His brief period of office as head of the university resulted only in some improvement in the intellectual level of the staff and their teaching, without introducing any ferment of critical inquiry. His brother, Ali Abdel Raziq, was then trying to apply the distinction between politics and religion to Islam, by showing that the Caliphate was not an integral part of Islamic doctrine and that it was contrary to its teaching to embody religious and political power in a single individual. As a result he was condemned by the Ulemas in 1925 and excluded from university office.[1] It was at that time that Taha Husain was mercilessly attacked by the Azharists for trying to introduce historical criticism into the study of the Koranic texts, in connexion with pre-Islamic poetry.

Since then 'religious' disputes have hardly gone beyond matters of practical ritual, unless we count the storm raised in 1946 by M. Khalafullah's thesis on 'tales in the Koran'. This thesis, like Taha Husain's, committed the 'error' of introducing a critical attitude to Koranic exegesis. In a period of over three years spent in Egypt (from 1953 to 1956), the authors of the present book witnessed only one dispute which involved both religious specialists and the opinion of a public that is reputed to 'live' its religion. It concerned the Ramadan fast.

Early in June, at the time of Ramadan, Sheikh Abdel Hamid Bekhit, a professor of Moslem theology at El Azhar University, published in the popular daily *El Akhbar* an article in which he argued that this fast is not absolutely binding on those who find it too painful an ordeal, such as workmen who have to work ten hours a day under the terrible Egyptian sun. He quoted the 'Sunna' to prove that God had no intention of inflicting 'unbearable suffering' on the faithful. Sheikh Bekhit was already regarded as an eccentric.

[1] This was because King Fuad was hoping, for his own advantage, to revive the Caliphate which Ataturk had abolished.

Only thirty-eight, he was known as the 'sheikh with the béret' on account of his headgear which looked out of place in old Cairo. His article caused some surprise but there were no strong reactions at first. Several days later the Pakistan Press referred to his article, pointing out indignantly that this Azhar teacher was undermining the faith. It was only then that the Ulemas in Egypt began to stir, feeling somewhat upset by this sermon from Indian Islam, which never loses an opportunity for stressing that it is the most powerful section of Islam, both in numbers and through the quality of some of its leaders such as Iqbal.

The Ulema Council at once adopted the role of an inquisition and called on the 'sheikh with the béret' to retract what he had written. Much to the disappointment of some of the Press who were ready to give him their strong support, the 'revolutionary' sheikh withdrew, saying that more had been ascribed to him than he had actually written, and that the rule of fasting was one of the fundamental duties of any good Musulman. Nothing could have been worse, for his former supporters turned against Bekhit, accusing him of 'base opportunism' and assuring him of their utmost contempt, while the Sheikh Tag, Rector of El Azhar, announced to the stupefaction of the 'heretic' and the world at large that his retraction was a 'proof of his guilt' and would be taken into account at his trial, which opened before the Ulema court on the 4th of July 1955.

Outraged and suddenly freed from his feelings of scruple or perhaps prudence, Bekhit meanwhile printed some explosive statements in the weekly *Rose el Yusuf*, saying that 'women must enjoy their full political rights', that 'they should have the same right as men to choose their partner and ask his hand in marriage', that 'Moslem professors were breaking the rules of the Koran by dressing differently from other believers', and so on. This is why the young lecturer's trial took on a symbolic significance. He was thrown out of El Azhar and further humiliated by being appointed to a job as a school-teacher in a little provincial school. Standing immediately afterwards in the University entrance, he said angrily, 'From now on young Islam will declare war on the Old Gang who are in power.' This frail-looking man with the face of an eagle made you think that Egypt had found its Lamennais. Was he going to be another Mohamed Abduh? Far from it. The Supreme Court (composed of lay judges) annulled the Ulema Council's sentence six months later,

435

and by restoring Bekhit to his university post apparently put an end to the whole affair and appeased the angry young man. Bekhit was not up to the challenge he had perhaps unthinkingly thrown down. Western minds might take the whole episode as being nothing more than a storm in a teacup, failing to realize that in Islam a dispute over ritual observances might appear even more important than one over doctrine. However, it proved an abortive revolution.

The most interesting aspect of the affair was the stand taken by the majority of the newspapers, if not in Bekhit's favour, at least on the side of an open debate on such a problem, and in support of the young sheikh's right to defend hisattitude, however right or wrong. It is to be noted that most of those who were at all versed in Koranic exegesis held the view that his thesis was no more than a rather lax interpretation of the spirit of the sacred texts: it is undeniable that social conditions have changed so much since seventh-century Medina that it is not easy to apply a rule which was intended for camel-drivers of the Hijaz, to the hard-pressed Egyptian proletariat of today. El Azhar's reaction was generally considered as dictatorial, narrow-minded and unfair, and its prestige was by no means strengthened because it announced that to fail to observe the fast is a less serious offence than to deny its necessity, 'a form of apostasy which should be punished by death'.[1]

Egyptian Islam is cruelly incapable of thinking for itself, for although it is often diluted with elements of the Pharaonic or Christian traditions in the country areas, it is faithfully observed among the poorer classes everywhere. (A sheikh told us that when he took it on himself to exempt the less robust fellahs from fasting, one hot summer when the Ramadan coincided with harvesting, hardly one out of twenty villagers broke the rule.) It has certainly suffered from the excesses of the Moslem Brotherhood, whose unexpected success was a kind of reply to other excesses, such as cosmopolitanism and the demoralizing conditions in the towns. But it suffers even more from the mediocrity of the great organizations for the study and application of the law which are offshoots of El Azhar and amount to nothing less than a hierarchized clergy with disciplinary powers of its own. No public opinion, being gradually enlightened as in the case of Egypt, could help breaking away unconsciously from a religion whose leaders, like the rector of the Azhar, never lose a chance of showing the most unsavoury sec-

[1] *A Rule of Fiqh*, quoted by G.-H. Bousquet.

tarianism and blindness to realities. The venerable Sheikh Abdel-Rahman Tag, rector of El Azhar, whose long stay at the Sorbonne seem to have left his mind as firmly closed as before, replied to a Cairo newspaper which had criticized polygamy, that this practice was the only one suitable for human nature 'because mankind contains more women than men' and 'what would become of a man suddenly a prey to violent desire when his wife is sick'. This raised a storm in the Press, the government newspaper *El Gumhuriya* answering irreverently that 'the violent desires on the part of wives should also be taken into consideration and tolerated likewise, especially in the absence of their husbands'. The newspaper *El Ahram* objected that the sheikh could just as well advise cannibalism when there is a shortage of mutton.[1] The same man, when questioned by another Cairo daily as to the causes of religious and moral decadence in the Arab world, could find no better explanation than the plotting of 'enemies of the East who are trying to divide and rule us'. As for Sheikh Hasan Mazlum, the Grand Mufti of Egypt, he was once asked what sanctions should be imposed on certain Egyptians, brought up as Christians, who became Moslems in order to put away their wives (some of them then proceeding to return to their original faith). He replied 'A Christian who embraces Islam is not an apostate; he is merely recognizing the Prophet in addition to his Christian faith. He is adding to and perfecting his faith. Whereas a Moslem who becomes a Christian is denying Mohamed: he is an apostate and deserves to be put to death.'

Such theologians who are spontaneously rejected by all active Egyptian minds, including the faithful, obviously appear inadequate to the enormous task which was none the less undertaken by the Christian thinkers, from Saint Thomas Aquinas to Teilhard de Chardin. They are unfit to

'bring about in Islam that revision of values which has been the hallmark of European thought since the Renaissance, or to shape the ideals and problems of the modern world in an Islamic mould which alone, so far, has been capable of striking a chord in the conscience of Moslem peoples . . . though this would have enabled

---

[1] This declaration by the sheikh of El Azhar aroused—among others—(a) his daughter's indignation, which she expressed in the weekly *Akhir Sa'a* 'in the name of all Egypt's women', and (b) the indignation of one of the members of the Junta who said to the present writers at the time, 'It is so stupid that there is no point in making a protest.'

them to canalize through the faith, that circulation of ideas within a society which is now stretched to breaking-point between the Middle Ages and the twentieth century'.[1]

Not the slightest sign or inkling of such a 'revision' can be found in the pronouncements or writings of the Egyptian Ulema.

And yet we of the West must avoid thinking, with a sense of superiority, that Islam *must* pass through the same stages as our Christian theologians have gone. Just as the Arabian bedouin takes more naturally to the aeroplane than a peasant from the Rouergue, yet is astonished by a bicycle, in the same way Islamic research can quite well throw up fresh concepts without having first digested or rejected the experiments of European philosophy and apologetics over the past seven hundred years. Historical or systematic parallels have to be avoided. H. A. R. Gibb, looking into the factors which might be misleading in any comparison between the European Renaissance and Moslem Reformism, particularly brings out the fact that

'In the Renaissance (as distinct from the Reformation) the chllaenge to the doctrines and culture of the mediaeval church came partly, it is true, from the subjectivism of the newly released sense of individuality, but also (and more effectively) from a relatively pure devotion to reason and a belief in its supremacy; whereas Islam and its culture are challenged today by a pseudo-rationalism (as clamorous in the West as in the East) which mistakes emotion for thought and propaganda for argument.'[2]

The Oxford and Harvard professor adds more precisely,

'Historical method in the West is still to a large degree under the influence of that scientific determinism which the Moslem mind has always rejected.[3] The Moslem historian, if he builds upon the foundations of Moslem thought, will not be tempted to reduce history to a pattern of abstract concepts; for him concrete facts are always to be viewed in their particular concrete relations.'

Remarking that Mohamed Abduh was deeply influenced by the great historian of the Berbers, Ibn Khaldun, Professor Gibb adds,

[1] Francis Bertier: 'Recontre de l'Islam et du monde moderne' in the review *Lettres Nouvelles*, 7 August 1956.
[2] *Modern Trends in Islam* (Chicago, 1947), p. 136, n. 7.
[3] In the past, yes. But will this be the case for long?

'In the teaching of his truest followers the evolutionary concept of historical development is slowly broadening out and overleaping the limitations set upon it by the traditional, orthodox doctrine'.[1]

Is this to be interpreted as one of the few signs of this 'tension' towards revival which these observers who are most favourably disposed towards Islam would like us to see? However much we ought to consider the European model and the Western experiment as a threat to the Egyptian imagination or intelligence, and however little value we have as teachers, yet we have to point out that in Egypt, at least, present researches hardly go any farther than an attempt to adapt their ritual technically to the rhythm of modern life. We have already mentioned the curious and perhaps important attempt on the part of a few young Azhar sheikhs, to reconcile the teachings of the Prophet with Marxism. Except for Khaled Mohamed Khaled, this amounts to nothing but hair-splitting in the spirit of the Jesuitry at which Pascal poked fun in the *Lettres Provinciales*, and a few grammatical subtleties.

When it comes to a 'Treason of the Intellectuals' it is surely the duty of the civil power to assume responsibility. And since that 'half of the Caliph' in which disciplinary power and control of the law is invested has proved itself inadequate, should not the other 'half of the Caliph', the dictator, come to the help of a paralysed religion?

When Gamal Abdel Nasser, immediately after their attack on him in October 1954, undertook the merciless struggle against the Moslem Brotherhood which led to the Association's collapse and the hanging of half a dozen of its leaders, one wondered whether that brutal repression was the first stage in a radical 'dis-Islamization' after the manner of Kemal Ataturk. That is the question we put, a few days after the Brotherhood paid the price, to Major Gamal Salim, Vice-Premier and president of the People's Court in which he had acted as a ruthless prosecutor rather than as a judge. We asked if this implied a step in the direction of secularization? We had to repeat the question, mentioning Ataturk. Gamal Salim started up and replied, 'There is no question of that. We are and remain Moslems, and it is precisely because we are faithful to Islam, a tolerant and liberal religion, that we had to condemn these imposters and assassins.' A few weeks later the army review *El Tahrir* carried an editorial on the same theme in which occurred the passage:

[1] Ibid., p. 128.

'The Egyptian régime of Gamal Abdel Nasser is not anti-religious like that of Kemal Ataturk in Turkey. It did not oppose the Moslem Brotherhood in order to strike at religion, but on the contrary to purge it of that charlatanism which would have taken the form of a new influx of imperialism and a further exploitation of the Egyptian proletariat. Every day our new government is working to put social justice more into effect, and is thus drawing closer to Islam.'

The majority of the Cairo officers are pious Moslems. Of modest country stock, they have been unaffected by the wave of modernist scepticism and demoralization which has been sweeping over the Egyptian upper classes for over half a century. These 'simple souls' are not ashamed of kneeling with their faces to the East, in the mosque, every Friday. When the régime was first set up, common prayers held perhaps a more important place in the government system than they do now. This was partly due to Neguib's influence, and partly to a desire to placate the Moslem Brotherhood, who were then their allies. Now they pray without being photographed at the same time, and have their minds on other things.

Between 1952 and 1956 the military Republic has struck blows against Islam which had every appearance of heralding a revolution. We have already mentioned such things as the suppression of the religious courts, the partial dissolution of El Azhar particularly in the creating in 1955 of an Institute of Islamic Research which is a dangerous rival, the extending of the vote to women who were already agitating for it. We have also drawn attention to the plan put forward for limiting polygamy, and for restricting unilateral repudiation to particular cases, which must now be approved by the 'Judge of personal status'. We have referred to the way in which the government's official newspaper, El Gumhuriya, never misses the chance of supporting the modernist view against that of El Azhar, as in the case of Bekhit and in the tussle over polygamy.

Even bolder is the government's experiment in creating twelve clinics to cater for what is modestly called 'family planning', but which are really birth-control centres. This problem, which would not have involved a second's hesitation among twenty Catholics, resulted in lively disputes among the learned doctors of Moslem law, and one in four of the sheikhs was found to admit it in principle.[1]

---

[1] See the chapter, 'The Problem of Overpopulation'.

Nasser himself does not appear to have made his line of conduct plain, being unwilling to adopt Malthusianism before exhausting all other ways of solving the problems arising from an increase of half a million new citizens a year in an already over-populated country. But the very fact that these clinics were opened at all was a profoundly revolutionary innovation which, for instance, any Catholic in this country can easily imagine, just as the alarm caused in the Egyptian peasantry by the attack on polygamy could be compared with what a Spanish rustic would think if divorce were suddenly allowed. Seen from Europe, such measures might appear rather timid and even somewhat conservative. But they represent a shaking of the foundations in the case of the closed society of Islam.

What was Nasser aiming at? Hanging Moslem Brothers, restricting polygamy, undermining El Azhar, suppressing religious courts, votes for women, questioning the Ramadan fast, the experiment of birth-control, all this is rather much from a pious Moslem. The 'miscreant' Mustafa Kemal hardly did much more in his first three years as dictator.[1] But let us examine the difference between their two policies. For Kemal, who was in a stronger position since he was a national hero, a victorious general, the 'Father of the Ottomans', Islam was no more than an old obstacle which had to be knocked down, a paltry hindrance to the total re-shaping of his country on the model of the West. He looked at the Moslem religion much as Lenin looked on Orthodoxy, with its clergy and customs. In both cases it was seen from the outside and condemned outright as the opium of the masses. Nasser, on the contrary, saw the problem from within, as a believer himself, and perhaps this is the best way of knowing what is wrong. It is not his aim to knock down Islam but to transform it and fit it into modern life for the purposes of government and diplomacy. It could be said that Nasser is out to 'neutralize' Islam in internal politics, while 'utilizing' it in foreign politics.

From the Western point of view the Nasser undertaking could rather be related to that of his opponents, the Moslem Brotherhood, while having more political intelligence. They have in common the idea of rebuilding a society which is impregnated with Islam, and completely freed from the apron-strings of foreign powers. But here again Nasser is different, for if he still regards the Koran as a useful

[1] The Caliphate was suppressed in 1924.

and respectable point of reference, it is incapable in any way of providing him with a plan of action, and even less a charter or Constitution. The colonel-president, who has certainly not read it, would appear to have been inspired by a curious book published in the late nineteenth century by Savvas Pasha and freely quoted from in M. Cherfils' book *Bonaparte et l'Islam*. In it he expounded, cynically enough, his theory of the 'islamization of truths', which may be summed up as follows. It is impossible to govern in the Moslem world in any way which offends the Koran or the Sunna.[1] But anything can be brought into line with the Koranic teaching, which is both adaptable and multiple. Thus any truth which is useful for political ends can be 'islamized'. Its immersion in the Koran will give it the necessary colour and give it both publicity and authority . . .

Thus the Bikbashi has tried to islamize modernism, in order to modernize and rearm Egyptian Islam. This looks to us like proposing one of the three solutions to the political problem which arises from the clash between Islam and modern life—the other two solutions being the cautious laicization of Bourguiba, and Russian Neo-Kemalism. Stalin, Kemal and even Bourguiba obtained and are obtaining striking results, but the Bikbashi has not used the methods of the first two of these, and the society on which it is working has none of the suppleness or variety of Tunisia.

To stretch Islam, even when already, so to speak, under an anaesthetic, on the operating-table in this way is inviting risks. The Ulemas' servility seems to have no limits so long as the political 'half-caliph' remains successful. In the past they have defended the principle of an hereditary Caliphate for the benefit of King Fuad and King Faruk, and then the 'sacred' character of the republican system for the benefit of the Society of Free Officers. It is more likely that the great mass of believers will give vent to the strongest protests, and their demand for integral Islam would put the régime in danger. Nor should we forget the reactions of the rest of the world to the government's measures, which in Damascus and Khartum are regarded as savouring of heresy. The new Saladin's prestige has so far given him plenty of rope, but Egyptian Islam is not what it was in the time of Saladin. There are other centres where the Prophet's teaching is taken more seriously, and the last opportunity for reforming Islam

[1] Cf. the interview quoted in the chapter, 'The Dictator as He Really Is': 'We are anxious not to do anything contrary to the Koran.'

might well come from the Maghrib, or from the Qarawiyin of Fez, for instance, rather than from El Azhar.

How then, in Egypt, could this headless religion give some shape to a people in search of its own soul? How can an arrested Islam give a sense of direction and a framework to such a crumbling society? Of course the Egyptian nation—wedged in the Nile Valley, descended from a race that was twenty times invaded and twenty times remade, this nation intent on a great undertaking, which is the exploitation of as much land as possible while using the least possible water, nine out of ten of them worshipping the same God and all frantically centralized on Cairo—this nation is rightly proud of a unity unknown to any other 'under-developed' country today. It is certainly a nation, self-contained and thoroughly 'nationalized', while being part of the Moslem Umma, which is a kind of International Association. But is it a *society*?

Political unity has been achieved. In spite of the incredible stupidity of public life at the town-council and provincial level, yet a state machine is working in the best modern style and very satisfactorily. But it is all based on a conception of a national State supported by European techniques, on the fringe of and even in contradiction with the total and universal religion of Islam, and the social and political teachings that go with it. All this has been built up in spite of Islam. But what has not yet been built up—because in this sphere Islam has not yet lost its grip, though this does not mean it has anything positive to offer—is a genuine Egyptian society, with its own system of rules and laws, its own system of relationships, its own system of spiritual life with its attendant moral code.

Agricultural Egypt still makes up a class-society, however bold it might seem to apply such a term to it. It still has its great land-owning capitalists, threatened or ruined though they be, who although they no longer have a free hand since the 1952 revolution —nor even their monopoly of such paths to power as education (revolution of 1919)—are still the most powerful element. It still has its rural *petite bourgeoisie*, straining for land, education and jobs in the civil service. There are still the small tenant-farmers who have been reprieved for a while by the Agrarian Reform, but are depressed to an almost proletarian level, while there are still the agricultural labourers, a sub-proletariat growing hungrier every day. But the urban population is nothing but a shapeless mass, with no clearly marked divisions. It is tending, with the decadence of the great cosmopolitan capital and the emergence of an organized proletariat, towards a kind of vertical breakdown of the poor, the only differentiations that one can make seeming to be according to income—those earning more than £100 a month, those between £100 and £10, those between £10 and £3, and those less than £3.

However, we are less interested in making such a classification than in some adequate and adaptable definition of a social life in the ant-hill cities of Egypt. There is no sign of anything but decomposition and stratification. To have genuine social classes there would need to be more cohesion in the different groups and less sense of isolation on the part of the ruling element.

There is, firstly, stratification as regards Islam, a whole layer of the population having nothing but irony or indifference for the 'men of religion', if not for the religion itself, while another layer objects to El Azhar's teaching being so different from what they themselves received in the State schools, and is thus becoming conscious of some kind of separation of Church from State. A third layer, which could be identified with those who earn less than £3 a month, clings to Islam as a drowning man clutches a straw, or regards it as a sedative or—if he is a Moslem Brother—as a kind of weapon. There is a fourth layer which rightly believes that the mosque is the only place where poverty is not considered to be shameful.

There is also a stratification as regards Western modernism. Some Egyptians master Western techniques and greedily enjoy all its comforts; others struggle frantically to gain admission to this paradise, going without food in order to pay hire-purchase for a symbolic refrigerator. Some see it as a hateful mirage, provokingly thrust at them from every side in the shape of films, cars and shop-windows. This permanent challenge of the Cadillac to mass poverty is not likely to go unanswered: on the 26th of January 1952 the revolutionaries were not slow in identifying themselves with this long-smouldering resentment.

We cannot overlook the sexual obsession to which the urban population seems to be a prey. In this they are all alike, at all levels of wealth and poverty. At the top level there is a minority who like to pretend that they are completely free to do what they like in such matters. Others are still strongly swayed by Moslem Puritanism. A young woman in the Cairo upper middle-class has far less opportunity of meeting young men of her own age than any London girl in the same position. She sees the same films and perhaps reads the same books, in the original or in translation. However small, this is the first stage at which private intentions and the 'rule' are at odds. It is even more marked lower down, where almost the entire middle-classes are victims of the strict inhibitions of an old society. They hesitate over introducing their sister or wife to their best friend. But it would be entirely wrong to imagine that this has anything to do with morality.

The truth is that the Egyptians, whatever their social group, are merely groping towards some sort of code of social behaviour, but not, as yet, a moral code. In Islam, as is well known, it is hard to regard as a 'morality' that body of rules, that code, which surrounds one's private existence and is particularly concerned with the relations between the two sexes. They learn 'thou shalt' and 'thou shalt not' as one might learn the rules of the road. It is in the domain of the private conscience, which still has some free play, that questions begin to arise, especially as circumstances, in everybody's daily life, tend to blur the distinctions between right and wrong, allowed or forbidden. An enormous re-assessment of behaviour is now going on. The freest and apparently most up-to-date newspapers, whose readers are drawn for the most part from the bewildered middle and lower-middle classes, hold stern inquiries into whether a young man can take his fiancée to the pictures, whether a brother can invite his sister to tea with his friends, or whether a husband can introduce his wife to other men. They are still in search of the most elementary principles of social behaviour.

Meanwhile, as they wait for some new definition of social inter-course and taboos, this baffled people is in the grip of a kind of inner fever. This is particularly true of the younger generation, since the market is so swamped with degrees and diplomas of all kinds that they are doomed to a depressing intellectual idleness. It is hardly surprising if the magistrates have invented the word 'louts' for those who take liberties with women in the street. The Egyptian penal code only had the word 'indecency' until 1956, but now there is a particular crime called caddishness. Groups of these young people, rather like Teddy Boys, stand linked together, barring the pavement to other people in Sulaiman Pasha or Fuad Street, or go off in gangs to the cinema, up to mischief. The police are on the look-out, so that they cannot go much farther than making furtive passes or muttering insults. They all hang together and seem to disappear together.

There are many different signs of Egypt's sexual feverishness: the burning of Cairo, starting with the cinemas and less public places of enjoyment; shortly afterwards the morbid interest that was taken in the trial of a pretty young woman whose car ran over three people, two of whom were children, and who said in evidence that she had not been driving. On that occasion the court was crowded with peeping Toms out for the accused woman's blood, she being a fashionable woman who took men out in her car. On another occasion when a film was shown of the typical American curvaceous blonde doing strip-tease, a deep, furious, panting reaction came spontaneously from the whole audience. When you add this sexual inhibition to all the resentment of hunger and nationalism, it is not surprising if urban Egypt strikes one as living in a state of crisis and indulges in certain excesses.

There was certainly an Egyptian *society* or social structure in the nineteenth century, with its Turkish overlords, Coptic executives and Moslem subjects. It was that society which Nerval, Gautier and Flaubert saw and described. It was still firmly in the grip of Islam, but already the Modernism introduced by Mohamed Ali and Isma'il was gnawing at the foundations. This society was rocked this way and that by British imperialism, Egyptian nationalism and Western techniques. It has been rocked out of existence, and is now in little pieces. The Moslem 'corset' is torn apart and cannot adapt itself to the task of creating a fresh unity. Yet it is better fitted for the task than most of the ideologies and recipes of the West; for can we regard nationalism as an ideology capable of filling the breach and renewing the whole structure of a society? If so, then Nasserism is right, but if not, a ruthless Leninism, quite capable of creating 'structures', will no doubt offer its solution.

With all its ups and downs Egypt is busy solving its national economic and political problems. Unity has been achieved on the national scale, the country has been pulled together, and the great problem of adapting the land to absorb its half a million new citizens every year is not technically impossible. Once it has overcome the dangers of agricultural speculation based on a single, staple crop, once the industrialization scheme is applied, real technicians produced and Egyptian capital invested in the national programme, Egypt will be a model of what a lethargic, colonized people can achieve in less than two hundred years. It will prove that an Oriental nation can turn itself into a modern state. Does this amount to saying that the Egyptian experiment is to be held up as an example?

Egypt is still far from solving its cultural, social and religious problems. To take the last of these, with the Wafd Egypt experimented in the direction of the greatest tolerance, allowing some power to the religious minority and showing signs of a discreet laicism. With Nasser it has made religion an integral part of the nationalist programme and begun a bold though dangerous drive for a modernized form of Islam. This is bold because a civilization cannot risk cutting itself off from its origins and sources before trying every possible means of infusing fresh life and values into them. It is dangerous because further islamization might result in a challenge to national unity, practically cutting Egypt off from its Christian and Jewish *élites* whose value was recognized by former governments although they appeared less 'progressive' than the present military rulers.[1] What makes it still more dangerous is the fact that, identifying itself with Arab aspirations, it means shouldering a still weak, peace-loving and unadventurous country with a crusading role which is beyond its powers. Maybe all Moslems ought to pull together, but all sorts of responsibilities will accrue if that is taken literally by a dictator. Where is he likely to draw the line? It might be heroic to fend for the Moslems of the Celebes or Melilla, like a modern Saladin, but it is too much for a nation which has as much as it can do to stand on its own feet. It also means alienating the Western world, which it cannot do without.

The Egyptian 'New Deal' is still in its crawling stage on the cultural plane. A few painters, two or three scenario-writers and producers, a handful of young novelists, journalists and poets are not enough for creating a new culture. What can be said for a nation which cannot give its neighbours and enemies a full expression of itself?

Yet Egypt is perhaps busy forging the essential instrument of its culture, in its loosening up of the Arabic language. Her neighbours will no doubt forgive Egypt many a piece of clumsy interference if she manages to adapt this tongue to the needs of the modern world.

[1] The recent tendency to exclude Copts from public employment, and the Jews from banking, can hardly be interpreted otherwise.

The Algerian writer Katib Yasin not so long ago condemned the way it is corrupted 'by aristocratic castes which have turned it into a snobbish, precious and exclusive jargon' in order to keep the masses in their present state of ignorance.[1]

This freeing of the Arabic tongue from mandarinism would be more than a cultural reform: it would amount to a social one. For the break-up or fragmentation we have noticed in Egyptian society is largely due to the small amount of communication that goes on, or is possible, between the higher and lower levels of the nation. There is hardly any provision for movement from one to the other, and this is not only because of differences of means or origin (whether Turkish or Syrian at the top, or rural down below). A common language is essential if there is to be any interchange within the country itself. For the past twenty-five years (at last!) those who have been in power have been Arabic-speaking. This is all to the good, but it will be better still once they can reach the masses by means of a language, formulas, images, a vocabulary as remote from mob-oratory as it is from the refined jargon of the chosen few. It is said that Zaghlul knew how to address all men. Once responsible Egyptians learn to talk in such a way that the masses can understand them (Nasser appears to have succeeded in this on the famous evening of the 26th of July 1956—but how much of that was due to hatred for the foreigner, how can one fail to be understood when it is a question of nationalizing and conquering?) and when those in power in Cairo have learnt how to convince the majority, then one of Egypt's fundamental problems will be solved.

But the greatest step of all would still remain to be taken: that is, to feed and support more than four men to an acre. All the foregoing is little when compared with this. All the other problems depend on this one. However, it is also an international problem. Egypt can only succeed here with the help of other nations, whether it be the Sudan and her share of the Nile, or those other nations which can provide new capital for her industrial programme. Egypt's convalescence needs all kinds of help. She must therefore seek and define some means of avoiding permanent hostility towards the rest of the world. Arab-Moslem sympathy with Egypt runs deep, and Cairo, where every strain of Eastern nationalism comes to earth, will never be able to forget the fact. What can a still-enfeebled country hope to

[1] *Lettres Nouvelles*, July–August 1956.

gain by adopting a hostile attitude? Can she really want to fan again the flames of hatred that were loosed against her from July 1956 onwards? For Egypt, feeding her people is not only a question of working, it is a question of relations with the rest of the world.

Part Five

THE GREAT TEST

I

Nasser as He Really Is

What first impresses you is his massive, thick-set build, the dazzlingly white smile in his dark face. He is tall, tough, African. As he comes towards you on the steps of his small villa on the outskirts of the city, or strides across his huge office at the Presidency, he has the emphatic gait of some Covent Garden porter or some heavy, feline creature, while he stretches his brawny hand out with the wide gesture of a reaper, completely sure of himself. His eyes have an Asiatic slant and almost close as he laughs. His voice is metallic, brassy, full, the kind of voice that would be useful on manœuvres in the open country. His English is remarkably correct and almost polished.

The impression of strength remains when he relaxes. He has an air of youthfulness, together with a certain timidity. He is grey at the temples but his hard face, that reminds you of a plough-share, sometimes takes on an adolescent look. This is especially the case when he is asked some awkward question, and he has the earnest expression of an undergraduate. He eyes you with a mixture of astonishment and uneasiness, wrinkles his brow, tightens his jaws, his nose seeming to become longer in the process. His reply, when it comes, astonishes you by its seeming frankness, and at the same time his face lights up with a kind of cunning joy. However his square head, set obliquely on powerful shoulders which he tends to bring up in a sort of shrug against the chair-back, is not quite so reassuring. Those frightening, hungry jaws seem to be looking for something to devour. Then on each side of his long nose—oddly Semitic, in that African face—the eyes, which are set too close together, are disturbingly intent. When he is angry, as sometimes happens during a badly organized meeting or when he is impatient with a foolish secretary, he shows signs of uncontrollable violence.

He is more agreeable in personal interviews. Admittedly he was more so in 1953, when this former leader of the 'conspirators', still

453

in the background but growing ripe for power, was not yet President. Embarrassed by his relative youth and the gaps in his education he tends to keep people at arm's length except at those moments when he lets himself go. His boyish smile was often seen whenever people compared him with Mustafa Kemal, Sun Yat Sen or Nehru, but it is less in evidence now. But he is still polite, poising his head over your questions like a collector over a medallion, seemingly intrigued and eager to keep on learning, no matter from whom. Nehru recently said of him, 'What I like about this young man is that he is always ready to learn.'

Gamal Abdel Nasser is extremely intelligent. Not, perhaps, in the way that Valéry or Aldous Huxley is, for he shows not an inkling of Socratic questioning, irony or deftness. His mind is rough and ready, rather slow and heavy. He has a kind of greedy impatience to penetrate people and things and size them up and weigh them, an animal-like sense of direction, a ruthless determination not to be taken in. All this goes with an ambitiousness which is the more inflexible the more it is disinterested, a Sandhurst kind of patriotism, and imagination worthy of an Arab tale-teller which he almost always manages to restrain but which sometimes runs away with him. His lectures at the Staff College were regarded as brilliant, long before the daring *coup* of the 23rd of July. Since he came to power he has out-manœuvred the wiliest tacticians in Egyptian politics, such as Ali Mahir, Sirag ud-Din and Hodeibi, with baffling virtuosity.

It might be replied that he has the 'intelligence' of a thousand or so bayonets behind him. That might be true in the last resort. But before falling back on such explanations we should recall some of his previous encounters, the cunning with which he constantly played off Mahir against Faruk, hamstrung the Wafd, set the Moslem Brotherhood factions at each others' throats, not to mention the various brands of communism, though that would be harder to demonstrate. He has the intelligence of a Saïdi fellah, particularly clever at dividing his neighbours in order to lay his hands on some disputed plot of land. He certainly has both finesse and flair, as is proved by his dealings with foreign diplomats, with Jefferson Caffery in order to make Churchill press on the evacuation, the way in which he has won over one ambassador or distinguished visitor after another, including the British Prime Minister, Labour delegates, the American candidate for the Presidency, the French Minister, the editors of important New York reviews.

Is there nothing but violence, megalomania, frenzy? Of all the Orientals we have ever met, this man answering in good staff-officer's English is the one who most—at least until recently—gives an impression of calmness and self-control. Is it only an enormous reserve of violence which he controls with great effort? He gives few outward signs of it, except in his hardening and narrowing eyes, or the set of his great jaw. There is a look of attention on his face, every evidence of concentration, as he is asked the most direct and leading questions about such things as his government's police-methods, its relations with Israel, or the problems facing North Africa. Perhaps only Mr Somerset Maugham or some other expert writer of adventure novels would put down the way he pulls sharply at his cigarette to nothing more than irritability, anger or anxiety. His bronzed face, with its strange greenish patches on the brow and cheeks, hardly moves a muscle.

No doubt all this can be put down to calculation. 'Oriental' cunning is not the word for it, for the Westerner can give points to any Oriental on this score. It is the cunning of the weak, rather, of those who at least have long been humiliated. It is the duplicity of the revolted peasant as he faces his master, that of coloured people towards some alien white overlord. This Upper-Egypt peasant was not, for nothing, an officer in an army of which one of its creators, the old General Aziz el Misri, said, 'It was a poor army, for it was to the advantage of the British to keep it that way'—or that he was the subject of a king who gave more cause for shame than for fear, or citizen of a country in which a Ruritanian atmosphere had as its background the hungry resignation of the masses as they toiled in the fields. It is owing to this that such a proud Egyptian shamelessly practises deceit and lying. He must have looked very frankly at Mr Baldwin, President of the League of the Rights of Man, when he assured him late in 1954 that none of the 'Zionist spies' would be sentenced to death. Marzuk and Azar were hanged a week later. He looked just as frankly at ambassador Du Chayla in the spring of 1956, when he assured him that there was no threat to the Suez Canal Company. It is not easy to say whether he was sincere or two-faced on those occasions. The trouble for dictators is that, unlike democratic rulers, they cannot lay the blame on anyone else when their promises are broken.

The Colonel-President is not just a self-educated man. He is a man without any real culture, who knows how to put together, most cunningly, any scraps of knowledge or information he can pick up from pamphlets, newspapers, films, in fact anywhere. From the time when the Officers' plot first started, down to the Suez negotiations, he has given about fifteen hours a day for about fifteen years to the problem of seizing and keeping power. He has had little time left over for Milton or *Horizon*. Incidentally he shows no eagerness to discuss artistic matters. He has to be questioned directly before he admits a taste for Beethoven, Rimsky-Korsakoff, Tewfik el Hakim and Russian films. His library consists mainly of works of biography, politics, history and strategy. *Mein Kampf* and *Das Kapital* are no doubt among them.[1] We have noticed Clausewitz, Liddell Hart and Wavell, also Aneurin Bevan's *In Place of Fear*, Toynbee's *Study of History* and the complete works of Nehru.

He gives over an hour a day to reading newspapers. He devours the English Press, the *New York Times*, the Syrian and Lebanese dailies, and, for reference, those which get by his own censors. Together with a few outings in his fast car, a few strolls on the government estate—The 'Barrage', not far outside Cairo—and some tussles at chess with his great friend General Abdel Hakim Amir, and an occasional respite at the cinema, this is the only time taken off by this tireless worker.

Gamal Abdel Nasser makes no secret of the pleasure he finds in entertaining foreign guests, and perhaps he has a weakness for giving interviews. Shy in public, and unable until his Alexandria speech on 26th of July 1956 to make any impression on crowds because they intimidated him, Nasser is quite at ease and almost convincing in private. But he also has an itch for writing, and this is a more serious matter. The day after the Suez *coup*, the European Press dug up his *Philosophy of the Revolution* which had been carefully dissected and reviewed when it appeared, by all those who had their eyes open in Cairo. They found it to be surprisingly awkward in style for a man who had so cleverly and cynically outwitted the plot against him by Neguib's supporters. How could such an immature work be produced by such a mature politician?

The optimists said at the time that once he was really in command, Egypt's new master, this empirical realist who had tried and thrown off the Moslem Brotherhood, the different brands of communism and the Green Shirt militia, was obliged to find himself a style, a

---

[1] It is particularly since 27 July that reporters say they have seen these books on his shelves.

history and the rudiments of a doctrine. With the help of his friend the journalist Hasanein Haykal he had patched together some odds and ends of articles from the newspapers, drafts for his own speeches, extracts from his notebooks, and thus produced this paltry *Philosophy*, hastening to add in a preliminary note that the term was rather an exaggeration. Pessimists saw it as an almost unconscious 'explosion' of his lust for power, while rescuing from the rest of his nonsense the concluding pages on pan-Arabism and pan-Islamism, which he expounded with alarming frankness.

Is there anything positive to be found in this bullied cadet's *Philosophy*? This chaotic work could be divided roughly into three parts. First come the confessions of a young nationalist, rebelling against dictatorship and the foreign occupation, gradually forging the means with which his country could be freed. Fairly long quotations have already been given from this section, in our chapter on the military movement. This is related, touchingly enough, with a typically Egyptian romanticism. No reader can despise a patriot who was ashamed of terrorist methods.

The second part contains some very interesting and very bitter remarks on the Egyptian people's attitude towards the military régime. Unaffected enthusiasm here gives way to a kind of clear-sighted gloom, of the kind which Gide termed frustrated fervour. This section could be called an Elegy on a Revolution. It tells how a number of illusions were lost. Perhaps this part contains the key to the Lieutenant-Colonel's evolution, beginning with hopes for Parliament to be reassembled, voting for the reprieve of the worker Khamis, and becoming only three months later the 'strong man' who was already declaring that any return to parliamentarianism was out of the question. These are significant or at least striking passages, the more so when they were written by a dictator—one who by definition is 'infinitely popular'. If the first part described a 'leader's childhood', the second shows a manly discovery of the mob's ingratitude. The third part contains the leader's 'dream', but he would have done better to remain fully awake in the first place.

This third part is full of crowds assembled for a pilgrimage, pledges of unity, statistics all tending to prove that the Arab countries contain most of the world's petrol, and therefore . . . Nothing but exclamations like 'This region is awaiting its hero—we have come in answer to its cry', or 'The Arab world, united from the Persian Gulf to the shores of the Atlantic . . .' The Egyptian government's leader, with his recent experience of relations between Arab states, can hardly read such words now without a certain feeling of irony.

It is perhaps true, as one of the dictator's closest collaborators recently told us, that Nasser said such things only in order to awaken the masses from their fearful lethargy, and that they were intended for Arab consumption and did not imply serious imperialist designs. This would certainly be more in accordance with Egypt's real capacities. However, such lyrical outpourings were all the more disappointing, as they came after a merciless analysis of the Egyptian people's attitude to its 'liberators'. There is as much realism in Nasser as there is romance.

Let us listen to him, as he leans with his elbows on his desk, his head bending forward a little, staring at us with dark eyes flecked with green, as is often the case with Upper Egyptians. The man of January 1954 (to begin with), who was to come into the open against Neguib a month later, was always in uniform and received visitors in a monk-like cell in Faruk's Admiralty building on the banks of the Nile, where the Revolutionary Council had installed itself the year before. He was now Vice-Premier, 'Neguib's Deputy', but it was common knowledge that he was really the country's master. He was isolated, unpopular (known as 'Colonel Jimmy') and quite aware of his semi-failure. His main aim at the time was to squeeze an 'honourable' evacuation-treaty from the British, and there is ample evidence that he would have been satisfied with obtaining Western financial and technical help towards modernizing his country. He had just dissolved the Moslem Brotherhood. Did this decision imply that the Officers had finally rejected the Brotherhood's ideal of making the Koran the Egyptian Constitution? On the wall behind his desk—where there was a little plaster bust of Neguib—was a large Arabic inscription—the word *Allah*. He drew twice on his cigarette and looked out of the window at the grey Nile.

'Frankly, after eighteen months in power, I still don't see how it would be possible to govern according to the Koran. Admittedly it is not only a spiritual book, like the Old or New Testaments. It lays down rules for public as well as those for private life. But it is open to so many interpretations! We are anxious to avoid contradicting it. You must also remember that however old and apparently inapplicable to modern life its commandments may be, they are more reasonable than some people try to make out. But they are wrapped up in so many conditions that they become impossible to carry out. Take for instance stoning, which is the punishment prescribed for woman in adultery. It looks and sounds horrible, but apart from that it is almost impossible to put into practice. There have to be four witnesses, who have to testify in court that the crime was committed. The Koran is a very general text, capable of interpretation, and that is why I don't think it is suitable as a source of policy or political doctrine. The Koran's teaching depends on the state of mind of whoever is to apply it.'

Asking him, as regards the Anglo-Egyptian problem, why Egypt was not content to wait until 1956, when the 1936 treaty was due to expire, he gave a broad laugh and said, 'We are quite aware that this treaty wouldn't just expire. The British would take it before some international tribunal and obtain permission for prolonging it. We smaller nations haven't much confidence in these tribunals, which we know full well to be nothing more than courts run by and for the big nations.'

'Do you think any of the plans for Arab unity can be put into practice?'

'At the moment, no. If only because of the rivalry of interests and prestige between the two ruling families, the Saudis and Hashimis, as well as the fact that several Arab states are still partly or entirely ruled by foreigners. But this unification could be started on a more modest scale through economic and defence agreements, of the same kind as in Europe.'

'Do you intend to restore constitutional government as soon as the British forces are withdrawn?'

'No. It would not be reasonable to expect that. A year and a half have not been enough in which to put an end to corruption. The Egyptian people has not yet recovered. If we restored the vote now, I'm afraid that the same landowners would be elected as before, and the new parliament would be no better than the last. Many of my fellow-citizens have failed to grasp this. This can be seen in the Liberation Rally, most of whose members only support us in order to obtain favours or to be excused for their past mistakes. We neither can nor will allow the capitalists and moneyed classes to regain power. If we gave them a chance to be elected now, it would be as if the Revolution had never happened.'

Before leaving him, we asked what books and studies had most helped him to become a leading politician.

'Leading politician? I only became mixed up in politics by

459

accident, or almost. I studied nothing but strategy, which I taught to the cadets at the military college. My teachers were such strategists as Napoleon, Clausewitz and Liddell Hart. I regard strategy as an integral part of politics. Egypt has never had any strategy, but we are trying to give it one now.

'But if you want me to name the writer whose works did a lot to turn me into a revolutionary, it was Tewfik el Hakim. That is why, when a month ago our Minister of Education wanted to dismiss Tewfik from his post as director of the National Library, I took steps to dismiss the Minister instead.' He gave a short laugh. 'Fancy trying to dismiss a man whose works are played at Salzburg and Paris, and who is the envy of Europe!'

One is impressed at first by such an appearance of reflection and clarity. But at that time we had no idea of the extent to which Nasser, like his fellow-Egyptians, indulges in the national vice of the 'looking-glass complex' which Gamal Salim poured scorn on in the case of Neguib. This means showing your visitor the face you imagine he will like best—not just out of a desire to deceive, or out of meanness of character, but out of friendliness, spontaneous 'niceness' and perhaps a certain sense of hospitality. They say to themselves that a French journalist is likely to be liberal in politics, to have been brought up a Christian: therefore they suddenly talk in the most broad-minded way about religion, soft-pedal pan-Arabism, are careful what they say about the English, and are as mild as lambs about North Africa. Nobody could be more sweetly reasonable, less fanatical than your Egyptian ...

However, there is no point in being systematically sceptical. A number of quite interesting points emerged from our interview with the deputy Premier, in spite of our host's skill and opportunism. He showed a respectful clarity on the question of Islam. His remarks on parliamentarianism showed more caution than was immediately necessary. With regard to Arab unity he showed a scepticism which was not entirely due to the fact that the plans then under discussion came from Iraq. As for the 'great powers', both their policies and methods filled him with what appeared to be long-founded suspicion. He laughed heartily enough when we mentioned the expiry of the 1936 treaty. He said it was the Chinese who invented the idea of 'unfair treaties'. But Egypt, and its present master, would gladly have been first in the field.

Allowing for first impressions, charm and the effects of his calm strength, Nasser remained for us a by no means ordinary personality, skilfully exploiting his power and showing that his athlete's brawn hid no mean order of cunning. At about the same date Adlai Stevenson told the Egyptian Press representatives, 'Nasser is the strongest personality of his generation. Only the small countries have the luck to find such remarkable rulers.' This remark must have been built up by the local Press: but it was not only the Americans who were impressed by the smiling 'Bikbashi', as he is called.

Two years later he was installed as Prime Minister, in an enormous office with pretentiously carved woodwork. He had consigned Neguib to house arrest,[1] signed the evacuation treaty with the British, crushed the Moslem Brotherhood, concluded the sensational bargain with Prague for armaments, and drawn up a truly Caesarean Constitution. He was no longer the quiet Lieutenant-Colonel playing the Grey Eminence to the General-President, the Junta and the government, playing his own hand only in the matter of obtaining the best possible terms for the evacuation of the Canal Zone. He had become an all-powerful chief of state, more feared than loved, more respected than supported, praised by all and yet alone. He had boldly snatched Egypt out of the Western diplomatic and strategic orbit, inserting it between Tito and Nehru in an orbit of neutrality. At last he had achieved that independence he passionately desired. There were only two flies in the the ointment. Israel, angered and convinced that Cairo intended aggression, was hesitating whether to attack first. And the three-quarters of a million men who are born every year, looked as though they would have a long time to wait before they would enjoy the advantages of the new Nile Dam, the only answer to Egypt's haunting problem of over-population.

Nasser has grown heavier. He is still athletic, but a bit flabby. He has given up his uniform in favour of suits which broaden his enormous shoulders still further, after the manner of the statues of the Pharaohs in olden days. He has gone greyer at the temples, but there is still energy in his hair. He smiles less than before, once polite formalities are over. He has also acquired a fixed smile for the public's benefit. There are still traces of awkwardness, shyness and military stiffness. Everything in his manner bears the marks of

---

[1] General Neguib, compromised (?) in the Moslem Brotherhood plot of 1954, was confined to a country residence at El Marg, near Heliopolis.

the enormous problems he has handled, the crowds he has had to face, the unpleasant experiments he has had to try. He has worked on and almost recast his own personality, he has hastily moulded himself anew. There are still some faults, cracks in the plaster, such as his bursts of artlessness or clumsiness. But the Colonel has thoroughly taken on the role of President, as the conspirator has become chief of state. He is now on the side of power—indeed he is *the* power.

We now come to late November 1955, three weeks after the Israeli attack on Sabha. While the fida'iyin from the Gaza sector were trying to avenge their comrades on Israeli civilians, Soviet arms were being unloaded off Alexandria. He assured us straight away that these supplies merely gave him parity of arms with Israel.

But, we asked, did the strong position he thought he had now gained, encourage him to start negotiations for a peaceful settlement?

'I consider the terms for discussion that were proposed on the 9th of November 1955 by Mr Eden—that is to say the United Nations' 1947 plan for frontier settlement—were the most satisfactory.'

'But don't you think that the Arabs, who rejected that plan in 1947 and made war in order to avoid its application, are rather badly placed for invoking it at present?' In asking this question we thought we might as well go straight to the point. Nasser's look of cool self-possession as he listened to us gravely from the other side of his big desk was decidedly encouraging. He took his time, eyed the smoke from his cigarette, then counter-attacked.

'It was not the Arabs who set Palestine on fire in order to stop the partition from coming into force: it was the British. Who received a mandate to administer and develop an Arab Palestine? Yet between 1920 and 1947 they encouraged Zionism. By withdrawing quickly in 1948 [14th May] they aimed at nothing more nor less than leaving the Zionists—who were arming quickly and making warlike preparations—face to face with the unarmed Arab peasants. It amounted to offering the whole of Palestine to Zionism, and it was against that violation of the very spirit in which the partition should have been made, that the Arabs took up arms in 1948.'

'It is now clear that the Israelis would like peace on the basis of the *status quo*, that of the Tripartite declaration of 1950; whereas certain Arabs, including the Egyptian government, want it to be on the basis of the partition of 1947. Is there no hope of finding some compromise, for instance by having a neutral strip along the Gulf of Akaba which would assist the unification of the Arab world by joining up Egypt and Jordan?'

'We can only have worth-while negotiations if two problems are settled: not only that of frontiers, but that of what happens to refugees. The expelling of a million inhabitants and replacing them by new tenants of the land has no precedent in history. Neither Genghis Khan nor Hitler ever dared to do that. The refugees must be given their right, either to return home or to receive proper compensation.'

'But they would all want to go back home!'

'No. The status of second-class citizen accorded to Arabs in Israel would hardly encourage them to return there. Many would prefer to settle in some other Arab state, given a good compensation.'

'But if the majority wanted to return, how is it physically or economically possible to fit such a huge mumber of people into a state of a mere million and a half inhabitants?'

'Do you remember Mr Ben-Gurion or Mr Sharett saying a few days ago that Israel must be prepared to absorb a million more immigrants in the future? Surely, in that case, the right of entry should go to those who were there before?'

'Speaking frankly, don't you think that all Arabs are convinced that sooner or later Israel has to be suppressed and cease to exist as a State, and be reduced to something like a Jewish Vatican City?' Again Nasser remained inscrutable and showed no haste to reply.

'No. As far as we in Egypt are concerned, we merely ask that the State of Israel should respect Arab rights. It has to recognize them the same as other states do.'

'Even at the price of peace in the Middle East—or shall we say world peace?' The green-flecked eyes glinted, but his voice remained calm.

'We want peace here and in the rest of the world, as you know perfectly well. But why should it always be the smaller nations that have to be sacrificed in the general interest?'

'As for North Africa, can we assume that Egypt is ready to declare its sympathy for a policy of "progressive stages" or stepping-stones in the development of the status and government of the various countries concerned, rather than encouraging extremist demands? From an Arab point of view, do you agree that the North African countries have special links with France, according to their different situations?'

463

'In such questions we base our stand on self-determination. If the North African countries choose to link themselves with France through special treaties, it would be wrong of us to interfere . . .'

'Arising from that, can it be said that the Tunisians showed their desire to maintain a special relationship with France, through the Bourguiba plebiscite at the Sfax Conference?'

'Yes, I think so.'

'Then is it not surprising that one of your Ministers, Sheikh Baquri, during his recent tour of Tunisia, insisted on dealing with the Opposition leader Salah Ben Yusuf on the same footing as the head of the government? It's like a French Minister coming here and advising your opponents just after visiting you, isn't it?'

'If that is the way the French side interpret the facts, then allow me to correct you. After we decided to accept Premier Bourguiba's invitation, I made it clear to Sheikh Baquri that the aim of his mission was to reconcile Bourguiba and Ben Yusuf. He didn't encourage the opposition, but was working for Tunisian unity in order to avert civil war. I don't think that can be interpreted as doing Tunisia a disservice. If we had wanted to harm Bourguiba and help the opposition, it would have been the easiest thing to refuse his invitation openly. By sending Baquri, we were *de facto* recognizing the Tunisian government.'

'Some observers predict that your closer relations with the Eastern countries, and especially the outcry this has caused in the West, might result in your seeking the support of Left elements in Egypt . . .'

'Left elements? Do you know any Left elements that have any strength in them? I don't. Where are they?' (cleverly feigning astonishment).

'In press circles, perhaps . . .'

'What newspaper, for instance?'

'*El Gumhuriya* . . .'

'But that is my own newspaper!'

'Yes, that's why it's interesting to see it carrying articles similar to those in the Polish newspapers . . .'

'You are mistaken. What you take for Leftism is nationalism in this case. It's not our fault if our country has always had to complain about the same powers, which are Western ones, and not of those which are in the East. But we are not communists. Our movement has been nationalist right from the beginning.'

464

'You have sometimes spoken about Socialism?'

'Well—as far as ideologies go we still have no final position. We are still at the formative stage. We haven't really made our choice between liberalism and controls in matters of economics and politics. Our decisions will be taken according to specific problems and needs.'

Before leaving him we tried to interest Nasser in the fate of a 'progressive' friend who was then interned. We suggested he should be allowed to leave Egypt and return to his study of Philosophy in France. Showing some interest, he asked us for details and took a note of the name. Then, quickly raising his head and showing his former smile, he said:

'Are you Left, like your friend?'

'Well, President—having certain social ideas . . .'

'You are really a nationalist,—like us?'

'That's more like it, Colonel.'

He laughed again, and said as we were leaving, 'Fancy them saying that we are communists—and you see for yourself how we treat communists!'

What kind of 'doctrine' emerges from all this? A personality, yes. A few main lines of policy, a few solid complexes. No attempt at hiding his fundamental empiricism. At the most he could only be called provisional, with so much groping and hoping. The socialism that comes out at his public gatherings melts away, quite literally, in interviews. As for his determination to ignore the Egyptian left-wing, which has its representatives, both open and otherwise, even in the offices in his own building, it gives less proof of the man's cleverness than of his habit of covering his tracks. How can he imagine that a journalist who has spent several years in Egypt, and particularly in 1955, could remain unaware of the existence and influence of the 'progressive' groups? Much more interesting is his effort to 'nationalize' the progressive elements. This is a clever move and is not without its justification. Perhaps he gives some clue to the increasing strength of left-wing elements in Egypt, in saying, 'It's not our fault if our country has always had to complain about the Western powers . . .'

Perhaps the way in which he talked about Israel and the Maghrib might cause some surprise. Concerning the Jewish State, even at the end of 1955, a painful enough year, he clearly admitted its right

465

to existence—the interview was censored in Egypt, but he knew it would be noticed in the world Press and would sooner or later be read in Damascus, Amman and Baghdad. He was well aware that the 1947 plan was unacceptable, but spoke of it as at least a basis for negotiations. His approach to the refugee problem surprised many specialists by its realism. He seemed to approach the Maghrib in the same spirit, though one point emerges here. As regards his Minister's trip to Tunis, Nasser completely failed to realize that his activities to 'avert civil war in Tunisia', however well meant, were the kind of interference in other people's affairs that he pretends to denounce. He sees it only as a quarrel between 'Arab brethren', and as an Arab feels himself responsible for patching up a family misunderstanding. As we know, that might lead rather a long way.

The dramas which have since unfolded in Egypt might appear to make the above declarations look somewhat out of date, for all their mixture of coolness and dialectical skill. His smooth remarks were followed, seven months later, by the sneering public speeches in Alexandria, boot-stamping and the shedding of blood which might have been avoided with a little more imagination. To us, however, they still appear to deserve some attention, for when things are at their worst there is something to be said for knowing whether the leader is a good hand at chess, and whether he knows how to keep his accounts straight or is anxious to get home . . . Since then there have been signs—for instance the way he received Mr Menzies —that the charming but realistic Colonel of yesterday tends more and more to hesitate between the role of Sergeant-Major and that of Field-Marshal. Have we to admit, as the English moralists say, that 'If power corrupts, absolute power corrupts absolutely'?

II

The Suez Crisis

On the 19th of July 1956 Gamal Abdel Nasser came back to Cairo after spending a week in Jugo-Slavia, where he attended the 'three neutrals' conference' together with Marshal Tito and Nehru. But as he left the plane that had brought him from Belgrade he showed no sign of the satisfaction that the head of a poor and until recently colonized state might be expected to feel after negotiating on equal terms with two of the most respected statesmen of the day. His face was expressionless and he refused to answer any questions before he quickly entered his car. His secretary, Ali Sabri, made no attempt to hoodwink the reporters, for everyone knew why they were upset and had been talking about it all day: 'Yes,' he said, 'the American withdrawal of their offer to finance the Aswan High Dam has completely upset our plans.' But giving a little smile which failed to hide his disappointment, he added, 'But we will build the Dam all the same.'

The crisis started off by the American State Department was undoubtedly the most serious one that the military government had so far had to face. Everyone in Cairo was asking the same question, which was whether the government would survive the death-sentence imposed from Washington. A list of names for a Neguib government was already being passed around. A change seemed the more certain as the publication two days earlier of Mr Dulles' department's communiqué—which was drawn up in the form of an indictment—had been preceded by the abrupt posting of Mr Byroade, United States Ambassador to Cairo, who was well known to have given stronger support to Nasser, so far as the American administration was concerned, than his duties warranted. While they did not create the 'Bikbashis' or officers' régime they were the first to protect it, though they were given little thanks. Now Washington had just inflicted the worst possible affront on Marshal Tito's guest, a material and moral snub such as could only have been administered by the enemies of neutrality and enemies of Arabism.

467

This was certainly what Mr Foster Dulles, in one of his pet phrases, called an agonizing re-appraisal of American policy. Washington made no secret of its irritation over the arms agreement between Egypt and the Czechs in September 1955. Yet the State Department subsequently gave a friendly reception to the Egyptian representatives when they came to negotiate the financing of the High Dam project by the American administration and the International Bank, and were particularly cordial to the Finance Minister, Mr Qaysuni, in November 1955. This was followed on the 19th of December of the same year by Washington offering Cairo 54 million dollars, after persuading Britain to put up a further 16 million dollars towards the first stages of building the barrage. In January 1956 Mr Eugene Black, President of the International Bank, went to Cairo, where on the 11th of February 1956 he signed, together with the Egyptian negotiators, an agreement 'in principle' for a loan of 200 million dollars, at $3\frac{1}{2}$ per cent, redeemable in twenty years. What seems rather odd—at first sight—is that this flood of dollars seemed to delight the lenders but was received with suspicion in Egypt, the signatories of the agreement making it clear, in the Arabic version of the text, that Egypt would only make use of the loan as the need arose.

We have already mentioned the panic caused in Egypt by the slightest signs of economic or financial control by some other power. The statutes of the International Bank expressly stated in Articles 13 and 14 that the borrower must allow some control of his budget by the lending organization, and is unable to borrow further without the Bank's agreement. Such guarantees are given and taken as a matter of course between such relatively independent nations as those in Europe. However, a country which has just emerged from semi-colonial status regards them as unbearable. This was especially the case as Moscow was wooing Nasser by holding out the hope, however vague, of an unconditional loan at 2 per cent, repayable in thirty years.

Accordingly Nasser hung fire, intending to go into the new proposals to be submitted in June 1956 by Mr Shepilov. Meanwhile the opponents of Egypt and its government were working at top pressure against them in Washington. Foremost among these were the British, who, convinced that the Colonel was reopening the 'Arab revolt' all over again for his own benefit, were blaming Nasser for the breakdown of the Baghdad Pact, the dismissal of

Glubb Pasha, and the disturbances in the Persian Gulf, and intended to get rid of him in the spring of 1956. Then M. Christian Pineau, who had showed every signs of friendship for the Egyptian Prime Minister during his visit to Cairo on the 14th of March 1956, blamed him for the blow given to his prestige in France by their fruitless interview. He particularly regretted the brilliant arguments which he, Pineau, had made in the *Chambre* in order to prove that it would be foolish to follow a hostile policy towards Egypt. Thus the Minister for Foreign Affairs declared publicly on his return from Washington in June 1956 that he had 'enlightened' Mr Dulles about Nasser. It appears that together with the British he had opposed continuing the National Bank's loan to Egypt. At the same time the Israeli 'lobbying' continued unabated—though this was unwise, since encouraging Egypt to build its great Dam in the south would have turned her attention from the north-eastern frontier and busied her with an enormous undertaking that would have put any 'revenge' in Palestine out of the question. There was also the 'cotton lobbying' from American growers; this was equally ill-advised because the new dam would have encouraged putting more acreage under rice, cereals and vegetables rather than under cotton. Finally there was the offensive of the 'right-thinking' senators who set their faces against the 'red dictatorship' of a man who was a friend of Tito and Shepilov.

Recalled to Cairo in June, Mr Ahmed Husain, Egyptian Ambassador in Washington, warned the Colonel-President that if the promised credits were not voted by Congress on the 1st of July, there was a danger that they might never be voted at all. The new law on American Aid laid down that 80 per cent of any funds advanced were repayable, whereas the International Bank insisted, on the contrary, that these funds should be handed over in the form of a gift, as the Egyptian public debt ran the risk, according to Western experts, of being too heavily mortgaged by such a debt. The financial committee of the Senate, which after a sharp battle with Mr Dulles had reluctantly agreed to maintain credits to Belgrade, did nothing to hide its dislike of giving financial aid to Egypt. Nasser heard this disturbing news at the moment when M. Shepilov informed him in Cairo that the U.S.S.R. was prepared to make a special effort towards industrializing Egypt, but could not commit itself to anything as ambitious as the Aswan Dam.

The Colonel-President at once understood that there was no way

out, and sent his ambassador back to Washington with instructions
to make a last effort to persuade the West to relax its harsh conditions. However, on the 10th of July, after a long interview with
President Eisenhower and the Republican leaders in the Senate,
Mr Foster Dulles said at a Press conference that 'it had become
improbable' that Egypt would receive the advances that had been
discussed. Nasser at once cabled to Ahmed Husain from Belgrade, urging him to accept the loan, whatever the terms. It was
on the very next day (18th of July) that he received a slap in the
face from the State Department. Not only had it announced to
the Press, before even informing Cairo, that Egypt was to be denied
the promised loan, but this announcement was accompanied by a
number of bitter 'explanations', in which attention was drawn to the
instability of the political régime and the country's economy, and
to the fact that the undertaking could not be put in hand without
the previous consent of the Sudan, Ethiopia and Uganda, which
also bordered and had claims on the River Nile. As soon as it was
publicized by the international news-agencies this statement was
interpreted, throughout the Middle East, as the end of Nasser's
political career. There was speculation as to why Washington had
thrust him so brutally into the arms of Russia.

Some explanation was given a few days later when Mr Shepilov,
Soviet Minister for Foreign Affairs, told a group of Western journalists that his government had 'no *immediate* intention' of financing
the High Dam project. Then it was obvious that Mr Dulles, already
under pressure from Congress to refuse credit to Egypt, had learnt
that the Russians were unable to step in, and that he had set out
to show the Arabs that for all its fine words Moscow could do
nothing for the poverty of the under-developed countries.[1] This
apparent master-stroke, which was described as a 'clever poker-
trick' in the Republican Press, was loudly acclaimed by London and
Paris, who had promoted it.[2] But the *New York Times* remarked
peevishly that 'when you make an enemy you must treat him as such'.
This advice was forgotten by the State Department in as short a time
as it had taken to break with Nasser.

The Colonel, who had returned to a stormy Cairo, remained

[1] This interpretation has been confirmed by Mr Beal in his recent book on J. F.
Dulles.
[2] In three Middle East states which we visited at that time, the American diplomats
were hard put to hide their embarrassment, whereas the French and British were
overjoyed.

behind locked doors for a few days with one or two of his closest advisers. Everyone was demanding his reply to the Americans. Would it take the form of a pact with Russia, or the dismissal of all 'Point Four' American organizations, or a break between Egypt and the International Bank, which had followed the State Department's example by cancelling the loan it had promised on the 11th of February? On the 22nd of July the President, now apparently recovered, gave a speech in the suburbs of Cairo in which he told the Americans, 'We'll find some way of building the Dam, even if it kills you!' The next day, which was the fourth anniversary of the Revolution, had all the appearance of an armed vigil. The topic of the moment was the speech, which was to be 'the most important in the last ten years', which the President was to give in Alexandria on the 26th of July—exactly four years, to the very hour, after Faruk's departure into exile.

At about seven o'clock that evening, as night began to fall on the huge Mohamed Ali Square, the great crowd was well contained by powerful detachments of police. A wonderful breeze literally revived all those who, like ourselves, had just survived one of the most stifling weeks Cairo had ever experienced. From the balcony from which Nasser was to give his address we could see, only twenty yards away, the point from which the Moslem Brother Abdel Latif had fired eight shots at the same Gamal Nasser, then denounced as an 'Anglo-American agent'. Nasser passed close by us as he made for the rostrum. He was smiling vaguely as if he had forgotten that incident of October 1954. He took the microphone in his hand and started his speech on a rather odd note. Whence this *baladi* language, this rather colloquial and slangy form of Egyptian? The entranced crowd reacted to every inflection in this jesting harangue. We came expecting to hear a tragic monologue, and instead he was giving us a humorous account of what had happened.

'Now I'll give you the dope about my adventures with the American diplomats . . .' There was the austere Gamal Nasser, former Staff College instructor, posing as a kind of Hyde Park orator and couching his message in the lingo of the East End. The crowd roared. 'An American diplomat came and told me, "If Mr Allen passes you a message from the State Department about Czech armaments, just you chuck him out of your office. But if he goes back without having given it you, then Mr Dulles will chuck him out." . . . What's to be done for poor Mr Allen?' The orator put on a comic act in mime, playing the part of the Egyptian comic, Goha, struggling against the foreign Goliaths, while all around us the Egyptian journalists, taken unawares by the novelty of Nasser's approach, were muttering 'Kuwayis 'awi' (Jolly good). The shy and awkward Nasser had suddenly discovered how to talk to the Egyptian people. Down below us, in the dark bowl of the Mohamed Ali Place, there was no longer seething anger, but an enormous laughter that had to be heard to believed.

But now the tone began to change. Telling of his difficulties with the president of the International Bank, Eugene Black, Nasser suddenly said, strangely, 'Mr Black suddenly reminded me of Ferdinand de Lesseps . . .' He pronounced the name 'de Lissipse' [sic], with a kind of hissing tone. This unleashed an unbroken denunciation—bitter, violent, finally furious—against what he called 'mortgage colonialism'. At first the crowd hardly reacted at all. It was obviously expecting the anti-American satire to develop into an announcement that measures would be taken for closer friendship with the Soviets. What had de Lesseps to do with all this? But Nasser was becoming interesting: 'All those benefits which were filched from us by that imperialistic company, that State within a State, at a time when we were dying of hunger, we are about to take back . . .' On the rostrum as well as in the 'pit' people began to clap their hands in surprise, to say the least. 'And I can announce that at the very moment when I am speaking to you, the government Journal is publishing a new Law nationalizing the Suez Company, and at this very moment our Government agents are taking over the Company's premises!' There was uproar all around us. Journalists whom we knew to be sceptical of the government were standing on their chairs, shouting enthusiastically, while Nasser—suddenly seized with a fit of laughing at his own cheek—continued, 'Well, the Canal will pay for the Dam. Four years ago today King Faruk fled from Egypt. Today, in the name of the people, I am taking over the Company. Tonight our Egyptian canal will be run by Egyptians. Egyptians!' His words and laughter were drowned in a great storm of applause, and he left the rostrum on which the few foreigners who were present looked at each other in amazement. Rarely has a man been seen to undertake such a dangerous task with such a happy look on his face.

Half an hour earlier, at the very moment when Nasser was saying and the wireless was broadcasting the sentence 'Mr Black reminded me of Ferdinand de Lesseps', Egyptian forces had taken over the headquarters of the Company in Cairo, together with their offices in Ismaïlia, Port Saïd, Port Tewfik and Suez. All this was done with a precision unusual for Egyptians. The managing director, M. Ménessier, had been invited to dinner by the governor of Ismaïlia, and learnt what had happened as he was listening to Nasser's speech on the wireless. Meanwhile all Alexandria was dancing with joy on the promenade, where mobile loud-speakers bellowed forth Nasser's words. The presence of the English cruiser *Jamaica*, which was lying off-shore on a 'courtesy' visit, restrained some people's enthusiasm. One of our Alexandrian friends murmured, 'It was a brave enough gesture, but God help us.'

We felt the full force of the people's frenzy in Cairo two days later, when the 'Bikbashi' came back, suddenly promoted to the status of national hero. You had to have seen the erstwhile timid staff-officer, the morose Gamal Nasser of yesterday, the timid technocrat, to see the change in him now as he was lifted above the heads of a howling mob, waving his arms like a drowning man on the boiling sea—a boxing champion returning in triumph to his native Chicago . . . There was the same approval in the poorer cafés and in society drawing-rooms —'He did the right thing, he has made a fool of the people who wanted to get rid of him, the whole country's been waiting for something like this for a long time and we'll have to see it through.' We heard almost the same words from Wafdists, sympathizers among the Moslem Brotherhood, landowners who had suffered through the Agricultural Reform, and from the entire Opposition. The communists and fellow-travellers were delighted. The only ones with any reservations were among those who were over fifty, those who read the British newspapers and were struck by the violent reactions coming from London. The Egyptians we spoke to all said, 'What else can be done about it?'—but with little or no sign of anxiety.

In the British and French parliaments Eden, Lloyd, Mollet and Pineau denounced this 'new Hitler' and warned the 'insolent thief', that 'apprentice-dictator now at bay', that they would force him to retract. In Cairo, Nasser's closest collaborator, Major Ali Sabri, said to us at the same moment, with startling calmness, 'Well, what's all the rumpus about? The Canal Company was Egyptian: we have nationalized it, and so what? What has France to lose? Your share-holders will be amply compensated. The freedom of the Canal? We guarantee it absolutely. In the past we had no direct interest in protecting navigation which paid us nothing. Now it is different. All the sanctions you can impose on us, such as boycotting the Canal or blocking accounts, will prove more costly for you than for us. And as you see the Americans are leaving you in the lurch. As for the employees, we are not sentencing them to work against their will. Those who want to leave can do so as long as they give a few days' notice. In the interests of users of the Canal, however, we would regard mass resignations as an act of sabotage and we are most anxious to avoid this . . .'

Was this serenity or a failure to realize all the implications? Somewhere between the demonic fury of one section—those in France who felt a certain satisfaction at finding an opportunity for revenging all the humiliations and disappointments of North Africa, on an enemy they were glad to hold responsible for them, believing him, also, to be disliked by the masses and therefore easy to liquidate —and the sneering complacency of the rest, could nobody at the time take an objective view of what had happened on the 26th of July? Who even set out to define that event, instead of shouting about a new Munich? It was certainly not a case of aggression like the attack on Abyssinia in 1935, or the occupation of the Rhine in 1936, or the invasion of Czecho-Slovakia in March 1939, or that of Southern Korea in June 1950. There was neither annexation of territory, nor blood spilt, nor the use of mustard-gas. No nation's independence had been threatened, nobody's life was in danger. The Canal itself, both before and after Nasser's sneering speech of the 26th of July, came under Egyptian sovereignty. Had there been anything illegal in the transfer, any broken contract or promise? This can be seen only by examining the undertakings and contracts then in force.

As regards the Canal, the Egyptian government was bound by two types of text. There were the 'firmans' or Ottoman decrees of 1854 and 1856 which conceded the exploitation of the Canal to a 'World Suez-Canal Company' for 99 years dating from the opening of the waterway, that is to say from 1869 to 1968. Then there was the International Convention of Constantinople of 1888, which laid down the most solemn undertaking—of the utmost international importance—that the passage of all ships of whatever nationality should be maintained without discrimination, even in times of war. This undertaking had been violated already by Great Britian, Egypt's 'protector', as regards German ships; then by Egypt herself, on many occasions since 1949, in connexion with Israeli shipping. The Security Council twice voted resolutions condemning Egypt's attitude but she refused to change her policy, invoking Article 10 of the Constantinople Convention to the effect that *Egypt alone* is the only sovereign power entitled to restrict the passage of ships, 'should it prove necessary to her defence or the maintenance of public order'. Egyptian lawyers considered Egypt as being well within her rights in asserting that a blockade of Israeli shipping was 'indispensable to the defence' of the country.

In any case one thing is quite certain: this attitude on Egypt's part had produced no reactions in Great Britain when, occupying the Canal Zone, she had the necessary means for obliging Cairo to obey the U.N.O. resolution. When, to that end, a group of Members of Parliament approached Mr Eden in 1955, he merely shrugged his shoulders. The above-mentioned texts, together with the Anglo-Egyptian Treaty of October 1954, make it clear that Egypt's sovereignty extends over the Canal. The events of 26th July changed nothing, while every speech made by the Egyptian Prime Minister at that time solemnly repeated Egypt's intention to respect freedom of transit through the Canal. This freedom was even extended to British and French ships which refused to pay Canal dues, as well as to ships chartered by Israelis or carrying Israeli cargoes.

While respecting the letter of the 1888 Convention, was not Egypt still infringing the spirit of it by ending the terms of concession twelve years before the expiry of the lease? This has been argued, notably in a memorandum published by the World Company itself on the 10th of October 1956. Referring to articles published in *Le Monde* a few days earlier by Professors Pinto and Goldmann, the Company's spokesman maintained that 'the *firmans* governing the lease had been incorporated into international law . . . and form part of Egypt's international obligations', and that 'the 1888 Convention implies international management vested in the Company until the lease expired'. M. de la Pradelle, a lawyer who disagreed with this interpretation, said that in his view 'the only question to be asked was whether the *firmans*, in so far as they conveyed a lease for the exploitation of the Canal to the World Company, were or were not an integral part of the Treaty of 1888' (in *Le Monde*, 6 October 1956).

If the answer is in the affirmative and if it follows that the Cairo Cabinet broke with the spirit of the Convention; if, above all, we recall that Egypt had just signed (on 21 June 1956) an agreement with the Company according to which the latter agreed to invest £21,000,000 in Egypt in the subsequent ten years and was thus confirmed in its rights and prerogatives, then it must be agreed that Nasser's act of 26th July was an illegal act carried out in an alarming manner, and that he had unjustly broken the terms of the lease and undermined Egypt's good faith and credit in international affairs. But at the very most it is impossible to regard his action as anything worse or more than *illegal*, or more than an unpleasant breach of confidence. To keep the matter at its legal level, one might say that it was a matter calling for legal action. But at the time everyone assumed the tone of a public prosecutor as well as polishing the hangman's axe. Perhaps the Islamic law is not the only one that cuts off a thief's hands . . .

Guilty of an infringement of rights but not of a crime on the legal plane, was Egypt sufficiently well equipped technically to ensure the actual freedom of passage of shipping? During the first few weeks this would have been out of the question without the help of the Company's personnel. It was this which led Nasser to incorporate in his nationalization law the extraordinary article (No. V) conscripting the labour of the Company's employees and forbidding them to leave their work 'under penalty of court-martial'. There has been much argument as to whether the pilots, especially those who made up the Company's outstanding team, could at all be replaced. We heard a discussion on these lines in the Company's club at Ismaïlia, only four days after the nationalization of the Canal. One pilot out of six and one officer in three raised doubts except for ships of over 15,000 tons—the case of which has now been settled by the facts. On the eve of the sabotage carried out in answer to the Franco-British expedition, Egypt had solved the problem by means of a fresh team drawn from different nationalities—the kind of solution that might be applied in other fields. It is by no means sure that such teams and crews will be as skilful as those in the past, in avoiding the hazarding of ships as a result of bad weather conditions (fog, etc.) which are frequent on the Canal in winter. If the new managers seem to have solved the secondary problem of piloting, it appears less well equipped for such essential tasks as planning the navigation, maintenance, dredging, and the constant deepening and broadening of the Canal in view of the increased volume or size of traffic.

As for the question of finance, which was originally the crux of the matter, since Egypt intended to make it pay for the Dam, it soon became obvious that there is little connexion between the two undertakings. Nasser referred in his speech to a revenue of £35 million, which indeed looked as though it would be enough for financing the Dam. But he should really have said £35 million by way of receipts. Taking into account the outgoings for maintenance, various financial charges and permanent works, the actual normal revenue would be about £20 million. If the development scheme already under way is to be carried on and if shareholders are to be compensated, the net profits are unlikely to exceed £8 or £10 million a year for the next ten years. The Cairo Government could reply that by comparison with the 7 per cent on dues which she had to be content with previously, plus the £3 or £4 million in customs and excise which the Company used to pay, Egypt's income has certainly benefited. But the profit is very low, when such a price has had to be paid for the whole operation in other directions.

The unpleasant way in which the change-over was announced and carried through, the whole atmosphere of conspiracy with which it was hatched, the Prime Minister's choice of language on the occasion, the way he gave it the appearance of a ferocious challenge, all served to deprive Egypt of the benefit of sound arguments which liberal-minded or progressive people abroad would have interpreted in her favour. They would have pointed out that if it is usual in international law for a new government, revolutionary or not, to take over its predecessor's obligations, it is not absolutely fair to apply this strictly to a state which has recently changed and become independent of treaties signed in its predecessor's name by a foreign 'protecting' power (which in this case was Turkey). This is especially true if such a treaty only came into being through the weakness of both 'protector' and 'protected' compared with the other signatories. To expect an independent Egypt, in the middle of the twentieth century, to put up with all the restrictions laid on her as a colony of the Ottoman Empire, and to continue paying a poor, under-equipped and over-populated country less than 10 per cent of the

[1] Note, however, that when he left Egypt on the 12th of September 1957 after directing operations for clearing the Canal, General Wheeler said that the plans for its exploitation drawn up by Mahmud Yunis, Egyptian director of the nationalized company, were 'fairly good'.

profits drawn from a partly Egyptian company, would be to ignore the change that has taken place in modern society and the way in which world Powers have changed in relation to one another. Was the precedent of Iran not sufficient warning?

However brilliant its organization might have been, however impressive the working of that great machine for shortening the voyage round the world, one can well imagine that the existence of a huge lavish, wealthy Society (alien in its way of life, style and profits, if not in any legal sense), in a poverty-stricken backward country, could not fail to produce some painful repercussions. The Company paid and looked after everyone, built houses, often played the part of fairy godmother in the poor little world of the Isthmus. But fairies can only go about gloriously arrayed, in Caliban's land, at their own risk.

Had it been dealt with on a technical and legal plane, the Suez affair would have given rise to litigation in Egypt, where its brutal and irresponsible nature would have made an impression on most observers and politicians both in Egypt and from Arab and Eastern countries. But the tone which was adopted and the rumbling of armed forces and communiqués could only make the dispute appear, in the East, as Mr Bevan then wrote, 'not as a conflict between Egyptian nationalism and the legitimate needs of world trade, but as a fresh example of the old sterile struggle between imperialism and nations which have only recently won self-government'. At the very moment when the Western statesmen were remembering that the dear colonel was nothing but a dictator, that same dictator was transformed by his action into the chosen leader of his people, the man who in the people's name was restoring its rightful resources to his country.

Our subject is Egypt, and not the policies of the Great Powers. Everyone knows what has been said and done since the 26th of July 1956. It is all too bitter for repetition.[1] From London to Cairo, on the tracks of Mr Menzies and then again in London, Franco-British diplomacy has seemed to be doing its utmost to dramatize the whole affair rather than to find a solution in which Western interests would be respected, keener on preparing Nasser's pyre than to

[1] 'There has been no war. Nasser has retreated a bit, the Americans have taken over. The French and British have yielded. Everybody has pulled the chestnuts out of the fire for the Russians. But these and least of all Nasser won't necessarily have the last word.' A. Fontaine, *Le Monde*, 25 September 1956. See also A. Frossard in *Le Monde*, 21 September 1956, and A. Fabre-Luce in the same journal, 9 October 1956.

exorcize the evil. Whereas on the 12th of October—at the United Nations meeting—logic and technical considerations seemed to outweigh the passions of the crusading spirit, the 6-Point agreement went back to the real problem, which is to ensure the proper use of the Canal to all and at all times, and not to teach the Arabs a lesson by bringing Nasser to London in an iron cage.

This ingenious plan for an agreement was, then, drawn up on the 12th of October. Seventeen days later a tripartite military operation was already in progress although no fresh fact or event of a decisive character had supervened. Neither the French navy's capture of the Egyptian cargo-boat *Athos II*, carrying arms for the Algerian rebels, nor the much publicized tightening of the military pact between Egypt, Jordan and Syria, nor Israeli–Arab tension on the Jordan, had in any way modified the problem of Suez.

Is that not enough for deciding that Nasser had won and that the Canal affair would remain a great victory for Egyptian nationalism and an important step forward for the under-developed nations? We have tried to show that the Suez *coup* was not a crime. Certainly, since the 27th of July the Egyptian President has not made many mistakes, and has given many proofs of that realism and caution which until recently appeared to be essential qualities of his personality. The operation carried out on the night of the 26th of July was handled with a skill worthy of Captain Roehm's assault troops. The Egyptian treasury is likely to benefit by several million pounds a year as a result. Egyptian strategy has gained several new methods of persuasion.

But what is all this worth by comparison with the friendships Egypt has lost, the credit that is now withdrawn, the fresh resistance that is likely to strengthen against other nationalist aspirations in places where, hitherto, the claims of the smaller nations were always defended? On that evening of the 26th of July the cause of the under-developed countries lost support and sympathy *which the Franco-British intervention in itself is not enough to restore.* As for Arab nationalism, the attitude it took that night is not likely to favour any demands it might make in the future. From the take-over of the Canal traffic to the discussions in the United Nations, Gamal Abdel Nasser no doubt won the overall battle. But he has certainly not won the war for equipping his country, nor for setting its independence on a firm footing, nor for guaranteeing its security. He has heaped up hatred on his own person and on his government. Too much hatred to be good for anybody. The atmosphere of adventure, the poker-trick stunting which characterized the whole move did not only disturb the enemies of his country and its government. 'He had no right to take such a risk with his country's very existence and all the benefits of thirty years' effort towards building up the State, and especially of the last four years of the revolution,' we heard the very day after the Alexandria speech, from an Egyptian civil servant who, not long after, became an ardent supporter of Nasser as a result of the attitude of the West. In the Suez affair, Egypt is certainly 'moving on', but it looks very like the wrong move . . .

III

The Franco-British Invasion

On the 29th of October 1956, at eight-thirty in the evening, two Israeli brigades crossed into Egyptian territory towards the small post at Kuntilla, not far from the Gulf of Akaba. This southern sector of the Negev was almost without Egyptian defences. Advancing at extraordinary speed across such sandy and broken country, they soon went beyond Nakhl and in less than twenty-four hours were within a few miles of the Suez Canal. While General Moshe Dayan was thus playing the Napoleon, enveloping a third of the Egyptian armed units in the south before folding back on the sea to cut their communications, disorder reigned in Cairo which had been completely taken by surprise by this lightning Israeli attack. London and Paris were much less surprised at the news and the two governments rapidly set in motion a plan which was calculated to 'bring the Egyptian dictator to his knees' in under a week. The preliminary phase had just been carried out with impressive thoroughness.

Mr Eden and M. Mollet announced to their respective parliaments in the course of that afternoon that they had sent an ultimatum to the two parties concerned calling on them to retire to a distance of ten miles on each side of the Canal. They were also to allow the installation of Franco-British forces at Port Saïd, Ismaïlia and Suez, otherwise those bases would be forcibly occupied 'in order to protect freedom of navigation'. The Israelis were only too ready to agree to this, as they had not yet even reached the point from which they were ordered to 'withdraw'. The Egyptians could only reject it, as they were called on to sacrifice even more than they had already lost through the attack. At the end of the following night French and British planes began bombarding Egyptian aerodromes, grounding or destroying machines which had recently been bought from the Soviet Union.

The discomfiture of Egypt appeared complete, there seemed no further hope for the Bikbashi and his Arab alliances. The London and Paris Cabinets had started what a French minister, in August, had called 'the stag-hunt' and were already in full cry. Whitehall and the Hôtel Matignon waited for a telephone-call from Cairo to say that the Egyptian people had come to its senses, overthrown the dictator and accepted the internationalization of the Canal.

Ever since the abrupt nationalization of the Canal Company it had been apparent that only two factors prevented London and Paris from armed retaliation which was foreshadowed by the highly-charged speeches by the heads of the two governments. These factors were American opposition and lack of military preparation. There was a strong current of public opinion urging the statesmen to take up the challenge from Alexandria, until the 5th of August when the Labour Party began its campaign against intervention. The High Commands wanted five or six weeks in which to make ready. As soon as, early in September, they made it known that the necessary forces were gathered in Cyprus, the politicians and diplomats who had supported the idea of military measures at the end of July felt that the opportunity was gone, and that both international and British opinion was against the use of force as a means of settling the Suez crisis.

Meanwhile diplomatic action was being taken, and despite the reluctance of the Franco-British side as well as the Egyptian, the American negotiators, together with Indian representatives and the Secretary-General of the United Nations, had persuaded Paris, London and Cairo on the 12th of October into a draft agreement based on six principles. This included the withdrawal, in practice, of the Franco-British demand for 'international management' and an implicit recognition of the nationalization of the Company. On the Egyptian side it involved the Egyptian recognition of the fundamental principle that 'the working of the Canal must not be dependent on the policy of any single power'. Acknowledging the scope of the concessions made by its opponents, the Egyptian government then tried to turn the proposals into realities, sending out strong rumours of a conference to be held in Geneva. But it fell into the capital error of not putting forward a counter-plan as its Indian and American sympathizers expected. Thus during the week of the 12th–19th of October it lost the opportunity for a friendly settlement which would have been in the interests of all concerned. While Colonel Nasser was thus throwing his chances away, Washington also made a capital mistake by diverting the Canal Users' Association —which had been founded on Mr Foster Dulles's initiative—from its real objectives. By insisting that the Association must repay Egypt 90 per cent of dues received, before beginning negotiations with Egypt, the Americans turned a weapon for economic pressure, designed to deprive Egypt of its profits from the July 'hold-up'—or at least a means of negotiation—into nothing more or less than a tool for capitulation. While America was busy 'playing' Egypt, Egypt was not sincerely playing peace-cards. The supporters of military intervention grouped round Mr Macmillan in London and round M. Bourgès-Manoury in Paris began to take heart.

Three factors were then in their favour. It is important to remember that the means for action had existed since September: four Franco-British divisions had been stationed in Cyprus, a Command had been created and the undertaking had even been given a code-name. It was to be called 'Hamilcar'—a name which was subsequently changed to 'Operation Musketeer'. Of course it was not openly talked about. But it was an open secret in Paris that more and more para-chutists were being sent to Cyprus, and that tank-formations were being assembled not far from Algiers and embarked for 'an unknown destination'. On the other hand, the seizure of the *Athos II*, a pirate-ship bringing the Algerian rebels seventy tons of Egyptian arms (loaded in the port of Alexandria with the utmost impudence and clumsiness), provoked a violent surge of anger against Egypt in French public opinion. In addition, the kidnapping of five leaders of the Algerian F.L.N. on the 22nd of October strengthened the idea that an 'energetic' policy paid dividends and that the time was coming for a counter-attack. Finally, the Middle East was itching for battle, and if Egypt appeared anxious to find a satisfactory solution to the Suez affair and to run the Canal properly and involve the French and British in prolonged discussions, at the same time Iraq, with London's blessing, was preparing to occupy eastern Jordan. Indeed, the Anglo-Iraq plan aimed not only at absorbing the larger part of that little kingdom, which pointedly anti-British elections and a series of frontier incidents with Israel were threatening to throw into chaos, but fulfil the old dream of the 'Fertile Crescent' which would link Iraq, Jordan, Syria and Lebanon in one great State closely linked with Great Britain.

British diplomacy believed that this achievement would compensate for its setback at Suez, and would also have the advantage of being a bitter pill for both Nasser and Egypt, relegating it to the status of a second-class Power in comparison with an expanded Iraq. But Mr Eden's French partners were much less enthusiastic. It is a fixed tenet of French diplomacy that the setting up of the 'Fertile Crescent' would mean its eviction from the Middle East, and that only its defence of Syrian and Lebanese independence keeps France its friends and customers and markets there. What was the point in losing in both Cairo and Baghdad? The French leaders also pointed out that the creation of such a great Arab State would threaten Israel, the 'best friend of the West in the Middle East', with extinction, adding that the Jerusalem government had made clear that it would resist rather than let itself be hemmed in.

Since the plucky Jewish State was ready to fight, and since the main aim after all was to humiliate Nasser and teach Pan-Arabism a lesson, why not redirect the Israel-Arab dispute over Jordan towards Sinai? The military experts were all agreed that in spite of Nasser's enormous efforts as regards armaments since September 1955, the Israeli army would easily crush the Egyptian forces, at least so long as the latter had not been trained in the use of their Soviet weapons, which would mean another two years. However, London hesitated. It was tempted to inflict a military defeat on Nasser, but to compromise oneself by coming out on the side of Israel and risk offending Iraq did not appeal to the Foreign Office, which still hugs the idea of a return of the Anglo-Arabism of 1918 and 1945.

All through the month of October the French and British governments therefore followed parallel courses. Eden and Selwyn Lloyd were mounting the Jordan operation with Baghdad while making more and more concessions over the Canal in order to lull Cairo's suspicions. Meanwhile the French Cabinet received numerous visits from delegates of the Israeli High Command. Was there any Franco-Israeli Treaty in the formal sense of the word? Proofs of this are still wanting. It has certainly been stated[1] that on a visit to London in the middle of October on the instructions of the President of the French Council, M. Albert Gazier communicated to or discussed with the British a certain document containing a formal guarantee of the State of Israel by the French. A few days earlier Mr Ben-Gurion had referred, in the Knesseth, to a 'great ally' whose name he would soon be in a position to disclose. In public declarations made by

[1] Bulletin of the *Centre d'Information du Proche-Orient* (*C.I.P.O.*), Paris.

MM. Mollet and Pineau in September and October, they hinted several times at a 'diplomatic secret' which allowed them to believe that 'the last word had not been said over the Suez Affair', and that 'the possibility of using force is not yet excluded'.

In the September the visit to France of Mr Menahem Begin, leader of the extreme Right party in Israel, the 'Herouth', and an open supporter of a preventive war against Egypt, and the contacts he then made in influential circles in France, encouraged the suspicion that some plan was being worked out. A great deal of movement between Paris and Israel went unnoticed at the time. In the event the real 'warning shot' addressed to Egypt was a surprising speech delivered by the President, Ben-Gurion, to the Knesseth on the 15th of October. While three serious incidents had occurred on the Israel-Jordan frontier, and while threats of the Iraqi *Anschluss* were being talked of in the world Press and the Amman elections suggested that there would be increased tension on the Jordan, the Jewish statesman said not a word against Iraqi troop-movements and turned all his eloquence against 'Israel's only real enemy', that is to say Egypt, on whose borders there had not been a serious incident since the Suez crisis began. What was the significance of all this? A few well-informed people gave this event the serious attention it deserved, but observers on the spot were content with noting the 'surprise' to public opinion in Israel, since everyone there was primarily concerned with Jordan and the eastern border.

Events now moved quickly. The next day, the 16th of October (or so it has been said[1]), MM. Mollet and Pineau and their British colleagues decided on their threefold operation directed at the Canal. Opinion in Paris was indignant at the first clear proof—the interception of the *Athos II*—of an intolerable intervention on Egypt's part in the Algerian conflict. The Mollet government was increasingly attacked for the contrast between his outspokenness and the diplomatic inertia into which his allies had dragged him, without wringing the slightest real concession from the stubborn Egyptian dictator. The Congress of the French Radical Party held in Lyons 'regretted' the Cabinet's behaviour, while both the M.R.P. and Independents made it plain that they would not allow this capitulation to Nasser to pass unchallenged. The anti-French demonstrations in Syria and Jordan after Ben Bella's arrest revived anti-Arab feeling in France. Thus it was enough for the Palestinian *fida'iyin* to commit one of the many

[1] H. de Galard in *France-Observateur*, 1 November 1956.

acts of aggression that had caused so much bloodshed on the frontier for the past two years, for the tripartite action to begin—large-scale Israeli attacks, followed by a 'pacifying' intervention by France and Britain. However, on the 21st of October the death of two Israeli soldiers near Gaza did not result in any retaliatory action. It was without any immediate provocation that General Dayan's forces, which four days earlier had been brought up secretly by bus to the southern Negev, started moving early on the night of the 29th October. Why? Everything suggests that the French wanted a few days longer, and that nothing was ready on the 21st or 29th. But it is not unlikely that the Israelis thought they would do well to strike before the American elections on the 6th of November, and that the new flare-up of the Russo-Hungarian crisis would distract world attention—including Russia's—away from the Middle East. Through Israel forestalling the agreed plan, the operation took both London and Paris by surprise, although it had been laid some time before.

But there were swift reactions. The day after the Israeli attack began the French and British governments sent out their ultimatum in spite of M. Mendès-France's warnings to M. Mollet[1] and those given to Mr Eden by the majority of the British Press and the Labour Opposition. The military intervention was generally unpopular in Britain from the outset; socialism, puritanism, a reliance on legal processes, and a sense of realism all uniting to denounce the undertaking as 'immoral and lunatic'.[2] But the French public, which had long been exasperated by Egyptian interference in North African problems, and enraged against the Cairo government by propaganda to which Nasser's behaviour only added more fuel, welcomed this curious form of arbitration by bombers as a necessary corrective. It must be said that apart from a few individuals who believed that eliminating one man was only a short-term solution, and in the end would only embitter Arab demands, and those on the other hand who thought that this 'throw of the dice' was more fraught with international perils than with benefits for France in the Maghrib, most French people's reaction was to say, 'Nasser has gone too far.'

The two government leaders had underestimated the risks. After the strong disapproval on the home front, violently and sharply expressed by the Labour Party chief, Mr Hugh Gaitskell, there came an American reaction of a bitterness and harshness that neither

[1] M. Mendès-France on the 30th demanded a four-power conference to preserve peace.   [2] *The Observer.*

London nor Paris had thought possible: 'So the French and British are going to Suez—via Dien-Bien-Phu . . .' declared a senior State Department official on the 30th of October.[1] This was followed by a series of condemnations against the two Powers from the Security Council and the U.N.O. General Assembly, in which they were called on to withdraw their troops from Egyptian territory and suggestions were made for hurriedly creating an international police force to take over from the invaders from Port Saïd to Gaza. Then the threatening Russian ultimatum of the 5th of November hinted at the outbreak of atomic warfare, giving the 'throw of the dice' of the 30th of October a far more tragic significance than Mendès-France or Gaitskell had thought of.

Indian and Canadian opposition within the Commonwealth, that of the Labour Party and the independent newspapers in London, together with warnings from Washington, Moscow and the 'anti-colonialist' majority in the United Nations thus brought about a cease-fire on the 7th of November. During the previous forty-eight hours British parachute troops, backed by a naval bombardment of Port Saïd, had installed themselves in the town after severe fighting. Meanwhile the French had taken the Gamil and Port Fuad airfield and were advancing along the Ismaïlia highroad in order to dominate the Canal. The cease-fire given during the night of the 6th–7th of November held up the whole operation only thirty-six hours before its completion, within three miles of El Kantara. The Franco-British troops were thus in control of less than a third of the Canal. However, the Egyptian High Command had already had time in which to increase the cost of the offensive by sinking forty ships which were to block the traffic for at least six months. Nothing remained for the invaders but to evacuate Port Saïd, where the international 'police-force' came in to take their place.

The balance-sheet of the offensive can be summed up as follows: the Egyptian army had been shattered by the Israeli attack and the French and British bombardments. But the Canal, which was supposed to have been 'liberated', was put out of service for months, with serious effects for the shipping of oil to Europe. Egypt's Arab alliances appeared to have broken down, but though Colonel Nasser's prestige suffered from the defeat of his Sinai army, it was restored by the solid international action in favour of Egypt. The defeated Colonel was now seen as the head of a small nation

[1] *Le Monde*, 31 October 1956.

attacked by two Great Powers, protected by the leaders of two great world empires and saved by the 'world conscience'. The result of Franco-British intervention had been to save Nasser's face, transforming his defeat at the hands of a small neighbouring state into 'imperialist aggression'.

We do not propose to look into the consequences of the third Egyptian expedition (the first of which destroyed Saint Louis and the second of which led Bonaparte to the seizure of power on the 18 Brumaire), so far as they affect France, Britain, Israel or the United States, but rather to give a rapid interpretation of its immediate effects in Egypt. The fact is that it simply prolonged and accentuated the effects of the initial Suez affair. It increased Nasser's popularity, confirmed now in his role of 'pilot' of the Arab peoples, sailing on in spite of 'imperialist' plots. It strengthened the anti-Western feeling among the Egyptian masses, now convinced by propaganda and the turn of events that the Western Powers had no intention of respecting the Eastern nations' independence. Together with this went a surge of feeling in favour of Soviet Russia, whose harsh notes of the 5th and 10th of November created a powerful impression. Though these came at the very moment when Hungary was being martyred, they gave Russia an immense prestige as 'protectors of the smaller nations' all over the Arab world. All who witnessed it were struck by the tremendous rise of the popularity of the Soviets with the Egyptian people. For instance, a neutral journalist who returned from Cairo to Paris in March 1957 wrote in the French weekly *Réforme* (26 July 1957):

'One had to be in Egypt during the nationalization of the canal, the Security Council debates and the armed intervention by Israel, France and Britain, in order to understand the prestige which the Russians were able to gain at no cost to themselves. The Russians— "El Rouss"—were regarded as supermen "flying to the victims' help". As a result the crushing of the revolt in Budapest was viewed as being to Russia's credit.'

This psychological drift towards the East, accompanied as it was by strong economic and industrial support, may be regarded as the decisive outcome of the chain-reaction crises from which Egypt has suffered. We need to be more cautious than before in estimating Nasser's popularity and his government's length of life. In spite of all the applause with which he is at present surrounded, yet we believe that a crack has shown in the 'Officers' republic'. The dictator is still playing his part with the same boldness and coolness. But if, as we have said, the whole régime is based on the army, it surely follows that the military breakdown during the Sinai conflict, in a matter of days, is bound to have a deep effect on the morale and efficiency of the ruling class of officers in spite of all the flashy declarations of victory that came over the wireless.

We have no desire to mock at troops which were outclassed by a bolder and better-trained force. But if it has been possible to delude the Egyptian public, the authority wielded by the 'Khaki shirts' in the various branches of state affairs is likely to be undermined by events at Sinai. What form will the army's dissatisfaction take, once the people responsible are made to give an account of themselves? Once again the Franco-British intervention helped the government by blinding people to the facts and turning inefficient and boastful leaders into martyrs.

However, the facts were not obscured to such an extent that the Egyptian people failed to realize their officers' true calibre. In Cairo in February 1957 an officer was trying to pass to the head of a queue, when a lower-class civilian shouted, 'You weren't in such a hurry in Sinai, Captain.' Only a year before nobody would have dared say such a thing, nor would an officer have let it pass: it shows a significant change in the public's attitude towards the army.

Another unpleasant outcome for the President is that the Sinai defeat and the army's general behaviour in the war confirm the arguments put forward not so long ago by General Neguib and especially his friend Colonel Ahmed Shawki, which was that an army which dabbles in politics becomes unfit for defending the country: 'they should stick to their barracks'. There is no doubt that one of the main reasons for the collapse at Sinai is that since the military government was formed the two or three hundred best officers in the Egyptian army have left their job and their troops in order to run a ministry, administer a province or run some public service or direct the police force. The 'Falluja tigers' of the past are now sitting behind office desks.

While the army 'cracked up' in October, the militia, which was hastily formed and called the 'Liberation Army', distinguished itself by the courage with which it resisted at Port Saïd. Observers on the spot regarded this as decisive, particularly Jean-Jacques Faust, the correspondent of the *Agence-France-Presse*, who gave a brilliant analysis of the masses' sudden awareness of their own importance at the time, in an article published in *Études méditerranéennes* in June 1957:

'Whatever might be said about this new "proletarian awakening", the testimony of those who live in contact with the lower classes—"poor whites", Greeks or Italians, Christian by faith—all points in the same direction. From the time when the government called on them to defend their country and enrolled and armed them, inviting them to unite in their hatred for the foreigner (and almost inevitably "the rich"), a radical change came over those "God-forgotten men" whom nobody had ever seemed to need before and who had always seemed doomed to the same lot, mere robots making the same gestures of toil from day to day. Only some change of consciousness, of self-awareness, can explain the seriousness and sense of self-imposed discipline of the Liberation Army volunteers. Though inadequately trained and equipped, there were few cases in which there was any attempt to profit personally, by murder or theft, from the confused situation. As a result it is impossible for the régime to go back to what it was before the Suez affair. In this sense the Suez expedition has weakened Nasser's position as much as strengthened it. It has obliged the dictator to run the risk of a "real revolution".'

But the main reason for Colonel Nasser's weakness is that he was saved thanks to Russian interference. He is beholden to Moscow. This awkward and distasteful fact is likely to be held against him: it is already making him enemies, especially in the Arab world, as was seen during the autumn crisis. Neutrality used to pay dividends. The Americans are now trying to offset the influence and prestige of Russia in Nasser's eyes, and the tug-of-war is likely to become more intense when it comes to discussing the financing of the High Dam project. Egypt's 'neutral' policy is now too compromised and committed for her to have any real independence or economic self-determination. Nasser owes too much to the authors of the Russian ultimatum for his fate not to depend on further Russian pressure in his favour. But should that pressure be relaxed for any reason, the Americans who are now wooing Egypt will drop him at once. He thus becomes the kind of item that is haggled over at Yalta ... Maybe the Colonel would be well advised to rediscover the caution which served him so well until the beginning of 1956. Will he have the sense to avoid—whatever the cost—the urge to take revenge for the humiliation he suffered at Sinai? In view of his statement, 'We are not at war with Israel,' which he made on the 4th of November, is he capable of seeking better and more permanent relations with the Jewish State? Can he not see that the only realistic solution is to cut his losses in the north and slash his heavy military commitments in order to set Egypt on its feet industrially?

Another thing which was shown by the violent weeks of autumn 1956 is that in spite of being egged on by propaganda the Egyptian people gave signs of such genuine human feeling. In such a crisis it was far more remarkable to see such people respecting foreign residents, most of whom were denounced as 'enemies', than to see them manning turrets and brandishing rifles. Port Saïd alone was the scene of pillage and brutality, directed against the Jews, while the 'cold pogrom' which was legalized against them was unworthy of Egypt.

But J.-J. Faust, who witnessed the event and was arrested and expelled from the country, says of the Egyptian people's behaviour: 'Many French and English nationals noticed during those unhappy days, that apart from a few profiteers who were eager to snap up the deportees' property for next to nothing, which they did with the utmost arrogance, many Egyptians were kinder to them than normally, going out of their way to make up for the brutality of the police. This is the more to their credit as a recent law made it a crime against State security to have any contact with enemy deportees.'

Costly as it was for all concerned—with the exception of the Russians—the Suez affair gives a clear demonstration of the changed relationship between colonizing and recently colonized nations. Have the Europeans really admitted that there is no further point in trying to manage Eastern states? The 'lesson' which was incompletely given in 1956 will not prevent the smaller countries, who are only too eager to put an end to every sign of foreign exploitation or control, scrapping the 'one-sided' treaties as soon as they see a way of having them revised or suspended. They are likely to oppose the righteous indignation of the Great Powers by invoking their right to take over what has always belonged to them, in much the same way as socialist theory in the nineteenth century justified the violence of the proletariat.

With its blustering language and its savagery on the technical plane, the seizure of the Canal is an important new step in the under-developed nations' will to inherit all the wealth which Western techniques have developed on their soil. It is an example of a bad solution to the problem, whether these poor countries can equip themselves without losing all or some of their newly-found independence. It is, of course, to be expected that Western capital as represented by the International Bank would insist on checking the use of funds advanced to Egypt towards the construction of the new Dam. It is no more surprising that a nation which is anxious to avoid the restrictions of 'financial imperialism' should try to pay for an undertaking on which its very life depends, by diverting to it the revenue from another undertaking which in many respects could be considered as a national property.

However, we are not obliged to accept such a harsh form of dialectic. It is not inevitable for the relations between rich and poor nations to consist of nothing but a see-saw of oppression on the part of the strong and banditry on the part of the weak. There is no reason why weak countries should have to ensure their liberty and survival by flouting laws made by Great Powers.

The course taken by the Suez affair can teach both sides what can and what cannot be done. In spite of his superficial success we can be sure that Nasser is by no means satisfied by the operation as a whole, or with the effect on his own reputation and on his relations with the West. Mr Dulles's tactical skill holds out no better prospects for Washington than for London and Paris: in any case, the State Secretary's balance-sheet is by no means the one he had expected on the 18th of July 1956. As for the Soviets, they have proved that they were really better prepared than their rivals for winning the confidence of the ex-colonial countries. Yet they had to admit their ineffectiveness when it came to taking over the financing of the Aswan project from the Western Powers. They know full well that their newly-established positions can have no lasting value unless they are backed by a genuine development within Egypt itself, involving a complete change in its economic structure, as well as a stabilizing of the Egyptian Left, which is far from being in sight.

IV

Egypt Carries On

Those who have recently been expelled from Egypt, as well as travellers, friends and enemies, all agree that the Cairo streets have returned to normal and show little sign of the drama that has been enacted. Life has hardly slowed down. Many familiar faces have gone but the shops are as busy as ever: the saleswomen behind the counter merely ask anyone at all foreign-looking, 'And when will you be leaving Egypt?' Outside the Semiramis Hotel, which now challenges the new Shepheard's which has been rebuilt on the Nile bank, pretty women sit out on the terrace in the evening, risking a chill while they show off their bare shoulders. In the Sporting Club, tall, tough-looking fair-haired young men, clean-shaven and probably from the North-East, have merely replaced the fair-haired young men with moustaches who have gone back to the North-West. On the newspaper stalls the *News of the Soviet Union* is displayed, hiding such magazines as *Confidential* and *Whisper*. For the passer-by, the new era has replaced the glamour-girl by the tractor.

Ten piastres (about two shillings) for either the propaganda-sheet or the glossy is beyond the average poor Egyptian's pocket, in any case. His choice won't be determined by the Press, whether illustrated or not. The faces in the street show no sign of the gleaming happiness of July 1956, nor the feverishness of the following November. Yet there is no doubt that nationalization was extremely popular and that the whole régime was admired, obeyed and backed to the hilt when things were at their worst in the November, as the whole population's dignity at that time proved. But for a considerable part of Cairo's poorer classes, the wholesale departure of foreigners and of middle-class Jewry has been a blow to their purse. Porters, dry-cleaners and pressers, car-minders and artisans have lost their best customers, while the new 'gentlemen' of the Egyptian *bourgeoisie*, which is slowly taking over from the old cosmopolitan society, have not yet learnt how to spend.

But Westerners are too inclined to take only material factors into account when assessing the opinion or outlook of the Eastern masses. 'They are a bit hungrier, therefore . . .' the argument runs. But we ought to pay more attention to the longing for dignity and the horror of being humiliated which have haunted Egyptians, Tunisians or Persians for so many generations.

Maybe they are a little hungrier than before. Maybe they are not altogether pleased with the present state of things, yet we must not forget that their judgement may be affected by other factors than hunger. Perhaps insight and common sense have something to do with their judgement of the régime and enables them to see the difference between the exciting months of 1956 and the realities of 1957, and to see that Egypt is only hurting herself in expelling so many foreigners and minority groups.

However, these expulsions have brought several social elements round in support of Nasser and his government, among others those employees who could never have hoped to become more than chief clerks but who are now managers or directors, or members of administrative committees. The cosmopolitan residents' withdrawal has left, like the Nile, a fertile soil behind it on which a new class of *bourgeois* is now rising. The industrialists have also benefited. Whether their funds and equipment are ample or inadequate, they are profiting fully from the suspension of trade between the Egyptian, French, English and American economies. Such things as nails, textiles or rope, which never found buyers on the home market because they were inferior to the foreign product, now fetch good prices.

Is the régime becoming more middle-class or *bourgeois* in its outlook? Is it likely to be captured, so to speak, by those whom it now favours, whether it wants to or not? On the contrary, some observers think that everything is pushing it towards the Left, towards a radicalism from which it has no escape. In a remarkable study published in the French review *Études méditerranéennes*,[1] Jean-Jacques Faust, who was in Cairo in November 1956 as correspondent for the France-Presse agency, argued that the 'artificial' Egyptian revolution of 1952–4 became a reality from the autumn of 1956 onwards.

Faust suggests that by appealing to the lower classes, arming them and using them to defend Port Saïd in support of a crumbling army, Nasser gave the Egyptian masses certain rights which cannot be with-

[1] No. 1, June 1957. Éditions de Minuit, Paris.

drawn. By having enough sense or dignity to refrain from using its strength for plundering and holding to ransom, the people proved its claim to those rights. From now on, Faust concludes, 'the way is open for social revolution, and the people's destiny now transcends that of the tyrant'. Such factors as the U.S.S.R.'s active friendship, the awakening of a sense of public responsibility among the un-educated classes, the rise to power—at least in the fields of publicity and economics—of such leftist officers as Lutfi el Wakid and Khalid Muhi ud-Din and other Marxist-trained intellectuals, the proletarian-ization which is following upon industrial development, are all calculated to incline the 'Bikbashi Republic' towards a popular democracy. Looked at historically, this analysis of the situation is acceptable enough; but seen politically, it would appear (at the end of 1957) to be rather premature.

Meanwhile, it might be asked whether the government has been able to keep the support of the masses which was partly won through Nasser's trip to Bandung, broadened by his purchase of Czech arms and which was in no doubt during the 1956 crisis. The *ra'is* or President still seems to enjoy all the prestige which is accorded to a man who takes risks and comes out successful. But certain symptoms (silence in the cinemas when his face appears in the news-reel, or the rare appearances he now makes in public) suggest that there is a return to the relationship that formerly existed between the people and the Colonel. That is, a cowed deference towards the chief who works hard and makes others work, who has covered Egypt with unexpected glory, who has bravely stood out against imperialism, but who rules with a heavy hand, whose acts of initiative are likely to be paid for dearly, and who has hardly touched the living conditions of the masses during his five years of power. Their reaction is made up of an Oriental romanticism together with peasant common sense.

The régime's popularity had to stand an interesting test in 1957, in the election of the Republic's first Parliament (which had been promised by the Officers as long ago as 1953), according to the Constitution of January 1956; then the assembling of the new Par-liament on the 23rd of July 1957, the fifth anniversary of Faruk's abdication.

We had expected little more than a formality ending in a complete victory for the existing government, basing this view on the Presi-dent's popularity after the Suez crisis, the Officers' dictatorial methods and the experiment of holding elections in Egypt. But we were in for a few surprises.

The first came before the appeal to the electorate. It had been arranged that the nominees for the 350 seats in the Assembly had to be examined and approved by a committee over which Nasser was to preside in person. Out of 3,000 nominations only 1,350 were approved. The exclusion of 55 per cent of the candidates showed an unusual degree of prudence, even if the reasons were as honest as they seemed, for instance for belonging to a middle-class family of cosmopolitan origin, or the lack of a genuine political consciousness. It was noted with some surprise that some candidates were refused because they had worked too closely with the Communist Party. One of these was the famous writer, Abdel Rahman Sharqawi, whose rejection raised a stir in the left-wing group among the Colonel's supporters. A further surprise was the number of candidates who had to face the second ballot, not having a sufficient majority at the first. Apart from seventy official candidates, mainly military, who were really elected automatically three weeks before the ballot because their opponents had been warned to hold off, two-thirds of the remaining supporters of the régime had to face the electors a second time, including one of the President's brothers and his closest private friend the civilian Ahmed Fuad, his economic adviser.

The third surprise was the defeat of several well-known figures belonging to the inner circle, namely Ahmed Fuad, already mentioned, who was beaten by a young Cairo schoolmistress, and Rashid Barawi, Director of the Republican Bank. The elimination, among others, of these two leading 'leftist' economic experts came as a shock—much as the rejection of a Pervukhin would be in Russia—and gave the impression that the President had no wish to see Marxism expressed anywhere except in his private company, and certainly not in Parliament.

Taking into account one or two checks administered by the dictatorial government, the Egyptian Republican Parliament, which was elected after a relatively open campaign, is fairly representative of the new Egyptian society's tendencies. It contains only two women, four working men and one man of religion. More or less Wafdist views are represented, timidly enough, by a few *bourgeois*, and about a dozen members have communist sympathies. Can it be expected to exert any pressure on those in power? We have not to forget that the

President has a constitutional right to dissolve Parliament, as the king had previously.

But this new factor in government must be taken seriously. Egyptian eloquence can go a long way. Also, when it came to a vote by applause for electing Major Abdel Latif Boghdadi, the government's chief town-planner, to be chairman, about ten members abstained. This does not give the impression that the Cairo Assembly will be content to remain a catspaw. But will it act as a brake or an accelerator on Colonel Nasser? The second seems more likely. Only a few months after the *coup d'état* in 1952, the malcontents were saying that the 'revolution' had merely replaced a king by twelve Faruks. In two or three years' time it will be clear whether the July 1957 elections merely replaced a dictator by 350 Nassers . . .

Egyptian foreign policy seems to have three main objects since the end of the storm in 1956. Colonel Nasser's first concern was naturally to make for a lessening of tension with the West, while taking care not to appear any the less victorious in the eyes of the Egyptian public. He made only one imprudent and brutal gesture, which was the sudden 'administrative' reoccupation of Gaza, in the spring. Otherwise his attitude towards the U.N.O. forces in Sinai, and especially concerning cargoes for Israel passing through the Canal (and which formerly had been refused transit), seemed to be governed by a desire for more peaceful relations, though that does not necessarily mean a political agreement with Israel, which is not yet in sight. Moreover, his negotiations with France in Geneva, and with Britain in Rome in autumn 1957, gave the impression that Egypt wanted, if not to forget the past, at least to let international relations take their normal course again, and no longer to be regarded as an outlaw even by the so-called imperialists.

A second Egyptian concern is to do everything to keep up the line of 'positive neutrality' which was followed from Bandung to Brioni—though this includes being able to denounce the United States every day while asking them for help, and applauding Russia at the same time.

As against the insults directed by the Press and radio against the U.S.A., Colonel Nasser regularly makes sensible and almost friendly declarations of policy in various American reviews and newspapers. The Egyptian President has also shown that he is in fine intellectual form in his shrewd analysis of Washington diplomacy during an interview given to *El Ahram* on the 9th of September 1957. As for his relations with the Soviet Union, China and their satellites, their cordiality has hardly been reduced by the fact that Moscow still has little to say, any more than in 1956, about helping Egypt with the Aswan Dam project.

Cairo's third aim in foreign policy is obviously to retain its leadership of the Arab world. This means bringing all the 'brother countries' into the neutral fold so as to impose an Arab solution on the Palestine problem, to raise as strongly as possible the whole question of profits from oil in the Middle East, and to replace the Baghdad Pact with a regional alliance centred on Cairo. In all this Cairo seems to show no restraint whatever, fanning every grudge and blindly encouraging every so-called popular and patriotic faction against monarchical, feudal or colonial governments. From the Persian Gulf to Morocco, from Oman to the Sahara, Nasser's Egypt seems to be doing its utmost to look like the scarecrow that Conservative peers and such French politicians as M. Soustelle have painted him to be. Acts of violence, consignments of weapons, appeals for support for 'The Voice of the Arabs', everything is grist to the Egyptian agents' mill. The campaign for the liberation of the Arab peoples, which has been so long exploited—and still is—by the Great Powers, is one which naturally rouses sympathy. But those who are well disposed to it become discouraged at the sight of such prolonged overstatement of claims, the endless nagging of those who, like Egypt up to the time of nationalization, know how to modify their demands on occasion, and keep the rhythm of their emancipation in step with realities. President Nasser has certainly acquired the stature of a liberator and hero in the eyes of the Arab masses. But he would be in no way diminished if Egyptian policy showed less tendency, throughout the Middle East, to substitute its own agents for other countries' governments, which are not all tools of imperialism.

The President has sustained some definite set-backs in the struggle for Arab leadership. King Saud, far from weakening his ties with America, has strengthened them, as well as drawing closer to Iraq. King Husain succeeded in bringing the pro-Nasser forces to heel in Jordan and exerted force to set the pro-Western Trans-Jordan minority above the Palestinian majority who were against the West. Thus there came into being, between Iraq and the neutralists of Cairo and Damascus, and according to the Eisenhower policy, a rather loosely-knit and not very strong group consisting of Lebanon, Saudi

Arabia and Jordan. The sharp change of direction towards Russia made by the Syrian army in August 1957 was hardly calculated to make up for Nasser's previous disappointments, for as the one who introduced 'positive neutrality' into the Middle East, he could not want to see the Syrians set themselves at the head of the movement and twist it leftwards. He had to content himself with a grudging approval.

As for the Sudan, its relations with Egypt have not recovered from the 1955 crisis. Abdullah Khalil does not behave any more like a British agent than his predecessor Ismail el Azhari behaved as an Egyptian one. But the Sudanese government does not forgive Egypt for trying to ferment opposition to it within the country, and has made up its mind to retaliate by playing the major trump-card it still holds, which is its power of veto over the building of the Aswan Dam. The meetings between Nasser and Khalil in October 1957 were significant in this respect. Khalil has the whip-hand.

Thus by autumn 1957 Egypt had reaped very meagre local advantages from its feverish 'diplomatic' activity. Only Syria remained faithful. But while the various Arab governments edged away from Cairo, the masses remained under Nasser's spell, particularly in Jordan. In this respect it could be said that the Officers' Republic is working in depth, for the benefit of the rising generation. But it is working for those who have an ideology, a plan, a real programme to put forward. Should Nasserism disappear, another 'ism' will have to be found—and it is already on the way.

There are two black spots to be noted in the life of this new Egypt: the treatment given to minorities, and the revival of extortion. The military government had found ways of dealing with the second of these, and while being unable to eradicate it completely, none the less harassed it and made it the exception rather than the rule. A new wave of corruption has swept over the administration, thanks to the social upheaval during the crisis, the unlimited power of the political police, problems coming in the wake of expulsion, repatriation, economic controls, confiscations. Visas, the right to exchange currency, permits for residence in the country or for leaving prison, all these have to be paid for under the counter. Has the régime failed to keep its promise in this direction also?

As for the minorities, we have already touched on the expulsion or imprisonment of Jews, which is not only cowardly but a great psychological mistake, whatever one might think of the Israeli attack or the sympathies which most of the large Jewish community in Egypt had for their 'Eretz Israel'—a sympathy which most often went hand in hand with scrupulous loyalty to the Egyptian State.

But little has been said of the increasing discrimination shown against the Copts in the past two or three years. These three million citizens have produced many outstanding personalities, and long gave Egypt its most conscientious and hard-working civil servants. Legally, there is no 'numerus clausus' against them, and the government at present has a Coptic minister. But in the University, the army and the administration alike, it would be instructive to compare the rate of promotion, all things being equal, of a Moslem and an Egyptian Christian. Yet so far as can be seen there was no difference in the two communities' reaction during the 1956 crisis.

One of the most important consequences of the operations in autumn 1956 was that a new myth had to be found to replace that of the Dam project. This one was more fascinating for most Egyptians and found an echo in all their oldest aspirations and deep-seated grudges: the economic grip in which foreigners held Egypt.

The liquidation of foreign interests had already been carefully studied and undertaken by the former régime. Laws concerning the residence of aliens, laws controlling labour and anonymous companies, the law on real estate, the strict currency laws controlling the capital of alien residents, were all worked out and often applied with unnecessary unpleasantness by all King Faruk's governments.

Although at the beginning Neguib's and Nasser's government insisted that they intended to collaborate closely with foreign minorities in Egypt, in practice the laws discriminating between alien residents, minorities and actual Egyptians were applied with increasing strictness. But the contradiction between the severity of those laws and Egypt's need for foreign capital and technicians was so harmful to the government that more generous regulations were introduced as to the residence and investments of foreign nationals.

The Franco-British attack suddenly stripped all the pretence away. 'They had better go, and let us be masters in our own country. They were too powerful, as their recent aggression proves.' Indeed, it appears as though the attack on Egypt was not so much the real cause of Nasser's decision to make short shrift of all foreign financial interests in the country, as an opportunity for him to create a new myth, calculated to please the *bourgeoisie*, businessmen and officers in the government. They could well be satisfied, as entire fortunes, thriving enterprises and important appointments could be taken over by them. Thus the 'egyptianization' process did much to rescue the government's popularity.

In order to make up for selfish interests reaping benefit from the huge liquidation that took place, and to give the new policy the appearance of a social reform, a large part of this foreign property was turned into joint-stock undertakings in which the State held the majority of shares and votes. This was also a means of balancing the public accounts, by including part of formerly foreign-controlled undertakings in the normal State Budget.

The only inconvenient thing about this new myth is that it cannot last very long, once the initial take-over is completed and no more funds flow in. The foreigners went, leaving everything behind. 'We are the sole masters of our national economy and are alone responsible.' Is Egypt likely to succeed, now that no 'colonialist' interests, such as those of the expelled foreigners, are there to affect its outlook and government?

Egypt still lacks the conditions, trained executives and labour traditions which are needed for running the great network of undertakings which it had taken several generations of foreign settlers to build up in the country. Egypt has some valuable trained men and staffs, but they are too few and inexperienced, so that the creative potential of the national surplus has hardly been developed at all since the crisis.

This revolutionary 'egyptianization' of the entire economy has had many repercussions. There has been a flight of capital, uneasiness (to say the least) among all the foreign communities concerned, a fall in the value of the Egyptian pound on foreign exchanges, the blocking of credit balances in London, Washington and Paris, and finally the creation of an 'end of the world' atmosphere and general sense of liquidation of which the Egyptians, happily seizing foreigners' money and jobs, are as yet hardly aware.

The scale of the operation was such that Egypt was able for a time to overlook the difficulties of overseas trade, arising particularly from deficits which had accumulated over a period of years and are now frozen in Egypt's accounts with a number of countries. There is a deficiency of foreign currencies which the new revenue from the Suez Canal will not be enough to cover.

Egypt could only look forward to an improved future so long as her deficits in overseas trade were justified by her extension of capital industrial equipment and her development of important new projects. But as soon as deficits abroad result in the arresting or slowing down of installations and plans for development, business comes to a standstill in almost every sphere of economic activity. In order to provide against this the Egyptian government announced a hundred new projects in 1957, for the most part designed to set up small or light industries with help and currency from the Eastern countries. But however interesting, such plans cannot be carried out for ten years or so. As things are in 1957 they imply more State control than before, and a kind of protectionism which can only result in an ingrown economy, in a country which has not yet the proper modern groundwork and preparation for the task.

According to Egyptian statistics, the economic balance-sheet of 1957 may be summarized as follows: a rise in State-revenue, thanks to its interest in a number of undertakings with guaranteed yearly dividends, as well as to the increase in direct taxation to make up for losses on customs and excise; a surplus in receipts from foreign trade for the first time for about fifteen years, obtained through the slowing-down of essential imports; a marked shrinking of the money in circulation owing to the sluggish state of business; a relative stability in the cost of living, brought about by a reduction of incomes.

At all events it must be recognized that nothing better could be achieved in view of the conditions in the country itself and the state of its relations with the outside world. The inflation which threatened during the Suez war and which had begun to be felt in the previous year has been checked, although the proportion of Treasury Bonds in the financial margin remains rather high. Public finances which recklessly tended to increase loans and indirect taxes have been partly steadied. The rise in the cost of living, which otherwise would have gone too far, has been checked in spite of under-stocking inessential goods.

What concerns us is whether this state of affairs can last, and whether it offers a basis for that policy of economic expansion which alone could justify a totalitarian government, in a country where politically informed circles stress the need for rapidly improving the masses' standard of living.

The answer is not far to seek. The Egyptian economy can neither survive nor develop in isolation from the rest of the world. This is why Egypt is being pressed to resume its discussions with the United States, Britain and France. Egypt will no doubt wish to avoid any final liquidation of its interests abroad, and to develop its commercial relations with all countries. The outcome of such a policy and a mark of its success would be a renewed effort to obtain foreign capital for the Dam project.

Once the government has exhausted the legend of the foreign economic grip on the country, it will soon be trying to find some new or renewed myth which will bring the same kind of short-term advantage. The financing of a new Aswan scheme could well, among other things, result in delaying some such compelling idea as the arabization of petrol in the 'brother' Moslem countries.

If Colonel Nasser were to start such a campaign with the same energy as he showed in 1956, he would not be slow in finding allies in the East, and no doubt elsewhere.

Budgets:

1956-7—Normal budget, 1 July, balanced at £E180,000,000
1957-8—Expenditure £183,000,000, revenue £300,000,000—an enormous fiscal effort

Note circulation:

6 June 1957: £205,644,000 (a national record)
6 June 1956: £171,500,000 (military outlay)
22 August 1957: (end of cotton season) £175,400,000—Deflation: poverty

Trade balance:

First 6 months of 1957: Exports £93,600,000
Imports, £87,100,000
Surplus: £6,500,000
12 months, 1956: Exports £140,000,000
Imports £186,000,000
Deficit £43,000,000 (including re-exports)
12 months, 1955: Exports £137,000,000
Imports £183,000,000
Deficit £44,000,000 (military equipment?)

Reserve of convertible foreign currency:

November 1956 (Franco-British attack): £8,000,000
June 1957   (Canal revenues)   £17,000,000

Egypt's great problem is, therefore, as before the 26th of July 1956, how to raise the standard of life of the masses. This problem cannot be isolated from its relationship with the West as regards technicians and finance. Egyptian independence and neutrality already owe much to the communist and Asiatic states. Yet they cannot be made really positive without co-operation from and with the Western nations, including those who were the victims of the seizure of the Suez Canal, or who came in as peacemakers at Port Saïd. Egypt wants both independence and food. It would be a poor look-out for the state of the world in the middle of the twentieth century if these two needs were regarded as incompatible. Nor should that 'independence' mean that relations between East and West should be based only on a spirit of reprisal or revenge, or on replacing domination by theft. There is no need, either, why relations between the Eastern countries themselves should mean that moderation is denounced as treason, or that the only virtues to be recognized should be extremism, intolerance and racial prejudice. Even more so than many other countries that have recently found their freedom and who sometimes take her as a model, *Egypt needs others*. It is outside her own frontiers that Egypt will and must find the means of saving some two thousand children a day. Her future depends above all else on solidarity with the rest of the world. Anything that threatens this solidarity is a danger to Egypt.

V

The 'United Arab State'

There is no longer an Egypt.

Since February 1958—and for how long?—the Nile Valley has become only the south-west region of the strangest State in the world, the only country whose three provinces have no common frontier, and which is made up of two republics and a kingdom—the Yemen. The United Arab State has come into being.

Even while it was ruled over by foreigners for three thousand years —by Ethiopians, Greeks, Arabs, Turks, Circassians and Albanians, Egypt remained Egypt. But no sooner have the men of the Nile Valley taken full power into Egyptian hands than they abolish the State itself. However, it is true that its integration with other Arab peoples gives it a status more like that of England within the United Kingdom than that of a Massachusetts absorbed into the United States.

Thothmes III, Saladin and Ibrahim Pasha had already extended their rules over Syria, but needless to say not one of them was begged to do so by ninety-nine per cent of the Barada valley people. On the 21st of February 1958 only about a hundred Syrian voters were against merging their own country into the new United Arab State. Even more surprisingly, in spite of appearances, there were hardly more Egyptians to raise their voice against this venture.

This fact alone would have been enough to make the 21st of February a significant date in Egyptian history. Yet it is even more remarkable that at the very moment when Egypt was thus extending her frontiers to Mesopotamia, the Sudan was lodging a protest against Cairo with the U.N.O. Security Council over a trivial frontier dispute. Was this in order to stress the fact that Egypt's thrust towards the North and towards Asia meant sacrificing its future southwards and in Africa? Whether deliberate or accidental, was Egypt now making the fundamental choice between its 'Arab' and 'African' destinies?

Suddenly faced by this daring act of initiative, European onlookers either sneered or panicked. Some made fun of this hasty marriage,

505

this sudden mingling of two, then three countries separated as they were by a more or less hostile state. This fusion which seemed to have no basis in any clear-headed view of the material and political realities appeared to them as a kind of conjuring trick, an improvisation. They laughed at the whole operation's simple-mindedness, the disregard for tradition and the short-sightedness it implied on the part of those who were rushing into it. So they refused to take it seriously.

Other observers, without lingering on that aspect of the question, saw it as the first stage in the regrouping of the Arab world, Pan-Arabism on the move, the birth of an empire. They had qualms for their oil, the Baghdad Pact, Algeria and the security of the 'southern bastion of Europe'.

Both these groups were overstating the case, the first of them unduly stressing obvious factors, the second making too much of a kind of pipe-dream. Such a political event can be neither understood nor judged without giving their proper place to a rational analysis of the facts as well as of popular myths or wishful thinking.

In some respects it is an extravagant solution.

One evening in January, General Afif Bizri, C.-in-C. of the Syrian Army and the real master of the country, together with a small group of staff officers including Sirag, Sabbagh, Enfuri Amdun and Kanut, left Damascus without warning and unknown to the legal government. He landed in Cairo and set out to persuade Nasser, head of the Egyptian State, that they must take immediate and radical measures to bring about the unification of Syria and Egypt, of which there had been some talk for the past three years. This would have to be not merely a federation but a straightforward merger of the two countries.

Two days later Salah ud-Din Bittar, the Syrian Foreign Minister, came to Cairo with his government's approval of this bold undertaking, and particularly the Socialist Party's support, he being one of its most respected leaders. Nasser took a further two days to make up his mind, when he announced that Egypt and Syria would from now on become 'a single State, a single army, a single party'.

What were the reasons for this 'anschluss' in reverse, demanded by the weaker partner? Why should Syria want to efface herself in the brother-state? Why should President Abdel Nasser, who in his cooler moments is such an astute politician, agree to take a hand in this impromptu game?

Behind it there is, of course, the Arab world's untiring hope for unity, part of that myth which will be discussed later. But the new partners seem to have been swayed by three more immediate reasons. For the Syrians—and for those excitable young Syrian officers who are often called 'the red colonels'—there was first and foremost a reflex in favour of defence against the communist threat.

These officers had been the masters of an uneasy Syria for almost two years. Sharing much the same ideas and reactions as the Socialist Party led by Akram Hurani, Salah Bittar and Michel Affak, like them they were the dispirited and anxious allies of the Communist Party which was led by Khaled Baghdash. His political background, experience and subtlety enabled this powerful demagogue to stand head and shoulders above his rivals, who finally took alarm at his influence, as well as at the prestige he drew from Soviet support, the rising progressive tendencies among the masses, and the possibility of the country being taken over from both without and within.

The communist leader had already, several months earlier, made Syrian-Egyptian *federation* one of the points in his propaganda campaign. The officers and their supporters replied with blunt talk about complete union. The communist newspaper *El Nasr* came out against the idea, protesting that it might lead Syria to take 'a step backwards from democracy' since it was in advance of Egypt in its respect for civil liberties. At this, Bizri at once rushed over to Cairo and the communist giant's power was undermined. It was announced ten days later that Khaled Baghdash and his family were leaving Damascus for Prague. This did not amount to formal exile. But the creation of a Syrian-Egyptian 'single-party government' based on Cairo's 'national union' system meant that the Syrian Communist Party was absorbed shortly afterwards.

The Egyptian President could not fail to be attracted by an anti-communist move of this sort. That is one of the reasons why he allowed his colleagues from the Damascus H.Q. to come and offer him the keys of Syria. Apart from Nuri Said, Baghdash is about the only man in the Arab world that he might have trouble in reckoning with. It was worth taking risks in order to remove him and all that he stood for—especially as, ever since the Afro-Asian conference held in Cairo in December 1957, when Moscow upset some of his plans, Nasser had felt himself hemmed in by communism. At the same time as he was signing an economic agreement with Moscow which looked like binding him to Soviet production, he had to swing to the Right and set up some sort of bulwark against the Marxist menace. Right

507

from the beginning of his political career Nasser has always founded his pendulum-policy on this technique of compensation.

But Gamal Abdel Nasser was swayed by another consideration. It is now obvious that for both Nasser and all the other Arab revolutionists, the nationalization of the Suez Canal Company can only be a prelude to the more rewarding but in any case complementary nationalizing of Middle-East petrol. This idea is implicit in *The Philosophy of the Revolution*, dating back to April 1954. At that time it was no more than a remote aim, the bee in the bonnet of the well-behaved lieutenant-colonel who was governing Egypt like some Arab Salazar. After the Suez 'sun-stroke', its victorious outcome and the Egyptian administration's success in running the Canal, the oil-fields already appeared to be within reach, though it was of the utmost importance not to lay hands on them too quickly in case the mirage should recede. By guaranteeing his control of the Syrian State, with its economy and communications, the Egyptian leader could already see himself master of four-fifths of the means for transporting petrol. The prospects for nationalization could hardly be rosier.

But in order to convince the Egyptian President (the 'raïs'), the Syrian officers and socialist leaders used another argument, which in substance was as follows: 'For three years now you have been turning your energies to the building of the Aswan barrage. In order to do so you have taken every risk and stood firm against every crisis. Why? Is it in order to find land for settling a million fellahs? Well, if we bring about Syrian-Egyptian unity, your million fellahs can easily be absorbed into the Gazira plains, which are under-populated and under-developed. Of course this cannot be done in a year, but in ten years, at the same rate as you complete your barrage scheme. We can take a hundred thousand Egyptian fellahs straight away.'

Was this the decisive factor for Abdel Nasser? This is not certain since, being himself of peasant stock, the President is fully aware of the realities of Egyptian rural life. He knows full well that the authorities will have their work cut out to uproot the Upper Egypt fellahs, the most stay-at-home people in the world, from their pathetic, over-populated strip of soil to which they cling with all their might. Will he have to use force? And for their part, will the masters of the 'Syrian province' be able to foist the Nile folk on the Gazira peasantry, who will naturally regard them as intruders? In any case it is safe to say that such a transfer of population is

508

the best justification that can be found for the merging of Egypt and Syria. This would provide an important economic and social policy, in line with Egypt's deepest and most lasting interests.

But the union of the two countries has more general and permanent reasons behind it. We have no need to recall the vague but stubborn Arab-Moslem ideal of recomposing the Umma, the community of the faithful. Sentiments of this kind are powerful and deep-rooted. But it is too indefinable to provide the motive-power for precise political action. Let us stress, rather, two of the elements that make up this inner urge for unification: the dawn of economic integration, and the development of a cultural community.

From Beirut to Cairo and from Damascus to Baghdad, over the past twenty years a network of commercial relations has emerged, a trade trend which has brought to light the existence of a coherent, trading *bourgeoisie* in each of those quarters. Exporters, middlemen, promoters together make up the beginnings of a certain class—however inappropriate or derogatory the term may sound—which perhaps will form the most reliable bond in this unification of the Arab countries. Something of much the same kind must have happened in Germany early in the nineteenth century, with the emergence of a shifting, trading middle-class which laid the foundations of the 'zollverein' and thus of German unity. Arab unity is bound to owe much to these businessmen who are travelling up and down the Middle East, filling the planes and hotels, calling on the same credit and speaking the same language—a language which is often a quaint cocktail of English and Arabic—or rather English, American, French and Arabic.

But there is no question of any such hybrid language being used by the writers and journalists who are also playing a vital part towards achieving Arab unity. After being until fairly recently more and more adulterated but without managing to adapt itself any better to the needs of modern life, the language of the Prophet is now being both modernized and reshaped. Whereas it used to be split into a number of local, old-fashioned dialects, Arabic is being broadened, rejuvenated, and is becoming a more pliable instrument altogether thanks to the 'Press-Arabic' which is exactly the same in Cairo, Damascus, Jerusalem and Beirut. Increasing numbers everywhere are reading the same articles—those of Ihsan Abdel Qudus (Cairo), Kamel Meruh (Beirut) and Michel Affak (Damascus)—and the same novels, for instance those of the Egyptian novelists Tewfik el Hakim and

Abdel Rahman Sharqawi, and listen to the same songs originating in Cairo, by Omm Kalthum, Mohamed Abdel Wahad and Farid el Attrash.

However many the reasons for the Damascus-Cairo merger, and however powerful they might be, they do not necessarily imply that the populations of the two countries concerned greet it with enthusiasm. In fact, contrary to what was thought in Europe, it was more favourably regarded in Syria than in Egypt. Apart from communist misgivings or those of the citizens of Aleppo (understandably more interested in Iraq and Turkey, so that their government's flirting with Africa must have baffled and upset them even more than they were two years ago in their relationship with the southern capital at Damascus), it was given a very warm welcome by two sections of the population, namely, the intellectuals and business people.

The intellectuals, who are almost all members of the Socialist *baath*, had already been hoping for this for some years. In 1954 Salah Bittar was already talking to us about reunification, with every sign of emotion. The Damascus newspapers had been full of the plan for some months. The Syrians now see themselves as members of a very large nation. Their horizon has suddenly opened out, and all the more so as they are convinced that, being subtler and politically more experienced than their newly-found fellow-countrymen in the south, sooner or later they will be able to hold key positions in the new State. This is the same kind of argument as was used before, by those who supported the merger with Baghdad. It may be asked whether these hopes have been dashed by the choice of the first joint Cabinet, in which the Syrians have only one Minister out of nine. Probably not. This is as much as the Syrians expect in the first stage, but they no doubt regard it as the thin end of the wedge.

The business people and tradesmen are delighted. Anyone would think the alliance had been arranged in the Damascus bazaars, in that half-light in which lengths of cloth, jewels, apricots and household gadgets change hands in a feverish, breathless bustle. Damascene trade was going through a lingering death, with its meagre home market and little or no outlet abroad. The sudden widening of the frontiers and the discovery of a new public, the adjustment of exchange-rates, new buyers and suppliers, all this new blood and fresh circulation is a blessing for the bazaar dealers. Does it spell their salvation? In any case they behave as though it did, especially as Khaled el Azam, one of the 'wise' who made his fortune long ago, is one of the union's strongest supporters.

Feelings are more divided in Cairo. An indefinable but lingering mistrust colours the admiration which the masses and large numbers of young people and intellectuals feel for Nasser. Damascus seems very remote to them, and the Syrians are noted for their cunning. They wonder whether Egypt isn't being taken in, whether it isn't something of a gamble, to rove so far away from the Nile Valley and set up frontiers on the borders of Mesopotamia and the Taurus.

Some liberal intellectuals think that if Egypt joins Syria, which has a more liberal-minded government, this will result in a more tolerant policy in Egypt itself. With a man like Shukri Kuwatli in power in Damascus, how could his friend and mentor Mustafa Nahas be held in semi-captivity in Cairo? Such hopes appear to be ill-founded, for after a few weeks of experience it became clear, as might have been foreseen, that the new alignment did not mean that the 'hard' system would yield to the 'soft'; but on the contrary, that semi-liberty would give way to something approaching dictatorship.

The February 'anschluss' was expected to result in extremely lively reactions in Israel as well as in the neighbouring Arab monarchies against the 'social-nationalism' and 'positive neutrality' as practised by Cairo and Damascus.

In the event, Jerusalem maintained an impressive level-headedness. Official statements and those made by the Press and the political parties all asserted that Arab unity could do no harm to peace in the Middle East and that Israel could only welcome everything making for stability in the Arab world, so long as the regrouping had some aim other than revenge. The Israeli leaders' sober attitude is based on three factors. First, they believe that they proved in October–November 1956 that it will be years before any Arab force can become a serious threat. Second, they believe that a United Arab State will be more mature in outlook and more capable of a realistic approach to the Palestine problem—and this is true. Third, that the Cairo-Damascus move will hold up communist infiltration in the Middle East, which gave some cause for anxiety.

Indeed, it was from the other part of the Arab world, that of the 'Petrol Kings' in which there is a complete divorce between the people and the exercise of power, that the most unfavourable reaction came. This was not so at the outset. The Hashimi kings replied to the Cairo-Damascus axis by setting up an 'Arab Federation' of Iraq and Jordan—much to the dismay of Israel, since this brought the Iraqi army down the Jewish State's frontiers while she was still in a state of war with Baghdad, though this was offset by formal reassurances from London and Washington.

For the first few weeks the United Arab State and 'Hashimi Federation' dealt with each other with cautious ceremony. They exchanged notes of congratulation in which their dislike for each other was politely veiled, while each side did its utmost to seduce the remaining neutrals, Sa'udi Arabia and Lebanon. Trouble started when Riyad opted for the Hashimi group of Iraq and Jordan. Damascus and Cairo now gave vent to their anger, denouncing a 'plot' on King Sa'ud's part to assassinate President Nasser, and waging verbal warfare on the 'traitor-kings who were betraying the Arab cause'.

Baghdad counter-attacked on the 10th of March, when Nuri Saïd, no friend of Nasser's, formed his fifteenth Cabinet containing four ex-Prime Ministers, every one of whom was a sworn enemy of the Egyptian dictator. This aggressive Cabinet promises that relations between the United Arab State and the Hashimite Federation are likely to be stormy. '*Baath*' and Nasserism are strong in Baghdad, especially in the University, and even more so among the refugees from Palestine who make up the majority of Jordan's population. But old Nuri Pasha, with King Sa'ud on his side, has it is in his power to make the going hard for the socialist colonels in Cairo and Damascus. He has many friends, or rather allies, in Khartum, Benghazi and Beirut. However much Nasser and Sirag are dreaming of nationalizing Arab petrol, Nuri Pasha is unlikely to allow Cairo to reap any benefit from the process.

This Arab unity, of which the Syro-Egyptian merger, together with the unexpected addition of the Yemen, is probably no more than the initial stage, is none the less an impressive idea.

Critics will go on talking about Pan-Arabism, racism, Islamic imperialism. They will not forget to mention Saladin. But it would be more accurate to speak in terms of a syndicalist or trade-union merger. The national movements in Africa and Asia, and that in the Middle East most of all, remind one more and more of proletarian associations. They have the same harshness and energy, caused by long years of waiting and a lasting sense of frustration. The Arabs as a whole are people who all complain in the same language of the same humiliation, the same hunger.

However unprogressive the uniformed creators of the Syro-Egyptian State may be at bottom, and however reactionary some of their unspoken thoughts, yet what they have done is not unlike the fusion of two workers' groups. Shall we say a union made up of steel and transport workers? They are making the same kind of claim, demanding their due. It is quite natural that this should fire the proletarian or, rather, sub-proletarian masses that make up the Arab peoples. Let us make no mistake about one thing: in spite of the somewhat stiff approval on the part of political leaders in Tunis or Rabat, the bulk of their population was deeply touched by these events. They are waiting for something to come out of them.

It is not certain whether this something can be provided from a hastily-patched-up union, held together by opportunism and under-the-counter agreements, and which looks like some bargain struck between Glasgow dockers, Pittsburgh metal-workers and Ruhr miners, on the initiative of Corsican police and Swiss customs officers. But hope is certainly there.

But for Egypt we can foresee more disappointments, bitterness and hazards than there will be fruits. No doubt there might be some imperialist wishful-thinking in the notion of isolating Egypt and containing the Nile folk within their narrow valley. But the country's and nation's originality was so striking by comparison with that of her neighbours, and Egypt's future seems to be so closely bound up with its main artery the Nile, that such a bold overflow eastwards and northwards looks like the kind of mistake from which a great statesman should protect his people. Even if Reza Shah had begged him on hands and knees (and the Iran sovereign was as close to him as Hurani is to Nasser), would Mustafa Kemal have agreed to sink Turkey's destiny into that of Persia? Never.

Must it already be said, alongside those who are well versed in Egyptian affairs, that Damascus will prove both an over-heavy burden and a dangerous source of weakness; that the worm is in the fruit and that the Nasser state, whose virtues as well as vices we have impartially described, is henceforth threatened with disequilibrium, elephantiasis and complete breakdown? Perhaps it is enough to say that the game that is being played is a dangerous gamble, and that Gamal

Abdel Nasser's hesitations in late January 1958 gave proof of his political vision. Is Egypt no more? It is too real to disappear. But the 'United Arab State' is perhaps too mythical to survive.

Ismaïlia—
La Sauvetat-du-Dropt, 1956
Paris, 1957–8

A Chronology of Modern Egypt

1798 Landing of Bonaparte's expeditionary force.

1801 Withdrawal, resulting from General Menou's defeat at Canopus.

1805 Mohamed Ali, an Albanian officer, acclaimed Pasha of Cairo.

1811 He had 400 Mamelukes massacred in the Cairo Citadel.

1820-3 Conquest of the Sudan by Mohamed Ali's troops.

1832 Mohamed Ali's son Ibrahim crushed the Turkish army at Koniya.

1839 Ibrahim's further victory over the Turks at Nizib.

1840 Mohamed Ali established hereditary rule in Egypt.

1849 Death of Mohamed Ali.

1854 Ali's second successor, Saïd, makes a concession to Lesseps, giving him the right to cut a canal.

1859 Work was begun on cutting through the isthmus.

1863 The Khedive Ismaïl succeeded Saïd.

1869 Opening of Suez Canal.

1876 Financial crisis in Egypt resulted in the floating of a Foreign Debt Control.

1879 Ismaïl deposed by the 'Sublime Porte' on the initiative of the Western Powers.

1881 A nationalist movement led by Colonel Arabi struck against foreign misrule and the new Khedive, Tewfiq.

1882 Great Britain intervened, the British fleet bombarding Alexandria. Arabi arrested and tried. The British 'provisional' occupation of Egypt began.

1885 Egypt driven from the Sudan by the Dervish revolt.

1899 After the re-conquest of the Sudan, London and Cairo establish a 'condominium'.

1914 Egypt became a British Protectorate.

1918 Sa'd Zaghlul led a delegation asking for Egypt's independence.

1919 London refused. Outbreak of revolution.

1922 Declaration of Egyptian independence.

1924 (April) Election of the first Parliament, with a large Wafdist majority.

1924 (November) Assassination of Sir Lee Stack, British head of the Egyptian army, resulting in a tightening of British control over Egypt.

1927 Death of the leader of the national movement, Sa'd Zaghlul.

1936 The Wafdist government of Nahas Pasha obtained the evacuation of Egypt by British forces, with the exception of the Canal Zone.

1937 At the Montreux Conference the same government obtained the annulment of the 'Capitulations' which limited Egyptian sovereignty.

1942 The British obliged King Faruk to recognize the Nahas Cabinet, which was anti-German.

1945 The creation of the Arab League (in Cairo), with Egypt as its leader.

Major Gamal Abdel Nasser began forming his small group of revolutionaries who were to call themselves the 'Free Officers'.

1946 Violent anti-British disturbances in Cairo and Alexandria.

1948 Palestinian War between the new Israeli State and the Arab States.

1949 Victory of Israel, which signed the Rhodes Armistice, mainly with Egypt.

1950 Wafd secured heavy voting at the polls and now controlled Parliament.

1951 The Nahas Cabinet denounced the 1936 Treaty with Britain and began the 'Battle of the Canal' against the British.

1952 (January) The Great Fire of Cairo, started by organized but unidentified groups.

(23 July) A group of officers led by Lieut.-Colonel Nasser seized the G.H.Q. and forced King Faruk to make General Neguib head of the army.

(26 July) Faruk forced to abdicate. Left Egypt.

(September) General Neguib became President of the Council.

1953 (June) Proclamation of the Republic. Neguib made President of the Republic and Premier, with Nasser as Vice-Premier.

1954 (February–March) Disagreement between Neguib and Nasser. After a month of political struggle the former remained President of the Republic, Nasser becoming Prime Minister.

1954 (July) Signature of a draft agreement between Britain and Egypt. The British undertake to evacuate the Canal within twenty months.

(November) Wholesale suppression of the terrorist organization of the Moslem Brotherhood. Neguib, compromised in the Brotherhood plot, was shorn of the Presidency and placed under house-arrest.

1955 (February) A raid by an Israeli commando force in Gaza left forty Egyptian dead.

(April) Colonel Nasser represented Egypt at the Bandung Afro-Asian conference. Leftist parties begin to support the military régime.

(September) It was announced that a contract had been signed for Egypt to obtain arms from Iron Curtain countries.

1956 (February) Signature of an 'in principle' agreement between the International Bank and Egypt, whereby Egypt would receive a loan of 200,000 million dollars for the construction of the High Dam above Aswan.

(18 July) The United States secured the withdrawal of this loan to Egypt.

(26 July) Colonel Nasser announced in Alexandria that the Suez Canal Company was being nationalized 'in order to make the Canal finance the Dam'.

(August) Nasser refused to take part in the London Conference on the status of the Canal.

(September) Mr Menzies, Prime Minister of Australia, acting as the Western delegate, left Cairo without obtaining satisfaction from Nasser.

(12 October) Tentative agreement reached at the United Nations on a six-point charter for the Canal.

(29 October) Israeli forces invaded Sinai.

(30 October) London and Paris intervened forcibly 'to separate the combatants'. A week later the two governments accepted a cease-fire.

1957 (March) The Suez Canal, sabotaged by the Egyptians in November 1956, was reopened to navigation.

(June) President Nasser declared 'the question of the passage of Israeli shipping through the Canal will be submitted to arbitration at the international court at The Hague'.

1957 (July) Election of the first Egyptian National Assembly. Several official candidates defeated.

(August) Anglo-Egyptian negotiations held in Rome, to clear up the Suez crisis.

(September) Franco-Egyptian negotiations in Geneva, with the same intention.

On leaving Egypt after directing the clearance of the Suez Canal, the American General Wheeler announced that the Egyptian plans for running the Canal and its further development were 'fairly good'.

1958 (February) The United Arab State established, consisting of Egypt, Syria and the Yemen.

Reading List

ABBAS, MEKKI. *The Sudan Question*. London, 1952

AMMAR, HAMED. *Growing up in an Egyptian Village*. International Library of Sociology and Social Reconstruction. London, 1954

AYROUT, HENRI HABIBI. *Fellahs d'Égypte*. Alexandria, 1953

BERQUE, JACQUES. 'Sur la structure sociale de quelques villages égyptiens' (Social Structure of some Egyptian Villages). In *Les Annales de Sociologie*, Paris, 1955, No. 2

CARRÉ, JEAN-MARIE. *Écrivains et voyageurs français en Egypte* (French Writers and Travellers in Egypt). French Institute of Archaeology in Cairo. 1956 edn.

COLOMBE, MARCEL. *L'Évolution de l'Égypte de 1924 à 1950* (The Development of Egypt between 1924 and 1950). Paris, 1951

COSSERY, ALBERT. Novels—*Les Hommes oubliés de Dieu* (The Men whom God forgot)
La Maison de la mort certaine (The House of Certain Death)
Mendiants et orgueilleux (The Poor and the Proud)

CROMER, EARL OF. *Modern Egypt*. 2 vols. London, 1908

FEDDEN, R. *The Land of Egypt*. London, 1939

FROMONT, PIERRE. *L'agriculture égyptienne et ses problèmes* (Egyptian Agriculture and its Problems). Extr. doctoral thesis. Paris, 1955

GIBB, H. A. R. *Modern Trends in Islam*. Chicago, 1947

GREITLY, ALI. 'The Structure of Modern Industry in Egypt.' In *L'Égypte contemporaine*, Cairo, 1947

GROUPE D'ÉTUDES D'ISLAM. *L'Égypte indépendante* (Independent Egypt). Paris, 1937

HANOTAUX, GABRIEL. *Histoire de la nation égyptienne* (A History of the Egyptian Nation). 7 vols. Paris, 1935–40

HENEIN, GEORGES. 'Inventaire contre le désespoir' (Stocktaking Against Despair). In *Études Méditerranéennes*, Paris, No. 1, summer 1957

HURST, H. E. *The Nile* (A General Account of the River and the Utilization of its Waters). London, 1952

519

ISSAWI, CHARLES. *Egypt at Mid-century.* London, 1954
 Egypt, an Economic and Social Analysis. (Royal Inst. of Internat.
 Affairs). London, 1947
JARVIS, H. W. *Pharaoh to Farouk.* John Murray, London, 1955
LANE, EDWARD. *The Manners and Customs of the Modern Egyptians.*
 London, 1860
LAQUEUR, WALTER Z. *Communism and Nationalism in the Middle
 East.* London, 1956
MARLOWE, JOHN. *Anglo-Egyptian Relations (1800–1953).* London,
 1954
MILNER, LORD. *England and Egypt.* London, 1892
LLOYD, LORD. *Egypt since Cromer.* London, 1933–4
NEGUIB, MOHAMED. *Egypt's Destiny.* London, 1955
NASSER, GAMAL ABDEL. *The Philosophy of the Revolution.* Cairo,
 1954
RIFAAT BEY, M. *The Awakening of Modern Egypt.* London, 1947
ROWLATT, MARY. *A Family in Egypt.* London, 1956
SABRI, MOHAMED. *La genèse de l'esprit national égyptien* (The Birth
 of the Egyptian Nationalist Outlook). Paris, 1924
SAMMARCO, A., and J. BAINVILLE, A. MORET, H. MUNIER. *Précis de
 l'Histoire de l'Égypte* (A Concise History of Egypt). 4 vols.
 Paris, 1930–5
SADAT, ANWAR EL. *Revolt on the Nile.* London, 1957
TAHA HUSAIN. *The Future of Culture in Egypt.* Cairo, 1957
 Le livre des jours (The Stream of Days)—autobiographical
TEWFIK EL HAKIM. *Le journal d'un substitut de campagne* (The Maze
 of Justice)—a novel
VAILLAND, ROGER. *Choses vues en Égypte* (Things Seen in Egypt).
 Paris, 1952
WARRINER, DOREEN. *Land Reform and Development in the Middle
 East.* London, 1957
WAVELL, A. P. *Allenby in Egypt.* London, 1943
YOUNG, SIR GEORGE. *Egypt.* London, 1927

Daily newspapers:
 La Bourse Égyptienne, Cairo
 Egyptian Gazette, Cairo
Weeklies:
 Actualités, Cairo
 Images, Cairo

Annuaire de la Fédération de l'Industrie (Industrial Federation Year-book). Cairo

Bulletin de la Banque belge et internationale, Cairo

Bulletin du Centre d'Information du Proche-Orient (C.I.P.O.), Paris

Quarterly Bulletin of the National Bank of Egypt, Cairo

Cahiers d'Histoire Égyptienne, Cairo

Cahiers de l'Orient contemporain, Paris

Index

Date Due

DEC 11 1970			
	PRINTED	IN U. S. A.	